박지성

고려대학교 언어학과 및 영어영문학 졸

현 | 해커스 편입 독해전임
　　마공스터디 온라인 강사
　　대치동 용인외대부고·휘문고·숙명여고 내신
　　목동 용인외대부고 내신

전 | 강창용편입 독해전임
　　이패스편입 독해전임
　　리스공 공무원 강사

저서 | 리딩이노베이터(기본편)「JH press」
　　　리딩이노베이터(실전편)「JH press」
　　　영어독해 개념이해「Jonghap Books」
　　　영어독해 문제원리·풀이이해「Jonghap Books」
　　　매그너스 MAGNUS 고등영어 서술형 기본편 6주완성「오스틴북스」
　　　매그너스 MAGNUS 서술형 시리즈 고등영어 서술형 실전편「오스틴북스」

퍼펙트 독해

발 행 일 2025년 11월 14일(개정2판 2쇄)
저　　자 박지성
발 행 인 이도경
발 행 처 JH press
주　　소 13558 경기도 성남시 분당구 판교공원로1길 65
홈페이지 www.booksellers.co.kr
전자메일 proper002@properenglish.co.kr
대표전화 070-4454-1340
팩　　스 031-718-0580

정가 24,800원

ISBN　　979-11-94493-00-6　　　　13740

※낙장 및 파본은 바꾸어 드립니다.

퍼펙트 독해
PERFECT READING

실전대비 능력 극대화! - 완벽을 추구한다!

지음 박지성

Perfect Reading

Prologue: 독해학습 접근 방법

책의 본문 학습에 앞서 다음 몇 가지를 당부하고자 한다.

첫째, 다양한 영어 원문으로 된 분야의 주제에 따른 문제들을 많이 푸는 것이 최선이라는 점에는 이의가 없다. 하지만 독해의 기본이 되는 글의 구성과 전개 방식에 대한 지식이 확실히 서 있지 않다면, 반드시 이 부분에 대한 점검이 필요하다. 기본기가 잘 다져 있지 않은 사람은 아무리 많은 문제를 풀어 본다 하더라도 모래 위에 쌓은 성처럼 여전히 불안할 뿐이다.

둘째, 위에서 언급한 글의 구성과 전개 방식에 관한 이야기를 좀 더 이어서 하자면, 모든 글은 주제가 있기 마련이며, 글쓴이는 자신이 전달하고자 하는 내용을 가장 효율적으로 전달할 방법을 생각한다. 다시 말해, 글의 구성과 전개 방식은 모든 글쓴이가 전달하고자 하는 요지를 위해 선택하는 도구나 마찬가지이다. 글의 구성과 전개 방식은 주제문의 위치, 문제 유형, 보기 항의 구성 등에 영향을 미치기 때문에 이러한 기본적인 요소를 철저하게 익힌 후 반복적인 문제 풀이를 통해 이를 적용함으로써 자신의 것으로 '체득'하는 것이 무엇보다 중요하다.

셋째, 많은 수험생이 해석과 독해를 동일한 것으로 보는데, 이는 엄연히 다른 말이다. 독해는 글을 이해하는 능력을 말한다. 수준 높은 독해란 글쓴이 자신의 주장을 논리적으로 통일성(Unity)과 응집성(Coherence)을 갖추어 전개하고 있는지를 비판적으로 판단할 수 있는 능력을 말한다. 이러한 맥락에서 특정 언어를 떠나 글을 분석하고 읽는 독해력이 절실히 필요하다. 이를 위해 틈나는 대로 신문 사설 및 교양서적을 읽어 두기를 권한다. 예를 들어, 서양 역사의 맥을 잡아 주는 책을 아침마다 조금씩 읽는다든지, 저녁에 하루 일과가 끝나면 신문의 사설을 한 번쯤 읽으면서 글쓴이의 주장은 무엇이며, 이를 뒷받침하는 내용이 적절한지를 비판적으로 생각해 보는 것도 좋은 방법 중 하나이다.

　넷째, 대부분의 공인 영어 시험에는 문제 유형이 대략 10개 내외로 정해져 있다. 편입도 예외는 아니다. 예를 들어, 거의 모든 학교에서 출제되는 주제, 제목, 요지, 내용 일치, 유추, 빈칸 문제와 일부 학교에서 나오는 글의 목적, 문장 배열, 문장 삽입, 글 전개 방법 등 학교마다 일관성 있게 매년 문제의 유형을 지켜 나가고 있다. 이를 다른 시각에서 본다면, 문제마다 나름의 접근 방법이 있다는 말이므로 이를 잘 활용할 필요가 있다. 단순히 지문을 읽고 그때그때 순간적인 생각에 문제를 풀기보다는 각 문제 유형마다 자신만의 접근 방법을 세우는 것이 중요하다.

　다섯째, 최근 배경지식에 관한 논의가 많은 듯하다. 배경지식과 문제 풀이는 다음과 같은 관점에서 바라보면 된다. 배경지식은 본문의 내용을 파악하는 데 도움을 주고, 문제의 답은 반드시 본문의 내용만을 바탕으로 이끌어내야 한다는 점이다. 문제에서 요구하는 근거는 언제나 본문에 있다는 것을 명심해야 한다.

　이상 각각의 사항을 염두에 두고 학습 시 참고·활용하기 바라며, 이 책을 통해서 조금이나마 자신이 원하는 목표에 다가갈 수 있기를 간절히 기원한다.

박지성

책의 구성과 특징

본책에는 '실전문제(Day 1 ~ Day 30)'를 다뤘으며, 별책을 두어 실전문제에 따른 해설 및 정답을 수록했다.

| 본책 | 실전문제 Day 1 ~ Day 30

전체 30 Day로 나눠 인문, 사회, 과학, 시사 등의 다양한 중·상급 지문을 섞어 구성하여 특정 분야에 치우친 '편식 독해'를 없앴다. 각 Day는 총 10개의 지문과 함께 적게는 24문제에서 많게는 30문제로 구성되어 있는데, 이는 서울 소재 상위권 학교의 평균을 고려한 문항 수이다. 또한 각 Day는 말 그대로 실제 시험에 나오는 1회분의 시험에 해당하는 것으로, 매번 문제를 풀 때마다 시간을 정해 놓고 실전과 같이 연습할 수 있도록 구성했으며, 각 지문에 배정된 문항 수는 최근 편입 경향을 반영한 2~4개 정도이다. 그리고 일반 시중에 나와 있는 토플, 고시, SAT 등의 문제를 짜깁기하거나 수정한 것이 아니라, 대학교 교양 수준에 상당하는 인문, 사회, 과학, 그리고 시사 내용을 반영하여 새롭게 구성한 지문과 문제만을 수록했다.

| 별책 | 실전문제 해설 및 정답

문제마다 해설 부분을 강화하여 혼자 공부하는 독학생들이 더욱 쉽게 이해할 수 있도록 배려했는데, 한편 필요 시 왜 답이 아닌지에 대한 오답 설명도 추가했으며, 또한 문제 구성 원리를 함께 제시하여 이해를 돕도록 했다.

Contents

Prologue: 독해학습 접근 방법 ·················· 4.P
책의 구성과 특징 ································ 6.P
Contents ·· 7.P

| 본 책 | **실전문제**

Day 1 ············ 10.p
Day 2 ············ 22.p
Day 3 ············ 31.p
Day 4 ············ 39.p
Day 5 ············ 48.p
Day 6 ············ 57.p
Day 7 ············ 66.p
Day 8 ············ 75.p
Day 9 ············ 84.p
Day 10 ············ 94.p
Day 11 ············ 102.p
Day 12 ············ 112.p
Day 13 ············ 120.p
Day 14 ············ 128.p
Day 15 ············ 135.p

Day 16 ············ 145.p
Day 17 ············ 155.p
Day 18 ············ 165.p
Day 19 ············ 173.p
Day 20 ············ 182.p
Day 21 ············ 192.p
Day 22 ············ 201.p
Day 23 ············ 210.p
Day 24 ············ 221.p
Day 25 ············ 232.p
Day 26 ············ 242.p
Day 27 ············ 252.p
Day 28 ············ 260.p
Day 29 ············ 269.p
Day 30 ············ 278.p

| 별 책 |
실전문제 해설 및 정답 ·· 2.P

PART 1

실전문제
Day 1 ~ Day 30

Day 1

★ Perhaps the most valuable result of all education is the ability to make yourself do the thing you have to do, when it ought to be done, whether you like it or not; it is the first lesson that ought to be learned; and however early a man's training begins, it is probably the last lesson that he learns thoroughly.

Thomas H. Huxley (1825 - 1895)

아마도 모든 교육의 가장 가치 있는 결과는 무엇인가를 해야 할 때, 그것이 하고 싶든 그렇지 않든 해야 하는 것을 스스로 할 수 있도록 하는 능력일 것이다. 이것은 배워야 하는 첫 번째 것이다. 그러나 아무리 일찍 인간의 교육이 시작된다 하더라도, 이것은 인간이 철저하게 배우는 마지막 교훈이다. (토마스 헉슬리)

[Challenge 1]

Nineteenth-century nature writing by women took various forms, but one theme that is seen in most of these works is the importance of the link between human beings and their natural surroundings. For most female writers, concern with the environment is not tied to a romantic longing for the openness of the rugged landscape or the withdrawal from society, which are common themes in men's nature writing. Rather, the earth is seen as the sustainer of human life and relationships, and the ____(a)____ boundary between nature and humanity is emphasized. Critics who study these women's writings have been particularly interested to show how the "gendered" female landscape that is central to nineteenth-century male writing about the environment is given more complex expression in works by women. They also show how female writing about the environment weaves together concerns about ordinary life and explores questions of community, gender, domination, and exploitation.

문제 1 What is the passage mainly about?
(1) Relationship between human beings and their nature
(2) How male writers are different from female writers
(3) Female literary standpoint on nature in 19C
(4) Female writing styles on nature

문제 2 Fill in blank (a).
(1) fragile
(2) spurious
(3) existing
(4) resilient

[Challenge 2]

As a general rule, we remember for a time the substance of what we have written, for the subject is generally new to us; but if we are writing what we have often written before, we lose consciousness of this too, as fully as we do of the characters necessary to convey the substance to another person, and we shall find ourselves writing on as it were ___(a)___ while thinking and talking of something else. So a paid copyist, to whom the subject of what he is writing is of no importance, does not even notice it. He deals only with familiar words and familiar characters without caring to go behind them, and thereupon writes on in a quasi-unconscious manner; but if he comes to a word or to characters with which he is but little acquainted, he becomes immediately ___(b)___ to the consciousness of either remembering or trying to remember. His consciousness of his own knowledge or memory would seem to belong to a period, so to speak, of twilight between the thick darkness of ignorance and the brilliancy of perfect knowledge; as colour which ___(c)___ with extremes of light or of shade. Perfect ignorance and perfect knowledge are alike unselfconscious.

문제 1 Fill in blank (a).
(1) consciously
(2) mechanically
(3) deliberately
(4) obliviously

문제 2 Fill in blank (b).
(1) underlined
(2) accustomed
(3) awakened
(4) known

문제 3 Fill in blank (c).
(1) contrasts
(2) vanishes
(3) protrudes
(4) materializes

[Challenge 3]

One of the first empiricists was (a) <u>Aristotle</u>. In fact, it's safe to say that it was Aristotle who made the empirical point of view a reality. Aristotle was the teacher of Alexander the Great. Aristotle had also been the pupil of Plato, who was in turn, the student of Socrates. Plato, simply stated, believed that universal ideas of things — like justice, beauty, truth — had an objective existence all their own. What this means is that (b) <u>these things existed whether men perceived (apprehended) them or not.</u> They had an independent reality which Plato believed men could come to grasp as knowledge. These ideas exist (c) "<u>apriori</u>," that is, they exist prior to experience and hence, transcend experience. For Plato, our senses are deceptive and what we experience in our daily lives is not reality but the shadow of reality. This is one of the messages of Plato's Republic, specifically (d) <u>THE ALLEGORY OF THE CAVE</u>. Plato's doctrine of the Forms (Ideas, or Universals) concerns itself with innate ideas — ideas which exist before men have experience of them. This philosophical school has come to be known as rationalism. So, between 384 and 330 B.C. in Athens, the two major western philosophical traditions of thought were born. For 2000 years, philosophers had to choose whether they followed Plato and his rationalism, or Aristotle and his empiricism. Indeed, Plato comes off as the first philosopher and Aristotle as his first critic. As Whitehead wrote in Process and Reality in 1929: The safest general characterization of the European philosophical tradition is that it consists of __(가)__ to Plato.

문제 1 According to the passage, which of the following is CORRECT?
(1) Aristotle was directly taught by Socrates.
(2) For Plato, justice, beauty and truth exist regardless of human experiences.
(3) The word 'apriori' is closely related to the idea of tabula rasa.
(4) Rationalism is more aligned with the scientific method than empiricism as represented by Aristotle.

문제 2 According to the passage, which of the following does NOT belong to the rest?
(1) (a)   (2) (b)
(3) (c)   (4) (d)

문제 3 Choose one that is most appropriate for blank (가).
(1) a series of footnotes   (2) a sting of pungent criticism
(3) a sense of unity   (4) a combination of black and white

[Challenge 4]

The Black Death reared its head sporadically in Europe over the next few centuries. But by 1352, it had essentially loosened its grip. Europe's population had been hard hit, which had an economic impact. The workforce had been destroyed — farms were abandoned and buildings crumbled. The price of labor skyrocketed in the face of worker shortage, and the cost of goods rose. The price of food, though, didn't go up, perhaps because the population had declined so much.

The Black Death did set the stage for more modern medicine and spurred changes in public health and hospital management. Frustrated with Black Death diagnoses that revolved around astrology and superstition, educators began placing greater emphasis on clinical medicine, based on physical science. (가) While schools initially had to close for lack of educators, the plague eventually drove growth in higher education. New schools were established, sometimes specifically mentioning in their charters that they were trying to address the decay in learning and gaps in education left by the Black Death.

People who survived the Black Death era generally suffered a communal crisis of faith. Rather than becoming more religious in thanksgiving to God for their survival, people harbored doubts. (나) They had turned to the church for an answer to the plague, and the church had been able to offer no help. Additionally, priests, who, along with doctors, had the highest rate of contact with the diseased, also had one of the highest rates of fatalities. Several new heretical movements sprang up. (다) Those who still clung to their faith were more likely to do so in a very personal manner. Many began to build private chapels. Feeling, essentially, that God had turned his back on them, the people reacted to the end of the Black Death by turning their backs on him. They engaged in wild debauchery to celebrate being alive. They held gluttonous banquets, drank, wore extravagant clothing and gambled. (라) The danse macabre, or dance of death, is an allegorical concept that was expressed in drama, poetry, music and visual art. The danse macabre usually shows a procession or dance between the living and the dead. The range of figures shown is meant to show that death will come for everyone, and the various activities depicted are a reminder that death could always be right around the corner.

문제 1   Which of the following is the best title for the passage?
(1) Why the Black Death Affected Europe the Most
(2) How the Black Death Changed the Way People Viewed Religion
(3) Effects of the Black Death
(4) God's Rage: the Black Death

문제 2 According to the passage, which of the following is CORRECT?

(1) Priests were relatively free from the impact of the black death when it reached its peak.

(2) The Black Death did not give in until the end of the Middle Ages.

(3) Among the most seriously affected areas by the Black Death was the price of food.

(4) The black death led to the dramatic changes in how people showed their faith toward God.

문제 3 Where does the sentence below best fit in the passage?

> It was clear through the art of the time, though, that people still had death on their minds.

(1) (가)   (2) (나)
(3) (다)   (4) (라)

[Challenge 5]

Paine's book followed in the tradition of early eighteenth-century British deism. These deists, while maintaining individual positions, still shared several sets of assumptions and arguments that Paine articulated in The Age of Reason. The most important position that united the early deists was their call for "free rational inquiry" into all subjects, especially religion. Saying that early Christianity was founded on freedom of conscience, they demanded religious toleration and an end to religious persecution. They also demanded that debate rest on reason and rationality. Deists embraced a Newtonian world-view, and they believed all things in the universe, even God, must obey the laws of nature. Without a concept of natural law, the deists argued, explanations of the workings of nature would descend into irrationality. This belief in natural law drove their skepticism of miracles. Because miracles had to be observed to be validated, deists rejected the accounts laid out in the Bible of God's miracles and argued that such evidence was neither sufficient nor necessary to prove the existence of God. Along these lines, deistic writings insisted that God, as the first cause or prime mover, had created and designed the universe with natural laws as part of his plan. They hold that God does not repeatedly alter his plan by suspending natural laws to (miraculously) intervene in human affairs. Deists also rejected the claim that there was only one revealed religious "truth" or one true faith; religion could only be "simple, apparent, ordinary, and universal" if it was to be the logical product of a benevolent God. They therefore distinguished between "revealed religions" (which they rejected), such as Christianity, and "natural religion", a set of universal beliefs derived from the natural world that demonstrated God's existence (they were, thus, not atheists). While some deists accepted revelation, most argued that revelation's restriction to small groups or even a single person limited its explanatory power. Moreover, many found the Christian revelations in particular to be contradictory and irreconcilable. According to these writers, revelation could reinforce the evidence for God's existence already apparent in the natural world, but more often it led to superstition among the masses. Most deists argued that priests had deliberately corrupted Christianity for their own gain by promoting the acceptance of miracles, unnecessary rituals, and illogical and dangerous doctrines (these accusations were typically referred to as "priestcraft"). The worst of these doctrines was original sin. By convincing people that they required a priest's help to overcome their innate sinfulness, deists argued, religious leaders had enslaved the human population. Deists therefore typically viewed themselves as __(a)__ .

문제 1 Which of the following is the topic of the passage?
(1) Characteristics of Eighteenth-Century British deism
(2) Christian Revelations Leading to Deism
(3) Heated Debates Over Usefulness of Deism
(4) Christianity vs Jewism

문제 2 Which of the following is NOT correct about the passage?
(1) Deists reject the account of 'selected people' based on the logical result of a benevolent God.
(2) Deists use inductive reasoning to prove the existence of God.
(3) Deists think of reason as the most important tool for understanding all things in the universe including religion.
(4) Deists do not believe in miracles because they are not for sure whether they are done by God or by human beings.

문제 3 Fill in blank (a).
(1) intellectual liberators
(2) slave drivers
(3) 'new' religious leaders
(4) men 'in chains'

[Challenge 6]

The single greatest weakness of American parties is their inability to achieve cohesion in the legislature. Although there is some measure of party unity, it is not uncommon for the majority to be unable to implement important legislation. The unity is strongest during election campaigns; after the primary elections, the losing candidates all promise their support to the party nominee. By the time Congress convenes, the unity has _____. This phenomenon is attributable to the fragmented nature of party politics. The national committees are no more than feudal lords who receive nominal loyalty from their vassals. A member of Congress builds power upon a local base. Consequently, a member is likely to responsive to local special interest groups. Evidence of this is seen in the differences in voting patterns between the Upper and Lower Houses. In the Upper House, where terms are longer, there is more party unity.

문제 1 Which of the following word best fills in the blank?
(1) fortified (2) dismissed
(3) dissipated (4) bolstered

문제 2 Which of the following, if true, would most weaken the author's argument?
(1) Members of Congress are more loyal to national party committees than to local constituencies.
(2) The Upper House members vote against the party leaders less often than the Lower House members.
(3) The primary duty of an officeholder is to be responsive to a local constituency rather than arty leaders.
(4) There is more unity among minority party members than among majority party members.

문제 3 Which of the following can be inferred about the passage?
(1) A majority of the ruling party members in the Lower House voted for the party leaders.
(2) A majority of the ruling party members in the Upper House voted for the party leaders.
(3) A minority of the ruling party members in the Upper House voted for the party leaders.
(4) A minority of the ruling party members in the Lower House voted against the party leaders.

[Challenge 7]

Learning can be defined as the process leading to relatively permanent behavioral change or potential behavioral change. ___(a)___ , as we learn, we alter the way we perceive our environment, the way we interpret the incoming stimuli, and therefore the way we interact, or behave. John B. Watson (1878~1958) was the first to study how the process of learning affects our behavior, and he formed the school of thought known as Behaviorism. The central idea behind behaviorism is that only observable behaviors are worthy of research since other abstraction such as a person's mood or thoughts are too subjective. This belief was dominant in psychological research in the United States for a good 50 years.

Perhaps the most well known Behaviorist is B. F. Skinner (1904~1990). Skinner followed much of Watson's research and findings, but believed that internal states could influence behavior just as external stimuli. He is considered to be a Radical Behaviorist because of this belief, although nowadays it is believed that both internal and external stimuli influence our behavior.

문제 1 What is the passage mainly talking about?
(1) Learning and Behaviorism
(2) History of Behaviorism
(3) Life of John B. Watson
(4) A Radical Behaviorist : B. F. Skinner

문제 2 Fill in blank (a).
(1) To sum up
(2) In other words
(3) On the other hand
(4) As a matter of fact

문제 3 Which of the following is TRUE of the passage?
(1) All behaviorists believe that our behavior is only triggered by external stimuli.
(2) B. F. Skinner did not agree with any of John B. Watson's theory because he thought internal factors as well as external stimuli could influence behavior.
(3) According to behaviorism, people are much like a machine that only responds to outer environments.
(4) John B. Watson thought human minds are not pertinent to objective research.

[Challenge 8]

The Greek word for a rite as already noted is dromenon, "a thing done" — and the word is full of instruction. The Greek had realized that to perform a rite you must do something, that is, you must not only feel something but express it in action, or, to put it psychologically, you must not only receive an impulse, you must react to it. The word for rite, dromenon, "thing done," arose, of course, not from any psychological analysis, but from the simple fact that rites among the primitive Greeks were things done, mimetic dances and the like. It is a fact of cardinal importance that their word for theatrical representation, drama, is own cousin to their word for rite, dromenon; drama also means "thing done." Greek linguistic instinct pointed plainly to the fact that art and ritual are near relations. But we have to note that the Greek word for rite, dromenon, "thing done," is not strictly adequate. It omits a factor of prime importance; it includes too much and not enough. All "things done" are not rites. You may shrink back from a blow; that is the expression of an emotion, that is a reaction to a stimulus, but that is not a rite. You may digest your dinner; that is a thing done, and a thing of high importance, but it is not a rite. One element in the rite we have already observed, and that is, that it be done ___(a)___ , by a number of persons feeling the same emotion. A meal eaten in common, under the influence of a common emotion, may, and often does, tend to become a rite.

問題 1 According to the passage, which of the following is NOT correct?
(1) The word rite has a practical undertone to it.
(2) The definition of rite as "thing done" is not sufficient to carry its full meaning.
(3) A meal digested alone is certainly no rite.
(4) A person doing impressions of others can be a rite.

問題 2 Fill in blank (a).
(1) psychologically
(2) collectively
(3) theatrically
(4) synonymously

[Challenge 9]

    Many prefer to live in that state of ___(a)___, which may be called tolerable health, a state in which they do not suffer, yet are not quite well. In this condition they have their little ups and downs and occasionally a serious illness, which too often proves fatal. Even such people ought to acquire health knowledge, for the time may come when they will desire to enjoy life to the fullest, which they can do only when they have health. Those who have this knowledge are often able to help themselves quickly and effectively when no one else can.

    I am acquainted with many who have been educated out of disease into health. Many of them are indiscreet, but they have learned to know the signs of approaching trouble and they ease up before ___(b)___. In this way they save themselves and their families from much suffering, much anxiety and much expense. Every adult should know enough to remain well. Every one should know the signs of approaching illness and how to abort it. The mental comfort and ease that come from the possession of such knowledge are priceless.

문제 1 What is the passage mainly talking about?
    (1) Suffering from Illness
    (2) Development of Illness into Incurable
    (3) Ways to Good Health
    (4) Importance of Health Knowledge

문제 2 Fill in blank (a).
    (1) uncertainty   (2) dichotomy
    (3) indecision   (4) aplomb

문제 3 Which of the following logically fills in blank (b)?
    (1) things get better
    (2) anyone else gets contaminated
    (3) they miss the chance to be educated
    (4) anything serious overtakes them

[Challenge 10]

Starbucks Coffee can be insanely busy. It is common practice for baristas to write customers' names or tag numbers in the U.S. Unlike the coffee branches in South Korea, most of them don't give out pagers to call the customer when their drinks are ready. Recently, two English speaking Koreans dropped by a Starbucks located in Georgia, and discovered that (a) they were served more than just coffee.

One employee decided to try something unique and different. Instead of writing down the names, the barista put his artistic skills to the test by drawing a caricature with slanted eyes to identify the two Korean customers.

Receiving a cup with a drawing of slanted eyes instead of their names, the two customers were shocked. They were surprised and offended, and immediately complained to the store manager. They were simply given a gift card. It was only a matter of time before the story got out. The incident spread like wildfire online and Starbucks indicated that the employee involved in the issue was asked to leave.

The incident is now rankling just about all Koreans since there was another racial controversy at Papa John's restaurant in the Big Apple. The popular U.S. pizza chain was under attack last month when an employee typed out "lady chinky eyes" on a receipt. Once again this was done to replace the customer's name. Unfortunately for Papa John's, the existence of social networking services made matters worse for them. The angry Korean woman took the issue to Twitter and instantly more than 100,000 people viewed her post and retweeted it.

"What's going on with all the racist slurs?" "This nonsense is truly annoying." "Do we still have discrimination based on color?" Countless people are posting messages on their Facebook and discussing the issue on Twitter, and these are only a few posts. Observers say that discrimination on the minorities has been an on-going problem in major cities in the U.S. Although messages of discrimination are no longer verbal in real life acts such as writing a comment on a receipt or drawing a picture on a disposable coffee cup are incidents that happen every day. The unfortunate factor is that they are happening so often that no one had paid any attention until recently.

To take immediate action a group of Korean-American housewives have decided to take the issue to the court. Three things are distinctively clear. One is that the existence of racial discrimination is evident. Second, racial discrimination has evolved. Finally, discrimination against Asians continues because the majority assumes Asian-Americans will stay quiet over these kinds of incidents. We must know that racial discrimination, bullying, and bigotry are unjust regardless of which race or ethnic group it is directed to.

문제 1 Which of the following can be the best title for the passage?
(1) Changing Environment for Baristas
(2) Revival of Racial Discrimination
(3) Violence of Work ethic
(4) Evolving Discrimination in the U.S.

문제 2 Given the context, which of the following best paraphrases the underlined (a)?
(1) People have been unwittingly paying more than they need to.
(2) Customers received a hospitable welcome from the baristas.
(3) Customers were given more coffee than what they paid for.
(4) Some customers experienced racial discrimination.

문제 3 Which of the following is TRUE of the passage?
(1) The fact that no one had paid any attention to racial discrimination until recently means that it is a new social issue.
(2) Social networking services can be used as a vehicle to express social issues.
(3) In the U.S. baristas usually use pagers to let customers know their order is ready to go.
(4) Asian-Americans have been quite active in fighting against social injustices.

Day 2

★ Men acquire a particular quality by constantly acting a particular way... you become just by performing just actions, temperate by performing temperate actions, brave by performing brave actions.

Aristotle (384 BC - 322 BC)

인간은 특정한 방식으로 지속적으로 행함으로 특정한 능력을 습득한다. 당신은 정당한 행위를 함으로 정당함을 얻고, 절제하는 행위를 함으로 절제함을 행하며, 용감한 행위를 보이며 용감해진다. (아리스토텔레스)

[Challenge 1]

The greatest of the three institutions affecting boy life, from the very fact that it is the primary one, is the home. The home is the basis of the community, the community merely being the aggregation of a large number of well-organized or ill-organized homes. The first impressions the boy receives are through his home life, and the bent of his whole career is often determined by the home relationships. The large majority of homes today are merely places in which a boy may eat and sleep. The original prerogatives of the father and mother, so far as they pertain to the physical, social, mental and moral development of boyhood, have been farmed out to other organizations in the community. The home life of today greatly differs from that of previous generations. This is very largely due to social and economic conditions. Our social and economic revolution has made vast inroads upon our normal home life, with the result that the home has been seriously weakened and the boy has been deprived of his normal home heritage.

문제 1 Which of the following is the best title for the passage?
 (1) Our Home In Crisis (2) Working Definition of Home
 (3) Changed Roles of Parents (4) Abnormal Child Development

문제 2 Which of the following can NOT be inferred from the passage?
 (1) The relationships at home can be detrimental to a boy's life, leaving a lasting impact on him.
 (2) A person's personality often forms early in life at home.
 (3) There has been a big shift in the role of home.
 (4) Nowadays kids learn their home heritage from other organizations in the community.

[Challenge 2]

We can learn without a teacher. Children learn hundreds of facts before they ever see a school, sometimes with the aid of parents or others, often by their own unaided efforts. In the greater part of our acquisitions we are self-taught, and it is quite generally conceded that knowledge is most permanent and best which is dug out by unaided research. Everything, at the outset, must be learned by the discoverer without an instructor, since   (a)   . If, then, we can learn without being taught, it follows that the true function of the teacher is to create the most favorable conditions for self-learning. Essentially the acquisition of knowledge must be brought about by the same agencies and through the use of the same methods, whether with or without a teacher.

문제 1   Which of the following can NOT be inferred from the passage?
(1) The fundamental role that teachers play in one's learning is to facilitate self-learning.
(2) Teachers have no place in one's learning.
(3) Children can be their own teachers.
(4) There are times when children need help from others for learning to occur.

문제 2   Fill in blank (a).
(1) some things can be understood without any knowledge
(2) everything reveals itself
(3) instructors who already know it are not always available
(4) no instructor knows it

[Challenge 3]

The most beautiful thing about youth is its power and eagerness to make ideals, and he is unfortunate who goes out into the world without some picture of services to be rendered, or of a goal to be attained. There are very few of us who, at some time or another, have not cherished these ideals, perhaps secretly and half ashamed as though to us alone had come an inspiration of a career that should touch the pulses of the world and leave it better than we found it. And in the making of youthful ideals we have changed very little with the passage of the centuries. The character of the ideals has changed with changing needs, but not we ourselves. Our young men still see visions; they still fill the future with conflict and with struggle and prospectively live out their lives with the crown of achievement in the distance. It is well that it should be so. The ideals of our youth are the motive-power of our lives, and even those of us who have lived far into the eras of disappointment would not willingly wipe from our memories even the most extravagant day dreams from which we drew energy and hope and fortitude and self-reliance.

문제 1 Which of the following is mainly talked about in the above passage?
    (1) Good Old Days   (2) Youthful Ideals
    (3) Public Services   (4) Characteristics of Youth

문제 2 According to the passage, the character of the ideals changes _____.
    (1) as the demands of the society change
    (2) the very person who owns them
    (3) only when there is a big change going on inside the person
    (4) the chance of achieving them

[Challenge 4]

In a little book on the snakes of India, published many years ago by Dr. Nicholson of the Madras Medical Service, the conviction was expressed that the snake-charmers of Burmah knew of some antidote to the poison of the cobra which gave them confidence in handling it. He said that nothing would induce them to divulge it, but that he suspected it consisted in gradual inoculation with the venom itself. Putting the question to himself why he did not attempt to attest this by experiment, he replied that there were two reasons, which, if I recollect rightly, were, first, that he had a strong natural repugnance to anything like cruelty to animals, and, secondly, that he had observed that as soon as a man got the notion into his head that he had discovered a cure for snake-bite, he began to show symptoms of insanity.

It is rather remarkable that, after so many years, another Scottish doctor, not in Madras, but in Edinburgh, has proved, by just such experiments as Dr. Nicholson shrank from, that an "aged and previously (a) <u>sedate</u> horse" may, by gradual inoculation with cobra poison, be rendered so thoroughly proof against it that a dose which would suffice to kill ten ordinary horses only imparts "increased vigour and liveliness" to it. Further, Dr. Fraser has found that the serum of the blood of an animal thus rendered proof against poison is itself an antidote capable of combating that poison after it has been at work for thirty minutes in the veins of a rabbit, and arresting its effects. And all this has been achieved __(b)__ the distinguished doctor's sanity.

문제 1 What is the passage mainly talking about?
    (1) Snake-charmers of Burmah   (2) Antidote to Snake Bite
    (3) Dr. Nicholson's Experiment   (4) Dilemma of Raising Cobras

문제 2 Which of the following is NOT correct about Dr. Nicholson?
    (1) He thought putting the venom itself in a body would make the body immune to it.
    (2) He tried to talk snake-charmers into revealing their secret of dealing cobras with confidence, only to fail.
    (3) He was afraid that he would go insane if he ever tried to find a cure for snake-bite.
    (4) He really liked animals such as snakes.

문제 3 Which of the following is closest in meaning to the underlined (a)?
    (1) calm   (2) flighty   (3) perturbed   (4) aggravated

문제 4 Fill in blank (b).
    (1) with the aid of   (2) in the same vein with
    (3) without apparent detriment to   (4) detrimental to

[Challenge 5]

Total economic enterprise in China is apportioned along lines of directive planning (mandatory), indicative planning (indirect implementation of central directives), and those left to market forces. In the early 1980s during the initial reforms enterprises began to have increasing discretion over the quantities of inputs purchased, the sources of inputs, the variety of products manufactured, and the production process. Operational supervision over economic projects has devolved primarily to provincial, municipal, and county governments. The majority of stateowned industrial enterprises, which were managed at the provincial level or below, were partially regulated by a combination of specific allocations and indirect controls, but they also produced goods outside the plan for sale in the market. Important, scarce resources — for example, engineers or finished steel — may have been assigned to this kind of unit in exact numbers. Less critical assignments of personnel and materials would have been authorized in a general way by the plan, arrangements left up to the enterprise management.

In addition, enterprises themselves are gaining increased independence in a range of activity. While strategically important industry and services and most of large-scale construction have remained under directive planning, the market economy has gained rapidly in scale every year as it subsumes more and more sectors. Overall, the Chinese industrial system contains a complex mixture of relationships. The State Council generally administers relatively strict control over resources deemed to be of vital concern for the performance and health of the entire economy. Less vital aspects of the economy have been transferred to lower levels for detailed decisions and management. Furthermore, the need to coordinate entities that are in different organizational hierarchies generally causes a great deal of informal bargaining and consensus building.

문제 1 Which of the following is the best title for the passage?
(1) Differences between Private and Public Sectors
(2) Changed Government Role under the Age of Economic Reformation
(3) 'Invisible Hand' Fully Employed in Modern China
(4) Increased Control of China over World Economy

문제 2 Which of the following is neither stated nor implied about the Chinese Economy?
(1) The whole policy-making process involves extensive consultation and negotiation.
(2) Direct control is exercised by designating specific physical output quotas and supplyallocations for some goods and services.
(3) Economic plans and policies are implemented by a variety of direct and indirect control mechanisms.
(4) Enterprises low in organizational hierarchies have no control over detailed decisions and management.

[Challenge 6]

While both Democrats and Republicans square off to discuss health care reform and how every person should be insured, I think the solution is simple: Let people pay the consequences of their own actions. My roommate works at the burn unit in Cook County Hospital in Chicago. Yesterday, a patient came into the ward with severe burns on the side of his face. The cause? He drank too much and fell on his car's radiator. The doctors there had to perform an emergency skin graft to save his face. Who paid for this? You and me, the American taxpayers. If someone chooses to smoke five packs of cigarettes a day, the burden of his health problems should not be placed on the shoulders of the public. If someone is fulfilling some wild fantasy and ends up injured somehow, that should not be something other people have to pay for. I think it's time that people relearn the most basic principle of karma — be ready to bear the consequences of your actions because you are responsible for your choices. If we stick to that simple mantra, perhaps a great many of our problems will be solved.

문제 1 Which of the following is the best title for the passage?
(1) What Drives People to Act Unscrupulously?
(2) Universal Health Care is the Answer!
(3) Lack of Hospital Staff Adds more to the Death Toll
(4) Consequences Should Drive Health Care

[Challenge 7]

Airplanes are such a common form of travel that it's easy to forget just how recently they were invented. Today, even a person in the middle of nowhere would not be surprised to see a plane in the sky. But before the Wright Brothers flew their plane at Kitty Hawk, North Carolina, in 1903, most scientists thought flight by heavier-than-air machines would never be achieved. Never. In fact, the word airplane didn't come into common usage until after 1945.

문제 1 The reference to the "person in the middle of nowhere" serves primarily to _____.
(1) indicate the scope of a change
(2) challenge common beliefs
(3) highlight the limitations of an accepted idea
(4) question modern morals

문제 2 The author of the passage would most likely agree with each of the following statements EXCEPT _____.

(1) airplanes are a relatively recent innovation
(2) the Wright Brothers took the first airplane flight
(3) air travel remains the privilege of the elite
(4) the word airplane was rarely used in the early twentieth century

[Challenge 8]

For years, American companies looking to reduce costs have found savings by looking overseas. Even those that lamented offshoring's effect on domestic employment couldn't deny its balance-sheet appeal. Once the offshoring trend hit critical mass, anyone who didn't join in was at a huge disadvantage: If all your competitors have moved their call centers to India, how could you afford not to?

But is offshoring always the best choice? A growing movement is questioning the knee-jerk assumption that sending manufacturing and service jobs overseas is the only way to stay competitive. One reason is that the costs of offshoring are rising: fuel prices are up (making shipping more expensive) and workers in developing countries are demanding steadily higher wages.

Proponents of reshoring say that factors other than price should also be taken into account. For Simple Wave, a California housewares company, bringing manufacturing to the U.S. from China had numerous benefits: It made the company more agile in adapting to customer needs; it allowed for better quality control; and it brought a huge amount of positive publicity within its industry. Just as importantly, it gave employees a sense of pride. "We wanted to do the right thing, and it felt good to make that decision," says co-founder Richard Stump.

Simple Wave's signature product is the CaliBowl, a bowl with an inward-curving lip that prevents food from spilling out. (a) <u>When the company was founded in 2008, the decision was made early on to manufacture the rubber bowls in China. "We went to China because that's what everyone else did," says Stump.</u>

But producing a precisely designed product far from the company's home base turned out to be harder than the founders expected. The curved lip of the bowls was difficult to mold, and quality control became a concern. There were worries about lead times and inventory. When a chocolate company requested 800 CaliBowls on short notice for its store displays, it became clear that it was time to move toward a just-in-time delivery model. "We needed to be able to adapt more quickly," says Stump. "You lose a lot of opportunities if you can't deliver."

Customer demand was another factor. About half the company's sales are overseas, and those customers wanted to buy CaliBowls that were actually made in California. "Our customers in Korea, Canada and even China wanted U.S.-made products," says Stump. "The Made-in-America brand has real value overseas." Manufacturing domestically also made sense for the green-friendly image of the CaliBowl itself.

From a _____(b)_____ standpoint, the move to the U.S. has clearly paid off. "We've gotten a lot of attention," says Stump. "We've had offers from chefs who want to work with us. We can hardly keep up with the opportunities that are being offered."

문제 1 The best title for the passage is _____.
(1) Offshoring Precedes Reshoring   (2) Going Back to Offshoring
(3) Benefits of 'Reshoring' Companies   (4) Staggering Labor Market Due to Reshoring

문제 2 Which of the following best describes the underlined (a)?
(1) To teach a fish how to swim.   (2) Monkey see, monkey do.
(3) A rags to riches story   (4) Pie in the sky.

문제 3 Which of the following is NOT mentioned as a benefit of bringing companies back to the U.S.?
(1) better quality control   (2) image competitive
(3) lead times   (4) positive publicity

문제 4 Fill in blank (b).
(1) financial   (2) quality control
(3) manufacturing   (4) marketing

[Challenge 9]

All religious principles are founded upon the idea of a God, but it is impossible for men to have true ideas of a being who does not act upon any one of their senses. All our ideas are but pictures of objects which strike us. What can the idea of God represent to us when it is evidently an idea without an object? Is not such an idea as impossible as an effect without a cause? An idea without a prototype, is it anything but a (a) <u>chimera</u>? Some theologians, however, assure us that the idea of God is _____(b)_____, or that men have this idea from the time of their birth. Every principle is a judgment; all judgment is the effect of experience; experience is not acquired but by the exercise of the senses: from which it follows that religious principles are drawn from nothing, and are not innate.

문제 1 Given the context, the underlined (a) means that _____.
(1) the idea of God is a delusion
(2) sensory organs can be illusory
(3) God is omnipotent
(4) God is the First Cause

문제 2 Which of the following is most appropriate for blank (b)?
(1) significant
(2) innate
(3) appropriate
(4) expedient

[Challenge 10]

The idea of the Middle Ages in general, and of the Dark Ages in particular, is specifically European in origin — or rather, Western European. In contrast to Western Europe, Eastern Europe experienced no dark age, and indeed became home to a splendid reminder of ancient Greek and Roman glory in the form of the Byzantine Empire. Nor did the Arabs of the Middle East view the period as a "dark age": beginning in the 600s, Arabia experienced a cultural flowering on a scale seldom equaled in human history. While the ancestors of the English and French were still mostly illiterate peasants living in drafty huts, the Arabs enjoyed a degree of civilization that easily put them on a level with ancient Rome. It is not surprising that when they first encountered Western Europeans during the Crusades beginning in 1095, the Arabs viewed them as ignorant, foul-smelling brutes.

문제 1 Which of the following best represents the main idea of the passage?
(1) The Arabs viewed Europeans as barbarians.
(2) The view of "the Middle Ages" as "dark ages" is mostly Western European in general.
(3) The Arabs of the Middle East enjoyed a splendid glory no less than the ancient Greeks.
(4) Arabia established the highest civilization in history.

문제 2 Which of the following can NOT be inferred from the passage?
(1) The view of the Middle Ages as "Dark Ages" has its own bias.
(2) Eastern Europe and Western Europe developed different courses of history respectively in the same period.
(3) The fact that Arabia experienced cultural exuberance in the same period contradicts the view that the Middle Ages was known as the "Dark Ages" by the Western Europeans.
(4) During the Crusades, the higher culture of the Europe passed onto the Arabs.

★ Fortune favors the brave.

Virgil (70 BC - 19 BC)

운명은 용감한 자의 손을 든다. (Virgil)

[Challenge 1]

　　The plague started in China and made its way west across Asia to the Black Sea by 1347. One theory is that a group of infected Tartars besieged a Genoese outpost on the coast. To harass the trapped townspeople, the Tartars used their catapults to hurl the dead bodies of their comrades over the town walls spreading the epidemic among the Genoese. The panicked inhabitants fled the scene by ship showing up in the ports of northern Italy and bringing the Black Death to Europe.

문제 1　Which of the following is the best title for the passage?
　　　(1) The Origin of the Black Death In Europe
　　　(2) The Cause of the Black Death
　　　(3) How China Affected the Economy of Europe
　　　(4) A Theory to Cure the Black Death

[Challenge 2]

　　Two things in nature impressed me more than any others in my childhood. One was the apparent motion of the moon, when I tried to walk or run away from it. To see it keep an equal pace with me, moving when I moved, stopping when I stopped, sometimes vexed me and more often amused me. The heavens are young when we are, close and companionable; they come down to the earth not more than two miles from where we stand. (a) I tried many experiments with the moon, when it was full, to see if I could not outrun the bright and tricksy traveller. My efforts were vain and only increased my wonder. I never spoke of it nor required an explanation from my elders. (b) Children ask no questions regarding those simple operations of nature which they first observe. (c) They remain deep in their silent consciousness. Such as they do ask are superficial, and are either a passing impulse of a dawning social nature or are impulsed by parents and teachers. (d) I have observed that when they ask these questions they care nothing and remember naught of the answers. What is deepest in them is growing in silence; it is not yet formed into conceptions, and has no language. The difference between the spoken questions of children and their impressions, as yet so undefined, is like that between pictures of the snapshot camera and the astronomer's plates which, for hours, gather and develop the figure of some distant, unseen star.

문제 1 Which of the following can NOT be true?
(1) The motion of the moon was actually in the mind of an observer.
(2) The child thought the moon was trying to copy whatever he did.
(3) Unsuccessful attempts of the child to outrun the moon discouraged his curiosity.
(4) The child kept the secret of his experience to himself.

문제 2 If required, at which letter should the paragraph be divided?
(1) (a)   (2) (b)
(3) (c)   (4) (d)

문제 3 Which of the following comes after this paragraph?
(1) Spoken questions of children   (2) Other childish observations
(3) Impressions on the Moon   (4) Observation of Stars

[Challenge 3]

There exists a natural, although, in point of number, a very unequal division amongst machines: they may be classed as; first, those which are employed to produce power, and as, secondly, those which are intended merely to transmit force and execute work. The first of these divisions is of great importance, and is very limited in the variety of its species, although some of those species consist of numerous individuals. Of that class of mechanical agents by which motion is transmitted it has been demonstrated, that no power is gained by their use, however combined. Whatever force is applied at one point can only be exerted at some other, diminished by friction and (a) <u>other incidental causes</u>; and it has been further proved, that whatever is gained in the rapidity of execution is compensated by the necessity of exerting additional force.

문제 1　According to the passage, which of the following is neither stated nor implied?
　　(1) There exists a division of the objects of machinery.
　　(2) During the process of transmitting force by the second type of machine there is some inevitable loss of energy.
　　(3) The machine that produces force can not perform work.
　　(4) The rapidity of execution affects the amount of energy loss caused by friction.

문제 2　Which of the following does NOT belong to the 'second' kind of machine in the passage?
　　(1) lever　　　　　　　　(2) pulley
　　(3) wedge　　　　　　　 (4) windmill

문제 3　Which of the following does NOT belong to the underlined (a)?
　　(1) abrasion　　　　　　 (2) lubrication
　　(3) wear and tear　　　　(4) resistance

[Challenge 4]

　　Let me give an illustration of the so-called "reforms" that are recklessly urged upon us to-day and that are to be found in operation here and there throughout the country. I refer to the matter of street franchises. Now it may be true, it probably is true, that in many cases these franchises have become of great value and that they ought not to be granted without adequate return. But would it not be just to remember that when these franchises were originally granted they provided a service that was absolutely essential to the growth of the community and that those who obtained the franchises faced a serious risk to their capital and practically threw in their lot with the prospective welfare of the city? It is hard to realize how serious that risk sometimes was and how problematical were the returns. The shareholders in these street traction corporations are spread over the population and every class of the population is represented in them. They invested their money in good faith at a time when no question had ever been raised as to the propriety of these franchises and at a time when these franchises were considered to be for the public good and indubitably were for the public good. And I will ask you if it is honest to use all the machinery of the government, all the artifices of the politician to depreciate the value of those franchises, to threaten their holders with confiscation, to hamper and harass them by all the ways that are open to a democratically governed people? I say unhesitatingly that it is dishonest to do these things, and I will go so far as to say — believing as I do in the good faith of the great majority — that most of those who noisily advocate such measures would be ashamed to do so if they would but face the facts and understand what it is that they are actually doing and the wrong that they are inflicting upon innocent men and women. If mistakes have been made in granting franchises, then take care to avoid such mistakes in the future, but do not enter into a bargain that seemed advantageous to yourselves and then repudiate it when you find that it is not so advantageous as you thought.

문제 1 What is the problem that the author is talking about in the passage?
(1) All the machinery of the government
(2) Repealing street franchises once granted
(3) Estimating the returns of street franchises
(4) Granting street franchises

문제 2 According to the passage, which of the following best represents the attitude of the government toward the street franchise?
(1) After rain comes fair weather.
(2) A lie travels round the world while truth is putting her boots on.
(3) Accidents will happen in the best regulated families.
(4) When needed, it's grateful, but once unneedful, it's useless and abandoned.

[Challenge 5]

If, as Matthew Arnold says, conduct is (a) <u>three-fourths</u> of life, then a careful inquiry into the laws of conduct is indispensable to the proper interpretation of the meaning and purpose of life. Conduct of itself, however, is merely the outward expression of character; and character again has its roots in personality; so that if we are to form a just conception of life, we have to examine the forces which shape __(b)__ and raise it to its highest power and efficiency. In estimating the value of man all the facts of consciousness and experience must be considered. Hence no adequate account of the end of life can be given without regard to that which must be the most stupendous fact of history — the fact of Christ.

문제 1 What can be inferred from the underlined (a)?
(1) Conduct consists of four components.
(2) Conduct needs no small amount of attention.
(3) Conduct can be calculated with numbers.
(4) Conduct has three layers of meaning.

문제 2 Fill in blank (b).
(1) character
(2) conduct
(3) value
(4) personality

[Challenge 6]

The chief difficulty in acquiring this happy and cheerful dignity comes from the desire to be admired, which is a tendency inborn in the great majority of women. It stands in the way of their greatest strength and usefulness, because it takes away their real independence and keeps them thinking about themselves instead of about others. It is a form of bondage which makes them vain and self-conscious and renders impossible the truest and happiest companionship between men and women friends.

문제 1 According to the passage, which of the following is the main obstacle that makes impossible the true friendship between men and women?
(1) Propensity to be admired from others
(2) Tendency to gain more power than men
(3) Disposition to obtain real independence
(4) Propensity to create a rift between men and women

[Challenge 7]

Despite the fact of the long-established and almost universal use of lime, it can scarcely be said that we as yet clearly understand the exact nature of its action. Much light, however, has been thrown of late years on the subject by the great advance which has been made in our knowledge of agricultural chemistry. _____(a)_____ , there are many points connected with the action of lime on the soil which are still obscure. Perhaps one reason for the conflicting ideas prevalent with regard to the value of this substance in agriculture is to be found in the fact that it acts in such a number of different ways, and that the nature of the changes it gives rise to in the soil is most complicated. The experience of agriculturists with lime in one part of the country often seems contradictory to the experience of those in other parts of the country. Its action on different soils is very dissimilar. For these reasons, therefore, the discussion of the value of lime as a manure is by no means an easy one.

문제 1 Which of the following is the topic of the passage?
(1) Effects of Lime on the Soil
(2) Perplexing Nature of Lime
(3) Development of the Soil
(4) Soil and Chemical Fertilizer

문제 2 Fill in blank (a).
(1) Nevertheless
(2) Therefore
(3) In short
(4) In fact

문제 3 According to the passage, Lime's action on different soils _____.
(1) is complicated
(2) proves effective
(3) is consistent
(4) varies to a great extent

[Challenge 8]

An emission cap and permit trading system is a quantity instrument because it fixes the overall emission level (quantity) and allows the price to vary. Uncertainty in future supply and demand conditions (market volatility) coupled with a fixed number of pollution credits creates an uncertainty in the future price of pollution credits, and the industry must accordingly bear the cost of adapting to these volatile market conditions. The burden of a volatile market thus lies with the industry rather than the controlling agency, which is generally more efficient. However, under volatile market conditions, the ability of the controlling agency to alter the caps will translate into an ability to pick "winners and losers" and thus presents an opportunity for corruption. In contrast, an emission tax is a price instrument because it fixes the price while the emission level is allowed to vary according to economic activity. A major ___(a)___ of an emission tax is that the environmental outcome (e.g. a limit on the amount of emissions) is not guaranteed. On one hand, a tax will remove capital from the industry, suppressing possibly useful economic activity, but conversely, the polluter will not need to hedge as much against future uncertainty since the amount of tax will track with profits. The burden of a volatile market will be borne by the controlling (taxing) agency rather than the industry itself, which is generally less efficient. An advantage is that, given a uniform tax rate and a volatile market, the taxing entity will not be in a position to pick "winners and losers." A third option, known as a safety valve, is a hybrid of the price and quantity instruments. The system is essentially an emission cap and permit trading system but the maximum (or minimum) permit price is capped. Emitters have the choice of either obtaining permits in the marketplace or purchasing them from the government at a specified trigger price. (b) The system is sometimes recommended as a way of overcoming the fundamental disadvantages of both systems by giving governments the flexibility to adjust the system as new information comes to light. It can be shown that by setting the trigger price high enough, or the number of permits low enough, the safety valve can be used to mimic either a pure quantity or pure price mechanism.

문제 1 Which of the following is NOT true of the passage?
(1) With the system of an emission tax the opportunity for corruption will be less.
(2) An emission tax can be used as an alternative to increase government revenues.
(3) The burden of market volatility is greater with the industry than with the government in an emission cap and permit trading system.
(4) The system of safety valve gives more flexibility to the industry than to the government in terms of the market volatility.

문제 2 Choose one that is most appropriate for blank (a).
(1) drawback   (2) deadlock
(3) standoff   (4) obstacle

문제 3 Which of the following is CORRECT about the underlined (b)?
(1) The industry itself sets the price of the permits by interacting with each other.
(2) Its system is completely based on the market mechanism.
(3) Within the system, the industry is in greater danger than in a cap and trade system as market volatility is not guaranteed.
(4) The government can rapidly react to the economic changes within the system.

[Challenge 9]

In most cases, cholera can be successfully treated with oral rehydration therapy (ORT), which is highly effective, safe, and simple to administer. Rice-based solutions are preferred to glucosebased ones due to greater efficacy. In severe cases with significant dehydration, intravenous rehydration may be necessary. Ringer's lactate is the preferred solution. Large volumes and continued replacement until diarrhea has subsided may be needed. Ten percent of a person's body weight in fluid may need to be given in the first two to four hours. If commercially produced oral rehydration solutions are too expensive or difficult to obtain, solutions can be made. One such recipe calls for 1 liter of boiled water, 1 teaspoon of salt, 8 teaspoons of sugar, and added mashed banana for potassium and to improve taste.

문제 1 Which of the following is the best title for the passage?
(1) How to Make Rehydration Solutions
(2) Treatment of Cholera
(3) Symptoms of Cholera
(4) Why Ringer's Lactate is Most Preferred

[Challenge 10]

With regard to the question whether inspiration should take place through the mouth or through the nostrils, I must enter my most decided protest against making it a practice to inhale through the mouth. There are, of course, (a) <u>occasions</u> when this is unavoidable. But complete inflation, or, "full breath," is not the work of a moment; it takes time, and must be done gradually, steadily, and without the slightest interruption. This should always be done through the nostrils. The mouth was never intended for breathing, while the nose is specially and admirably adapted for this purpose. Not only can the lungs be well and quickly filled through this channel, but it is so cunningly devised that it acts at the same time as a "respirator," both _____(b)_____ the air before it touches the more delicate parts of the vocal organ. On the other hand, when inhaled through the mouth, the air carries with it, sometimes right into the voicebox, dust and other impurities, and its temperature is not materially altered. The consequence is that the throat and voice-box, when heated by singing or talking, or by hot rooms, are often exposed to cold, raw, and foggy winter air, and serious derangements of the respiratory organs are the natural consequence. If, moreover, this pernicious habit of breathing be once contracted, we shall soon also sleep with open mouths, thus parching our throats, and sowing the seeds of many a serious disorder.

문제 1 Which of the following is the best title of the passage?
(1) Two sides of Mouth-Breathing
(2) Types of Breathing
(3) Which is Better, through Mouth or Nose?
(4) Workings of Mouth-Breathing

문제 2 Which of the following can be an occasion such as the underlined (a)?
(1) A person resuscitates his companion who is undergoing a heart attack.
(2) A person who has a stage fright has butterflies in his stomach.
(3) A singer has rapidly to take what is called a "half breath."
(4) A yogi takes a deep breath before he does his routines.

문제 3 Choose one that is most appropriate for blank (b).
(1) clarifying and cooling
(2) richening and fortifying
(3) purifying and warming
(4) disinfecting and sustaining

★ Having once decided to achieve a certain task, achieve it at all costs of tedium and distaste. The gain in self-confidence of having accomplished a tiresome labor is immense.

Arnold Bennett

일단 어떤 일을 성취하기로 마음을 먹었으면, 아무리 지루하고, 싫더라도 그것을 감수하고 성취해라, 힘든 노동을 성취한 자신감에서 얻는 것은 엄청나다. (Arnold Bennett)

[Challenge 1]

(a) Making a study schedule is one important step in becoming a successful student in college. Students should schedule one hour of study time for every one hour of class time. (b) At exam time, more study time may be necessary. Also, students must study in an appropriate place. It is important to study in a quiet place away from the distraction of other people and such things as the television and the radio. Students should find a comfortable place with plenty of space for all the necessary study supplies. (c) Then, students need to study the information in small amounts. It is a good idea to learn the required concepts slowly and thoroughly instead of trying to learn everything on the evening before the exam. (d) Students who want to be successful in college should remember these three helpful study strategies.

문제 1 Which of the following is the topic sentence of the passage?
(1) (a)   (2) (b)
(3) (c)   (4) (d)

[Challenge 2]

With modern appliances, within the means of the average farmer, the generation of electricity, with its unique conveniences, becomes automatic, provided some dependable source of power is to be had — such as a water wheel, gasoline (or other form of internal combustion) engine, or the ordinary windmill. The water wheel is the ideal prime mover for the dynamo in isolated plants. Since water-power is running to waste on tens of thousands of our farms throughout the country, much attention is needed to this. The tiny unconsidered brook that waters the farm pasture frequently possesses power enough to supply the farmstead with clean, cool, safe light in place of the dangerous, inconvenient oil lamp; a small stream capable of developing from twenty-five to fifty horsepower will supply a farmer (at practically no expense beyond the original cost of installation) not only with light, but with power for even the heavier farm operations, as threshing; and in addition will do the washing, ironing, and cooking, and at the same time keep the house warm in the coldest weather. Less than one horsepower of energy will light the farmstead; less than five horsepower of energy will provide light and small power, and take the drudgery out of the kitchen.

문제 1 Which of the following is the best title of the passage?
(1) Difficulty of Generating Electricity in Farmstead
(2) Difference Between Water Power and Horsepower
(3) The Power of Water
(4) Alternatives to Energy in the Farmstead

문제 2 Which of the following is NOT true of the passage?
(1) In the farmstead, the generation of electricity through water has already become automatic throughout the nation.
(2) The tiny unconsidered brook is well enough to provide the farm with necessary light.
(3) The prime mover for the dynamo is water-power in secluded plants.
(4) A small stream can be equivalent to the power of twenty-five to fifty horsepower.

[Challenge 3]

The commerce of the United States is essential, ____(a)____ , at least to their comfort, their growth, prosperity, and happiness. The genius, character, and habits of the people are highly commercial. Their cities have been formed and exist upon commerce. Our agriculture, fisheries, arts, and manufactures are connected with and depend upon it. ____(b)____ , commerce has made this country what it is, and it can not be destroyed or neglected without involving the people in poverty and distress. Great numbers are directly and solely supported by navigation. The faith of society is pledged for the preservation of the rights of commercial and sea faring no less than of the other citizens. Under this view of our affairs, I should hold myself guilty of a neglect of duty if I forbore to recommend that we should make every exertion to protect our commerce and to place our country in a suitable posture of defense as the only sure means of preserving both.

문제 1 Which can NOT be inferred from the passage?
(1) The author feels responsible for taking every action to protect the commerce of the United States
(2) The author thinks the rights of commercial faring is important enough to surpass those of citizens.
(3) Ignoring the importance of the commerce may put the country in poverty.
(4) The character of the Americans is mercantile.

문제 2 Fill in blank (a).
(1) if not to their national defense
(2) if not to their existence
(3) if not to their political purpose
(4) if not to their financial status

문제 3 Fill in blank (b).
(1) In short
(2) Still
(3) Nevertheless
(4) For instance

[Challenge 4]

When first we meet Hannah, the wondrously mopey mid-20s heroine of HBO's new hit series "Girls," she seems to have more strikes against her than a bowling alley at Fenway Park. Her parents have cut off her monthly stipend. Her literary-magazine boss refuses to turn her unpaid internship into a real job. She lives in New York City. She majored in English.

Yet offsetting all those slings and risk factors is a powerful defense system: girlfriends. Hannah has a tight-knit network of three female confederates, one best friend and two sturdy runners-up; and while none of the girl-women can offer much material support, no spare bedroom in a rent-controlled apartment, they are each other's emotional tourniquets. While her titular characters may all date men, female friendship is "the true romance of the show."

As in urban jungles, so too in jungle jungles. Researchers have lately gathered abundant evidence that female friendship is one of nature's preferred narrative tools. In animals as diverse as African elephants and barnyard mice, blue monkeys of Kenya and feral horses of New Zealand, affiliative, longlasting and mutually beneficial relationships between females turn out to be the basic unit of social life, the force that not only binds existing groups together but explains why the animals' ancestors bothered _____ in the first place.

Scientists are moving beyond the observational stage — watching as a couple of female monkeys groom each other into a state of hedonic near-liquefaction — to quantifying the benefits of that well-groomed friendship to both picking partners. Researchers have discovered that female chacma baboons with strong sororal bonds have lower levels of stress hormones, live significantly longer and rear a greater number of offspring to independence than do their less socialized peers.

Similarly, wild mares with female friends are harassed less often by stallions and have more surviving foals than do mares that lack social ties. Female mice allowed to choose a friend as a nesting partner will bear more pups than females forced to share straw space with a mouse they dislike. Researchers have determined that a female baboon with a small but devoted core of grooming companions will be less prone to jagged spikes of the stress hormone cortisol than a female who casts her social net wide but not deep.

문제 1 The best title for the passage is _____.
(1) Jungles Among Jungles
(2) Nature's Defense System: The Spirit of Sisterhood
(3) Differences between Female and Male Friendships
(4) Types of Friendship between Female Animals

문제 2 Which of the following is CORRECT about the passage?
(1) The benefits from having a tight female relationship only apply to animals.
(B) Less socialized people can become more social by developing a tight-knit friendship with others.
(C) Those who share intimate friendships with chums tend to be less stressed out than those who don't.
(D) The number of friends is more important than the quality of the friendship.

문제 3 Fill in the blank to the passage.
(1) being divided   (2) getting tightened up
(3) getting scattered   (4) going herd

문제 4 Which of the following is most likely to be followed immediately after the above passage?
(1) benefits of having more friends
(2) ideal buddy count
(3) tendency of girls to get together
(4) characteristics of men's friendship

[Challenge 5]

Of all the influences that through these wandering and desolate ages had sustained humanity and helped it onward, the mightiest has been left to speak of last. It was Christianity, a Christianity which had by now taken definite form as the Roman Catholic Church. (a) Strongest of all the institutions bequeathed by the ancient empire to her conquerors was this Church. (b) Indeed, it has been said that Rome had influenced Christianity quite as much as Christianity did Rome. (c) They lent the weight of law to what had been but individual belief and impulse. (d) Thus the Church grew hard and strong.

In the same manner that the early emperors had ordered the persecution of Christianity, so the later ones ordered the persecution of heathendom, nor had the Church grown civilized or Christian enough to oppose this method of conversion. Luckily for all parties, however, (e) the heathen were scarcely sufficiently enthusiastic to insist on martyrdom, and so the persecuting spirit which man ultimately imparted to even the purest of religions remained latent.

문제 1 Which of the following is NOT true of the passage?
(1) There was a time when Christianity went through persecution.
(2) Christianity is one of the mightiest influences on humanity.
(3) Rome and Christianity had a mutual influence on each other.
(4) Christianity has never persecuted others because of the philanthropic teachings of Jesus.

문제 2 In the above passage, where does the sentence below in the box best fit?

> The legal-minded Romans insisted on the laying out of exact doctrines and creeds, on the building of a definite organization, a priesthood, a hierarchy.

(1) (a)   (2) (b)   (3) (c)   (4) (d)

문제 3 Which of the following can be inferred from the underlined (e)?
(1) Pagans thought of martyrdom as the ultimate way to show their faithfulness.
(2) The spirit of Christianity changed when it was under severe persecution.
(3) Fortunately, there were no human massacres of pagans.
(4) Pagans all denied the conversion to Christianity.

[Challenge 6]

It is curious that knowing so much of Thomas Paine, we also know so little of him. For every friend, he had an enemy; he was loved greatly and hated violently, praised and slandered, mocked and revered. The only emotion he failed to provoke was ___(a)___ . He was a volatile, angry, and outspoken man. When he believed something, he was incapable of hiding such belief or even tempering it. He worshipped reason and logic, and despised the absence of these qualities in others; and he himself loved and hated with the same intensity he provoked in others

문제 1 Which of the following is NOT true about Thomas Paine?
(1) He was a mysterious person.
(2) He seems to have had two opposite personalities.
(3) He was so emotional that he lacked logical thinking.
(4) He had a firm faith in what he believed.

문제 2 Fill in blank (a).
(1) courtesy   (2) indifference
(3) animosity   (4) rancor

[Challenge 7]

What then is this logical connection between the physical and the mental? This question can best be answered by reflecting, for example, on how a cartoonist might go about showing that a particular table was angry or in pain. Now as indicated above, it is impossible to attach literal meaning to the assertion that a given inanimate object is angry or in pain, but clearly a certain imaginative latitude may be allowed for specific purposes, and a cartoonist might conceivably want to picture a table as being angry for humorous reasons. What is significant in this connection, however, is the fact that to achieve this effect, the cartoonist must picture the table as having human features—the pictured table will appear angry to us only to the extent to which it possesses the natural human expression of anger; the concept of anger can find purchase in relation to the table only if it is represented as possessing something like a human form.

문제 1 According to the passage, how can an object function as something that has 'emotions'?
(1) by ascribing human features to the object
(2) by reflecting on the nature of the object
(3) by considering the object to be physically-bound
(4) by abstracting human characteristics from the object

[Challenge 8]

"Big Brother Is Watching You" was the pervasive punch-line in British writer George Orwell's classic novel "1984." _____(a)_____. Revelations that Rupert Murdoch's News International Corp. for years has conducted massive hacking into British cell phone information are truly shocking. Alleged targets include cell phones of a murdered young girl and relatives of soldiers killed in action. Britain's political parties have united in Parliament, an unusual move, to condemn the company. The scandal includes allegations of police payoffs. Murdoch's political influence in Britain has been enormous. Politicians across the spectrum fear his power to embarrass or endorse, and have assiduously courted his favor. Orwell, one of the greatest writers of the 20th century, was a committed socialist. Unlike many on the left, however, he had personal involvement with working people, because he was one. He stressed egalitarianism, while warning about the dangers of concentrated power in government as well as corporations. The Murdoch snooping scandal is particularly grotesque, and may bring down that media empire. However, guarding individual freedom, including privacy, from intrusive power structures inevitably is a challenge.

문제 1 1 Fill in blank (a).
  (1) The writer turned out to be wrong about his forecast about the future
  (2) Now we know Big Brother is listening too
  (3) The punch line has become "powerless" in an information age
  (4) The novel has recently been bombarded with condemnations

문제 2 What can be inferred from the passage?
  (1) The British government assumes the attitude of an on-looker about the scandal.
  (B) For now, it seems that Murdoch could get away with deserve condemnation, and prosecution.
  (C) Guarding individual freedom is almost impossible, if not at all, even with the extensive and consistent regulation of government toward institutional intruders.
  (D) George Orwell was a man of foresight good enough to see even big companies could get engaged in the snooping on personal information.

[Challenge 9]

In the Tungus creation myth there was once only water everywhere. Buga, the central deity, issued forth the fire against this water. Following a long struggle much of the water was consumed and thus land emerged. Then Buga created the light and separated it from darkness, and descended to the newly created land. There (a) he confronted Buninka, the devil, and a dispute arose between them over who had created the world. Buninka was spiteful and tried to injure Buga's creation. (b) He broke Buga's twelve-stringed lyre, and Buga angrily challenged Buninka to make a fir-tree and raise it to stand fast and firm in the middle of the sea. Buga agreed (c) he would bow to Buninka's powers if he could do so, but if he failed then Buga would subject himself to the same challenge. If Buga were then to succeed, Buninka must concede to Buga that (d) he was the most powerful creator. Buninka agreed to the challenge and commanded a fir-tree to rise from the sea. The tree grew, but it was weak and bobbed to and fro. Buga then created a second tree but it thrived and grew into a stately tree. Buninka was forced to acknowledge Buga's greater power and bowed in homage. Buga put his hand to Buninka's head and turned it to iron. This caused so much pain in Buninka that he begged Buga for release, and Buga relented-Buninka was then allowed to roam the earth. Buga collected materials to make mankind. From the east he gathered iron; from the south fire; the west, water; and from the north, earth. From the earth he made flesh and bone; from the iron he made heart; from the water he made blood; and from the fire he gave them vitality, and thus he made two beings, a man and a woman. Buninka was strictly forbidden to do mankind any injury, but after they had increased in numbers, he wanted to claim half as his own. Buga refused to give him any of the living. But Buninka was granted the vicious men and women after they had died, Buga keeping the virtuous to himself. So after death, the evil join Buninka in hell, which is in the center of the earth, where they are punished.

문제 1 Which of the following is the best title for the passage?
(1) The Creation Myth of Tungus
(2) Characteristics of the Tungus Myth
(3) How Buninka Submitted Himself to Buga
(4) Different Gods of the World

문제 2 Which of the following is CORRECT from the passage?
(1) Buga and Buninka had a dispute over the domination of the world when they first met.
(2) When Buga created land through the fire against the water, there was no one on the entire world.
(3) Buga took different materials to make each part of human bodies.
(4) Buninka was in charge of all the dead people.

문제 3 Which of the following does not refer to the same entity?
(1) (a)   (2) (b)   (3) (c)   (4) (d)

[Challenge 10]

It was early spring in 1777 before John Jay, withdrawing to the country, began the work of drafting a constitution. His retirement recalls Cowper's sigh for

"... a lodge in some vast wilderness,
Some boundless contiguity of shade,
Where rumours of (a) oppression and deceit,
Of unsuccessful and successful war,
Might never reach me more."

Too much and too little credit has been given Jay for his part in the work. One writer says he "entered an almost unexplored field." _____(b)_____ , John Adams wrote Jefferson that Jay's "model and foundation" was his own letter to George Wythe of Virginia. Neither is true. The field was not unexplored, nor did John Adams' letter contain a suggestion of anything not already in existence, except the election of a Council of Appointment, with whose consent the governor should appoint all officers. His plan of letting the people elect a governor came later. "We have a government to form, you know," wrote Jay, "and God knows what it will resemble. Our politicians, like some guests at a feast, are perplexed and undetermined (c) which dish to prefer;" but Jay evidently preferred the old home dishes, and it is interesting to note how easily he adapted the laws and customs of the provincial government to the needs of an independent State.

문제 1 Which of the following can NOT be inferred from the passage?
(1) On the one hand, John Jay has not been appreciated properly for his role in drafting a constitution.
(2) John Jay seemed to be at a loss for which laws and customs to follow at first.
(3) John Jay was in favor of the concept of popular sovereignty.
(4) John Jay was a radical liberalist from the beginning.

문제 2 According to the context, what kind of "oppression and deceit" does the underlined (a) imply?
(1) theological   (2) economical   (3) social   (4) political

문제 3 Which of the following best fills in blank (b)?
(1) On the other hand   (2) Thereafter   (3) In fact   (4) And

문제 4 According to the passage, what does the word "dish" in the underlined (c) mean?
(1) laws and customs   (2) governors
(3) states   (4) independence

Day 5

★ Getting ahead in a difficult profession requires avid faith in yourself. That is why some people with mediocre talent, but with great inner drive, go much further than people with vastly superior talent.

Sophia Loren

어려운 직업에서 앞서 가는 것은 자신에 대한 열렬한 믿음을 요구한다. 그렇기에 재능은 별로이나 내면의 강한 추진력으로 훨씬 뛰어난 재능을 가진 사람보다 훨씬 더 나아갈 수 있는 것이다. (Sophia Loren)

[Challenge 1]

Since the child is immature in the use of all his capacities, it is the first business of education to give such training as will bring them to full development. This training may be physical, mental, or moral. Since the child is ignorant, it is the business of education to communicate to it the experience of the race. This is properly the work of teaching. Considered in this light, the school is _____(a)_____ , since we continue throughout our lives to acquire experience. The first object of teaching, then, is to stimulate in the pupil the love of learning, and to form in him habits and ideals of independent study. These two, the cultivation of capacities and the transmission of experience, together make up the teacher's work. All organizing and governing are subsidiary of this twofold aim. The result to be sought is a full-grown physical, intellectual, and moral manhood, with such resources as are necessary to make life useful and happy and as will enable the individual to go on learning from all the activities of life.

문제 1 Which of the following is the topic sentence of the passage?
    (1) The Object of Education
    (2) Being a Good Teacher
    (3) The Role of the School
    (4) Life-long Learning

문제 2 Fill in blank (a).
    (1) where the child spends most of the time
    (2) a place where most of the teaching in one's life is carried on
    (3) not as important as it is considered to be
    (4) but one of the agencies of education

[Challenge 2]

Here is a man who is wretchedly poor. He is extremely anxious that his surroundings and home comforts should be improved, yet all the time he shirks his work, and considers he is justified in trying to deceive his employer on the ground of the insufficiency of his wages. (a) Such a man does not understand the simplest rudiments of those principles which are the basis of true prosperity, and is not only totally unfitted to rise out of his wretchedness, but is actually attracting to himself a still deeper wretchedness by dwelling in, and acting out, indolent, deceptive, and unmanly thoughts. (b) Here is a rich man who is the victim of a painful and persistent disease as the result of gluttony. (c) He is willing to give large sums of money to get rid of it, but he will not sacrifice his gluttonous desires. (d) He wants to gratify his taste for rich and unnatural viands and have his health as well. Such a man is totally unfit to have health, because he has not yet learned the first principles of a healthy life.

* viands 음식

문제 1   When the passage is divided into two, where does the second paragraph begin?
(1) (a)   (2) (b)
(3) (c)   (4) (d)

문제 2   Which of the following is NOT true of the person in the first paragraph?
(1) He is negligent in his duties at work.
(2) He thinks he should get a raise because of his hard work.
(3) He does not understand that true prosperity comes from being industrious.
(4) He is ignorant that his indolent thought is actually the source of his misery.

문제 3   Which of the following would be the most reasonable advice to the man in the second paragraph?
(1) Human beings never get satisfied.   (2) Money and health come and go.
(3) Voracity and health do not go hand in hand.   (4) What is done can not be undone.

[Challenge 3]

Proxemics is the study of how people use and perceive the physical space around them. The space between the sender and the receiver of a message influences the way the message is interpreted. The perception and use of space varies significantly across cultures and different settings within cultures. Space in nonverbal communication may be divided into four main categories: intimate, social, personal, and public space. The distance between communicators will also depend on sex, status, and social role. Proxemics was first developed by Edward T. Hall during the 1950s and 60s. Hall's studies were inspired by earlier studies of how animals demonstrate territoriality. The term territoriality is still used in the study of proxemics to explain human behavior regarding personal space. Hargie & Dickson identify 4 such territories:

1. Primary territory: this refers to an area that is associated with someone who has exclusive use of it. (a) For example, a state-run park that people cannot enter without tickets.
2. Secondary territory: unlike the previous type, there is no "right" to occupancy, but people may still feel some degree of ownership of a particular space. (b) For example, someone may sit in the same seat on a train every day and feel (e) <u>aggrieved</u> if someone else sits there.
3. Public territory: this refers to an area that is available to all, but only for a set period, such as a parking space or a seat in a library. Although people have only a limited claim over that space, they often exceed that claim. (c) For example, it was found that people take longer to leave a parking space when someone is waiting to take that space.
4. Interaction territory: this is space created by others when they are interacting. (d) For example, when a group is talking to each other on a footpath, others will walk around the group rather than disturb it.

문제 1   Which of the following is the topic of the above passage?
(1) Four Types of Territory
(2) Proxemics
(3) Effects of Different Cultures on Space
(4) Importance of Personal Space

문제 2   Which of the following is not an appropriate example to each category identified by Hargie & Dickson?
(1) (a)   (2) (b)   (3) (c)   (4) (d)

문제 3   Choose one that is closest in meaning to the underlined (e).
(1) trespassed upon
(2) distressed
(3) lamented over
(4) vexed

[Challenge 4]

Let us consider what those who teach about technology could gain from the philosophy of technology. There are at least four reasons for technology educators to get acquainted with this discipline. The philosophy of technology can be a source of inspiration for determining the content of a curriculum, it can yield insights into how to construct teaching and learning situations, it can provide a conceptual basis and proper understanding of technology which can help technology educators respond to unforeseen situations while teaching about technology, it can help to position the teaching of technology among other subjects, and it can help identify the research agenda for educational research in technology education.

문제 1   Which of the following is the topic of the passage?
(1) Integrating Technology into the School Curriculum
(2) How to Discipline Students
(3) Why We Need Philosophy of Technology
(4) Four Reasons to Learn Technology

[Challenge 5]

A neuron is a special type of cell that is found in the bodies of most animals (all members of the group Eumetazoa, to be precise — this excludes only sponges and a few other very simple animals). The features that define a neuron are electrical excitability and the presence of synapses, which are complex membrane junctions used to transmit signals to other cells. The body's neurons, plus the glial cells that give them structural and metabolic support, together constitute the nervous system. In vertebrates, the majority of neurons belong to the central nervous system, but some reside in peripheral ganglia, and many sensory neurons are situated in sensory organs such as the retina and cochlea.

문제 1   Which of the following is the topic of the passage?
(1) The Overview of the Neuron
(2) The Function of the Neuron
(3) Different Looks of the Neuron in Animals
(4) Types of the Neuron

문제 2   Which of the following is neither stated nor impiled?
(1) Synapses are neuronal junctions which relay signals to other cells.
(2) A neuron is a chemical substance that can be found in most animals.
(3) Sponges do not have neurons.
(4) Neurons are positioned in different parts of the body according to their functions.

[Challenge 6]

For Confucius, what characterized superior rulership was the possession of "virtue." Conceived of as a kind of moral power that allows one to win a following without recourse to physical force, such "virtue" also enabled the ruler to maintain good order in his state without troubling himself and by relying on loyal and effective deputies. Confucius claimed that, "He who governs by means of his virtue is, to use an analogy, like the pole-star: it remains in its place while all the lesser stars do homage to it." (Lunyu 2.1) The way to maintain and cultivate such royal "virtue" was through the practice and enactment of "rituals" — the ceremonies that defined and punctuated the lives of the ancient Chinese aristocracy. In an influential study, Herbert Fingarette argues that the performance of various ceremonies, when done correctly and sincerely, involves a "magical" quality that underlies the efficacy of royal "virtue" in accomplishing the aims of the ruler.

문제 1 From what is stated or implied, which of the following is NOT correct?
(1) Confucius denies the very idea of hierarchical organization in forming the government.
(2) Virtue can be cultivated through the practice of rituals.
(3) Properly performed rituals have a function of maintaining social order.
(4) People pay great trust to their ruler when he is vested with virtue.

[Challenge 7]

Sweden, since 1991 has banned all advertising during children's prime time due to findings that children under 10 are incapable of telling the difference between a commercial and a program, and cannot understand the purpose of a commercial until the age of 12. In the US, research from the American Psychological Association (APA) shows that children under the age of eight are unable to critically comprehend televised advertising messages and are prone to accept advertiser messages as truthful, accurate and unbiased. This can lead to unhealthy eating habits as evidenced by today's youth obesity epidemic. For these reasons, a task force of the American Psychological Association (APA) is recommending that advertising targeting children under the age of eight be restricted.

The research on children's commercial recall and product preferences confirms that advertising does typically get young consumers to buy their products. Findings show that children recall content from the ads to which they've been exposed and preference for a product has been shown to occur with as little as a single commercial exposure and strengthened with repeated exposures. _____(a)_____ , these product preferences can affect children's product purchase requests, which can put pressure on parents' purchasing decisions and instigate parent-child conflicts when parents deny their children's requests. There are concerns regarding certain commercial campaigns primarily targeting adults that pose risks for child-viewers. For example, beer ads are commonly shown during sports events and seen by millions of children, creating both brand familiarity and more positive attitudes toward drinking in children as young as 9-10 years of age. Another area of sensitive advertising content involves commercials for violent media products such as motion pictures and video games. Such ads contribute to a violent media culture which increases the likelihood of youngsters' aggressive behavior and desensitizes children to real-world violence.

문제 1   Which of the phrases best represents the theme of the passage?
　　　(1) A Huge Industry Recently Targeting Children's Eating Habit
　　　(2) Violence Creeping into the Family
　　　(3) Advertising to Children Considered Harmful
　　　(4) Effects of TV on Children under 10

문제 2   Which of the following is CORRECT about the passage?
　　　(1) Children under 8 uncritically take things which they are exposed to on TV.
　　　(2) Sweden used to ban all the advertisements targeting Children under the age of 10.
　　　(3) In the U.S advertising targeting children under the age of eight is strictly restricted now.
　　　(4) TV commercials are the main culprit for today's youth obesity epidemic.

문제 3   According to the passage, one time exposure to harmful Commercials _____.
　　　(1) has little impact on children but it strengthens as the number of exposures increases.
　　　(2) is still powerful as it affects children's preference for a certain product
　　　(3) is equivalent to the power of repeated exposure
　　　(4) has no effect on children's preference for a certain product

문제 4   Fill in the blank (a).
　　　(1) In fact　　　　　　　　　　(2) On the other hand
　　　(3) Furthermore　　　　　　　 (4) Nonetheless

[Challenge 8]

I led the horse to the stable, when a fresh perplexity arose. I removed the harness without difficulty; but, after many strenuous attempts, I could not remove the collar. In despair, I called for assistance, when aid soon drew near. Mr. Wordsworth brought his ingenuity into exercise; but, after several unsuccessful efforts, he relinquished the achievement, as a thing altogether impracticable. Mr. Coleridge now tried his hand, but showed no more grooming skill than his predecessors; for, after twisting the poor horse's neck almost to strangulation and the great danger of his eyes, he gave up the useless task, pronouncing that the horse's head must have grown since the collar was put on; for he said 'it was a downright impossibility for such a huge head to pass through so narrow a collar!' Just at this instant, a servant-girl came near, and, understanding the cause of our (a) <u>consternation</u>, 'La! master,' said she, 'you don't go about the work in the right way. You should do like this,' when, turning the collar completely upside down, she slipped it off in a moment, to our great humiliation and wonderment, each satisfied afresh that there were heights of knowledge in the world to which we had not yet attained.

문제 1 Which of the following best presents the title for the above passage?
(1) Admiration of Simplicity
(2) A Girl's Baffled Face
(3) Three Men in a Puzzle
(4) Training of a Horse

문제 2 Which of the following best describes the situation (a)?
(1) Where a huge head is stuck in a collar
(2) Where three men can not get the collar out of a horse
(3) Where three men can not find a right person to help with a horse
(4) Where a horse is strangled almost to death

문제 3 What was Mr. Coleridge's analysis of 'the useless task'?
(1) His physical strength had gotten too week to pull the horse's head out of his collar.
(2) The collar had gotten too small for the horse's head to come out of.
(3) He did have a grooming skill that could solve the problem.
(4) His impracticability led to the task unworkable.

[Challenge 9]

Birds of a feather flock together. A man is known by his friends. It is of great importance therefore that (a) your friends should be such as will show that you yourself are of the right sort. A boy, unless he is a particularly disagreeable one, will probably have a fair number of friends, that is to say, of fellows that he knows and associates with, but above and beyond these he will probably have some one particular chum, one who shares in all his plans, one with whom to talk over all his schemes, one often with whom to join in some piece of mischief. Chums to do one another much good should be about the same age. There may be a friendship between an elder and a younger boy, or between a boy and a man, but they will not be exactly chums. A friendship of this sort is very useful if the elder is one who will lead aright, but if the elder is the weaker of the two, or still more if the elder is viciously inclined, such an acquaintance is one of the worst possible things for a lad. A young boy, hanging on to an elder one, learning all his bad habits, is only too likely to prove an apt pupil, and come utterly to grief. Remember no one is worthy of the name of friend who would ever counsel you to do anything wrong, or who would (b) not give you a word in season when he found you were going on a wrong tack. A chum of one's own age is quite a different article. Very often they are not lads of the same dispositions and tastes, and are drawn to one another by these very differences. It not unfrequently happens that a bright active lad will chum with a very quiet meditative one. The one doing the thinking and the other the acting. Such friendships will last on sometimes through life, but generally well through boyhood.

문제 1 Which of the following is the best title for the above passage?
  (1) Characteristics of Good Friendship
  (2) Kinds of Friendship
  (3) A Real Chum
  (4) Difference between Friendship and Acquaintance

문제 2 Choose one that is neither stated nor implied in the passage.
  (1) A young boy is vulnerable to the bad habits of people around him.
  (2) Men usually come to make friends with one particular person, called a 'chum'.
  (3) A friendship where one person is older than the other does not always turn out to be a good one.
  (4) A person must be judged by whom he is with.

문제 3 Which of the following best displays the same meaning as the underlined (a)?
(1) A friend is a mirror of yourself.
(2) A friend to all is a friend to none.
(3) A fair-weather friend goes away when the weather is not good.
(4) A friend in need is a friend indeed.

문제 4 Which of the following best paraphrases the underlined (b)?
(1) not give you a heads-up
(2) make no promise
(3) make no effort
(4) take a different path

[Challenge 10]

   Nor can I ascertain that all people lose their minds and their sense of fashion when they have children. My husband, for instance, has never forgotten to button his shirt or worn two different colored shoes. So the answer must lie in the fact that, as women, we are wired differently. The men in our lives can happily scoot off to work with all their clothes perfectly coordinated despite the screaming children in tow. However, we sympathetic women want to do more than drop the children off at childcare. We want to find out why they are crying and somehow make it all better. Amidst the nose wiping, hugging, and comforting, we occasionally forget small items such as the car keys we locked in the house.

문제 1 The development of the above writing is _____.
(1) cause and effect
(2) spacial contrast
(3) comparison and contrast
(4) chronical order

★ A timid person is frightened before a danger, a coward during the time, and a courageous person afterward.

Jean Paul Richter (1763 - 1825)

소심한 자는 위험이 다가 오기 전에 겁을 먹고, 겁쟁이는 위험이 다가왔을 때 겁을 먹으며, 용감함 자는 위험이 지나간 후 겁을 먹는다 (Jean Paul Richter)

[Challenge 1]

Most singular _____ of opinion prevails in the community in regard to the pleasantness of the business of teaching. Some teachers go to their daily task merely upon compulsion; they regard it as intolerable drudgery. Others love the work: they hover around the school-room as long as they can, and never cease to think, and seldom to talk, of their delightful labors. Unfortunately, there are too many of the former class, and the first object which, in this work, I shall attempt to accomplish, is to show my readers, especially those who have been accustomed to look upon the business of teaching as a weary and heartless toil, how it happens that it is, in any case, so pleasant. The human mind is always essentially the same.

That which is tedious and joyless to one, will be so to another, if pursued in the same way, and under the same circumstances. And teaching, if it is pleasant, animating, and exciting to one, may be so to all.

문제 1 Which of the following can NOT be inferred from the passage?
 (1) The author tries to show how pleasant teaching can be.
 (2) Not all people think teaching is exciting work to do.
 (3) Some people like teaching so much that they keep talking about it.
 (4) The author thinks under a certain situation, teaching can be very grueling and energyconsuming.

문제 2 Fill in the blank to the passage.
 (1) counterpoise   (2) consistency
 (3) contrariety   (4) congruity

57

[Challenge 2]

The peculiar mission of woman, it has been said, is to be a wife and mother. Is it not as truly the peculiar mission of man to be a husband and father? If she is called to add to the happiness and worth of her husband, he is called to add to the happiness and worth of his wife. They are alike bound to protect and educate their children. And the other duties, the private improvement of self and the public improvement of society rest on them in common. The assertion, then, that the distinctive Office of woman is to be the helpmeet of man, does not imply that she ought to be legally or morally any more subservient to him than he to her; for the supreme duty of a woman, as of every other human being, is, through the perfecting of her own nature as a child of God, to fulfil her personal destiny in the universe. To love, to marry, to rear a family, is by no means an entire statement of the obligations and privileges of women: because no woman always has lover, husband, or children; many fail to have all of them in succession; and a few never have either of them.

문제 1   Which of the following can NOT be inferred from the passage?
   (1) Taking care of the children is not the office that only women participate in.
   (2) There is a widespread belief that women are treated as supplements to men.
   (3) Women have a higher duty of perfecting her nature other than just doing house chores.
   (4) Managing household affairs with sacrifice is the single most important job for every woman.

문제 2   Raising children is not an absolute mission of women because _____.
   (1) not all women are qualified to raise children.
   (2) there are other important things to do at home.
   (3) some women don't even have a chance to get married.
   (4) some women prefer doing outdoor activities rather than raising children.

[Challenge 3]

The complete science of 'politics' falls into two parts which may for convenience be called ethics and politics. Aristotle's ethics, no doubt, are social, and his politics are ethical; he does not forget in the Ethics that the individual man is essentially a member of society, nor in the Politics that the good life of the state exists only in the good lives of its citizens. Still, he has no doubt that there is a difference between the two enquiries. About the nature of the relationship between them he is not so clear. At the outset of the Ethics he describes the good of the state as 'greater and more perfect' than that of the individual, and the latter as merely something _____ which we may have to put up if we cannot attain the former. But his sense of value of the individual life appears to grow as he discusses it, and at the end of the work he speaks as if the state were merely ancillary to the moral life of the individual, supplying the element of compulsion which is needed if man's desires are to be made subservient to his reason.

문제 1 According to the passage, which of the following statements is true?
 (1) Aristotle wrote the Ethics, but not the Politics.
 (2) Aristotle didn't distinguish between ethics and politics which constitute social science.
 (3) Aristotle didn't lucidly specify the nature of the relationship between ethics and politics.
 (4) Aristotle criticized politicians, in the Politics, for pursuing a policy of conciliation.

문제 2 According to the passage, what does Aristotle think at the end of the Ethics about the relationship between the state and the individual?
 (1) Man's desires are more important than the state's future.
 (2) The individual must work hard to build up the power of the state.
 (3) The state must provide the individual with wealth and power.
 (4) The state is subsidiary to the moral life of the individual.

문제 3 Fill in the blank to the passage.
 (1) for (2) with
 (3) of (4) under

[Challenge 4]

"When you leave here, if you love art, surround yourselves with little reverences. I wish you all a questful life." Max Weber, his bright face illumined by the circle of a bonfire radiance interlacing the circle of student faces lifted toward him, was but echoing for his class, his own rich philosophy. His quest is still fruitful, his eye, keen, his language of art and man holding a fullness of that true (a) sap of past treasure, while (b) his hand still breaks ground.

Twice within the past five years he has left his home and studio at Long Island to teach; to give, abundantly, "I go a little further, I give you myself. Teaching is more than imparting knowledge. It is a kind of _____(c)_____ ." His inspiration has the sure quality of lifting the questful ones out into the mainstream where lies, "the greatest companion you have in life-the elan-and that is art."

Max Weber is an articulate teacher. The authority of his faithful study of art at its highest levels, rings through his smallest sentence. When he shows slides, darting exuberantly from one point of exciting form to another, he says, "It is my opera. I know these works like I know my little pocket here." He touches his shirt. "You have to study these things. Those beautiful hours when you hide from the world and study."

There is a direct simplicity in his manner and method. "I am here to call your attention to things. I say humbly of myself I am not one to solve their needs. I can help. I have a greater experience."

문제 1 Which of the following is most appropriate for the topic of the above passage?
    (1) Life of Max Weber (2) Max Weber as a Good Teacher
    (3) Secrets of Weber's Teaching (4) Max Weber as a Friend to his Pupils

문제 2 Which of the following is neither stated nor implied?
    (1) Max Weber knows how to humble himself, which in turn makes him a greater teacher.
    (2) Max Weber thought there is more to teaching than cramming information into students' minds.
    (3) He knows what he is doing like the back of his hand.
    (4) He is always there to solve students' needs for them.

문제 3 Choose one that is closest in meaning to the underlined (a).
    (1) elan (2) backbone
    (3) affection (4) legitimacy

문제 4   Which of the following best paraphrases the underlined (b)?
　　　　(1) he digs his heels in   (2) he takes a different path
　　　　(3) he blazes a trail   (4) he puts himself on firm ground

문제 5   Choose one that is closest in meaning to the underlined (a).
　　　　(1) elan   (2) backbone
　　　　(3) affection   (4) legitimacy

[Challenge 5]

　　Ice cream prices could be on the verge of a price increase, The London Daily Telegraph reports. (a) <u>The problem</u>? Apparently production is down worldwide, from India to Mexico, leading to grim predictions for the ice cream eaters of the world. Vanilla prices are already up from $25 per kilogram to nearly $40 a kilogram, but so far ice cream producers are ___(b)___. Nick Peksa, a Mintec market analyst, thinks it will affect ice cream across the board. He explained, "The stocks in the world are being run down, and we are getting to a point now where we are likely to see the price suddenly shoot upwards. It is the most expensive ingredient in ice cream production per kilogram, so it is highly likely that some producers will not be able to absorb the extra cost. It could push the price of ice cream up by around 10 per cent."

문제 1   Given the context, which of the following refers to the underlined (a)?
　　　　(1) Vanilla pod shortages
　　　　(2) Raised price of ice cream
　　　　(3) Irrational distribution structure of the ice cream industry
　　　　(4) Market instability

문제 2   Fill in blank (b).
　　　　(1) taking the hit
　　　　(2) hitting below the belt
　　　　(3) hitting home
　　　　(4) hitting the spot

[Challenge 6]

The effects of Twittering have found successfully their way, albeit relative, into the hearts and minds of the political pundits and reporters as they Twitter away, sharing their views with high-powered politicians. President Obama quite successfully maneuvered the social networking stratosphere with Facebook, MySpace and Twitter and with its help, cinched the presidency. He was able to gather large, massive followings, many of which are still growing even until today. He has used these platforms to further his agenda and to share his political message. Since what he has done with these platforms is such a success, many other politicians are taking note of it and using it for their own purposes.

Obama's staunch political opponent, John McCain, seemed to have been reluctant who did not go as far as Obama did in finding and securing the online vote like Barack did. Could he have increased his chances had he embraced social media? No one can say for sure whether or not heavy networking on these social scenes could have helped, or even hurt his chances. But one thing is for sure and that is that social networking works, it works well and it's here to stay. Suggestion: _____(a)_____ !

문제 1 Which of the following is CORRECT about the passage?
  (1) The majority of political intellectuals are now using social networking programs to share their political views with others.
  (2) The author is not quite sure of the power of Twittering.
  (3) President Obama was at first unwilling to use online networking but later found it useful in sharing his political views with others.
  (4) Online votes were not at the center of MaCain's concern at the time of the election.

문제 2 Choose one that is most appropriate for blank (a).
  (1) get on the social networking train
  (2) learn how social networking works psychologically
  (3) take classes about social networking
  (4) try to keep updated with how social networking evolves

[Challenge 7]

Representatives need money to have any chance of winning an election. Thomas Ferguson calls this the "campaign cost condition," and places it at the center of his theory of the dynamics of American politics. There are two additional aspects of Ferguson's theory worth pointing out. The first is the claim that competition among moneyed interests is unlikely to solve the problem of access to the agenda. Ferguson calls this the "principle of noncompetition across investor blocs," noting that "on all issues affecting the vital interests that major investors have in common, no party competition will take place." Second, Ferguson argues that although elections do not simply go to the highest bidder, only access to money from investors makes a real campaign possible. Since representatives need money to get elected, they can't take positions unpopular with moneyed interests, though those positions would win in the "perfectly informed voters" world of the median-voter theorem. Voters cannot overcome the transaction costs of pooling their resources, so they must accept the choices offered.

문제 1 According to the passage, which of the following is correct?
   (1) 'Principle of noncompetition' represents the desired realization of democracy.
   (2) The amount of money poured in the campaign is in inverse proportion to the chance of getting elected due to the iniquity in it.
   (3) Among the upmost important facts of winning an election is access to money.
   (4) Competition among moneyed interests usually leads to the settlement of the disputed issues.

[Challenge 8]

Ethics in ancient times signified moral philosophy generally, which was also called the doctrine of duties. Subsequently it was found advisable to confine this name to a part of moral philosophy, namely, to the doctrine of duties which are not subject to external laws (for which in German the name Tugendlehre was found suitable). Thus the system of general deontology is divided into that of jurisprudence, which is capable of external laws, and of ethics, which is not thus capable, and we may let this division stand.

문제 1 Which of the following can NOT be inferred from the passage?
   (1) Moral responsibility is more like something that is internal in the mind.
   (2) Germans needed to coin a new word for the doctrine of duties.
   (3) Deontology has two different levels under it.
   (4) Jurisprudence and ethics deal with two different realms.

[Challenge 9]

The Jewish town is quite distinct from that of the Moors; but the difference between them is very little: the streets are equally narrow and dirty, and the houses have no windows on the outside; the roofs are also quite flat; the only variation is, that the streets are covered with a roof extending from the houses on each side, and _____(a)_____ . There is a regular communication between the houses at the top, which is the favourite scene of recreation. Some of the women scarcely ever take the air, excepting on these flat roofs: in short, the inhabitants, both Jews and Moors, dance, sing, and take all their amusements on them. The rooms of the Jewish houses (as well as of the Moors) are long, narrow, and lofty, resembling galleries. Most of the houses are occupied by several families, which are generally large. Those inhabited by the more opulent are kept tolerably neat, and are adorned with rich and curious furniture; but they are, for the most part, exceedingly dirty; and the exhalations from the garlic and oil, which they use in great quantities in frying their fish, are enough to suffocate a person not entirely divested of the sense of smelling. Their taste is so exquisitely refined, in regard to the oil they use, that they prefer our lamp-oil to any other, on account of its high flavor.

문제 1   Which of the following is the topic of the above passage?
(1) Characteristics of the Jewish Town
(2) Conditions of the Jewish Houses
(3) Exceptional Features of the Roof Structure
(4) Differences between the Jew and the Moors

문제 2   Which of the following best fills in blank (a)?
(1) are packed with women doing house chores
(2) have a couple of doors on each side of the roofs
(3) are apropos for cars to go through
(4) have the appearance of subterraneous passages

문제 3   Which of the following is NOT true of the passage?
(1) The overall impression of the Jewish houses is dirty.
(2) To a new comer, the town might smell quite different.
(3) Jewish houses inhabited by rich people are flawlessly immaculate.
(4) On the flat roofs are women seen talking to each other.

[Challenge 10]

It happened one afternoon, in those years when Cowper's accomplished friend, Lady Austen, made a part of his little evening circle, that she observed him sinking into increased dejection; it was her custom, on these occasions, to try all the resources of her sprightly powers for his immediate relief. She told him the story of John Gilpin, (which had been treasured in her memory from her childhood), to dissipate the gloom of the passing hour. Its effects on the fancy of Cowper had the air of enchantment. He informed her the next morning that (a) <u>convulsions of</u> laughter, brought on by his recollection of her story, had kept him waking during the greatest part of the night! and that he had turned it into a ballad. So arose the pleasant poem of John Gilpin.

문제 1   What is the most appropriate for the title for the passage?
(1) Origin of Cowper's 'John Gilpin'
(2) Out of Depression
(3) Impacts of A Small talk
(4) Fancy of Cowper

문제 2   Which of the following is NOT true of the passage?
(1) Cowper burst into laughter the whole night after hearing the story of John Gilpin.
(2) Lady Austen liked helping people out of distress.
(3) Cowper was helped by his friend with his depression.
(4) The poem John Gilpin greatly helped Cowper out of his dejection.

문제 3   Choose one that best paraphrase the underlined (a).
(1) bits of   (2) herds of
(3) fits of   (4) breaks of

★ Courage and perseverance have a magical talisman, before which difficulties disappear and obstacles vanish into air.

John Quincy Adams (1767 - 1848)

용기와 인내는 부적과 같은 힘을 가지고 있다. 이것 앞에선 어려움은 사라지고, 장애물은 허공에 사라진다. (John Quincy Adams)

[Challenge 1]

"There is work enough in the world for every one to do something. There is no proper place for idle people." This is what old Michael the basket maker used to say to his children; and as they grew up, they found reason enough to thank him for the lesson.

(a) By this time he had got two children, and the eldest was old enough to learn to read. She used to sit by him with her book as he worked, and he taught her when she wanted help. His wife was in the mean time doing something in the house, or working for some of the farmers who lived near.

(b) Michael had been a sailor in his youth, but when he married, he settled in a country place, and took up the trade of a basket maker. At first, he could hardly get money enough to buy rods: but by working very hard, he soon got money and credit too. No one in the village was now up before Michael, and most people went to bed before he left off work.

(c) As for Michael himself, though he was well off, he kept on his old trade, and went on in his old habits. The last time I saw him before I left the place in which he lived, he was teaching his youngest child to read while he was at work, just as he had taught his eldest. I have often thought of Michael's words, "There is no place in the world for idle people."

(d) Small as was the sum of money that he could earn in a week, he would always put by something, if it was but a penny. Every month he put these savings into the savings' bank; and in the course of the first six years, he found he had got twenty-five pounds.

(e) Michael now bought a cow and two pigs, and made some profit by them. In six years more he bought the cottage he lived in; and twelve years after this, that is twenty-four years after he was married, he rented a little farm. By this time he had seven children; and as he had made his cottage larger, they all lived at home and helped him. His eldest boys worked at the farm, and the girls milked the cows and made the butter, under the care of their mother, and kept the poultry.

문제 1 Which of the following is the subject matter of the above passage?
(1) Industry   (2) Frugality
(3) Prudence   (4) Enterprise

문제 2 Choose one that is put in the right sequence.
(1) (b) - (d) - (a) - (e) - (c)   (2) (d) - (a) - (e) - (c) - (b)
(3) (c) - (a) - (b) - (e) - (d)   (4) (a) - (b) - (d) - (e) - (c)

[Challenge 2]

In all your actions, in all your dealings, let strict and rigid honesty guide you. Never be tempted to swerve from its dictates, even in the most trivial degree. There will be strong allurements to entice you from this path. The appetite for gain — the voice of avarice — will often whisper that honesty may be violated to advantage. There will be times when it will seem that its dictates may be placed aside — that a little dishonesty will be greatly to your benefit. Believe not this siren song. (a) Although there may be occasions when you will seem actually to lose by adhering to honesty, yet you should not shrink a hair's breadth. (b) Whatever you may lose, in a pecuniary point of view, at any time, by a strict submission to honesty, you will make up an hundred-fold in the long-run, by establishing and preserving a reputation for integrity. (c) Looking at it in simply a pecuniary point of view, community will give their countenance, their patronage, and business, much quicker to a man who has established a reputation for honesty, than to one who is known, or suspected of being fraudulent in his dealings. (d) Every consideration which can bear upon the young, religious, moral and pecuniary, unite to urge them to establish, in the outset of life, the rule of unswerving honesty and integrity, as their constant guide. Let it not be forgotten, that in every possible point of view, and in every conceivable condition of things, it will always be true, that "Honesty is the best policy."

문제 1 Where does the sentence below in the box best fit in the above passage?

This is the time you are in the most danger of being deceived to your serious injury.

(1) (a)   (2) (b)   (3) (c)   (4) (d)

문제 2 Which of the definitions of the underlined words in the passage is NOT correct?
(1) siren - seductive
(3) pecuniary - distinct
(2) a hair's breadth - even a tiny bit
(4) countenance - support

문제 3 Which of the following is neither stated nor implied?
(1) The appetite for pecuniary gain may look more advantageous in the moment than adhering to the policy of honesty but in the long run it does not guarantee the ultimate success of life.
(2) Anyone walking the path of 'honesty' may encounter the temptation of lust for money.
(3) There comes a time when people with great honesty may seem to lose in terms of money.
(4) Money is a necessary evil. It is not everything about life, but without it you can not make your wishes fulfilled.

[Challenge 3]

Sterne's sermons are, in general, ____(a)____, which circumstance gave rise to the following joke at Bull's Library, at Bath: A footman had been sent by his lady to purchase one of Smallridge's sermons, when, by mistake, he asked for a small religious sermon. The bookseller being puzzled how to reply to his request, a gentleman present suggested, "Give him one of Sterne's."

문제 1 Which of the following best fills in blank (a)?
(1) figurative
(2) succinct
(3) allegoric
(4) representative

[Challenge 4]

The best Eskimo carvings of all ages seem to possess a powerful ability to reach across the great barriers of language and time and communicate directly with us. The more we look at these carvings, the more life we perceive hidden within them. We discover subtle living forms of the animal, human, and mystical world. These carvings are not the cold sculptures of the frozen world. Instead, they reveal to us the passionate feelings of a vital people well aware of all the joys, terrors, tranquility, and wildness of life around them. Eskimo carvers are people moved by dreams. In spite of all their new contacts with outsiders, they are still concerned with their own kind of mystical imagery.

문제 1   The author is primarily concerned with _____.
(1) showing how Eskimo carvings achieve their effects
(2) describing how Eskimo artists resist the influence of outsiders
(3) discussing a significant characteristic of Eskimo art
(4) explaining how Eskimo carvers depict animals and humans

문제 2   Which of the following is CORRECT about the passage?
(1) Eskimo carvings are time-limited.
(2) There's more to Eskimo carvings than what appears on the surface.
(3) Human beings would never understand the depths of Eskimo carvings.
(4) Eskimo sculptures have been intact because of little or no contact with the outside world.

[Challenge 5]

(a) The grave defect in our American life is not that we are hero worshipers, but rather that we worship but one type of hero; we recognize but one type of achievement; we see but one sort of genius. For two generations our youth have been led to believe that there is only one ambition that is worth while, — the ambition of property. Success at any price is the ideal that has been held up before our boys and girls. And today we are reaping the rewards of this distorted and unjust view of life.

I recently met a man who had lived for some years in the neighborhood of St. Paul and Minneapolis, — a section that is peopled, as you know, very largely by Scandinavian immigrants and their descendants. This man told me that he had been particularly impressed by the high idealism of the Norwegian people. His business brought him in contact with Norwegian immigrants in what are called the lower walks of life, — with workingmen and servant girls, — and he made it a point to ask each of these young men and young women the same question. "Tell me," he would say, "who are the great men of your country? Who are the men toward whom the youth of your land are led to look for inspiration? Who are the men whom your boys are led to imitate and emulate and admire?" And he said that he almost always received the same answer to this question: the great names of the Norwegian nation that had been (b) burned upon the minds even of these workingmen and servant girls were just four in number: Ole Bull, Bjö̈rnson, Ibsen, Nansen. Over and over again he asked that same question; over and over again he received the same answer: Ole Bull, Bjö̈rnson, Ibsen, Nansen. A great musician, a great novelist, a great dramatist, a great scientist.

문제 1 Which of the following is the best title for the passage?
(1) Who is a True Hero?
(2) A True Ambition in Life for the Youth
(3) Different Types of Heros
(4) Material Life in the U.S.

문제 2 Which of the following is the best explanation for the underlined (a)?
(1) They have set too idealistic an ambition for life.
(2) They have been led to believe that there is only one worthy ambition in life, which is accumulating more and more.
(3) They have been infused into the idea that material conditions are better than spiritual well-being in life.
(4) They only follow what they are told to do; therefore they lack initiative.

문제 3 Which of the following can be replaced with the underlined word (b)?
(1) engraved
(2) imparted
(3) incinerated
(4) brainwashed

[Challenge 6]

Experiment in non-human primates suggests that monkeys can track the displacement of invisible targets, that invisible displacement is represented in prefrontal cortex, and that development of the frontal cortex is linked to the acquisition of object permanence. Various evidence from human infants is consistent with this. For example, the formation of synapses in the frontal cortex peaks during human infancy, and recent experiments using near-infrared spectroscopy to gather neuroimaging data from infants suggest that activity in the frontal cortex is associated with the successful completion of object permanence tasks.

문제 1 Which of the following is the topic of the passage?
(1) Formation of Object Permanence
(2) Reflections of Object Permanence on the Brain
(3) Ability of Non-human Primates for Object Permanence
(4) Frontal Cortex and Object Permanence

[Challenge 7]

There is a great difficulty in the way of a writer who attempts to sketch a living Constitution — a Constitution that is in actual work and power. The difficulty is that the object is in constant change. An historical writer does not feel this difficulty: he deals only with the past; he can say definitely, the Constitution worked in such and such a manner in the year at which he begins, and in a manner in such and such respects different in the year at which he ends; he begins with a definite point of time and ends with one also. But a contemporary writer who tries to paint what is before him is puzzled and perplexed: what he sees is changing daily. He must paint it as it stood at some one time, or else he will be putting side by side in his representations things which never were contemporaneous in reality. The difficulty is the greater because a writer who deals with a living Government naturally compares it with the most important other living Governments, and these are changing too; what he illustrates are altered in one way, and his sources of illustration are altered probably in a different way.

문제 1 Which of the following is the passage mainly talking about?
  (1) Traits of contemporary governments
  (2) Governments in different perspectives
  (3) The dilemma of writing a living constitution
  (4) Workings of a constitution

문제 2 The difficulty that the author is discussing in the above passage mainly derives from _____.
  (1) the complex structures of the object   (2) the changing qualities of the object
  (3) the profundity of the object   (4) the incomparable nature of the object

[Challenge 8]

Ferguson's Essay on the History of Civil Society (1767) drew on classical authors and contemporary travel literature, to analyze modern commercial society with a critique of its abandonment of civic and communal virtues. Central themes in Ferguson's theory of citizenship are conflict, play, political participation and military valor. He emphasized the ability to put oneself in another's shoes, saying "fellow-feeling" was so much an "appurtenance of human nature" as to be a "characteristic of the species." Like his friends Adam Smith and David Hume as well as other Scottish intellectuals, he stressed the importance of the spontaneous order; that is, that (a) coherent and even effective outcomes might result from the uncoordinated actions of many individuals.

Ferguson saw history as a two-tiered synthesis of natural history and social history, to which all humans belong. Natural history is created by God; so are humans, who are progressive. Social history is, in accordance with this natural progress, made by humans, and because of that factor it experiences occasional setbacks. But in general, humans are empowered by God to pursue progress in social history. Humans live not for themselves but for God's providential plan. He emphasized aspects of medieval chivalry as ideal masculine characteristics. British gentleman and young men were advised to dispense with aspects of politeness considered too feminine, such as the constant desire to please, and to adopt less superficial qualities that suggested inner virtue and courtesy toward the 'fairer sex.'

Ferguson was a leading advocate of the Idea of Progress. He believed that the growth of a commercial society through the pursuit of individual self-interest could promote a self-sustaining progress. Yet ___(b)___ Ferguson also believed that such commercial growth could foster a decline in virtue and thus ultimately lead to a collapse similar to Rome's. Ferguson, a devout Presbyterian, resolved the apparent paradox by placing both developments in the context of a divinely ordained plan that mandated both progress and human free will. For Ferguson, the knowledge that humanity gains through its actions, even those actions resulting in temporary retrogression, forms an intrinsic part of its progressive, asymptotic movement toward an ultimately unobtainable perfectibility.

문제 1 Which of the following is the best title for the passage?
  (1) How Ferguson Interprets History
  (2) Social Thought of Adam Ferguson
  (3) Ferguson and the Idea of Progress
  (4) Relative Merits about the Pursuit of Individual Self-Interest

문제 2 Which of the following phrases best represents the underlined (a)?
  (1) paradoxical phenomena   (2) unintended consequences
  (3) invisible hands   (4) self interests

문제 3 Fill in blank (b).
  (1) hyperbolically   (2) metaphorically
  (3) paradoxically   (4) conversely

[Challenge 9]

Rome had passed the (a) summits and stood looking into the dark valley of fourteen hundred years. Behind her the graves of Caesar and Sallust and Cicero and Catullus and Vergil and Horace; before her centuries of madness and treading down; round about her a multitude sickening of luxury, their houses filled with (b) spoil, their mouths with folly, their souls with discontent; above her only mystery and silence; in her train, philosophers questioning if it were not better for a man had he never been born -deeming life a misfortune and extinction the only happiness; poets singing no more of "pleasantries and trifles," but seeking favor with poor (c) obscenities. Soon they were even to celebrate the virtue of harlots, the integrity of thieves, the tenderness of murderers, the justice of oppression. Leading the caravan were types abhorrent and self-opposed — (d) effeminate men, masculine women, cheerful cynics, infidel priests, wealthy people with no credit, patricians, honoring and yet despising the gods, hating and yet living on the populace. Here was the spectacle of a republican empire, and an emperor gathering power while he affected to disdain it.

문제 1 Which of the following is the passage mainly talking about?
(1) Disgusting Corruption of the Roman Government
(2) Weakling Leaders of Rome
(3) The Disintegrating Aura of Rome
(4) Good Old Days of Rome

문제 2 The tone of the passage is _____.
(1) dismal   (2) cryptic
(3) obscure   (4) baffling

문제 3 Which of the following is NOT the synonym of each underlined word in the passage?
(1) (a) summits - zenith
(2) (b) spoil - pillage
(3) (c) obscenities - indecency
(4) (d) effeminate - virile

[Challenge 10]

Lovelock was shocked at public reaction to Gaia: A New Look at Life on Earth (his initial book on the subject, first published in 1979): "I had no inkling that it would be taken as a religious book," he admitted in his 1988 follow-up, The Ages of Gaia. "Two-thirds of the letters received, and still coming in, are about the meaning of Gaia in the context of religious faith." A review of the history of the Gaia theory and Earth Day suggests that some go too far in condemning the annual observance as being rooted in the unabashed celebration of an ancient pagan deity, but the fact that some do make a religious connection is undeniable. That connection prevented many scientists from taking Lovelock's theory seriously. Eventually, however, he realized that (a) their objections "were less about the science of Gaia than the semantics and the use of metaphor". "Neo-Darwinist biologists had had their own difficult times fending off creationists, traditionalists and proponents of group selection." He recounted that one critic told him "Gaia had seemed at first just another of these false theories: the New Age religious faith in an Earth Mother was anathema to him." "Now," wrote Lovelock in the 2000 edition of Gaia: A New Look at Life on Earth, "most scientists appear to accept Gaia theory and apply it to their research, but they still reject the name Gaia and prefer to talk of Earth System Science, or Geophysiology, instead."

문제 1   Which of the following is CORRECT about the passage?
(1) Lovelock wrote Gaia: A New Look at Life on Earth wholly within the context of religion.
(2) Lovelock wanted to tell people that the Earth was created by Gaia, only to be ridiculed before the public.
(3) Many scientists were captivated by the fact that there is a connection between the Gaia theory and a pagan god.
(4) Even after the 2000 Edition of Gaia by Lovelock, scientists are reluctant to use the name Gaia because of its connection with a pagan deity.

문제 2   The underlined (a) implies that _____.
(1) the church rejected the theory of Gaia because of its profane nature that it contains
(2) scientists think the theory of Gaia is a total mistake of pseudo-science
(3) scientists objected to the theory of Gaia due to its analogy to a pagan god the word has
(4) scientists are less creative in using metaphorical uses of a word than religious writers

★ Concentration comes out of a combination of confidence and hunger.

Arnold Palmer

집중력은 자신감과 배고픔의 조화에서 발생한다. (Arnold Palmer)

[Challenge 1]

So a key to success in creative thinking is clarity. Take the time to think through, discuss and ask questions that help you to clarify exactly what you are trying to accomplish and exactly what problems you are facing at the present moment. Just as fuzzy thinking leads to fuzzy answers, clear thinking leads to clear answers. A second key is concentration. (a) <u>Put everything else aside</u>, and concentrate single-mindedly on focusing all your mental powers on solving one single problem, overcoming one particular obstacle or achieving one important goal. The ability to concentrate on a single subject without diversion or distraction is a hallmark of the superior thinker. A third key is an open mind. The average person tends to be rigid and fixed in his thinking about getting from where he is to where he wants to go. The creative thinker, however, tends to remain very flexible and open to a variety of ways of approaching the problem. The average person has a tendency to leap to conclusions and determine that there is only one way to achieve a particular goal. The superior thinker, on the other hand, tends to be more patient and willing to consider a variety of options before moving toward a conclusion.

문제 1   What is the topic of the passage?
(1) Asking Questions in Time
(2) Importance of Clarity
(3) Keys to Creative Thinking
(4) Difference between creative thinkers and average persons

문제 2   Which of the following best paraphrases the underlined (a)?
(1) Put less important things on the back burner   (2) Save everything else
(3) Search every nook and cranny   (4) Put things asunder

문제 3   Which of the following is LEAST likely to be the hallmark of superior thinkers?
(1) Openness   (2) Concentration   (3) Flexibility   (4) Fast decision-making

[Challenge 2]

We are Americans working to create a fair and inclusive society. Our members represent the diversity of thought, background, and circumstance that is found in the cities, towns, and neighborhoods of our country. We are a meeting place for Americans seeking common ground and collective action to strengthen our democracy. We maintain our independence from all political parties and labels. Yes, we are non-partisan, but being non-partisan does not mean we will not take positions. It means that Coffee Party members will arrive at positions based on principles and facts; not on __(a)__. By seeking and spreading accurate information, we empower ourselves to take action and participate in government based on __(b)__ decisions. The Coffee Party provides a place where men and women of all ages, races, physical abilities, and orientations can come together for a respectful and honest exchange of ideas. We believe that by talking and learning together—we can take action to solve the problems facing our nation. Along with national goals, we encourage Coffee Party chapters across the country to pursue local and regional projects chosen by their members. As voters and grassroots volunteers, we understand that the federal government is not our enemy, but the expression of our collective will—and we pledge to both support leaders who work toward positive solutions, and hold __(c)__ those who obstruct them. The Coffee Party USA believes that the influence of money, and the politics of fear and exclusion, __(d)__ in the way of a government "of, by and for the people."

문제 1 The tone of the passage is _____.
 (1) pacific (2) skeptical (3) idyllic (4) assertive

문제 2 Choose one that is appropriate for each blank.

	(a)	(b)	(c)	(d)
(1)	party affiliation	informed	accountable	stand
(2)	political sects	assorted	good	thwart
(3)	party affiliation	objective	good	thwart
(4)	political sects	written	accountable	stand

[Challenge 3]

The Mazengarb Committee was of opinion that there should be a long-term study of the problem of delinquency. As a matter of fact the present Committee heard evidence on this suggestion from several witnesses, and we were greatly impressed by what we heard. It goes without saying that if one would seek a remedy for a given problem a thorough diagnosis of the problem itself is a fundamental prerequisite. First let us find the facts; let us know what is the nature and extent of the evil; let us get as much data as to its causes and incidence. With that material in hand we should be in a better position to search for useful methods of treatment. This task of fact finding would be a long and arduous one; it would need to be entrusted to experts of wide knowledge and experience. A start has already been made by the setting up of the Inter-Departmental Committee referred to earlier in this report. We strongly recommend the Government to give very favourable consideration to this particular proposal, and we hope that ways and means will be found of giving effect to it. We think that this suggestion is of fundamental importance in any approach to the problem, and we consider it should be given consideration by the Government.

문제 1 According to the passage, which of the following is the very first step to come up with useful methods of treatment to a ceratin problem?
(1) Figuring out the implications of the problem
(2) Finding the nature of the problem
(3) Collecting facts about the problem itself
(4) Seeking the causes of the problem

문제 2 Which of the following is NOT mentioned in the passage?
(1) The suggestion of the Mazengarb Committee is supported by the witnesses of the delinquent problem.
(2) Searching for the facts is time-consuming and energy-consuming.
(3) Fact-finding is such a simple matter as requires no expertise.
(4) The Committee which suggested a long-term study of the problem of delinquency requests the government to take a serious look at the problem.

[Challenge 4]

U.S. painting has a native and singular flavor that sets it apart. True enough, some painters like Whistler, Sargent, and Mary Cassatt belong to the English or French school, but they are the exceptions. Almost all U.S. artists have developed on their own. They have been self-taught artists who have perfected their talents to a greater or lesser degree. Those who felt the imperious need to visit Europe did so when they had already achieved maturity. For them the (a) Old World influence served more to improve their techniques than to modify their already existing styles. For some artists, for example Grant Wood, a European tour stimulated awareness of their own national roots, and convinced them that their true place was in their own country and in their own setting.

문제 1 The author maintains that Whistler, Sargent, and Mary Cassatt are exceptions because _____.
(1) they developed on their own in isolation
(2) their styles were influenced by their European contacts
(3) they became aware of their national roots
(4) they were immature when they visited Europe

문제 2 The Old World in the underline (a) refers to which of the following?
(1) Europe   (2) England   (3) America   (4) Greek

[Challenge 5]

(a) At one time or another, humans have turned to just about every viable option on the planet for new means of destroying one another. We've leveled forests, plundered the elements and diverted religion, philosophy, science and art to fuel humanity's desire for bloodshed. Along the way, we've even weaponized some of nature's most formidable viral, bacterial and fungal foes.

(b) The first half of the 20th century saw the use of the biological weapon anthrax by both the Germans and Japanese, as well as the subsequent development of biological weapons programs in nations such as the United States, the United Kingdom and Russia. Today, biological weapons are outlawed under 1972's Biological Weapons Convention and the Geneva Protocol. But while a number of nations have long destroyed their stockpiles of bioweapons and ceased research into their proliferation, the threat remains.

(c) The use of biological weapons, or bioweapons, dates back to the ancient world. As early as 1,500 B.C. the Hittites of Asia Minor recognized the power of contagions and sent plague victims into enemy lands. Armies, too, have long understood the power of bioweapons, catapulting diseased corpses into besieged fortresses and poisoning enemy wells. Some historians even argue that the 10 biblical plagues Moses called down against the Egyptians may have been more of a concentrated campaign of biological warfare rather than the acts of a vengeful god.

(d) Since those early days, advances in medical science have led to a vastly improved understanding of harmful pathogens and the way our immune systems deal with them. But while these advancements have led to vaccinations and cures, they have also led to the further weaponization of some of the most destructive biological agents on the planet.

문제 1 What is the purpose of the passage?
(1) To tell the reader about the brief history of biological weapons
(2) To discuss the harmful effects of biological weapons
(3) To make a comparison between conventional weapons and biological weapons
(4) To introduce a new weapon to the reader

문제 2 The logical sequence of the passage is _____.
(1) (b) - (a) - (c) - (d)
(2) (a) - (c) - (d) - (b)
(3) (c) - (b) - (a) - (d)
(4) (d) - (a) - (c) - (b)

[Challenge 6]

In the first place, the main principle of action in that society rests wholly on a false deduction from past experience. Experience has shown, that when certain moral evils exist in a community, efforts to awaken public sentiment against such practices, and combinations for the exercise of personal influence and example, have in various cases tended to rectify these evils. Thus in respect to intemperance; — the collecting of facts, the labours of public lecturers and the distribution of publications, have had much effect in diminishing (a) <u>the evil</u>. So in reference to the slave-trade and slavery in England. The English nation possessed the power of regulating their own trade, and of giving liberty to every slave in their dominions; and yet they were entirely unmindful of their duty on this subject. Clarkson, Wilberforce, and their coadjutors, commenced a system of operations to arouse and influence public sentiment, and they succeeded in securing the suppression of the slave trade, and the gradual abolition of slavery in the English colonies. In both these cases, the effort was to enlighten and direct public sentiment in a community, of which the actors were a portion, in order to lead them to rectify an evil existing among THEMSELVES, which was entirely under their control.

*coadjutor 조수, 보좌

문제 1 Which of the following best represents the main idea of the passage?
(1) Public awareness of slave-trade and slavery in England was high enough to rectify the problems at hand.
(2) The English nation has the power to make slaves both in the country and in its colonies.
(3) An attempt to arouse and direct public sentiment against an existing evil practice is the first step to rectify the evil.
(4) The abolition of the slave trade in the English is a first and foremost important thing to be done at the moment.

문제 2 Which of the following is NOT a part of the methods that does away with the evil in the underlined (a)?
(1) Awakening public sentiment against it
(2) Public lectures on it
(3) Issuing a pamphlet that tells about the vice of it
(4) Aggregating information about it

[Challenge 7]

Computers were originally just supposed to be number-crunchers, but now their number-crunching has been harnessed in a thousand imaginative ways to create new virtual machines, such as video games and word processors, in which the underlying number-crunching is almost invisible, and in which new powers seem quite magical. Our brains, _____(a)_____, weren't designed (except for some very recent peripheral organs) for word processing, but now a large portion — perhaps even the lion's share — of the activity that takes place in adult human brains is involved in a sort of word processing: speech production and comprehension, and the serial rehearsal and rearrangement of linguistic items. And these activities magnify and transform the underlying hardware powers in ways that seem quite magical.

문제 1 Which of the following is CORRECT about the passage?
  (1) Virtual reality driving simulator can be a fine example of number-crunching.
  (2) Computers are way advanced now than when they were first invented.
  (3) Human brains have limited functions in terms of number-counting.
  (4) Intellectual evolution does not apply to human brain.

문제 2 Fill in blank (a).
  (1) otherwise
  (2) on the other hand
  (3) similarly
  (4) on the flip side

[Challenge 8]

The new cameras, which have started to catch on in the last few years, are meant for shooting video and photos while skiing, surfing and doing other sports. Likewise, many cyclists use them to memorialize their rides. GoPro and Contour make popular models; GoPro says sales through bike retailers have nearly doubled so far this year from the same period last year. One of the most prominent bicycle crash videos so far was recorded in April by two Brazilian riders who were climbing the hills of Berkeley when a black car knocked them down and sped off. Neither bicyclist was seriously injured, according to the Berkeley police. The video of the crash has been viewed more than 362,000 times on YouTube. The Berkeley police identified the car's license plate and later found the man the vehicle was registered to. They believe he falsely reported his car stolen to cover up for the driver of the car and are still investigating the incident, said Capt. Andrew Greenwood, a spokesman for the police.

On a recent Friday evening, as the streets of downtown Washington were jammed with cars heading home, Mr. Wilder pedaled away wearing a camera on his forehead, looking like a spelunker wearing a headlamp. He scooted between parked cars and traffic on the road, sometimes with less than a foot of space between him and moving vehicles. The video Mr. Wilder shot of his crash in Washington, which occurred last August, at first did not seem as if it would help much in tracking down the motorist who had struck him. But Mr. Wilder, who works in the photography department of National Geographic, examined the video frame by frame until he discovered a clear picture of the vehicle's license plate, captured while he was lying on the ground. The District of Columbia's office of the attorney general charged the motorist, John W. Diehl, with leaving the scene of an accident. Federal prosecutors, who handle felony cases in the district, are also looking into the case.

Mr. Diehl's lawyer, Adam R. Hunter, declined to comment. Mr. Diehl has pleaded not guilty, said a spokesman for the attorney general. Mr. Wilder said, "Most cyclists don't use cameras so Mr. Diehl may have assumed he could assault and drive away anonymously."

문제 1   The best title for the passage is _____.
(1) Cameras On Wheels
(2) Uphill Battles Between Bicycles and Cars
(3) Bicycles Pushing Cars Out of the Road
(4) More People Switching to Bicycles

문제 2   Which of the following is neither stated nor implied in the passage?
(1) At the time of the accident, Mr. Wilder didn't have time to notice the license plate of the car.
(2) The video camera Mr. Wilder had strapped to his head caught the episode of the accident.
(3) Video from these cameras has begun to play an invaluable role in police investigations of a small number of hit-and-runs and other incidents.
(4) Motorists and pedestrians have a confrontational attitude toward cyclists.

문제 3   According to the passage, small cameras serve as _____.
(1) a life jacket of a cyclist
(2) the cycling equivalent of the black box on an airplane
(3) a flak jacket of a cyclist in the car crash
(4) air bags in a car

[Challenge 9]

In reviewing the literature on who gets access to rigorous curricula in schools, it appears that, on the basis of standardized test results, a disproportionate number of racial and ethnic minority individuals, particularly those from low-income backgrounds, are judged as "low ability" and assigned to low-track or remedial classes. In contrast, individuals of European descent, particularly those from high-income backgrounds, are more likely to be considered "gifted and talented" and placed in enriched or accelerated programs. (a) Because track enrollment determines the level of courses students take and the quality of the curriculum and instruction to which they are exposed, this means that minority students, on average, are less likely than their majority peers to engage in high-caliber curricula. (b) Diminished opportunity to learn high-level material results in low academic achievement. (c) Well-equipped libraries, mentoring, tutoring, quality teaching, rigorous curricula, low counselor-student and teacher-student ratios, small class sizes, extracurricular experiences, and computer and other technologies are examples of key resources in education that may be viewed as preconditions for enabling high levels of academic achievement. (d) Unfortunately, a disproportionate number of individuals from certain minority groups (e.g., African Americans, Latinos, and Native Americans), particularly those from low-income backgrounds, are likely to attend schools with limited access to these resources, thus minimizing their opportunity to do well academically. ___(e)___, many of these individuals live in economically distressed communities where they experience poor health and inadequate nutrition, factors that place them further at risk educationally.

문제 1   If the passage is divided into two, where does the second paragraph begin?
   (1) (a)   (2) (b)
   (3) (c)   (4) (d)

문제 2   Which of the following shows the topic of the passage?
   (1) Limited Opportunities to Learn
   (2) Factors of Low Minority Achievement
   (3) Limited Access to Institutional and Other Resources
   (4) Relationship between Public Education and Overall Achievement

문제 3 Which of the following is neither stated nor implied?
(1) There is a stereotypical thought that children from low-income families tend to be low in academic achievement.
(2) Low academic achievement can result from limited access to high-level material.
(3) Poor health puts students vulnerable to life-threatening situations.
(4) The quality of the curriculum and instruction is one factor that could affect the students' achievement.

문제 4 Fill in blank (e).
(1) On the other hand
(2) Moreover
(3) Accordingly
(4) Then

[Challenge 10]

Adam Ferguson's main thesis was that differences in status in the workplace, and in the community based on wealth, extend to differences in power in the political and social setting in which work takes place. Thus, the accumulation of wealth, from whatever source, creates a demand for perpetuation of privilege. Wealth also affords a disproportionate influence over government policy. People with money share interests with the other wealthy, and recognize the need to use their power to make sure those interests are protected.

문제 1 Which of the following is neither stated nor implied from the passage?
(1) People with money tend to exert more political impact on others than those without it.
(2) Wealth can create certain social privileges in the person who owns it.
(3) Money has nothing to do with political influences.
(4) The wealthy tend to create a 'bloc' to protect their interests, thus blocking others from invading their interests.

Day 9

★ I was always looking outside myself for strength and confidence, but it comes from within. It is there all the time.

Anna Freud (1895 — 1982)

나는 항상 힘과 자신감을 나 자신 밖에서 찾았지만, 정작 이것은 나의 내면에서 오는 것이다. 이것은 언제나 거기에 항상 존재하고 있는 것이다. (Anna Freud)

[Challenge 1]

　　For several years I had been subject to attacks of the singular disorder which physicians have agreed to term catalepsy, in default of a more definitive title. Although both the immediate and the predisposing causes, and even the actual diagnosis, of this disease are still mysterious, its obvious and apparent character is sufficiently well understood. Its variations seem to be chiefly of degree. Sometimes the patient lies, for a day only, or even for a shorter period, in a species of exaggerated (a) lethargy. He is senseless and externally motionless; but the pulsation of the heart is still faintly perceptible; some traces of warmth remain; a slight color lingers within the centre of the cheek; and, upon application of a mirror to the lips, we can detect a torpid, unequal, and vacillating action of the lungs. Then again the duration of the (b) trance is for weeks — even for months; while the closest scrutiny, and the most rigorous medical tests, fail to establish any material distinction between the state of the sufferer and what we conceive of absolute death. Very usually he is saved from premature interment solely by the knowledge of his friends that he has been previously subject to catalepsy, by the consequent suspicion excited, and, above all, by the non-appearance of decay. The advances of (c) the malady are, luckily, gradual. The first (d) manifestations, although marked, are equivocal. The fits grow successively more and more distinctive, and endure each for a longer term than the preceding. In this lies the principal security from inhumation. The unfortunate whose first attack should be of the extreme character which is occasionally seen, would almost inevitably be consigned alive to the tomb.

문제 1 What is the passage mainly talking about?
(1) Causes of a Disease
(2) Overall Characteristics of a Disease
(3) When to Bury the Patient
(4) Ways to Prevent a Disease

문제 2 Which of the following is neither stated nor implied from the passage?
(1) The patient under the influence of catalepsy might seem to be in a coma.
(2) The disease in the passage has no definite title.
(3) A close examination can definitively determine whether a person with catalepsy is alive or not.
(4) The advances of the disease take place at a slow speed.

문제 3 Which of the following does NOT refer to the same item?
(1) (a)
(2) (b)
(3) (c)
(4) (d)

[Challenge 2]

Franklin was naturally disputatious. With his keen intellect, he was pretty sure to come off as victor, at least in his own judgment, in discussions with his associates. But the Socratic method of argumentation, so different from that in which he had been accustomed to indulge, at once secured his approval and admiration. Socrates was never guilty of the discourtesy of assailing an opponent with flat contradiction or positive assertion. With a politeness which never failed him, and a modesty of demeanor which won the regard of all others, he would lead his fellow disputant, by a series of questions, to assent to the views which he advocated. Franklin immediately commenced practicing upon this newly discovered art. He was remarkably successful, and became one of the most agreeable and beloved of companions. But before long he became satisfied of the folly of these disputations, in which each party struggles, not for truth, but for victory. It is simply an exercise of _____(a)_____, in which the man who has the most skill and muscle discomfits his antagonist. Jefferson warned his nephew to avoid disputation. He says, "I have never known, during my long life, any persons' engage in a dispute in which they did not separate, each more firmly convinced than before of the correctness of his own views."

문제 1 Which of the following would be the best title for the passage?
(1) Franklin and Socratic Method of Argumentation
(2) Contentious Characteristic of Franklin
(3) How Socratic Method of Argumentation is developed by Franklin
(4) Common Features between Socrates and Franklin

문제 2 Which of the following is NOT true of the passage?
(1) Jefferson knew disputations could lead two different views of opinion to more disparity.
(2) Franklin was fond of arguing.
(3) Franklin was at first defensive toward Socrates's method of argumentation but soon was fascinated by it.
(4) Socrates did his method of argumentation for the search of truth.

문제 3 Fill in blank (a).
(1) unsolvable labyrinth   (2) intellectual gladiatorship
(3) physical tug-of-war   (4) brainteaser

[Challenge 3]

After having an abortion, many women feel a sense of relief at having avoided the stress and responsibility of pregnancy and a baby, but abortions eventually cause serious emotional damage in millions of women. The American Psychiatric Association has identified abortion as one of the stressor events that can trigger post-traumatic stress disorder (PTSD). Many of us associate PTSD with Vietnam Veterans suffering from the effects of the war; but post-abortion syndrome is a form of PTSD that affects women who have had abortions. The death of a child is one of the biggest stress points a person can experience in life. Post-abortion syndrome is the emotional stress of not grieving, not letting ourselves feel the pain and suffering that is part of a loss. To be emotional healthy, we all have to grieve through our losses; but what do you do when society tells you there's nothing to grieve about? If a woman does not recognize her need to grieve for her baby, or if she does not allow it to occur, that emotional pain is going to go somewhere. Frequently, following a woman's abortion, she goes into what one CPC counselor described as "self-destruct mode": getting pregnant again, having an affair, punishing herself, and generally showing all the variations that severe depression can take. Women experiencing post-abortion syndrome generally feel a confusing and overwhelming sense of guilt. One study reported that 92 percent of women who have had an abortion feel guilt. One woman who is now involved in a post-abortion healing group reports that after her abortion, the memory __(a)__ her. She heard this little voice in her head: "Abortion, abortion; you're a terrible, awful person." For many women, the guilt and shame is expressed through a deep anger at the doctors and abortion counselors for hurting her and her baby, at her husband, boyfriend, or parents for pressuring her into an abortion, and at herself for getting pregnant and having the abortion.

문제 1   Which of the following would be the best title for the passage?
(1) Why Women Get Abortions (2) Characteristics of Abortion
(3) How to Evade Post-Abortion Syndrome (4) Post-Abortion Syndrome

문제 2   Which of the following is TRUE of the passage?
(1) According to the American Psychiatric Association, women whose husbands participated in the Vietnam War have a higher chance of getting an abortion than those who did not.
(2) Women who have had abortions might go through the same symptoms as those who went through horrible events such as war and terrorist attacks.
(3) Women who have had abortions all showed the same patterns of emotional disorders.
(4) So-called self-destruct mode regarding post-abortion syndrome rarely takes place in cases of abortion-on-demand.

문제 3   Given the context, which of the following best fills in the blank (a)?
(1) exasperated (2) plagued
(3) haunted (4) perplexed

[Challenge 4]

Industry and thrift are closely allied. Economic studies show clearly that ninety-five per cent of the employers are employers because they systematically saved money. Any man who systematically saves money from early youth automatically becomes an employer. He may employ thousands or he may have only two or three clerks in a country store, but he nevertheless is an employer. These same studies show that ninety-five per cent of the wage workers are wage workers because they have systematically spent their money as fast as they have earned it. They of necessity remain wage workers. These are facts which no labour leader can disprove and which are exceedingly significant. This is especially striking when one considers that the employer often started out at the same wages and in the same community as his wage workers. The employer was naturally industrious and thrifty; while those who remained wage workers were not.

문제 1   Which of the following is the topic of the above passage?
(1) Differing Characteristics of Employers and Wage Workers
(2) How to Remain Employers
(3) Factors telling Good Employers Apart from Bad Employers
(4) Reasons why Employers are Richer than Wage Workers

[Challenge 5]

Even if eligibility for free lunch is problematic, students can always brown-bag it, right? That's not what I've seen in school cafeterias across the country. In the USDA's most recent comprehensive study of school food, 62 percent of students chose the school lunch and about 10 percent of the students brought lunch from home on the day being surveyed. What happened to everyone else? Some did not eat lunch (4 percent of elementary students and 8 percent of high school students). Others bought food from a la carte options in the cafeteria, left the campus to purchase food, or bought from vending machines or school stores. What they were getting on their own was typically not as healthy as the school lunch that met the federal nutrition guidelines, known as the reimbursable meal. According to one recent nutrient assessment, high school students who participated in the lunch program consumed significantly greater amounts of Vitamins A and B12, calcium, potassium and other nutrients than non-participants did. Other studies have found that kids in the national school lunch program drink more milk and eat fewer snack foods, sweets and sweetened beverages than others. While certainly some households send carefully crafted healthy lunches, far too many children arrive at school with a brown bag containing a sweet drink and a bag of chips.

문제 1   Which of the following is CORRECT about the passage?
   (1) Most students who don't participate in the National School Lunch Program eat a healthy lunch brought from home.
   (2) Most students think they are eating healthy food at school because of the state-run lunch program.
   (3) According to the USDA's study, more than half of the students surveyed came to school with brown-bag lunches.
   (4) High school students who participate in the lunch program are eating healthier food than those who do not.

[Challenge 6]

An advance-fee fraud is a confidence trick in which the target is persuaded to advance sums of money in the hope of realizing a significantly larger gain. Among the variations on this type of scam, are the Nigerian Letter (also called the 419 fraud, Nigerian scam, Nigerian bank scam, or Nigerian money offer), the Spanish Prisoner, the black money scam as well as Russian/Ukrainian scam (also widespread, though far less popular than the former). The so-called Russian and Nigerian scams stand for wholly dissimilar organised-crime traditions; they therefore tend to use altogether ____(a)____ breeds of approaches. Although similar to older scams such as the Spanish Prisoner, the modern 419 scam originated in the early 1980s as the oil-based Nigerian economy declined. Several unemployed university students first used this scam as a means of manipulating business visitors interested in shady deals in the Nigerian oil sector before targeting businessmen in the west, and later the wider population. Scammers in the early-to-mid 1990s targeted companies, sending scam messages via letter, fax, or Telex. The spread of e-mail and easy access to e-mail-harvesting software significantly lowered the cost of sending scam letters by using the Internet. In the 2000s, the 419 scam has spurred imitations from other locations in Africa, Asia and Eastern Europe, and, more recently, from North America, Western Europe (mainly United Kingdom and Netherlands), and Australia.

문제 1 Which of the following is NOT correct about the passage?
(1) Email beats scam letters in terms of cost.
(2) In the early 1980s, scammers first used the modern 419 scam to frame up visitors who were interested in the government oil project.
(3) The Internet served as a tool for Nigerians to get easier access to their targets.
(4) The development of the modern 419 scam has to do with the Nigerian economy at the time.

문제 2 Choose one that is most appropriate for blank (a).
(1) several
(2) different
(3) miscellaneous
(4) coinciding

[Challenge 7]

Much of the controversy surrounding social capital has to do with its application to different types of problems and its use in theories involving different units of analysis. The original theoretical development of the concept by the French sociologist Pierre Bourdieu and the American sociologist James Coleman centered on individuals or small groups as the units of analysis. With some significant variations, both scholars focused on the benefits accruing to individuals or families by virtue of their ties with others. (가) Bourdieu's treatment of the concept, in particular, was instrumental, going as far as noting that people intentionally built their relations for the benefits that they would bring later. (나) In a few brilliant pages, the French sociologist dealt with the interaction between money capital, social capital, and cultural capital, the latter defined as the formal educational credentials that an individual possesses and the more intangible complex of values and knowledge of cultural forms in his or her demeanor. (다) Bourdieu's key insight was that forms of capital are ____(a)____, that is they can be traded for each other and actually require such trades for their development. (라)

문제 1 Which of the following is the best explanation of cultural capital depicted in the passage?
(1) It is a form of knowledge, education, and advantages that a person has, which give them a higher status in society.
(2) It refers to all resources that determine the value and the competitiveness of an enterprise.
(3) It refers to connections within and between social networks.
(4) It is resources based on group membership, relationships, networks of influence and support.

문제 2 Fill in blank (a).
(1) fungible
(2) identical
(3) inexplicable
(4) analogous

문제 3 Where does the sentence below best fit in the passage?

> Social capital of any significance can seldom be acquired, for example, without the investment of some material resources and the possession of some cultural knowledge, enabling the individual to establish relations with others.

(1) (가) (2) (나)
(3) (다) (4) (라)

[Challenge 8]

(a) <u>Last month North Korea dramatically raised tensions in east Asia when it shelled the island of Yeonpyeong, hitting a South Korean military base and killing four people. South Korea said it was conducting military exercises at the time but insists test firings were not directed toward North Korea.</u> "In Japan we have a strong sense of crisis over the North Korean artillery attack on the island of Yeonpyeong," Hajime Hirota, parliamentary vice-minister of defense said. "It is an act that we in Japan we cannot tolerate ... For other countries of northeast Asia, including Japan, this act is seen as a large threat." Hirota said the attack would see Japan forging stronger ties with South Korea and the United States and that the key was to avoid further escalation. "We don't know how North Korea will react to the situation going forward," he said. Japan has long taken a hard-line stance against Pyongyang over its nuclear and missile programs and its kidnappings of Japanese nationals in the 1970s and 80s to train North Korean spies — still a highly emotive issue among the public. The country has pledged to cooperate closely with South Korea and the United States and said it is discussing with them on how to deal with the issue in the U.N. Security Council. Japan should also increase its defense budget given the growing uncertainty in Asia, Hirota said. A week after North Korea's shelling of Yeonpyeong, Pyongyang announced it had made advances in its nuclear program. Japan's ties with China and Russia also remain fragile after a flare-up in long-standing territorial feuds. "My personal view is that Japan should increase its defense budget but at the same time Japan's fiscal condition is the worst among the advanced countries," he said at the Manama Dialogue meeting of the International Institute for Strategic Studies, a London-based think-tank. "The environment in Asia surrounding Japan has seen an enhanced level of uncertainty and therefore as a nation we have to have the will to secure a necessary budget."

問題 1　The function of the underlined (a) in the passage is to _____.
　　　　(1) elucidate a certain natural disaster that has recently happened before going into the details of the cause
　　　　(2) show the contrasting ideas of a certain phenomenon
　　　　(3) demonstrate how one country can start a war with another
　　　　(4) provide the overall background before going into the details of the passage

問題 2　Which of the following best represents the title for the passage?
　　　　(1) North Korea should stop international terrorist activities.
　　　　(2) South Korea and Japan will launch a joint military exercise soon.
　　　　(3) South Korea calls for immediate actions against North Korea.
　　　　(4) Japan feels sense of crisis over North Korea.

문제 3 Which of the following is NOT correct about the passage?

(1) After the attack, Japan would build up stronger ties with South Korea.

(2) North Korean abducted Japanese nationals who were spying on them.

(3) Japan's ties with China and Russia is on the rocks due to the territorial conflicts.

(4) The increased uncertainty in Asia is encouraging Japan to think that increasing its defense budget is a necessary step for now.

[Challenge 9]

Plato says somewhere in his "Republic" that things will go well only when those men shall govern the state who do not desire to govern. The idea is probably that, assuming the necessary capability, a man's reluctance to govern affords a good guarantee that he will govern well and efficiently; whereas a man desirous of governing may very easily either abuse his power and become a tyrant, or by his desire to govern be brought into an unforeseen situation of dependence on the people he is to rule, so that his government really becomes an illusion.

문제 1 Which of the following can NOT be inferred from the passage?

(1) A man aspiring to attain to power may ill-use his position.

(2) People with the necessary capability to govern sometimes do not engage themselves in political circles.

(3) If someone shows reluctance in dealing with something, it is safe to say that he or she is not competent enough to handle it.

(4) A man's desire to govern does not mean that he is well-equipped to govern well.

[Challenge 10]

Global carbon dioxide (CO2) emissions — the main contributor to global warming — show no sign of abating and may reach record levels in 2010, according to a study led by the University of Exeter (UK). The study, which also involved the University of East Anglia (UK) and other global institutions, is part of the annual carbon budget update by the Global Carbon Project. In a paper published November 21 in Nature Geoscience, the authors found that despite the major financial crisis that hit the world last year, global CO2 emissions from the burning of fossil fuel in 2009 were only 1.3 per cent below the record 2008 figures. This is less than half the drop predicted a year ago. The global financial crisis severely affected western economies, leading to large reductions in CO2 emissions. _____(a)_____, UK emissions were 8.6% lower in 2009 than in 2008. Similar figures apply to USA, Japan, France, Germany, and most other industrialised nations. However, emerging economies had a strong economic performance despite the financial crisis, and recorded substantial increases in CO2 emissions (e.g. China +8 per cent, India +6.2 per cent). Professor Pierre Friedlingstein, lead author of the research, said: "The 2009 drop in CO2 emissions is less than half that anticipated a year ago. This is because the drop in world Gross Domestic Product (GDP) was less than anticipated and the carbon intensity of world GDP, which is the amount of CO2 released per unit of GDP, improved by only 0.7 per cent in 2009 — well below its long-term average of 1.7% per year." The poor improvements in carbon intensity were caused by an increased share of fossil-fuel CO2 emissions produced by emerging economies with a relatively high carbon intensity, and an increasing reliance on coal. The study projects that if economic growth proceeds as expected, global fossil fuel emissions will increase by more than 3% in 2010, approaching the high emissions growth rates observed through 2000 to 2008.

문제 1   According to the passage, which of the following is CORRECT about the passage?
(1) It is said that a recent rise in levels of CO2 is soon to change its course downward.
(2) The major financial crisis in 2008 led to a dramatic drop in CO2 consumption in developing countries.
(3) The carbon intensity has been improved dramatically due to an increased use of fossilfuels.
(4) Most of the economic powers experienced a drop in the amount of CO2 used after the global financial crisis.

문제 2   Fill in blank (a).
(1) In the same way   (2) In addition
(3) For example   (4) Given that

Day 10

★ They always say time changes things, but you actually have to change them yourself.
  Andy Warhol (1928 - 1987), *The Philosophy of Andy Warhol*

사람들은 시간이 흐르면 사태가 바뀔 것이라고 말하지만, 사실 네 스스로 바꿔야만 한다. (Andy Warhol)

[Challenge 1]

The Observatory was like most approved recreation spots — large and raucous, selling unrationed food and drink and amusement at uncontrolled prices of which (a) the government took its usual lion's share. The angle in this place was astronomy. The ceiling was a blue haze a-glitter with slowly wheeling constellations, and the strippers began with (b) make-believe spacesuits. There were some rather good murals on the walls depicting various stages of the conquest of space. Lancaster was amused at one of them.

문제 1 According to the passage, which of the following refers to the 'Observatory' in the above passage?
  (1) A club   (2) A monitor station
  (3) A refectory   (4) A cafeteria

문제 2 Which of the following best paraphrases the underlined (a)?
  (1) The government took austere control of the people using the Observatory.
  (2) The government took possession of the best portion of the returns from the Observatory.
  (3) The government strictly controlled the process of price decision-making.
  (4) The government sometimes stripped the Observatory of the right to sell.

문제 3 Find one that is closest in meaning to the underlined (b).
  (1) vacillating   (2) allegiant
  (3) steadfast   (4) spurious

[Challenge 2]

It is sometimes difficult to see the difference between a fad and a trend. A fad lasts a very short time and is not very important, while a trend lasts much longer. A recent trend is the interest in good health, but many fads come from this trend: aerobic exercise, cholesterol counting, and the like. Trendspotting is the ability to identify a trend at an early stage — an extremely important skill in the business world. The first company that can correctly identify a new trend has a competitive edge — an advantage — over other companies. The person who founded the Starbucks chain of coffeehouse was able to find _____ — interest in quality and variety in coffee. Today, people buy Starbucks products in shopping centers, airports, and supermarkets everywhere. But when a development in popular culture is new, it's difficult to distinguish between a fad and a trend. People who invested their funds in Green Peace swimsuits probably regret their decision. Clearly, they mistook a fad for a trend.

문제 1 Which of the following would best fit in the blank?
(1) a fad   (2) a trend   (3) a business   (4) a company

문제 2 Which of the following can be inferred from the passage?
(1) People aren't really concerned about environmental problems.
(2) The founder of Starbucks does not have an ability to find a fad.
(3) Anyone who can identify a new trend is likely to make a lot of money in business.
(4) People who have invested into Green Peace swimsuits are soon to see great returns.

[Challenge 3]

Nathaniel Bowditch, the translator of Laplace's Mécanique Céleste, displayed in very early life a taste for mathematical studies. In the year 1788, when he was only fifteen years old, he actually made an almanack for the year 1790, containing all the usual tables, calculations of the eclipses, and other phenomena, and even the customary predictions of the weather. (a) Bowditch was bred to the sea, and in his early voyages taught navigation to the common sailors about him.(b) Captain Prince, with whom he often sailed, relates, that one day the supercargo of the vessel said to him, "Come, Captain, let us go forward and hear what the sailors are talking about under the lee of the long-boat." (c) They went forward accordingly, and the captain was surprised to find the sailors, instead of (e) <u>spinning their long yarns</u>, earnestly engaged with book, slate, and pencil, discussing the high matters of tangts and secants, altitudes, dip, and refraction. (d) Two of them, in particular, were very zealously disputing, — one of them calling out to the other, "Well, Jack, what have you got?" "I've got the sine," was the answer. "But that ain't right," said the other; "I say it is the cosine."

문제 1 When the passage is divided into two, where does the second paragraph begin?
(1) (a)   (2) (b)
(3) (c)   (4) (d)

문제 2 Which of the following is neither stated nor implied in the passage?
(1) Nathaniel Bowditch was a marvel even from his early days.
(2) Nathaniel Bowditch probably had an ability to deliver complexity of math in straightforward and plain terms.
(3) Nathaniel Bowditch made his own calendar, which is quite elaborate in its content.
(4) In Nathaniel Bowditch's day, ordinary sailors knew a lot about math.

문제 3 Give the context, which of the following best paraphrases the underlined (e)?
(1) taking a short nap
(2) talking about small talks
(3) working on a mill
(4) engaging in rowing

[Challenge 4]

After ratifying the Convention on the Rights of the Child on 16 July 1995, the architects of the new South Africa embedded its precepts into their country's constitution. Section 28 of South Africa's Bill of Rights guarantees children's right to an identity, basic services, education and protection within the legal system. Other key legislation to protect the rights of children introduced during the post-apartheid era includes the Basic Conditions of Employment Act, the Domestic Violence Act, the Child Justice Act and the Sexual Offences Act. The most comprehensive addition to the child rights framework is the 2005 Children's Act and Amendment, which reinforces provisions in the Bill of Rights and details the responsibilities of parents and guardians. Important provisions include the right of access to state grants for children over age 16 who head households, and greater access to health care for young people, including the right of consent to HIV testing and treatment.

문제 1 Which of the following is most appropriate for the title for the passage?
(1) Child rights at the heart of the post-apartheid constitution
(2) South Africa's Bill of Rights
(3) The History of South Africa's Constitution
(4) Unprecedented Changes in South Africa's Constitution

Day 10

[Challenge 5]

Chinese scientists may have to learn to _____(a)_____ the "Great Firewall" if they want to visit the official Web site of the Nobel Prize. Within China, typing the site's URL into a browser's address bar yields a blank screen with the words "the connection has been reset." The block comes in the wake of the Norwegian Nobel Committee's decision to award this year's peace prize to Chinese dissident Liu Xiaobo. The Chinese government did not permit Liu, who is in prison, or his family members to travel to Oslo to accept the award at a ceremony held earlier today. Such a "simplistic and crude blockade" is akin to "refusing to eat for fear of choking," Yan Ning, a biology professor at Tsinghua University in Beijing, lamented in her blog on ScienceNet.cn. Yan says she used to visit the Nobel site regularly to download lectures as reading material for her students, before discovering last month that the Web site was no longer accessible.

문제 1 Which of the following is the best title of the passage?
　　　　(1) The "Great Firewall" in Comparison with The Great Wall
　　　　(2) China's Great Firewall Blocking the Nobel Site
　　　　(3) Call for the New Qualifications of the Nobel Peace Price
　　　　(4) The Chinese Government's Crack Down on Illegal Web Sites

문제 2 Which of the following would be most appropriate for the blank (a) to the passage?
　　　　(1) decimate　　　(2) concoct　　　(3) scale　　　(4) dwindle

[Challenge 6]

Over the past several days, the anti-secrecy Web site WikiLeaks has been hit with a series of blows that have seemed to threaten its survival. Its primary Web address was deactivated, its PayPal account was frozen, and its Internet server gave it the boot. The result: WikiLeaks is now stronger than ever, at least as measured by its ability to publish online. Blocked from using one Internet host, WikiLeaks simply jumped to another. Meanwhile, the number of "mirror" Web sites — effectively clones of WikiLeaks' main contents pages — grew from a few dozen last week to 200 by Sunday. By early Wednesday, the number of such sites surpassed 1,000. At the same time, WikiLeaks' supporters have apparently gone on the offensive, staging retaliatory attacks against Internet companies that have cut ties to the group amid fears they could be associated with it. On Wednesday, hackers briefly shut down access to the Web sites for MasterCard and Visa, both of which had announced they had stopped processing donations to WikiLeaks. WikiLeaks' long-term survival depends on a number of unknowns, including the fate of its principal founder, Julian Assange, who is being held in Britain while awaiting possible extradition to Sweden related to sexual-assault allegations. But the Web site's resilience in the face of repeated setbacks has underscored a lesson already absorbed by more repressive governments that have tried to control the Internet. "The Internet is an extremely open system with very low barriers to access and use," said Vint Cerf, Google's vice president. "The ease of moving digital information around makes it very difficult to suppress once it is accessible."   (a) , despite the global uproar over the release of sensitive U.S. diplomatic cables, Assange's Web site remained defiantly intact Wednesday. Over the past week it has continued to publish a steady stream of leaked State Department documents with little visible evidence of injury from repeated, anonymous cyber-attacks or the multiple attempts to cut off its access to funding and Web resources.   (b) , companies that have pulled the plug on WikiLeaks have suffered publicly, with cyber-attacks rendering their Web sites inaccessible for hours at a time. While a group of "hacktivists" targeted MasterCard and Visa — part of "Operation Payback," they called it — anonymous assailants have also in recent days attacked PayPal, which severed relations with WikiLeaks citing violations of its terms of service.

문제 1 Which of the following is NOT correct about the passage?
(1) WikiLeaks has recently been under criticism due to the release of sensitive information.
(2) Julian Assange is now in Sweden waiting for the ruling related to sexual-assault allegations.
(3) Companies that have cut ties with WikiLeaks have been under cyber-attacks.
(4) The number of "mirror" Web sites has soared lately.

문제 2 What can be inferred from the underlined sentence in the passage?
(1) Governments tend to keep all the online activities under control.
(2) An attempt to regulate the Internet is nearly impossible to do.
(3) A Web site's resilience gets exacerbated by the number of attacks it gets.
(4) Internet is an open system full of destructive information.

문제 3 Fill in blanks (a) and (b).
(1) For this reason — So   (2) In reality — Futhermore
(3) Thus — By contrast   (4) However — In other words

[Challenge 7]

Confucianism was the most influential Chinese religion. It was founded by Confucius or Kung-fu-tzu. Confucianism was the state religion from the establishment of the Han Dynasty in 202 B.C. to the end of the imperial epoch in 1911. Confucian teachings were the subject of civil service examinations for more than 2,000 years. Confucianism maintains that people should embrace their station in life to preserve social harmony. It identifies five cardinal relationships between intrinsically superior and inferior beings. The inferior must avow complete loyalty and obedience to the superior and superior beings must be benevolent and compassionate toward the inferior. Filial piety was one of the most important qualities stressed by Confucius.

문제 1   Which of the following can be inferred from the passage?
(1) The civil service examination was first suggested by Confucius.
(2) Confucianism was the only influential religion in China over 2,000 years.
(3) Under confucianism social mobility was greatly increased.
(4) Confucianism can be used to intensify the class consciousness.

[Challenge 8]

The grave question now is, How far will this peculiar old system continue and how far will it be altered? I am afraid I must put aside at once the idea that it will be altered entirely and altered for the better. I cannot expect that the new class of voters will be at all more able to form sound opinions on complex questions than the old voters. There was indeed an idea that there then was an unrepresented class of skilled artisans who could form superior opinions on national matters, and ought to have the means of expressing them. We used to frame elaborate schemes to give them such means. _____(a)_____ the Reform Act of 1867 did not stop at skilled labour; it enfranchised unskilled labour too. And no one will contend that the ordinary working man who has no special skill, and who is only rated because he has a house, can judge much of intellectual matters. The messenger in an office is not more intelligent than the clerks, not better educated, but worse; and yet the messenger is probably (b) a very superior specimen of the newly enfranchised classes. The average can only earn very scanty wages by coarse labour. They have no time to improve themselves, for they are labouring the whole day through; and their early education was so small that in most cases it is dubious whether even if they had much time, they could use it to good purpose.

문제 1   Choose the transition that best fits in blank (a).
(1) And   (2) But   (3) Therefore   (4) In addiction

문제 2 Which of the following can be inferred from the underlined (b)?
(1) Only when most of the workers are enfranchised is the real democracy realized.
(2) Most of the unskilled workers newly given the right to vote probably do not show a required ability to make an intellectual decision.
(3) Unskilled workers are great examples which show that educated people do not always make right political decisions.
(4) Most of the messengers working in the office are now enfranchised.

문제 3 Which of the following is not one of the reasons for the author to say that unskilled average workers are not intellectual enough to make good judgement?
(1) Physical weaknesses   (2) Poor early education
(3) Low income   (4) Long work hours

[Challenge 9]

There was a poor woman named Rachel Jenkins, who lived in a very little cottage at some distance from any other house. She was a widow, and very poor, but she was very clean and careful; so that her cottage had always a look of neatness and comfort. She used to spend most of her time in spinning. She had one son, whose name was Harry. He was twelve years old, and used to carry a basket filled with tapes and thread, pins and needles, and other things of that sort, which he sold to people who lived near. He used to go out in the morning and return in the evening; and you may be sure his mother was always glad when the time came for him to come home. One evening, as he was on his way home, about half a mile from his mother's house, he saw an old man sitting by the way-side, who was very tired, and seemed as if he was not able to walk any further. His hair was quite white, and his face and hands were thin and wrinkled. Harry said to him in a kind voice, "You seem tired, father; have you got much further to walk." The old man told him that he had to go to the next town, which was twelve miles further; but that he was so tired, he was sure that he should not be able to get there that night. On this, Harry said, "I wish you would go home with me; for I am sure my mother would be very glad that you should sleep in our house." The old man thanked him and said he would go with him. So he rested his hand upon Harry's shoulder, and walked slowly towards the house. Harry's mother met them at the door; and when Harry had told her how he had met with the old man, she said she was glad to see him, and asked him to walk in to take some tea. After tea, the old man told Sarah Jenkins that he was going to see his son, who was laid up in a hospital in the town to which he was going. His son was a soldier, and had been in the West Indies for some years; but he caught the yellow fever, and was sent home sick. The next morning the old man went on his way, and blessed Sarah Jenkins and Harry, because they had done good to him who could make no other return than to thank them and pray for them.

문제 1 Which of the following best describes the lesson shown through the act of Harry?
(1) Hospitality   (2) Fortitude
(3) Perseverance   (4) Infirmary

문제 2 Which of the following is NOT true of the passage?
(1) Rachel Jenkins managed her cottage in a clean way.
(2) Harry, son of Rachel Jenkins used to vend sewing items to neighbors.
(3) The old man who Harry met on the way home had a son, who was in the army at the time.
(4) The old man thanked the kindness of Rachel Jenkins and her son and made the best of his way after spending the night at their home.

[Challenge 10]

In conversation people often unconsciously modify their own speech to conform to the speech of others. This type of adjustment linguists call accommodation. Ethnographers (cultural anthropologists) concerned with language socialization (acquiring the rules for using language) describe the important role of accommodation in cross-cultural studies of language use. (가) Infants, children, and young adults in all societies model their speech after that of adults and their peers. (나) Thus, the differences in the way language is used to reinforce various cultural ideas (especially when emphasizing differences in status by age, gender, and experience) are, at least in part, learned through modeling language and speech behavior. (다) Accommodation also refers to the adjustments or adaptations made by an entire speech community for the benefit of new members who speak a different language from that of the larger group. (라) Accommodation of this kind typically occurs in contact situations where language-minority speakers are present. Often members of the larger speech community use more nonverbal cues (exaggerated hand, arm, and facial gestures) as a way of organizing communication with the newer members.

문제 1 When the above passage is divided into two, where would be the best boundary?
(1) (가)   (2) (나)
(3) (다)   (4) (라)

문제 2 Which of the following is TRUE of the passage?
(1) In general, accommodation is used to discriminate against minorities by larger groups.
(2) Accommodation can be used as a tool to emphasize or minimize the social differences.
(3) In normal conversation, nonverbal cues do not usually occur.
(4) Accommodation is an important concept when forming a new community.

Day 11

★ It's not that some people have willpower and some don't. It's that some people are ready to change and others are not.

James Gordon, M.D.

어떤 이는 의지력이 있고, 어떤 있는 의지력이 없는 그런 것이 아니다. 이것은 어떤 이는 변화할 준비가 되어 있는 반면, 어떤 이는 그렇지 않을 뿐이다. (James Gordon, M.D.)

[Challenge 1]

If there is any one thing in the world that seems utterly chaotic, it is the way in which the mind wanders from one subject of thought to another. It requires but a moment for it to flash from New York to San Francisco, from San Francisco to Tokyo, and around the globe. Yet mental processes are as law-abiding as anything else in Nature. So much is this true, that if we knew every detail of your past experience from your first infantile sensation, and knew also just what you are thinking of at the present moment, we could predict to a mathematical certainty just what ideas would next appear on the kaleidoscopic screen of your thoughts. This is due to laws that govern the association of ideas. These laws are, in substance, that the way in which judgments and ideas are classified and stored away, and the order in which they are brought forth into consciousness depends upon what other judgments and ideas they have been associated with most habitually, recently, closely and vividly.

문제 1 Which of the following is the best title of the passage?
(1) A Chaotic Nature of Mind   (2) Laws of Association of Ideas
(3) Four Prime Laws of Association (4) Classification of Thoughts

문제 2 According to the passage, which of the following is NOT correct about the mind?
(1) It is spaceless.   (2) It is timeless.
(3) It obeys certain laws. (4) It is disorganized.

[Challenge 2]

Some may think there is danger of setting too high a standard of action. I have heard teachers contend that a child will learn to write much faster by having an inferior copy, than by imitating one which is comparatively perfect; "because," say they, "a pupil is liable to be discouraged if you give him a perfect copy; but if it is only a little in advance of his own, he will take courage from the belief that he shall soon be able to equal it." I am fully convinced, however, that this is not so. The more perfect the copy you place before the child, the better. For it must always be possible in the nature of things, for the child to imitate it; and what is not absolutely impossible, every child may reasonably be expected to aspire after, on the principle, that whatever man has done, man may do. So in human conduct, generally; _____. I might show that it is a part of the divine economy to place before his rational creatures a perfect standard of action, and to make it their duty to come up to it.

문제 1 Which of the following is the topic of the passage?
 (1) Importance of Aiming High   (2) Effects of Imitation on Children
 (3) Principles of Writing   (4) Role Models for Children

문제 2 Fill in the blank to the passage.
 (1) whatever is possible should be aimed at
 (2) what is possible can or can not be pursued
 (3) things should be considered in consideration of the circumstances
 (4) getting things done is the best policy one can take

[Challenge 3]

The linear arrangement of words into a logical or coherent pattern (a sentence) is grammar. Developing an understanding of grammar — or syntax, as it is sometimes called — is important to linguists because through grammatical organization language has coherence. Coherence refers to the logical binding together of word types (parts of speech) to produce low-level meaning. For example, consider the following sentence: "We took the kites out and flew them all day." For English speakers the arrangement of these words into a recognizable pattern (such as the noun phrase "the kite" and verb phrases "we took" and "flew them") allows listeners to obtain the general meaning of the sentence. If the word order is randomized, the sentence loses coherence: "Day and all we flew them out took kites the." Grammar, therefore, is the glue that holds sentences together as logical structures. The linguist Noam Chomsky illustrates the idea of coherence with his famous sentence: "Colorless green ideas sleep furiously." Although this sentence contains contradictions ("colorless green" and "sleep furiously") and thus has little practical meaning, the sentence ____(a)____ because the various parts of speech are arranged in a sequential logical manner.

*low-level: occurring or operating at the phonetic level of linguistic representation or analysis

문제 1 Which of the following is correct about the passage?
(1) Not every language has its own syntax.
(2) Syntax is a more complex form of grammar.
(3) Coherence organizes words and phrases into logical structures.
(4) It is coherence that gives meaning to sentences.

문제 2 Choose one that is most appropriate for blank (a).
(1) does not carry any coherence
(2) still has coherence
(3) is still meaningful
(4) is not practical

[Challenge 4]

It is assumed, I suppose, that contradictions among ideas and beliefs are of various degrees and of various modes besides that specific one which we call logical incompatibility. _____(a)_____ A perception may be pictorially inconsistent or tonically discordant with another perception; a mere faith unsupported by objective evidence may be emotionally antagonistic to another mere faith, as truly as a judgment may be logically irreconcilable with another judgment. And this wide possibility of contradiction is particularly to be recognized when the differing ideas or beliefs have arisen not within the same individual mind but in different minds, and are therefore colored by personal or partisan interest and warped by idiosyncrasy of mental constitution. The contradictions of, or rather among, ideas and beliefs, with which we are now concerned, are more extensive and more varied than mere logical duels; they are also less definite, less precise. In reality they are culture conflicts in which the opposing forces, so far from being specific ideas only or pristine beliefs only, are in fact more or less bewildering complexes of ideas, beliefs, prejudices, sympathies, antipathies, and personal interests.

문제 1 Which of the following is the topic of the passage?
(1) Discrepancy of Ideas and Beliefs (2) Kinds of Ideas and Beliefs
(3) Characteristics of Perception (4) Cultural Conflicts

문제 2 According to the passage, contradictions among ideas and beliefs get more distinctive when _____.
(1) a faith is not supported by objective material
(2) personal or partisan interests are involved
(3) the difference in ideas happens among people with different mind-sets
(4) beliefs are culture-related

문제 3 Fill in blank (a).
(1) However (2) for example
(3) Nevertheless (4) In addition

[Challenge 5]

Hero makes no suggestions as to application of any of the devices he describes to a useful purpose. From the time of Hero until the late sixteenth and early seventeenth centuries, there is no record of progress, though evidence is found that such devices as were described by Hero were sometimes used for trivial purposes. To the next contributor, Edward Somerset is apparently due the credit of proposing, if not of making, the first useful steam engine. In the "Century of Scantlings and Inventions," published in London in 1663, he describes devices showing that he had in mind the raising of water not only by forcing it from two receivers by direct steam pressure but also for some sort of reciprocating piston actuating one end of a lever, the other operating a pump. His descriptions are rather obscure and no drawings are extant so that it is difficult to say whether there were any distinctly novel features to his devices aside from the double action. _____ there is no direct authentic record that any of the devices he described were actually constructed, it is claimed by many that he really built and operated a steam engine containing pistons. In 1675, Sir Samuel Moreland was decorated by King Charles II, for a demonstration of "a certain powerful machine to raise water." Though there appears to be no record of the design of this machine, the mathematical dictionary, published in 1822, credits Moreland with the first account of a steam engine, on which subject he wrote a treatise that is still preserved in the British Museum.

문제 1 Which of the following is the topic of the passage?
    (1) How the Steam Engine Works   (2) Preceeding Inventors of Steam Engine
    (3) Inventions of Early Originative People   (4) Features of the Steam Engine

문제 2 Which of the following is NOT correct from the passage?
    (1) Before the invention of a steam engine containing pistons, there is no direct record of practical and effective steam engines being invented.
    (2) Devices Hero described never applied to any part of daily life until the late sixteenth and early seventeenth centuries.
    (3) Edward Somerset deserved to be called to propose the first useful steam engine.
    (4) Moreland's treatise on the steam engine is extant.

문제 3 Which of the following is most appropriate for the blank?
    (1) While   (2) Therefore
    (3) And   (4) In fact

[Challenge 6]

If there is one subject which, above all others, may be regarded as of national interest at the present time, it is the subject of Slavery. Wherever we go, north or south, east or west, at the fireside, in the factory, the rail-car or the steamboat, in the state legislatures or the national Congress, this "(가) ghost that will not down" obtrudes (a) itself. The strife has involved press, pulpit, and forum alike, and in spite of all compromises by political parties, and the desperate attempts at non-committal by religious bodies, (b) it only grows wider and deeper. But the distinctive feature of (c) this, as compared with other questions of national import, is, that here both parties draw their principal arguments from the Bible as a common armory of weapons for attack and defense. On the one side, (d) it is claimed that slavery, as it exists in the United States, is not a moral evil; that it is an innocent and lawful relation, as much as that of parent and child, husband and wife, or any other in society; that the right to buy, sell, and hold men for purposes of gain, was given by (나) express permission of God, and sanctioned by Christ and his apostles; that this right is founded on the golden rule; and says Dr. Shannon of Bacon College, Ky., "I hardly know which is most unaccountable, the profound ignorance of the Bible, or the sublimity of cool impudence and infidelity manifested by those who profess to be Christians; and yet dare affirm that the Book of God gives no sanction to slaveholding." All these affirmations are fairly summed up thus: "As slavery was practiced by the patriarchs, received sanction and legality from God in the Mosaic law, and was not denounced by Christ and his apostles, it must have been right. If right then, it is so still; therefore Southern slavery is right." On the other hand, it is contended that chattel slavery is nowhere warranted or sanctioned by the Bible, but is totally opposed both to its spirit and teachings.

문제 1 What is the passage mainly talking about?
(1) Secular Views on Slavery
(2) What the Bible says about Slavery
(3) Slavery in Different Perspectives
(4) Slavery as a Moral Evil

문제 2 According to the passage, which is NOT true?
(1) Slavery is one of the trickiest issues across the country.
(2) Dr. Shannon acknowledges the sanction of slavery by the Bible.
(3) Slavery in the South is likely to have been .
(4) There is one interpretation on slavery in the Bible.

문제 3 What can be inferred from the underlined (가)?
(1) It is omnipresent.   (2) It is illusory.
(3) It is omnipotent.   (4) It is invisible.

문제 4 Which of the following does NOT refer to the same item?
  (1) (a)   (2) (b)
  (3) (c)   (4) (d)

문제 5 Which of the following is closest in meaning to the underlined (나)?
  (1) explicit   (2) implicit
  (3) unstated   (4) tacit

[Challenge 7]

Great confusion and diversity of opinion prevail as to the real views of the man whose writings have agitated the whole world, scientific and religious. If a man says he is a Darwinian, many understand him to avow himself virtually an atheist; while another understands him as saying that he adopts some harmless form of the doctrine of evolution. This is a great evil. It is obviously useless to discuss any theory until we are agreed as to what that theory is. The question, therefore, What is Darwinism? must take precedence of all discussion of its merits. The great fact of experience is that the universe exists. The great problem which has ever pressed upon the human mind is to account for its existence. What was its origin? To what causes are the changes we witness around us to be referred? As we are a part of the universe, these questions concern ourselves. What are the origin, nature, and destiny of man? Professor Huxley is right in saying, "The question of questions for mankind — the problem which underlies all others, and is more interesting than any other — is the ascertainment of the place which Man occupies in nature and of his relation to the universe of things. Whence our race has come, what are the limits of our power over nature, and of nature's power over us, to what goal are we tending, are the problems which present themselves anew and with undiminished interest to every man born into the world." Mr. Darwin undertakes to answer these questions. He proposes a solution of the problem which thus deeply concerns every living man. Darwinism is, therefore, a theory of the universe, at least so far as the living organisms on this earth are concerned.

문제 1 What is the purpose of the passage?
  (1) To elucidate a clear definition of a theory before going further into discussion about it
  (2) To explain the differences between a new theory and an existing one
  (3) To ascertain that human beings are the products of the evolutionary process
  (4) To explain scientifically how human beings react to the surrounding environments in the process of evolution

[Challenge 8]

Negotiators from different cultures may tend to view the purpose of a negotiation differently. For deal makers from some cultures, the goal of a business negotiation, first and foremost, is a signed contract between the parties. Other cultures tend to consider that the goal of a negotiation is not a signed contract but rather the creation of a relationship between the two sides. _____(a)_____, the essence of the deal is the relationship itself. For example in my survey of over 400 persons from twelve nationalities, reported fully in The Global Negotiator, I found that whereas 74 percent of the Spanish respondents claimed their goal in a negotiation was a contract, only 33 percent of the Indian executives had a similar view. The difference in approach may explain why certain Asian negotiators, whose negotiating goal is often the creation of a relationship, tend to give more time and effort to negotiation preliminaries, while North Americans often want to rush through this first phase of deal making. The preliminaries of negotiation, in which the parties seek to get to know one another thoroughly, are a crucial foundation for a good business relationship. They may seem less important when the goal is merely a contract. It is therefore important to determine how your counterparts view the purpose of your negotiation.

問題 1 Which of the following is the best title for the passage?
　　　(1) Stalemates of Deal Makers
　　　(2) Requirements of a Good Negotiator
　　　(3) Negotiating Goal: Contract or Relationship?
　　　(4) Foundations for a Good Business Relationship

問題 2 Which of the following best fills in blank (a)?
　　　(1) Although the written contract expresses the relationship
　　　(2) Although the deal makers from the parties disagree with each other
　　　(3) Because business negotiations are nothing but a contract
　　　(4) Since the contract from the parties does not come into effect right after

問題 3 Based on the above passage, which of the following is NOT correct?
　　　(1) If relationship negotiators sit on the other side of the table, merely convincing them of your ability to deliver on a low-cost contract may not be enough to land you the deal.
　　　(2) You may have to persuade relationship negotiators, from the very first meeting, that your two organizations have the potential to build a rewarding relationship over long term.
　　　(3) If the other side is basically a contract deal maker, trying to build a relationship may be a waste of time and energy.
　　　(4) The contract between negotiators from different cultures in all probability comes to a deadlock.

[Challenge 9]

In China, red is the symbol of fire and the south (both south in general and Southern China specifically). It carries a largely positive connotation, being associated with courage, loyalty, honor, success, fortune, fertility, happiness, passion, and summer. In Chinese cultural traditions, red is associated with weddings (where brides traditionally wear red dresses) and red paper is also frequently used to wrap gifts of money or other things. Special red packets in Mandarin are specifically used during the Chinese New Year to give monetary gifts. _____(a)_____, obituaries are traditionally written in red ink, and to write someone's name in red signals either cutting them out of your life, or that they have died. Red is also associated with both the feminine and the masculine (yin and yang respectively).

In Japan, red is a traditional color for a heroic figure. In the Indian Sub-continent, red is the traditional color of bridal dresses, and is frequently represented in the media as a symbolic color for married women. The color is associated with purity, sexuality in marriage relationships through its connection to heat and fertility. It is also the color of wealth, beauty, and the goddess Lakshmi. In Central Africa, Ndembu warriors rub themselves with red during celebrations. Since their culture sees the color as a symbol of life and health, sick people are also painted with it. Like most Central African cultures, the Ndembu see red as ambivalent, better than black, but not as good as white. In other parts of Africa, however, red is a color of mourning, representing death. Because of the connection red bears with death in many parts of Africa, the Red Cross has changed its colors to green and white in parts of the continent.

문제 1 Which of the following is the best title for the passage?
  (1) Ways to Interpret the Color Red
  (2) Meaning of Red In African Countries
  (3) Eastern and African Traditions Regarding Red
  (4) Why Chinese People Wear Red

문제 2 Choose one that is most appropriate for blank (a).
  (1) Put in a simpler way   (2) On the more negative side
  (3) On a broader sense   (4) With such a meaning in red

문제 3 What can be inferred from the passage?
  (1) In china, writing someone's name in red means he will make a lot of money in the near future.
  (2) In china, women who like dressing in red will have a better chance of getting married than those who do not.
  (3) In Central Africa, the color red only carries a bad connotation.
  (4) Color does not have a specific intrinsic meaning to it.

[Challenge 10]

According to Kuhn the development of a science is not uniform but has alternating 'normal' and 'revolutionary' (or 'extraordinary') phases. The revolutionary phases are not merely periods of accelerated progress, but differ qualitatively from normal science. Normal science does resemble the standard cumulative picture of scientific progress, on the surface at least. Kuhn describes normal science as 'puzzle-solving' (1962/1970a, 35-42). While this term suggests that normal science is not dramatic, its main purpose is to convey the idea that like someone doing crossword puzzles or chess puzzles or jigsaws, the puzzle-solver expects to have a reasonable chance of solving the puzzle, that his doing so will depend mainly on his own ability, and that the puzzle itself and its methods of solution will have a high degree of familiarity. A puzzle-solver is not entering completely ____(a)____ territory. Because its puzzles and their solutions are familiar and relatively straightforward, normal science can expect to accumulate a growing stock of puzzle-solutions. Revolutionary science, however, is not cumulative in that, according to Kuhn, scientific revolutions involve a revision to existing scientific belief or practice. Not all the achievements of the preceding period of normal science are preserved in a revolution, and indeed a later period of science may find itself without an explanation for a phenomenon that in an earlier period was held to be successfully explained. This feature of scientific revolutions has become known as "____(b)____."

문제 1 What is the passage mainly talking about?
   (1) Kuhn's Model of the Development of a Science
   (2) The Rise and Fall of Science
   (3) How Normal Science Becomes Revolutionary Science
   (4) The Advent of the Scientific Revolution

문제 2 Which of the following is NOT related to "normal science" in the passage?
   (1) Under normal science, researchers have a perfect explanation for every phenomenon in nature unlike revolutionary science.
   (2) Science progresses incrementally and cumulatively during the stage of normal science.
   (3) Kuhn describes normal science as a game in which the player knows what he is doing with familiarity.
   (4) Under normal science, solutions to scientific problems are understood as "relatively straightforward."

문제 3 Fill in blank (a).
   (1) acclaimed   (2) versed   (3) uncharted   (4) acquainted

문제 4 Fill in blank (b).
   (1) Kuhn-loss   (2) Kuhn-fiasco   (3) Kuhn-ism   (4) Kuhn-structure

Day 12

★ Any transition serious enough to alter your definition of self will require not just small adjustments in your way of living and thinking but a full-on metamorphosis.

Martha Beck

자신의 정체성을 바꿀 만큼의 심각한 어떤 변화는 단지 당신의 생활과 사고방식의 작은 부분의 변화를 요구하는 것이 아니라 전면적인 변화를 요구하는 것이다. (Martha Beck)

[Challenge 1]

The biggest emerging market question mark is China, of course. China's economy has been among the principal engines of global growth, and its expansion roared to near 11% this year. But observers are growing increasingly fearful that the Chinese government will be unable to contain inflation without producing a too-rapid growth slowdown, which could harm rich world economies. Here's the New York Times:

But a growing number of economists now worry that China — the world's fastest growing economy and a pillar of strength during the global financial crisis — could be stalled next year by soaring inflation, mounting government debt and asset bubbles.

Two credit ratings agencies, Moody's and Fitch Ratings, say China is still poised for growth, yet they have also recently warned about hidden risks in its banking system. Fitch even hinted at the possibility of another wave of nonperforming loans tied to the property market...

A sharp slowdown in China, which is growing at an annual rate of about 10 percent, would be a serious blow to the global economy since China's voracious demand for natural resources is helping to prop up growth in Asia and South America.

And because China is a major holder of United States Treasury debt and a major destination for American investment in recent years, any slowdown would also hurt American companies.

And so on. Is there cause for worry? Well, there's always cause for worry, but I am less fearful about a China (a) <u>implosion</u> than some others, for a couple of reasons. One is that it's easy to overstate the extent to which Chinese property markets are experiencing a bubble. In some coastal regions, ratios of prices to incomes and rents are clearly in bubble territory, but elsewhere housing isn't much more expensive than it was in 2007 or has become more affordable relative to incomes. Another is that China's government has the financial and political ability to cushion its economy against negative shocks. It's not impossible to imagine the Chinese economy producing destabilising shocks in the next year, but China is better positioned to handle them than most.

문제 1 Which of the following is the best title for the passage?
(1) New Emerging Markets for China
(2) Are Worries about China based on the Solid Explanation?
(3) China's Growing Roar of Economic Growth
(4) Effects of China's Inflation on the Global Economy

문제 2 The underlined (a) refers to _____.
(1) China's voracious demand for natural resources
(2) slowdown induced by the bubbles of property markets
(3) debacle of stock markets
(4) imbalance of incomes between property owners and tenants

[Challenge 2]

That there had once been a time of heroes and heroines few Greeks ever doubted. They knew all about these epic figures: their names, their genealogies, and their exploits. Homer was the most authoritative source of information about them, but by no means the only one. Unfortunately, neither Homer nor other early Greek poets had the slightest interest in history as we understand it. The poets' concern was with certain events of the past, not with their relationship to other events, past or present, and in the case of Homer, not even with the consequences or dates of those events. The outcome of the Trojan War, the fall and destruction of Troy, and the fruits of Greek victory would have been of prime importance to a historian of the war. But Homer, the poet of the Iliad, was indifferent to all that; he gives no indication of the date of the Trojan War other than "once upon a time."

문제 1 According to the passage, early Greek poets were most concerned with which of the following?
(1) Portrayal of heroic virtue
(2) Proof of military exploits
(3) The dates of past events
(4) The connection between past and present events

문제 2 By saying that for Homer the Trojan War began "once upon a time," the author implies that Homer's treatment of past events is _____.
(1) historically imprecise
(2) morally neutral
(3) highly formulaic
(4) excessively prosaic

[Challenge 3]

Dissatisfied with a too-rigid, overrefined standard curriculum, _____(a)_____ some educational philosophers have swung sharply to an espousal of "life experience" as the sole source of learning. They argue that only through "dong" can learning take place. Spouting such phrases as "Teach the child, not the subject," they demand, without seeing its absurdity, an end to rigorous study as a means of opening the way to learning. While not all adherents to this approach would totally eliminate a study of great books, the influence of this philosophy has been felt in the public school curricula, as evidenced by the gradual subordination of great literature.

Then, why teach literature? Why read, if life alone is to be our teacher? Aristotle states that the artist reveals the human situation by re-creating life out of life. The great writer, consciously or unconsciously, reveals the human situation most tellingly, extending our understanding of ourselves and our world. Thus, the fuction of literature, the enlarging of our own life sphere, is of itself of major importance. If so, what we have to do is to convince our dissenters that far from being separate, literature is that part of life which illumines life.

문제 1 Which of the following is CORRECT about the underlined (a)?
(1) They espouse that the "life experience" approach can also be achieved through literature.
(2) They feel sorry about the current trend of the gradual subordination of great literature.
(3) Through rigorous study, one can really understand how life is really working.
(4) They probably argue that if you want to build a house, you have to go out and build it yourself.

문제 2 Which of the following is the main idea of the passage?
(1) The best way to learning is to go out there and experience it yourself.
(2) The real education takes place when one can really absorb himself in someone else's life through literature.
(3) Literature as a tool to better understand ourselves and our world should not be separated from the school curriculum.
(4) Re-creating 'life out of life' through literature does not come from just sitting in the classroom.

[Challenge 4]

The Irish government has increased its funding for research in 2011 by 12.5% despite being forced to make 16 billion in cuts following its recent bailout. The budget, which passed in the Da´il yesterday by a margin of four votes, came following an 185 billion International Monetary Fund-E.U. rescue package announced last month. Measures included increased taxes, specific targets for reducing the numbers employed by the state, reductions in social welfare payments, reductions in the minimum wage, and reductions in pension payments to former state employees. But amid the _____(a)_____, Ireland decided not only to protect its science and research budget but also to increase it by one-eighth. Conor Lenihan, the minister responsible for science, technology and innovation, and the brother of the Finance Minister Brian Lenihan, said: "The budget for high-tech start-ups and focused commercial research is up for the first time in 3 years." That emphasis on "commercial research" has some scientists concerned that funding for basic science will suffer as Ireland's research portfolio becomes even more focused and applied. They're also worried about a policy change announced in March following a cabinet reshuffle. The move gave total control of the lucrative Programme for Research run by the Higher Education Authority (HEA) — one of two main public bodies funding science in Ireland — to Minister Lenihan's new department. Science Foundation Ireland (SFI), the other major funding body in Ireland, meanwhile has survived, and seen its budget increased slightly for 2011. SFI has been associated with funding people, while HEA tends to fund infrastructure. Do´il Leech, former secretary of the now-defunct Irish Research Scientists' Association said: "The cumulative effect of the past 2 years has been a cut of over 30% in the research budget of funders, mostly SFI." Science Foundation Ireland is the main public body funding science in Ireland.

문제 1 Which of the following is the best title for the passage?
   (1) Importance of Encouraging Commercial Research Investment
   (2) Amidst Bailout, Ireland Increases Science Budget
   (3) Is Our Current Science Curriculum Competitive?
   (4) Pros and Cons of Increased Funding for Basic Science

문제 2 Fill in blank (a).
   (1) black-ink balance
   (2) belt-tightening
   (3) bullish market
   (4) stock market crash

[Challenge 5]

Thus also, those ancient cities which, from being at first only villages, have become, in course of time, large towns, are usually but ill laid out compared with the regularity constructed towns which a professional architect has freely planned on an open plain; so that although the several buildings of the former may often equal or surpass in beauty those of the latter, yet when one observes their indiscriminate juxtaposition, there a large one and here a small, and the consequent crookedness and irregularity of the streets, one is disposed to allege that chance rather than any human will guided by reason must have led to such an arrangement.

문제 1   What is the passage mainly talking about?
(1) Irregularity of Ancient Cities   (2) Different Kinds of Towns
(3) Act of Chance   (4) Importance of Planning

문제 2   According to the passage, which of the following is NOT logically paired as cause and effect?
(1) Regularity - Constructed towns   (2) Indiscriminate juxtaposition - Irregularity
(3) Chance - Ancient Towns   (4) Reason - Large Towns

[Challenge 6]

Reviving the practice of using elements of popular music in classical composition, an approach that had been in hibernation in the United States during the 1960s, composer Philip Glass (born 1937) embraced the ethos of popular music without imitating it. Glass based two symphonies on music by rock musicians David Bowie and Brian Eno, but the symphonies' sound is distinctively his. Popular elements do not appear out of place in Glass's classical music, which from its early days has shared certain harmonies and rhythms with rock music. Yet this use of popular elements has not made Glass a composer of popular music. His music is not a version of popular music packaged to attract classical listeners; it is high art for listeners steeped in rock rather than the classics.

문제 1   Which of the following is NOT correct about the passage?
(1) Glass's work shows such a great level of integrity that it sounds like one genre of music.
(2) Glass's work incorporates elements from two apparently disparate musical styles.
(3) Glass used popular elements in his classical compositions.
(4) Glass's work displays a return to the use of popular music in classical compositions.

[Challenge 7]

Modern science takes its starting point from the Renaissance, that marvellous period of spiritual and intellectual rebirth, which put an end to the thousand year reign of ignorance and superstition. Humanity once again looked to nature with eyes unblinkered by dogma. They rediscovered the wonders of classical Greek philosophy, directly translated from reliable versions which reached Italy after Constantinople was taken by the Turks. The materialist world outlook of the old Ionians and the atomists pointed science onto the right path.

문제 1 Which of the following can NOT be inferred from the passage?
(1) The Renaissance is a resurrection of the classics from the old Greeks.
(2) In the center of the Renaissance is humanity with the eyes of reason.
(3) The rediscovery of classical Greek philosophy was triggered by the Turks' conquest over Constantinople.
(4) Italy was the main country that translated the Greek philosophical writings.

[Challenge 8]

A cow's horn is supposed to furnish a correct indication of the age of the animal, but this is not always true. For ordinary purposes, however, the following will be found approximately correct: At two years of age a circle of thicker matter begins to form on the animal's horns, which becomes clearly defined at three years of age, when another circle begins to form, and an additional circle every year thereafter. The rings on a bull's horns do not show themselves until he is five years old — so in the case of a bull five must be added to the number of rings. Unless the rings are clear and distinct these rules will not apply. Besides, dishonest dealers sometimes file off some of the rings of old cattle.

문제 1 Which of the following is the title for the passage?
(1) Evasive Nature of Cow's Age   (2) Age of Cattle
(3) How to Tell Bulls from Cows   (4) Functions of Bull's Horns

문제 2 In the case of a cow, the maximum number of circles that can be seen at the age of 4 is _____.
(1) 0   (2) 1   (3) 2   (4) 3

문제 3 In the case of a bull, the maximum number of circles that can be seen at the age of 4 is _____.
(1) 0   (2) 1   (3) 2   (4) 3

[Challenge 9]

The introduction and spread of Buddhism were hastened by the decline of Confucianism and Taoism. The Han dynasty (206 B.C.~221 A.D.) established a government founded on Confucianism. It reproduced the classics destroyed in the previous dynasty and encouraged their study; it established the state worship of Confucius; it based its laws and regulations upon the ideals and principles advocated by Confucius. The great increase of wealth and power under this dynasty led to a gradual deterioration in the character of the rulers and officials. The Confucian regulations became burdensome to the people who ceased to respect their leaders. Confucianism lost its hold as the complete solution of the problems of life. ___(a)___ Taoism had become a veritable jumble of meaningless and superstitious rites which served to support a horde of ignorant, selfish priests. The high religious ideals of the earlier Taoist mystics were abandoned for a search after the elixir of life during fruitless journeys to the isles of the Immortals which were supposed to be in the Eastern Sea.

문제 1   What is the passage mainly talking about?
     (1) The Wane of Confucianism and Taoism
     (2) Favorable Background for the Spread of Buddhism
     (3) The Origin of Buddhism in China
     (4) The Core Doctrines of Confucius

문제 2   Choose one that is most appropriate for blank (a).
     (1) In fact   (2) In general
     (3) However   (4) At the same time

[Challenge 10]

The problem of affluent self-employed people free riding on the national health insurance system is well known. To avoid paying contributions commensurate with their large personal wealth, these people manage to put their names on company payrolls and register themselves as employees. To curb these practices, the National Health Insurance Corp. has begun to levy extra contributions on employees with income other than their monthly salaries. A recent report shows that the free rider problem is not limited to wealthy self-employed people but is also serious among low-income people. According to the report, some 5 million wage earners have registered themselves either as self-employed people or dependents to reduce their insurance contributions or pay no contribution at all. As the contribution of a person in self-employment is computed based on his assets, such as property and vehicle, as well as his income, an employee with little property can lower his premium by posing as a self-employed person.

문제 1 What is the passage about?
(A) Ways to Avoid Health Care Fees
(B) National Health Care in Crisis
(C) New Direction For Health Care System
(D) Health Care Free Riders

문제 2 It can be inferred from the passage that people put their names on payrolls because _____.
(1) they get paid more than they employ themselves
(2) contributions are computed based on their monthly wages
(3) they want their premium to rise
(4) they can't afford to employ themselves

Day 13

★ Change has a considerable psychological impact on the human mind. To the fearful it is threatening because it means that things may get worse. To the hopeful it is encouraging because things may get better. To the confident it is inspiring because the challenge exists to make things better.

King Whitney Jr.

변화는 인간의 마음에 심리적으로 상당한 영향을 미친다. 두려운 자에게 이것은 위협적인 존재인데, 이는 상황이 나빠질 것을 의미하기 때문이다. 희망을 품는 자에게 이것은 희망을 주는데, 이는 상황이 좋아질 것을 의미하기 때문이다. 자신감 있는 자에게 이것은 고무적인데, 이는 도전이란 상황을 더 좋게 만들기 위해 존재하기 때문이다. (King Whitney Jr.)

[Challenge 1]

Who knows what evil lurks in the hearts of men? Dr. Prabir Bhattacharya and his computers might. He and Concordia graduate student Abu Sayeed Sohail are developing a computer image processing system that detects and classifies human facial expressions. The aim of this system is to take and analyze photos of individuals. If one could take random photos of the crowd and process them fast enough, there is the potential to identify those individuals who might be problematic. Facial expressions do not actually involve the entire face, but rather specific sets of muscles under the face near the eyes, nose and mouth. Bhattacharya and Sohail's system measures 15 key points on the face and then compares these measures against images of identifiable facial expressions. Although there is great variety in expression across both individuals and cultures, the pair has identified seven basic expressions that seem to be relatively universal.

문제 1 Which of the following is CORRECT from the passage?
  (1) The image processing system is designed to search the whole face of a person and spot 15 key points.
  (2) The image processing system could be used in areas of high traffic where security is a primary concern, such as an airport.
  (3) Bhattacharya and Sohail are anthropologists.
  (4) Since facial expressions are fairly fixed in numbers across cultures, Bhattacharya and Sohail were able to come up with 7 basic expressions.

[Challenge 2]

I don't wish to deny that the flattened, minuscule head of the large-bodied "stegosaurus" houses little brain from our subjective, top-heavy perspective, but I do wish to assert that we should not expect more of the beast. First of all, large animals have relatively smaller brains than related, small animals. (a) The correlation of brain size with body size among kindred animals (all reptiles, all mammals, for example) is remarkably regular. (b) As we move from small to large animals, from mice to elephants or small lizards to Komodo dragons, brain size increases, but not so fast as body size. (c) In fact, brains grow only about two-thirds as fast as bodies. (d) Since we have no reason to believe that large animals are consistently stupider than their smaller relatives, we must conclude that large animals require relatively less brain to do as well as smaller animals. If we do not recognize this relationship, we are likely to underestimate the mental power of very large animals, dinosaurs in particular.

문제 1　Where does the sentence below best fit in the passage?

> In other words, bodies grow faster than brains, and large animals have low ratios of brain weight to body weight.

(1) (a)　　　　(2) (b)　　　　(3) (c)　　　　(4) (d)

[Challenge 3]

Although Elizabeth H. Bradley and Lauren Taylor never use the words "social determinants of health," they are illustrating the profound truth that it is the circumstances in which people live and work that determine the health status of any population, in any nation. Along with that come some counterintuitive truths. First, that health care, while crucial to individual survival, makes at best a modest contribution to population health. Second, that most social and economic policies are in effect health policies because of their impact on those social determinants. Even a perfect American health care system (let alone what we have now) cannot by itself fix our abysmal maldistribution of health. When my colleagues and I worked at the nation's first community health center in the Mississippi Delta in the 1960s, our doctors saved many lives and eased much suffering. We repaired collapsing plantation shacks. We built sanitary privies. In the face of devastating poverty, unemployment and malnutrition, we organized a cooperative farm where residents grew tons of vegetables, and we found pathways to jobs and education. Those interventions did far more to save lives, ease suffering and improve our target population's health than our medical care did.

문제 1 Which of the following is the main idea of the passage?
(1) Medical care does not work without the government help.
(2) The improvement of the environment in which people live and work is what makes the health status of a country better.
(3) Most social and economic policies are in effect health policies.
(4) We should go back to the way we lived in 1960s.

문제 2 The attitude of the author toward health care can best be described as _____.
(1) necessary   (2) positive
(3) secondary   (4) negative

[Challenge 4]

U.S. President Barack Obama Tuesday called for the United States to look to South Korea in adopting longer school days and after-school programs for American children to help them survive in an era of keen global competition. He said our children spend over a month less in school than children in South Korea every year. "That's no way to prepare them for a 21st-century economy." Obama made the remarks while emphasizing the need for sweeping reform of the U.S. education system for which he earmarked $41 billion out of the $787 billion stimulus package to cope with the worst recession in decades. "We can no longer afford an academic calendar designed for when America was a nation of farmers who needed their children at home plowing the land at the end of each day," he said. The U.S. president called for Americans "not only to expand effective after-school programs but to rethink the school day to incorporate more time, whether it's during the summer or through expanded-day programs for children who need it." Obama's remarks came as a surprise to many South Koreans as the country's education system has been under constant public criticism due to its lack of creativity and heavy dependence on private tutoring.

문제 1 From what is stated or implied, which of the following is NOT correct?
(1) Obama thinks the US school calendar may have once made sense, but today it puts American children at a competitive disadvantage.
(2) Obama lauds Korea's education of children.
(3) American education has been under great pressure due to its lack of creative power.
(4) American children currently spend less time in school than children in South Korea.

[Challenge 5]

Addiction affects someone's personality and behavior in a variety of ways although this very much depends upon the type of substance used and the amount. Some substances have a greater effect than others upon mental health, for example, heroin is stronger than nicotine and will have a bigger impact upon the brain. Added to that is the fact that all of us are different in regard to our psychological makeup which means that no two people are affected in the same way. So, one person may experience a greater level of "damage" than another person using the same substance, mainly due to their brain chemistry. So what does an addiction do to someone's mental health and behavior? The most obvious sign is the fact that they behave in ways which are totally out of character. They may become secretive or deliberately offensive; self-harm; lie, cheat or steal; or place their need for their addiction above their family and friends. Other examples including paranoia, restlessness, low self-esteem or a lack of trust in themselves and anyone else. On the other hand they may behave in an arrogant and uncaring manner as if only their needs matter and no-one else's. As the addiction worsens they may start to withdraw from their family and friends or spend time with people who you don't know. The chemistry of the brain is affected by addiction, for example, taking crystal meth, amphetamines, cannabis, ecstasy and excessive alcohol use. These have the power to change certain structures of a person's brain which have a dramatic effect upon that person's personality.

문제 1 Which of the following is the best title for the passage?
  (1) Effects of Addiction on Personality   (2) Families in Danger of Addiction
  (3) Types of Addiction   (4) Addiction and the Functions of the Brain

문제 2 Which of the following is neither stated nor implied in the passage?
  (1) Heroin is the most noxious substance in terms of brain damage.
  (2) People respond to a certain type of substance in a different way.
  (3) An Addict may look like a totally different person than usual.
  (4) Drug abusers are likely to have a hard time adapting to a normal social life.

[Challenge 6]

Jere Cohen's article in the AJS, "Rational Capitalism in Renaissance Italy," represents an important new challenge to the much debated connection that Max Weber drew between Protestantism and the development of the spirit of modern capitalism. Cohen's intention is not to claim that capitalism in some unspecified general sense is older than Protestantism, but to show "that modern capitalism, in Weber's sense, existed in pre-Reformation Catholic countries." This challenge rests not so much on the conceptual analysis and reworking of such notions as "capitalism" or "rationality" as on the deployment of a vast mass of data drawn from historical studies of pre-Reformation Italy.

문제 1 According to the passage, what can be inferred from Max Weber's theory of Capitalism?
  (1) The development of capitalism has something to do with the ethics of Protestantism.
  (2) Capitalism occurred much earlier than the Reformation.
  (3) Max Weber based his work on a vast amount of date from historical studies from pre-Reformations Italy.
  (4) Max Weber conflated capitalism with the literary revival in Italy.

문제 2 Which of the following is TRUE of the passage?
  (1) Jere Cohen's article dates back to the Reformation.
  (2) Max Weber's argument on the relationship between Protestantism and the spirit of modern capitalism is controversial from Jere Cohen's point of view.
  (3) Max Weber bases his work on a vast mass of data drawn from historical studies of pre-Reformation Italy.
  (4) In fact, modern capitalism has nothing to do with the spirit of modern capitalism.

[Challenge 7]

Habitus is arguably the lynchpin concept of Bourdieu's entire corpus, the one, at the very least, for which he is best known. In Bourdieu's writings there are countless definitions and formulations of the term. _____(a)_____ most simply put, habitus is an internalized structure or set of structures (derived from pre-existing external structures) that determines how an individual acts in and reacts to the world, serving, as Thompson phrases it, to "generate practices, perceptions and attitudes which are regular without being consciously co-ordinated or governed by any "rule." In Outline of a Theory of Practice, Bourdieu defines habitus as a generative system of "durable, transposable dispositions" that emerges out of a relation to wider objective structures of the social world. As an internalized collection of durable dispositions and structured proclivities to think, feel, and act, habitus is characterized as a "conductorless orchestration" that serves to give systematicity, coherence, and consistency to an individual's practices.

문제 1 Which of the following is neither stated nor implied?
(1) Habitus is the main concept in Bourdieu's Theory of Practice.
(2) According to the concept of "habitus," a person internalizes a certain structure that unconsciously determines his action in a certain situation.
(3) The generative nature of "habitus" reproduces a structure that ensures the continuity of the "habitus" itself.
(4) Once a person is disconnected from the existing "habitus," he would never have access to it again.

문제 2 Choose the conjunction that best fills in blank (a).
(1) Therefore   (2) Nevertheless
(3) In contrast   (4) However

문제 3 What is the topic of the above passage?
(1) Definition of Habitus   (2) Kinds of Habitus
(3) Two Perspectives in Habitus   (4) Theory of Practice

[Challenge 8]

Jeffrey T. Kuhner seems to overlook the real drivers in postponing the much-debated, snowed-out NFL game to a different time — the NFL lawyers and the concession merchants. The lawyers examine the risk of lawsuits from people who get into accidents on the way to an event. They thus poison their organization's own purpose. As for the concession vendors looking at reduced attendance, and therefore sales, they would lobby strongly for postponement to a time that would bring more people to the event.

문제 1 Which of the following is CORRECT about the passage?
(1) The chances are that the event will eventually be held as planned.
(2) The concession vendors are well aware of the fact that the cancelation of the event would damage the organization's well-meaning.
(3) The concession merchants are fundamentally money-driven in lobbying for the delay.
(4) People do not go to national sports events when there is snow.

[Challenge 9]

Corruption is not an absolute condition. It can range from the acts of violence perpetrated by outright dictators to rules being bent and a blind eye turned to acts that a completely moral society would consider offensive. Political corruption can mean anything from buying votes or obtaining financial support by giving rewards only accessible by governments, to the elimination of people standing in the way of those in power.

In 1993 serious allegations of corruption, involving varying levels of government, surfaced in countries as diverse as Australia, Bolivia, Brazil, Bulgaria, France, Haiti, India, Italy, Japan, Malaysia, Paraguay, South Africa, Spain, and the USA. In Brazil, the allegations caused the president's resignation and a subsequent action for impeachment. In Italy, political leaders resigned and a major judicial inquiry was instigated as links were alleged between politicians, including former prime ministers, and the Italian Mafia. In Japan, the prime minister was discredited and removed from office.

문제 1 Which of the following best represents the topic of each of the paragraphs above?
(1) Conditions of Corruption - Degrees of Corruption
(2) Varieties of Corruption - Government Corruption
(3) Political Corruption - Mafia-related Corruption
(4) Corruption - Ways to Impeach the President

문제 2 According to the passage, which of the following is NOT likely to be considered as political corruption?
(1) Judicial inquiry
(2) Illegal fund-raising
(3) A frame-up ballot
(4) A purge of dissident members

[Challenge 10]

A considerable difference exists between the terms making and manufacturing. The former refers to the production of a small, the latter to that of a very large number of individuals; and the difference is well illustrated in the evidence, given before the Committee of the House of Commons, on the Export of Tools and Machinery. On that occasion Mr. Maudslay stated, that he had been applied to by the Navy Board to make iron tanks for ships, and that he was rather unwilling to do so, as he considered it to be out of his line of business; ____(a)____, he undertook to ____(b)____ one as a trial. The holes for the rivets were punched by hand-punching with presses, and the 1680 holes which each tank required cost seven shillings. The Navy Board, who required a large number, proposed that he should supply forty tanks a week for many months. The magnitude of the order made it worth his while to commence ____(c)____, and to make tools for the express business. Mr Maudslay therefore offered, if the Board would give him an order for two thousand tanks, to supply them at the rate of eighty per week. The order was given: he ____(d)____ tools, by which the expense of punching the rivet-holes of each tank was reduced from seven shillings to ninepence; he supplied ninety-eight tanks a week for six months, and the price charged for each ____(e)____ from seventeen pounds to fifteen.

문제 1 Which of the following is the topic of the passage?
 (1) A Great Offer from the Navy Committee
 (2) Difference between Making and Manufacturing
 (3) A Lucrative Business of Making Ship Tanks
 (4) Mr. Maudslay's Experiment with Ship Tanks

문제 2 Choose the transition word that best fills in blank (a).
 (1) however (2) therefore
 (3) in addition (4) on the other hand

문제 3 Which of the following is NOT the appropriate word for each blank from the passage?
 (1) (b) - make (2) (c) - manufacture
 (3) (d) - manufactured (4) (e) - was reduced

문제 4 Which of the following is NOT true of the passage?
 (1) The terms making and manufacturing are not synonymous.
 (2) At first Mr. Maudslay was not willing to accept the offer from the Navy Board.
 (3) The magnitude of the order by the Board made him change his mind and set out to make tanks.
 (4) The more tools he made for the tanks, the less expensive the cost became.

Day 14

★ Destiny is no matter of chance. It is a matter of choice. It is not a thing to be waited for, it is a thing to be achieved.

William Jennings Bryan (1860 - 1925).

운명이란 우연의 문제가 아니다. 이것은 선택의 문제이다. 운명을 오기를 기다리는 것이 아니라, 성취하는 것이다. (William Jennings Bryan)

[Challenge 1]

Crows don't forget a face especially one they're afraid of. Now, images of the birds' brain activity reveal what happens neurologically when they see a familiar face. Researchers from the University of Washington donned identical masks and captured 12 wild American crows. The scientists kept the birds in captivity for a month and fed them while wearing a different, "caretaker" mask. Afterward, the team showed the birds humans wearing the two different masks and monitored the crows' brain activity using positron emission tomography. The "threatening" mask the researchers wore to capture the birds activated brain regions associated with fear. The caretaker mask worn to feed the birds, on the other hand, activated another set of regions associated with reward and motivation.

문제 1 These results suggest that American crows, like humans, distinguish faces by _____.
   (1) recognizing subtle changes in the face
   (2) combining visual information with preexisting memories
   (3) using a "hunch" they are born with
   (4) getting accustomed to a certain face

[Challenge 2]

There exists, perhaps, no single circumstance which distinguishes our country more remarkably from all others, than (a) <u>the vast extent and perfection</u> to which we have carried the contrivance of tools and machines for forming those conveniences of which so large a quantity is consumed by almost every class of the community. The amount of (b) <u>patient thought</u>, of

(c) <u>repeated experiment</u>, of happy exertion of genius, by which our manufactures have been created and carried to their present excellence, is scarcely to be imagined. If we look around the rooms we inhabit, or through those storehouses of every convenience, of every luxury that man can desire, which deck the crowded streets of our larger cities, we shall find in the history (d) <u>a series of failures</u> which have gradually led the way to excellence; and we shall notice, in the art of making even the most insignificant of them, processes calculated to excite our admiration by their simplicity, or to rivet our attention by their unlooked-for results.

문제 1   Which of the following is neither stated nor implied?
　　　(1) The country in the passage has achieved greatness in tools and machines, thus creating a
　　　　 great deal of usefulness in every field of society.
　　　(2) Dust Storms and Life of farmers In the Great Depression
　　　(3) Failures are positive forces leading to a greater level of success than it is now.
　　　(4) Sometimes technology creates something unnecessary such as luxuries.

문제 2   Which of the following does NOT refer to the same item?
　　　(1) (a)　　　　　(2) (b)　　　　　(3) (c)　　　　　(4) (d)

[Challenge 3]

　　In previous depressions, farmers were usually safe from the severe effects of a depression because they could at least feed themselves. Unfortunately, during the Great Depression, the Great Plains were hit hard with both a drought and horrendous dust storms. Years and years of overgrazing combined with the effects of a drought caused the grass to disappear. With just topsoil exposed, high winds picked up the loose dirt and whirled it for miles. The dust storms destroyed everything in their paths, leaving farmers without their crops. Small farmers were hit especially hard. Even before the dust storms hit, the invention of the tractor drastically cut the need for manpower on farms. These small farmers were usually already in debt, borrowing money for seed and paying it back when their crops came in. When the dust storms damaged the crops, not only could the small farmer not feed himself and his family, he could not pay back his debt. Banks would then foreclose on the small farms and the farmer's family would be both homeless and unemployed.

문제 1   Which of the following is the best title for the passage?
　　　(1) The Great Depression
　　　(2) Dust Storms and Life of farmers
　　　(3) Life of Farmers in the Great Depression
　　　(4) Life In and Out of the Great Depression

[Challenge 4]

Civilization, I apprehend, is nearly synonymous with order. However much we may differ touching such matters as the distribution of property, the domestic relations, the law of inheritance and the like, most of us, I should suppose, would agree that without order civilization, as we understand it, cannot exist. Now, although the optimist contends that, since man cannot foresee the future, worry about the future is futile, and that everything, in the best possible of worlds, is inevitably for the best, I think it clear that within recent years an uneasy suspicion has come into being that the principle of authority has been dangerously impaired, and that the social system, if it is to cohere, must be ____(a)____.

문제 1   According to the passage, which of the following is NOT true?
(1) People are of different opinions about the law of inheritance.
(2) The optimist always tries to see the bright side of things.
(3) The optimist thinks since we can not see what's coming in the future, it is better to dwell on the past.
(4) The foothold of authority has recently been shaken.

문제 2   Fill in blank (a).
(1) invigorated   (2) abraded
(3) strengthened   (4) reorganize

[Challenge 5]

The qualifications of those who might vote for members of the Legislature greatly restricted suffrage. Theoretically every patriot believed in the liberties of the people, and the first article of the Constitution declared that "no authority shall, on any pretence whatever, be exercised over the people of the State, but such as shall be derived from and granted by them." This highsounding (a) <u>exordium</u> promised the rights of popular sovereignty; but in practice the makers of the Constitution, fearing the passions of the multitude as much as the tyranny of kings, deemed it wise to keep power in the hands of a few. A male citizen of full age, possessing a freehold of the value of twenty pounds, or renting a tenement of the yearly value of forty shillings, could vote for an assemblyman, and one possessing a freehold of the value of one hundred pounds, free from all debts, could vote for a senator.

문제 1   Which of the following is the topic of the passage?
(1) Makers of the Constitution
(2) Theoretical Idea of Suffrage
(3) Conditions of Popular Sovereignty
(4) Criterion of Suffrage

문제 2 Which of the following is neither stated nor implied in the passage?
(1) It has existed for a long time, potentially as long as humans have been around.
(2) In the Constitution, it is said that people can participate in electing their representatives regardless of their social and economical backgrounds.
(3) While the Constitution theoretically supports popular sovereignty, in practice, voting was heavily restricted based on property ownership and economic status.
(4) Lawmakers wanted to keep their exclusive prerogatives of controlling the country in the hands of a few.

문제 3 Which of the following does the underlined (a) refer to?
(1) the first article   (2) the Constitution
(3) the authorities   (4) the Legislature

[Challenge 6]

One advantage of living in water is the water's ability to easily support body weight. So, a fish in water is most weightless. This 'weightlessness' in turn means two things: one, a fish can get along with a light weight and simple bone structure, and two, limitations to a fish's size are practically removed. Yet there is one basic difficulty to living in water. For a fish to move through water, it must actually shove it aside. Most can do this by wiggling back and forth in snakelike motion. Next, the water flows back along the fish's narrowing sides, closing in at the tail, thus helping the fish propel itself forward. A flat and angular shape can be moved through water only with difficulty. And for this reason, fish have a basic shape that is beautifully adapted to deal with this peculiarity.

문제 1 What is the passage mainly about?
(1) a comparison of fish to warm-blooded animals
(2) the difference between saltwater and freshwater environments
(3) the importance of fish to human beings
(4) how water has affected the development of fish

[Challenge 7]

It is not known when people began to dance. However, it is possible that dance developed along with the evolution of our species. Many animals perform dance-like movements in situations similar to human courtship and play. These movement rituals, however, lack the conscious use of symbols that is present in human dance. There are several primitive groups that we can refer to today for information about this type of dance. Among Australian aborigines and several African tribes, for example, skilled individuals perform various dances. At times their dances may look simple to an outsider, but often they are not. Usually they form part of complicated rituals that involve highly sophisticated religious or philosophical ideas.

문제 1 What would be the best title of the passage?
   (1) the athleticism of dance
   (2) modern dance forms
   (3) romantic symbolism of dance
   (4) early forms of dance

문제 2 What does the passage imply about the origins of dance?
   (1) It has existed for a long time, potentially as long as humans have been around.
   (2) Many ancient people did hardly approve of it.
   (3) It did not develop until the ancient civilizations formed.
   (4) Prehistoric dances surely had some practical meaning.

[Challenge 8]

Having received a classical education in England, he returned home and entered the University of Virginia, where, after an extravagant course, followed by reformation at the last extremity, he was graduated with the highest honors of his class. Then came a boyish attempt to join the fortunes of the insurgent Greeks, which ended at St. Petersburg, where he got into difficulties through want of a passport, from which he was rescued by the American consul and sent home. He now entered the military academy at West Point, from which he obtained a dismissal on hearing of the birth of a son to his adopted father, by a second marriage, an event which cut off his expectations as an heir. The death of Mr. Allan, in whose will his name was not mentioned, soon after relieved him of all doubt in this regard, and he committed himself at once to authorship for a support.

문제 1 Which of the following is NOT true of 'he' in the above passage?
   (1) He took an intensive course.
   (2) He joined the insurgent Greeks.
   (3) He got help from the American consul at West Point.
   (4) He got discharged from the military academy because of his adopted father.

문제 2 Why was 'he' cut off from his expectations as an heir to his adopted father?
   (1) Because 'he' disgracefully dropped out of the military school.
   (2) Because 'he' joined the army so the adopted father did not feel he had to give 'him' his fortune.
   (3) Because now the adopted father had his own son to inherit his fortune.
   (4) Because by law if the adopted father gets remarried, he naturally loses his right to the inheritance.

[Challenge 9]

The married women among the Aztecs were treated kindly and respectfully by their husbands. The feminine occupations were spinning and embroidery, etc., as among the ancient Greeks, while listening to ballads and love stories (a) <u>related</u> by their maidens and musicians. In banquets and other social entertainments the women had an equal share with the men. Sometimes the festivities were on a large scale, with costly preparations and numerous attendants. The Mexicans, ancient and modern, have always been passionately fond of flowers, and on great occasions not only were the halls and courts strewed and adorned in profusion with blossoms of every hue and sweet odor, but perfumes scented every room. The guests as they sat down found ewers of water before them and cotton napkins, since washing the hands both before and after eating was a national habit of almost religious obligation. Modern Europeans believe that tobacco was introduced from America in the time of Queen Isabella and Queen Elizabeth, but ages before that period the Aztecs at their banquets had the "fragrant weed" offered to the company, "in pipes, mixed up with aromatic substances, or in the form of cigars, inserted in tubes of tortoise-shell or silver." The smoke after dinner was no doubt preliminary to the siesta or nap of "forty winks." It is not known if the Aztec ladies, like their descendants in modern Mexico, also appreciated the yet, as the Mexicans called "tobacco."

문제 1 Which of the following is neither stated nor implied in the above passage?
(1) Aztec men were nice to their wives.
(2) In the ancient Greeks, spinning and embroidery were common chores among females.
(3) The Mexicans really like flowers.
(4) Modern Europeans know that tobacco originally came from the culture of the Aztecs.

문제 2 Choose one that is closest in contextual meaning to the underlined (a).
(1) integrated   (2) regarded   (3) communicated   (4) associated

문제 3 The act of Mexicans' washing their hands before and after eating has do to with _____.
(1) a kind of spiritual practice   (2) a sense of social obligation
(3) a form of family tradition   (4) a form of secular affair

[Challenge 10]

Medical inspection is an extension of the activities of the school in which the educator and the physician join hands to insure for each child such conditions of health and vitality as will best enable him to take full advantage of the free education offered by the state. Its object is to better health conditions among school children, safeguard them from disease, and render them healthier, happier, and more vigorous. It is founded upon a recognition of the intimate relationship between the physical and mental conditions of the children, and the consequent dependence of education on health conditions. In Cleveland, the value of medical inspection was recognized while the movement was still in its infancy in America. Here, as elsewhere, this sudden recognition of the imperative necessity for safeguarding the physical welfare of school children grew out of the discovery that (a) <u>compulsory education under modern city conditions meant compulsory disease</u>. The state, to provide for its own protection, has decreed that all children must attend school, and has put in motion the all-powerful but indiscriminating agency of compulsory education, which gathers in the rich and the poor, the bright and the dull, the healthy and the sick. The object was to insure that these children should have sound minds. One of the unforeseen results was to insure that they should have unsound bodies. Medical inspection is the device created to remedy this condition. Its object is prevention and cure. Ever since its establishment the good results of medical inspection have been evident. Epidemics have been checked or avoided. Improvements have been noted in the cleanliness and neatness of the children. Teachers and parents have come to know that under the new system it is safe for children to continue in school in times of threatened or actual epidemic.

문제 1 What is the main theme of the passage?
(1) Medical Check for Children before Attending School
(2) Requirement for Medical Inspection
(3) Setting up the Right Target for Medical Inspection
(4) Establishing the Good Environments for Students

문제 2 Which of the following is neither stated nor implied in the above passage?
(1) Without health, students can not make the most out of state-run free education.
(2) Medical inspection is an integrated part of school activity.
(3) The efforts of medical inspection in school did not pay off until teachers and parents had actively participated in the new system.
(4) Indiscriminating policy of education is a necessary condition for equal treatment of all children.

문제 3 Which of the following best paraphrases the underlined (a)?
(1) The current conditions of compulsory school education now inevitably lead to the disease.
(2) Education under modern city has inherent defects in terms of health for children.
(3) Modern city has become vulnerable to disease.
(4) Conditions of modern city are only suitable for healthy children to study at school.

문제 4 Which of the following is NOT mentioned as the result of medical inspection?
(1) Suppression of the current epidemics
(2) Increased acknowledgement of its necessity
(3) Physically unsound
(4) An increase in the cleanliness and neatness of the children

Day 15

★ Men are not prisoners of fate, but only prisoners of their own minds.

Franklin D. Roosevelt (1882 - 1945)

인간은 운명의 노예가 아니다. 단지 자신의 마음의 노예일 뿐이다. (Franklin D. Roosevelt)

[Challenge 1]

There are ways in which we may use gestures and body movements to greater effect. When using any particular gesture, we should consider carefully the context in which we use this gesture to make sure the gesture is appropriate. Some body language expressions are universal whilst culture and convention dictate others. We must bear in mind that people from other cultures than our own may understand a gesture to mean something radically different from what we intended; and no culture can claim to be more right or wrong than another. Sometimes it may serve us well to avoid gestures, simply because they are open to misinterpretation, not because they're wrong in any sense. _____(a)_____, women, who cross their legs, revealing an expanse of thigh in the process, may convey a message they do not intend. Gestures may also provide an observer with a leakage of feelings and emotions we may prefer, or have an advantage, of concealing.

Before we (b) <u>fall a verdict on</u> someone, it is crucial to be sure, that that person displays an unequivocal pattern of behavior. A loud, boisterous man may be considerate, and a quiet man might not be listening to a conversation simply because he is tired. We must always look out for more than one expression, more than one symptom. We need to interpret behavior, but to avoid over-interpretations.

문제 1 Which of the following is NOT inferred from the above passage?
   (1) Culture affects the way people behave.
   (2) Behavior is a relative concept.
   (3) Cultural relativism is required when understanding cultures other than my own.
   (4) People are born to over-interpret other behaviors.

문제 2   Fill in blank (a).
   (1) In addition (2) For example
   (3) Still (4) In other words

문제 3   Which of the following best paraphrases the underlined (b)?
   (1) fall back on (2) jump to the conclusion about
   (3) fall victims of (4) lay our eyes on

[Challenge 2]

Despite Alfred Wegener's wonderful evidence in support of his continental drift hypothesis, he was lacking the mechanism to explain how continents actually move. This information did not surface until after Wegener's death. Wegener originally believed that the continents plowed through the ocean floor as a result of either centrifugal forces caused by the rotation of the earth, or because of the gravitational forces caused by the sun and moon (Weil, 1997). These ideas were rejected by geologists of the time, but after Wegener's death more research was done into one of his hypotheses that the mantle undergoes thermal convection. The resulting convection currents are caused by the very hot magma at the deepest part of the mantle rising, then _____(a)_____, and then heating, rising and repeating the cycle over again. Arthur Holmes suggested that the thermal convection currents were like a conveyor belt and that the upwelling pressure could break a continent apart, forcing the broken continent in opposite directions (Weil, 1997). This idea received very little attention at the time, but now convection currents are accepted as the mechanism that drives continental drift.

문제 1   Which of the following is most appropriate for the title for the passage?
   (1) Alfred Wegener's Evidence for Continental Drift
   (2) More Evidence for Continental Drift
   (3) Arthur Holmes's Theory of Continental Drift
   (4) Wegener's Death and Demise of Continental Drift

문제 2   Fill in blank (a).
   (1) cooling and bursting (2) cooling and sinking
   (3) bursting and sinking (4) cooling and melting

[Challenge 3]

The Framers of the American Constitution did not include a bill of rights in that document. The reason for this omission was not indifference to fundamental rights, but a feeling that as the Constitution did not specifically grant authority over such matters as freedom of the press or assembly, there was no need whatsoever to state that this authority did not exist. This position was logically sound, but not psychologically; Americans generally wanted their rights specially set forth in the Constitution. Shortly after the first Congress met, James Madison introduced a long Bill of Rights as amendments to the Constitution. Twelve of these were passed by the Congress. However, only ten were ratified by the States, and became part of the Constitution on December 15, 1791. They became known as the Bill of Rights. Most of them are stated as limitations on government things the National government may not do. Eventually they came to be interpreted to apply, in a general way, to State governments as well. As almost every State has a bill of rights either as part of the State Constitution or as amendments, it is correct to say that all Americans everywhere enjoy protection of such bills of rights against all governments, local, State, and National.

문제 1 Which of the following is the topic of the passage?
 (1) New Amendments to the Constitution
 (2) James Madison's Theory of Justice
 (3) American Bill of Rights
 (4) Limitations over the Power of the States

문제 2 According to the passage, which of the following is CORRECT?
 (1) Americans did not want a bill of rights to be set forth in the Constitution.
 (2) The Architects of the American Constitution accidently omitted include a bill of rights in the charter.
 (3) Freedom of the press or assembly were taken for granted so that the Framers of the American Constitution did not think it was necessary to put them in the Constitution.
 (4) The bill of rights of the U.S. was the direct influence from that of Britain in 1689.

[Challenge 4]

The relentless assault on [U.S.] military aid restrictions that began shortly after the September 11th attacks ... has continued unabated. This spring the [Bush] administration attempted yet again to win (a) <u>blanket</u> exemptions for aid distributed as part of the "war on terror" by including the FY2002 supplemental appropriations bill that _____(b)_____ most existing restrictions and reporting requirements. The administration's second attempt was more successful. Two key Defense Department funding allocations — $390 million to reimburse nations providing support to U.S. operations in the war on terror and $120 million "for certain classified activities" — can now be delivered "notwithstanding any other provision of the law." This means there will be none of the normal restrictions placed on this large sum of military aid.

The provision on "classified activities" is especially troubling because it permits "projects not otherwise authorized by law," in other words, covert actions. Not only is the language in the Supplemental opaque, attempts to get more information from a defense committee staffer led nowhere. He refused to answer questions about the intended use of the funds, the applicability of foreign aid restrictions, and reporting requirements on the grounds that all of that information is "classified." In other words, there will be no public scrutiny of this aid, and that's just fine with Congress.

문제 1 Which of the following is CORRECT about the passage?
    (1) U.S. military aid restrictions are not likely to be lifted in the near future.
    (2) The Pentagon is more than ready to talk to the press about the so-called "covert actions."
    (3) The September 11th attacks serve as a good excuse for the U.S. to expand military aid to other nations providing support to U.S. operations in the war on terror.
    (4) The United States is currently sitting on the fence about whether or not it will take a firm action against international terrorism.

문제 2 Which of the following is closest in meaning to the underlined (a)?
    (1) covert   (2) surreptitious
    (3) over-all   (4) insular

문제 3 Fill in blank (b).
    (1) distorts   (2) classifies
    (3) reinforces   (4) waives

[Challenge 5]

The Democrats lack a winning platform on estate taxes — work hard, save, invest and after death, Uncle Sam gets half. Why would anyone in their right mind put any effort into work or take any chances on starting a new business if they knew half was going to the government? It shows hard work and risk-taking isn't all it's cracked up to be. Democrats don't realize that unlike the Joe Kennedys of this world, children might not keep accumulating wealth. Taking half of what someone put his life into might end up ripping that life apart. The whole process smacks of that old Marxist slogan, "From each according to his ability, to (a) each according to his needs."

문제 1 What is the author's tone about the underlined (a)?
(1) critical   (2) supportive
(3) unbiased   (4) neutral

[Challenge 6]

In the beginning of the year 1856 I commenced business on my own account, as a merchant in a Northern City. Previous to that time I had been engaged in an unsuccessful partnership, but I paid my creditors in full with the small capital (a) advanced to me by my friends for the purpose of my new adventure. When I began operations, therefore, (b) I was literally without a shilling in the world, but I had a spotless character, enjoyed good credit, and possessed a thorough knowledge of my business; advantages which I easily persuaded myself would enable me to succeed without the actual possession of capital. My business connections were scattered over various parts of the world, and generally ranked among the very best class of foreign merchants. I usually received orders by letter, sometimes I gave open credits to houses whose orders I could not otherwise secure, but frequently I had remittances long before the merchandise could arrive at its destination. The trade was one of confidence, requiring both character and position for its development, and had I been prudent enough to confine myself strictly to this branch of the business, I would now, without doubt, have been a wealthy and successful merchant. At the end of my first year's operations my ledger showed a satisfactory balance to my credit. The year 1857 opened auspiciously, and I continued to prosper almost to the end of it, when a storm swept over the commercial world, which involved hundreds of firms in bankruptcy and ruin.

문제 1   Which of the following is NOT true about 'I' in the above passage?
(1) He was in dept when his previous business went bankrupt.
(2) He ran a business in partnership with someone else before he launched his own business.
(3) He is a man of character.
(4) His possession of capital helped him to establish good business connections.

문제 2   Which of the following can be replaced with the underlined word (a)?
(1) elevated   (2) fostered
(3) loaned   (4) progressed

문제 3   Which of the following best describes the underlined (b)?
(1) I had no one to depend on.   (2) I was penniless.
(3) I had a pretty penny.   (4) I broke bread with him.

문제 4   Which of the following is neither stated nor implied?
(1) The protagonist thinks good character and a thorough knowledge of his field are more important than capital in doing business.
(2) The new business was smooth sailing even after 1857.
(3) The protagonist was willing to offer business on credit.
(4) In the beginning of 1857 the protagonist enjoyed much success in his new enterprise.

[Challenge 7]

In addition to depleting resources, overpopulation increases environmental problems. Pollution is an environmental problem whose magnitude is increased by overpopulation. As more people drive more cars, use more electricity, throw away more trash, and cut down more trees, the environmental problems we experience are greatly increased. The earth could easily sustain a small population of highly polluting people. But as more people such as ourselves pollute, massive problems occur. Pollution is magnified in developing nations. As those nations with larger growing populations become richer, their pollution increases with their wealth. Developing nations often promote industries that pollute to compete economically. These industries are less tightly regulated in order to stimulate growth.

Besides causing the environmental strains on the earth, overpopulation causes a large number of the social problems in today's society. One example of this is described in the recent study by Ohio State University showing that children whose family sizes were larger did worse in school. "The research, to be published in October's American Sociological Review, found that as family size increases, parents talk less to each child about school, have lower education expectations, save less for college and have fewer educational materials available" (CAPS).

Each individual's political power is reduced with increased population. As the population increases, each representative in the US and state congresses (as well as senators) represents a wider segment of the population. This problem was initially addressed by increasing the number of representatives. However, when the number of US representatives reached 435, the sheer numbers became unimaginable and led to a cap on the number of representatives. In Lincoln's time, there were 185,000 residents in a congressional district. Today, there are about 600,000 people in each district. The only alternative would be increasing the number of representatives, however this would only decrease congresses' efficiency.

문제 1 What is likely to be discussed before the above passage?
(1) social maladjustments of children from poor families
(2) malnutrition and its related diseases due to the food shortage
(3) animals in danger of extinction due to reckless human hunting
(4) increased social funding per capita due to overpopulation

문제 2 Which of the following is the best title for the passage?
(1) Causes of Overpopulation
(2) Effects of Overpopulation
(3) Political Consequences of Overpopulation
(4) Increased Environmental Strains on the Earth

문제 3 From what is stated or implied, which of the following is CORRECT?
(1) As people in developing countries get richer, they become more aware of the environmental problems.
(2) Ironically, overpopulation gives representatives more power to exercise their influence on the public.
(3) Increasing the number of representatives impedes congresses' efficiency.
(4) A nuclear family is more effective in dealing with family matters than a large family.

[Challenge 8]

We may have high-speed information at our disposal, but our basic grammar skills are regressing. A recent study released by the English Spelling Society reveals that the Web has not only wholly altered the English language, but has turned us into a culture of misspellers. "The increasing use of variant spellings on the internet has been brought about by people typing at speed in chat rooms and on social networking sites where the general attitude is that there isn't a need to correct typo's or conform to spelling rules," the paper says, meaning our attitude toward grammar has become increasingly ___(a)___. ut the real harm in a commonplace Web speak shorthand? If correct grammar continues on a path to irrelevancy, children won't bother to correct themselves, ___(b)___ learn it in the first place.

The study, which focused in on the burgeoning Internet generation reported that one in five 18-to-24 year-olds say they would not feel confident enough to write an important e-mail without a dictionary or spell checker acting as an aid, a scary stat seeing as this is the just the tip of the population who can't remember a time before computers. Though nearly a third of the those surveyed for the study claimed that alt-spellings common in Internet chatter are "completely unacceptable," the other two-thirds expressed support for these rebel words to be included in the dictionary. "Accurate spelling is of the utmost importance, but from this most recent survey we can conclude that the unprecedented reach and scale of the internet has given rise to new social practices and it is now an agent in spelling change," Jack Bovill, Chair of the English Spelling Society, said in the paper. _____(c)_____.

문제 1 Which of the following best represents the main idea of the passage?
   (1) Kids are naturally born as bad spellers.
   (2) The Internet was intrinsically designed to be the hotbed for typos.
   (3) Alt-spellings are in great demand due to the problems of the current spelling system.
   (4) The Internet turns kids into terrible spellers.

문제 2 Choose a pair that is most appropriate for the blanks (a) and (b).
   (1) sensitive - not to mention   (2) lenient - let alone
   (3) intricate - much less   (4) sympathetic - still more

문제 3 Which of the following best fills in blank (c)?
   (1) Traditional ways of spelling words should be adopted into cyber space immediately.
   (2) Measures such as giving on-line users spelling classes are just an option.
   (3) Chatting on-line is a necessary evil.
   (4) Maybe grammar could use a reboot.

[Challenge 9]

Miss B. was, on one occasion, walking in company with another young lady through a field, when a bull came running up to them with all the marks of malevolence. Her friend began to run towards the stile, but was prevented by Miss B., who told her, that as she could not reach the stile soon enough to save herself, and as it is the nature of these animals to attack persons _____(a)_____, her life would be in great danger if she attempted to run, and would be inevitably lost if she chanced to fall; but that, if she would steal gently to the stile, she herself would take off the bull's attention from her, by standing between them. Accordingly, turning her face towards the animal (b) <u>with the firmest aspect</u> she could assume, she fixed her eyes steadily upon his. It is said by travellers, that a lion itself may be controlled by _____(c)_____; but that, no sooner a man turns his back, than the beast springs upon him as his prey. Miss B., to whom this property of animals seems to have been known, had the presence of mind to apply it to the safety of her friend and of herself. (d) <u>By her steady aspect</u> she checked the bull's career; but he showed the strongest marks of indignation at being so controlled, (e) <u>by roaring and tearing the ground</u> with his feet and horns. While he was thus engaged in venting his rage on the turf, she cautiously retreated a few steps, without removing her eyes from him. When he observed that she had retreated, he advanced till she stopped, and then he also stopped, and again renewed his frantic play. Thus by repeated degrees she at length arrived at the stile, where she accomplished her safety; and thus, (f) <u>by a presence of mind</u> rarely seen in a person of her youth and sex, she not only saved herself, but also, at the hazard of her own life, protected her friend. Some days afterwards, this bull gored its master.

문제 1 Which of the following is the best title for the above passage?
(1) The Nature of Bulls
(2) Remarkable Instance of Courage in a Lady
(3) How to Avoid Bulls in the First Place
(4) Taming of the Bull

문제 2 Choose one that best fills in blank (a).
(1) in anger   (2) in flight   (3) off guard   (4) on duty

문제 3 Choose one that best fills in blank (c).
(1) a carrot-and-stick policy
(2) walking up to him with your eyes on him
(3) turning your back on him
(4) the steady looks of a human being

문제 4 Which of the following does NOT refer to the same state of mind from the rest?
(1) (b)   (2) (d)   (3) (e)   (4) (f)

문제 5　When you chance to meet a bull on the street, which of the following is the smartest move according to the passage?

(1) Watchfully step back with a steady look on the bull.

(2) Run for our life with no looking-back.

(3) Confront the bull if there is no other way to get around it.

(4) Look around and search for a fence and rush to it.

[Challenge 10]

　　Let me give you an example of how workplaces foster ineffectiveness. It's almost impossible to keep a healthy perspective on life and very difficult to have the emotional presence needed for healthy relationships if you're constantly working 50 or 60 hours a week and, more importantly, constantly tethered to all the electronic devices that keep us connected to one another. New brain research tells us that when we're on cognitive overload, dopamine and other brain chemicals are released, and they give us a false sense of confidence. So we're under the illusion that multitasking will make us more productive and more effective. In all the research on multitasking that I'm aware of, some groups of people are given several tasks and told, "You can multitask; do it any way you want to do it." Other groups are told to complete the same tasks in consecutive order, one task being completed before the next is begun. In every one of the studies I've looked at, they find that the groups that work linearly complete all of the tasks more quickly and with less error than the multitaskers. But when the multitaskers are interviewed, they're quite sure they've outperformed the linear group. _____(a)_____ . The brain says, "If I give you some dopamine, you're going to feel confident to deal with this amount of stress." The problem is, dopamine makes us feel smart when we may be doing something stupid. That's why decisions under stress are always risky.

문제 1　Which of the following is TRUE of the passage?

(1) Not a lot of people realize multitasking is what makes them more effective.

(2) People are more connected due to all the electronic devices, which strengthens collaboration.

(3) Getting things done in a linear way is actually more effective than doing several things at the same time.

(4) The more dopamine you get, the more efficient you are.

문제 2　Which of the following is most appropriate for blank (a)?

(1) It's a brain trick to help us deal with overload

(2) The brain is resistant to new environments

(3) Human beings are programmed to do one thing at a time

(4) Stress can be a positive factor in the workplace

Day 16

★ I am still determined to be cheerful and happy, in whatever situation I may be; for I have also learned from experience that the greater part of our happiness or misery depends upon our dispositions, and not upon our circumstances.

Martha Washington (1732 - 1802)

나는 어떠한 상황에 내가 처하더라도 여전히 기쁘고 행복하다. 왜냐하면, 나는 경험을 통해서 우리가 겪는 행복 또는 불행의 대부분은 우리가 처한 환경에 의해서가 아니라 우리의 내면의 성향에 의해 영향을 받는 다는 것은 경험으로 배웠기 때문이다.
(Martha Washington)

[Challenge 1]

We live in a new age, a time Sir Ian Wilmut calls the "age of biological control," where he believes the notion of something being biologically impossible is _____(a)_____. Wilmut in 1996 created the first mammal cloned from an adult body cell. Although there were several others (lambs that were not only cloned but genetically modified as well), Dolly became the best known. She proved that a totally differentiated adult cell contained a complete genome. Of course, it was the ideas of creating duplicates and cloning people that spawned the greatest intrigue. Surely by now, however, we all understand that even though a clone may share the donor's genetic make-up, every individual is, well, individual — the unique product of genetic, environmental and experiential inputs. Cloning is not going to be a good hedge against the things we fear most: disease and death. _____(b)_____, when the topics of gene engineering, chromosome-making, stem-cell injection and genomic analysis are jumbled together, almost anything seems possible. Of course, all things are not yet possible. Even the most likely stem-cell-based regenerative medicine remains a long-range goal with many short-term research objectives still to be met. These include understanding how the cells work to generate healing from a biological perspective, and how they perform in patients. "You have to be pragmatic in your approach, as well as apply the best and most rigorous science that you can," says Clive Svendsen, director of the Cedars-Sinai Regenerative Medicine Institute in Los Angeles. There is one group of people that says, 'We need to know everything about this before we can possibly touch a patient.' And there is another that says, 'I don't care about anything; put the cells in, because the patient is dying.' I say, let's have a rational plan backed up by statistical evidence that something has an effect; but once we get to a certain point, let's proceed with that 'something' to a clinical trial.

문제 1 Fill in blank (a).
　　　(1) sound　　　　(2) epoch-making　　　(3) self-professed　　　(4) obsolete

문제 2 Fill in blank (b).
　　　(1) Nevertheless　(2) In addition　　　(3) Otherwise　　　　(4) For this reason

문제 3 Which of the following can be inferred from the passage?
　　　(1) People consider cloning to be 'something impossible.'
　　　(2) Dolly is the only cloned sheep that turned out to be successful.
　　　(3) A clone is virtually a copy of the donor with the same genetic constitution.
　　　(4) There will be more human efforts to understand how biology works.

문제 4 Which of the following phrases best represents the author's attitude toward 'stem-cellbased regenerative medicine'?
　　　(1) Crying Over Spilled Milk　　　　(2) A Bull in a China Shop
　　　(3) Speaking of the Devil　　　　　(4) Just Getting On With Business

[Challenge 2]

　　The specimens of native Egyptian Literature printed herein are taken from tombs, papyri and other monuments, and, with few exceptions, each specimen is complete in itself. Translations of most of the texts have appeared in learned works written by Egyptologists in English, French, German, and Italian, but some appear in English for the first time. In every case I have collated my own translations with the texts, and, thanks to the accurate editions of texts which have appeared in recent years, it has been found possible to make many hitherto difficult passages clear. The translations are as literal as the difference between the Egyptian and English idioms will permit, but it has been necessary to insert particles and often to invert the order of the words in the original works in order to produce a connected meaning in English. The result of this has been in many cases to break up the short abrupt sentences in which the Egyptian author delighted, and which he used frequently with dramatic effect. Extraordinarily concise phrases have been paraphrased, but the meanings given to several unknown words often represent guess-work.

문제 1 Which of the following is neither stated nor implied?
　　　(1) Some of the unidentified words have been given educated guesses in translation by the author.
　　　(2) The author solely depended on his own translations from the original texts in dealing with the translation.
　　　(3) The author admitted some of the limitations that he encountered in doing the work.
　　　(4) Some of the expressions between two different languages can not be translated through one to one correspondence.

[Challenge 3]

The right of petition is founded in the very institution of civil government, and has from time immemorial been acknowledged as among the unquestionable privileges of our English ancestors. This right springs from the great truth that government is established for the benefit of the governed; and it forms the medium by which the people acquaint their rulers with their wants and their grievances. So accustomed were the Americans to the exercise of this right, even during their subjection to the British crown, that, on the formation of the Federal Constitution, the Convention _____(a)_____, made no provision for its security. But in the very first Congress that assembled under the new Government, the omission was repaired. It was thought some case might possibly occur, in which this right might prove troublesome to a dominant faction, who would endeavor to stifle it. An amendment was therefore proposed and adopted, by which Congress is restrained from making any law abridging "the right of the People, peaceably to assemble, and to petition the Government for a redress of grievances."

문제 1 The right of petition stems from the fact that _____.
    (1) it is an inevitable component of the civil government
    (2) the government exists for the people
    (3) a clone is a perfect copy of the donor, including their exact personal experiences and memories.
    (4) the unquestionable privileges of English ancestors said so

문제 2 Fill in blank (a).
    (1) not conceiving that it could be endangered
    (2) not conceiving that it could not be endangered
    (3) conceiving that it could be endangered
    (4) conceiving that it could not be endangered

문제 3 According to the passage, which of the following is NOT true of the right of petition?
    (1) The right of petition allows the people to have their needs addressed by the government.
    (2) The right of petition can sometimes be inconvenient for the ruling party.
    (3) The provision for the right of petition was accidentally omitted by the framers of the new American government.
    (4) The right of petition is a power derived from the people who established the nation.

[Challenge 4]

One of the most common forms of relaying gossip or scandalous information is the "he said, she said" method. The danger of this practice, of course, is the potential for unreliability: The person telling a story wasn't actually present when the story was unfolding. Often, a story can pass around a circle of friends and end up as a mangled form of the truth. It's a lot like the game "Telephone." In a circle of players, one person whispers a sentence to a neighbor. The neighbor attempts to whisper the same sentence to the next player and so on until the phrase finally reaches its original source. (a) The point of the game is to compare the original sentence with its final version, and chances are the two are quite different. (b) If you've ever played, you might understand the delicate nature of the spoken word and how __(가)__ hearsay can be. (c) Gossip may be fine in the office or at school, but it's a different matter in the courtroom. When lawyers need to convince a judge or jury of the truth or falsity of something, they often provide evidence to back up their claim. (d) Although almost anything can be considered evidence, whether or not a court gets to contemplate a statement or an object during a trial actually depends on a set of rules. In the United States, The Federal Rules of Evidence, set by Chief Justice Earl Warren in 1965 and made law by Congress in 1975, lay out what makes evidence admissible or inadmissible in court. Although states have their own, slightly different rules regarding evidence, they generally follow the federal guidelines.

문제 1 What is the passage mainly talking about?
 (1) Who determines the final decision of a trial?
 (2) What is the function of gossip in court?
 (3) What makes evidence inadmissible in court?
 (4) How does the idea of hearsay relate to the rules of evidence in court?

문제 2 When the passage is divided into two, where does the second paragraph begin?
 (1) (a)　　　　　　　　　　　(2) (b)
 (3) (c)　　　　　　　　　　　(4) (d)

문제 3 Choose one that is most appropriate for blank (가).
 (1) unreliable　　　　　　　　(2) helpless
 (3) robust　　　　　　　　　　(4) critical

[Challenge 5]

Communism collapsed suddenly and unexpectedly in Eastern Europe at the end of 1989. In the Soviet Union, the Communist Party still rules, but the extraordinary social and economic chaos gripping the country suggests that _____(a)_____. In the West, many commentators acclaim the triumph of capitalism over communism. However, neither the success nor the survival of capitalism is guaranteed by the failure and demise of Soviet communism. Capitalism is a legal system that safeguards private property and permits free trade in competitive markets. Individuals are free to pursue their self-interest. As long as self-interest is restrained by competition, society benefits from lower prices and greater choices. The problem is that the powerful forces of self-interest have a natural tendency to collusion and corruption. In other words, capitalists tend to seek power and to use it to rig the market in their favor to the detriment of society.

The intellectual father of capitalism is Adam Smith. He observed over 200 years ago that the competitive market, as if by an "invisible hand," transforms self-interest into a force for public good. Smith explained how competition maximizes productivity and social welfare by assuring the optimal allocation of capital and labor in the overall economy. Yet, always a pragmatist, he recognized that capitalists could corrupt the system: "People of the same trade seldom meet together, even for merriment and diversion, but the conversation ends in a conspiracy against the public, or in some contrivance to raise prices."

문제 1 Which of the following is TRUE of the passage?
   (1) Individuals are checked by their government to enhance their self-interest in capitalism.
   (2) The Communist Party has vanished.
   (3) When self-interest is restrained by competition, customers gain benefits from it.
   (4) The demise of Soviet communism helped to guarantee the success of capitalism.

문제 2 Fill in blank (a).
   (1) the party's days are numbered
   (2) the party is ready to take active intervention in the nation's economy
   (3) the party will be more likely to take the form of capitalism
   (4) the party is willing to bail out the entire economy

문제 3 According to Adam Smith, which of the following is NOT correct about the competitive market?
   (1) Competition drives people to the maximization of productivity.
   (2) In the competitive market, self-interest is a driving force for public good.
   (3) Capitalists tend to devise ways to increase prices.
   (4) Capitalism is, by its very nature, bound to corrupt the economic system.

[Challenge 6]

Every young woman should have some avocation, or calling. The Jews formerly had a proverb, that whoever of their sons was not bred to a trade, was (a) bred to the gallows; and both Mohammedans and Pagans have maxims among them which amount to the same thing. True it is, and deeply to be regretted, that there is a fashionable feeling abroad, which is the reverse of all this. Both men and women, in fashionable life, are apt to regard all labor — not only manual, but mental — as mere drudgery. They will labor, perhaps, if they cannot help it; but seldom, if they can. Or at least, this seems to be their feeling when they begin a course of industrious action. Some, it is confessed, finally become so much accustomed to action, that they continue it, either as a matter of mere habit, or because its discontinuance would now render them as miserable as they were in breaking up their natural indolence, and in forming their present industrious habits.

문제 1 What can be inferred from the underlined (a)?
(1) the importance of having jobs
(2) the sternness of the Jews
(3) A wide variety of jobs that the Jews have
(4) the elusive nature of calling

문제 2 Which of the following is neither stated nor implied in the passage?
(1) Young people think of work as a mere habit.
(2) Maxims reflect how people perceive things.
(3) The author feels sorry that young people think of labor as a toil.
(4) These days people tend to prefer mental work to physical work.

[Challenge 7]

The American belief in "free enterprise" has not precluded a major role for government, however. Americans at times have looked to government to break up or regulate companies that appeared to be developing so much power that they could defy market forces. They have relied on government to address matters the private economy overlooks, from education to protecting the environment. And despite their advocacy of market principles, they have used government at times to nurture new industries, and at times even to protect American companies from competition.

As the sometimes ___(a)___ approach to regulation demonstrates, Americans often disagree about the appropriate role of government in the economy. In general, government grew larger and intervened more aggressively in the economy from the 1930s until the 1970s. But economic hardships in the 1960s and 1970s left Americans skeptical about the ability of government to address many social and economic issues. Major social programs — including Social Security and Medicare, which, respectively, provide retirement income and health insurance for the elderly — survived this period of reconsideration. But the growth of the federal government slowed in the 1980s.

문제 1 Which of the following can be inferred from the passage?
(1) In general, Americans want the pure mechanism of 'laissez-faire.'
(2) Americans want their government to exercise absolute power over the market.
(3) The role of the American government in the social and economic sector has gone through changes in the past century.
(4) Since the 1980s, America has focused more on funding welfare policies than on financing various economic stimulus packages.

문제 2 Fill in blank (a).
(1) concordant   (2) combined
(3) inconsistent   (4) kaleidoscopic

[Challenge 8]

    Friedrich Engels has often been credited in composing the first drafts, which led to The Communist Manifesto. In July 1847, Engels was elected into the Communist League, where he was assigned to draw up a catechism. This became the Draft of a Communist Confession of Faith. The draft contained almost two dozen questions that helped express the ideas of both Engels and Karl Marx at the time. In October 1847, Engels composed his second draft for the Communist League entitled, The Principles of Communism. The text remained unpublished until 1914, despite its basis for The Manifesto. From Engels's drafts Marx was able to write, once commissioned by the Communist League, The Communist Manifesto, where he combined more of his ideas along with Engels's drafts and work, The Condition of the Working Class in England. Although the names of both Engels and Karl Marx appear on the title page alongside the "persistent assumption of joint-authorship", Engels, in the preface introduction to the 1883 German edition of the Manifesto, said that the Manifesto was "essentially Marx's work" and that "the basic thought belongs solely and exclusively to Marx." Engels wrote after Marx's death, "I cannot deny that both before and during my forty years' collaboration with Marx I had a certain independent share in laying the foundations of the theory, but the greater part of its leading basic principles belong to Marx. Marx was a genius; we others were at best talented. Without him the theory would not be by far what it is today. It therefore rightly bears his name."

문제 1 Which of the following is the best title for the passage?
　　　(1) Engels: the Hero of Marx
　　　(2) Authorship of The Communist Manifesto
　　　(3) How The Communist Manifesto Came into Being
　　　(4) Beliefs Manifest in The Communist Manifesto

문제 2 Which of the following is NOT true of the passage?
　　　(1) The Draft of a Communist Confession of Faith was written as questions and answers.
　　　(2) Friedrich Engels was able to finish writing The Communist Manifesto after a series of revisions from the first drafts.
　　　(3) The Condition of the Working Class in England was written by Friedrich Engels.
　　　(4) Engels thought the real authorship of The Communist Manifesto should go to Marx.

[Challenge 9]

　　Raymond de Roover expanded on Schumpeter's observation, writing a series of pathbreaking articles for academic journals on the subject of these neglected figures. De Roover punctured substantial holes in the received view of late medieval and early modern economic thought, particularly when it came to the subject of the just price. Prior to de Roover's work, the Scholastic conception of the "just price" had been grotesquely misinterpreted; the Scholastics were said to have believed that certain objective criteria could help determine a good's "just price." To the contrary, de Roover showed, for the Scholastics the just price was the market price, the price arrived at by the interaction of buyers and sellers on the market. (This statement was subject to a proviso: if the state should impose a price, the state-imposed price would be considered the just one. Even here, though, some of the Scholastics remained skeptical of nonmarket prices and of the state's ability to ascertain and impose an objectively just price.) Previous work in this area, de Roover showed, had placed altogether too much emphasis on the idiosyncratic views of the relatively unimportant Heinrich von Langenstein at the expense of the broader consensus of the Scholastics and canonists. The view of medieval economic thought held by nineteenth- and twentieth-century romantics and corporatists, in which theologians encouraged the setting of "just prices" by the public authority and recommended the guild system as a vehicle for promoting justice for buyers and sellers alike, did not survive de Roover's re-evaluation. On the latter point, it turns out that the Scholastics, in those rare instances when they mentioned the guilds at all, chided them for their ___(a)___ behavior. "I do not find evidence in their treatises that they favored the guild system," wrote de Roover, "which is so often pictured as an ideal organization for Christian society or is recommended as a panacea against the evils of modern industrialism."

문제 1 What is the purpose of the above passage?
(1) To clarify misinterpreted notions
(2) To reinforce and add up to the existing concepts
(3) To contrast one theory with another
(4) To compare different concepts

문제 2 The following is a summary of the reevaluation of "Just Price" mentioned in the text. Which of the following best fills in the blank?

> De Roover's central argument revolves around the Scholastics' conception of the "just price." Contrary to earlier interpretations, which suggested that the Scholastics believed in an objective, state-determined price, de Roover shows that they actually saw the just price as the market price—determined by the free interaction of buyers and sellers. This finding is significant because _____.

(1) it contradicts the idea that prices should be set by religious authorities according to moral criteria.
(2) it suggests that the state has a crucial role in determining fair market prices.
(3) it emphasizes the importance of guilds in regulating economic activity to ensure just prices.
(4) it aligns medieval economic thought more closely with modern market theories, particularly those related to supply and demand.

문제 3 Fill in blank (a).
(1) philanthropic   (2) monopolistic
(3) obstructive   (4) cooperative

[Challenge 10]

It is no doubt owing to the conversion of the entire Armenian nation under the passionate preaching of Gregory the Illuminator that most of the literary products, of primitive Armenia — the mythological legends and chants of heroic deeds sung by bards — are ____(a)____. The Church would have none of them. Gregory not only destroyed the pagan temples, but he sought to (b) stamp out the pagan literature — the poetry and recorded traditions that celebrated the deeds of gods and goddesses and of national heroes. (c) He would have succeeded, too, had not the romantic spirit of the race clung fondly to their ballads and folk-lore. Ecclesiastical historiographers in referring to those times say quaintly enough that in spite of their great religious advantages the Armenians persisted in singing some of their heathen ballads as late as the twelfth century. _____(d)_____, we owe the fragments we possess of early Armenian poetry to these same ecclesiastical critics. These fragments suggest a popular poesy, stirring and full of powerful imagery, employed mostly in celebrating royal marriages, religious feasts, and containing dirges for the dead, and ballads of customs.

문제 1 Choose one that is most appropriate for blank (a).
(1) engrossed
(2) lost
(3) irreclaimable
(4) astray

문제 2 Choose one that best replaces the underlined (b).
(1) root out
(2) drive out
(3) compensate for
(4) take up

문제 3 Which of the following is NOT true of the above passage?
(1) The preaching of Gregory the Illuminator had so enormous an impact that the nation converted to the Christian Church.
(2) Gregory the Illuminator was not in favor of pagan religions.
(3) The deeds of national heroes were much celebrated in the time of Gregory the Illuminator.
(4) It was ecclesiastical historiographers that kept early Armenian poetry from vanishing.

문제 4 What can be inferred from the underlined (c)?
(1) Some of the pagan literature survived in spite of the persecution.
(2) Gregory eliminated most of the folk-lore.
(3) The human race always likes the romantic love-stories.
(4) National heroes defeated Gregory at the last minute.

문제 5 Choose one that best fills in blank (d).
(1) Frankly speaking
(2) Generally speaking
(3) Fairly enough
(4) Curiously enough

Day 17

★ The greatest discovery of my generation is that a human being can alter his life by altering his attitudes of mind.

William James (1842 - 1910)

우리 세대의 가장 위대한 발견은 바로 인간은 자신의 내면의 태도를 바꿈으로 삶을 바꿀 수 있다는 것이다. (William James)

[Challenge 1]

The infant seeks to grasp the burning lamp; — the parent endeavors to dissuade him from it. At length he grasps it, and suffers the consequences. Finally, however, if the parent manages him properly, he learns to follow his advice, and obey his indications, in order to avoid pain. Such, at least, is the natural result of rational management. And the habit of seeking parental counsel, once formed, is not easily eradicated. It is true that temptation and forgetfulness may lead some of the young occasionally to grasp the lamp, even after they are told better; but the consequent ____(a)____ generally restores them to their reason. It is only when the parent neglects or refuses to give advice, and for a long time manifests little or no sympathy with his child, that the habit of filial reliance and confidence is destroyed.

In fact there are very few children indeed, however improperly managed, who do not in early life acquire a degree of this confiding, inquiring, counsel-seeking disposition.

문제 1 What is the passage mainly talking about?
(1) Parental Management   (2) Child Exploration
(3) Formation of Habits   (4) Importance of Sympathy

문제 2 Fill in blank (a).
(1) scolding   2) rational management   (3) counsel-seeking   (4) suffering

문제 3 Which of the following can NOT be inferred from the passage?
(1) Habits, once formed hardly cease.
(2) Temptation sometimes outdoes reason.
(3) Infants have natural curiosity to explore things surrounding them.
(4) Sometimes infants seem to enjoy pain.

[Challenge 2]

Faith and vision do not come from the wealth of a nation. It's the faith and vision which produce the wealth. (a) Raw materials are to a certain extent essential and to a great extent valuable; but the nations which to-day are richest in raw materials are the poorest in wealth. (b) Even when considering one country — the United States — the principle holds true. (c) The coal and iron and copper have been here in this country for thousands of years, but only within the last fifty years have they been used. Water-powers exist even to-day absolutely unharnessed. Look the whole world over and there has been no increase in raw materials. (d) There existed one thousand years ago more raw materials than we have to-day, but we then lacked men with a vision and the faith to take that coal out of the ground, to harness the water-powers, to build the railroads and to do other things worth while. So I say, the great fundamental of prosperity is Faith.

문제 1   Which of the following is the topic of the passage?
(1) From Raw Materials to Prosperity
(2) The Fundamental Factor of Prosperity
(3) Characteristics of Faith
(4) Conditions for Being a Wealthy Country

문제 2   Where does the sentence below best goes?

> The wealth of a country does not depend on its raw materials.

(1) (a)   (2) (b)
(3) (c)   (4) (d)

[Challenge 3]

One of the least appealing aspects of corporate leadership is the delusion held by many corporate executives that they are 'special' people, somehow 'better' than normal humans. This confuses power with efficiency. Just because a person can make big changes does not mean they are 'clever', such power comes with the position—it is not an intrinsic feature of the (a) 'bum on seat'. In today's ego-tripping society merging companies is assumed however to make CEOs themselves more successful, presumably because they accidentally then 'own' more assets and people! The ability to engineer massive change by edict however conceals the fact that such changes are usually also massively destructive to areas of society not related to the corporation 'bottom-line'. The responsibility for (b) these negative overall changes is strangely never claimed by such executives. The capitalist scheme of values in fact transformed five of the seven deadly sins of Christianity—pride, envy, greed, avarice and lust into—positive social virtues, treating them as necessary incentives to all economic enterprise; whilst the cardinal virtues, beginning with love and humility, were rejected as bad for business. (c)

Even considering only the intended narrow purpose of such boardroom instigated changes, history tells (가) us that failure is much more common than success here. (d) Additionally this delusion of grandeur prevents the (나) 'boss' listening to any expertise from other members of the company. (e) The negative effects of these arrogant behaviours actually lead to the failure of many firms, so far from being the (다) "God's gift to humanity" that these people imagine themselves, in reality (라) they are often amongst the most ignorant, small-minded and unimaginative people on the planet! (f)

문제 1 The underlined (a) refers to which of the following?
(1) corporate executives
(2) normal humans
(3) big changes
(4) factors of corporate leadership

문제 2 Negative overall changes by corporate executives in the underlined (b) can be said _____.
(1) changes without effects
(2) responsibility outside one's authority
(3) power without responsibility
(4) abuse of authority

문제 3 It can be inferred from the passage that power requires responsibility because _____.
(1) it can bring about enormous changes
(2) it corrupts the mind of a person who possesses it
(3) it is immunized from outside criticism
(4) it is reduced to

문제 4 Which of the following is different from the rest?
(1) (가)   (2) (나)   (3) (다)   (4) (라)

문제 5 Where does the sentence below best fit in the passage?

> Additionally many successes are in fact incidental to any boardroom action (e.g. share price improvements when the whole market has risen anyway!) and easily reversed if the contingent factors don't play ball

(1) (c)   (2) (d)   (3) (e)   (4) (f)

[Challenge 4]

(A) Genetic engineering can introduce a known or unknown allergen into a food that previously did not contain it. For example, a soybean engineered to contain genes from a brazil nut was found to produce allergic reactions in blood serum of individuals with nut allergies. (B) Allergic reactions to nuts can be serious and even fatal. Researchers were able to identify the danger in this particular case because nut allergies are common and it was possible to conduct proper tests on blood serum from allergic individuals. (C) In other cases, testing for allergenic potential can be much more difficult. (D) When genetic engineering causes a familiar food to start producing a substance previously not present in the human food supply, it is impossible to know who may have an allergic reaction.

문제 1 Which of the following is the topic sentence of the passage?
(1) (A)   (2) (B)
(3) (C)   (4) (D)

문제 2 The author's attitude toward genetic engineering is _____.
(1) impartial   (2) promising
(3) subjective   (4) disapproving

[Challenge 5]

John Abercromby gives a list of food-vessels found with cremated burials in Ireland, and to these must be added a food-vessel of early type found in 1912 in a quarry at Crumlin, County Dublin. (a) It must, however, be left for future excavations to decide many questions to which at present no answer, or only a doubtful one, can be given. (b) Scandinavian influences can be detected in the great tumuli of the New Grange group; and Iberian influence is discernible in some of the later types of bronze implements. (c) Ireland was, during the Bronze Age, a kind of western ____(가)____, owing to her great richness in gold; Irish gold ornaments have been found both on the Continent and in Scandinavia; while Scandinavian amber has been found in Ireland. (d) The Bronze-Age people were acquainted with the art of weaving; and fine ornaments of horse-hair were sometimes used. The art of making pottery by hand was carried to a high degree of excellence. Shaving must have been fairly common, judging by the number of bronze razors found.

문제 1   Where does the sentence below best fit in the passage?

> This, however, is certain — Ireland during the Bronze Age was not isolated, but stood in direct communication with the Continent.

(1) (a)   (2) (b)   (3) (c)   (4) (d)

문제 2   Which of the following is most appropriate for blank (가)?
(1) El Dorado   (2) Salt Lake
(3) Black See   (4) Gold Rush

[Challenge 6]

I see the evidence for a moribund housing market every time I drive through my neighborhood. I can count four houses for sale in less than a quarter of a mile (I haven't done a complete count further back into my subdivision). And these houses have been on the market for many months. The odd thing is that ours is not a part of the country plagued by foreclosures. Three of these houses are owned by people who had to move for various reasons. One was owned by an elderly man who died eight months ago. They can't sell their homes because no one is buying. Make no mistake, this is a tremendous drag on the economy. Hey, here's a thought. You think the (a) <u>superrich oligarchs</u> who just got a tax break will spread the wealth around and buy up these homes? You know, as a patriotic gesture. Love of country and all.

문제 1   Which of the following is CORRECT about the passage?
   (1) The current housing market is seeing the light at the end of the tunnel.
   (2) The current housing crisis is mainly caused by foreclosures.
   (3) The neighborhood the author lives around does not have many houses.
   (4) The housing market is not in good shape now.

문제 2   The author's attitude toward the underlined (a) is _____.
   (1) idyllic   (2) indecisive
   (3) positive   (4) negative

[Challenge 7]

Recent years have brought minority-owned businesses in the United States unprecedented opportunities—as well as new and significant risks. Civil rights activists have long argued that one of the principal reasons why Blacks, Hispanics, and other minority groups have difficulty establishing themselves in business is that they lack access to the sizable orders and subcontracts that are generated by large companies. Now Congress, in apparent agreement, has required by law that businesses awarded federal contracts of more than $500,000 do their best to find minority subcontractors. Indeed, some federal and local agencies have gone so far as to set specific percentage goals for apportioning parts of public works contracts to minority enterprises. Corporate response appears to have been substantial. According to figures collected in 1977, the total of corporate contracts with minority businesses rose from $77 million in 1972 to $1.1 billion in 1977. The projected total of corporate contracts with minority businesses for the early 1980's is estimated to be over 53 billion per year with no letup anticipated in the next decade.

Promising as it is for minority businesses, this increased patronage poses dangers for them, too. First, minority firms risk expanding too fast and overextending themselves financially, since most are small concerns and, unlike large businesses, they often need to make substantial investments in new plants, staff, equipment, and the like in order to perform work subcontracted to them. If, there after, their subcontracts are for some reason reduced, such firms can face potentially crippling fixed expenses. A second risk is that White-owned companies may seek to cash in on the increasing apportionments through formation of joint ventures with minority-owned concerns. Of course, in many instances there are legitimate reasons for joint ventures; clearly, White and minority enterprises can team up to acquire business that neither could acquire alone. But civil rights groups and minority business owners have complained to Congress about minorities being set up as "fronts" with White backing, rather than being accepted as full partners in legitimate joint ventures. Third, a minority enterprise that secures the business of one large corporate customer often runs the danger of becoming—and remaining—dependent. Even in the best of circumstances, fierce competition from larger, more established companies makes it difficult for small concerns to broaden their customer bases.

Day 17

문제 1 The primary purpose of the passage is to _____.
(1) present a commonplace idea and its inaccuracies
(2) describe a situation and its potential drawbacks
(3) propose a temporary solution to a problem
(4) analyze a frequent source of disagreement

문제 2 The passage supplies information that would answer which of the following questions?
(1) What federal agencies have set percentage goals for the use of minority-owned businesses in public works contracts?
(2) How widespread is the use of minority-owned concerns as "fronts" by White backers seeking to obtain subcontracts?
(3) How many more minority-owned businesses were there in 1977 than in 1972?
(4) What is one set of conditions under which a small business might find itself financially overextended?

문제 3 According to the passage, civil rights activists maintain that one disadvantage under which minority-owned businesses have traditionally had to labor is that they have _____.
(1) been especially vulnerable to governmental mismanagement of the economy
(2) been denied bank loans at rates comparable to those afforded larger competitors
(3) not had sufficient opportunity to secure business created by large corporations
(4) not been able to advertise in those media that reach large numbers of potential customers

문제 4 The author implies that a minority-owned concern that does the greater part of its business with one large corporate customer should _____.
(1) avoid competition with larger, more established concerns by not expanding
(2) concentrate on securing even more business from that corporation
(3) try to expand its customer base to avoid becoming dependent on the corporation
(4) pass on some of the work to be done for the corporation to other minority-owned concerns

[Challenge 8]

The pioneers of the teaching of science imagined that its introduction into education would remove the conventionality, artificiality, and backward-lookingness which were characteristic of classical studies, but they were gravely disappointed. So, too, in their time had the humanists thought that the study of the classical authors in the original would banish at once the dull pedantry and superstition of mediaeval scholasticism. (a) The professional schoolmaster was a match for both of them, and has almost managed to make the understanding of chemical reactions as dull and as dogmatic an affair as the reading of Virgil's Aeneid.

The chief claim for the use of science in education is that it teaches a child something about the actual universe in which he is living, in making him acquainted with the results of scientific discovery, and at the same time teaches him how to think logically and inductively by studying scientific method. A certain limited success has been reached in the first of these aims, but practically none at all in the second. Those privileged members of the community who have been through a secondary or public school education may be expected to know something about the elementary physics and chemistry of a hundred years ago, but they probably know hardly more than any bright boy can pick up from an interest in wireless or scientific hobbies out of school hours. As to the learning of scientific method, the whole thing is palpably a farce. Actually, for the convenience of teachers and the requirements of the examination system, it is necessary that the pupils not only do not learn scientific method but learn precisely the reverse, that is, to believe exactly what they are told and to reproduce it when asked, whether it seems nonsense to them or not. The way in which educated people respond to such quackeries as spiritualism or (b) astrology, not to say more dangerous ones such as racial theories, shows that fifty years of education in the method of science in Britain or Germany has produced no visible effect whatever. The only way of learning the method of science is the long and bitter way of personal experience, and, until the educational or social systems are altered to make this possible, the best we can expect is the production of a minority of people who are able to acquire some of the techniques of science and a still smaller minority who are able to use and develop them.

문제 1 Which of the following is CORRECT about professional schoolmaster in the underlined (a)?
  (1) He has been a pioneer in both science and humanities.
  (2) He has thwarted attempts to enliven education.
  (3) He has aided true learning.
  (4) He has supported the humanists.

문제 2 The author's attitude to secondary and public school education in the sciences is
_____.

(1) ambivalent (2) neutral
(3) supportive (4) contemptuous

문제 3 The author blames all of the following for the failure to impart scientific method through the education system except _____.

(1) poor teaching
(2) lack of interest on the part of students
(3) lack of direct experience
(4) the social and education systems

문제 4 If the author were to study current education in science to see how things have changed since he wrote the piece, he would probably be most interested in the answer to which of the following questions?
(1) Do students know more about the world about them?
(2) Can students apply their knowledge logically?
(3) Have textbooks improved?
(4) Do they respect their teachers?

문제 5 Astrology in the underlined (b) is mentioned as an example of _____.
(1) a science that needs to be better understood
(2) a belief which no educated people hold
(3) something unsupportable to those who have absorbed the methods of science
(4) the gravest danger to society

[Challenge 9]

Does it inevitably corrupt? In 1887 the English historian Lord Acton wrote, in a letter to Bishop Mandell Creighton, a sentence set to become one of the world's most familiar quotations: 'Power tends to corrupt and absolute power corrupts absolutely.' The link between power and corruption had long been recognized. William Pitt, Earl of Chatham, in a speech in the House of Lords in 1770, said: 'Unlimited power is apt to corrupt the minds of those who possess it'. In the 4th century BC, the Greek philosopher, Plato, argued in The Republic that only politicians who would gain no personal advantage from the policies they pursued would be fit to govern. This is recognized also in the aphorism that those who want to hold power are most likely those least fit to do so. The present century has produced numerous examples of corrupt political leaders: Erich Honecker of East Germany; Jean-Bedel Bokassa of the Central African Republic; Joseph Stalin of the former USSR. There are many more examples.

The world's liberal democracies were thought to be relatively immune from corruption of the sort found in less developed politics, but revelations of widespread Mafia corruption in Italy, involving some of the country's most respected politicians, have brought the problem to light again right at the centre of European life.

문제 1   Which of the following is the best title for the passage?
  (1) The Historical Relationship Between Power and Corruption
  (2) Plato's View on Political Leadership
  (3) The Rise and Fall of Political Leaders
  (4) The Inescapable Corruption of Absolute Power

문제 2   Which of the following is neither stated nor implied?
  (1) The connection between power and corruption has long been in the history of human beings.
  (2) The more absolute the power is, the more corrupt it becomes.
  (3) According to Plato, personal advantage tends to make politicians go astray.
  (4) Liberal democracies are immune from political corruption.

[Challenge 10]

There are some terrible robbers in the pond world, and, in our aquarium, we may witness all the cruelties of an embittered struggle for existence enacted before our very eyes. If you have introduced to your aquarium a mixed catch, you will soon see an example of such conflicts, for, amongst the new arrivals, there will probably be a larva of the water beetle Dytiscus. Considering their relative size, the voracity and cunning with which these animals destroy their prey eclipse the methods of even such notorious robbers as tigers, lions and wolves. These are all as lambs compared with the Dytiscus larva.

문제 1   In referring to the "terrible robbers in the pond world," the author uses which literary technique?
  (1) personification   (2) hyperbole
  (3) understatement   (4) metaphor
  (5) simile

문제 2   The author's attitude in describing the Dytiscus larva can best be described as _____.
  (1) disinterest   (2) abhorrence
  (3) grudging admiration   (4) fascination
  (5) mild disapproval

Day 18

★ Eccentricity is not, as dull people would have us believe, a form of madness. It is often a kind of innocent pride, and the man of genius and the aristocrat are frequently regarded as eccentrics because genius and aristocrat are entirely unafraid of and uninfluenced by the opinions and vagaries of the crowd.

Edith Sitwell (1887 - 1964)

기행(奇行)이란 어리석은 사람들이 우리를 믿게 만드는 것처럼 일종의 광기가 아니다. 이것은 종종 일종의 순수한 자존심이다. 천부적인 재능을 가진 사람과 귀족은 종종 괴짜라고 불리는데, 이는 천재와 귀족은 군중의 변덕스러운 견해를 전혀 놀라지도 영향을 받지 않기 때문이다. (Edith Sitwell)

[Challenge 1]

To a plant, sunbathing is life. Literally. In fact, plants have evolved all sorts of ways to maximize their exposure to the sun while at the same time preventing loss of critically needed water. Plants, as well as some algae and bacteria, perform photosynthesis, a process that involves the capture and use of the Sun's energy to create biological compounds. Photosynthetic organisms generate these compounds using carbon dioxide (CO2) and water (H2O), and the products they release are oxygen (O2) and carbohydrates as byproducts.

Plants provide us with the oxygen we breathe. Now that you know this tidbit of info, you may have a little better understanding of why environmentalists freak out over the rapid destruction of rainforests, wetlands, and natural habitat. The lower the number of plants on the planet, the less O2 produced for important things like, say breathing.

Photosynthesis can be divided into two processes: the first requires light, and the second does not. In the first phase of photosynthesis, cellular protein pigments called chloroplasts are excited by light that propels them into high-energy states. The chloroplasts then transfer this energy through electrons to other protein complexes. This group of proteins is called the electron transport chain. The proteins operate similarly to _____(a)_____ : after the first one has been pushed, each protein transfers energy to each member along down the line. Water (H2O) is split in this process, releasing oxygen (O2) and hydrogen ions (H+). The electrons from the electron transport chain combine with these H+ ions and NADP+ to form adenosine triphosphate (ATP) and a reduced unit of NADP+, called NADPH. These energy storage forms, ATP and NADPH, are used to convert carbon dioxide (CO2) to build carbohydrates during the second phase of photosynthesis. Plants can then break down these carbohydrates to fuel their existence.

문제 1 The topic of the passage is _____ .
(1) Photosynthesis (2) Life of Plants
(3) Mainspring of Human Activity (4) Importance of Plants

문제 2 Which of the following can be inferred from the passage?
(1) Some proteins stick together to form a group.
(2) Light is critical in the second process of photosynthesis.
(3) Oxygen and hydrogen ions are produced after the process of photosynthesis is complete.
(4) Carbohydrates form during the first process of photosynthesis.

문제 3 Fill in blank (a).
(1) a bridge between two cities (2) buildings abreast each other
(3) a group of dominoes (4) a range of mountains

[Challenge 2]

The consumption of a food typically leads to a decrease in its subsequent intake through habituation — a decrease in one's responsiveness to the food and motivation to obtain it. We demonstrated that habituation to a food item can occur even when its consumption is merely imagined. Five experiments showed that people who repeatedly imagined eating a food (such as cheese) many times subsequently consumed less of the imagined food than did people who repeatedly imagined eating that food fewer times, imagined eating a different food (such as candy), or did not imagine eating a food. They did so because they desired to eat it less, not because they considered it less palatable. These results suggest that mental representation alone can engender habituation to a stimulus.

문제 1 Which of the following is the best title for the passage?
(1) Reinforcement of Food Consumption Through Imagination
(2) Imagined Consumption Reduces Actual Consumption
(3) Breaking out of a Bad Food Habit
(4) Direct Proportion between Food Consumption and Imagination

[Challenge 3]

An analysis of worldwide political corruption reveals common factors. First, in many cases a person, regime or party has been continuously in power for a long period. Second, and flowing from the first, power rather than public service has become the main purpose of political life. Third, with the retention of power the main objective, virtually any action is acceptable if it furthers this end. In other words, morality and probity take second place to the essential objective of maintaining power. Inevitably, this involves politicians granting favours to win votes ((a) 'pork barrel' politics), or granting favours to obtain money to finance their parties. It is an ____(b)____ process, with one favour demanding another and one shady deal leading to the next.

문제 1   Which of the following is the topic of the passage?
   (1) Features of Politics
   (2) Corruption of Power
   (3) Common Factors of Political Corruption
   (4) Abuse of Authority

문제 2   According to the passage, which of the following best describes the term of the underlined (a)?
   (1) A political metaphor for the appropriation of government spending for projects that are intended primarily to benefit particular constituents or campaign contributors.
   (2) Situations where the advancement of a qualified person within the hierarchy of an organization is stopped at a lower level because of some form of discrimination.
   (3) Policies that take "race, color, religion, sex or national origin" into consideration.
   (4) Language, ideas, policies, and behavior seen as seeking to minimize social and institutional offense in occupational, gender, racial, cultural, sexual orientation, disability, and age-related contexts.

문제 3   Choose one that is most appropriate for blank (b).
   (1) imperceptible   (2) conspicuous
   (3) overt   (4) insidious

[Challenge 4]

So it would seem that Lord Acton was right, (a) <u>human nature being what it is</u>. The evidence is there for all to see, right across the world. There are probably few politicians whose hands are absolutely clean. Is there an answer? There is certainly not a simple or instant one.

In most countries it will be a long-haul process. The theory of multiparty politics, in which there is always an effective opposition ready to take over should the party in power ___(b)___, should be made more of a reality. Government should be opened up much more to public scrutiny and this should include the accountability of political parties for their funds. Most important of all, however, public esteem for politicians should be restored. This can only be done by the politicians themselves, demonstrating by deeds that they see themselves as elected to serve, rather than to profit.

문제 1 What is the purpose of the passage?
(1) To elucidate a problem
(2) To offer a solution to a problem
(3) To elaborate on something
(4) To analyse a certain event

문제 2 According to the passage, which of the following best describes the underlined (a)?
(1) Men are born to attain power.
(2) Not every one is born to be a politician.
(3) A man in power tends to corrupt.
(4) Serving for the public is against man's nature.

문제 3 Choose one that is most appropriate for blank (b).
(1) perpetrate
(2) perpetuate
(3) alter
(4) falter

[Challenge 5]

The theory of "Socialism in One Country" was conceived by Stalin as a response to (a) this theory, rejecting the Soviet Union's dependence on fostering international Marxism. In Stalin's first treatment on the subject, "The October Revolution and the Tactics of the Russian Communists," Stalin clearly expressed the opinion that Trotsky's theory of Permanent Revolution ran counter to Lenin's theory of the proletariat revolution, going so far as to claim that "Trotsky's theory of 'permanent revolution' is a variety of Menshevism." Thus, the theory of "Socialism in One Country" was created in direct opposition to Trotsky's theory. Trotsky acknowledged as much in his often quoted passage declaring that, "the theory of socialism in one country…… is the only theory that consistently and to the very end opposes the theory of the permanent revolution."

문제 1 Which of the following would mostly likely refer to the underlined (a)?
(1) Socialism in One Country
(2) Theory of the Permanent Revolution
(3) Menshevism
(4) Lenin's Theory of the Proletariat Revolution

[Challenge 6]

The so called "baby blues" happen in many women in the days right after childbirth. (a) A new mother can have sudden mood swings, such as feeling very happy and then feeling very sad or angry. (b) She may cry for no reason and can feel impatient, irritable, restless, anxious, lonely, and sad. (c) The baby blues may last only a few hours or as long as one to two weeks after delivery. (d) The baby blues always require treatment from a health-care provider. Often, joining a support group of new moms or talking with other moms helps.

문제 1 Which of the underlined sentences is not cohesive to the overall passage?
(1) (a)   (2) (b)
(3) (c)   (4) (d)

[Challenge 7]

True statesmanship is the masterful art. Poetry, music, painting, sculpture and architecture please, thrill and inspire, but the great statesman and diplomatist and leader in thought and action convinces, controls and compels the admiration of all classes and creeds. Logical thought, power of appeal and tactfulness never fail to command attention and respect. It has always been thus, and it will unquestionably so remain. Many really able and brilliant men, however, lack balance and the faculty of calculation. They are too often swayed by emotions, and their intellectual powers, which ____(a)____ might exert a controlling influence, are thus weakened, and often result in failure. True greatness in a man is gauged by what he accomplished in life, and the impress he left upon his fellow-men. It does not consist of one act, or even of many, but rather their effect upon the times in which he lived, and how long they endure after the actor is gone from the throng of the living.

문제 1 Which of the following can NOT be inferred from the passage?
(1) The statesman with logical thought, power of appeal and tactfulness is sure to make a difference in others' lives.
(2) The author thinks highly of the art of true statesmanship.
(3) The great statesman has a tremendous impact on people in every walk of life.
(4) The value of a statesman can be judged not by his achievements but by his genuine motives.

문제 2 Choose one that is most appropriate for blank (a)?
(1) though   (2) at once
(3) otherwise   (4) nonetheless

[Challenge 8]

Officials with the oil company BP say a large containment chamber designed to cap a leaking underwater oil well is now suspended over the target site in the Gulf of Mexico. BP officials say the device has been lowered close to the leaking well, 1,500 meters below the surface of the gulf. They expect the dome to be in place over the main leak by the end of the day Friday. The officials say a device of this type has never been used at this depth and they are offering no guarantees it will work. But if all goes well, they hope the dome could be ready by next week to funnel oil to a boat on the gulf's surface. The damaged oil well has been spilling hundreds of thousands of liters per day, since an oil rig exploded and sank two weeks ago. Oil reached barrier islands off southern Louisiana's coast Thursday, where there are many fragile animal habitats.

U.S. Interior Secretary Ken Salazar told reporters Thursday there would be no new U.S. offshore drilling permits issued until a federal investigation into the oil spill is completed May 28. He also said BP and its partners made "some very major mistakes," and that the company's "life is on the line." Salazar did not elaborate on those comments. Among BP's other efforts to contain the spill, the company is drilling a relief well to pump the leaking reservoir. But BP says the well will take about three months to prepare.

문제 1 Which of the following is NOT correct from the passage?
(1) The oil company BP made such a huge mistake that the life of the company is unpredictable.
(2) The success of the dome is undecided.
(3) The containment chamber is not yet in place to contain the oil leak.
(4) New offshore drilling permits are being issued under strict regulations.

문제 2 According to the passage, which of the following is the most urgent thing to be done?
(1) Getting the oil rig fixed
(2) Controlling new drilling permits
(3) Getting the dome to be in place over the leakage
(4) Providing a relief well

[Challenge 9]

His licentiousness having now (가) become more unbounded, the Caesar began to be burdensome to all virtuous men. (a) And discarding all moderation, he harassed every part of the East, sparing neither those who had received public honours, nor the chief citizens of the different cities; nor the common people. (b) At last by one single sentence he ordered all the principal persons at Antioch to be put to death. (c) Being exasperated because when he recommended that a low price should be established in the market at an unseasonable time, when the city was threatened with a scarcity, they answered him with objections, urged with more force than he approved. (d) This circumstance was also a proof of the cruelty of his nature, that he took delight in cruel sports, and in the circus he would rejoice as if he had made some great gain, to see six or seven gladiators killing one another in combats which have often been forbidden.

문제 1 Which of the following is the best title for the passage?
(1) Domestic Policies of Ruthless Caesar
(2) Caesar, The Tyrant
(3) Exotic Propensities of Caesar
(4) Economic Policies of Caesar

문제 2 Which of the following best paraphrases the underlined (가)?

(1) get out of control
(2) become contained
(3) get subdued
(4) go shackled

문제 3 Where does the sentence below best fit in the above passage?

> And they would all have been put to death to a man, if Honoratus, who was at that time count of the East, had not resisted him with pertinacious constancy.

(1) (a)
(2) (b)
(3) (c)
(4) (d)

[Challenge 10]

Human knowledge has two forms: it is either intuitive knowledge or logical knowledge. In ordinary life, constant appeal is made to intuitive knowledge. It is said to be impossible to give expression to certain truths; that they are not demonstrable by syllogisms; that they must be learnt intuitively. The politician finds fault with the abstract reasoner, who is without a lively knowledge of actual conditions; the pedagogue insists upon the necessity of developing the intuitive faculty in the pupil before everything else; the critic in judging a work of art makes it a point of honour to set aside theory and abstractions, and to judge it by direct intuition; the practical man professes to live rather by intuition than by reason. ____(a)____ this ample acknowledgment, granted to intuitive knowledge in ordinary life, does not meet with an equal and adequate acknowledgment in the field of theory and of philosophy.

문제 1 What is the passage mainly talking about?
(1) The limitations of logical knowledge compared to intuitive knowledge
(2) The preference for intuitive knowledge in practical life over logical knowledge
(3) The development of logical reasoning skills in education
(4) The challenges of applying intuitive knowledge in theoretical contexts

문제 2 Choose one that is most appropriate for blank (a).
(1) Therefore
(2) But
(3) In addition
(4) Otherwise

Day 19

★ Wisdom doesn't automatically come with old age. Nothing does - except wrinkles. It's true, some wines improve with age. But only if the grapes were good in the first place.

Abigail Van Buren

지혜는 나이를 먹어감에 따라 저절로 생겨나지 않는다. 주름살 외에는 어떤 것도 생기지 않는다. 어떤 와인은 시간이 지나면서 질이 좋아지는 것은 사실이다. 그러나 이것 또한 단지 포도가 처음부터 좋았을 때의 이야기다. (Abigail Van Buren)

[Challenge 1]

When forming personal convictions, we often interpret factual evidence through the filter of our values, feelings, tastes, and past experiences. Hence, most statements we make in speaking and writing are assertions of fact, opinion, belief, or prejudice. The usefulness and acceptability of an assertion can be improved or diminished by the nature of the assertion, depending on which of the following categories it falls into: A fact is verifiable. We can determine whether it is true by researching the evidence. This may involve numbers, dates, testimony, etc. (Ex.: "World War II ended in 1945.") The truth of the fact is beyond argument if one can assume that measuring devices or records or memories are correct. Facts provide crucial support for the assertion of an argument. However, facts by themselves are worthless unless we put them in context, draw conclusions, and, thus, give them meaning. An opinion is a judgment based on facts, an honest attempt to draw a reasonable conclusion from factual evidence. (For example, we know that millions of people go without proper medical care, and so you form the opinion that the country should institute national health insurance even though it would cost billions of dollars.) (가) An opinion is potentially changeable — depending on how the evidence is interpreted. By themselves, opinions have little power to convince. You must always let your reader know what your evidence is and how it led you to arrive at your opinion. (나) Unlike an opinion, a belief is a conviction based on cultural or personal faith, morality, or values. (다) Statements such as "Capital punishment is legalized murder" are often called "opinions" because they express viewpoints, but they are not based on facts or other evidence. (라) They cannot be disproved or even contested in a rational or logical manner. Since beliefs are inarguable, they cannot serve as the thesis of a formal argument. (Emotional appeals can, of course, be useful if you happen to know that your audience shares those beliefs.)

문제 1 Which of the following is the topic of the passage?
(1) How to Convince People
(2) Distinguishing Between Fact, Opinion, Belief, and Prejudice
(3) How Not to Make Biased Opinions
(4) Differences between Fact and Opinion

문제 2 Which of the following will be discussed in the next paragraph?
(1) How to tell the difference between opinion and belief
(2) Another kind of assertion based on insufficient or unexamined evidence
(3) Additional information about opinions
(4) How to form the thesis of a formal argument

문제 3 When the passage is divided in 3 different paragraph, where does the third one begin?
(1) (가)   (2) (나)   (3) (다)   (4) (라)

[Challenge 2]

Man is a product of the (a) earth's surface. This means not merely that he is a child of the earth, dust of her dust; but that the earth has mothered him, fed him, set him tasks, directed his thoughts, confronted him with difficulties that have strengthened his body and sharpened his wits, given him his problems of navigation or irrigation, and at the same time whispered hints for their solution. (b) She has entered into his bone and tissue, into his mind and soul. On the mountains she has given him leg muscles of iron to climb the slope; along the coast she has left these weak and flabby, but given him instead vigorous development of chest and arm to handle his paddle or oar. In the river valley she attaches him to the fertile soil, circumscribes his ideas and ambitions by a dull round of calm, exacting duties, narrows his outlook to the cramped horizon of his farm. Up on the wind-swept (c) plateaus, in the boundless stretch of the grasslands and the waterless tracts of the desert, where he roams with his flocks from pasture to pasture and oasis to oasis, where life knows much hardship but escapes (d) the grind of drudgery, where the watching of grazing herd gives him leisure for contemplation.

문제 1 Which of the following is the main idea of the passage?
(1) Man is a product of the earth's surface.
(2) The earth's surface was not always beneficial to man.
(3) Man are helpless to the powers of nature.
(4) Man and nature are in a reciprocal relationship.

문제 2 Which of the following is CORRECT about the passage?
(1) Man is given abilities to overcome his weaknesses.
(2) Nature does not provide any help to mankind.
(3) Nature only provides material needs to man.
(4) Man sometimes goes against the will of Mother Nature.

문제 3 Which of the following does not imply the same meaning?
(1) (a)   (2) (b)
(3) (c)   (4) (d)

[Challenge 3]

The effects of the Black Death had not yet subsided, and the graves of millions of its victims were scarcely closed, when a strange delusion arose in Germany, which took possession of the minds of men, and, in spite of the divinity of our nature, hurried away body and soul into the magic circle of hellish superstition. It was a(an) ____(a)____ which in the most extraordinary manner infuriated the human frame, and excited the astonishment of contemporaries for more than two centuries, since which time it has never reappeared. It was called the dance of St. John or of St. Vitus, on account of the Bacchantic leaps by which it was characterized, and which gave to those affected, whilst performing their wild dance, and screaming and foaming with fury, all the appearance of persons possessed. It did not remain confined to particular localities, but was propagated by the sight of the sufferers, like a demoniacal epidemic, over the whole of Germany and the neighbouring countries to the north-west, which were already prepared for its reception by the prevailing opinions of the time.

문제 1 Which of the following is the topic of the passage?
(1) St. John's Dance   (2) The Black Death
(3) A Hellish Superstition   (4) Possessed Minds of Men

문제 2 According to the passage, which of the following is most appropriate for blank (a)?
(1) adoration   (2) wonder
(3) convulsion   (4) deification

문제 3 Which of the following is TRUE of the passage?
(1) The origin of the name, Dance of St. John was derived from some of the symptoms of it.
(2) The dance of St. John was the real effects of demonic powers.
(3) The effects of the Black Death were no longer in effect.
(4) The neighbouring countries affected by the dance of St. John were caught off guard by the sudden attach of it.

문제 4 According to the passage, how was the dance of St. John diffused?
(1) by the touch of it   (2) by the spectacle of it
(3) by the contact with it   (4) by the imagination of it

[Challenge 4]

Adorno (1903-69) argued that capitalism fed people with the products of a "culture industry" — the opposite of "true" art — to keep them passively satisfied and politically apathetic. Adorno saw that capitalism had not become more precarious or close to collapse, as Marx had predicted. Instead, it had seemingly become more entrenched. Where Marx had focussed on economics, Adorno placed emphasis on the role of culture in securing the status quo. Popular culture was identified as the reason for people's passive satisfaction and lack of interest in overthrowing the capitalist system. Adorno suggested that culture industries churn out a debased mass of unsophisticated, sentimental products which have replaced the more 'difficult' and critical art forms which might lead people to actually question social life. False needs are cultivated in people by the culture industries. These are needs which can be both created and satisfied by the capitalist system, and which replace people's "true" needs — freedom, full expression of human potential and creativity, genuine creative happiness. Commodity fetishism (promoted by the marketing, advertising and media industries) means that social relations and cultural experiences are objectified in terms of money. We are delighted by something because of how much it costs. Popular media and music products are characterized by standardization (they are basically formulaic and similar) and ____(a)____ (incidental differences make them seem distinctive, but they're not). Products of the culture industry may be emotional or apparently moving, but Adorno sees this as cathartic — we might seek some comfort in a sad film or song, have a bit of a cry, and then feel restored again. Boiled down to its most obvious modern-day application, the argument would be that television leads people away from talking to each other or questioning the oppression in their lives. Instead they get up and go to work (if they are employed), come home and switch on TV, absorb TV's nonsense until bedtime, and then the daily cycle starts again.

문제 1 According to Adorno's argument, which of the following is NOT correct about the capitalist system?
(1) People under capitalism are manipulated to pay much of their attention to the culture industries.
(2) People think they are enjoying products that seem to be customized to their own needs but they are unconsciously accustomed to standardized commodities.
(3) He thought capitalism is bound to fall apart because it puts too much emphasis on economic values.
(4) TV deprives family members of the chances to have meaningful conversations with each other.

문제 2 Fill in blank (a).

(1) a blank and white division

(2) pseudo-individualization

(3) an age of materialism

(4) unrealistic obsession

[Challenge 5]

In view of this apparent change in the attitude of people toward the farm problem, it may not be (a) <u>idle</u> to suggest some possible errors that should be avoided when we are thinking of rural society. The student will doubtless approach his problem against misconceptions — he probably has thoughtfully established his view-point. But the average person in the city is likely to call up the image of his ancestral home of a generation ago, if he were born in the country, or, if not, to draw upon his observations made on a summer vacation or on casual business trips into the interior. Or he takes his picture from Shore Acres and the Old Homestead. In any case it is not improbable that the image may be faulty and as a consequence his appreciation of present conditions wholly inadequate. Let us consider some of these possible sources of misconception.

In the first place it is not fair to compare country life as a whole with the best city conditions. This is often done. The observer usually has education, culture, leisure, the experience of travel, more or less wealth; his acquaintance is mostly with people of like attainments. When he fails to find a rural environment that corresponds in some degree to his own and that of his friends, he is quick to conclude that the country has nothing to offer him, that only the city ministers to the higher wants of man. He forgets that he is one of a thousand in the city, and does not represent average city life. He fails to compare ___(b)___, manifestly the only fair basis for comparison. Or he may err still more grievously. He may set opposite each other the worst country conditions and the better city conditions. He ought in all justice to balance country slum with city slum; and certainly so if he insists on trying to find palaces, great libraries, eloquent preachers, theaters, and rapid transit in each rural community. City life goes to extremes; country life, while varied, is more even. In the country there is little of large wealth, luxury, and ease; little also of extreme poverty, reeking crime, unutterable filth, moral sewage. Farmers are essentially a middle class and no comparison is fair that does not keep this fact ever in mind.

문제 1 Which of the following is the topic of the passage?

(1) Different Conditions between Rural and Urban Societies

(2) Solutions to Distorted Pictures of the Rural Society

(3) Conditions of Rural Societies

(4) Misconceptions about Rural Communities

문제 2 The paragraph that immediately follows the above passage is probably about _____.
(1) Another inadequate source of information about the country
(2) Rural conditions of Poverty
(3) Rural communities in rapid transition
(4) Characteristics of middle-class farmers

문제 3 Which of the following is synonymous with the underlined (a)?
(1) lethargic   (2) resting   (3) futile   (4) pivotal

문제 4 Fill in blank (b).
(1) the average country conditions with those of a specific person from the city
(2) himself with one individual person from the country
(3) himself with the average country conditions
(4) the average country conditions with the average city conditions

[Challenge 6]

Third among the colonists in order of numerical importance were the Germans. From the very beginning, they appeared in colonial records. A number of the artisans and carpenters in the first Jamestown colony were of German (a) descent. Peter Minuit, the famous governor of New Motherland, was a German from Wesel on the Rhine, and Jacob Leisler, leader of a popular uprising against the provincial administration of New York, was a German from Frankfort-on-Main. The wholesale migration of Germans began with the founding of Pennsylvania. (b) Penn was diligent in searching for thrifty farmers to cultivate his lands and (c) he made a special effort to attract peasants from (d) the Rhine country. A great association, known as the Frankfort Company, bought more than twenty thousand acres from (e) him and in 1684 established a center at Germantown for the distribution of German immigrants. In old New York, Rhinebeck-on-the-Hudson became a similar center for distribution. All the way from Maine to Georgia inducements were offered to the German farmers and in nearly every colony were to be found, in time, German settlements. _____(f)_____ the migration became so large that German princes were frightened at the loss of so many subjects and England was alarmed by the influx of foreigners into her overseas dominions. Yet nothing could stop the movement. By the end of the colonial period, the number of Germans had risen to more than two hundred thousand.

문제 1 What is the passage mainly talking about?
(1) Progress of the German Immigration
(2) Immigration of the Germans
(3) Conditions of the German Settlements in the Early Colonies
(4) Great Figures of the Early Colonies

문제 2 Which of the following is the synonym for the underlined word (a)?
(1) inclination (2) extraction
(3) slant (4) career

문제 3 Which of the following does NOT refer to the same object?
(1) (b) (2) (c)
(3) (d) (4) (e)

문제 4 Choose the right transition that best fills in blank (f).
(1) Nevertheless (2) However
(3) In fact (4) Therefore

[Challenge 7]

The great idealistic philosophers of Germany, Schelling and Hegel, understood the insufficiency of the human nature point of view. Hegel, in his "Philosophy of History," makes fun of the Utopian bourgeoisie in search of the best of constitutions. German Idealism conceived history as a process subject to law, and sought the motive-power of the historical movement outside the nature of man. This was a great step towards the truth. But the Idealists saw this motive-power in the absolute idea, in the "Weltgeist" and as their absolute idea was only an abstraction of "our process of thinking," in their philosophical speculation upon history, they reintroduced the old love of the Materialist philosophers — human nature — but dressed in robes worthy of the respectable and austere society of German thinkers. (a) Drive nature out of the door, she flies in at the window! Despite the great services rendered to social science by the German Idealists, the great problem of that science, its essential problem, was no more solved in the time of the German Idealists than in the time of the French Materialists.

문제 1 Which of the following is NOT the characteristics of German Idealism depicted in the above passage?
(1) Objection to the Utopian bourgeoisie
(2) Understanding history as a law-bound process
(3) Praise for Austerity
(4) Love for Materialistic ideas

문제 2 Which of the following best paraphrases the underlined (a)?
(1) Human nature is 'omnipresent' found anywhere on earth.
(2) Human nature only stays in the home of the human mind.
(3) It is not easy to understand the historical movement outside the nature of man.
(4) Human nature is the door or the window to understanding history.

[Challenge 8]

According to ancient Chinese (a) <u>metaphysics</u>, as recorded some 4000 years ago in I ching or the Book of changes, when the un-differentiated universe (symbolized by an empty circle) moved, light or Yang was produced; when movement ceased, dark or Yin appeared. The continuous (b) <u>interplay</u> between these primal bipolar forces of Yang and Yin (symbolized by a circle of interwound white and black segments) creates stress, change, and harmony in the universe as humans know it. At the beginning of the Great Commentary on I ching, (c) <u>attributed to</u> Confucius, we find the following: 'Heaven is high, the earth is low; thus the Creative and the Receptive are determined. In correspondence with this difference between low and high, inferior and superior places are established. Movement and rest have their definite laws; according to these, firm and yielding lines are differentiated... The way of the Creative brings about the male; the way of the Receptive brings about the female.' The underlying polarity of Yang and Yin thus begins with light vs. dark and extends not only into high vs. low, creative vs. receptive, firm vs. (d) <u>yielding</u>, moving vs. resting, and masculine vs. feminine, but also into many other areas of human concern, including the sun and the moon, the weather, the parts of the body, and even the distinction between gods (all Yang) and ghosts (all Yin).

문제 1 Which of the following is neither stated nor implied in the above passage?
(1) The book I ching is based on the notion of dichotomy.
(2) The book I ching is about two forces bringing the world into existence.
(3) Confucius wrote the Great Commentary on I ching.
(4) The underlying polarity of Yang and Yin tells on almost every field of the universe.

문제 2 Which of the following is not an appropriate synonym in the given context for the underlined expression?
(1) (a) metaphysics - ontology
(2) (b) interplay - action and reaction
(3) (c) attributed to - credited to
(4) (d) yielding - subject to change

[Challenge 9]

Men are anxious to improve their circumstances, but are unwilling to improve themselves; they therefore remain bound. The man who does not shrink from self-crucifixion can never fail to accomplish the object upon which his heart is set. This is as true of earthly as of heavenly things. Even the man whose sole object is to acquire wealth must be prepared to make great personal sacrifices before he can accomplish his object; and how much more so he who would realize a strong and well-poised life?

문제 1 Which of the following is neither stated nor implied in the passage?
   (1) Men who are eager to enhance their surroundings may not try to improve themselves.
   (2) Personal sacrifices are required to reach the goal one sets on his heart.
   (3) Earthly matter needs personal sacrifices to achieve.
   (4) A strong and well-poised life naturally comes from within one's heart.

[Challenge 10]

The secret of Alexander's success was his character. He possessed a certain combination of mental and personal attractions, which in every age gives to those who exhibit it a mysterious and almost unbounded ascendency over all within their influence. Alexander was characterized by these qualities in a very remarkable degree. He was finely formed in person, and very prepossessing in his manners. He was active, athletic, and full of ardor and enthusiasm in all that he did. At the same time, he was calm, collected, and considerate in emergencies requiring caution, and thoughtful and   (a)   in respect to the bearings and consequences of his acts. He formed strong attachments, was grateful for kindnesses shown to him, considerate in respect to the feelings of all who were connected with him in any way, faithful to his friends, and generous toward his foes. In a word, he had a noble character, though he devoted his energies unfortunately to conquest and war.   (b)   he lived in an age when great personal and mental powers had scarcely any other field for their exercise than this. He entered upon his career with great ardor, and the position in which he was placed gave him the opportunity to act in it with prodigious effect.

문제 1 What is the topic of the passage?
   (1) Two Sides of Alexander   (2) Alexander's Enthusiasm in War
   (3) Character of Alexander   (4) Conditions of Success

문제 2 Fill in blank (a).
   (1) far-seeing   (2) consolable
   (3) expedient   (4) opportune

문제 3 Choose one that best fills in blank (b).
   (1) In fact   (2) Therefore
   (3) On the other hand   (4) In the same vein

Day 20

★ You ask me why I do not write something....I think one's feelings waste themselves in words, they ought all to be distilled into actions and into actions which bring results.

Florence Nightingale (1820 - 1910)

나에게 왜 무엇인가를 쓰지 않고 있냐고 물으시나요. 나는 한 사람의 감정은 말 속에서 낭비될 뿐이라고 생각합니다. 이러한 감정은 결과를 낳는 행위로, 행위로 모두 흡수되어야 합니다. (Florence Nightingale)

[Challenge 1]

But necessary as is better public sentiment, we must also have practical machinery for enforcing the laws and for stopping the fires that do start. Just as a city is safeguarded best by an organized fire department, so the forest can be protected effectively only by trained men who know the work. And the man who prevents the most fires is the man who is looking for them, not the man who goes after the fire is under way. Theodore Roosevelt says: "I hold as first among the tasks before the states and the nation in their respective shares in forest conservation the organization of efficient fire patrols and the enactment of good fire laws on the part of the states." The National Conservation Commission reports: "Each state within whose boundaries forest fires are working grave injury, and that means every forest state, must face the fact squarely that to keep down forest fires needs not merely a law upon the statute books, but an effective force of men actually on the ground to patrol against fire." We all know that few disastrous fires start under conditions which prevent their control. Usually they spring from some of the many small, apparently innocent fires which burn unnoticed until wind and hot weather fan them into action. (a) <u>It is far cheaper to put them out in the incipient stage than to fight them later</u>, perhaps unsuccessfully until after great damage has been done. And if fighting is necessary, it is of the highest importance to have it led by competent, experienced men. Moments count, and bad judgment is expensive. Most western states already have laws regulating the use of fire for clearing during the dry season. To accomplish this with safety and without hardship requires fire wardens to issue permits and help with the burning if necessary.

문제 1 What is the passage mainly about?
  (1) Laws of Forest Conservation   (2) Danger of Forest Fires
  (3) Necessity of Patrol Service   (4) Financial Disasters of Forest Fires

문제 2 Which of the following can NOT be inferred from the passage?
  (1) Most of the forest fires start as minor but turn into grave if not controlled right away.
  (2) Theodore Roosevelt wanted to establish machinery for effective fire control only at the federal level.
  (3) When controlling the fires, to have competent, experienced men is of great importance.
  (4) The use of fire for clearing may lead to a forest fire if not accompanied by the permits of fire wardens.

문제 3 Which of the following best describes the situation of the underlined (a)?
  (1) Forewarned is forearmed.
  (2) Do to others as you would have done to yourself.
  (3) Teach an old dog new tricks.
  (4) Garbage in, garbage out

[Challenge 2]

The aphorism, "As a man thinketh in his heart so is he," not only embraces the whole of a man's being, but is so comprehensive as to reach out to every condition and circumstance of his life. A man is literally what he thinks, his character being the complete sum of all his thoughts. As the (a) plant springs from, and could not be without, the seed, so every act of a man springs from the (b) hidden seeds of thought, and could not have appeared without them. This applies equally to those acts called "spontaneous" and "unpremeditated" as to (c) those, which are deliberately executed. Act is the blossom of thought, and joy and suffering are its fruits; thus does a man garner in the sweet and bitter (d) fruitage of his own husbandry.

문제 1 Which of the following can NOT be inferred from the passage?
  (1) The epigram in the passage suggests the importance of thought.
  (2) The best way to judge a person is to look inside his mind.
  (3) The seeds of thought bloom into the form of action.
  (4) Spontaneous acts bear bad consequences.

문제 2 Which of the following does NOT refer to the same item?
  (1) (a)   (2) (b)
  (3) (c)   (4) (d)

[Challenge 3]

A final reason for the growing interest in Confucianism in particular is that an increasing number of Westerners, not only philosophers and academics, have themselves challenged key assumptions of Western morality in ways that might naturally suggest the possibility of Confucianism as a viable alternative. According to one kind of challenge, the centrality accorded to individual rights and autonomy in Western morality has resulted in a stunted understanding of responsibilities the individual has to others. The United States in particular is often presented as the preeminent case in point: the world's most affluent country and yet one of the most unequal, failing to provide basic necessities in health and education for all its members. According to another related challenge, Western morality provides ineffective grounding for duties to others because it cannot show the individual how the performance of these duties is related to achieving a specific conception of the good and worthwhile life. MacIntyre has been among the most influential critics in this regard. (a) At the same time, critics of Confucianism often flip this apparent strength into a moral failing: that it neglects individual rights and autonomy in favor of a life of relationship. (b) Moreover, the favored set of relationships is frequently criticized as patriarchal and oppressively hierarchical, reputedly stifling the self. (c) By contrast, one of the strengths of Confucianism is frequently thought to lie in the way it conceives a fully human life in terms of relationship to others, structured by a set of duties to them that realize the self rather than constrain it.

문제 1 Which of the following is NOT mentioned in the passage?
(1) Problems of the key assumptions of Western morality
(2) Confucianism as a viable alternative to Western morality
(3) Growing interest in Confucianism in Asian countries
(4) Moral failures of Confucianism

문제 2 Which of the following is neither stated nor implied?
(1) Western morality has been shaken to its foundations.
(2) Not only specialists but also ordinary people think confucianism is the only solution to the problems they are now facing.
(3) In the United States, not all people have access to health and education.
(4) MacIntyre has criticized the ineffectiveness of Western Morality to provide the grounding for duties to others.

문제 3 Which of the following is the best order?
(1) (a) - (b) - (c)   (2) (c) - (a) - (b)
(3) (b) - (a) - (c)   (4) (b) - (c) - (a)

문제 4 Which of the following is NOT suitable to the criticism of Confucianism?
(1) Usually males are the decision-makers and hold positions of power and prestige, and have the power to define reality and common situations.
(2) People are organized into ranks, and social mobility is highly restricted.
(3) A fully human life is considered in terms of relationship to others.
(4) Decisions of the elderly are considered more important than those of the young.

[Challenge 4]

Cognitive psychology is one of the more recent additions to psychological research, having only developed as a separate area within the discipline since the late 1950s and early 1960s following the "cognitive revolution" initiated by Noam Chomsky's 1959 critique of behaviorism and empiricism more generally. The origins of cognitive thinking such as computational theory of mind can be traced back as early as Descartes in the 17th century, and proceeding up to Alan Turing in the 1940s and '50s. The cognitive approach was brought to prominence by Donald Broadbent's book Perception and Communication in 1958. Since that time, the dominant paradigm in the area has been the information processing model of cognition that Broadbent put forward. This is a way of thinking and reasoning about mental processes, envisioning them as software running on the computer that is the brain. Theories refer to forms of input, representation, computation or processing, and outputs. Applied to language as the primary mental knowledge representation system, cognitive psychology has exploited tree and network mental models. Its singular contribution to AI and psychology in general is the notion of a semantic network. One of the first cognitive psychologists, George Miller is well-known for dedicating his career to the development of WordNet, a semantic network for the English language. Development began in 1985 and is now the foundation for many machine ontologies.

문제 1 Which of the following is the topic of the passage?
(1) Cognitive Psychologists in History
(2) Workings of Cognitive Thinking
(3) History of Cognitive Psychology
(4) Noam Chomsky and his Theories

문제 2 Based on the passage, which of the statements has something to do with cognitive psychology?
  (1) Knowledge that arises from evidence gathered via sense experience is the only reliable source that humans can resort to.
  (2) A theory should be based upon observable behaviors, so it is easier to quantify and collect data and information when conducting research.
  (3) Language is a set of habits that can be acquired by means of conditioning.
  (4) Unlike psychoanalysis, which relies heavily on subjective perceptions, cognitive psychology uses scientific research methods to study mental processes.

문제 3 Which of the following can be inferred from the WordNet George Miller developed?
  (1) The concept of WordNet is based on the fact that machines can also develop a humanlike ability to talk.
  (2) Cognitive psychologists must be a Native English speaker.
  (3) Cognitive psychologists and linguists may work together as a team.
  (4) Cognitive psychology has nothing to do with the brain.

[Challenge 5]

There's nothing stimulating about the current state of the global economy. Job creation is on the decline in the United States, and the European Union is in the third year of a worsening debt crisis. Growth is nowhere to be found on either side of the Atlantic.

With interest rates close to zero, there's nothing left in the monetary-policy bag of tricks. Printing up more money is not the answer. Keynesians like Larry Summers, the chief White House economist under President Clinton, recognize this and insist the solution is to borrow more money to stimulate the economy — as if the federal government has been practicing austerity for the past few years.

Mr. Summers argues private businesses haven't borrowed enough to invest and jump-start the economy. Thus, the government must do so because interest rates remain remarkably low. The nominal interest rate on 10-year bonds is a low 1.5 percent, and close to zero for shorter-maturity bonds.

We're borrowing so much already that the deficit this year is expected to be $1.2 trillion. That is more than the $831 billion spent under President Obama's American Recovery and Reinvestment Act (ARRA), the so-called stimulus. If the big spenders were right, that should have been plenty to get the economy moving, yet our annual growth rate is a paltry 1.9 percent and the rate of job creation has been falling.

Even if the government chose to increase borrowing simply because it's a bargain, there is little reason to believe that taking on more public debt would reinvigorate the economy. As Stanford economist John Taylor estimated, at the height of the Obama administration's stimulus spending binge, ARRA reached 0.21 percent of gross domestic product, and federal infrastructure spending was 0.05 percent of GDP, (a) only to come with a price.

Debt is 100 percent of U.S. GDP now and projected to explode to 180 percent by 2035, according to estimates by the Congressional Budget Office. That will exact a long-term cost on economic growth. Moreover, maintaining near-zero interest rates ____(b)____ savers, the retirees and others who depend on their holdings of Treasury bonds and government securities for their incomes.

There's nothing productive about the government sector. The solution to America's economic woes won't be found in what government can do, but what the private sector is allowed to do. It's time to return to the limited-government principles that allow entrepreneurs to succeed.

문제 1 Which of the following is TRUE of the passage?
(1) The government sector has not really done anything at all to help the staggering economy stand on its own feet.
(2) Deficit financing caused interest rates to rise.
(3) The nation has seen its economy growth without government pump priming.
(4) The easy money, borrow-and-spend policies haven't gotten the economy going.

문제 2 What can be inferred from the underlined (a)?
(1) Obama administration's stimulus package increased the hope of economic recovery.
(2) The prices are now on the downside.
(3) That spending spree didn't get the economy going.
(4) John Taylor does not think that the Obama administration is doing enough.

문제 3 Which of the following is most likely to be the one that the author would agree to perk up the economy?
(1) government-induced job creation
(2) increased money supply
(3) going back to small government
(4) increasing leading conglomerates' grip over the economy

문제 4 Fill in blank (b).
(1) encourages   (2) mollifies
(3) hurts   (4) placates

[Challenge 6]

Not all Social Darwinists were quite so extreme, and Social Darwinism was not the only justification of colonialism, imperialism, and other intrusive exploits (the "white man's burden" was another, almost completely opposite, justification). In fact, the early Social Darwinists, who regarded the theory as a logical extension of laissez-faire capitalism, would have been appalled at the use of the concept to promote state-run eugenics programs. Though its moral basis is now generally opposed, Social Darwinism did have some favorable effects. Belief in Social Darwinism tended to discourage wanton handouts to the poor, favoring instead providing resources for the fittest of all walks of life to use, or choosing specific, genuinely deserving people as recipients of help and support. Some major capitalists, such as Andrew Carnegie, combined philanthropy with Social Darwinism; he used his vast fortune to set up hundreds of libraries and other public institutions, including a university, for the benefit of those who would choose to avail themselves of such resources. He opposed direct and indiscriminate handouts to the poor because he felt that this favored the undeserving and the deserving person equally.

문제 1 Which of the following is the best title for the above passage?
  (1) Definition of Social Darwinism
  (2) Limitations of Social Darwinism
  (3) Who Benefits from Social Darwinism
  (4) Positive Results of Social Darwinism

문제 2 From what is stated or implied, which of the following is NOT correct?
  (1) Social darwinism was used to justify imperialism.
  (2) Social darwinism was promoted to justify the Anglo-Saxon expansion and domination of other peoples.
  (3) The early Social darwinists maintained that the state-run eugenics programs are based on scientific research.
  (4) Andrew Carnegie felt that helping the poor without reservation is not right.

[Challenge 7]

Error analysts distinguish between errors, which are systematic, and mistakes, which are not. They often seek to develop a typology of errors. (a) Error can be classified according to basic type: omissive, additive, substitutive or related to word order. (b) They can be classified by how apparent they are: overt errors such as "I angry" are obvious even out of context, whereas covert errors are evident only in context. (c) Errors may also be classified according to the level of language: phonological errors, vocabulary or lexical errors, syntactic errors, and so on. (d) They may be assessed according to the degree to which they interfere with communication: global errors make an utterance difficult to understand, while local errors do not. In the above example, "I angry" would be a local error, since the meaning is apparent.

문제 1 Which of the following is the topic of the passage?
 (1) Classification of Errors
 (2) Identifying Systematic Errors
 (3) Global and Local Errors
 (4) Difference between Errors and Mistakes

문제 2 Where would the following sentence best fit in?

> Closely related to this is the classification according to domain, the breadth of context which the analyst must examine, and extent, the breadth of the utterance which must be changed in order to fix the error.

 (1) (a) (2) (b)
 (3) (c) (4) (d)

문제 3 Choose one that is different from the error of the rest of the sentences?
 (1) A strange thing happen to me yesterday.
 (2) I love the London.
 (3) I stayed there during five years ago.
 (4) The books is here.

[Challenge 8]

The ultimate aim of Socialism is the nationalization of all land, industry, transportation, distribution and finance and their collective administration for the common good as a governmental function and under a popular government. It involves the abolition of private profit, rent and interest and especially excludes the possibility of private profit by increase of values resulting from increase or concentration of population. The majority of Socialists would reach this end gradually, by successive steps, and with compensation to existing owners. A violent minority would reach it per saltum, by bloodshed if necessary, and by confiscation — "expropriation" they call it. All alike conduct their propaganda by endeavoring to create or accentuate the class consciousness of manual workers who constitute the majority of human beings and whose condition, it is insisted, would be improved under a Socialistic regime. The violent wing promotes not merely class consciousness but class hatred.

문제 1 Which of the following is neither stated nor implied in the passage?
(1) The control over all the functions of society is an important part of Socialism.
(2) The legitimacy of the collective administration arises from the fact that manual workers are the majority of human beings.
(3) Two fractions of socialism are quite different in terms of their respective approaches to the ultimate goal.
(4) Class consciousness originates from the existing owners in power.

문제 2 Which of the following can NOT be the characteristics of Socialism?
(1) Abrogation of private property
(2) Class consciousness
(3) Control of population increase
(4) Hostility towards existing owners

[Challenge 9]

Others give prominence to the role of the intellect. God is the most reasonable explanation of the facts of life. Religious truths and men's minds harmonize as though they had been made for each other. The thought of Deity gives them perfect mental satisfaction. Dante tells us: "The life of my heart, that of my inward self, was wont to be a sweet thought which went many times to the feet of God, that is to say in thought I contemplated the kingdom of the Blessed." And a present-day English thinker, Mr. F. H. Bradley, writes: "All of us, I presume, more or less are led beyond the region of ordinary facts. Some in one way and some in another, we seem to touch and have communion with what is beyond the visible world. In various manners we find something higher which both supports and humbles, both chastens and transports us. And, with various persons, the intellectual effort to understand the universe is a principal way of their experiencing the Deity."

문제 1   Which of the following is the main idea of the passage?
(1) The best way to get to know the presence of God is through intellectual activity.
(2) Nothing on Earth can provide the comfort to human beings.
(3) God is a spiritual being so man can not have access to him whatsoever.
(4) Even the greatest writers in history are nothing but a humble being in the presence of God.

[Challenge 10]

It is often said that Judaism left belief free while it put conduct into fetters. Neither half of this assertion is strictly true. Belief was not free altogether; conduct was not altogether controlled. In the Mishnah certain classes of unbelievers are pronounced portionless in the world to come. (a) Among those excluded from Paradise are men who deny the resurrection of the dead, and men who refuse assent to the doctrine of the Divine origin of the Torah, or Scripture. (b) Thus it cannot be said that belief was, in the Rabbinic system, perfectly free. (c) Equally inaccurate is the assertion that conduct was entirely a matter of prescription. (d) Not only were men praised for works of supererogation, performance of more than the Law required; not only were there important divergences in the practical rules of conduct formulated by the various Rabbis; but there was a whole class of actions described as "matters given over to the heart," delicate refinements of conduct which the law left _____ and were a concern exclusively of the feeling, the private judgment of the individual.

문제 1   What is the purpose of this passage?
(1) To explain two different perspectives on Judaism
(2) To correct the misconception about an assertion by Judaism
(3) To analyze a certain phenomenon in Judaism
(4) To consolidate two different Rabbinic concepts

문제 2   If you devide the passage into two, where would it be?
(1) (a)   (2) (b)   (3) (c)   (4) (d)

문제 3   Fill in the blank to the passage.
(1) untouched   (2) unattended   (3) unnoticed   (4) uncharted

Day 21

★ Young men's minds are always changeable, but when an old man is concerned in a matter, he looks both before and after.

Homer (800 BC - 700 BC)

젊은이의 마음은 항상 변하기 쉽지만, 어떤 일에 있어 나이든 사람은 이전과 이후를 모두 살핀다. (Homer)

[Challenge 1]

For my own part I speak of the only field of success I know — the world of ordinary affairs. And I start with a contradiction in terms. Success is a constitutional temperament bestowed on the recipient by the gods. And yet you may have all the gifts of the fairies and fail utterly. Man cannot add an inch to his stature, but by taking thought he can walk erect; all the gifts given at birth can be destroyed by a single curse. Like all human affairs, success is partly a matter of predestination and partly of free will. You cannot make the genius, but you can either improve or destroy it, and most men and women possess the assets which can be turned into success. But those who possess the precious gifts will have both to hoard and to expand them.

문제 1 Which of the following best represents the main idea of the passage?
 (1) Freewill will eventually lead to success regardless of one's predetermined conditions.
 (2) The gifts that lead to success are twofold. That is, it is something you are born with at first and something you are to make good use of.
 (3) Those who are given all the possible gifts man can possess are more likely to fall the victims to them.
 (4) Under no circumstances should men succumb to any temptation that easy life can offer.

[Challenge 2]

There was once a little Scotch boy named James Watt. He was not a strong child, and could not always run and play with other boys, but had often to amuse himself at home. One holiday afternoon little James amused himself in this way. He held a saucer over the stream of steam which came from the spout of a boiling kettle, and as he watched he saw little drops of water forming on the saucer. He thought this was very strange, and wondered why it happened, for he did not know that steam is just water changed in form by the heat, and that as soon as it ____(a)____ it turns again into water. He asked his aunt to explain it, but she only told him not to waste his time. If she could have foreseen the work which her nephew would do when he became a man, she would not have thought he was wasting his time. When James Watt grew up, he was as much interested in steam and its wonderful power, as he had been as a boy. He was sure it could be made of great service to men. It was already used for driving engines, but the engines were not good, and it cost much money to work them. Watt thought they could be improved, but it was long before he found out the way to do this. Often, he sat by the fire watching the lid of the kettle as it was made to dance by the steam, and thinking of many plans; and at last a happy thought came to him. His plan enabled great improvements to be made in the working of engines, and now steam drives our trains and ships, our mills and factories, and is one of our most useful servants.

문제 1 Which of the following is the best title for the above passage?
　　　(1) Watt and the Kettle　　　(2) Curiosity and Its Characteristics
　　　(3) Biography of James Watt　　(4) The Workings of Steam Engines

문제 2 Which of the following is neither stated nor implied?
　　　(1) Watt's aunt was so near-sighted that she could not see his curiosity as the seed of inventions in the future.
　　　(2) Watt's physical weakness somehow helped him pay more attention to the surroundings around him than playing with kids outdoors.
　　　(3) Watt was the first to invent steam engines.
　　　(4) His inquisitive propensity stayed with him even when he was an adult.

문제 3 Fill in blank (a).
　　　(1) changes its form　　　　(2) touches something cold
　　　(3) condenses to something solid　(4) is absorbed in the air

[Challenge 3]

The earliest symptom is a dragging sensation in the back when the child is in the act of sucking, and an exhausted feeling of sinking and emptiness at the pit of the stomach afterwards. (a) This is soon followed by loss of appetite, costive bowels, and pain on the left side; then, the head will be more or less affected, sometimes with much throbbing, singing in the ears, and always some degree of giddiness, with great depression of spirits. (b) Soon the chest becomes affected, and the breathing is short, accompanied by a dry cough and palpitation of the heart upon the slightest exertion. (c) As the disease advances, the countenance becomes very pale, and the flesh wastes, and profuse night perspirations, great debility, swelling of the ankles, and nervousness ensue. (d) All that it will be useful to say in reference to treatment, is this; that, although much may be done in the first instance by medicine, change of air, cold and sea bathing, yet the quickest and most effectual remedy is to wean the child, and thus remove the cause.

문제 1 When the passage is divided in two, where does the second paragraph begin?
  (1) (a)   (2) (b)   (3) (c)   (4) (d)

문제 2 According to the passage, which is the best remedy to the problem at hand?
  (1) Take a walk for a change.   (2) Stop breast-feeding.
  (3) Take a sea bath.   (4) Take medicine.

[Challenge 4]

Plants have a very complex and diverse influence on the climate system. Plants take carbon dioxide out of the atmosphere, but they also have other effects, such as changing the amount of evaporation from the land surface. It's impossible to make good climate predictions without taking all of these factors into account. Plants give off water through tiny pores in their leaves, a process called evapotranspiration that cools the plant, just as perspiration cools our bodies. On a hot day, a tree can release tens of gallons of water into the air, acting as a natural air conditioner for its surroundings. The plants absorb carbon dioxide for photosynthesis through the same pores. But when carbon dioxide levels are high, the leaf pores shrink. This causes less water to be released, diminishing the tree's cooling power. The warming effects of carbon dioxide as a greenhouse gas have been known for a long time but it is not as widely recognized that carbon dioxide also warms our planet by its direct effects on plants.

문제 1 Which of the following is NOT correct about the passage?
(1) Tree's cooling power can be enhanced by making holes in the leaves of trees.
(2) An increase in carbon dioxide levels could affect the ability of trees to release water into the air.
(3) Trees release water into the air, therefore cooling the surroundings.
(4) If the leaf pores shrink, the rate of evapotranspiration will decrease.

[Challenge 5]

In Canada, the oil industry is transforming boreal forests and wetlands — one of the world's last remaining intact ecosystems — into America's gas tank. Alberta's boreal forest is home to a diverse range of animals, including lynx, caribou and grizzly bears, as well breeding grounds for many North American songbirds and waterfowl. Oil companies are scraping up hundreds of thousands of acres of this wildlife haven to mine tar sands — silty deposits that contain small amounts of crude bitumen. Mining and drilling tar sands, and turning bitumen into crude oil, uses vast amounts of energy and water, and causes significant air and water pollution, putting Canada's forests and wetlands at risk. For aboriginal peoples, mining in the region reduces local water supplies, and increases exposure to toxic substances. To top it off, the production of synthetic crude oil from tar sands causes three times the global warming pollution of conventional crude oil production. The rush to strip-mine and drill tar sands in the boreal will destroy and fragment millions of acres of this wild forest for low-grade petroleum fuel. At a time when we must embrace a clean energy future, _____(a)_____. The United States should instead implement a comprehensive oil savings plan and reduce oil consumption by increasing fuel efficiency standards, hybrid cars, renewable energy, environmentally sustainable biofuels, and smart growth to meet our transportation needs.

문제 1 Which of the following is the best title for the passage?
(1) Alberta's Boreal Forest in Great Danger
(2) Oil Savings Plan
(3) Endangered Animals in Canada
(4) Aboriginal Peoples Suffering from Global Warming

문제 2 Choose an expression that is most appropriate for blank (a).
(1) tar sands take us far into the wrong direction
(2) you have everything to gain and nothing to lose with tar sands.
(3) anything that uses petroleum fuel needs to be eradicated.
(4) a comprehensive study of boreal forests and wetlands is where the most attention needs to be paid.

[Challenge 6]

Only recently have attempts to actually measure creative aptitude in music begun. Much of this work has focused on young children, ages six to ten, and has sought to identify divergent and convergent thinking skills in music using musical tasks in game-like contexts. For example, a measure I developed uses an amplified voice, a round sponge ball with a piano, and a set of temple blocks to engage children in musical imagery. The tasks begin very simply and progress to higher levels of difficulty in terms of divergent thinking. _____(a)_____.

The first section of this evaluation procedure is designed to help the children become familiar with the instruments used and how they are arranged. The children explore the parameters of "high/low", "fast/slow", and "loud/soft" in this section and throughout the measure. The way they manipulate these parameters is, in turn, used as one of the bases for scoring. They are given tasks that involve images of rain in a water bucket, magical elevators, and the sounds of trucks.

The middle section asks the children to engage in more challenging activities with the instruments and to focus on the creation of music using each of the instruments singly. Children enter into a kind of musical question/answer dialogue with the mallet and temple blocks, and they create songs with the round ball on the piano and with the voice and the microphone. They use images that include the concept of (b) "frog" music and that of a robot singing in the shower (realized with the child's voice through the microphone).

In the last section of the procedure, the children are encouraged to use multiple instruments in tasks whose settings are less structured. They tell a space story in sounds, using drawings as a visual aid. The final task asks the children to create a composition that uses all the instruments and that has a beginning, a middle, and an end.

This measure, and others like it, yields scores for such factors as musical originality, extensiveness, and flexibility, as well as musical syntax. Measurement strategies are based on the careful analysis of video or audio tapes of children actually engaged in the activities. Objective criteria as well as rating scales are used: musical extensiveness, for example, is measured by the time involved in the creative tasks, while evaluators rate originality by observing the manner in which pitch, tempo, and dynamics are manipulated.

문제 1   Which of the following is the passage mainly talking about?
　　(1) Obstacles to Creative Musical Imagination
　　(2) Measures of Creative Aptitude in Music
　　(3) A Step-by-step Approach to Musical Composition
　　(4) Conventional Ways to Teach Musical Imagination
　　(5) Types of Musical Instruments and Ways to Master Them

문제 2 Fill in blank (a).
(1) There is no limited time for the tasks
(2) There are no right or wrong answers to the tasks
(3) There is one and only one answer to each task
(4) There is no helper around the children
(5) There are always two answers to the tasks

문제 3 Which of the following best describes the underlined (b)?
(1) It is accomplished by hopping and rolling the ball on the piano.
(2) It is accomplished by making frogs jump on the piano.
(3) It is accomplished by having the children play with frogs.
(4) It is accomplished by letting frogs play with the ball on the piano.
(5) It is accomplished by making a song with the theme of frogs.

[Challenge 7]

We have certain qualities in common with inanimate matter, such as weight, opacity, resilience. It is clear that these are not human. We have other qualities in common with all forms of life; cellular construction, for instance, the reproduction of cells and the need of nutrition. These again are not human. We have others, many others, common to the higher mammals; which are not exclusively ours — are not distinctively "human." What then are true human characteristics? In what way is the human species distinguished from all other species?

(a) That degree of development which gives us the human mind is a clear distinction of race. The savage who can count a hundred is more human than the savage who can count ten.

(b) Human life of any sort is dependent upon what Kropotkin calls "mutual aid," and human progress keeps step absolutely with that interchange of specialized services which makes society organic. The nomad, living on cattle as ants live on theirs, is less human than the farmer, raising food by intelligently applied labor; and the extension of trade and commerce, from mere village market-places to the world-exchanges of to-day, is extension of human-ness as well.

(c) More prominent than either of these is the social nature of humanity. We are by no means the only group-animal; the ant, and even the well-worn bee, are social creatures. But insects of their kind are found living alone. Human beings never. Our human-ness begins with some low form of social relation and increases as that relation develops.

(d) Our human-ness is seen most clearly in three main lines: it is mechanical, psychical and social. Our power to make and use things is essentially human; we alone have extra-physical tools. We have added to our teeth the knife, sword, scissors, mowing machine; to our claws the spade, harrow, plough, drill, dredge. We are a protean creature, using the larger brain power through a wide variety of changing weapons. This is one of our main and vital distinctions. Ancient animal races are traced and known by mere bones and shells, ancient human races by their buildings, tools and utensils.

문제 1 Which of the following is the best title for the passage?
(1) Development of Human Tools
(2) True Human-ness
(3) Difference between Humans and Great Apes
(4) Sociality of Human Beings

문제 2 Choose one that is in the right sequence.
(1) (a) - (b) - (c) - (d)   (2) (d) - (a) - (c) - (b)
(3) (b) - (d) - (a) - (c)   (4) (c) - (b) - (a) - (d)

[Challenge 8]

In the breeding of animals closest inbreeding is frequently resorted to in order to improve the stock, and many examples can be given of the closest possible inbreeding for generations without apparent detriment, but it is universally admitted that the animals selected for such inbreeding must be sound constitutionally, and free from disease. After a certain number of generations however, degeneration apparently sets in. The number of generations through which inbreeding may be carried varies with the species, and the purpose for which the animals are bred. (a) Where they are bred primarily for their flesh, as for beef, mutton or pork, it can be pursued farther and closer than where they are bred for achievement in which a special strength is required — for instance in the breeding of race horses.

In man, however, freedom from hereditary taint cannot so easily be secured. Individuals cannot be selected scientifically for breeding purposes. Furthermore, the human body is more delicately constructed than that of the lower animals, and the nervous system is more highly developed and specialized, so that it is reasonable to suppose that in man degeneration would ____(b)____ in the process of inbreeding, and that it would be impossible to breed as closely as with the lower animals. Instances are well known, however, where incestuous unions have been productive of healthy offspring, and successive generations of offspring of incestuous connection are not unknown; but, although statistics are lacking, it seems to be very often true that children of such unions are degenerate.

문제 1 Which of the following is NOT mentioned in the first paragraph?
(1) The Effects of Close Inbreeding in Animals
(2) The Purpose of Close Inbreeding in Animals
(3) The Conditions of Close Inbreeding in Animals
(4) The Types of Close Inbreeding in Animals

문제 2 According to the passage, which of the following is most likely to be inferred from the underlined (a)?
(1) Horses are naturally born to be 'fit' for the race so they don't have to be crossbred.
(2) The more delicate brain and nervous system is sooner affected than the lower bodily functions.
(3) Degeneration in close inbreeding of the horse takes place a few generations later than as in cows.
(4) There is practically no detrimental effect to the close inbreeding of the lower animals.

문제 3 Which of the following is most appropriate for blank (b)?
(1) come to a steady stop   (2) set in earlier
(3) disappear faster   (4) occur more systematically

[Challenge 9]

Austrian School principles advocate strict adherence to methodological individualism — analyzing human action exclusively from the perspective of an individual agent. Austrian economists also argue that mathematical models and statistics are an unreliable means of analyzing and testing economic theory, and advocate deriving economic theory logically from basic principles of human action, a method called praxeology. Additionally, whereas experimental research and natural experiments are often used in mainstream economics, Austrian economists contend that testability in economics is virtually impossible since (a) it relies on human actors who cannot be placed in a lab setting without altering their would-be actions. Mainstream economists are generally critical of methodologies used by modern Austrian economists; in particular, a primary Austrian School method of deriving theories has been criticized by mainstream economists as a priori "non-empirical" analysis and differing from the practices of scientific theorizing, as widely conducted in economics.

Austrian School economists generally hold that the complexity of human behavior makes (가) mathematical modeling of an evolving market extremely difficult (or undecidable) and advocate a (나) laissez faire approach to the economy. They advocate the strict enforcement of voluntary contractual agreements between economic agents, and hold that commercial transactions should be subject to the smallest possible imposition of (다) coercive forces. In particular, they argue for an extremely limited role for (라) government and the smallest possible amount of government intervention in the economy.

문제 1 Which of the following can be inferred from the underlined (a)?
  (1) Limitations of Austrian School principles
  (2) Uncertainty of human action
  (3) Accumulative nature of human action
  (4) Needs of scientific theorizing

문제 2 Given the context, which of the following does NOT belong to the same category?
  (1) (가)   (2) (나)
  (3) (다)   (4) (라)

[Challenge 10]

 Walking is another example of the rapid exercise of volition with but little perception of each individual act of exercise. We notice any obstacle in our path, but it is plain we do not notice that we perceive much that we have nevertheless been perceiving; for if a man goes down a lane by night he will stumble over many things which he would have avoided by day, although he would not have noticed them. Yet time was when walking was to each one of us a new and arduous task — as arduous as we should now find it to wheel a wheelbarrow on a tight-rope; whereas, at present, though we can think of our steps to a certain extent without checking our power to walk, we certainly cannot consider our muscular action in detail without having to come to a dead stop.

문제 1 Which of the following is neither stated nor implied from the passage?
  (1) Walking is a type of habit which takes place to a certain extent under unconsciousness.
  (2) The action of human beings is affected by visual limitations.
  (3) Human beings are born with the ability to walk with no conscious exercise.
  (4) When somebody in a certain motion needs to stop doing it, he needs to think about that motion whether it is a conscious or unconscious one.

★ Don't be too timid and squeamish about your actions. All life is an experiment. The more experiments you make the better.

Ralph Waldo Emerson (1803 - 1882)

자신의 행위에 너무 소심하고, 까다롭게 굴지마라. 인생은 실험이다. 더 많은 실험을 할수록 더 나은 너를 발견한다.
(Ralph Waldo Emerson)

[Challenge 1]

A good criterion of the purity of water fit for domestic purposes, is (a) <u>its</u> softness. This quality is at once obvious by the touch, if we only wash our hands in it with soap. Good water should be beautifully transparent; a slight opacity indicates extraneous matter. To judge of the perfect transparency of water, a quantity of (b) <u>it</u> should be put into a deep glass vessel, the larger the better, so that we can look down perpendicularly into a considerable mass of the fluid; we may then readily discover the slightest degree of muddiness much better than if the water be viewed through the glass placed between the eye and the light. (c) <u>It</u> should be perfectly colourless, devoid of odour, and its taste soft and agreeable. It should send out air-bubbles when poured from one vessel into another; it should boil pulse soft, and form with soap an uniform opaline fluid, which does not separate after standing for several hours. (d) <u>It</u> is to the presence of common air and carbonic acid gas that common water owes its taste, and many of the good effects which it produces on animals and vegetables.

문제 1   Which of the following is the topic of the passage?
 (1) Water in Black and White   (2) Different kinds of Good Water
 (3) Characters of Good Water   (4) Ways to Make Good Water

문제 2   Which of the following does NOT refer to the same item?
 (1) (a)   (2) (b)
 (3) (c)   (4) (d)

[Challenge 2]

　　Deflation, a sustained decline in prices across the economy, remains merely a threat, with overall prices still rising mildly. For some of the nation's largest industries, though, falling prices are a reality. "More goods are chasing less money," said a research director, "instead of more money chasing fewer goods." U.S. officials say deflation remains unlikely but, because it is so hard to stop once it starts, they are considering taking preventive measures. The lack of pricing power has been forcing executives to cut costs even as they increase production, and it has led to job cuts in the current economic recovery. Almost two hundred thousand jobs were eliminated across the country in November and December. The biggest culprit is the 1990's bubble that left many industries with more goods than they could profitably sell and more capacity than they could use. But the surge of imports from low-cost countries like China, the rise in American productivity, and the continuing trend toward deregulation and market-determined prices are all playing roles. Faced with stagnant revenue, many companies are aggravating their industries' troubles by further reducing prices to (가) grab pieces of a shrinking pie. Today's wave of price cutting - stemming mainly from economic weakness - continues to bring benefits for consumers, but there is little that is virtuous about it for companies caught in its vise.

문제 1　Which of the following is closest in meaning to (가)?
　　(1) hold on to their business interests in the confectionary industry
　　(2) secure income from an increasingly worsening market
　　(3) market their products quickly at increasingly low prices
　　(4) gain advantage in profitable chain-restaurant businesses

문제 2　Which of the following is NOT among the major causes of the recent increase in unemployment?
　　(1) Government officials implemented measures for fear of the detrimental effects of deflation
　　(2) Some of the largest industries had production capacity beyond what they could make use of.
　　(3) The 1990's bubble left many industries with more products than they could sell at a profit.
　　(4) Market-determined prices are affected by products from low-cost countries that have advantages in pricing over U.S. goods.

문제 3　Which of the following is NOT true of the passage?
　　(1) The prices in general are still rising, if not sharply.
　　(2) Reducing regulations and interference in the market is a current trend.
　　(3) Despite the current economy recovery, many people have become unemployed.
　　(4) Price-cutting is beneficial to consumers as well as to industries with surplus stock.

[Challenge 3]

Several features are found in all creation myths. They are all stories with a plot and characters who are either deities, human-like figures or animals who often speak and transform easily. They are set in a dim and nonspecific past. And all creation myths speak to deeply meaningful questions held by the society that shares them, revealing their central world-view and the framework for the self-identity of the culture and individual in a universal context. Common motifs include the fractionation of the things of the world from a primordial chaos; the separation of the mother and father gods; and land emerging from an infinite and timeless ocean.

문제 1 Which of the following is the topic of the passage?
   (1) Contents of Creation Myths
   (2) Common Attributes of Creation Myths
   (3) Reasons for Creating Creation Myths
   (4) Human Desire for Creation Myths

문제 2 Which of the following can NOT be inferred from the passage?
   (1) People want to get some important answers through creation myths.
   (2) Creation myths from different countries have had mutual influences on each other.
   (3) Creation myths have a form of story in them.
   (4) A world in a creation myth goes from a state of disorder into order.

[Challenge 4]

Poe was born in poverty at Boston, January 19, 1809, dying under painful circumstances at Baltimore, October 7, 1849. His whole literary career of scarcely fifteen years a pitiful struggle for mere subsistence was malignantly misrepresented by his earliest biographer, Griswold. For "The Raven," first published in 1845, and, within a few months, read, recited and parodied wherever the English language was spoken, the half-starved poet received $10! Less than a year later his brother poet, N. P. Willis, issued this touching appeal to the admirers of genius on behalf of the neglected author, his dying wife and her devoted mother, then living under very straitened circumstances in a little cottage at Fordham, N. Y. : "Here is one of the finest scholars, one of the most original men of genius, and one of the most industrious of the literary profession of our country, whose temporary suspension of labor, from bodily illness, drops him immediately to a level with the common objects of public charity. There is no intermediate stopping-place, no respectful shelter, where, with the delicacy due to genius and culture, he might secure aid, till, with returning health, he would resume his labors, and his unmortified sense of independence."

문제 1 Which of the following is neither stated nor implied in the passage?
　　　(1) Poe was interspersed with struggles for mere sustenance throughout his entire life.
　　　(2) Griswold's interpretation about Poe inadequately portrays the reality that Poe was put in.
　　　(3) N. P. Willis was willing to help Poe financially but he refused it.
　　　(4) Ironically, the reputation Poe earned after the publication of "The Raven" did not really help him improve the bad situation.

문제 2 Which of the following is NOT true of N. P. Willis?
　　　(1) He felt sorry for Poe.
　　　(2) He knew about Poe's situation fairly well.
　　　(3) He thought highly of Poe's literary talent.
　　　(4) He was worried that the bad health might take away Poe's literary talent.

[Challenge 5]

　　The damage to art is irreparable. As a result of death in the church, written language was almost lost and whole churches were abandoned. Carving was changed. Coffins had pictures of corpses on the lid. Some of these dated around 1400 showed bodies with about half of their flesh and shredded garments. A few of the sculptures showed worms and snails munching on the diseased. Painting was effected by the black death too. There are a number of paintings containing people socializing with skeletons. These paintings were made on a powerful person's command, and called "danse macabre". Artists abandoned old ways of painting things idolized by the Christian religion. They were so depressed by the death that surrounded them that they began to paint pictures of sad and dead people.

문제 1 Which of the following is the best title for the passage?
　　　(1) The Origin of Danse Macabre
　　　(2) Different Views on Funeral Sculptures
　　　(3) Forms of Art at the Time of the Black Death
　　　(4) Effects of the Black Death on Art

Day 22

[Challenge 6]

Diplomacy depends on truth, trust, information and good communication. All of these elements were ignored by the Germans and Austrians once they had decided they were going to war. German diplomatic staff were not truthful about their knowledge of the content of the Austrian diplomatic note threatening Serbia, and they did all they could to throw up a smoke screen as to the real activities and intentions for war. Serbians, for their part, were assured of Russia's help and were not truthful about their knowledge of certain activities that occurred on their own side. Deliberately poor communication by all involved was at the crux of the problem. Ultimatums were issued as late as possible in order to minimize time for considering responses. Diplomatic moves by the Allied powers to prevent the expansion of a local Balkan war were dismissed. The Allied powers made their own mistakes. They had no idea that Germany had an aggressive action plan for war on two fronts and that it was prepared to carry it out. The Germans expressed amazement when the British supported France and Belgium, and claimed to have totally misread the earlier British diplomatic signals that this would be the obvious British response — though Britain could certainly have made it clearer that a breach of Belgian neutrality would be punished. _____(a)_____ to the problem was the fact that German generals were dismissive of the threat from the British army because of its small size in comparison to the million men — plus steamroller that was their own army. _____(b)_____, despite the blood ties of the royal families of Britain, Russia and Germany, the diplomatic efforts of the British and Russian monarchs did not prevent conflict. Mistakes, blunders, poor communication, lies, distrust, tensions, the desire for recognition, revenge: are these not all part of the human condition? These forces affect nations, neighborhoods, families and individuals, and it is within the human heart that they begin. _____(c)_____, and ultimately war on any scale is the result.

問題 1 Which of the following is the main cause of the war in the passage?

(1) Unforgiveness

(2) Aggressiveness of Human Nature

(3) Bad Communication

(4) Bottomless Desire for Wealth

問題 2 Fill in blanks (a) and (b).

(1) Contributing - Ironically

(2) Oblivious - Paradoxically

(3) Prior - correspondingly

(4) Impervious - congruously

205

문제 3 Choose one that is most appropriate for blank (c).

(1) Let human beings be in shackles
(2) Let them all be under human control
(3) Learn to fight against them
(4) Leave them unchecked

[Challenge 7]

Treviranus (1776-1837), whom Huxley ranked beside Lamarck, was on the whole Buffonian, attaching chief importance to the influence of a changeful environment both in modifying and in eliminating, but he was also Goethian, for instance in his idea that species like individuals pass through periods of growth, full bloom, and decline. "Thus, it is not only the great catastrophes of Nature which have caused extinction, but the completion of cycles of existence, out of which new cycles have begun." A characteristic sentence is quoted by Prof. Osborn: "In every living being there exists a capability of an endless variety of form-assumption; each possesses the power to adapt its organization to the changes of the outer world, and it is this power, put into action by the change of the universe, that has raised the simple zoophytes of the primitive world to continually higher stages of organization, and has introduced a countless variety of species into animate Nature."

문제 1 Which of the following is NOT true of the passage?
(1) Treviranus assumed that changes in the environment are of great importance in the modifications of species.
(2) Huxley thought highly of Treviranus.
(3) The cycle of existence that Treviranus maintained not only causes extinction of a species but also leads to a new cycle.
(4) Buffon and Huxley shared many of the same evolutionary ideas.

문제 2 According to the passage, the basic mechanism that raises simple creatures to more complex ones is a(an) _____ to the changes of the outer world.
(1) adaptability
(2) flexibility
(3) susceptivity
(4) vulnerability

[Challenge 8]

That the Divine, that is, God, is not in space, although omnipresent and with every man in the world, and with every angel in heaven, and with every spirit under heaven, cannot be comprehended by a merely natural idea, but it can by a spiritual idea. It cannot be comprehended by a natural idea, because in the natural idea there is space; since it is formed out of such things as are in the world, and in each and all of these, as seen by the eye, there is space. In the world, everything great and small is of space; everything long, broad, and high is of space; in short, every measure, figure and form is of space. This is why it has been said that it cannot be comprehended by a merely natural idea that the Divine is not in space, when it is said that the Divine is everywhere. Still, by natural thought, a man may comprehend this, if only he admit into it something of _____(a)_____. For this reason something shall first be said about spiritual idea, and thought therefrom. Spiritual idea derives nothing from space, but it derives its all from state. State is predicated of love, of life, of wisdom, of affections, of joys therefrom; in general, of good and of truth. An idea of these things which is truly spiritual has nothing in common with space; it is higher and looks down upon the ideas of space which are under it as heaven looks down upon the earth.

문제 1 According to the passage, which of the following is NOT the characteristic of God?
(1) Widespread (2) Spatial
(3) Celestial (4) Immateiral

문제 2 Fill in blank (a).
(1) spiritual light (2) natural dimension
(3) worldly matter (4) intuitive nature

[Challenge 9]

Among the earliest and most important attempts made to solve the problem of plant-growth was that by Jean Baptiste Van Helmont, one of the best known of the alchemists, who flourished about the beginning of the seventeenth century. Van Helmont believed that he had proved by a conclusive experiment that all the products of vegetables were capable of being generated from water. The details of this classical experiment were as follows: "He took a given weight of dry soil — 200 lb. — and into this soil he planted a willow-tree that weighed 5 lb., and he watered this carefully from time to time with pure rain-water, taking care to prevent any dust or dirt falling on to the earth in which the plant grew. He allowed this to go on growing for five years, and at the end of that period, thinking his experiment had been conducted sufficiently long, he pulled up his tree by the roots, shook all the earth off, ___(a)___ the earth again, weighed the earth and weighed the plant. He found that the plant now weighed 169 lb. 3 ounces, whereas the weight of the soil remained very nearly what it was — about 200 lb. It had only lost 2 ounces in weight." The conclusion, therefore, come to by Van Helmont was that the source of plant-food was . ___(b)___

문제 1 Which of the following is the best title for the passage?
  (1) The Secret of Willow-Tree
  (2) Alchemists and Plant Growth
  (3) The Effects of Weight on Plant Growth
  (4) Van Helmont's Theory

문제 2 Fill in blank (a).
  (1) dried   (2) watered
  (3) prevented   (4) absorbed

문제 3 Fill in blank (b).
  (1) the weight of soil   (2) earth
  (3) water   (4) rain

[Challenge 10]

This war has justified both the Old Pacifism and the New. By universal admission events have proved that the Pacifists who opposed the Crimean War were right and their opponents wrong. Had public opinion given more consideration to those Pacifist principles, (a) <u>this country</u> would not have (b) "<u>backed the wrong horse,</u>" and this war, two wars which have preceded it, and many of the abominations of which the Balkan peninsular has been the scene during the last 60 years might have been avoided, and in any case Great Britain would not now carry upon her shoulders the responsibility of having during half a century supported the Turk against the Christian and of having tried uselessly to prevent what has now taken place — the break-up of the Turk's rule in Europe.

The fundamental causes of this war are economic in the narrower, as well as in the larger sense of the term; in the first because conquest was the Turk's only trade — he desired to live out of taxes wrung from a conquered people, to exploit them as a means of livelihood, and this conception was at the bottom of most of Turkish misgovernment. And in the larger sense its cause is economic because in the Balkans, remote geographically from the main drift of European economic development, there has not grown up that interdependent social life, the innumerable contacts which in the rest of Europe have done so much to attenuate primitive religious and racial hatreds.

문제 1   What does the underlined (a) refer to?
   (1) Turk   (2) Great Britain   (3) the Balkans   (4) None of above

문제 2   According to the passage, what can be inferred from the underlined (b)?
   (1) "This country" was discreet enough to choose the right country to work with.
   (2) "This country" did not back up Turk with horses suitable for war.
   (3) "This country" supported the Turk's conquest but it turned out to be wrong.
   (4) "This country" saved the tide and conquered the Balkans.

문제 3   What is the topic of the second paragraph?
   (1) Causes of the Crimean War
   (2) Tax Policy in a Conquered State
   (3) Reasons for European Economic Development
   (4) Europe as a Kingpin Town

문제 4   Which of the following can NOT be inferred from the second paragraph?
   (1) The cause of the war was mostly economic.
   (2) The Balkans were geographically inferior.
   (3) Turk performed an appeasement policy in its conquered states.
   (4) Europe was a multi-racial continent.

Day 23

★ The superior man is modest in his speech, but exceeds in his actions.

Confucius (551 BC - 479 BC)

군자는 언행에 조심스럽고, 행위에 담대하다. (Confucius)

[Challenge 1]

Not all parents are comfortable with the idea of using medications to treat a baby's pain and suffering. Medicines are often applied to the baby's gums to relieve swelling and pain. These gels are similar to the toothache gel that is used by adults for sore gums and toothaches, but is administered in much smaller doses. Teething gels work as a _____(a)_____ to dull the nerves in the gums so that the pain is less noticeable. It is important to follow the directions on the package to ensure that the correct amount of medication is administered and that proper techniques are used to reduce the risk for infection. It is important not to let the medicine numb the throat as it may interfere with the normal gag reflex and may make it possible for food to enter the lungs.

Acetaminophen and ibuprofen are also recommended to treat the pain and swelling that babies experience, but should not be administered to babies under six months of age. It should only be used a few times a day so that it does not _____(b)_____ symptoms that are being experienced due to other medical conditions and not because of teething. Products that contain aspirin should not be given to a child unless directed by a pediatrician. A teething ring is generally a soft plastic device that can be chewed on and allows the baby to break down some of the gum tissue which promotes the growth of the teeth out of the gum. Some teething rings can easily be broken or damaged, so other types of teething devices can be made from household items. Placing a wet washcloth in the freezer for a few minutes and then applying it gently to the gums can be effective, but care must be taken not to expose a baby's gums to coldness for too long.

문제 1 Which of the following is the best title for the passage?
  (1) Determining When to Apply Medications
  (2) Treatment of Teething
  (3) Types of Teething Rings
  (4) Effectiveness of Teething Rings

문제 2 Fill in blank (a).
  (1) numbing agent   (2) dissolvent
  (3) catalytic agent   (4) defending mechanism

문제 3 Which of the following is TRUE of the passage?
  (1) If you want to apply any products that contain aspirin, you'd better consult a pediatrician.
  (2) Acetaminophen and ibuprofen can only be applied to babies every other day.
  (3) A teething ring can be too hard on the gums so a cold wet washcloth is recommended more often.
  (4) Teething gels are usually infectious.

문제 4 Fill in blank (b).
  (1) develop   (2) mask
  (3) exhibit   (4) show off

[Challenge 2]

Integrity is the mother of knowledge. (a) The desire for truth is the basis of all learning, the value of all experience and the reason for all study and investigation. (b) Without integrity as a basis, our entire educational system would fall to the ground; all newspapers and magazines would become sources of great danger. (c) Our whole civilization rests upon the assumption that people are honest. With this confidence shaken, the structure falls. And it should fall, for, unless the truth be taught, the nation would be much better off without its schools, newspapers, books and professions. (d) Better have no gun at all, than one aimed at yourself. The cornerstone of prosperity is the stone of Integrity.

문제 1 Where does this sentence below best fit in?

| And the publication of books would have to be suppressed. |

  (1) (a)   (2) (b)
  (3) (c)   (4) (d)

[Challenge 3]

The first thing to be aimed at by the young, should be the establishment of a good character: In all their plans, anticipations, and prospects for future years, this should form the grand starting-point! — the chief corner-stone! It should be the foundation of every hope and thought of prosperity and happiness in days to come. It is the only basis on which such a hope can mature to full fruition. A good character, established in the season of youth, becomes a rich and productive moral soil to its possessor. Planted therein, the "Tree of Life" will spring forth in a vigorous growth. Its roots will strike deep and strong, in such a soil, and draw thence the utmost vigor and fruitfulness. Its trunk will grow up in majestic proportions — its wide-spreading branches will be clothed with (a) <u>a green luxuriant foliage</u>, "goodly to look upon" — the most beautiful of blossoms will in due time, blush on every twig — and at length each limb and bough shall bend beneath the rich, golden fruit, ready to drop into the hand. Beneath its grateful shade you can find (b) <u>rest and repose</u>, when the heat and burden of life come upon you. And of its delicious fruit, you can pluck and eat, and obtain (c) <u>refreshment and strength</u>, when the soul becomes wearied with labor and care, or (d) <u>the weight of years</u>. Would you behold such a tree? Remember it grows alone on ___(가)___ ! Labor to prepare such a soil.

문제 1 Which of the following is the passage talking about?
(1) The Formation of Character
(2) Conditions of Trees for the Upmost Fruitfulness
(3) Ways to Lift Up the Burdens of Life
(4) Physical Conditions for Good Character

문제 2 Which of the following does NOT fall under the same category?
(1) (a)   (2) (b)
(3) (c)   (4) (d)

문제 3 Choose one that best fills in blank (가).
(1) sufficient nutrition
(2) the soil of a good reputation
(3) the optimal combination of labor and care
(4) the intrinsic tolerance to its environments

문제 4 The tone of the passage is _____.
(1) prophetic   (2) admonitory
(3) expositive   (4) analytical

[Challenge 4]

Object permanence refers to the ability of the brain to retain and utilize visual images. It develops at about eight months of age. This faculty is distinct from a baby's recognition memory. For example, a baby is able to recognize and prefers to look at its mother by the third day of life. However, it will not cry upon being left by mother; "_____(a)_____." At around eight months, the child will exhibit signs of separation anxiety when mother leaves the room. This is because the child can now appreciate what he has just lost — the presence of his mother. Another sign of the attainment of object permanence is baby's delight at the game of "peek-a-boo," which demonstrates graphically that the child appreciates that just because Mother is out of direct view she is still in the world and can be recalled by moving the hands or blanket out of the way.

문제 1 Which of the following is the topic of the passage?
(1) Object Permanence
(2) The Workings of Object Permanence
(3) Types of Object Permanence
(4) Recognition Memory and Object Permanence

문제 2 Which of the following is most appropriate for blank (a)?
(1) Out of sight, out of mind
(2) Nothing ventured, nothing gained
(3) No use crying over spilt milk
(4) A bird in the hand is worth two in the bush.

문제 3 According to the passage, which of the following is CORRECT?
(1) Babies go through two different kinds of object permanence.
(2) The time of occurrence of object permanence varies depending on the child.
(3) Object permanence and separation anxiety take place around the same time.
(4) Babies' ability to retain information dramatically increases during the first year.

[Challenge 5]

While the time of man's first knowledge and use of the expansive force of the vapor of water is unknown, records show that such knowledge existed earlier than 150 B.C. In a treatise of about that time entitled "Pneumatica," Hero, of Alexander, described not only existing devices of his predecessors and contemporaries but also an invention of his own which utilized the expansive force of steam for raising water above its natural level. He clearly describes three methods in which steam might be used directly as a motive of power; raising water by its elasticity, elevating a weight by its expansive power and producing a rotary motion by its reaction on the atmosphere.

문제 1 Which of the following is the topic of the passage?
(1) Records of the Use of Steam
(2) Three Methods to Produce Steam
(3) The Workings of the Steam Engine
(4) Characteristics of the Vapor of Water

문제 2 Which of the following is NOT true of the passage?
(1) The knowledge of the expansive force of the steam existed earlier than 150 B.C.
(2) Pneumatica contains information about the expansive force of steam.
(3) Hero was the only person who used the expansive force of steam at the time.
(4) Hero knew how to use steam as a motive of power.

[Challenge 6]

Society exists through a process of transmission quite as much as biological life. This transmission occurs by means of communication of habits of doing, thinking, and feeling from the older to the younger. Without this communication of ideals, hopes, expectations, standards, opinions, from those members of society who are passing out of the group life to those who are coming into it, social life could not survive. If the members who compose a society lived on continuously, they might educate the new-born members, but it would be a task directed by personal interest rather than social need.

If a plague carried off the members of a society all at once, it is obvious that the group would be permanently done for. Yet the death of each of its constituent members is as certain as if an epidemic took them all at once. But (a) the graded difference in age makes possible through transmission of ideas and practices the constant reweaving of the social fabric. Yet this renewal is not automatic. Unless pains are taken to see that genuine and thorough transmission takes place, the most civilized group will relapse into barbarism and then into savagery. In fact, the human young are so immature that if they were left to themselves without the guidance and succor of others, they could not acquire the rudimentary abilities necessary for physical existence. The young of human beings compare so poorly in original efficiency with the young of many of the lower animals, that even the powers needed for physical sustentation have to be acquired under tuition. How much more, then, is this the case with respect to all the technological, artistic, scientific, and moral achievements of humanity!

문제 1 Which of the following is the topic of the passage?
(1) Effects of Natural Disaster on Human Society
(2) Nature of Animal Transmission
(3) Continuity of Society through Transmission
(4) Human Intervention in Nature

문제 2 Which of the following is CORRECT about the passage?
(1) Unlike society, human beings exist without a process of transmission.
(2) Transmission of human knowledge takes place just like natural selection.
(3) In general, the young of the lower animals are superior to those of human beings in physical sustentation.
(4) Transmission of human knowledge from one group to another occurs with no conscious effort of the former.

문제 3 Which of the following refers to the underlined (a)?
(1) Some enjoy longevity.
(2) Some age faster than others.
(3) Some are born as some die.
(4) People age as they get older.

[Challenge 7]

Galileo Galilee was born in 1564 into a Europe wracked by cultural ferment and religious strife. The popes of the Roman Catholic Church, powerful in their roles as both religious and secular leaders, had proven vulnerable to the worldly and decadent spirit of the age, and their personal immorality brought the reputation of the papacy to historic lows. In 1517, Martin Luther, a former monk, attacked Catholicism for having become too worldly and politically corrupt and for obscuring the fundamentals of Christianity with pagan elements. His reforming zeal, which appealed to a notion of an original, "purified" Christianity, set in motion the Protestant Reformation and split European Christianity in two.

In response, Roman Catholicism steeled itself for battle and launched the Counter-Reformation, which emphasized orthodoxy and fidelity to the true church. The Counter-Reformation reinvigorated the church and, to some extent, eliminated its excesses. But the Counter-Reformation also contributed to the decline of the Italian Renaissance, a revival of arts and letters that sought to recover and rework the classical art and philosophy of ancient Greece and Rome. The popes had once been great patrons of Renaissance arts and sciences, but the Counter-Reformation put an end to the church's liberal leniency in these areas. Further, the church's new emphasis on religious orthodoxy would soon clash with the emerging scientific revolution. Galileo, with his study of astronomy, found himself at the center of this clash.

Conservative astronomers of Galileo's time, working without telescopes, ascribed to the ancient theory of egocentricity. This theory of astronomy held that the earth lay at the center of the solar system, orbited by both the sun and the other planets. Indeed, to the casual observer, it seemed common sense that since the sun "rose" in the morning and "set" at night, it must have circled around the earth. Ancient authorities like Aristotle and the Roman astronomer Ptolemy had championed this viewpoint, and the notion also coincided with the Catholic Church's view of the universe, which placed mankind, God's creation, at the center of the cosmos. Buttressed by common sense, the ancient philosophers, and the church, the geocentric model of the universe seemed secure in its authority. The Ptolemaic theory, however, was not impervious to attack. In the 16th century, astronomers strained to make modern observations fit Ptolemy's geocentric model of the universe.

Nicholas Copernicus, a Polish astronomer, openly questioned the Ptolemaic system and proposed a heliocentric system in which the planets "including Earth" orbited the sun. This more mathematically satisfying way of arranging the solar system did not attract many supporters at first, since the available data did not yet support a wholesale abandonment of Ptolemy's system. By the end of the 16th century, however, astronomers like Johannes Kepler had also begun to embrace Copernicus's theory.

Ultimately, Galileo's telescope struck a fatal blow to the Ptolemaic system. But, in a sense, the telescope was also nearly fatal to Galileo himself. The Catholic Church, desperately trying to hold the Protestant heresy at bay, could not accept a scientific assault on its own theories of the universe. The pressures of the age set in motion a historic confrontation between religion and science, one which would culminate in 1633 when the church put Galileo on trial, forced him to recant his stated and published scientific beliefs, and put him under permanent house arrest.

문제 1 The term "ferment" most closely means _____.
  (1) alienation   (2) turmoil
  (3) consolidation   (4) decomposition
  (5) stagnation

문제 2 Which of the following was NOT a reason for Martin Luther's attack on the Catholic Church?
(1) pagan elements in its practices
(2) the amorality of its leadership
(3) its excessive attention to piety
(4) its corruption and worldliness
(5) the political involvement of the popes

문제 3 Which of the following best explains why the Catholic Church started the Counter-Reformation?
(1) to fight scientific heresy
(2) to clean out its own ranks
(3) to reinvigorate artists and intellectuals
(4) to elect a new pope
(5) to counter Protestant challenges

문제 4 In the second paragraph, the passage implies that during the Renaissance, the Catholic Church _____.
(1) saw little conflict between its own goals and those of the arts and sciences
(2) promoted the arts as a way to limit the social influence of scientists
(3) supported Martin Luther's views on religion and the church
(4) had limited interaction with the religious affairs of commoners
(5) focused on spirituality as opposed to worldly matters

문제 5 The author's description of Galileo's telescope as having "struck a fatal blow" is an example of _____.
(1) simile
(2) metaphor
(3) personification
(4) allusion
(5) irony

문제 6 Which of the following best states the main idea of the passage?
(1) Science always conflicts with religion.
(2) Science is vulnerable to outside social forces.
(3) Ideally, scientific theories should reinforce religious doctrine.
(4) Science operates in a vacuum.
(5) Advanced technology is the only route to good scientific theories.

[Challenge 8]

The most memorable example of what has been advanced is (a) <u>afforded</u> by a great pestilence of the fourteenth century, which desolated Asia, Europe, and Africa, and of which the people yet preserve the remembrance in gloomy traditions. It was an oriental plague, marked by inflammatory boils and tumors of the glands, such as break out in no other febrile disease. On account of these inflammatory boils, and from the black spots, indicative of a putrid decomposition, which appeared upon the skin, it was called in Germany and in the northern kingdoms of Europe the Black Death, and in Italy, la mortalega grande, the Great Mortality.

Few testimonies are presented to us (b) <u>respecting</u> its symptoms and its course, yet these are sufficient to (c) <u>throw light upon</u> the form of the malady, and they are worthy of credence, from their coincidence with the signs of the same disease in modern times. The imperial writer, Kantakusenos, whose own son, Andronikus, died of this plague in Constantinople, notices great imposthumes of the thighs and arms of those affected, which, when opened, afforded (d) <u>relief</u> by the discharge of an offensive matter. Buboes, which are the infallible signs of the oriental plague, are thus plainly indicated, for he makes separate mention of smaller boils on the arms and in the face, as also in other parts of the body, and clearly distinguishes these from the blisters, which are no less produced by plague in all its forms. In many cases, black spots broke out all over the body, either single, or united and confluent.

＊boil(impostume) 종기 bubo 림프선종(참고: bubonic plague 선페스트)

문제 1 Which of the following is the topic of the first paragraph?
(1) Deadly Disease in the Orient
(2) Symptoms of the Black Death
(3) A Great Pestilence, the Black Death
(4) Examples of the Black Death

문제 2 According to the passage, which of the following is NOT true of the Black Death?
(1) The impact of the Black Death in the 14th century was a formidable danger to people in many parts of the world.
(2) For all the notorious symptoms of the Black Death, its mortality rate was relatively low.
(3) The name Black Death is attributed to one of its symptoms.
(4) Kantakusenos differentiated buboes from blisters.

문제 3 Which of the following is NOT the synonym of each underlined word in the passage?
(1) (a) afforded - paid for
(2) (b) respecting - regarding
(3) (c) throw light upon - lay open
(4) (d) relief - alleviation

[Challenge 9]

Let's start with a closer look at what 'power' is. Power is typically thought of having a certain attribute which gives one person more influence over another. This attribute could be intelligence or experience, it could be job title, or perhaps money. According to most social psychologists, there are five types of power: coercive, reward, legitimate, expert, and referent. (a) Coercive power means the power punish. Parents are said to have coercive power because they can place their child in time-out, for example; bosses have coercive power because they can fire an employee or assign an employee a less pleasing job. (b) Reward power is almost the opposite; it is the power to reward. ___(가)___ parents and bosses have this type of power as well, as do many others in our lives. (c) Legitimate power refers to the power granted by some authority, such as the power a police officer has due to the local or state government or the power a professor has due to the rules of a college or university. (d) Expert power results from experience or education. Those individuals with more knowledge tend to have more power in situations where that knowledge is important. For instance, the physician will have more power in a medical emergency than the plumber. But, when the pipes explode and the house is being flooded, the physician is not the person to call. Finally, referent power refers to admiration or respect. When we look up to people because of their accomplishments, their attitude, or any other personal attribute, we tend to give them more power over us. Imagine being asked to do something by your "hero" or your favorite movie star; we are very likely to comply out of admiration or respect.

문제 1 If the passage is divided in two, where does the second paragraph begin?
　　　(1) (a)　　　　　　　　　　　(2) (b)
　　　(3) (c)　　　　　　　　　　　(4) (d)

문제 2 Fill in blank (가).
　　　(1) In that sense　　　　　　(2) However
　　　(3) On the flip side　　　　　(4) On the same level

문제 3 Which of the following is CORRECT about the passage?
　　　(1) Power tends to flow from the privileged few to the masses.
　　　(2) Expert power has more to do with knowledge rather than a job title.
　　　(3) In a medical situation, doctors have more power than plumbers because of their power granted by some authority.
　　　(4) Parents can punish their children because of the power that comes from admiration or respect.

[Challenge 10]

An external event often seems to initiate an episode of depression. Thus, a serious loss, chronic illness, difficult relationship, financial problem, or any unwelcome change in life patterns can trigger a depressive episode. Very often, a combination of genetic, psychological, and environmental factors is involved in the onset of a depressive disorder. Stressors that contribute to the development of depression sometimes ___(a)___ . For example, minority groups who more often feel impacted by discrimination are disproportionately represented. Socioeconomically disadvantaged groups have higher rates of depression compared to their advantaged counterparts. Immigrants to the United States may be more vulnerable to developing depression, particularly when isolated by language.

문제 1 Which of the following is the topic of the passage?
(1) Anomalous Episodes of Depression
(2) Depression and Minorities
(3) Causes of Depression
(4) Depression Presented by Immigrants in the US

문제 2 Given the context, choose one that fits in blank (a).
(1) can be fuel by economical factors
(2) can only be found in minority groups
(3) affect some groups more than others
(4) vary from group to group

Day 24

★ In the field of observation, chance favors only the prepared mind.

Louis Pasteur (1822 - 1895)

관찰력의 분야에서, 우연은 단지 준비된 자에게만 호의를 보인다. (Louis Pasteur)

[Challenge 1]

(a) <u>A good character cannot be inherited, as the estate of a father descends to his heirs</u>. However respectable and worthy parents may be, their children cannot share in that respect, unless they deserve it by their own merits. Too many youth, it is to be apprehended, are depending upon their parents' reputation as well as their parents' property, for their own (b) <u>standing</u> and success in life. This is an insecure foundation. In our republican land, every individual is estimated by his or her own conduct, and not by the reputation of their connections. It is undoubtedly an advantage in many points of view, for a young person to have respectable parents. But if they would inherit their parents' good name, they must imitate their parents' virtues.

A good character cannot be purchased with gold. Though a man or a woman may have all the wealth of the Indies, yet it cannot secure a worthy name — it cannot buy the esteem of the wise and good, without the merit which deserves it. The glitter of gold cannot conceal an evil and crabbed disposition, a selfish soul, a corrupt heart, or vile passions and propensities. Although the sycophantic may fawn around or bow obsequiously before them, on account of their riches, yet, in fact, they are despised and condemned in the hearts even of their hangers-on and followers.

A good character cannot be obtained by simply wishing for it. The Creator has wisely provided, that the desire for a thing does not secure it. Were it to be thus, our world would soon present a strange aspect. It is, undoubtedly, much better than it should be as it is. We have the privilege to wish for whatever we please; but we can secure only that which we labor for and deserve. Were the traveller to stand throughout the day, at the foot of the hill, wishing to be at the summit, his simple desire would not place him there. He must allow his wishes to _____**(c)**_____. It is only by persevering industry, and patient toil, contented to take one step at a time; that his wish is gratified, and he finds himself at length upon the brow of the eminence.

문제 1 Choose the rhetorical device that is used in the underlined (a)?
(1) Repetition   (2) Metaphor   (3) Simile   (4) Hyperbole

문제 2 Which of the following is neither stated nor implied?
(1) Pulling strings to one's advantage to some degree can help him to achieve what he wants but is not a secure foundation for the ultimate goal of his life.
(2) The 'halo' of parents' reputation can not ensure that their children will get the same degree of respect from their followers if they don't imitate their parent's virtues.
(3) There are things that money can not buy and there is more to life than just making money.
(4) A good character is more likely to be fostered in a family whose parents are respected by others.

문제 3 Which of the following gives the best definition of the word (b)?
(1) Uprightness of one's character   (2) Establishment of oneself in life
(3) Good opportunities in life   (4) Unchanging point of view

문제 4 Fill in blank (c).
(1) prompt him to proper exertion   (2) be fulfilled by proper thinking
(3) be made with some realistic quality   (4) build up in size as time goes by

[Challenge 2]

Mr. Samuel Ireland, originally a silk merchant in Spitalfields, was led by his taste for literary antiquities to abandon trade for those pursuits, and published several tours. One of them consisted of an excursion upon the river Avon, during which he explored, with ardent curiosity, every locality associated with Shakspeare. He was accompanied by his son, a youth of sixteen, who imbibed a portion of his father's Shakspearean mania. The youth, perceiving the great importance which his parent attached to every relic of the poet, and the eagerness with which he sought for any of his MS. remains, conceived that it would not be difficult to gratify his father by some productions of his own, in the language and manner of Shakspeare's time. The idea possessed his mind for a certain period; and, in 1793, being then in his eighteenth year, he produced some MSS. said to be in the handwriting of Shakspeare, which he said had been given him by a gentleman possessed of many other old papers. The ecstasy expressed by his father urged him to the fabrication of other documents, described to come from the same (a) quarter. Emboldened by success, he ventured upon higher compositions in prose and verse; and at length announced the discovery of an original drama, under the title for Vortigern, which he had written in the period of two months. Having provided himself with the paper of the period and with ink prepared by a bookbinder, ___(b)___. The father, who was a maniac upon such subjects, gave such (c) éclat to the supposed discovery, that the attention of the literary world, and all England, was drawn to it.

＊MS 원고(pl. MSS)

문제 1 Which of the following is mainly talked about in the passage?
(1) Mr. Samuel Ireland's Literary Tour   (2) Life of Mr. Samuel Ireland
(3) Shakspeare Forgeries   (4) Excavation of Shakspeare's MSS

문제 2 Which of the following is neither stated nor implied?
(1) Mr. Samuel Ireland was looking for any relic of Shakspeare.
(2) Mr. Samuel Ireland was rubbing off on his son.
(3) Mr. Samuel Ireland urged him to fabricate more of Shakspeare's work.
(4) The son of Mr. Samuel Ireland was organized and smart enough to deceive his father with his concocted work of Shakspeare.

문제 3 Given the context, choose one that is closest in meaning to the underlined (a).
(1) source   (2) portion   (3) share   (4) parcel

문제 4 Given the context, which of the following best fills in blank (b)?
(1) writing was much easier than before
(2) he did not have to worry about the supplies of his work
(3) financial pressure was off his mind immediately
(4) no suspicion was entertained of the deception

문제 5 Given the context, choose one that is closest in meaning to the underlined (c).
(1) reprobation   (2) ovation   (3) opulence   (4) nefariousness

[Challenge 3]

At birth we have no self-image. We can not distinguish anything from the confusion of light and sound around us. From this beginning of no-dimension, we gradually begin to differentiate our body from our environment and develop a sense of identity, with the realization that we are a separate and independent human being. We then begin to develop a conscience, the sense of right and wrong. Further, we develop social consciousness, where we become aware that we live with other people. Finally, we develop a sense of values, which is our overall estimation of our worth in the world. _____.

문제 1 Fill in the blank to the passage.
(1) The sum total of all these developments is called the self-image.
(2) This estimation of worth is only relative to our value system.
(3) Therefore, our conscience keeps our sense of values in perspective.
(4) The sum total of living with other people makes us a total person.

문제 2   According to the passage, which of the following is CORRECT?
(1) Conscience allows one to differentiate between right and wrong.
(2) Social consciousness is our most important awareness.
(3) Heredity is predominant over environment in development.
(4) The ability to distinguish between moral issues depends on the dimension of selfdevelopment.

[Challenge 4]

The early years of Galileo were, like those of almost all great experimental philosophers, spent in the construction of instruments and pieces of machinery, which were calculated chiefly to amuse himself and his schoolfellows. (가) And though, from the (a) <u>straitened</u> circumstances of his father, he was educated under considerable disadvantages, yet he acquired the elements of classical literature, and was initiated into all the learning of the times. (나) Music, drawing, and painting were the occupations of his leisure hours; and such was his proficiency in these arts, that he was reckoned a skilful performer on several musical instruments, especially the lute; and his knowledge of pictures was _____(b)_____ by some of the best artists of his day. (다)

Galileo seems to have been desirous of following the profession of a painter: but his father had observed decided indications of early genius; and, though by no means able to afford it, he resolved to send him to the university to pursue the study of medicine. (라) He accordingly enrolled himself as a scholar in arts at the university of Pisa, on the 5th of November, 1581, and pursued his medical studies under the celebrated botanist Andrew Cæsalpinus, who filled the chair of medicine from 1567 to 1592.

In order to study the principles of music and drawing, Galileo found it necessary to acquire some knowledge of geometry. His father seems to have foreseen the consequences of following this new pursuit, and though he did not prohibit him from reading Euclid under Ostilio Ricci, one of the professors at Pisa, yet he watched his progress with the utmost (c) <u>jealousy</u>, and had resolved that it should not interfere with his medical studies. The demonstrations, however, of the Greek mathematician had too many charms for the ardent mind of Galileo. His whole attention was engrossed with the new truths which burst upon his understanding; and after many fruitless attempts to check his ardour and direct his thoughts to professional objects, his father was obliged to surrender his parental control, and allow the fullest scope to the genius of his son.

문제 1 Which of the following is TRUE of the passage?
(1) Galileo's father did not see education as an important factor for success in life.
(2) Galileo was skillful with his fingers.
(3) Galileo wanted to pursue the profession of a painter but he gave up his passion for it because of his father.
(4) Euclid was a great painter so that Galileo set him as his role model.

문제 2 Where can the sentence below be best inserted in the passage?

> This employment of his hands, however, did not interfere with his regular studies.

(1) (가)   (2) (나)   (3) (다)   (4) (라)

문제 3 Which of the following is closest in meaning to the underlined (a)?
(1) parsimonious   (2) destitute   (3) miserly   (4) avaricious

문제 4 Fill in blank (b).
(1) held in great esteem
(2) looked down on
(3) greatly expanded
(4) directly handed down

문제 5 Which of the following is closest in meaning to the underlined (c)?
(1) vigilance
(2) covetousness
(3) resentment
(4) mistrust

[Challenge 5]

Man can no more be scientifically studied apart from the ground which he tills, or the lands over which he travels, or the seas over which he trades, than polar bear or desert cactus can be understood apart from its habitat. Man's relations to his environment are infinitely more numerous and complex than those of the most highly organized plant or animal. So complex are they that they constitute a legitimate and necessary object of special study. The investigation which they receive in anthropology, ethnology, sociology and history is piecemeal and partial, limited as to the race, cultural development, epoch, country or variety of geographic conditions taken into account. Hence all these sciences, together with history so far as history undertakes to explain the causes of events, _____(a)_____ a satisfactory solution of their problems largely because the geographic factor which enters into them all has not been thoroughly analyzed. Man has been so noisy about the way he has "conquered Nature," and Nature has been so silent in her persistent influence over man, that the geographic factor in the equation of human development has been overlooked.

225

문제 1 Which of the following is the main idea of the passage?
(1) It is necessary to study geography in the history of human development.
(2) All sciences have their own limitations.
(3) The relationship between man and his environments is complex.
(4) Man has mastered nature, thus influencing a great deal on it.

문제 2 Which of the following is most appropriate for blank (a)?
(1) mingle with	(2) fail to reach	(3) render	(4) get rid of

[Challenge 6]

We have now (a) reached the stage where the world is a single economic unit and every group has access to the product of all other groups. There is no way of overestimating the importance of this. We live in a time when the problems and dangers humanity faces are worldwide. The dangers of nuclear war, of chemical pollution, of overpopulation, and of the greenhouse effect are global. No nation can escape.

Efforts to solve these problems must also be global. No nation by itself can effectively deal with any one of them if other nations do not cooperate. There are continuing international meetings on all such problems, for that reason.

How can we persuade nations, divided by thousands of years of national traditions that dictate rivalries, suspicions, hatreds, and wars, (b) to cooperate? We must find some common interest. Language, religion, culture in general are all divisive. Science is a unifying factor, but few people feel an overwhelming interest in science.

That leaves business. These days, anything that interrupts free international trade harms everyone. Most of the world is aware of the danger of protectionism, and objections arise (c) to forms of protectionism that still exist in Japan and elsewhere.

Already large business firms are multinational and are forced to think in global terms. Narrow considerations of nationalism and patriotism simply don't make sense. This must continue if we are to survive, and anything that facilitates trade and continues to make business more international necessitates a further increase in global thinking. This must make it easier to solve the world's problems, (d) if they are to solve at all.

문제 1 What is the main idea of the passage?
(1) Nations should abandon protectionism to enjoy common economic prosperity.
(2) National traditions may get in the way of promoting international understanding.
(3) Business helps persuade nations to cooperate to cope with the world's problems.
(4) Business firms should be multinational to survive in the fierce competition.

문제 2 Among the underlined (a)~(d), which of the following is NOT grammatically correct?
(1) (a)   (2) (c)   (3) (c)   (4) (d)

[Challenge 7]

(a) <u>Most economists in the United States</u> seem captivated by the spell of the free market. Consequently, nothing seems good or normal that does not accord with the requirements of the free market. A price that is determined by the seller or, for that matter, established by anyone other than the aggregate of consumers seems pernicious. Accordingly, it requires a major act of will to think of price-fixing (the determination of prices by the seller) as both "normal" and having a valuable economic function. In fact, price-fixing is normal in all industrialized societies because the industrial system itself provides, as an effortless consequence of its own development, the price-fixing that it requires. Modern industrial planning requires and rewards great size. Hence, a comparatively small number of large firms will be competing for the same group of consumers. That each large firm will act with consideration of its own needs and thus avoid selling its products for more than its competitors charge is commonly recognized by advocates of free-market economic theories. But each large firm will also act with full consideration of the needs that it has in common with the other large firms competing for the same customers. Each large firm will thus avoid significant price-cutting, because price-cutting would be prejudicial to the common interest in a stable demand for products. Most economists do not see price-fixing when it occurs because they expect it to be brought about by a number of explicit agreements among large firms; it is not.

Moreover, those economists who argue that allowing the free market to operate without interference is the most efficient method of establishing prices have not considered the economies of non-socialist countries other than the United States. These economies employ intentional price-fixing, usually in an overt fashion. Formal price-fixing by cartel and informal price-fixing by agreements covering the members of an industry are commonplace. Were there something peculiarly efficient about the free market and inefficient about price-fixing, the countries that have avoided the first and used the second would have suffered drastically in their economic development. There is no indication that they have.

Socialist industry also works within a framework of controlled prices. In the early 1970's, the Soviet Union began to give firms and industries some of the flexibility in adjusting prices that a more informal evolution has accorded the capitalist system. Economists in the United States have hailed the change as a return to the free market. But Soviet firms are no more subject to prices established by a free market over which they exercise little influence than are capitalist firms; rather, Soviet firms have been given the power to fix prices.

문제 1   The primary purpose of the passage is to _____.
   (1) refute the theory that the free market plays a useful role in the development of industrialized societies
   (2) suggest methods by which economists and members of the government of the United States can recognize and combat price-fixing by large firms
   (3) show that in industrialized societies price-fixing and the operation of the free market are not only compatible but also mutually beneficial
   (4) explain the various ways in which industrialized societies can fix prices in order to stabilize the free market
   (5) argue that price-fixing, in one form or another, is an inevitable part of and benefit to the economy of any industrialized society

문제 2   The author's attitude toward "Most economists in the United States" in underlined (a) can best be described as _____.
   (1) spiteful and envious   (2) scornful and denunciatory
   (3) critical and condescending   (4) ambivalent but deferential
   (5) uncertain but interested

문제 3   It can be inferred from the author's argument that a price fixed by the seller "seems pernicious" because _____.
   (1) people do not have confidence in large firms
   (2) people do not expect the government to regulate prices
   (3) most economists believe that consumers as a group should determine prices
   (4) most economists associate fixed prices with communist and socialist economies
   (5) most economists believe that no one group should determine prices

문제 4   The suggestion in the passage that price-fixing in industrialized societies is normal arises from the author's statement that price-fixing is _____.
   (1) a profitable result of economic development
   (2) an inevitable result of the industrial system
   (3) the result of a number of carefully organized decisions
   (4) a phenomenon common to industrialized and nonindustrialized societies
   (5) a phenomenon best achieved cooperatively by government and industry

문제 5   According to the author, price-fixing in nonsocialist countries is often _____.
   (1) accidental but productive   (2) illegal but useful
   (3) legal and innovative   (4) traditional and rigid
   (5) intentional and widespread

228

문제 6 According to the author, what is the result of the Soviet Union's change in economic policy in the 1970's _____.

(1) Soviet firms show greater profit
(2) Soviet firms have less control over the free market
(3) Soviet firms are able to adjust to technological advances
(4) Soviet firms have some authority to fix prices
(5) Soviet firms are more responsive to the free market

문제 7 In the passage, the author is primarily concerned with _____.

(1) predicting the consequences of a practice
(2) criticizing a point of view
(3) calling attention to recent discoveries
(4) proposing a topic for research
(5) summarizing conflicting opinions

[Challenge 8]

We must reflect that we are not to deal with some new race, but with the same race that inhabited Europe at the close of Neolithic times. The people who had triumphed over nature with their implements of stone were now put in possession of weapons and implements of greatly increased efficiency. The results could not fail to advance their culture. We would not expect any great change in the houses. They would, however, be much better built. The metallic tools were certainly a long ways ahead of the best stone implements. With the aid of metallic axes, knives, saws, gouges, and chisels, their cabins could be increased in size and appearance. They still built settlements over the lakes, but the Bronze Age settlements were more substantially built, and placed farther out from shore. Fortified places were still numerous; the remains of thousands of them of this age have been found in Ireland. But the forests were cleared, wild animals disappeared, society became more settled, and we may be sure that an increasing number of little hamlets were scattered over the country.

Caves were resorted to during this epoch only in times of danger. One at Heathbury Burn, in England, contained portions of the skeletons of two individuals, surrounded by many articles of bronze and a mould for casting bronze axes. It is not difficult to read the story. In some time of sudden danger workers in bronze fled hither with their stores, but owing to some cause were unable to escape the death from which they were fleeing, and their bodies _____(a)_____ until the modern explorer made them a subject of scientific speculations.

문제 1 Which of the following sentence would be the most appropriate beginning for the first paragraph?
(1) What dramatic changes would be brought about in every sector of society by the use of stone?
(2) Think about the social impacts of the implements of the stone in the period of the Stone Age.
(3) Let us now see what change in the home life, in the culture of the people, would be brought about by the use of bronze.
(4) What consequences of bronze have been brought about because of the use of the bronze?

문제 2 According to the passage, which of the following is CORRECT?
(1) In Bronze Age, many little communities were converging into one big city.
(2) There were great changes inside the houses as well as outside.
(3) The people at the close of Neolithic times overcame the hardships of nature by making tools of stone.
(4) Even in Bronze Age, caves were used as a main source for dwelling.

문제 3 Choose one that best fills in blank (a).
(1) were kept in an open place
(2) disintegrated apart
(3) were lost to sight
(4) were all together decomposed

[Challenge 9]

　Man is to be contemplated as an intellectual, and as a moral being. By his intellectual powers, he acquires the knowledge of facts, observes their connexions, and traces the conclusions which arise out of them. These mental operations, however, even in a high state of cultivation, may be directed entirely to truths of an extrinsic kind, — that is, to such as do not exert any influence either on the moral condition of the individual, or on his relations to other sentient beings. They may exist in an eminent degree in the man who lives only for himself, and feels little beyond the personal wants, or the selfish enjoyments of the hour that is passing over him. ___(a)___, when we contemplate man as a moral being, new relations open on our view, and these are of mightier import. We find him occupying a place in a great system of moral government, in which he has an important station to fill and high duties to perform. We find him placed in certain relations to a great moral Governor, who presides over this system of things, and to a future state of being for which the present scene is intended to prepare him. We find him possessed of powers which qualify him to feel these relations, and of principles calculated to guide him through the solemn responsibilities which attend his state of moral discipline.

문제 1 Which of the following is the topic of the passage?
(1) Two Parts of Man's Mental Constitution
(2) Man's Relation with the Moral Governor
(3) A Reciprocal Relationship between Man's Intellectual and Moral Status
(4) Man's Duty to Perform Moral Responsibilities

문제 2 Choose one that best fills in blank (a).
(1) Nonetheless   (2) In fact
(3) Moreover   (4) But

[Challenge 10]

Religion unites man with God or puts them in communication; but do you say that God is infinite? If God is infinite, no finite being can have communication or any relation with Him. Where there are no relations, there can be no union, no correspondence, no duties. If there are no duties between man and his God, there exists no religion for man. Thus by saying that God is infinite, you annihilate, from that moment, all religion for man, who is a finite being. The idea of infinity is for us an idea without model, without prototype, without object.

문제 1 Which of the following statements is most related to the passage?
(1) Man should learn the way God communicates to understand him.
(2) God is as much time-bound as human beings are.
(3) Every religion is an absurdity.
(4) In order to establish a true communication with God, man needs to be 'infinite.'

Day 25

★ Books...are like lobster shells, we surround ourselves with 'em, then we grow out of 'em and leave 'em behind, as evidence of our earlier stages of development.

Dorothy L. Sayers (1893 - 1957)

책은 로브스터의 껍질과 같다. 우리는 이것을 둘러싸고, 이것을 먹고 자란 후, 마친 우리의 초기 단계의 증거로서 이것을 남기고 떠난다. (Dorothy L. Sayers)

[Challenge 1]

You must try to understand that when I finished school I was as raw as raw could be. I had never travelled anywhere on my own, never purchased a train ticket, since like most kids my age I had only travelled with my parents or relatives and they made all the decisions. I had no experience of how to handle money (my knowledge being limited to spending the 50 paise or one rupee I would receive as pocket money now and then). So while I had set my sights on travelling far and wide my parents wisely thought that I should begin by learning to manage on my own within Goa itself. It was also the rainy season and travelling around the country would be much more difficult they explained. So I started out by helping at an aquarium shop in Mapusa, the town nearest my village. The proprietor of the shop is Ashok D'Cruz, a college friend of my father's. I must tell you about Ashok. He is no ordinary businessman: keeping fish is a passion with him. He is far more interested in chatting with his customers about fish than making money selling them. I have never seen him forcing any of his customers to buy from his stock of aquarium fish.

문제 1 According to the passage, which of the following is NOT true of 'I'?
(1) His parents gave him a piece of advice about his planned travel.
(2) When he got out of school, he did not know much of the world.
(3) He made up his mind to travel by himself but then decided not to after all.
(4) He earned 50 paise or 1 rupee through doing work in the aquarium shop.

문제 2　What is NOT true of Ashok D'Cruz?
(1) He ran a fish shop.
(2) He had an enthusiasm about what he was doing.
(3) His honesty policy with his customers made him earn a fortune.
(4) Selling fish is not his top priority.

[Challenge 2]

It is plain enough that the memory seems decidedly limited in its scope. This is because our power of voluntary recall is decidedly limited. But it does not follow simply because we are without the power to deliberately recall certain experiences that all mental trace of those experiences is lost to us. Those experiences that we are unable to recall are those that we disregarded when they occurred because they possessed no special interest for us. They are there, but no mental associations or connections with power to awaken them have arisen in consciousness.

문제 1　Which of the following is the topic of the passage?
(1) Workings of Recall
(2) Effects of Oblivion on Health
(3) Causes of Forgetfulness
(4) Experiences and Memory

[Challenge 3]

What babies know fascinates doctors, researchers and parents. With technology that can measure brain waves and other indicators, what researchers are finding is that babies know more than we suspect. What do they know and when do they know it? (a) Such questions have researchers monitoring babies' brains to find out. At Northwestern University, researchers recently concluded that well before babies start to speak, they recognize words and can link them to the things they represent. At four and a half months, Finn is not talking, but he definitely responds to what his mother says. The Northwestern study and others indicate that one of the best things parents can do is talk to their babies. Covington Campbell started talking to her baby even before he was born. "I spoke to Finn all the time. I sort of narrated what I was doing," Campbell said, (b) Campbell was in law school when she was pregnant with Finn. "I was finishing my last semester of law school, so, I guess, check back with me in 30 years and see if he's a litigator, because he would definitely come alive in my corporations classes and he always heard my professors speaking," she said. Professor Kathy Hirsh-Pasik directs the Infant Language Laboratory at Temple University in Philadelphia. "We think the very first processes of language development are actually starting in the womb because they are overhearing their mother's speech," she said. Researchers say that is when babies pick up the melodies of language.

문제 1   Which of the following is neither stated nor implied from the passage?
(1) The fact that babies can not talk does not mean that they can not 'hear' words.
(2) In the womb babies start picking up the 'song' of their mother's tongue.
(3) The main source of babies' linguistic input is from their mother's speech.
(4) It is a good idea that parents take language classes when they are pregnant.

문제 2   Which field of study does the underlined (a) most likely belong to?
(1) Linguistic Anthropology   (2) Cognitive Science
(3) Classical Linguistics   (4) Neurology

문제 3   Which of the following can be the premise of what Campbell believes in the underlined (b)?
(1) Babies begin developing language skills while they are in the womb.
(2) What babies hear in the womb determines the future of the baby.
(3) The best time to get pregnant is when someone is in school.
(4) Even babies in the womb can understand what professors are talking about.

[Challenge 4]

My political ideal is democracy. Let every man be respected as an individual and no man idolized. It is an irony of fate that I myself have been the recipient of excessive admiration and reverence from my fellow-beings. The cause of this may well be the desire, unattainable for many, to understand the few ideas to which I have with my feeble powers attained through ceaseless struggle. I am quite aware that for any organization to reach its goals, one man must do the thinking and directing and generally bear the responsibility. But the led must not be coerced, they must be able to choose their leader.

문제 1   Which of the following is neither stated nor implied from the passage?
(1) Leaders must be held accountable for his or her own action.
(2) The author is suggesting the right of resistance in case of dictatorship.
(3) People should be able to choose their own leaders.
(4) Leadership is required for an organization to attain its goal.

[Challenge 5]

The man that is governed by self, and not by a principle, (가) <u>changes his front when his selfish comforts are threatened</u>. Deeply intent upon defending and guarding his own interests, he regards all means as lawful that will subserve that end. (a) He is continually scheming as to how he may protect himself against his enemies, (나) <u>being too self-centered to perceive that he is his own enemy</u>. Such a man's work crumbles away, for it is divorced from Truth and power. (b) All effort that is grounded upon self, perishes; only that work endures that is built upon an indestructible principle. (c) The man that stands upon a principle is the same calm, dauntless, self-possessed man under all circumstances. (d) When the hour of trial comes, and he has to decide between his personal comforts and Truth, he gives up his comforts and remains firm. Even the prospect of torture and death cannot alter or deter him. The man of self regards the loss of his wealth, his comforts, or his life as the greatest calamities which can befall him. The man of principle looks upon these incidents as comparatively insignificant, and not to be weighed with loss of character, loss of Truth. To desert Truth is, to him, the only happening which _____(다)_____.

문제 1   Which of the following best paraphrases the underlined (가)?
  (1) saves his face
  (2) adopts a new line
  (3) turns over a new leaf
  (4) changes his face

문제 2   Where is the paragraph best divided in half?
  (1) (a)   (2) (b)
  (3) (c)   (4) (d)

문제 3   According to the passage, what can be inferred from the underlined (나)?
  (1) One's selfishness makes him easy to perceive his enemy.
  (2) Selfishness does not actually protect one's interests.
  (3) One's self-centeredness makes him oblivious to the fact that he is the source of his enemy.
  (4) Selfishness makes enemies.

문제 4   Choose one that best fills in blank (다).
  (1) can really be called a calamity
  (2) can make him turn back to his self
  (3) makes him pay more attention to his surroundings
  (4) helps him better focus on himself

[Challenge 6]

The fact that natural science emphasizes the abstract and history the concrete will become clearer if we compare the results of the researches of the two sciences. However finespun the conceptions may be which the historical critic uses in working over his materials, the final goal of such study is always to create out of the mass of events a vivid portrait of the past. And what history offers us is pictures of men and of human life, with all the wealth of their individuality, reproduced in all their characteristic vivacity. Thus do the peoples and languages of the past, their forms and beliefs, their struggles for power and freedom, speak to us through the mouth of history. How different it is with the world which the natural sciences have created for us! However concrete the materials with which they started, the goal of these sciences is theories, eventually mathematical formulations of laws of change. Treating the individual, sensuous, changing objects as mere unsubstantial appearances (phenomena), scientific investigation becomes a search for the universal laws which rule the ____(a)____ changes of events. Out of this colorful world of the senses, science creates a system of abstract concepts, in which the true nature of things is conceived to exist — a world of colorless and soundless atoms, ____(b)____ all their earthly sensuous qualities. (c) Such is the triumph of thought over perception. Indifferent to change, science casts her anchor in the eternal and unchangeable. Not the change as such but the unchanging form of change is what she seeks.

문제 1 Which of the following does NOT belong to the characteristics of natural science?
    (1) Forming abstract, universal laws
    (2) Unsusceptible to change
    (3) Perceiving concrete objects as abstract entities
    (4) Vivid presentations of what natural science pursues

문제 2 Which of the following best fills in blank (a)?
    (1) unpredictable   (2) timeless
    (3) palpable   (4) transient

문제 3 Which of the following best fills in blank (b)?
    (1) despoiled of   (2) under the impact of
    (3) indispensible to   (4) derived from

문제 4 What does the underlined (c) imply?
    (1) Perception derives its origin from thought.
    (2) Sensuous objects are under the rule of the universal laws.
    (3) Earthly perception sometimes avoids scientific investigation.
    (4) Thought is of greater importance than perception.

[Challenge 7]

Socio-linguistic studies attempt to describe the human ability to use the rules of speech appropriately in different situations, e.g. when it is suitable to address a person as Ms., Mrs., Mary, Doctor, or simply as "you." Choice of terms, accent, or pronunciation may induce a greater empathy and understanding. ____(a)____, in certain dialects of American English, the pronunciation of the r-sound is linked to social class. In expressions such as "fourth floor," some people pronounce the r and others do not, and the usage of the r-sound is claimed to be consistent within a given socioeconomic niche. According to one study of English, as used in New York City, people aspiring to move from the lower middle class to the upper middle class attach prestige to pronouncing the r. Sometimes they even overcorrect their speech to pronouncer where those they emulate may not.

문제 1 The author's purpose is _____.
  (1) to argue   (2) to refute
  (3) to persuade   (4) to inform

문제 2 Which of the following can NOT be inferred from the passage?
  (1) A person can be referred to as different names of title in different situations.
  (2) Accent can serve as an indicator differentiating social classes.
  (3) People in a given area tend to show the same linguistic pattern of language.
  (4) People in New York City exclusively use the 'r' sound in their English.

문제 3 Fill in blank (a).
  (1) In addition   (2) For example
  (3) However   (4) There fore

[Challenge 8]

President Obama today brought out former president and Democratic heavyweight Bill Clinton for an impromptu press conference to tout his tax cut deal with Republicans that has earned the ____(a)____ of many liberal Democrats. "The agreement, taken as a whole," Clinton said, "is, I believe, the best bipartisan agreement we can reach to help the largest number of Americans, and to maximize the chances that the economic recovery will accelerate and create more jobs, and to minimize the chances that it will slip back, which is what has happened in other financial collapses." The payroll tax credit will "actually create a fair number of jobs," he added. "I expect it to lower the unemployment rate and keep us going." In the briefing room today, a seemingly comfortable Clinton, who stumped for the health care bill by President Obama before pushed his fellow Democrats dubious of the deal to support the president. Obama's deal with Republicans entails new tax credits and tax cut extension for all income groups for two years. It also includes an estate tax provision that would lower taxes on inherited income. Democrats charge that the president caved in too quickly to Republican demands and that he should have stuck with his original argument to extend tax cuts only for lower- and middle-income groups. On Thursday, House Democrats passed a resolution overwhelmingly rejecting the deal and highlighting the growing ____(b)____ inside the president's own party. In the Senate today, Sen. Bernie Sanders railed against the bill for more than eight full hours, saying that the president made a "bad compromise." Obama has argued that he had to find a compromise to make sure middle-class Americans weren't slapped with tax hikes in 2011. The White House also got some concessions, including an extension of several tax credits and unemployment benefits for another 13 months that are expected to help about 9 million Americans.

문제 1 Which of the following is the best title for the passage?
(1) Millions of Americans in Economic Jeopardy
(2) Obama-GOP Tax Cut Deal
(3) Clinton's Attempt to Run for President
(4) Increased Feuds between the President and the Republicans

문제 2 Fill in blanks (a) and (b).
(1) ire - rift   (2) seconding - solidarity
(3) fury - unity   (4) compromise - flare-up

문제 3 According to the passage, new tax credits and tax cut extension will _____.
(1) create a fair number of jobs
(2) backfire, increasing the unemployment rate
(3) release tensions between the President and his own party
(4) increase economic inequality between the lower-income groups and middle-class

[Challenge 9]

How many really suffer as a result of labor market problems? This is one of the most critical yet contentious social policy questions. In many ways, our social statistics exaggerate the degree of hardship. Unemployment does not have the same dire consequences today as it did in the

1930's when most of the unemployed were primary breadwinners, when income and earnings were usually much closer to the margin of subsistence, and when there were no countervailing social programs for those failing in the labor market.

Increasing affluence, the rise of families with more than one wage earner, the growing predominance of secondary earners among the unemployed, and improved social welfare protection have unquestionably mitigated the consequences of joblessness. Earnings and income data also overstate the dimensions of hardship. Among the millions with hourly earnings at or below the minimum wage level, the overwhelming majority are from multiple-earner, relatively affluent families.

Most of those counted by the poverty statistics are elderly or handicapped or have family responsibilities which keep them out of the labor force, so the poverty statistics are by no means an accurate indicator of labor market pathologies. Yet there are also many ways our social statistics underestimate the degree of labor-market-related hardship. The unemployment counts exclude the millions of fully employed workers whose wages are so low that their families remain in poverty.

Low wages and repeated or prolonged unemployment frequently interact to undermine the capacity for self-support. Since the number experiencing joblessness at some time during the year is several times the number unemployed in any month, those who suffer as a result of forced idleness can equal or exceed average annual unemployment, even though only a minority of the jobless in any month really suffer.

For every person counted in the monthly unemployment tallies, there is another working part-time because of the inability to find full-time work, or else outside the labor force but wanting a job. Finally, income transfers in our country have always focused on the elderly, disabled, and dependent, neglecting the needs of the working poor, so that the dramatic expansion of cash and in-kind transfers does not necessarily mean that those failing in the labor market are adequately protected.

문제 1 Which of the following is the principal topic of the passage?
  (1) What causes labor market pathologies that result in suffering
  (2) Why income measures are imprecise in measuring degrees of poverty
  (3) Which of the currently used statistical procedures are the best for estimating the incidence of hardship that is due to unemployment
  (4) Where the areas of agreement are among poverty, employment, and earnings figures
  (5) How social statistics give an unclear picture of the degree of hardship caused by low wages and insufficient employment opportunities

문제 2   The author uses "labor market problems" to refer to which of the following?

(1) The overall causes of poverty

(2) Deficiencies in the training of the work force

(3) Trade relationships among producers of goods

(4) Shortages of jobs providing adequate income

(5) Strikes and inadequate supplies of labor

문제 3   The author contrasts the 1930's with the present in order to show that _____.

(1) more people were unemployed in the 1930's

(2) unemployment now has less severe effects

(3) social programs are more needed now

(4) there now is a greater proportion of elderly and handicapped people among those in poverty

(5) poverty has increased since the 1930's

문제 4   Which of the following proposals best responds to the issues raised by the author?

(1) Innovative programs using multiple approaches should be set up to reduce the level of unemployment.

(2) A compromise should be found between the positions of those who view joblessness as an evil greater than economic control and those who hold the opposite view.

(3) New statistical indices should be developed to measure the degree to which unemployment and inadequately paid employment cause suffering.

(4) Consideration should be given to the ways in which statistics can act as partial causes of the phenomena that they purport to measure.

(5) The labor force should be restructured so that it corresponds to the range of job vacancies.

문제 5   The author's purpose in citing those who are repeatedly unemployed during a twelve-month period is most probably to show that _____.

(1) there are several factors that cause the payment of low wages to some members of the labor force

(2) unemployment statistics can underestimate the hardship resulting from joblessness

(3) recurrent inadequacies in the labor market can exist and can cause hardships for individual workers

(4) a majority of those who are jobless at any one time do not suffer severe hardship

(5) there are fewer individuals who are without jobs at some time during a year than would be expected on the basis of monthly unemployment figures

문제 6 The author states that the mitigating effect of social programs involving income transfers on the income level of low-income people is often not felt by _____.
(1) the employed poor
(2) dependent children in single-earner families
(3) workers who become disabled
(4) retired workers
(5) full-time workers who become unemployed

문제 7 According to the passage, one factor that causes unemployment and earnings figures to over predict the amount of economic hardship is the _____.
(1) recurrence of periods of unemployment for a group of low-wage workers
(2) possibility that earnings may be received from more than one job per worker
(3) fact that unemployment counts do not include those who work for low wages and remain poor
(4) establishment of a system of record-keeping that makes it possible to compile poverty statistics
(5) prevalence, among low-wage workers and the unemployed, of members of families in which others are employed

[Challenge 10]

In the United States today more people are interested in Buddhism and Taoism than in Confucianism. In fact, most people only know Confucius from silly puns or jokes that are told "in his words." (a) A pun is a play on words and it is usually humorous because there are two meanings for one word in a saying that gives a totally different meaning to the saying as a whole. When these sayings are attributed to Confucius, the grammar of the saying is usually incorrect in some way to make the saying sound like a foreigner said it. Confucius never really said any of these thing, but part of the joke is also that these silly saying came from a wise man. For example, look at the following saying: "Confucius say he who sleep with head on railroad track wake up with splitting headache." The humor in this saying comes from the phrase "splitting headache." Usually this phrase means a headache that hurts a lot. But if a train comes along the track, the man's head will be split into two pieces, thus a "splitting headache." Grammatically, this saying should also be written as "Confucius says that a man who sleeps with his head on a railroad track will wake up with a splitting headache."

문제 1 Choose TWO examples that contain a pun described in the underlined (a)
(1) Confucius say a man who wants a pretty nurse must be patient.
(2) Confucius say a relationship is the opportunity to do something you hate with someone you love.
(3) Confucius say war does not determine who is right, war determines who is left.
(4) Confucius say a tattoo is permanent proof of temporary insanity.

Day 26

★ Character cannot be developed in ease and quiet. Only through experience of trial and suffering can the soul be strengthened, ambition inspired, and success achieved.

Helen Keller (1880 - 1968)

성품이란 쉽게 조용히 개발되지 않는다. 단지 도전과 시험을 경험하면서 영혼은 강해지고, 야망은 불붙으며, 성공이 따라온다. (Helen Keller)

[Challenge 1]

Writings on hygiene and health have been accessible for centuries, but (a) never before have books and magazines on these subjects been as numerous as they are today. Most of the information is so general, vague and indefinite that only a few have the time and patience to read the thousands of pages necessary to learn what to do to keep well. The truth is to be found in the archives of medicine, in writings covering a period of over thirty centuries, but it is rather difficult to find the grains of truth.

Health is the most valuable of all possessions, for with health one can attain anything else within reason. A few of the great people of the world have been sickly, but it takes men and women sound in body and mind to do the important work. Healthy men and women are a nation's most valuable asset.

It is natural to be healthy, but we have wandered so far astray that disease is the rule and good health the exception. Of course, most people are well enough to attend to their work, but nearly all are suffering from some ill, mental or physical, acute or chronic, which deprives them of a part of their power. The average individual is of less value to himself, to his family and to society than he could be. His bad habits, of which he is often not aware, have brought weakness and disease upon him. These conditions prevent him from doing his best mentally and physically.

문제 1 Which of the following best paraphrases the underlined (a)?
(1) Accessibility to writings on hygiene and health is much better than the previous ages all combined.
(2) There are thousands of books and magazines on health in this age.
(3) No other age has ever exceeded the number of books on hygiene and health than in this age.
(4) Books on health in this age are no less than those in the past three centuries.

문제 2 According to the passage, which of the following is neither stated nor mentioned?
(1) Bad habits can invite weakness and disease on an unconscious basis.
(2) Promoting health among men and women is an important job that a country should pay no small amount of attention to.
(3) There has never been any one who could achieve larger-than-life goals without health.
(4) People with afflictions, mentally or physically are unlikely to perform themselves to the fullest.

[Challenge 2]

Things are continually happening all around us that we see with but "___(a)___." They are in the "fringe" of consciousness, and we deliberately ignore them. Many more things come to us in the form of sense-impressions that clamorously assail our sense-organs, but no effort of the will is needed to ignore them. We are absolutely ___(b)___ to them and unconscious of them because by the selection of our life interests we have closed the doors against them. In either case, whether in the "fringe" of consciousness or entirely outside of consciousness, these unperceived sensations will be found to be sensory images that have no connection with the present subject of thought. They therefore attract no part of our attention. Just as each of our individual sense-organs selects from the multitude of ether vibrations constantly beating upon the surface of the body only those waves to the velocity of which it is attuned, so each one of us as an integral personality selects from the stream of sensory experiences only those particular objects of attention that are in some way related to the present or habitual trend of thought.

문제 1 Which of the following is NOT true of the passage?
(1) Things that are on the "fringe" of consciousness do not really catch our attention.
(2) To ignore uninteresting things does not take any conscious effort.
(3) Things that are in the present subject of thought catch the attention of ours.
(4) Human beings are in control of sense-organs by which information around them is amassed.

문제 2 Which of the following best fills in blank (a)?
(1) the corner of our eyes   (2) half an eye
(3) suspicious eyes   (4) an attitude

문제 3 Which of the following best fills in blank (b)?
(1) impervious   (2) accessible
(3) alert   (4) obedient

[Challenge 3]

A creation myth or creation story is a symbolic narrative of a culture, tradition or people that describes their earliest beginnings, how the world they know began and how they first came into it. They are stories expressing, usually through metaphor and imagery, how the world came to be and what humanity's place and role is in it. Creation myths develop in oral traditions, and are the most common form of myth, found throughout human culture. In the society in which it is told, a creation myth is usually regarded as conveying profound truths, although not necessarily in a historical or literal sense. They are commonly, although not always, considered cosmogonical myths — that is they describe the ordering of the cosmos from a state of chaos or _____(a)_____. They are also commonly, although not always, considered sacred accounts, and can be found in nearly all known religious traditions.

문제 1 Which of the following is the topic of the passage?
(1) Who Creates Creation Myth
(2) Effects of Creation Myth on Humanity
(3) What is Creation Myth?
(4) How the World Came Into Existence

문제 2 Which of the following is NOT correct from the passage?
(1) Through creation myths man-kind tries to know where its place is in the universe.
(2) Creation myths usually develop from mouth to mouth.
(3) Creation myths commonly have a cosmogonical nature in them.
(4) A creation myth does not carry any historical or literal sense in it.

문제 3 Which of the following is most appropriate for blank (a)?
(1) repugnance   (2) amorphousness
(3) revulsion   (4) upheaval

[Challenge 4]

Two of the little boys are playing at snowball. Although it may be hotter in the summer in their country than it is here, the winter is as cold as you feel it. Like our own boys, these lads enjoy a fall of snow, and still better than snowballing they like making a snowman with a charcoal ball for each eye and a streak of charcoal for his mouth. The shoes which they usually wear out of doors are better for a snowy day than your boots, for their feet do not sink into the snow, unless it is deep. These shoes are of wood, and make a boy seem to be about three inches taller than he really is. The shoe, you see, has not laces or buttons, but is kept on the foot by that thong which passes between the first and second toe. The thong is made of grass, and covered with strong paper, or with white or black. The boy in the check dress wears his shoes without socks, but you see the other boy has socks on. His socks are made of dark blue calico, with a thickly woven sole, and a place, like one finger of a glove, for his big toe. If you were to wear Japanese shoes, you would think the thong between your toes very uncomfortable. Yet from their habit of wearing this sort of shoe, the big toe grows more separate from the other toes, and the skin between this and the next toe becomes as hard as the skin of a dog's or a cat's paw.

문제 1 Which of the following is NOT true of the passage?
(1) In Japan, when they make a snowman, they use charcoal balls for each eye.
(2) The reason why the author says Japanese shoes are better in the winter is that they prevent the feet from sinking into the snow."
(3) In general, the thong comes in several different colors.
(4) Kids in Japan they wear shoes with and without socks.

문제 2 According to the passage, the skin between the first tow and the next gets as hard as that of a dog because the shoes have _____.
(1) laces   (2) a thong
(3) charcoals   (4) calico

[Challenge 5]

"Worthy of mention in the context of euthanasia and suicide is the samurai tradition of seppuku, a form of ritual suicide. Most samurais were Zen Buddhists, and their general philosophy was one in which length of life was regarded as far less important than honor. Seppuku was practiced by samurai "to avoid the dishonour of capture, show loyalty to one's lord by following him into death, or atone for failure." Involuntary seppuku was also the means of capital punishment for the Samurai class.

To commit seppuku, the samurai would first quiet his mind, then slit his stomach open from right to left with a ritual knife. This violent method served to demonstrate the samurai's strength and courage, but would lead to a long, painful death. Thus the ritual seppuku usually included a second samurai, an attendant, who would mercifully behead the one practicing seppuku shortly after he had slit open his own stomach.

Not only the merciful actions of the second samurai, but the practice of seppuku itself has been compared to the modern-day practice of euthanasia: The reasons for a samurai's suicide were either (1) to avoid an inevitable death at the hands of others, or (2) to escape a longer period of unbearable pain or psychological misery, without being an active, fruitful member of society. These are exactly the sorts of situations when euthanasia is desired today.

The samurai ritual of seppuku came very close to euthanasia indeed — an assistant would behead the suicide after the suicide had fatally stabbed themselves in order to bring death swiftly and reduce the time the suicide was in pain. The samurai motivation for suicide was similar to (a) that of the person seeking euthanasia: either they had lost a battle and would be killed by their enemies or they had been so badly wounded that they could no longer be useful members of society.

문제 1 Which of the following is the best title for the passage?
(1) Types of Ritual Suicide in Japan
(2) How Seppuku Turns Into Modern-Day Euthanasia
(3) The Samurai Ritual of Seppuku and Euthanasia
(4) Socioeconomic Factors of Seppuku

문제 2 Which of the following is CORRECT about the samurai tradition of seppuku?
(1) Longevity is considered to be one of the greatest virtues.
(2) The samurai ritual of seppuku is solely based on personal interests.
(3) Being captured by the enemies can sometimes make the captured a war hero.
(4) The process of seppuku was so unbearably painful that the merciful intervention of an attendant was included.

문제 3 Which of the following best describes the situation of (a) in the passage?
(1) The patients have become so used to the pain that they would not feel any of it.
(2) The patients have lost their battle against the disease, and it will kill them.
(3) People still believe that the patients in great pain could regain their strength and stand on their own two feet.
(4) The patients do not want to bring their families dishonor by being a tremendous economic burden.

Day 26

[Challenge 6]

From this analysis we observe that the nitrogenous matter is to the carbonaceous in the proportion of one-sixth, which is the composition of a perfect food. Besides taking part in this composition, the bran, being in a great measure insoluble, passes in bulk through the bowels, assisting daily laxation — a most important consideration. If wheat is such a perfect food, it must follow that wholemeal bread must be best for our daily use. That such is the case, evidence on every side shows; those who eat it are healthier, stronger, and more cheerful than those who do not, all other things being equal. Wholemeal bread comes nearer the standard of a perfect food than does the wheaten grain, as in fermentation some of the starch is destroyed, and thus the proportion of nitrogen is slightly increased.

The next question is, how shall we prepare the grain so as to make the best bread from it? This is done by grinding the grain as finely as possible with stones, and then using the resulting flour for bread-making. The grain should be first cleaned and brushed, and passed over a magnet to cleanse it from any bits of steel or iron it may have acquired from the various processes it goes through, and then finely ground. To ensure fine grinding, it is always advisable to kiln-dry it first. When ground, nothing must be taken from it, nor must anything be added to the flour, and from this bread should be made.

문제 1 Which of the following is immediately dealt with prior to this passage?
(1) Ways to make wheat more nutritious   (2) The average composition of wheat
(3) The characteristics of wheat   (4) How wheat can be made

문제 2 Which of the following is NOT mentioned as the merit of wheat?
(1) healthful   (2) laxative
(3) nutritious   (4) constipation

문제 3 Which of the following is the topic of the second paragraph?
(1) Preparation of the Grain
(2) Making of the Whole-Meal Bread
(3) Process of Making the Grain
(4) Kinds of Grain

문제 4 Which of the following is neither stated nor implied?
(1) Wholemeal bread is healthier than white bread.
(2) The bran helps one go to the bathroom.
(3) Due to fermentation, the proportion of nitrogen in Wholemeal bread increases.
(4) The use of magnet dramatically increases the quality of the grain.

247

[Challenge 7]

Many United States companies have, unfortunately, made the search for legal protection from import competition into a major line of work. Since 1980 the United States International Trade Commission (ITC) has received about 280 complaints alleging damage from imports that benefit from subsidies by foreign governments. Another 340 charge that foreign companies "dumped" their products in the United States at "less than fair value." Even when no unfair practices are alleged, the simple claim that an industry has been injured by imports is sufficient grounds to seek relief.

Contrary to the general impression, this quest for import relief has hurt more companies than it has helped. As corporations begin to function globally, they develop an intricate web of marketing, production, and research relationships. The complexity of these relationships makes it unlikely that a system of import relief laws will meet the strategic needs of all the units under the same parent company.

Internationalization increases the danger that foreign companies will use import relief laws against the very companies the laws were designed to protect. Suppose a United States-owned company establishes an overseas plant to manufacture a product while its competitor makes the same product in the United States. If the competitor can prove injury from the imports and that the United States company received a subsidy from a foreign government to build its plant abroad the United States company's products will be uncompetitive in the United States, since they would be subject to duties.

Perhaps the most brazen case occurred when the ITC investigated allegations that Canadian companies were injuring the United States salt industry by dumping rock salt, used to de-ice roads. The bizarre aspect of the complaint was that a foreign conglomerate with United States operations was crying for help against a United States company with foreign operations. The "United States" company claiming injury was a subsidiary of a Dutch conglomerate, while the "Canadian" companies included a subsidiary of a Chicago firm that was the second-largest domestic producer of rock salt.

문제 1   The passage is chiefly concerned with _____.
   (1) arguing against the increased internationalization of United States corporations
   (2) warning that the application of laws affecting trade frequently has unintended consequences
   (3) demonstrating that foreign-based firms receive more subsidies from their governments than United States firms receive from the United States government
   (4) advocating the use of trade restrictions for "dumped" products but not for other imports
   (5) recommending a uniform method for handling claims of unfair trade practices

문제 2 It can be inferred from the passage that the minimal basis for a complaint to the International Trade Commission is which of the following?
(1) A foreign competitor has received a subsidy from a foreign government.
(2) A foreign competitor has substantially increased the volume of products shipped to the United States.
(3) A foreign competitor is selling products in the United States at less than fair market value.
(4) The company requesting import relief has been injured by the sale of imports in the United States.
(5) The company requesting import relief has been barred from exporting products to the country of its foreign competitor.

문제 3 The last paragraph performs which of the following functions in the passage?
(1) It summarizes the discussion thus far and suggests additional areas of research.
(2) It presents a recommendation based on the evidence presented earlier.
(3) It discusses an exceptional case in which the results expected by the author of the passage were not obtained.
(4) It introduces an additional area of concern not mentioned earlier.
(5) It cites a specific case that illustrates a problem presented more generally in the previous paragraph.

문제 4 The passage warns of which of the following dangers?
(1) Companies in the United States may receive no protection from imports unless they actively seek protection from import competition.
(2) Companies that seek legal protection from import competition may incur legal costs that far exceed any possible gain.
(3) Companies that are United States-owned but operate internationally may not be eligible for protection from import competition under the laws of the countries in which their plants operate.
(4) Companies that are not United States-owned may seek legal protection from import competition under United States import relief laws.
(5) Companies in the United States that import raw materials may have to pay duties on those materials.

[Challenge 8]

The origin of matter out of non-matter is clearly not one of these natural events, because it is an inconceivable phenomenon for which we have no experience whatever that would serve as a guide to understanding it by analogy. It is inconceivable to us that matter never had a beginning; and it is equally inconceivable to us that matter came suddenly into being out of nothing. These are really the only two alternatives, and both are simply inconceivable. Yet one of them must be true.

So scientists accept what amounts to the eternity of matter, inconceivable though that is, simply because the only alternative, direct creation, is clearly incredible to them. In other words, they accept what is inconceivable rather than what is incredible, because they prefer a non-supernatural explanation to what they view as a supernatural one. Having started along this route, they are bound to follow it consistently and thereafter to reject any concept of divine interference unequivocally — indeed, dogmatically. They really have no choice.

문제 1 What is the passage mainly talking about?
    (1) How science understands the origin of matter
    (2) The origin of matter in different academic circles
    (3) Divine interference into the formation of nature
    (4) Pros and Cons of Direct Creation

문제 2 Which of the following is neither stated nor implied in the passage?
    (1) Two different views on the origin of matter are equally inconceivable to human minds.
    (2) A something-out-of-nothing theory has something to do with the concept of divine interference.
    (3) Scientists seek to find a non-supernatural explanation to a phenomenon even if it looks quite supernatural to them.
    (4) Scientists accept findings that can only be 'felt' by any faculty of perception.

[Challenge 9]

Are Aristotle's theories intrinsically gendered and sexist, so that gender cannot be removed without altering the theories themselves? Several feminist philosophers have developed this thesis. For example, in "Woman Is Not a Rational Animal," Lynda Lange argues that Aristotle's theory of sex difference is implicated in every piece of Aristotle's metaphysical jargon, and she concludes that "it is not at all clear that it [Aristotle's theory of sex difference] can simply be cut away without any reflection on the status of the rest of the philosophy." Elizabeth Spelman has argued that Aristotle's politicized metaphysics is reflected in his theory of soul, which, in turn, is used to justify the subordination of women in the Politics. And, finally, Susan Okin has argued that Aristotle's functionalist theory of form was devised by Aristotle in order to _____(a)_____ the political status quo in Athens, including slavery and the inequality of women.

문제 1 Which of the following is the best title for the passage?
(1) An Ardent Advocate of Slavery
(2) Gendered Interpretations of Aristotle
(3) Aristotle's Theory of Politics
(4) Misinterpretations of Aristotle

문제 2 Fill in blank (a).
(1) symbolize
(2) exonerate
(3) fabricate
(4) legitimate

[Challenge 10]

Erik Erikson was born in Frankfurt, Germany and studied psychology under Anna Freud (Sigmund Freud's daughter) at the Vienna Psychoanalytic Institute. He moved to the United States and became a U.S. citizen in 1939 where he taught at several major universities including Harvard, Yale, and the University of California at Berkley. He is most well known for his writings on child psychology. He developed a stage theory much like Sigmund Freud's Stages of Psychosexual development, but rather than sexual impulses, Erikson was concerned more with the social aspects of development. He developed his theory of Psychosocial Development where he divides the human lifespan into eight stages. Through his theories, the term 'identity crisis' was derived, as he saw each stage as having both a negative or a positive outcome, constituting a crisis at each stage of development.

문제 1 What type of writing is the above passage?
(1) Narrative
(2) Biography
(3) Fiction
(4) Obituary

문제 2 According to the passage, which of the following is TRUE of the passage?
(1) Erik Erikson served his apprentice under Sigmund Freud.
(2) Erikson was not on good terms with Sigmund Freud.
(3) Erik Erikson was forced to move to the U.S. by The Nazi.
(4) Erik Erikson coined the word 'identity crisis.'

Day 27

★ God loved the birds and invented trees. Man loved the birds and invented cages.

Jacques Deval

신은 새를 사랑하여 나무를 창조하셨다. 인간은 새를 사랑하여, 새장을 만들었다. (Jacques Deval)

[Challenge 1]

(a) If we were asked to name the most interesting country in the world, I suppose that most people would say Palestine — not because there is anything so very wonderful in the land itself, but because of all the great things that have happened there, and above all because of its having been the home of our Lord. But after Palestine, I think that Egypt would come next. For one thing, it is linked very closely to Palestine by all those beautiful stories of the Old Testament, which tell us of Joseph, the slave-boy who became Viceroy of Egypt; of Moses, the Hebrew child who became a Prince of Pharaoh's household; and of the wonderful exodus of the Children of Israel.

(b) The Pyramids, for instance, those huge piles that are still the wonder of the world, were far older than any building now standing in Europe, before Joseph was sold to be a slave in Potiphar's house. Hundreds of years before anyone had ever heard of the Greeks and the Romans, there were great Kings reigning in Egypt, sending out their armies to conquer Syria and the Soudan, and their ships to explore the unknown southern seas, and wise men were writing books which we can still read. When Britain was a wild, unknown island, inhabited only by savages as fierce and untaught as the South Sea Islanders, Egypt was a great and highly civilized country, full of great cities, with noble palaces and temples, and its people were wise and learned.

(c) But besides that, it is a land which has a most strange and wonderful story of its own. No other country has so long a history of great Kings, and wise men, and brave soldiers; and in no other country can you see anything to compare with the great buildings, some of them most beautiful, all of them most wonderful, of which Egypt has so many. We have some old and interesting buildings in this country, and people go far to see cathedrals and castles that are perhaps five or six hundred years old, or even more; but in Egypt, buildings of that age are looked upon as almost new, and ____(가)____. For the great temples and tombs of Egypt were, many of them, hundreds of years old before the story of our Bible, properly speaking, begins.

문제 1 Choose the right sequence for the above passage.
(1) (a) - (c) - (b)   (2) (b) - (c) - (a)
(3) (c) - (a) - (b)   (4) (b) - (a) - (c)

문제 2 Which of the following is most appropriate for the title for the passage?
(1) Great Cities in Palestine
(2) A Land of Old Renown
(3) Civilized People of Egypt
(4) The Seven Wonders of the World

문제 3 Choose one that is most appropriate for blank (가).
(1) people consider them useless
(2) Egyptians have just built them
(3) nobody pays very much attention to them
(4) they no longer try to build new buildings any more

[Challenge 2]

Exchange is the principal department of political economy, because it is by far the most frequent method of transmitting property, according to the free and voluntary agreements of the laws and effects of which this science treats. Properly speaking, exchange is the reciprocity of services. The parties say between themselves, "Give me this, and I will give you that;" or, "Do this for me, and I will do that for you." It is well to remark (for this will throw a new light on the notion of value) that the second form is always implied in the first. When it is said, "Do this for me, and I will do that for you," an exchange of _____(a)_____ is proposed. Again, when it is said, "Give me this, and I will give you that," it is the same as saying, "I yield to you what I have done, yield to me what you have done." The labour is past, instead of present; but the exchange is not the less governed by the comparative valuation of the two services: so that it is quite correct to say that the principle of value is in the services rendered and received on account of the productions exchanged, rather than _____(b)_____.

문제 1 The intent of the author in the above passage is _____.
(1) To give contrasting ideas of a concept
(2) To remark on the laws of a concept
(3) To give examples of a concept
(4) To offer an alternative definition of an existing concept

253

문제 2 Which of the following is most appropriate for blank (a)?
(1) service for production
(2) service for service
(3) production for service
(4) production for production

문제 3 Which of the following best fills in blank (b)?
(1) in the efforts put into the productions
(2) in the productions themselves
(3) through the contract between the parties
(4) by the prices of each production

[Challenge 3]

Because the spine is made of little bones with cushions between them, it bends easily, and children sometimes bend it more than they ought. If you lean over your book or your writing or any other work, the elastic cushions may get so pressed on the inner edge that they do not easily spring back into shape. In this way, you may grow round-shouldered or hump-backed. This bending over, also cramps the lungs, so that they do not have all the room they need for breathing. While you are young, your bones are easily bent. One shoulder or one hip gets higher than the other, if you stand unevenly. This is more serious, because you are growing, and you may grow crooked (a) before you know it. Now that you know how soft your bones are, and how easily they bend, you will surely be careful to sit and stand erect. Do not twist your legs, or arms, or shoulders; for you want to grow into straight and graceful men and women, instead of being round-shouldered, or hump-backed, or lame, all your lives.

문제 1 Which of the following best represents the title for the passage?
(1) How to Reshape Bad Posture
(2) Care of the Spine
(3) Elasticity of Bones
(4) Bones of Human Beings

문제 2 Which of the following is neither stated nor implied?
(1) Too much bending could cause a breathing problem.
(2) Bones have cushions in them.
(3) It can be said that it is important to educate children on how careful they should be when sitting and standing erect.
(4) Bad posture leads your body to grow crooked.

문제 3 Which of the following best paraphrases the underlined (a)?
(1) ignorantly
(2) illiterately
(3) unwittingly
(4) willingly

[Challenge 4]

Some types of depression run in families, indicating that a _____(a)_____ vulnerability to depression can be inherited. This seems to be the case, especially with bipolar disorder. Families in which members of each generation develop bipolar disorder have been studied. The investigators found that those with the illness have a somewhat different genetic makeup than those who do not become ill. However, _____(b)_____. That is, not everybody with the genetic makeup that causes vulnerability to bipolar disorder will develop the illness. Apparently, additional factors, possibly a stressful environment, are involved in its onset and protective factors are involved in its prevention.

문제 1 Which of the following best fits in blank (a)?
  (1) ecological   (2) biological
  (3) physiological   (4) domestic

문제 2 Which of the following will best fit in blank (b)?
  (1) there is another factor to contribute to it
  (2) this is not the case
  (3) the reverse is not true
  (4) there is a more serious case here

[Challenge 5]

A church, according to Locke, is "a free and voluntary society"; its purpose is the public worship of God; the value of worship depends on the faith that inspires it: "all the life and power of true religion consists in the inward and full persuasion of the mind;" and these matters are entirely outside the jurisdiction of the civil magistrate. Locke therefore (to use later language) was a voluntary in religion, as he was a(an) ____(a)____ on questions of state interference. There is an exception, however, to his doctrine of the freedom of the individual in religious matters. The toleration extended to all others is denied to papists and to atheists; and his inconsistency in this respect has been often and severely criticized. But it is clear that Locke made the exception not for religious reasons but on grounds of state policy. He looked upon the Roman Catholic as dangerous to the public peace because he professed allegiance to a foreign prince; and (b) <u>the atheist was excluded because, on Locke's view, the existence of the state depends upon a contract, and the obligation of the contract, as of all moral law, depends upon the divine will.</u>

문제 1 Fill in blank (a).
    (1) individualist   (2) fundamentalist
    (3) dualist   (4) pluralist

문제 2 Which of the following will best fit in blank (b)?
    (1) there is another factor to contribute to it
    (2) this is not the case
    (3) the reverse is not true
    (4) there is a more serious case here

문제 3 Which of the following is NOT true of the passage?
    (1) A church is a place where people get together on their own initiative.
    (2) The civil magistrate is not in a position to make judgements on church matters.
    (3) There was an exception in his theory of religious toleration.
    (4) His reason to deny atheists is solely based on a religious one.

[Challenge 6]

The discovery of America and the sea route to the East Indies opened up new horizons for trade and exploration. But even vaster horizons came into view in the field of the intellect. The old narrow one-sidedness became impossible. It was necessary to break down all the old barriers in order to get at the truth. As in all revolutionary epochs, at this time there was a burning desire to know.

문제 1 Which of the following is LEAST likely to be inferred from the passage?
    (1) Many of the goods from the Ease Indies might have flooded into Europe at the time.
    (2) A big change happened in the field of the intellect.
    (3) The old way of thinking was confronted with new ideas.
    (4) All the people, regardless of their color and social background, went to the school to learn new ideas.

[Challenge 7]

For Locke, civil and political rights accrued to human beings as gifts from their Creator. But God is seldom invoked today to justify first-generation rights. Instead, they are grounded in the view that human beings are basically autonomous individuals. And if I am indeed essentially an autonomous individual, it is easy to understand and appreciate my demands that ceteris paribus neither the state nor anyone else abridge my freedom to choose my own ends and means, so long as I similarly respect the civil and political rights of all others. But on what grounds can autonomous individuals demand a job, or health care, or an education — the second-generation rights — from other autonomous individuals? There is a logical gap here, which no one has successfully _____(a)_____ yet: from the mere premise of being an autonomous individual, no conclusion can follow that I have a right to employment. Something more is needed, but it is by no means clear what that something might be, unless it conflicted with the view of human beings as basically autonomous individuals.

문제 1 Which of the following best represents the main idea of the passage?
(1) Locke's concept of civil and political rights as gifts from God is well-grounded.
(2) The premise of being autonomous individuals does not provide an effective grounding for civil and political rights.
(3) Under no circumstances can my freedom to choose my own ends and means be abridged.
(4) No one can deprive the right to employment from any autonomous individuals.

문제 2 Which of the following is NOT true of the passage?
(1) There is a logical flaw in asking for a right to employment from others based on autonomous individuals.
(2) For Locke, all human beings are born with civil and political rights.
(3) With the assumption that human beings are autonomous, no one can deprive me of my freedom to choose my ends and means under any situation.
(4) Today, Locke's concept of civil and political rights as gifts from God is seldom used

문제 3 Which of the following best fills in blank (a)?
(1) made   (2) widened
(3) paid   (4) bridged

[Challenge 8]

Federal bankruptcy laws govern how companies go out of business or recover from crippling debt. A bankrupt company, the "debtor," might use Chapter 11 of the Bankruptcy Code to "reorganize" its business and try to become profitable again. Management continues to run the day-to-day business operations but all significant business decisions must be approved by a bankruptcy court. Most publicly-held companies will file under Chapter 11 rather than Chapter 7 because they can still run their business and control the bankruptcy process. Chapter 11 provides a process for rehabilitating the company's faltering business. Sometimes the company successfully works out a plan to return to profitability; sometimes, in the end, it liquidates. Under a Chapter 11 reorganization, a company usually keeps doing business and its stock and bonds may continue to trade in our securities markets.

문제 1   Which of the following can be inferred from the passage?
(1) The business which files chapter 7 is most likely to cease operations.
(2) Companies under chapter 7 still run the business operations.
(3) Companies under chapter 11 can not perform any business transactions unless the Federal bankruptcy laws permit.
(4) Firms which filed under Chapter 11 are usually considered as "unrecoverable status."

[Challenge 9]

A-not-B error is a phenomenon uncovered by the work of Jean Piaget in his theory of cognitive development of children. The A-not-B error is a particular error made by infants during sub-stage 4 of their sensorimotor stage. A typical task goes like this: An experimenter hides an attractive toy under box "A" within the baby's reach. The baby searches for the toy, looks under box "A", and finds the toy. This activity is usually repeated several times (always with the researcher hiding the toy under box "A"). Then, in the critical trial, the experimenter moves the toy under box "B", also within easy reach of the baby. Babies of 10 months or younger typically make the perseverance error, meaning they look under box "A" even though they saw the researcher move the toy under box "B", and box "B" is just as easy to reach. This demonstrates a lack of, or incomplete, schema of object permanence. Children of 12 months or older typically do not make this error.

문제 1   Which of the following is correct about the error in the above passage?
   (1) This phenomenon explains why the child sees an image and remembers where it was, rather than where it is.
   (2) A-not-B error without exception happens to every single child.
   (3) A-not-B error is so critical that if a child forms a negative image of this, he or she will be 'stuck' with this stage and never move on to the next one.
   (4) To experiment the error, it needs at least two experimenters to perform it at different times.

[Challenge 10]

Durkheim's views on crime were a departure from conventional notions. He believed that crime is "bound up with the fundamental conditions of all social life" and serves a social function. He stated that crime implies, "not only that the way remains open to necessary change, but that in certain cases it directly proposes these changes... crime [can thus be] a useful prelude to reforms." In this sense he saw crime as being able to release certain social tensions and so have a cleansing or purging effect in society. He further stated that "the authority which the moral conscience enjoys must not be excessive; otherwise, no-one would dare to criticize it, and it would too easily congeal into an immutable form. To make progress, individual originality must be able to express itself...[even] the originality of the criminal... shall also be possible."

문제 1   What is the purpose of the passage?
   (1) To explain a new understanding of an existing concept
   (2) To introduce a new phenomenon
   (3) To make a comparison between the existing concept and the new one
   (4) To explain the importance of discussing the topic

문제 2   Which of the following is NOT correct from the passage?
   (1) Individual originality must be expressed freely to provide the basis for social progress.
   (2) Durkheim went further by saying crime can be a positive social force to serve as a prelude to reforms.
   (3) The level of tension that is immanent in a society can be measured by the number of and the degree of crimes that society has.
   (4) Since crimes have a cleansing or purging effect in a society, they need to be encouraged.

Day 28

★ The more alternatives, the more difficult the choice.

Abbe' D'Allanival

대안이 많을수록, 선택은 더욱 어려워진다. (Abbe' D'Allanival)

[Challenge 1]

Economists have urged the use of "market-based" instruments such as emissions trading to address environmental problems instead of _____(a)_____ "command and control" regulation. Command and control regulation is criticized for being excessively rigid, insensitive to geographical and technological differences, and for being inefficient. However, emissions trading requires a cap to effectively reduce emissions, and the cap is a government regulatory mechanism. After a cap has been set by a government political process, individual companies are free to choose how or if they will reduce their emissions. Failure to reduce emissions is often punishable by a further government regulatory mechanism, a fine that increases costs of production. Firms will choose the least-costly way to comply with the pollution regulation, which will lead to reductions where the least expensive solutions exist, while _____(b)_____ emissions that are more expensive to reduce.

문제 1 According to the passage, which of the following is CORRECT about the passage?
  (1) Each economic entity has to pay a fine everytime they produce pollution.
  (2) Emissions trading is a market-based approach to reducing the amount of CO_2 produced in the market.
  (3) The government will use the fine collected from polluters to improve the existing air purification system.
  (4) The increased costs of production will make a firm comply more with the government policy of reducing emissions.

문제 2 Choose one that is most appropriate for blanks (a) and (b).
  (1) prescriptive - allowing
  (2) selective - permitting
  (3) fastidious - denying
  (4) discerning - reducing

[Challenge 2]

The existentialists' lack of interest in poetry (which, in the case of Sartre especially, turns into outright dismissal) is based on their view that poets make a misguided use of language. For the same reason, the other non-discursive arts attract almost as little interest as poetry. Yet, when they are discussed, they are treated more favourably than poetry, since they do not have language as their medium, and this means that the accusation against poetry becomes irrelevant. The emphasis on language as the eminent medium for the representation of human freedom reproduces a classical argument that is already at the heart of Hegel's aesthetics (a fact that the existentialists are fully aware of). The implication for the other arts is that they are able to produce and convey ideal contents, meaning and beauty, but that these are never as transparently accessed as in linguistic expression. Rather, the ideal content in non-linguistic art-forms remains trapped in the materiality of the artwork. Notes, colours, and forms are not signs. They refer to nothing exterior to themselves. As Merleau-Ponty has pointed out in The Phenomenology of Perception, "the dim little meaning which dwells within it remains immanent or trembles about like a mist; it is colour or sound."

문제 1 According to the view of existentialists, which of the following is the best medium to express human freedom?
(1) emblems
(2) visuality
(3) actions
(4) words

문제 2 Which of the following is most relevant to the argument of existentialists?
(1) Non-discursive arts can reach a higher level of aesthetics when accompanied by poetry.
(2) Paintings are better qualified to express one's thought since actions speak louder than words.
(3) Non-linguistic arts can be as expressive as language.
(4) It is one thing to work with colour and sound, and another to express oneself by means of words.

[Challenge 3]

Some thought that moderate living and the avoidance of all superfluity would preserve them from the epidemic. They formed small communities, living entirely separate from everybody else. They shut themselves up in houses where there were no sick, eating the finest food and drinking the best wine very temperately, avoiding all excess, allowing no news or discussion of death and sickness, and passing the time in music and suchlike pleasures. Others thought just the opposite. They thought the sure cure for the plague was to drink and be merry, to go about singing and amusing themselves, satisfying every appetite they could, laughing and jesting at what happened. They put their words into practice, spent day and night going from tavern to tavern, drinking immoderately, or went into other people's houses, doing only those things which pleased them. This they could easily do because everyone felt doomed and had abandoned his property, so that most houses became _____(a)_____ and any stranger who went in made use of them as if he had owned them. And with all this bestial behaviour, they avoided the sick as much as possible. Many others adopted a course of life midway between the two just described. They did not restrict their victuals so much as the former, nor allow themselves to be drunken and dissolute like the latter, but satisfied their appetites moderately. They did not shut themselves up, but went about, carrying flowers or scented herbs or perfumes in their hands, in the belief that it was an excellent thing to comfort the brain with such odours; for the whole air was infected with the smell of dead bodies, of sick persons and medicines.

문제 1 Which of the following is the best title for the passage?
　　　　(1) Sure Cures for the Plague
　　　　(2) Varying Reactions to Disaster
　　　　(3) Why People Abandon Themselves to Liquor
　　　　(4) How the Disaster Changed the Way People Think about Life

문제 2 Fill in blank (a).
　　　　(1) subsequently haunted　　　　(2) severely infected
　　　　(3) the hotbed of crime　　　　(4) common property

[Challenge 4]

　In 1837, my father being a member of the school committee of the Union township, Washington county, secured equal salaries for women; and in spite of steady opposition, there was no difference made for four years. The women who taught the schools in the summer were paid the same as the men who taught in the winter. At the death of my father the board returned to the old system of half pay for women; the result was "incompetent teachers," furnishing the opposition with just the plea they desired — that women were not fit for school teachers. My mother (a) <u>remonstrated</u>, but in vain. They replied, "women never received as much as men for any work" and moreover, these school matters belonged to men, and women had no right to interfere. In 1842, my mother offered to board the teacher in her district, gratis, if the board would raise her salary proportionally. They received her proposition with scorn. She then refused to pay her taxes. Such was the respect for her in the community, and the sense of justice in regard to the teachers, that the authorities _____(b)_____, and at the end of the year accepted the proposition, and for many years after, she boarded the teacher in her district, making the woman's net salary equal to that of the man.

문제 1 According to the passage, which of the following is neither stated nor implied?
(1) It was not uncommon in 1837 for women to be paid less than men at the same workplace.
(2) For at least four years starting from 1837 there was a sense of equality in salary for men and women across the board.
(3) In 1837 in the United States patriarchism was well spread across the country.
(4) In the early 1800s, there was significant opposition to women being teachers, reflecting a broader belief that women's involvement in school matters was inappropriate.

문제 2 Choose one that is closest in meaning to the underlined (a).
(1) picketed   (2) manifested
(3) demoted   (4) protested

문제 3 Choose one that best fills in blank (b).
(1) warned her to get the things right   (2) had her pay the tax
(3) suffered the tax to go unpaid   (4) paid extra respect to her

[Challenge 5]

(가) The New York floated toward the White Star ship, and would have rammed the new ship had not the tugs Vulcan and Neptune stopped her and towed (a) her back to the quay. When (b) the mammoth ship touched at Cherbourg and later at Queenstown she was again the object of a port ovation and thousands gazed in wonder at her stupendous proportions.

(나) After taking aboard some additional passengers at each port, the Titanic headed (c) her towering bow toward the open sea and the race for a record on her maiden voyage was begun.

(다) The big vessel had, however, a touch of evil fortune before (d) she cleared the harbor of Southampton.

(라) As she passed down stream, her immense bulk drew the waters after her with an irresistible suction that tore the American liner New York from her moorings; seven steel hawsers were snapped like twine.

문제 1 Choose one that is put in order.
(1) (다) – (라) – (가) – (나)   (2) (라) – (다) – (가) – (나)
(3) (라) – (가) – (나) – (다)   (4) (가) – (나) – (다) – (라)

문제 2 Which of the following does NOT refer to the same item?
(1) (a)   (2) (b)
(3) (c)   (4) (d)

[Challenge 6]

The history of mathematics may be instructive as well as agreeable; it may not only remind us of what we have, but may also teach us how to increase our store. Says De Morgan, The early history of the mind of men with regard to mathematics leads us to point out our own errors; and in this respect it is well to pay attention to the history of mathematics. It warns us against hasty conclusions; it points out the importance of a good notation upon the progress of the science; it discourages ___(a)___ specialization on the part of investigators, by showing how apparently distinct branches have been found to possess unexpected connecting links; it saves the student from wasting time and energy upon problems which were, perhaps, solved long since; it discourages him from attacking an unsolved problem by the same method which has led other mathematicians to failure.

문제 1 What is the best title for the passage?
(1) The Usefulness of The History of Mathematics
(2) Pros and Cons of Mathematics
(3) Dangers to Being too "Mathematical"
(4) Achievements of De Morgan In The History of Mathematics

문제 2 Which of the following best describes the development of the passage?
(1) General statements are presented and illustrated with specific details.
(2) In details, two conflicting ideas are presented and discussed in what way they are different.
(3) A specific story of a person is put forth at first and generalization is made at the end of the story.
(4) The cause of something is analyzed and the results of the occurrence are described.

문제 3 Fill in blank (a).
(1) disinterested   (2) excessive
(3) poised   (4) unbiased

[Challenge 7]

Learning can be defined as the process leading to relatively permanent behavioral change or potential behavioral change. _____(a)_____, as we learn, we alter the way we perceive our environment, the way we interpret the incoming stimuli, and therefore the way we interact, or behave. John B. Watson (1878-1958) was the first to study how the process of learning affects our behavior, and he formed the school of thought known as Behaviorism. The central idea behind behaviorism is that only observable behaviors are worthy of research since other abstraction such as a person's mood or thoughts are too subjective. This belief was dominant in psychological research in the United Stated for a good 50 years.

Perhaps the most well known Behaviorist is B. F. Skinner (1904-1990). Skinner followed much of Watson's research and findings, but believed that internal states could influence behavior just as external stimuli. He is considered to be a Radical Behaviorist because of this belief, although nowadays it is believed that both internal and external stimuli influence our behavior.

문제 1 What is the passage mainly talking about?
  (1) Learning and Behaviorism   (2) History of Behaviorism
  (3) Life of John B. Watson   (4) A Radical Behaviorist: B. F. Skinner

문제 2 Fill in blank (a).
  (1) To sum up   (2) In other words
  (3) On the other hand   (4) As a matter of fact

문제 3 Which of the following is TRUE of the passage?
  (1) All behaviorists believe that our behavior is only triggered by external stimuli.
  (2) B. F. Skinner did not agree with any of John B. Watson's theory because he thought internal factors as well as external stimuli could influence behavior.
  (3) According to behaviorism, people are much like a machine that only responds to outer environments.
  (4) John B. Watson thought human minds are not pertinent to objective research.

[Challenge 8]

To say that the American is an idealist is to commit a thoroughgoing platitude. Like most platitudes, the statement is annoying because from one point of view it is indisputably just, while from another it does not seem to fit the facts. With regard to our tradition, it is indisputable. Of the immigrants who since the seventeenth century have been pouring into this continent a proportion large in number, larger still in influence, has been possessed of motives which in part at least were idealistic. If it was not the desire for religious freedom that urged them, it was the desire for personal freedom. And of course all these motives were strongest in that earlier immigration which has done most to fix the state of mind and body which we call being American. I need not labor the argument. Our political and social history support it; our best literature demonstrates it, for no men have been more idealistic than the American writers whom we have consented to call great. Emerson, Thoreau, Hawthorne, Whitman — was idealism ever more thoroughly incarnate than in them?

And this idealism has been in the air of America. It has permeated our religious sects, and created several of them. It has given tone to our thinking, and even more to our feeling. But optimism, muck-raking (not all of its manifestations are pretty), social service, religious, municipal, democratic reform is evidence of the vigor, the bumptiousness of the inherited American tendency to pursue the ideal. No one can doubt that in 1918 we believed, at least, in idealism. Nevertheless, so far as the average individual is concerned, with just his share and no more of the race-tendency, this idealism has been suppressed, and in some measure perverted.

문제 1 The author thinks that _____.
(1) on an individual level, idealism is shown much stronger than on a national level
(2) the current warped idealism was fostered by some of the writers the people think highly of
(3) it is no doubt that the idealism was clearly embodied in American literature
(4) the fraction within the religious sects caused the country to be in divisiveness

문제 2 According to the passage, which of the following is the main cause of the distorted idealism?
(1) selfishness   (2) altruism
(3) philanthropism   (4) atheism

[Challenge 9]

There are two major ways people become infected with MRSA. The first is physical contact with someone who is either infected or is a carrier of MRSA. The second way is for people to physically contact MRSA on any objects such as door handles, floors, sinks, or towels that have been touched by a MRSA-infected person or carrier. Normal skin tissue in people usually does not allow MRSA infection to develop; however, if there are cuts, abrasions, or other skin flaws such as psoriasis (a chronic inflammatory skin disease with dry patches, redness, and scaly skin), MRSA may proliferate. Many otherwise healthy individuals, especially children and young adults, do not notice small skin imperfections or scrapes and may be lax in taking precautions about skin contacts. This is the likely reason MRSA outbreaks occur in diverse types of people such as school team players (like football players or wrestlers), dormitory residents, and armed-services personnel in constant close contact.

People with higher risk of MRSA infection are those with obvious skin breaks (for example, patients with surgical or traumatic wounds or hospital patients with burns, or skin ulcers) and people with (a) <u>depressed</u> immune systems (infants, the elderly, or HIV-infected individuals) or those with chronic diseases (diabetes or cancer). People with pneumonia (lung infection) due to MRSA can transmit MRSA by airborne droplets. Health-care workers as a group are repeatedly exposed to MRSA-positive patients and can have a high rate of infection if precautions are not taken. Consequently, health-care workers and patient visitors should use disposable masks, gowns, and gloves when they enter the MRSA-infected patient's room.

문제 1 Which of the following is the best title for the passage?
(1) How is MRSA Infection Transmitted or Spread?
(2) Characteristics of MRSA
(3) Effects of MRSA on Healthy People
(4) Ways to Prevent the Deadly Infection, MRSA

문제 2 Which of the following is CORRECT about MRSA?
(1) There are people who are not infected but rather colonized with the bacteria on their body.
(2) Most people are well aware of the deadliness of MRSA so they usually take precautions against it.
(3) People get infected by physical contact but not through the air.
(4) The outbreak usually takes place even by one-time exposure to MRSA-positive people.

문제 3 Choose one that is closest in meaning to the underlined (a).
(1) weakened   (2) constrained
(3) oppressed   (4) contained

[Challenge 10]

Forty years ago, before I read any of the works mentioned here or conducted any interviews for television on environmental issues, I was introduced to organic gardening and farming as a student. In the United Kingdom I had the privilege of studying agronomy and working as a gardener and composter with men dedicated to the organic tradition. The people I learned from did what they did because it had a biblical basis. For example, the farming program included the observance of the sabbatical year — a year of rest for the land every seventh year. This is an ecological law established long ago. Further, it demands faith to deliberately avoid planting or harvesting with only the promise that there will be sufficient food in the sixth year to cover the seventh and eighth years. Chapter 25 of the book of Leviticus spells out the law and the promised benefits. As Berry indicates above, there are biblical precepts that require of us conservation, care for the environment, love of land, balance, harmony and personal growth. His mention of the instruction to Adam to dress and keep the garden in which he had been placed is a reference to one of the first ecological principles in the Bible. It's significant that this book of human origins has a statement about how we should relate to the natural world around us. The Hebrew words for dress (abad) and keep (shamar) indicate working and guarding, cultivating and protecting. Certainly there is no suggestion of exploiting and ruining. The often-quoted reference to Genesis 1:26 about humans being given dominion over all of creation is to a beneficent leadership role, not a dominating or domineering one. They are expected to do so with care and love and wisdom.

문제 1 Which of the following is the best theme of the passage?
(1) How Environmentalists Interpret God's Instruction to Adam
(2) Biblical Basis of Environmentalism
(3) Books On Environmentalism
(4) Different Understandings of Genesis 1:26

문제 2 Which of the following is CORRECT about the passage?
(1) The depiction of human beings as 'exploiter' is not correct.
(2) God's instruction to Adam concerning the environment is vague.
(3) If there is not enough food, the Bible allows men to plant and harvest even on the seventh year.
(4) Methods of organic gardening and farming are well instructed in the Bible.

Day 29

★ If you limit your choices only to what seems possible or reasonable, you disconnect yourself from what you truly want, and all that is left is a compromise.

Robert Fritz

만약 당신이 가능하거나 이성적으로 보이는 것에만 선택의 범위를 제한 한다면, 당신은 진정으로 원하는 것을 놓치게 되고, 남은 것은 타협뿐이다. (Robert Fritz)

[Challenge 1]

Religion is experience. It is the response of man's nature to his highest inspirations. It is his intercourse with Being above himself and his world. Religion is normal experience. Its enemies call it "an indelible superstition," (a) and its friends assert that man is born believing. That a few persons, here and there, appear to lack the sense for the Invisible is like the fact that occasionally a man is found to be _____(b)_____. Mr. Lecky has written, "That religious instincts are as truly part of our natures as are our appetites and our nerves is a fact which all history establishes, and which forms one of the strongest proofs of the reality of that unseen world to which the soul of man continually tends." Some have sought to discredit religion as a surviving childishness. A baby is dependent upon its parents; and babyish spirits, they say, never outgrow this sense of dependence, but transfer that on which they rely from the seen to the unseen. While, however, other childish things, like ghosts and fairies, can be put away, man seems to be "incurably religious," and the most completely devout natures, although childlike in their attitude towards God, give no impression of immaturity. Its indestructible vitality is evidence that it is an inherent element in human nature, that the unbeliever is a subnormal man.

문제 1 Which of the following sentences contains the same function as the underlined (a)?

(1) There are some indispensible things <u>and</u> others that can be done without.
(2) I cooked lunch. <u>And</u> I made a cake.
(3) I like city life but there are cities <u>and</u> cities.
(4) Go <u>and</u> get me a pen please.

문제 2 Which of the following phrases is most appropriate for blank (b)?

(1) completely dependent on himself

(2) color-blind or without an ear for music

(3) deprived of his intellect to recognize the presence of God

(4) religious to the concept of God

문제 3 Which of the following would be the least likely comment the author would make concerning religion?

(1) Man is born with a disposition to walk with God in every moment of his life.

(2) Religion is a kind of bridge that connects human beings to the Omnipotent.

(3) Religion is an indispensible part of human nature.

(4) Religion is not a reality but rather has some profound impact on human beings.

[Challenge 2]

Robert Bruce, King of Scotland, sad and weary, lay upon the floor of a lonely cave among the hills. His mind was full of anxious thoughts, for he was hiding from the English soldiers (a) who sought to take him — alive or dead — to their king. The brave Scots had lost many battles, and Bruce began to fear that he would never make his dear country free. "I will (b) give up try," said he. Just then a spider, hanging from the roof of the cave, by a long thread, swung before the king's eyes, and he left his gloomy thoughts to see what the little creature would do. The spider began to climb its thread slowly, pulling itself up little by little; but it had gone only a short way, when it slipped and fell to the end once more. Again and again it started to climb, and again and again it slipped back, until it had fallen six times. "Surely the silly little creature will now give up trying to climb (c) a so fine thread," thought Bruce. But the spider did no such thing. It started on its upward journey yet a seventh time, and this time it did not fall. Up it went, inch by inch, higher and higher, until at last it reached the roof, and was safely at home. "Bravo!" cried the king. "The spider has taught me a lesson. I too will try until I win." Bruce kept his word. He led his brave men to battle, again and again, until at last the English (d) were driven back to their own land, and Scotland was free.

문제 1 Which of the following is the best title for the above passage?

(1) A Country At a Crisis   (2) The Miracles of the Spider

(3) Bruce and the Spider   (4) Reclaim for the Lost Country

문제 2 The tone of the passage is _____.

(1) didactic   (2) advisory   (3) explanatory   (4) analytic

문제 3 Which of the underlined expressions is awkward when revised?
(1) (a) who sought to take him — ,who sought to take him
(2) (b) give up try — give up trying
(3) (c) a so fine thread — so fine a thread
(4) (d) were driven back to — was driven back to

[Challenge 3]

The mind's ability to "think in sound" has been an important issue for musical achievement for some time. For example, the private trumpet teacher might encourage a student to "hear" a musical line internally before playing it to improve the quality of performance. A general music specialist can often encourage a sixth grade class to "remember" a musical passage during a listening lesson in order to compare the passage to an occurrence later. Conducting teachers encourage students to "imagine" the sound of a score before rehearsal. This ability to internally imagine sound meaningfully is not only important for music achievement and convergent tasks (tasks designed to yield a single right answer), but is also critical for creative thinking ability and specifically for divergent tasks (tasks for which several answers are possible). What is of interest is the encouragement of imaginative, divergent thinking in the classroom, rehearsal hall and the private studio. It is this imaginative problem solving with musical sound that plays such an important role in the creative process and that has captured the attention of many music professionals interested in the formal study of creativity. Ironically, it is precisely this kind of thinking that is so often not stressed by music teachers — often ignored in favor of factual or skill-oriented content. Factual information is, of course, critical for imaginative thinking, but we must provide students with opportunities for applying this conceptual understanding in creative tasks.

문제 1 What is the passage mainly talking about?
(1) Difference between Factual and Imaginative Information
(2) Musical Imaginative Thinking
(3) Imagination in Classroom
(4) Results of Musical Thinking

문제 2 Which of the following are NOT typical questions and statements that encourage imaginative, divergent thinking?
(1) Imagine what it would sound like without the strings — with just the tuba and piccolo playing together.
(2) Clarinets, imagine what that fugue subject would sound like if it had been written a century later.
(3) Play the piece repetitively so that you can later play it by ear.
(4) Think of what it would sound like without the strings — with just the tuba and piccolo playing together.

[Challenge 4]

Most of the literature that has its origin in the life and career of a great man may be grouped and classified under two heads: history and biography. The part that relates to the man's actions, and to the influence that such actions have had in shaping the destinies of peoples and states, belongs in the one class; while the part that derives its interest mainly from the man's personality, and deals chiefly with the mental and moral characteristics of which his actions were the outcome, goes properly into the other. The value of the literature included in these two classes depends almost wholly upon truth; that is, upon the precise ____(a)____ of the statements made with the real facts of the man's life and career. History is worse than useless if it does not accurately chronicle and describe events; and biography is valueless and misleading if it does not truly set forth individual character.

문제 1 When the passage is divided into two, what is the topic of the second paragraph?
(1) Moral Characteristics of Biography
(2) A Man's Action and its Consequences
(3) Absolute Condition of History and Biography
(4) Factors Affecting History

문제 2 Fill in blank (a).
(1) correspondence   (2) consequence
(3) equivocation   (4) elusion

[Challenge 5]

In his theoretical writings, Bourdieu employs some terminology of economics to analyze the processes of social and cultural reproduction, of how the various forms of capital tend to transfer from one generation to the next. For Bourdieu, formal education represents the key example of this process. Educational success, according to Bourdieu, entails a whole range of cultural behaviour, extending to ostensibly non-academic features like gait, dress, or accent. Privileged children have learned this behaviour, as have their teachers. Children of unprivileged backgrounds have not. The children of privilege therefore fit the pattern of their teachers' expectations with apparent 'ease'; they are 'docile'. The unprivileged are found to be 'difficult', to present 'challenges'. Yet both behave as their upbringing dictates. Bourdieu regards this 'ease', or 'natural' ability — distinction — as in fact the product of a great social labour, largely on the part of the parents. It equips their children with the dispositions of manner as well as thought which ensure they are able to succeed within the educational system and can then reproduce their parents' class position in the wider social system.

문제 1 Which of the following is the main idea of the passage?
(1) Social and cultural reproduction is maintained through formal education.
(2) Educational success is the most desirable goal of all human beings.
(3) The children of privilege have a better understanding of reality than the unprivileged.
(4) The current educational system is only geared toward perpetuating the existing social structure that feeds the avarice of the privileged.

문제 2 Which of the following is neither stated nor implied in the passage?
(1) The entitlement of higher education serves to maintain the social position of the privileged.
(2) Social and cultural reproduction is a product of social labour.
(3) Formal education plays a significant role in reproducing a certain class position in the social system.
(4) Educational success facilitates social mobility.

[Challenge 6]

Each of these facts — the child's immaturity and his ignorance — might serve as a basis for a science of education. The first would emphasize the capacities of the human being, their order of development and their laws of growth and action. The second would involve _____(a)_____, and how they are discovered, developed, and perfected. Each of these sciences would necessarily involve the other, as a study of powers involves a knowledge of their products, and a study of effects includes a survey of causes.

문제 1 Which of the following best fills in blank (a)?
(1) the child's obliviousness to his surroundings
(2) a study of the various branches of human knowledge
(3) the intervention of the parents to give knowledge to the child
(4) perfecting developmental milestones of each stage of growth

[Challenge 7]

At the beginning of this book a reference was made to the great upheaval in European history called the "Renaissance" or Revival of Learning. In 1453 the Turks took Constantinople, driving the Greek scholars to take refuge in Italy, which at once became the most civilized nation in Europe. Poetry, philosophy, and art thence found their way to France, England, and Germany, being greatly assisted by the invention of printing, which just then was beginning to make books cheaper than they ever had been. At the same time feudalism was ruined, because the invention of gunpowder had previously been changing the art of war. _____(a)_____, the King of France, Louis XI, as well as the King of England, Henry VII, had entire disposal of the national artillery; and therefore overawed the barons and armored knights. Neither moated fortresses nor mail-clad warriors, nor archers with bows and arrows, could prevail against powder and shot. The middle ages had come to an end; modern Europe was being born. France had become concentrated by the union of the south to the north on the conclusion of the "Hundred Years' War," the final expulsion of the English, and the abolition of all the great feudatories of the kingdom. England, at the same time, had entirely swept away the rule of the barons by the recent "Wars of the Roses," and Henry had strengthened his position by alliance with France, Spain, and Scotland. Spain, by the expulsion of the Moors from Granada in A. D. 1492, was for the first time concentrated into one great state by the union of Isabella's Kingdom of Castile-Leon to Ferdinand's Kingdom of Aragon-Sicily.

문제 1   Which of the following is the best title for the passage?
   (1) Quickening of a New World
   (2) Rebuilding of Feudalism
   (3) Abolition of Centralization
   (4) Wars in Europe

문제 2   According to the passage, which of the following is neither stated nor implied?
   (1) The Turks' ruling in Constantinople favorably served Italy because of the Greek Scholars from Constantinople.
   (2) The invention of printing made books available to more people than before.
   (3) The invention of gunpowder changed the whole face of warfare, which gave rise to the breakdown of feudalism.
   (4) Henry tried to strengthen his position by means of decentralization of power.

문제 3   Fill in blank (a).
   (1) In other words   (2) For example
   (3) On the other hand   (4) In a nutshell

[Challenge 8]

Anything we do to change ourselves, which makes us more productive employees in the future, or that we benefit from in other ways in the future, is an investment in human capital. An obvious example is education. Another example is preventive health care. When we get health care that keeps us healthy in the future, so that we miss fewer days of work and are more productive (and enjoy life more in the future), that is an investment in human capital. One way to increase production is to increase the quantity of resources available. Of these (가) three resources, the supply of labor and capital can be increased. By contrast, the quantity of land and natural resources on the planet cannot be increased. It is true that we can discover more natural resources — even if we cannot, like Columbus, discover a new supply of agricultural land on this planet. Discovery is not quite the same thing as creation, though; we can discover, but cannot create, more land and natural resources. We can create more capital and give birth to more labor. An increase in the population increases the supply of labor, but, as the saying goes, every additional person is also an additional mouth to feed. So increase of the population will not lead to a higher standard of living — a more wealthy nation — in and of itself. It may lead to a declining standard of living instead. __(나)__, an increase in the supply of capital means that each worker has more tools to work with, and can be more productive. That can lead to a higher standard of living — to economic growth.

문제 1 Which of the following is NOT the best way to improve a standard of living mentioned in the passage?
(1) Health care
(2) Education
(3) Higher quality of labor
(4) Increase of the population

문제 2 Out of the three sources in the underlined (가), which of the following best promotes the economic growth?
(1) An increase in the quantity of land
(2) An increase in population
(3) An increase in the supply of capital
(4) An increase in natural resources

문제 3 Fill in blank (나).
(1) On the other hand
(2) Therefore
(3) Still
(4) In addition

[Challenge 9]

　According to Chinese historians Buddhism was officially recognized in China about 67 A.D. A few years before that date, the emperor, Ming-Ti, saw in a dream a large golden image with a halo hovering above his palace. His advisers, some of whom were no doubt already favorable to the new religion, interpreted the image of the dream to be that of Buddha, the great sage of India. Following their advice the emperor sent an embassy to study into Buddhism. (가) It brought back two Indian monks and a quantity of Buddhist classics. (나) These were carried on a white horse and so the monastery which the emperor built for the monks and those who came after them was called the White Horse Monastery. (다) Its tablet is said to have survived to this day.

　This dream story is worth repeating because it goes to show that Buddhism was not only known at an early date, but was favored at the court of China. (라) This is not at all surprising, because an acquaintance with Buddhism was the inevitable _____(b)_____ of the military campaigning, the many embassies and the wide-ranging trade of those centuries. But the introduction of Buddhism into China was especially promoted by reason of the current policy of the Chinese government of moving conquered populations in countries west of China into China proper. The vanquished peoples brought their own religion along with them. At one time what is now the province of Shansi was populated in this way by the Hsiung-nu, many of whom were Buddhists.

문제 1　Which of the following is CORRECT about the passage?
　　(1) Buddha welcomed the embassy from China and sent them back with many of his classics.
　　(2) Buddhism was an indigenous religion of China.
　　(3) It was the people of China that welcomed Buddhism, not the court of China.
　　(4) The immigrant policy of China helped spread Buddhism in China.

문제 2　Where does the sentence below best fit in the passage?

> In fact, the same history which relates the dream contains the biography of an official who became an adherent of Buddhism a few years before the dream took place.

　　(1) (가)　　　　　　　　　　(2) (나)
　　(3) (다)　　　　　　　　　　(4) (라)

문제 3　Choose one that is most appropriate for blank (b)?
　　(1) integration　　　　　　(2) concomitant
　　(3) convergence　　　　　 (4) atrocity

[Challenge 10]

People who wonder if they should talk to their health professional about whether or not they have depression may consider taking a depression self-test, which asks questions about depressive symptoms. In thinking about when to seek medical advice about depression, the sufferer can benefit from considering if the sadness lasts more than two weeks or so or if the way they are feeling significantly interferes with their ability to function at home, school, or work and in their relationships with others. The first step to obtaining appropriate treatment is accurate diagnosis, which requires a complete physical and psychological evaluation to determine whether the person may have a depressive illness, and if so, what type. As previously mentioned, certain medications, as well as some medical conditions, can cause symptoms of depression. _____(a)_____, the examining physician should rule out (exclude) these possibilities through an interview, physical examination, and laboratory tests. Many primary-care doctors use screening tools for depression, which are usually (b) <u>questionnaires</u> that help identify people who have symptoms of depression and may need to receive a full mental-health evaluation.

문제 1 What is the passage mainly talking about?
   (1) Types of Diagnosis
   (2) How is Depression Diagnosed?
   (3) Steps to Cure Depression
   (4) Benefits of Depression Self-Test

문제 2 Choose one that best fits in blank (a)?
   (1) However
   (2) In addition
   (3) Therefore
   (4) As a matter of fact

문제 3 Which of the following questions would be inappropriate for the questionnaires as in the underlined (b)?
   (1) When did the symptoms start, and have they gotten any worse since then?
   (2) Why did you not contact your health professional when you knew you had the symptoms?
   (3) How severe are the symptoms now?
   (4) Have the symptoms occurred before, and if so, were they treated and what treatment did they receive?

Day 30

★ All truths are easy to understand once they are discovered; the point is to discover them.

Galileo Galilei (1564 - 1642)

모든 진실은 일단 그것이 발견되고 나면 이해하기 쉽다. 중요한 것은 이것을 (먼저) 발견하는 것이다. (Galileo Galilei)

[Challenge 1]

Bears will often continue on the road in front of the palanquin for a mile or two, tumbling and playing all sorts of antics, as if ____(a)____. But I believe it is their natural disposition; for they certainly are the most amusing creatures imaginable in their wild state. It is no wonder that with monkeys they are led about to amuse mankind. It is astonishing, as well as ludicrous, to see them climb rocks, and tumble or rather roll down precipices. If they are attacked by any person on horseback, they stand erect on their hind legs, showing a fine set of white teeth, and making a cackling kind of noise. If the horse comes near them, they try to catch him by the legs, and if they miss him, they tumble over and over several times. They are easily speared by a person mounted on a horse that is bold enough to go near them.

＊palanquin 1인용 가마

문제 1 Which of the following is the best title for the passage?
  (1) Capture of Bear   (2) Training of Bear
  (3) The Bear   (4) Ludicrousness of Bear

문제 2 Which of the following best fills in blank (a)?
  (1) they got the hang of it
  (2) they did not do it on purpose
  (3) they understood what they were doing
  (4) they were taught to do so

Day 30

[Challenge 2]

The garden must have a liberal supply of moisture. The first effort toward securing this supply should be the saving of the rainfall water. Proper preparation and tillage put the land in such condition that it holds the water of rainfall. Land that is very hard and compact may shed the rainfall, particularly if it is sloping and if the surface is bare of vegetation. If the hard-pan is near the surface, the land cannot hold much water, and any ordinary rainfall may fill it so full that it overflows, or puddles stand on the surface.

문제 1 Which of the following is NOT true of the passage?
(1) The garden should be prepared so as to hold water in it.
(2) The saving of the rainfall water is the only way to supply water to the land.
(3) If the land is sloping or bare of trees, it is likely to lose much rainfall.
(4) The hard-pan is a soil that is impervious to water.

[Challenge 3]

Therefore hastening with all speed, in order by their exceeding celerity of movement to anticipate all rumour of their motions, (a) <u>trusting to</u> their strength and activity of body, they travelled by winding roads until they reached the high ground on the tops of the mountains, the steepness of which delayed their march more than they had expected. And when at last, having surmounted all the difficulties of the mountains, they came to the (b) <u>precipitous</u> banks of the Melas, a deep river and one full of dangerous currents, which winds round the district, protecting the inhabitants like a wall, the night which had overtaken them increased their fears, so that they halted for a while awaiting the daylight. For they expected to be able to cross without hindrance, and then, in consequence of the suddenness of their inroad, to be able to ravage all the country around; but they had _____(c)_____.

문제 1 Which of the following is NOT mentioned in the above passage as the cause of the delay during their march?
(1) The steepness of the mountains   (2) The fear of the night
(3) The rushing torrents of the river   (4) A big wall in their way

문제 2 Which of the following can NOT replace the underlined (a)?
(1) presuming on   (2) resorting to
(3) falling back on   (4) putting on

문제 3 Choose one that is closest in meaning to the underlined (b).
(1) impetuous
(2) perpendicular
(3) hotheaded
(4) agitated

문제 4 Which of the following best fills in blank (c)?
(1) had no other way to get to their destination
(2) pillaged only a few quarters of the country
(3) incurred great toil to no purpose
(4) ended up somewhere unknown

[Challenge 4]

All bodies fall with the same velocity, when there is no resistance from the atmosphere, as is shown by the experiment of letting fall, from the top of a tall exhausted receiver, a feather and a guinea, which reach the bottom at the same time. The velocity of falling bodies is one that is accelerated uniformly, according to a known law. When the height from which a body falls is given, the velocity acquired at the end of the descent can be easily computed. It has been found by experiment that the square root of the height in feet multiplied by 8.021 will give the velocity.

문제 1 Which of the following can NOT be answered by the above passage?
(1) With what velocity does air rush into a vacuum?
(2) Under what condition do bodies with different weights fall with the same velocity?
(3) How do you determine the velocity of a body falling from a certain height?
(4) Do a feather and a guinea fall with the same velocity in a tall exhausted receiver?

[Challenge 5]

Starting out with splendid natural advantages — a wide range of soils of great fertility, (a) <u>indigenous</u> grasses of high food value, and a congenial climate — the dairying industry in Australia has _____(b)_____. The establishment throughout the chief districts of co-operative factories, owned and managed by the farmers themselves, and the introduction of cold storage greatly stimulated its growth. During the last decade its advancement has been remarkable. The Australian dairy industry is based on the world's markets. Every year the demand in various countries for Australian and other dairy and farmyard products increases, and the large home market is also expanding. The facilities for supervision, handling, and transportation are improving, and Australian dairymen today obtain high prices in both local and outside markets for their produce.

문제 1 Which of the following best represents the topic of the passage?
(1) Fabulous Natural Conditions for Dairy Industry
(2) Australia's Advancement in Farming Industry
(3) A Phenomenal Growth in Australian Dairy Industry
(4) A Sudden Demand for Dairy Products in Both Local and Overseas Markets

문제 2 Which of the following is closest in meaning to the underlined (a)?
(1) endemic   (2) ingenuous
(3) abortive   (4) remunerative

문제 3 Given the context, which of the following is most appropriate for blank (b)?
(1) taken a different path than the previous one to overcome the inferior environments for the industry
(2) taken a dramatic change for a better future
(3) long been the center of the world market for dairy products
(4) made phenomenal strides

문제 4 Which of the following is NOT true of the passage?
(1) Australia is favored by nature.
(2) The dairy industry in Australia is directly managed by farmers.
(3) The local market for the dairy products is relatively small, thus creating the demand for the world markets.
(4) The dairy industry in Australia is a lucrative one.

[Challenge 6]

Without a large degree of maternal rest there can be no day nursery. The task of creating a man needs the whole of a woman's best energies, more especially during the three months before birth. It cannot be subordinated to the tax on strength involved by manual or mental labor, or even strenuous social duties and amusements. (a) The numerous experiments and observations which have been made during recent years in Maternity Hospitals, more especially in France, have shown conclusively that not only the present and future well-being of the mother and the ease of her confinement, but the fate of the child, are immensely influenced by rest during the last month of pregnancy. (b) "Every working woman is entitled to rest during the last three months of her pregnancy." (c) For it is not enough to say that a woman ought to rest during pregnancy; it is the business of the community to ensure that that rest is duly secured. (d) The woman herself, and her employer, we may be certain, will do their best to cheat the community, but it is the community which suffers, both economically and morally, when a woman casts her inferior children into the world, and in its own interests the community is forced to control both employer and employed. We can no longer allow it to be said, in (e) Bouchacourt's words, that "to-day the dregs of the human species — the blind, the deaf-mute, the degenerate, the nervous, the vicious, the idiotic, the imbecile, the cretins and epileptics — are better protected than pregnant women."

*dreg: the basest or least desirable portion (ex.) the dregs of humanity

문제 1 Which of the following is the main idea of the passage?
(1) Newborns are healthier when mothers are in better health at the time of birth.
(2) The health of the mother comes first even before that of her baby.
(3) The fundamental need of the pregnant woman is rest.
(4) The race of human beings for the future is better secured with more intelligent babies.

문제 2 Where can the sentence below be best inserted in the passage?

> This formula was adopted by the International Congress of Hygiene in 1900, but it cannot be practically carried out except by the cooperation of the whole community.

(1) ingenuous   (2) endemic
(3) abortive   (4) remunerative

문제 3 Which of the following best refers to the situation of Bouchacourt's words in underlined (e)?
(1) Talk of the devil and you'll hear the flutter of his wings.
(2) Mend the barn after the horse is stolen.
(3) A stitch in time saves nine.
(4) The pot calls the kettle black.

[Challenge 7]

There is a broad measure of agreement among professional geologists that the evidence points to an orderly succession of stages through which the surface features of the earth have passed to reach their present form, and that this probably took a very long time to come about. (a) It was matched by an orderly succession of living forms, which began to appear rather later in the presently accepted time frame but has nevertheless been going on for a very long time relative to the span of human history. (b) These two broad conclusions, based on an enormous amount of research into the earth's past history, are accepted both by a very large number of informed Christians and by the vast majority of qualified geologists and biologists. (c) The universe is probably very old, and life began a very long time ago and shows an orderly progression from simple to complex. (d) We are talking only about the matter of a succession of forms; we are not talking about any linear evolution of these forms from one another. (e) When we come to consider the how of these immensely drawn out sequences of geological and paleontological events, we find somewhat less agreement among the scientists themselves, and even less among informed Christian people. (f) The fact is that the evidence can be interpreted in more than one way, and the preferred interpretation always depends upon certain basic and usually unstated assumptions. These assumptions hinge upon the question of whether natural laws are sufficient to account for all past events or only for some of them.

문제 1 Where can the sentence below be best inserted in the above passage?

> This does not by any means guarantee that they are true: but it certainly represents the present consensus of opinion in both circles.

(1) (a) (2) (b)
(3) (c) (4) (d)

문제 2 When the passage is divided in two, where does the second paragraph begin?
(1) (c) (2) (d)
(3) (e) (4) (f)

[Challenge 8]

One of Thomas Paine's great gifts was a sensitivity to currents of thought and action already present among the people. He could take the inchoate longings and aspirations of an inarticulate mass and make these beginnings whole and marvelously articulate. The superstructure of scholarship and experience upon his own poverty enabled him to talk to plain and often barely literate people, to expound the most complex of political ideas in straightforward, understandable, and dramatic language. He did this ___(a)___; he simplified by going directly to the heart of the matter, to the crux of the issue, not by writing in pidgin English.

문제 1 Which of the following can NOT be inferred from the passage?
(1) His experience of poverty made him more easy to sympathize with illiterate people.
(2) Thomas Paine was keen to the wants of the people.
(3) He had an ability to make budding longings of the masses come into full bloom.
(4) His political writings were simple enough for the masses to understand.

문제 2 Which of the following best fills in blank (a)?
(1) with much care   (2) with no efforts
(3) without writing down (4) without hesitation

[Challenge 9]

Looming in the backdrop is a European debt debacle that seems to get more convoluted by the week. Just two days after Ireland's parliament approved an $85 billion rescue from the European Union and the International Monetary Fund, the IMF warned the country still faces big risks that could affect its ability to repay the loan. Moody's, the ratings agency, slashed Dublin's credit grade and European banks warned of future losses on Irish assets. Investors' concern about the credit-worthiness of highly indebted euro zone countries will make it hard for some states to finance hefty debt repayments in the first half of 2011, even as new issuance in the bloc falls. Euro zone countries are expected to borrow less in the bond markets in 2011 than they did this year, but the interest rates investors are demanding pose a burden that may become unsustainable for the likes of Spain and Portugal. Unlike in the spring, when Europe's problems disrupted interbank lending and dented U.S. growth, such effects have not been felt in the latest. But analysts say the threat remains very real.

문제 1   Which of the following is the best title for the passage?
(1) Europe's Financial Morass
(2) Ireland Finding a Way Out of Depression
(3) Effects of the World's Economy Crisis on Ireland
(4) Ireland on the Brink of Bankruptcy

문제 2   Which of the following is not stated nor implied?
(1) The U.S. growth can be affected by the soundness of the European economy.
(2) The chances are that some of the European countries will not be able to make debt repayments in the near future.
(3) Spain and Portugal are relatively free from the current crisis.
(4) Ireland's credit grade has been downrated.

[Challenge 10]

U.S. researchers said that instead of a deep sleep, general anesthesia is more like a reversible drug-induced coma. General anesthesia is pharmacological coma, not sleep. Their findings, published in the New England Journal of Medicine, represent a three-year exploration of the similarities and differences of sleep, anesthesia and coma. They said while doctors and patients commonly describe general anesthesia as going to sleep, there are significant differences between the states, with only a bit of overlap between the deepest states of sleep and the very lightest phases of anesthesia. While sleeping usually involves moving through a series of phases, in general anesthesia, patients are typically taken to a specific phase or state and kept there during the surgery. This phase most closely resembles a coma. "The brain is becoming very, very quiet. The activity of the neurons is being dampened dramatically," Schiff said in a telephone interview. "That is also true in coma." Schiff, an expert in coma recovery, said while no two brain injuries are alike, studying the way people come out of anesthesia could be used as a model for _____(a)_____. That could lead to monitoring tools and diagnostics to assess what stage of recovery a person with a coma is in, and it could be used to develop new strategies to help doctors bring patients back to consciousness. Knowing more about the brain circuit mechanisms may also help researchers develop drugs to tweak specific brain circuits, Schiff said. And the study should lend new insight into understanding general anesthesia, Brown, an expert in general anesthesia, said in a statement.

문제 1 Which of the following is the best title for the passage?
(1) How to Recover from General Anesthesia
(2) Anesthesia Closer to Coma than Sleep
(3) Differences between Coma and Anesthesia
(4) New Findings about Coma and Sleep

문제 2 Choose an expression that is most appropriate for blank (a).
(1) curing patients with sleep problems
(2) developing a new method of putting patients to sleep
(3) keeping the patient from waking up during the operation
(4) predicting the stages of emerging from a coma

문제 3 According to the findings in the passage, which of the following is CORRECT about the person who is in general anesthesia?
(1) The patient is going through a complex train of stages.
(2) The activity of the brain changes slowly from idle to active.
(3) The activity of the brain is identical to that of the sleeping person.
(4) The patient stays in a certain stage all throughout the operation.

지음
박지성

퍼펙트 독해
PERFECT READING
실전대비 능력 극대화! - 완벽을 추구한다!

Perfect Reading

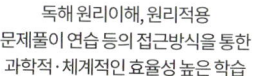
박지성 지음

독해 원리이해, 원리적용
문제풀이 연습 등의 접근방식을 통한
과학적·체계적인 효율성 높은 학습

인터넷 등, 어디서나 흔하게 볼 수 있는
문제들이 아닌 질 높은
다양한 실제 유형 문제구성

왜 답이 아닌지의 설명과 문제
구성원리 제시 등으로 독학생을
배려한 문제해설 강화

독학 가능한
완벽한 해설
부가 학습 자료 제공

실전문제
해설 및 정답

Day 1

[Challenge 1]

문제 1

답 (3)

해설 영어권의 글은 언제나 첫 번째 문장을 놓쳐서는 안 된다. 주제문(Topic Sentence)이 제시될 경우 본문에 기술될 중심 내용을 바탕으로 주제를 설정할 수 있으며, 글의 도입부에서 주제문이 나오지 않더라도 포괄적 주제인 중심 소재와 글의 방향성을 설정할 수 있다는 점에서 첫 번째 문장을 집중해서 읽어야 한다.

본문의 첫 번째 문장을 살펴보자.

> Nineteenth-century nature writing by women took various forms, but one theme that is seen in most of these works is the importance of the link between human beings and their natural surroundings.

일반적으로 'but' 뒤에 글쓴이가 전달하고자 하는 내용이 등장한다. 무엇에 관한 글인가? '19세기 여성이 쓴 자연에 관한 문학작품'에 관한 글이며, 이를 바탕으로 좀 더 구체적으로 전개하는 궁극적 내용은 무엇인가? 19세기 여성의 작품 속에 드러나는 "인간과 자연 사이에 존재하는 연결, 결합의 중요성"을 다루고 있다. 주제는 "19세기 문학에 나타난 자연에 대한 여성의 관점"이다. 박스 내용 이후 남자와 달리 여성의 작품 속에 드러난 자연에 대한 관점이 구체적으로 기술될 것을 예측할 수 있다.

문제 2

답 (1)

해설 빈칸문제는 글의 주제를 감안하면서 주어진 빈칸의 앞 뒤의 문맥적 내용을 살펴 가장 적절한 표현을 골라야 한다. 본 문의 주제가 "19세기 문학을 통해 나타난 자연에 대한 여성의 관점"이라는 점을 고려하면서 아래 본문을 살펴보자.

> Rather, the earth is seen as the sustainer of human life and relationships, and the _____ boundary between nature and humanity is emphasized.

우선 제시된 문장이 누구의 관점인지 파악한다. 여성의 글에서 나타나는 특성은 인간과 자연을 따로 보는 것이 아니라 그 경계가 불분명한, 즉 둘을 동일한 연장선에 보고 있다는 점이다. 'fragile'이란 단어는 '깨지기 쉬운' 또는 '미묘한, (금방 경계가) 무너지는, 덧없는' 등의 다양한 뜻을 가진다. 다른 선택지에 단어가 너무 동떨어져 있기에 'fragile'의 1차적 의미로 추론이 가능하다.

해석 19세기 여성이 쓴 자연에 관한 글은 다양한 형태를 취하고 있지만, 대부분의 작품에서 볼 수 있는 하나의 주제는 인간과 그를 둘러싼 주위 환경과의 관계의 중요성이다. 대부분의 여성 작가들의 경우 자연과의 관계는 그 당시 남성들의 자연에 관한 글에 주로 등장하는 주제인 거친 자연 광경의 광활함에 대한 로맨틱한 갈망 또는 사회로부터의 자연에의 회기와 관계가 없다. 그렇기 보다는, 지구는 인간 삶과 관계를 유지시켜 주는 것으로 간주되고 자연과 인간의 이런 미묘한 경계가 강조된다. 이런 여성에 대한 글을 연구한 비평가들은 특히나 19세기 환경에 관한 남성의 글에 핵심적인 '여성화 된' 자연의 광경이 어떻게 여성에 의한 작품에 더욱 복잡하게 표현되어지는지를 보여주는데 관심이 있었다. 이들은 또한 자연에 관한 여성들의 글이 일상의 삶에 대한 관심을 함께 엮어내, 공동체, 성, 지배 그리고 착취에 대한 문제를 탐구하는지 보여준다.

어휘

link *n.* 고리; 유대(bond) human being *n.* 인간
surroundings *n.* (주위) 환경; 주위의 상황
female *a.* 여성의 concern *n.* 관계
environment *n.* (주위를 에워싸는 것(상황, 정황); (생태학적, 문화적, 사회적) 환경
tie to ~에 결부시키다 longing for ~에 대한 동경, 갈망
openness *n.* 개방성; 솔직함, 관대
rugged *a.* 울퉁불퉁한, 조야한 landscape *n.* 풍경, 경치
withdrawal *n.* 물러남; 철수; 취소; 철회
sustainer *n.* 떠받치는(버티는) 사람, 물
boundary *n.* 경계선 (*pl.*) 한계, 범위, 영역
emphasize *v.* 강조하다; 역설하다 gender *n.* 성(性)
central *a.* 중심의 중앙의 기본적인, 중요한
complex *a.* 복잡한; (문제가) 어려운, 복합체의(composite)
weave *v.* 짜다, 뜨다, (이야기, 계획 등을) 만들어내다
concern about ~에 관심을 갖다; 염려하다
ordinary *a.* 보통의; 통상의; 평범한
explore *v.* 탐험[탐구]하다
domination *n.* 지배, 권세, 우월
exploitation *n.* 착취

[Challenge 2]

문제 1

답 (2)

해설 이미 알고 있는 정보를 다룰 때 우리는 이를 의식적으로 생각하지 않고 다룬다고 했다. 고로 습관적으로 생각 없이 하는 것과 같은 맥락의 보기 항(2)가 가장 적절하다.

문제 2

답 (3)

해설 본문 초반에 언급된 사항을 구체적 예를 통해서 전달하고 있다. 카피이스트의 경우 자신에게 익숙한 문장의 경우 아무런 의식 없이 기계처럼 다루지만, 만약 새로운 문자나 내용을 다룬다면 이는 본문 초반에 언급된 '새로운 정보(the subject is new)'가 되므로 주의를 가진다는 내용이다. 보기 항(3)이 가장 적절하다.

문제 3

답 (2)

해설 비유적 표현이 사용되고 있다. 본문의 내용을 바탕으로 유추할 수도 있지만, 빈칸이 들어간 문장의 수식 관계를 통해서 답에 접근하는 방법을 살펴보자.

as colour which _____(c)_____ with extremes of light or of shade

너무 밝고 또는 너무 어두울 경우 색상은 당연히 보이지 않게 된다. 즉, 빈칸을 수식하는 내용은 'with extremes of light or of shade'이다. 수식하는 내용은 수식 받는 내용을 한정하므로 '아주 밝은 빛과 아주 어두운 것에선' 색이 보이지 않게 된다.

해석 일반적으로 우리는 우리가 쓴 것의 내용을 일정 시간 기억한다(시간이 지나면 잊는다). 이는 이 주제가 일반적으로 우리에게 새롭기 때문이다. 그러나 만약 이전에 자주 쓰던 것을 쓸 경우, 우리는 이 또한 의식하지 않게 되는데, 다른 사람에게 이 내용을 전달하는 데 필요한 문자를 전혀 의식하지 않는 것과 마찬가지이며, 우리는 다른 것을 생각하고 말하는 동안 말하자면 기계적인 것처럼 쓰고 있게 된다. 그래서 돈을 받고 하는 카피이스트는 그에게 자기가 쓰는 것의 주제가 중요하지 않으면 그 자체를 인식하지 않는다. 그는 단지 익숙한 말과 문자를 다룰 뿐이지 이 이상의 관심을 두지 않으며, 그래서 반 무의식의 상태에서 글을 쓴다. 그러나 만약 그에게 익숙하지 않은 말이나 문자를 다루게 되면, 그는 즉시 기억 또는 기억하려는 의식으로 깨어나게 된다. 자신의 지식 또는 기억의 의식은 두터운 무지의 어둠과 완벽한 지식의 화려함 사이의 말하자면 황혼의 시기에 해당하는 것처럼 보인다. 마치 극단의 빛 또는 극단의 어두움에 사라지는 색상처럼. 완벽한 무지와 완벽한 지식은 모두 부지중에 일어난다.

어휘

as a general rule 대략, 대개는
substance n. 내용, 실체, 본질; 물질
consciousness n. 의식, 자각   fully ad. 완전히, 충분히
character n. 문자; 개성, 특징, 인물
necessary a. 필요한   convey v. 전달하다
notice v. 의식하다, 주목하다   familiar a. 친밀한, 친숙한
thereupon ad. 그러자 곧, 그 직접적인 결과로
quasi-unconscious 반 무의식적인
manner n. 방법, 태도   but little 거의 없는
acquaint v. 익히다, 숙지하다
belong to ~에 속하다   period n. 기간, 시기, 시대
so to speak 말하자면   twilight n. 황혼, 쇠퇴기
thick a. 두꺼운, 두터운   darkness n. 어둠, 암흑
ignorance n. 무지, 무식   brilliancy n. 광명, 탁월, 걸출
extreme n. 극단, 극도   shade n. 그늘
ignorance n. 무지, 무식

[Challenge 3]

문제 1

답 (2)

해설 소크라테스의 사제는 플라톤이고, 플라톤의 사제가 바로 아리스토텔레스라고 본문에 명시되어 있다. 보기 항 (1)은 틀리다. 보기 항 (3)의 경우 apriori는 선험을 나타내고, 백지 설인 tabula rasa는 경험주의 관점을 드러낸다. 합리주의보다는 관측에 기반을 둔 경험주의가 과학적 방법과 일치하므로 틀린 진술이다. 참고로 그리스 철학자의 사제 관계 중에서 다음 사실은 종종 지문에 등장하므로 알아두자. '소크라테스 — 플라톤 — 아리스토텔레스 — 알렉산더 대왕'

문제 2

답 (1)

해설 아리스토텔레스는 경험주의자이고, 나머지 선택 항은 플라톤과 관련된 선험적 지식을 드러내는 말이다.

문제 3

답 (1)

해설 빈칸 앞에 진술된 내용은 서양 철학 전통은 '플라톤' 또는 '플라톤을 비판한 아리스토텔레스'라는 두 양대 산맥으로 나뉜다고 하면서 이후 서양 철학자들은 이 둘 중 하나를 선택해야 한다고 말했다. 즉, 플라톤의 이론을 받아들일 것인가 아니면 그것을 비판한 아리스토텔레스를 이을 것인가를 선택해야 했다. 고로, 서양 철학은 플라톤의 이론에 관한 나름의 주석, 즉 그의 이론을 어떻게 받아들일 것인지의 문제로 볼 수 있다.

해석 초창기 경험주의자 중의 한 명은 바로 아리스토텔레스였다. 사실 경험주의적 관점을 실체로 만든 사람이 바로 아리스토텔레스라고 말해도 지나치지 않다. 아리스토텔레스는 알렉산더 대왕의 스승이었다. 아리스토텔레스는 또한 플라톤의 제자로, 플라톤은 역으로 소크라테스의 제자였다. 플라톤은 간단히 말해 모든 사물의 보편적 지식 - 예를 들어 정의, 아름다움, 진리 - 은 그 자체로 객관적 존재를 지닌다고 믿었다. 이것의 의미는 이러한 것들은 인간이 이들을 인식하는 것과 관련 없이 존재했다는 것을 의미한다. 이들은 독립적인 실체이며 플라톤은 인간이 이들을 지식으로 이해하게 될 수 있다고 믿었다. 이 사상은 '선험적'으로 존재하는데, 다시 말해 이들은 경험 이전에 존재하기에 경험을 초월한다는 의미이다. 플라톤의 경우, 우리의 감각은 기만적이기에 우리가 일상에서 경험하는 것은 현실이 아니라 현실의 그림자일 뿐이라고 말한다. 이것이 바로 플라톤의 공화국에서 전달하는 메시지 중의 하나인데, 특히 동굴의 비유를 말하는 것이다. 플라톤의 형상(이데아 또는 보편자) 이론은 내재적 사상과 관련이 된다. 이것은 인간이 이것을 경험하기 전 존재하는 개념이다. 이러한 철학 학파는 나중에 합리론자로 알려지게 된다. 그래서 기원전 384년에서 330년 사이 아테네에서 두 주된 철학 사상의 전통이 세워지게 된 것이다. 2000년 동안 철학자들은 플라톤을 따라 그의 합리론을 선택할 것인지 아니면 아리스토텔레스와 그의 경험론을 따를 것인지 선택해야 했다. 실로 플라톤은 첫 번째 철학자로 성공하고 아리스토텔레스는 그의 첫 번째 비평가로 드러나게 된다. Whitehead가 1929년에 진보와 현실에서 쓴 것과 같이 유럽의 철학 전통의 특징을 규정하는 가장 일반적 특징은 바로 이 유럽의 철학 전통은 플라톤에 대한 일련의 각주일 뿐이다.

어휘

empiricist *n.* 경험주의자

pupil *n.* 학생(흔히 초등학생 중학생); 제자

perceive *v.* ① (오관으로) 지각(知覺)하다, 감지하다; ~을 눈치 채다, 인식하다 ② 이해하다, 파악하다

grasp *v.* ① 꽉 잡다, 움켜잡다 ② 완전히 이해하다, 파악하다

transcend *v.* (경험·이해력 등의 범위·한계를 넘다; (우주·물질적 존재 따위를) 초월(超絶)하다; 능가하다, ~보다 낫다

deceptive *a.* (사람을 현혹시키는, 거짓의; 사기; 믿지 못할; 실망을 주는

doctrine *n.* ① 교의, 교리 ② 주의, 정치·종교·학문상의) 신조, 학설

school *n.* 파, 학파, 유파(派)

rationalism *n.* 이성주의

[Challenge 4]

문제 1

답 (3)

해설 흑사병이 다양한 사회 분야에 미친 영향력을 문단별로 다루고 있는 지문이다. 주의할 점은 소단락의 주제를 전체 주제로 파악하지 말아야 한다. 본문에서 발췌한 아래 부분을 확인해 보자.

> The Black Death reared its head sporadically in Europe over the next few centuries. But by 1352, it had essentially loosened its grip. Europe's population had been hard hit, which had an economic impact.

첫 번째 문단에선 인구와 경제적 측면에서 큰 타격을 입었다는 점을 알 수 있다.

> The Black Death did set the stage for more modern medicine and spurred changes in public health and hospital management.

두 번째 문단에선 현대 의학의 토대와 공중 건강 및 병원 관리에 큰 영향을 미쳤음을 알 수 있다.

> People who survived the Black Death era generally suffered a communal crisis of faith.

세 번째 문단에선 살아남는 사람들이 흑사병으로 인해 공동체적 신앙의 위기를 경험하게 되었음을 알 수 있다.

> Feeling, essentially, that God had turned his back on them, the people reacted to the end of the Black Death by turning their backs on him. They engaged in wild debauchery to celebrate being alive. They held gluttonous banquets, drank, wore extravagant clothing and gambled.

네 번째 문단에선 일반 사람들의 사고와 생활에 미쳤음을 알 수 있다.

문제 2

답 (4)

해설 세 번째 문단에서 보기 항 (4)에 대한 내용을 확인할 수 있다.

문제 3

답 (4)

해설 제시된 문장에서 최대한의 힌트를 찾도록 한다.

> It was clear through the art of the time, though, that people still had death on their minds.

흑사병으로 인한 수많은 피해가 당시 예술에도 영향을 미쳤다는 말을 하고 있다. 뒷받침 문장으로 예술에 관한 내용이 등장하는 곳은 바로 (라)이다.

해석 흑사병은 유럽에서 다음 몇 세기 동안 간헐적으로 고개를 드러냈다. 그러나 1352년 즈음 흑사병은 근본적으로 그 영향력이 수그러들었다. 유럽의 인구는 심각한 타격을 받고, 경제에 큰 영향을 미쳤다. 노동력이 줄어들고, 사람들은 농업을 버리고, 건물은 붕괴되었다. 노동 가치는 노력의 부족으로 인해 하늘을 치솟았고, 물가 또한 올랐다. 그러나 음식 가격은 오르지 않았는데, 이는 인구의 급격한 감소의 영향으로 보인다. 흑사병은 현대 의학의 초석을 쌓았으며, 공중 위생과 병원 경영에 변화를 일으켰다. 점성학과 미신에 맴돌던 흑사병에 대한 진단에 좌절한 교육자들은 물리학에 기초한 임상 의학에 더 강조점을 두기 시작했다. 학교는 처음에 교육자의 부족으로 문을 닫을 수밖에 없었지만, 역병으로 인해 결국 더 많은 교육 성장의 동력으로 작용했다. 새로운 학교를 설립하고, 때로 흑사병으로 인해 발생한 배움의 쇠퇴와 교육의 격차에 언급하고 해결하려고 한다는 점을 헌장에 특별히 언급했다. 흑사병 시대에 살아남은 사람들은 일반적으로 신앙의 공동체적 위기를 경험했다. 이들은 자신의 생존에 대해 하나님께 감사하는 의미로 더욱 종교적이기보다는, 사람들은 의심을 했다. 이들은 역병의 원인에 대한 답변을 얻기 위해 교회로 향했지만, 교회는 어떠한 도움을 제공할 수 없었다. 게다가, 의사와 함께 병에 가장 높은 접촉을 한 신부 또한 가장 높은 치사율을 보였다. 새로운 이단 운동이 여기저기 발생했다. 신앙을 여전히 고수하던 사람들은 지극히 개인적인 형태로 신앙을 지켰다. 많은 이들이 개인 교당을 세우기 시작했다. 근본적으로 하나님이 자신을 배반했다고 느낀 사람들은 반대로 하나님께 등을 돌리며 흑사병의 종식에 반응했다. 이들은 아주 방탕하게 생존을 축하했다. 이들은 아주 성대한 연회를 열고, 술을 마시며 아주 사치스러운 옷과 도박을 즐겼다. 그러나 그 당시 예술을 보면 이들은 자신의 마음 속에 여전히 죽음을 생각하고 있었다는 점은 분명했다. 죽음의 춤은 드라마, 시, 음악 그리고 시각 예술에 표현된 비유적인 개념이었다. 죽음의 춤은 일반적으로 죽은 자와 생존자 사이의 행렬 또는 춤을 드러낸다. 예술에서 보이는 다양한 층의 사람은 죽음이 모든 사람에게 올 것이라는 것을 의도한 것이며, 묘사된 다양한 활동은 죽음이 언제나 바로 앞에 있다는 것을 알려주는 것이다.

어휘

rear one's head 머리를 쳐들다; 《비유적》 (나쁜 마음 따위가) 고개를 쳐들다, (사람이) 두각을 나타내다

loosen v. ① 풀다 ② 늦추다, 느슨하게 하다
grip n. ① 꽉 쥠, 파악(grasp, clutch) ② 지배(통제)력, (남의) 주 의를 끄는 힘
workforce n. (국가·지역·산업체 등의) 총 노동력, 노동 인구
crumble v. 빻다 부수다, 가루로 만들다
skyrocket v. 급히 상승(출세)하다(시키다); 《구어》 급히 증대하 다, (물가 따위가) 급등하다(시키다)
spur v. ① ~에 박차를 가하다; 질주하게 하다 ② 몰아대다(drive), 자극(격려) 하다
revolve v. ① 회전(공전)시키다 ② 운행시키다 ③ 궁리하다, 곰곰 이 생각하다
astrology n. 점성학 [술]
place[put] (great) ~ on[upon] ~에 (큰 비중을 두다; ~을 (크게) 역설(강조)하다
plague n. ① 역병(病), 전염병 ② (흔히 the ~) 페스트, 흑사병
address v. ① ~에게 이야기를(말을) 걸다, ~에게 연설(인사)하 다, (~를 ...라고) 부르다 ② (문제를 역점을 두어 다루다
communal a. 자치 단체의, 시읍면(邑面)의 공공의
harbor v. ① 피난[은신]처를 제공하다; 감추다, (죄인 등을) 숨기다 ② (악의 따위를) 품다
priest n. 성직자 (감독 교회의) 목사; [가톨릭] 사제
heretical n. 이교의, 이단의 반대론자의
chapel n. 채플, 예배당(학교·병원·병영·교도소의), (교회의) 부속 예배당 2 〈영국〉 (영국 비국교도의) 교회당
debauchery n. 방탕, 도락 (pl.) 유흥, 야단법석
gluttonous a. 많이 먹는, 게걸들린(greedy); 골똘한, ~을 탐하는
banquet n. 연회(특히 정식의), 향연, 축연(祝)
danse macabre = dance of death 죽음의 무도
depict v. (그림·글·영상으로) 그리다: 묘사[서술, 표현]하다

[Challenge 5]
문제 1

답 (1)

해설 도입부에서 주제문이 등장하고, 이후 뒷받침 문장이 전개되는 전형적인 '일반 진술 → 구체적 진술'이다.

> Paine's book followed in the tradition of early eighteenth-century British deism. These deists, while maintaining individual positions, still shared several sets of assumptions and arguments that Paine articulated in The Age of Reason.

'18세기 이신론자들이 공유하는 신념과 주장'을 다루는 글로, 이후 이들의 주장에 대한 내용이 나열을 통해 기술되고 있다.

문제 2

답 (4)

해설 보기 항 (1)은 '만약 하나님이 모든 이에게 자비를 베푸는 분이시라면, 이성을 가진 모든 인간을 구원하실 터, 특정 민족만을 선택했다는 것은 옳지 않다.'고 말하고 있으므로 옳은 진술이다(religion could only be "simple, apparent, ordinary, and universal" if it was to be the logical *product of a benevolent God*). 이신론자들은 자연과학의 기반이 되는 귀납적 방법을 통해 하나님의 존재를 증명한다(a set of universal beliefs derived from the natural world that demonstrated God's existence). 고로 보기 항 (2)도 옳다. (3)의 경우 이신론에서 가장 강조하는 것이 바로 '이성'이라고 여러 번 본문에서 언급되었으므로 옳다. 보기 항 (4)의 경우 이신론자들은 기적의 경우 증명할 수 없는 것이기에 성경의 기적을 믿지 않았다.

문제 3

답 (1)

해설 결과를 이끄는 'therefore'가 들어간 문장이다. 앞에서 진술된 내용을 이유/근거로 삼아 적절한 답을 넣어야 한다. 'religious leaders had enslaved the human population'로 보아, 이신론자들 종교 지도자들이 '원죄'를 이용, 자신의 배를 채우기 위해 인간을 노예화시킨 것에 반대하는 사람이므로 이러한 '속박된 인간'을 자유롭게 한 사람들이 부른 보기 항 (1)이 가장 적절하다.

해석 Paine의 책은 초기 18세기 영국의 이신론의 전통을 따른다. 이러한 이신론자들은 개인적인 입장을 주장하는 반면 여전히 Paine이 『The Age of Reason』에서 명료하게 설명한 여러 가정과 주장을 고유하고 있다. 초기 이신론자들을 통합한 가장 중요한 입장은 모든 주제, 특히 종교를 포함한 모든 주제에 "자유로운 이성적 탐구"에 대한 요구였다. 초기 기독교가 양심의 자유에서 세워졌다고 말하면서 이들은 종교적 관용과 종교 박해의 종식을 요구했다. 이들은 또한 논쟁은 이성과 합리성에 기초해야 한다고 주장했다. 이 신론자들은 뉴턴식의 세계관을 받아들이고, 이들은 우주의 모든 것, 하나님조차 자연의 법칙을 따라야 한다고 믿었다. 자연의 법칙의 개념이 없이는 이신론의 주장에 따르면 자연이 어떻게 움직이는지에 대한 어떠한 설명도 불합리하게 될 뿐이라고 했다. 자연 법칙에 대한 이러한 믿음은 기적에 대한 회의주의로 이르게 했다. 기적을 증명할 수 있게 관측하려고 했기에, 이신론자들은 성경에 나온 기적에 대한 설명을 거부했으며, 이러한 증거는 하나님의 존재를 증명하기에 충분하지도 필수적인 요소도 아니라고 주장했다. 이런 맥락에 맞게, 이신론자의 글은 첫 번째 원인 또는 주된 운행자로서의 하나님은 그의 계획의 일환으로 자연 법칙에 따라 우주를 만들고 설계했다고 주장했다. 이들은 하나님은 자연의 법칙을 중단하면서 인간사에 (기적적인 면으로) 간섭하기 위해 자신의 계획을 반복적으로 바꾸지 않는다고 주장했다. 이신론자들은 또한 유일한 계시 종교적 "진실" 또는 하나의 진정한 진실만이 있다고 주장하는 것을 거부한다. 종교는 선한 하나님의 논리적 산물일 경우 "간단하고, 분명하며 일반적이고 보편적인" 수 있다. 그래서 이들은 기독교와 같은 "계시 종교"(이들이 거부한)와 하나님의 존재를 증명한 자연 세계에서 이끌어 낸 보편적 믿음이란 "자연 종교"(이들은 이런 의미에서 무신론은 아니다)를 구분했다. 어떤 이 신론자들은 계시를 받아들이지만, 대부분은 특정 단체 또는 심지어 한 사람에게 드러나는 계시의 제한은 그 설명적 능력에 제한을 가한다고 주장했다. 게다가 많은 이들은 특정 기독교의 계시가 모순적이고 대립된다는 것을 알아냈다. 이 작가들에 따르면, 계시는 자연 세계에 이미 분명히 드러나는 하나님의 존재에 대한 증거를 강화하기도 하지만, 더욱 종종 이것은 사람들 사이에 미신을 조장한다고 말했다. 대부분의 이신론자들은 주장하길 성직자는 기적, 불필요한 의식과 비논리적이고 위험한 이론(이러한 규탄은 일반적으로 "priestcraft"라고 일컬어졌다)을 받아들이는 것을 조장하면서 자기 자신의 득을 위해 기독교를 의도적으로 부패시켰다고 했다. 이런 이론 중 가장 최악의 경우는 바로 원죄이다. 사람들에게 자신의 내재적 죄악을 극복하는 데 성직자의 도움이 필요하다고 설득함으로 종교 지도자들은 인간을 자신의 노예로 삼았다고 이신론자들은 주장했다. 그래서 이 신론자들은 스스로 지적 해방자로 바라보는 것이 일반적이다.

어휘

deism *n.* 이신론(理神論)
articulate *v.* 똑똑히 발음하다; 분명히 말하다
conscience *n.* ① 양심, 도의심, 도덕관념 ② 의식, 자각
persecution *n.* ① (특히 종교상의) 박해 ② 성가시게[끈질기게] 졸라댐, 괴롭힘
embrace *v.* (주의·신앙 따위를) 채택하다, 신봉하다(adopt)
descend *v.* (이야기 등이) (~에) 미치다
drive *v.* (특정 행동을 하도록) 몰아가다
validate *v.* (법률상) 유효하게 하다; 정당함을 인정하다, 확인하다; 비준하다
prime *a.* ① 첫째의, 수위의, 가장 중요한 ② 최초의 원시적인 ③ 기초적인, 근본적인
alter *v.* (모양·성질 등을) 바꾸다, 변경하다; (집을) 개조하다
suspend *v.* 중지하다, 일시 정지하다, 한때 멈추다, 연기하다
intervene *v.* ① 사이에 끼다 ② (사이에 들어) 방해하다 ③ (사이에 들어) 조정[중재]하다
apparent *a.* ① (눈에) 또렷한, 보이는 ② 명백한, 곧 알 수 있는
benevolent *a.* 자비심 많은, 호의적인, 친절한, 인정 많은
derive *v.* (결론 따위를) 논리적으로 도출하다, (연역적으로) 추론하다
atheist *n.* 무신론자; 무신앙자
revelation *n.* 천계(天啓), 묵시, 계시(啓示), 계시된 것, 신탁(神託); 성서
irreconcilable *a.* 화해할 수 없는 조화되지 않는 대립[모순]된
superstition *n.* 미신; 미신적 관습
ritual *n.* (종교적) 의식, 예배식; 제식
innate *a.* (성질 따위가) 타고난, 생득의, 천부의
enslave *v.* 노예로[포로로] 하다, 예속시키다

[Challenge 6]

문제 1

답 (3)

해설 본문에서 언급하고 있는 것은 바로 당의 통합(unity)인데, 미국의 경우 당의 통합을 이끌어내지 못하는 단점이 있다고 했으므로 이와 같은 맥락에서 빈칸에 들어갈 표현은 "선거 기간에는 통합이 잠시 이뤄졌다가, 국회가 시작될 즈음에는 이러한 통합은 사라진다"는 내용이 적절하다.

문제 2

답 (1)

해설 "A member of Congress builds power upon a local base. Consequently, a member is likely to responsive to local special interest groups."에서 파악할 수 있듯이 국회의원은 지역에 기반을 두고 권력을 형성하기에 지역의 특수한 이익 집단의 요구에 적극적으로 대응하므로 (1)는 본문과 일치하지 않는다.

문제 3

답 (2)

해설 상원의 경우 통일성을 이루기 쉽다고 했으므로 특정 결의안에 찬반을 할 경우 다수가 함께 움직일 가능성이 크다. 고로 보기 (2)가 본문을 통해서 추론할 수 있는 가장 적절한 상황이다.

해석 미국 정당들의 한 가지 최대 약점은 입법부에서 통합을 이루지 못한다는 점이다. 비록 일정 수준의 통합성이 존재한다고 해도, 다수가 중요한 법안 시행을 성사시키지 못하는 것이 흔치 않은 일은 아니다. 통합성은 선거 운동 기간 중에 최고에 달한다. 예비 선거 이후 패배한 후보자들은 모두 당선자에 대한 지원을 약속한다. 의회가 개원할 무렵에는 이러한 통합성이 사라지게 된다. 이러한 현상은 정당 정치의 분열적인 속성에 그 원인이 있다. 미국의 의회는 그들의 가신들로부터 명목상 충성을 받는 단지 봉건 영주일 뿐이다. 의회의 구성원은 지역적 기반을 기초로 권력을 형성하게 된다. 따라서 그들은 지역의 특수한 이익 집단들의 요구에 반응할 가능성이 크다. 이러한 현상에 대한 증거는 상원과 하원의 투표 행태 상의 차이에서 찾아볼 수 있다. 의원들의 임기가 (하원보다) 긴 상원에서 정당의 통합성이 (하원보다) 더 많이 발휘된다.

어 휘

cohesion *n.* 통합, 단결, 결합, 유대
legislature *n.* 입법부
majority *n.* 다수당
implement *v.* 이행하다, 시행하다
nominee *n.* 지명된 사람
be attributable to ~의 탓이다
no more than 단지, 겨우
feudal lord 봉건영주
the Upper and Lower House 상원과 하원

[Challenge 7]

문제 1

답 (1)

해설 본문은 첫 번째 문장에서 보시다시피 '학습(learning)'의 정의를 시작으로 어떻게 행동주의가 형성되게 되었는지를 기술하고 있다. 이러한 행동주의가 미국의 주된 학문적 주류가 되었다는 점과 대표적인 사상가를 함께 거론하고 있다. 이 글은 주로 '학습과 행동주의'에 관한 이야기이다.

문제 2

답 (2)

해설 빈칸에 들어갈 접속사를 넣는 문제이다. 일반적으로 접속사는 앞 문장과 접속사에 걸리는 문장과의 관계를 파악하면 답 접근이 용이해진다. 빈칸 이후의 진술은 바로 앞에 전개된 내용에 대한 재진술에 해당함으로 (B)가 가장 적절하다.

문제 3

답 (4)

해설 내용일치 문제이다. 본문을 처음 읽을 때 중요한 사항에 미리 표시를 해 두지 않을 경우 상당한 시간적 소모가 있기에, 답을 맞힌다 하더라도 다른 문제에 심리적으로 압박을 주게 되어 오답률을 높이는 요인이 된다. 일반적으로 특정 사상학파가 나올 경우 특징을 정리해가면서 읽고, 만약 상대적으로 다른 주장을 펼친 학자가 비교/대조되고 있을 경우, 공통점과 차이점을 명확하게 정리하면서 학자들 각각의 특징을 파악해 둘 필요가 있다.

해석 학습이란 상대적으로 영구적인 행동 변화 또는 그럴 가능성이 농후한 행동 변화를 이끌어내는 과정으로 정의할 수 있다. 다른 말로 하자면, 우리는 배우면서 주변을 인식하고, 거기서 들어오는 자극을 해석한 후 상호작용 또는 행동하는 방법을 바꾸게 된다. John B. Watson은 학습 과정이 우리의 행동에 어떻게 영향을 미치는지를 연구한 첫 번째 사람이었으며, 그는 행동주의라는 사상학파를 창설하게 된다. 행동주의 이면의 핵심 사상은 단지 관측할 수 있는 행위만이 연구의 가치가 있다는 것인데, 이는 사람의 마음과 생

각과 같은 추상적인 것은 너무 주관적이기 때문이라는 것이다. 이러한 사상은 미국에서 자그마치 50년간이나 심리학 연구의 주류를 이루었다. 아마도 행동주의자 중에 가장 유명한 사람은 B. F. Skinner일 것이다. 그는 Watson의 대부분의 연구와 발견을 따랐지만, 내적 상태 또한 외적 자극과 마찬가지로 영향을 미칠 수 있다고 믿었다. 그는 이러한 신념으로 인해 극단적 행동주의 학자라고 간주되지만, 오늘날에는 내외적인 자극 모두가 우리의 행동에 영향을 미친다고 간주된다.

어휘

permanent *a.* 영구적인
stimuli *n.* 자극
abstraction *n.* 관념, 추상적 개념
dominant *a.* 지배적인
good *a.* 자그마치
internal *a.* 내적인
state *n.* 상태

[Challenge 8]

문제 1

답 (4)

해설 본문은 그리스 단어의 의식에 해당하는 'rite'의 의미를 전반부에서 밝히면서, 이후 단순히 '행하는 것'이란 의미에 추가적으로 집단적 감정과 행위가 포함되어야 한다는 다른 요소를 밝히고 있다. 보기 항 (3)은 후반부의 '공통된 집단적 행위'를 드러내지 못하기에 의식이라 볼 수 없다는 말은 옳다. 하지만 보기 항 (4)는 한 사람이 다른 삶의 흉내를 내는 행위이므로 'drama'의 성격을 가지곤 있지만 집단적 의식이 표현되지 않기에 'rite'라고 볼 수는 없다.

문제 2

답 (2)

해설 바로 뒤에 이어지는 부연설명을 통해서 알 수 있다. 'in common' 여러 사람이 공통으로 식사를 하는 경우 의식이라 말할 수 있다는 것에서 '집단적' 성격이 나타난다는 것을 알 수 있다.

> One element in the rite we have already observed, and that is, that it be done (a), by a number of persons feeling the same emotion. A meal eaten in common, under the influence of a common emotion, may, and often does, tend to become a rite.

해석 rite에 해당하는 그리스 단어는 이미 언급했듯이, dromenon로 '이루어진 것'이란 뜻이며, 이 단어는 지시의 의미를 가득 담고 있는 말이다. 그리스인들은 의식을 행하기 위해서, 뭔가를 해야 한다는 것을 깨닫게 되는데, 다시 말해 단지 뭔가를 느끼는 것만이 아닌 행위로 표현하는 좀 더 심리학적으로 말해 단순히 마음속에 충동을 느끼는 것이 아니라 이것에 반응해야 한다는 것이다. '뭔가를 행하다'라는 dromenon란 의식을 나타내는 말은 물론 어떤 심리학적 분석에서 발생한 것이 아니라 원시 그리스인들이 행한 의식은 모방을 하는 춤과 같이 실질적으로 뭔가를 행하는 단순한 의미이다. 연극의 표현인 drama라는 말은 dromenon라는 의식의 단어의 직접적으로 상응하는 말로, drama 또한 '뭔가를 행하다'의 의미한다. 그리스 언어적 직감에서 예술과 의식은 가까운 관계성을 지닌다는 것을 명백하게 가리키는 것을 알 수 있다. 그러나 그리스 단어의 '행위를 하다'의 dromenon라는 의식의 그리스 단어는 엄격하게 말해 적절한 것은 아니다. 이것에 아주 중요한 요소가 빠져 있다. 이것은 많은 것을 포함은 하지만 아주 충분하진 못하다. 모든 '행한 것'이 다 의식은 아니다. 당신은 주먹이 날아오는 것에서 뒤로 주춤할 것이다. 이것은 감정의 표현으로, 자극에 대한 반응을 말하지만 의식이라 말할 수 없다. 식사를 한다고 했을 때, 행위를 한 것이며 아주 중요한 것이지만 의식이라 할 수 없다. 우리가 이미 관찰한 의식의 한 요소로, 다시 말해 동일한 감정을 느끼는 수많은 사람들에 의한 집단적으로 행해진 것을 말한다. 공통적인 감정의 영향 아래서 먹는 식사는 종종 의식이 되면 그런 경향을 지닐 수도 있다.

어휘

rite *n.* 의례; 의식
note *v.* 언급하다
perform *v.* 실행하다; 연주하다; 이행하다
psychologically *ad.* 심리학상
impulse *n.* 충동; 충격
primitive *a.* 원시의; 야만적인
cardinal *a.* 주요한 기본적인; 선홍빛의
theatrical *a.* 극장의; 연극의
representation *n.* 표시; 표현, 상연; 설명
cousin *n.* 형제, 친척
instinct *n.* 본능 직관; 천성
plainly *ad.* 분명히; 명백히
adequate *a.* 어울리는; 적당한; 적임의
omit *v.* 빼다; 빠뜨리다
emotion *n.* 감동; 감격
stimulus *n.* 자격; 격려 고무
digest *v.* 소화하다; 요약하다
observe *v.* 관찰하다; 진술하다

[Challenge 9]

문제 1
답 (4)
해설 아래 본문 분석 참조.

문제 2
답 (1)
해설 빈칸은 계속적 관계대명사 바로 앞에 위치하고 있다. 관계대명사의 계속적 용법이 기본적으로 부연 진술인 점을 안다면, 이후 진술을 보고 빈칸의 단어를 유추해야 한다.

> which may be called tolerable health, <u>a state in which they do not suffer, yet are not quite well</u>.

밑줄 친 부분을 보게 되면, '아픈 것도 그렇다고 아주 건강한 것도 아닌 상태'를 드러냄으로 이를 가장 잘 표현한 단어는 'uncertainty'이다.

문제 3
답 (4)
해설 앞뒤의 문맥을 통해 빈칸에 들어갈 표현을 이끌어낼 수 있다. 본 문제의 경우 빈칸이 들어간 문장 내 논리 관계를 통해서도 접근이 가능하다.

> they have learned to know the signs of approaching trouble and they ease up before _____ (b) _____.

즉, 다가오는 병의 징조에 대해서 미리 예방한다고 했다. 고로 '큰 병이 발생하기 전'이라는 내용이 빈칸에 들어가야 한다.

본문분석

> 1) Many prefer to live in that state of uncertainty, which may be called tolerable health, a state in which they do not suffer, yet are not quite well. In this condition they have their little ups and downs and occasionally a serious illness, which too often proves fatal. Even such people ought to acquire health knowledge, for the time may come when they will desire to enjoy life to the fullest, which they can do only when they have health. Those who have this knowledge are often able to help themselves quickly and effectively when no one else can.
>
> 2) I am acquainted with many who have been educated out of disease into health. Many of them are indiscreet, but they have learned to know the signs of approaching trouble and they ease up before anything serious overtakes them. In this way they save themselves and their families from much suffering, much anxiety and much expense. Every adult should know enough to remain well. Every one should know the signs of approaching illness and how to abort it. The mental comfort and ease that come from the possession of such knowledge are priceless.

두 문단으로 나눠져 있다. 각 문단이 주로 무엇에 관한 글인지 그 주제를 밝히면서 읽도록 한다.

1) 첫 번째 문단

본문의 Key Word는 '건강(Health)'이다. 이후 파악해야 하는 점은 이것(건강)을 가지고 무슨 이야기를 하는지 즉, 무엇에 관한 글(what the text is about)을 파악하는 것이다. 첫 번째 문단에 마지막에서 알 수 있듯이 건강하지 못할 경우 삶을 충분히 즐길 수 없다고 말하고 있다. 즉, 건강한 삶의 중요성이 중요하다는 내용과 함께 이러한 건강을 위해 건강과 관련된 지식을 가진 사람의 도움을 언급하고 있다.

2) 두 번째 문단

글쓴이는 자신의 경험담을 통해 건강한 지식을 가진 사람이 병에 걸리지 않는다는 이야기를 하고 있다. 즉, 건강한 지식이 있을 경우 병을 미리 예방할 수 있다는 내용을 전개하고 있다. 본문 마지막 문장에서도 알 수 있듯이, 건강 지식에서 비롯된 정신과 육체의 안락함을 강조하고 있다.

주제 : 건강 지식 습득의 중요성

해설 많은 이는 반신반의한 상태에서 사는 것을 선호하는데, 이것은 웬만한 건강이라 부를 수 있는데, 사람들이 고통을 받지는 않지만 그렇다고 아주 건강이 좋은 상태는 아닌 것을 말한다. 이러한 상태에서 사람들은 자신이 건강할 때와 그렇지 않은 때를 맞이하고 때로는 아주 심각한 병에 걸리는데 종종 치명적으로 밝혀지는 경우도 있다. 이런 사람조차 건강의 지식을 습득해야 하는데, 왜냐하면 이들이 삶을 정말 최대한 누리고자 하는 욕망의 때가 오는데, 이것은 이들이 건강할 때만 할 수 있기 때문이다. 이 지식을 가진 사람은 다른 사람이 할 수 없는 상황에서도 <u>스스로 재빨리 효과적으로 자신을 도울 수 있게 된다</u>.

나는 교육을 통해서 병에서 건강한 상태를 찾은 사람을 많이 알고 있다. 많은 이들이 무분별하지만, 이들은 다가오는 질병의 문제의 징조를 아는 방법을 배웠기에 어떤 심각한 것이 이들을 덮치기 전에 사태를 완화시킨다. 이런 식으로 이들은 많은 고통과 근심 그리고 비용으로부터 자신과 가족을 구한다. 모든 어른은 건강을 계속 유지할 만큼 알아야 한다. 모든 이는 다가오는 질병의 징조와 이것을 막는 방법을 알아야 한다. 이러한 지식의 소유에서 오는 정신적 안정과 평정은 돈으로 살 수 없다.

어휘

prefer v. 좋아하다; 선호하다
state n. 상태, 형편, 지위; 신분; 계급. 진술하다
tolerable a. 참을 수 있는 웬만한
ups and downs 성하였다가 쇠하였다가 함; 성쇠
occasional a. 가끔의
fatal a. 치명적인, 운명의
acquire v. 획득하다, 습득하다
be acquainted with ~에 정통하다; ~을 잘 알고 있다
disease n. 병; 불건전; 퇴폐
indiscreet a. 무분별한; 경솔한
approach v. 접근하다; (아무에게) 이야기 꺼내다
ease up (근심 등을) 제거하다
anxiety n. 걱정; 근심, 염원; 열망
abort v. (계획 등을) 좌절시키다; 유산하다
mental a. 마음의, 정신의
comfort n. 위안
possession n. 소유; (pl.) 재산
priceless a. 돈으로 살 수 없는; 대단히 귀중한

[Challenge 10]

문제 1
답 (4)
해설 본문 초반에 기술되는 구체적 사례(인종차별)를 통해 미국 내에서 여전히 존재하는, 이전(verbal)과는 다른 형태의 인종차별을 비판하는 글이다.

문제 2
답 (4)
해설 뒤에 이어지는 내용으로 비추어볼 때 밑줄 친 내용은 스타벅스의 손님이 인종차별을 받았다는 의미이다.

문제 3
답 (2)
해설 본문 중반에 사회 문제를 퍼트리는 도구로 SNS를 활용하고 있는 내용이 등장한다.

해석 스타벅스 커피는 미칠 정도로 바쁠 때도 있다. 미국에선 바리스타가 손님의 이름 또는 숫자를 붙이는 것이 일반적인 관행이다. 한국의 커피 가맹점과는 달리 이들은 대부분 손님이 주문한 음료가 준비되었을 때 부르는 호출기를 주지 않는다. 최근 영어를 할 줄 아는 두 한국인이 조지아에 있는 한 스타벅스 매장에 들렀다가 커피 이상의 서비스를 받았다. 한 종업원이 뭔가 독특하고 색다른 것을 시도해보기로 했다. 이름을 쓰는 대신, 이 바리스타는 두 명의 한국 손님을 알아보기 위해 찢어진 눈을 가진 캐리커쳐를 그림으로 자신의 예술적 기교를 시험해 본 것이다.

자신의 이름 대신 찢어진 눈이 그려진 그림이 있는 컵을 받은 두 한국 손님은 충격을 받았다. 놀란 동시에 기분이 상한 이들은 즉시 가게 매니저에게 항의했다. 이들이 받은 것은 고작 기프트 카드 한 장이었다. 이 이야기가 퍼지는 것은 단지 시간 문제였다. 이 사건은 온라인에서 급속하게 퍼졌고, 스타벅스는 이 문제와 관련된 직원을 해고 조치시키도록 했다고 밝혔다.

이 사건은 이제 전체 한국인의 신경을 곤두서게 하고 있다. 뉴욕에 있는 파파존스의 한 레스토랑에서 또 다른 인종 관련 논쟁이 있었기 때문이다. 이 미국의 유명 피자 체인은 지난 달 한 직원이 영수증에 눈이 찢어진 여인'이라고 쓴 바람에 맹렬한 비판을 받았다. 이것 역시 손님의 이름을 바꾼 것에서 발생했다. 불행히도 파파존스 사태는 소셜 네트워킹 서비스의 존재로 인해 더욱 악화되었다. 화가 난 한국 여성이 이 문제를 트위터로 가져가, 즉시 10만 명 이상의 사람들이 그 녀가 올린 글을 보고 리트윗한 것이다.

"이 모든 인종 차별적 모함이 어떻게 돌아가는 것인가?", "이런 말도 안 되는 일이 정말 짜증이 난다.", "우리가 아직도 피부색으로 차별을 하는가?" 등등 수없이 많은 이들이 자신의 페이스북에 이러한 메시지를 올리고 있고, 트위터 상에 서 이 문제를 논의하고 있지만, 이는 단지 몇 개의 예에 해당 하는 글들일 뿐이다. 누리꾼들은 소수민족에 대한 차별은 미국의 대도시에서 지금도 계속해서 일어나는 문제라고 말한 다. 비록 실생활에서는 차별적인 메시지가 말로 표현되는 일 은 이제 없지만, 영수증에 글을 적거나 일회용 컵에 그림을 그리는 이러한 사건들은 매일 같이 일어난다. 유감스러운 점 은 이런 일이 너무 자주 일어나 어느 누구도 최근까지 관심 을 보이지 않았다는 점이다.

즉각적인 조치를 취하기 위해 한국계 미국인 주부단체는 이 문제를 법정에 가져가기로 했다. 세 가지는 아주 분명하다. 하나는 인종 차별이 여전히 분명하게 존재한다는 점. 두 번째로, 인종 차별은 진화했다는 점. 그리고 아시아인에 대한 차별이 지속적으로 이루어지고 있는 것인데, 이유는 대부분의 미국인이 아시아계 미국인들이 이러한 종류의 사건에 침묵할 것이라고 생각하기 때문이다. 우리는 어느 인종에게 적용되든지 간에 인종 차별, 괴롭힘 그리고 편협과 같은 것은 불의한 것이라는 것을 알아야 한다.

어휘

insanely ad. 미칠 정도로
barista n. 커피 만드는 전문가
paper n. 삐삐
drop by 잠깐 들르다 (= swing by, come by)
put sth to the test ~을 실험하다
offend v. 기분을 상하게 하다
manner of time 시간문제
get out 퍼지다

Day 1

spread like wildfire 급속히 퍼지다

rankle *v.* (불쾌한 감정 따위가) 끊임없이 마음을 괴롭히다, (원한따위가) 마음에 사무치다, 가슴에 맺히다

chinky eyes (가느다란) 찢어진 눈

social networking services 소셜 네트워킹 서비스

post *v.* (인터넷 상의) 글(을 올리다)

slur *n.* 중상, 모함

on-going *a.* 지속되는, 현재 일어나는

verbal *a.* 말의, 구두의

take action 조치를 취하다

take sth to the court ~을 법정에 부치다

bigotry *n.* 편협

Day 2

[Challenge 1]

문제 1

답 (1)

해설 본문은 현대 사회/경제 혁신으로 인해 가정의 기능이 약화되고 아이들은 자신들이 물려받아야 할 가정의 전통(유산)을 빼앗기고 있다는 문제점을 지적한 글이다. 참고, 주제나 제목은 언제나 Key Word를 반영하고 있는데, 본문의 Key Word가 '가정'이라는 점을 감안할 때, 보기 항 (1)과 (2)로 답안이 좁혀진다. Key Word와 Topic의 관계성을 정확히 모른다면, 본 책 독해의 기본과 적용에서 다루고 있으니 반드시 이해하고 넘어가도록 한다.

문제 2

답 (4)

해설 보기 (4)와 같은 표현은 주의해야 한다. 본문에서 현 가정의 문제점으로 지적하고 있는 부분을 보면 다음과 같다.

> The original prerogatives of the father and mother, so far as they pertain to the physical, social, mental and moral development of boyhood, have been farmed out to other organizations in the community.

즉, 현재 가정에서 아이에 관해 가지는 특권, 특히 신체, 사회, 정신, 도덕 발달을 공동체의 다른 기관에 맡겼다고 했다. 보기 항 (4)의 내용은 다른 공동체로부터 아이들 자신의 가족 유산을 배운다고 하는데, 이는 본문의 내용과 일치하지 않는 다. 본문 마지막에서도 알 수 있듯이, 이러한 가족 내 내려오는 유산은 그 가정 내 부모의 역할이 약화하면서 아이들이 물려받지 못한다고 나와 있다.

해석 아이의 삶에 영향을 미치는 3가지 조직 중에서 가장 크게 미치는 것은 그것이 가장 주된 것이라는 점에서 바로 가정이다. 가정은 공동체의 기본이 되며, 이 공동체는 단지 잘 조직된 또는 그렇지 않은 수많은 가정의 집합체일 뿐이다. 아이가 갖는 첫 번째 인상은 그의 가정생활을 통해서이며, 그의 전체의 생애 (career)의 성향은 바로 집안의 관계에 의해서 결정이 된다. 오늘날 대부분의 가정은 아이가 단지 먹고 자는 장소가 되었다. 부모는 아이의 신체, 사회, 정신 그리고 도덕적 발달에 관련한 과거에 원래 누리던 특권을 공동체의 다른 조직에 떠맡겼다. 오늘날의 가정생활은 이전 세 대의 그것과는 너무나 다르다. 이것은 주로 사회와 경제 형편이 만든 것이다. 우리의 사회와 경제의 혁신은 우리의 일 상가정생활 깊숙이 침투했으며, 이 결과로 가정은 심각하게 약화하고 아이들은 일반 가정의 전통을 잃어버리게 되었다.

어휘

institution *n.* 기관[공공] 시설, 기관, (확립된) 제도: 관례
primary *a.* 첫째의; 최초의 주요한
basis *n.* 기초: 기저 원칙: 이유, 근거
community *n.* 사회; 공동체; 공통성
aggregation *n.* 집합, 집성; 집단
organize *v.* 조직하다: 체계화하다
bent *n.* 성향, 취향   career *n.* 경력; 생애
original *a.* 최초의 고유의 독창적인; 색다른, 별난
prerogative *n.* (관직, 직위에 따르는) 특권
pertain *v.* 속하다; 관계하다; 적합하다, 어울리다 (to)
moral *a.* 도덕상의 훈계적인
boyhood *n.* 소년기
farm somebody out (사람을 보살피도록) (~에게) ~를 맡기다
organization *n.* 조직(화); 구성; 기구
revolution *n.* 혁명, 변혁
vast *a.* 광대한 거대한, 《구어》 대단한, 비상한
inroad *n.* 침입; 침략; (건강, 권리의) 침해
normal *a.* 정상의, 표준적인   weaken *v.* 약하게 하다
deprive *v.* (~에게서) (~을) 빼앗다; 박탈하다 (of)
heritage *n.* 상속, 재산, 유산, 전통

[Challenge 2]

문제 1

답 (2)

해설 배움은 반드시 선생이 있어야 발생하는 것이 아니라고 본문 초반에 나온다. 이때, 주의할 것은 본문에서 선생은 말 그대로 학교에서 가르치는 사람을 가리킨다는 점이다. 보기 항 (4)의 경우 'sometimes with the aid of parents or others' 에서 추론할 수 있으며, 보기 항 (3)의 경우 바로 뒤 따라 나오는 표현 (by their own unaided efforts)에서 알 수 있다. 보기 항 (1)의 경우 If, then, we can learn without being taught, it follows that the true function of the teacher is to create the most favorable conditions for self-learning.'에 잘 드러나 있다. 보기 항 (2)는 기본적으로 선생의 존재에 대해서 부정 하는 내용인데 이는 본문의 내용과 일치하지 않는다. 본문은 '배움이란 스스

로 발견하는 과정'임을 주장하는 내용이다.

문제 2

답 (4)

해설 빈칸이 들어간 문장에서 충분히 추론해 낼 수 있다. 전체 문장의 의미를 한정하는 부사구가 'at the outset'이라는 점을 활용한다.

> Everything, at the outset, must be learned by the discoverer without an instructor, since ___(a)___.

모든 것의 초창기에는 다른 사람의 도움 없이 발견자가 스스로 알게 되는 것인데, 이는 당연히 그것을 아는 사람이 없기 때문이다.

해석 우리는 선생이 없어도 배울 수 있다. 아이는 학교를 들어가기 전에 수백 가지 사실을 배우는데, 때로는 부모나 다른 이의 도움을 통해서이고, 나아가 자기 스스로 다른 이의 도움 없이 배우기도 한다. 우리가 습득하는 많은 것들은 사실 스스로 깨우치는 것이며, 지식은 스스로의 연구를 통해 발견했을 때 영속적으로 자신의 것이 된다는 것은 꽤 잘 알려졌다. 모든 것은 그 초창기에 그것을 아는 사람이 없기에 가르쳐 주는 사람 없이 발견자가 스스로 배우게 되어 있다. 그럼 만약 가르침 없이 배울 수 있다면, 교사의 진정한 기능은 자기 배움을 위한 가장 이상적인 조건을 만들어 주는 것이다. 근본적으로 지식의 습득은 선생의 유무와 관계없이 동일한 기능과 동일한 방법의 사용에 의해서 얻어지게 된다..

어 휘

fact *n.* 사실 실제 현실   aid *n.* 원조: 조력: 도움
effort *n.* 노력: 수고   acquisition *n.* 취득: 획득: 습득
concede *v.* 인정하다: 시인하다: 용인하다, 부여하다
knowledge *n.* 지식 학식, 인식
permanent *a.* 영구하는: 불변의
dig *v.* (노력해서) 발견하다, 찾아내다
outset *n.* 착수: 시작: 최초   discoverer *n.* 발견자
function *n.* 기능, 구실, 작용, 직무
condition *n.* 조건: (*pl.*) 주위의 상황, 상태: 지위: 신분 조건: 규약
agency *n.* 기능: 대리   method *n.* 방법: 순서

[Challenge 3]

문제 1

답 (2)

해설 본문은 젊은이들이 가지는 이상에 관한 내용을 주로 다루고 있다. 첫 번째 문장을 놓쳐서는 안 된다. 이는 첫 번째 문장이 글 전체의 내용이 어떤 식으로 전개될지 그 이정표 역할을 하기 때문이다. 굳이 주제문이 뒤따르지 않더라도, 중심 소재 설정은 대부분 첫 번째 문장에서 이루어지기 때문에 매우 중요하다.

> The most beautiful thing about <u>youth</u> is its power and eagerness to make <u>ideals</u>, and he is unfortunate who goes out into the world without some picture of services to be rendered, or of a goal to be attained.

문제 2

답 (1)

해설 본문에 언급된 구체적 사실을 확인하는 문제이다.

> <u>The character of the ideals has changed with changing needs</u>, but not we ourselves.

위의 내용에서 알 수 있듯이, 사회의 요구가 변하면서 우리의 이상의 성격도 변화한다.

해석 젊음에 관해 가장 아름다운 것은 바로 이상을 추구하려는 젊음이 가진 힘과 열정이며, 이루려고 하는 어떤 특정한 봉사나 성취하려는 목적에 대한 청사진 없이 세상에 나아가는 사람은 불운한 사람이다. 한 번도 이런 이상을 소중히 여기지 않은 사람은 우리 중 거의 없으며, 아마도 비밀스럽게 또는 마치 우리 혼자인 것처럼 부끄러움을 가진 채 세상의 고동치는 심장을 느끼고 우리가 이전에 발견한 세상보다 더 나은 세상으로 만들겠다는 영감의 직업을 떠올렸을 것이다. 수많은 시간이 흘렀지만 젊은 이상을 실현하는 데 있어 우리는 거의 변함이 없었다. 이상의 성격은 변화의 필요성에 따라 변하지만 우리 자신은 변하지 않는다. 우리의 젊은이들은 여전히 비전을 바라보면서 이들은 여전히 충돌과 투쟁으로 미래를 채우면서 장래의 먼 미래에 성취의 면류관과 함께 살아간다. 이렇게 된다면 정말 좋다. 우리의 젊음의 이상은 우리에게 삶의 동기를 제공하며, 실망의 시대 아주 깊숙이 살아온 우리조차도 우리의 기억 속에서 우리가 힘과 희망, 그리고 용기와 자기 독립을 이끌어 낸 가장 화려한 날들의 꿈을 버리려 하지 않는다.

어 휘

youth *n.* 어린 시절, 젊음   eagerness *n.* 열의, 열심
ideal *n.* 이상   unfortunate *a.* 불행한, 유감스러운
service *n.* 봉사   render *v.* 만들다, 주다, 제공하다
attain *v.* 이르다, 획득하다   cherish *v.* 소중히 여기다, 아끼다
secretly *ad.* 비밀히, 내밀히
ashamed *a.* 부끄러운, 창피스러운   inspiration *n.* 영감
pulsen *n.* 맥박, 맥   youthful *a.* 젊음의, 특유의
passagen *n.* (시간의) 흐름   vision *n.* 이상적인 상), 환상
conflict" *n.* 갈등, 물리적 충돌 *v.* 상충하다
struggle *n.* 투쟁   prospectively *ad.* 장래에 관하여
achievement *n.* 성취   distance" *n.* 거리, 먼 곳
eran *n.* 시대, 대   disappointment *n.* 실망, 낙담
willingly *ad.* 자진해서, 기꺼이   wipe *v.* 닦다, 훔치다

extravagant *a.* 낭비하는, 낭비력 있는
fortitude *n.* 불굴의 용기 **self-reliance** *n.* 자기 독립

[Challenge 4]

문제 1
답 (2)
해설 코브라의 독을 단계적으로 접종함으로써, 코브라를 부리는 사람들이 코브라에 물려도 죽지 않는다는 Dr. Nicholson의 가설을 Dr. Fraser가 증명하는 내용이다.

문제 2
답 (4)
해설 Dr. Nicholson과 Dr. Fraser에 관한 내용을 혼동해서는 안 된다. 첫 번째 문단에서 Dr. Nicholson은 동물에게 실험을 위해 잔인한 행위를 하는 것을 아주 싫어한다고 했다. 그렇다고 그가 뱀과 같은 동물을 아주 좋아한다고 말한 부분은 본문에서 찾을 수 없다. 고로 보기 항 (4)는 옳지 않다. 보기 항 (1)은 Dr. Nicholson이 생각한 가설이다. 그리고 'nothing would induce them to divulge it'로 보아 보기 항 (2)는 옳은 표현이다. 보기 항 (3)도 첫 번째 문단 마지막에서 확인할 수 있다.

문제 3
답 (1)
해설 'sedate'는 '차분한'이란 뜻이다.

문제 4
답 (3)
해설 첫 번째 문단에서 Dr. Nicholson은 코브라 해독제를 찾은 한 사람이 미친 것을 본 것을 보고 자신도 그렇게 될까봐 실험을 하지 않았는데, 두 번째 문단의 실험을 통해서 그의 실험의 정당성과 함께 이러한 사실이 정신병과 전혀 관련이 없다는 내용이 전개되고 있다. 보기 항 (3)이 가장 적절하다.

해석 Madras Medical Service의 Dr. Nicholson이 수년 전에 출판한 인도 뱀에 대한 한 작은 책자에서 Burmah의 뱀을 부리는 사람들은 코브라의 독에 특정한 해독제를 알기에 코브라를 다루는데 자신이 있다는 확신이 표현되어 있다. 그는 어떤 것도 이들이 이것을 밝히도록 꾀 낼 수 없다고 말했지만, 그는 코브라 독 그 자체를 단계적으로 접종하는 것이 아닌가 의심했다. 실험을 통해 이것을 증명하려는 시도를 하지 않은 이유에 대한 질문에, 내가 기억한 게 맞다면, 그는 우선 동물을 잔인하게 다루는 어떤 것에 본성적으로 강한 혐오감을 가지고 있다는 점과, 한 남자가 뱀에 물린 치료제를 발견했다는 생각을 하자마자 그는 정신병자의 증세를 보인 것을 보았기 때문이라는 두 가지 이유로 답변을 했다.

다소 주목할 만한 건 시간이 흐른 후에 스코틀랜드의 또 다른 의사가 Madras가 아닌 Edinbur에서 Dr. Nicholson이 꺼렸던 바로 그런 실험을 통해 "늙고 이전에 얌전하던 말을 코브라의 독에 조금씩 접종을 시키면서, 그것에 아주 철저하게 저항하는 것을 보였는데, 10마리의 일반 말을 죽이고도 남을 양이 단지 그 말에게는 "더욱 높은 활력과 생기를 심어주었다는 것을 증명했다는 것이다. 게다가 Dr. Fraser는 독에 저항하는 성질을 가진 한 동물의 혈청이 그 독약에 싸울 수 있는 해독제 자체가 되는 것을 확인하였으며 한 토끼의 혈관에 30분 동안 작용한 후 그 독약의 영향력을 저지시키는 점을 발견했다. 그리고 이 모든 것은 그 유명한 의사의 온전한 정신에 손상을 주지 않고도 이루어졌다.

어휘

conviction *n.* 신념; 확신; 유죄판결
antidote *n.* 해독제 **poison** *n.* 독; 폐해
confidence *n.* 신용; 신뢰; 자신 **handle** *v.* 취급하다; 다루다
induce *v.* 꾀다; 야기하다 **divulge** *v.* 누설하다 밝히다
gradual *a.* 단계적인; 점차적인 **inoculation** *n.* (예방) 접종
venom *n.* 독액; 독설 **attest** *v.* 증명하다; 입증하다
recollect *v.* 생각해내다; 회상하다
repugnance *n.* 질색; 강한 반감
cruelty *n.* 잔학함; 무자비함 **notion** *n.* 관념; 개념; 생각
symptom *n.* 징후; 조짐 **insanity** *n.* 광기
shrink *v.* 오그라들다, 수축하다 **sedate** *a.* 침착한, 조용한
render *v.* 만들다; 주다; 보답하다
proof *n.* 증명, 증거, 시험 **suffice** *v.* 족하다; 충분하다
impart *v.* 나누어 주다(give), 전하다, 알리다 **vigour** *n.* 활력
liveliness *n.* 원기; 활기 **serum** *n.* 장액; 혈청
combat *n.* 전투; 결투; 논쟁 **vein** *n.* 정맥; 기질; 특징
arrest *v.* 체포하다; 검거하다; 방해하다
sanity *n.* 제정신; 건전함

[Challenge 5]

문제 1
답 (2)
해설 1980년대 이후 초기 경제 개혁 이후 현재까지 경제 변혁에 따른 정부와 경제 주체 간의 역할 변화를 주로 다루고 있다.

문제 2
답 (4)
해설 아래 본문에서 알 수 있듯이 기업들은 1980년대 이후 원자재 구입의 양부터 다양한 제조 상품에 이르기까지 상당한 독립적 재량권을 누리기 시작했다고 말하고 있으므로, 보기 항 (4)는 옳지 못하다.

> enterprises began to have increasing discretion over the quantities of inputs purchased, the sources of inputs, the variety of products manufactured, and the production process ..... Less vital aspects of the economy have been transferred to lower levels for detailed decisions and management.

해석 중국의 전체주의적 경제 운영은 직접적 계획경제(의무), 간접적 계획경제(중앙정부의 명령을 간접적으로 실행), 그리고 시장의 요소에 맡긴 세 가지 노선에 따라 배분된다. 1980년대 초 초기 개혁 당시 기업들은 구입한 원자재의 투입량과 재료, 생산할 수 있는 다양한 제조 상품, 그리고 생산 과정에 대한 재량권을 점차 늘려가기 시작했다. 경제 계획에 대한 운영관리는 주로 주, 자치 도시, 그리고 군 정부로 이전되었다. 주 정부 또는 하위 단위로 운영되는 대부분의 국영 산업기관은 구체적 할당량과 간접적인 통제로 규제되었지만, 이들은 또한 시장 판매를 위해 국가 계획 외의 상품을 생산했다. 예를 들어, 엔지니어나 철강 완제품과 같이 희소성이 높은 자원은 정확한 수에 따라 이러한 종류(앞에서 언급한 시장 판매를 위한 정부 외 계획)의 계획에 할당되었다. 덜 중요한 인사와 물질에 대한 할당은 정부 계획에 따라 일반적인 방법으로 정부의 허가를 받았지만, 분배는 기업 경영에 맡겨졌다.

게다가, 기업 자체는 다양한 활동에 있어 상당한 독립성을 얻어가고 있다. 전략적으로 중요한 사업과 서비스, 그리고 대부분의 대규모 건설은 정부의 직접적인 계획 아래 여전히 운영이 되었지만, 시장 경제는 더욱더 많은 부분을 포섭하면서 매년 그 규모가 급격히 커지고 있다. 전반적으로 중국의 산업 체제는 아주 복잡한 관계가 혼합되어 있다. 국무회의에서 일반적으로 전체 경제에 대한 실행과 안정에 극히 중요하다고 간주되는 자원에 대해선 상대적으로 엄격한 통제를 행사한다. 덜 중요한 경제의 측면은 세부적인 결정과 운영이 낮은 단위로 전가되었다. 게다가, 다양한 조직적 위계질서를 이루고 있는 단체들을 통섭하기 위해 비공식적 교섭과 합의가 필요하게 되었다.

어휘

apportion *v.* 할당하다, 나누다; 배분[배당]하다
mandatory *a.* 명령의, 지령의; 위탁의 위임의; 의무적인, 강제적인 (obligatory)
implementation *n.* 이행, 수행; 완성, 성취
discretion *n.* 결정권, (자유) 재량, 참작
operational *a.* 조작상의
devolve *v.* (직책 따위가 남의 손에 넘어가다, 맡겨지다, (~에게) 귀속하다 (to; upon); (재산 등이) 계승되다, 이전되다
provincial *a.* 지방의, 시골의; 지방민의
municipal *a.* 시(市)의, 도시의
state-owned *a.* 국유의

regulate *v.* ① 규정하다; 통제[단속]하다 ② 조절하다, 정리하다
scarce *a.* 부족한, 적은   **finished** *a.* 끝낸, 완성된
assign *v.* ① 할당하다, 배당하다(allot) (to)
② (임무·일 따위를) 부여하다, 주다
personnel *n.* (*pl.*) (관청·회사 따위의) 전 직원, 인원; (회사·관청 등의) 인사부
authorize *v.* ① ~에게 권한을 주다, 위임하다(empower)
② 인가[허가]하다
strategically *ad.* 전략적으로   **scale** *n.* 규모, 정도
subsume *v.* 포섭[포함]하다; 규칙을 적용하다
deem *v.* (~으로) 생각하다(consider), ~로 간주하다
transfer *v.* ① 옮기다, 이동[운반]하다 ② (재산·권리를) 양도하다, 명의 변경하다 ③ (책임 등을) 전가하다 ④ (~로) 바꾸다, 변화 [변형]시키다 (into)
coordinate *v.* 조정[통합]하다
hierarchy *n.* 계급 제도; 권력자 집단
bargaining *n.* 거래, 교섭; 계약
consensus *n.* (의견, 증언 따위의) 일치; [법률학] 합의; 여론

[Challenge 6]

문제 1

답 (4)

해설 본문에서 건강 문제에 대한 해결책은 자기 자신, 바로 자신의 행위에 대한 책임감이라고 글쓴이는 강조하고 있다. 이러한 글쓴이의 주장을 가장 잘 드러내는 보기 항은 (4)이다.

해석 민주당과 공화당 모두 건강 보험 개혁과 모든 사람이 어떻게 보험을 받을지에 대해 논의하기 위해 공격 자세를 취 하지만, 해결책은 아주 단순하다고 나는 생각한다. 사람들이 자신의 행동에 대한 결과에 책임을 지도록 하는 것이다. 나의 룸메이트는 시카고의 Cook County Hospital 화상 치료 센터에서 일한다. 어제 한 환자가 얼굴 한쪽에 심각한 상처 를 입고는 병동에 들어왔다. 원인은? 그가 술을 너무 많이 마셔서 자동차 라디에이터에 넘어진 것이다. 거기 의사는 그의 얼굴을 되살리기 위해 긴급 피부 이식을 해야만 했다. 누가 이것을 지불해야 하는가? 당신과 나 우리 납세자이다. 만약 누군가가 하루에 다섯 갑을 피우기로 한다면, 그의 건강 문 제에 대한 부담은 모든 사람의 어깨에 놓여서는 안 된다. 만약 누군가가 말도 안 되는 공상을 일삼다 어떻게 다치게 된다면, 이것 또한 다른 사람이 지불해야 하는 것이 아니다. 나는 사람들이 가장 기본적인 카르마의 법칙을 다시 배워야 한다고 생각한다. 자신의 행동에 책임을 질 준비를 해야 한다. 이는 본인 자신의 행동에 책임을 져야 하기 때문이다. 우리가 이러한 단순한 진리를 고수한다면, 우리가 직면한 많은 문제들이 해결될 것이다.

어휘

Democrat *n.* 《미국》 민주당원
Republican *n.* 《미국》 공화당원

square off 싸울 자세를 취하다
insured *a*. 보험에 들어 있는, 보험이 걸린
consequences *n*. ① 결과; 결말 ② 영향(력) ③ (영향의) 중대성, 중요함; (사람의 사회적 지위[중요성], 실력, 오만함, 자존
burn unit 화상전문 치료센터
ward *n*. 병실, 병동
fulfill *v*. ① (약속·의무 따위를) 이행하다, 다하다, 완수하다 ② (일 을) 완료하다, 성취하다
karma *n*. ①【힌두교】업(業), 카마;【불교】인과응보, 업보(業報), 숙명(론); 인연 ②【미국 구어】(사람·물건·장소에서 나오는, 직감 적으로 느껴지는 특징적인 분위기
bear *v*. (의무·책임을) 지다, 떠맡다 (비용을 부담하다); (손실 따위에) 견디다, (손실을) 입다, (비난·벌을) 받다, 경험하다
stick to ~을 고집하다; ~을 굳게 지키다
mantra *n*.【힌두교】만투라, 진언(眞言)

[Challenge 7]

문제 1

답 (1)

해설 "person in the middle of nowhere"은 "외진 곳에 떨어진 사람"이란 뜻이다. 이는 이전과 달리 오늘날에는 비행기 가 그만큼 더 널리 활용되고 있다는 것을 뜻한다. 고로, 보기 (1) 이 가장 적절하다.

문제 2

답 (3)

해설 글의 주된 내용은 비행기가 발명이 된 지 얼마 되지 않았지만, 일반적으로 널리 사용된다는 점이다. 보기 (3)은 틀린 진술이다.

해석 비행기는 아주 흔한 여행 수단이라 그런지 이 비행기라는 게 최근에 발명이 되었다는 사실을 쉽게 잊고 만다. 오늘날에는 외진 곳에 사는 사람들도 하늘을 날아다니는 비행기를 보고 놀라지 않는다. 하지만 1903년 라이트 형제가 North Carolina의 Kitty Hawk에서 자신들이 만든 비행기를 타고 날기 전에는 대부분 과학자들이 공기보다 무거운 기계에 의한 비행은 절대 불가능하리라고 보았다. 절대로. 사실 비행기란 말은 1945년 이후가 되어서야 일반적으로 사용이 되었다.

어 휘

in the middle of nowhere 외진 곳에 있는
come into common usage 일반적으로 쓰이게 되다

[Challenge 8]

문제 1

답 (3)

해설 최근 일어나는 현상인 리쇼어링(Reshoring)에 관한 글로, 한 회사를 중심으로 그 장점을 기술하고 있다.

문제 2

답 (2)

해설 누구나 하기에 따라 하는 현상을 가장 잘 드러내는 속담은 (2)이다.

문제 3

답 (3)

해설 보기 (3)의 리드 타임(lead time)은 특정 물건을 만들어서 최종적으로 완성하는 데 걸리는 시간을 말한다. "There were worries about lead times and inventory."과 앞뒤 문맥으로 보아 오프쇼어링의 단점으로 리드 타임을 언급하고 있다.

문제 4

답 (4)

해설 바로 이어지는 내용을 보면, 리쇼어링을 통해서 회사는 더 많은 offer를 받게 되었다고 하고 있다. 즉, 리쇼어링의 마케팅 측면의 이야기임을 알 수 있다.

해석 수년간, 비용을 줄이려고 애쓰던 미국 회사들은 해외로 눈을 돌려 비용 절감을 모색해왔다. 오프쇼어링(해외업무 위탁)이 국내 고용에 미치는 영향에 대해 불만을 갖는 이들조차 이것의 대차대조표의 매력을 부정하지는 못했다. 일단 오프쇼어링이 임계 수준에 이르는 추세가 되자 여기에 참여 하지 않았던 사람들은 큰 손해를 보게 되었다. 당신의 경쟁사들이 모두 콜 센터를 인도로 이전하는데, 당신도 어떻게 그렇게 하지 않을 수 있겠는가?

그러나 오프쇼어링이 항상 최상의 선택인가? 점차 확산되는 움직임은 제조업 및 서비스업 일자리가 경쟁력을 갖기 위한 유일한 방법이라는 자동반사적인 가정에 의문을 제기하고 있다. 이러한 이유 중 하나는 오프쇼어링의 비용이 증가하고 있다는 점이다. 연료비가 오르고 (운송비를 비싸게 하는) 개발도상국 노동자들의 임금 인상 요구가 꾸준히 높아지고 있다. 리쇼어링을 지지하는 사람들은 가격 외의 다른 요소 또한 고려해야 한다고 말한다. 캘리포니아에 위치한 가정용품 회사인 Simple Wave는 중국에서 미국으로 제조 공장을 이전해 오면서 수많은 혜택을 누리게 되었다. 이로 인해 회사는 고객의 요구에 더욱 신속하게 반응할 수 있게 되었고, 더 나은 품질 관리가 가능해졌다. 그리고 자사가 속한 업계에서 많은 긍정적인 평판을 가져왔다. 그에 못지않게 중요한 것은 직원들에게 자부심을 심어주었다는 점이다. "우리는 옳은 일을 하기를 원했다. 그리고 이러한 결정을 내리게 되어 기분이 좋다."라고 공동 창업자인 Richard Stump는 말했다.

Simple Wave의 대표 상품은 CaliBowl로, 음식이 흘러 넘치는 것을 막아주는, 가장자가 안쪽으로 휜 그릇이다. 2008년 회사 창립 당시 초기에는 중국에서 고무 그릇을 제조하기로 했었다. "우리는 중국으로 갔는데, 이유는 다른 사람들도 다 그렇게 했기 때문이었다."라고 Stump는 말했다. 하지만 회사의 본거지에서 멀리 떨어진 곳에서 정확하게 설계된 제품을 생산하는 것은 설립자들이 기대했던 것보다 훨씬 어려웠다. 테두리가 휜 그릇을 만드는 것은 쉽지 않았으며, 품질 관리도 염려가 되었다. 리드 타임(생산 소요 시간)과 재고 조사를 하는 것도 걱정거리였다. 한 초콜릿 회사에서 상품 진열을 위해 800개의 CaliBowls를 급히 생산해 달라고 요청했을 때, 적시 공급 모델 쪽으로 방향을 틀어야 할 때가 되었음이 분명해졌다. "우리는 더욱 빨리 적응할 수 있어야 했다."라며 "배달을 못하면 많은 기회를 놓치게 된다."고 Stump는 말했다.

어 휘

lament *v.* 슬퍼하다, 비탄하다
offshoring *n.* 오프쇼어링 (해외로의 아웃소싱(outsourcing))
balance-sheet *n.* 대차 대조표
knee-jerk *a.* 자동적인 (반응)
proponent *n.* 제안자, 옹호자
reshoring *n.* 리쇼어링 (제조업 기업들이 생산시설을 본국으로 되돌리는 현상)
agile *a.* 몸이 재빠른, 민활한
signature product 특정회사 고유상품
lead time 리드 타임 (제품의 고안에서 완성, 사용까지의 시간)
pay off 이익을 가져오다; 성과를 올리다, 잘 되다
green-friendly *a.* 환경 친화의

[Challenge 9]

문제 1

답 (1)

해설 밑줄 친 '키메라'는 그리스 신화에 나오는 사자의 머리, 염소의 몸, 뱀의 꼬리를 한 불을 뿜는 괴물로, 실제가 아닌 환영 이다. 본문은 감각적 지식에 의존할 수 없는 신의 개념은 허상일 뿐이라며 '키메라'에 비유(metaphor)하면서 설명하고 있다.

문제 2

답 (2)

해설 'or'의 기능에 「환언·설명·정정·보완」 즉 바꿔 말하면'의 뜻이 있다는 것을 꼭 기억하자. 다시 말하면, 'A or B'라고 할 때, B는 A를 다른 말로 고쳐 쓴 것이다.

필수암기사항 – or의 활용

글쓴이는 자신이 전달하고자 하는 바를 어떻게 하면 좀 더 명확하고 쉽게 쓸 수 있을까를 고민한다. 수험생의 입장에 오래 있으면 문제를 꼬아내는(변별력을 위해) 출제자와 글쓴이를 동일하게 간주하는 경향이 있다. 그렇지만 우리가 읽는 글은 문제를 꼬아내는 출제자의 글이 아니다. 글쓴이는 독자에게 자신이 전달하고자 하는 바를 어떻게 하면 좀 더 명확하고 쉽게 할 수 있는지를 고민한다. 간혹, 수험생의 입장에 오래 있다 보니 문제를 꼬아내는(변별력을 위해) 출제자와 글쓴이를 동일하게 간주하는 경향이 있다. 그렇지만 우리가 읽는 글은 문제를 꼬아 만들려고 출제자가 쓴 글이 아니다.

문제화되는 지문(원문)은 대부분 정형화된 글의 구조를 따르는데, 논리적 글 전개뿐 아니라 독자의 이해를 돕기 위해 여러 가지 논리정보 장치를 활용한다. 논리정보 장치로 가장 많이 활용되는 것 중 하나인 'or'의 용례를 살펴보자.

or의 기능

1. 둘 또는 그 이상의 선택해야 할 어, 구절을 동격으로 결합한다.

    ① 긍정/의문문의 선택
    Which do you like better, apples or oranges?
    사과와 오렌지 중 어느 것을 좋아합니까?
    Will you be there or not?
    거기에 가시겠습니까, 안 가시겠습니까?

    ② either와 상관적으로 써서 either A or B로 쓰임 (일 반적으로 시험에서는 A와 B의 관계는 A↔B인 경우 가 많음)
    Either take it or leave it.

    ③ 부정문에서 '~도 없다'는 의미로 쓰임
    He cannot read or write.
    읽지도 쓰지도 못한다.
    He has no bothers or sisters.
    그는 형제도 자매도 없다.

④ 선택의 뜻이 약해지고 수 등의 불확실함을 나타내는 경우에 써서 ..정도, 약 ..., 거의, ...내지, ...이나'
a mile or so   1마일 정도, 거의 1마일
there or thereabout(s)   어딘가 그 근처
A day or two are needed.   하루나 이틀이 필요하다.
He is ill or something.   그는 아프거나 무슨 일이 있다.

2 A or B가 A = B로 쓰이는 경우:
앞의 진술한 내용을 다시 말할 때
psychology, or the science of the mind
심리학, 즉 마음의 과학

3 기본적으로 A≠ B이며, A ≒ B(비슷함)와 A ↔ B가 있다:
앞말의 정정 또는 바꾸어 말할 때(종종 rather를 동반)
She is, or was, a very beautiful woman.
그녀는 대단한 미인이다, 아니, 미인이었다. (말 정정)
His autobiography, or rather memoirs, will be published soon.
그의 자서전, 아니 회고록이 곧 출판될 것이다. A ≒ B
I've cleaned it all up, or at least most of it.
나는 다 치웠다. 아니 적어도 거의 다 치웠다. A ↔ B
I've met him somewhere. Or have I?
어딘가에서 그를 만난 적이 있다, 아니, 만났던가? A ↔ B

4 A. −B로 구분 가능
명령문 뒤에서, 때때로 else를 동반하여 부정 조건의 결과를 나타내어 '그렇지 않으면'의 의미로 쓰인다.
Go at once, or (else) you will miss the train.
지금 당장에 가거라, 그렇지 않으면 기차를 놓칠 거다.
You must hurry, or you'll be late.
서둘러야 한다, 그렇지 않으면 늦는다.
* Go at once (당장 가면 기차를 잡을 수 있다.)
→(or) you will miss the train.

or의 모든 용도가 다 자주 쓰이고 중요하지만, 시험과 관련하여 중요한 사항은 별색으로 표시한 부분이므로 반드시 기억하고 넘어가야 하며, 무엇보다 두 번째 기능인 A or B가 A =B인 것을 활용할 수 있어야 한다.

예 1.

> We use trees and plants for homes, paper, furniture, heat, food and even recreation. It's obvious that if we plan to support the world's rapidly growing population, we must manage our natural resources wisely. Many people in the sports industry are trying to set an example by "going green," or taking actions that are good for the environment. At the annual exhibit of the latest sports products, the venue used electricity produced by wind energy.

> The sellers used only recycled paper products and recycled plastic bags. Many of the major sports brands offered products made of earth-friendly materials, such as organic cotton t-shirts and running shoes.

본문에서 or가 활용된 문장을 살펴보자.

> Many people in the sports industry are trying to set an example by "going green," or taking actions that are good for the environment.

본문의 or는 A = B로 활용되고 있다. 다시 말해,

> 'going green = taking actions that are good for the environment'

'going green' 과 같은 맥락의 표현이 바로 이어지고 있다.

예 2.

> They are **either** based on real occurrences **or** fantasy materials. Such family storytelling is shown to have numerous advantages.

본문에 등장하는 or는 either A or B 형태로 A과 B가 A ↔ B의 관계를 지닌다.

real occurrences ↔ fantasy materials

해석 모든 종교적 원칙은 유일신의 개념에 기반을 두지만, 인간이 자신의 감각 중 어느 하나에 의존하지 않고 행하는 존재에 대한 진정한 개념을 형성하는 것은 불가능하다. 우리의 모든 생각은 우리에게 떠오르는 사물의 형상일 뿐이다. 신이 구체적 물체의 개념이 없는 것일 때 이 개념이 우리에게 어떤 의미가 있을 수 있겠는가? 이러한 생각은 원인이 없는 결과와 같이 불가능한 것이 아닌가? 본보기가 없는 생각은 키메라(허상) 외의 아무것도 아니지 않는가? 그러나 어떤 신학자들은 하나님의 개념은 내재적인 것, 다시 말해, 인간이 태어날 때부터 이러한 개념을 가진다고 말한다. 모든 원칙은 하나의 판단이다. 모든 판단은 경험의 결과이다. 경험은 감각의 실천을 통해서만 얻을 수 있다. 이것으로부터 종교적 원칙은 무에서 발생한 것(곧 허상이란 말임)이며 내재적인 것이 아니라는 결론이 나온다.

어 휘

religious a. 종교의, 독실한   principle n. 원리, 원칙
act upon ~에 따라 행동하다, 조치하다
sense n. 감각   picture n. 모습, 형상
strike v. 치다, 부딪치다   represent v. 나타내다, 묘사하다
evidently ad. 분명히, 눈에 띄게
prototype n. 원형   chimera n. 키메라, 불가능한 생각(희망)
theologian n. 신학자   assure v. 장담하다, 확언하다

judgment *n.* 판단, 심판, 심사　　acquire *v.* 얻다, 획득하다
exercise *n.* 실행, 실천　　draw from ~에서 …을 얻다
innate *a.* 타고난, 선천적인

[Challenge 10]

문제 1

답 (2)

해설 중세의 역사가 일반적으로 'dark ages'의 관점에서 해석되는 것은 서양 전반의 역사가 아닌 서유럽에만 해당한다는 것이 본문 내용의 골자이다. 부분적인 사실을 글 전체의 요지로 생각해서는 안 된다.

문제 2

답 (4)

해설 보기 항 (4)는 본문의 내용과 정반대된다. 본문 마지막 참조.

해석 일반적으로 중세라는, 특히나 'Dark Ages'라는 개념은 유독 그 기원이 유럽, 아니 서유럽의 개념이다. 서유럽과 대조적으로 동유럽은 어두움의 시대를 경험하지 않은데다 비잔틴 제국이라는 형식 아래 고대 그리스와 로마의 찬란한 영광을 떠오르게 하는 고장이 되었다. 중동의 아랍 또한 이 시기를 "어둠의 시대"로 보지 않는다. 600년을 기점으로 아라비아는 인간 역사에서 좀처럼 비교되지 못할 정도의 문화적 번성을 이뤘다. 영국과 프랑스의 조상은 여전히 대부분 바람이 새어 들어오는 오두막에 사는 문맹의 소작농이었던 반면, 아랍 사람들은 고대 로마의 수준에 버금가는 문화를 누렸다. 1095년에 시작한 십자군 전쟁 중에 처음 서유럽 사람을 만났을 때, 아랍인이 이들을 무식하고 냄새가 지독한 괴수로 바라본 것도 놀랄 일이 아니다.

어휘

Middle Ages *n.* 중세　　dark ages *n.* 암흑 시기
European *a.* 유럽의　　origin *n.* 기원
in contrast to ~와 대조가 되어
splendid *a.* 운이 좋은, 훌륭한
reminder *n.* 상기시키는 것　　ancient *a.* 고대의
glory *n.* 영광, 영예　　form *n.* 형성, 모양
the Byzantine Empire *n.* 비잔틴 제국
cultural *a.* 문화적인　　equal *v.* 맞먹다, 필적하다
illiterate *a.* 글을 모르는, 문맹의
peasant *n.* 소작농　　drafty *a.* 외풍이 있는
hut *n.* 오두막　　civilization *n.* 문명
encounter *v.* 맞닥뜨리다
crusade *n.* 운동, 십자군 전쟁　　view *v.* (~으로) 간주하다
ignorant *a.* 무지한　　brute *n.* 짐승, 야수

Day 3

[Challenge 1]

문제 1

답 (1)

해설 특정 이론을 통해 흑사병이 어떻게 중국에서 유럽으로 퍼지게 되었는지 설명하고 있다. 본문 중반에 나오는 타타르족과 관련된 부분적인 이야기를 주제로 삼아서는 안 된다. 참고로 앞에서 설명했듯이, 영어권의 글은 첫 번째 문장에서 중심 소재를 설정할 수 있다. 그리고 주제에는 반드시 이 중심소재 또는 이와 동일한 의미를 전달하는 표현이 들어가야 한다. 본문을 보면서 이를 한 번 적용해 보자.

> **The plague** started in China and made its way west across Asia to the Black Sea by 1347.

무엇을 가지고 이야기하는가? 바로 역병이라는 흑사병을 가지고 이야기하고 있다. 다시 말해, 이 글의 주제에는 반드시 이 흑사병이란 단어 또는 이것을 드러내는 표현이 들어가야 한다. 고로, 보기 항 (3)은 절대 답이 될 수 없다는 것을 알 수 있다. 일반적으로 이런 소거법을 쓸 경우, 쉽게 답에 접근할 수 있을 때도 있으므로 중심 소재와 주제와의 관계를 반드시 기억해 두자.

해설 흑사병은 중국에서 발생하여 아시아를 거쳐 서쪽으로 이동해 1347년 흑해에 이르렀다. 한 이론에 따르면, 감염된 타타르족이 제노바 해안의 어떤 작은 마을을 포위했다고 한다. 갇힌 그 마을 사람들을 공격하기 위해, 타타르족은 투석기를 이용해 죽은 동료의 시체를 성벽으로 넘겨 제노바에 병이 퍼지도록 했다. 공포에 질린 거주민들은 모두 배를 타고 그곳을 빠져나가 북부 이탈리아의 항구에 나타났는데, 이들이 유럽에 흑사병을 퍼뜨리게 되었다는 것이다.

어 휘

plague *n.* 역병, 전염병   the Black Sea 흑해
theory *n.* 이론   infect *v.* 감염시키다
besiege *v.* 포위하다   outpost *n.* 전초지
harass *v.* 괴롭히다   trapped *a.* 갇힌
catapult *n.* 투석기   hurl *v.* 날려 보내다
body *n.* 시체   comrade *n.* 동지
spread *v.* 퍼지게 하다   epidemic *n.* 유행병, 전염병
panicked *a.* 공포에 질린   inhabitant *n.* 거주민
flee *v.* 달아나다   scene *n.* 장소   by ship 배를 타고

[Challenge 2]

문제 1

답 (3)

해설 보기 항 (3)의 내용은 본문의 아래 내용과 일치하지 않는다.

> They remain deep in their silent consciousness.... when they ask these questions they care nothing and remember naught of the answers. What is deepest in them is growing in silence

문제 2

답 (2)

해설 달에 대한 글쓴이의 개인적인 경험과 일반 진술로 이어지는 부분을 찾아 문단을 나누면 된다. 두 개의 문단으로 나눠진 지문 중 'Specific General'의 경우는 다음과 같다. 첫 번째 지문에서 구체적인 경험 또는 현상을 제시하고, 이후 이를 일반화하여 글쓴이가 궁극적으로 이야기하려는 내용을 전개하고 있다. 일반적으로 첫 번째 문단에서 구체적 경험이나 현상이 제시될 경우 '글쓴이는 구체적 경험과 현상을 제시하면서 궁극적으로 무엇을 전달하려고 하는가?'라는 질문을 끊임없이 해야 한다. 이를 바탕으로 글쓴이가 다음 문단에서 전개할 일반 진술을 미리 예측할 수 있게 된다.

문제 3

답 (2)

해설 일반적으로 영어권의 글은 첫 번째 문장에서 주제문을 제시하고 이후 뒷받침 문장이 전개된다. 주제문은 중심 소재와 함께 글의 주제와 본문에서 주로 다뤄질 요지가 함께 제시될 수 있다. 첫 번째 문장이 모두 주제문은 아니지만 60~70%는 첫 번째 문장으로 글이 어떤 방향으로 나아갈지 설정할 수 있다. 본문의 첫 번째 문장을 살펴보자.

> Two things in nature impressed me more than any others in my childhood.

어린 시절 저자에게 인상 깊었던 자연의 두 가지에 대해서 언급했다. 바로 이어서 첫 번째에 대한 설명(달에 대한 글쓴이의 어린 시절 관측)이 이어지고 있다. 이후 두 번째에 해당하는 내용이 다음 소 문단을 형성하게 된다. 고로 보기 항 (2)가 가장 적절하다.

해석 내가 어렸을 때, 다른 어떤 것보다 자연의 두 가지가 나에게 깊은 인상을 주었다. 하나는 내가 걷거나 달아나려 할 때 달이 나를 따라오는 것처럼 보인다는 것이었다. 나와 항상 보조를 맞추어 내가 움직이면 움직이고 내가 멈추면 멈추었는데, 때로 이것이 나를 짜증나게도 하였지만, 대개는 기쁨을 주었다. 하늘은 우리가 친근하고 사교적일 때 어린아이와 같다. 하늘은 우리가 서 있는 곳에서 고작 2마일 떨어진 곳까지 지구로 내려온다. 달이 만삭일 때 내가 이 밝고 장난스러운 여행자를 앞지를 수 있을지 달을 가지고 여러 실험을 했다. 나의 노력은 늘 수포로 돌아갔지만 궁금증은 더해갔다. 나는 이에 관해 말한 적이 없으며, 어른들에게 이에 대한 설명을 요구한 적도 없다. 아이들은 처음 관측하는 이러한 간단한 자연의 섭리에 관한 질문을 하지 않는다. 이런 것들은 아이의 조용한 의식 깊이 남아 있다. 이들이 실제로 질문하는 것은 피상적이고, 서서히 나타나는 사회성의 일시적 충동이거나 아니면 부모나 선생님에 의해서 영감을 받은 것이다. 아이들이 이러한 질문을 할 때 이들은 전혀 신경을 쓰지 않으며 어떠한 답변도 기억하지 못하는 것을 알게 되었다. 아이들의 마음속에 깊이 자리잡은 것은 조용히 자란다. 이것은 아직 개념으로 형성되거나 말로 표현되지 않는다. 아이들이 말로 하는 질문과 아이들이 받은 막연한 인상과의 차이는 스냅 사진 카메라로 찍은 사진과 어떤 멀리 있는, 처음 보는 별의 모습을 천문학자가 오랜 시간 관찰하고 현상한 감광판의 차이와 같다.

어휘

impress v. 감동시키다; 깊은 인상을 주다
childhood n. 유년 시절
apparent a. 또렷한, 명백한, 외견만의
motion n. 운동, 동작
equal a. 같은, 동등한; 감당할 수 있는
vex v. 짜증 나게 하다, 화나게 하다
amuse v. 즐겁게 하다; 재미나게 하다
tricky a. 장난 좋아하는; 처리하기 힘든
vain a. 헛된, 공허한   **explanation** n. 설명; 해설; 대화
regarding prep. ~에 관해서는
operation n. 가동, 작업; 효력, 효과
observe v. 지키다; 준수하다, 관찰하다
silent a. 침묵하는; 무언의; 잠잠한
consciousness n. 자각, 의식
superficial a. 표면상의; 피상적인; 천박한
impulse n. 추진, 충격; 충동   **naught** n. 제로, 무
silence n. 침묵, 고요함   **conception** n. 개념; 구상; 착상
snapshot n. 스냅(사진)

[Challenge 3]

문제 1

답 (3)

해설 (3)번과 같이 동력을 만들어내는 기계가 작업을 수행할 수 없다는 이야기는 없다.

문제 2

답 (4)

해설 힘을 만들어내지 못하고 전달하는 것은 바로 두 번째 정의에 해당하는 기계인데, (4)번은 힘을 만들어내는 요인(agent)에 해당한다.

문제 3

답 (2)

해설 (2)번은 마찰을 감소해 주는 '윤활유'이다.

해석 비록 수의 관점이긴 하나 기계 사이에 아주 불공평한, 그렇지만 자연스러운 구분이 존재한다. 이것은 다음과 같이 구분된다. 우선, 힘을 만들어내는 것에 도입된 기계이며, 둘째는 힘을 단순히 전달하는 일을 수행하도록 도입된 기계이다. 이러한 구분의 첫 번째 기계는 아주 중요한데, 그 종류의 다양성은 아주 한정되어 있지만, 이러한 종류 중 어떤 것들은 수없이 많은 개별적 부품으로 이루어져 있다. 운동을 전달하는 종류의 기계 중에서 아무리 조합을 하더라도 이것을 사용하여 힘을 만들어내지 못한다는 것이 증명되었다. 한 시점에 적용된 힘은 무엇이든 마찰과 다른 부차적인 원인에 의해서 감소된 형태로 다른 시점에 실행된다. 그리고 아무리 빠른 실행에 의해서 얻어진 것은 무엇이든 추가적인 힘의 실행의 필요에 의해서(잃은 힘의) 보상이 이루어진다는 것도 증명이 되었다.

어휘

unequal a. 같지 않은; 불공평한
division n. 분할; 분배   **employ** v. 쓰다; 종사하다; 고용하다
transmit v. 보내다; 전도하다   **force** n. 힘; 세력; 기세
execute v. 실행하다; 실시하다; 처형하다
variety n. 변화; 변이; 가지각색의 것   **species** n. 종류; 종
numerous a. 다수의; 수많은
individual a. 개개의; 특유한; 고유한
agent n. 매개물   **demonstrate** v. 증명하다; 설명하다
gain v. 획득하다; 얻다 n. 이익; 증가
combine v. 결합시키다; 연합시키다
exert v. 발휘하다; 쓰다   **diminish** v. 줄이다; 감소시키다
friction n. 마찰; 불화   **incidental** a. 부차적인
further ad. 더 한층   **rapidity** n. 신속; 급속; 민첩함
execution n. 실행; 실시; 집행; 사형
compensate v. 보상하다; 변상하다
additional a. 부가의; 추가의

[Challenge 4]

문제 1

답 (2)

해설 본문은 한 때 정부가 수익을 바라보고 인정했던 거리 판매점을 철폐하려는 시도를 비판하는 내용의 글이다. '현상 – 문제점 지적 – 글쓴이의 주장(대안)'으로 이어지는 패턴을 파악한다.

문제 2

답 (4)

해설 본문 마지막 부분에서 글쓴이가 정부의 태도에 대해서 비판하고 있다.

> do not enter into a bargain that seemed advantageous to yourselves and then repudiate it when you find that it is not so advantageous as you thought

즉, 처음에는 득이 되는 것으로 보여서 참여했는데, 이후 생각만큼 득이 되지 않는다 하여 철폐하는 그런 행위를 비판하고 있다. 이러한 점을 가장 잘 반영한 보기 항은 (4)이다.

해석 오늘날 우리에게 분별 없이 촉구되고 전국 어디서나 여기저기 실행되고 있는 소위 말하는 "개혁"이라는 것에 대한 설명을 하려 한다. 나는 거리의 판매권에 대한 문제를 말하는 것이다. 이제 여러 경우 이런 판매권은 아주 가치 있는 것이 되었으며, 이것이 적절한 수익률이 보장이 안 된다면 허가가 되지 않을 것이라는 점은 사실이다. 그러나 이러한 판매권이 초기에 인정되었을 때, 이것이 공동체 성장에 절대적으로 필수적인 서비스를 제공했다는 것과 이 판매권을 획득한 사람들이 자신의 자본에 심각한 위험이 되는 상황에 직면하면서도 실질적으로 도시 미래의 복지에 자신의 운명을 함께 던진 것을 기억하는 것은 공정하지 아니한가? 때로 이러한 위기가 얼마나 심각한지와 이 수익이 얼마나 문제가 되는지를 깨닫는 것은 쉽지 않다. 거리의 사업의 주주는 전 인구에 퍼져 있으며, 모든 계층의 인구에 상당하다. 이들은 이러한 판매권의 적절성에 대한 문제가 제기되지 않고, 공공의 선으로 간주되고, 의심 없이 그러했을 때 선한 믿음 안에서 자신의 돈을 투자했다. 그리고 나는 만약 정부의 모든 조직과 정치인의 모든 책략을 사용해 이러한 판매권의 가치를 평가 절하하고 압수하겠다고 이들의 주주를 협박하며, 민주적으로 통치되는 사람들에게 열려 있는 모든 방법으로 이들을 방해하고 괴롭히는 것이 정직한지를 물어보겠다. 나는 주저 없이 이렇게 하는 것이 부당하다고 말하는 바이며, 다수의 선한 믿음으로 이렇게 함을 믿으며 이러한 수단을 격렬히 옹호하는 대부분 사람들은 만약 이들이 사실에 직면하고, 자신들이 하고 있는 행동이 무엇이며, 선량한 사람들에게 가하는 잘못된 행위를 이해한다면 (자신의) 이런 행위를 수치스럽게 느낄 것이라고까지 말하는 바이다. 만약 판매권을 인정하는 데 실수를 범했다면, 앞으로는 이러한 실수를 번복하지 말도록 조심해야 하고, 자신들에게 이롭게 보였는데, 생각한 것보다 그다지 이롭지 않다는 것을 발견하곤 거부하려는 그런 거래에는 발을 들이지 말아야 한다.

어 휘

illustration *n.* 삽화; 예증; 실례
reform *v.* 개혁[개정]하다; 개심시키다 *n.* 개혁, 개선
reckless *a.* 분별없는; 무모한
urge *v.* 재촉하다; 강력하게 추진하다
operation *n.* 가동; 효과; 조작; (사업 따위의) 운영
refer *v.* 언급하다; 인용하다
franchise *n.* 선거권; 관할권; 특권; 독점 판매권
return *n.* 이익, 수익   absolutely *ad.* 절대적으로; 정말로
essential *a.* 근본적인; 본질적인; 정말 중요한
prospective *a.* 예기되는; 장래의; 선견지명이 있는
welfare *n.* 복지; 후생
realize *v.* 실현하다; 현실화하다, (이득을) 얻다
shareholder *n.* 주주   traction *n.* 끌기; 견인; 매력
corporation *n.* 법인; 주식회사
spread *v.* 펴다; 펼치다; 흩뿌리다
represent *v.* ~에 상당[해당]하다
invest *v.* 투자하다; (권력, 지위, 성질, 직직을) 주다
propriety *n.* 타당; 적당; 예의바름
indubitable *a.* 의심의 여지가 없는; 명백한
machinery *n.* 조직, 기관   artifice *n.* 고안; 교묘한 솜씨
depreciate *v.* 평가절하 하다; 얕보다
holder *n.* (권리, 관직, 토지 등의) 소유자
confiscation *n.* 몰수   hamper *v.* 방해하다; 훼방하다
harass *v.* 괴롭히다; 애먹다   democratically *ad.* 민주주의로
unhesitating *a.* 주저하지 않는
inflict *v.* (타격, 상처, 고통 따위를) 주다, 가하다
innocent *a.* 무구한; 순결한; 결백한   bargain *n.* 매매, 거래
advantageous *a.* 유리한; 형편이 좋은
repudiate *v.* 거부하다; 부인하다

[Challenge 5]

문제 1

답 (2)

해설 바로 뒤에 이어지는 내용에서 문제를 해결할 수 있다. 행위가 인생의 많은 부분을 차지하기에 행위의 법칙을 발견하는 것이 곧 인생의 중요한 의미와 목적을 알맞게 해석해 내는 데 없어서는 안 될 것이라고 말하고 있다. 보기 항 (2)가 이를 가장 잘 반영하고 있다.

Day 3

문제 2

답 (4)

해설 바로 앞에 이어지는 인과의 내용을 바탕으로 빈칸의 단어를 추론할 수 있다.

> conduct = the outward expression of character → character has roots in personality

즉, 행위는 성품의 외적 표현이며, 성품은 다시 개인의 성격에 뿌리를 둔다고 했다. 고로, 인생의 바른 개념(행위로 드러나는)을 세우기 위해선, 가장 기본이 되는 **성격**에 영향을 미치는 요소를 잘 살펴볼 필요가 있게 된다.

해석 Matthew Arnold가 말한 것처럼 만약 행위가 인생의 4분의 3이라면 행동 규범에 대한 자세한 연구는 인간의 의미와 목적을 적절하게 이해하는 데 없어서는 안 된다. 그러나 행위 자체는 단지 성격이 외부로 나온 표현일 뿐이다. 그리고 다시 이 성격은 그 뿌리가 사람의 됨됨이에 있다. 그래서 만약 우리가 인생의 올바른 개념을 형성하기 원한다면 인간의 됨됨이를 형성하는 데 미치는 영향력을 검토해 이 됨됨이를 가장 잘 활용할 수 있고 효율적인 단계까지 올려야 한다. 인간의 가치를 평가할 때, 의식과 경험의 모든 측면이 고려되어야 한다. 그러므로 예수 그리스도의 가장 놀라운 역사적 사실을 고려하지 않고는 삶의 목적에 대한 어떠한 정의도 내릴 수 없다.

어 휘
conduct n. 행위; 행동; 지도   inquiry n. 문의; 조사; 연구
indispensable a. 불가결의; 없어서 안 될
proper a. 적당한; 고유의; 올바른
interpretation n. 해석; 설명
outward a. 밖을 향한; 외부의; 외관의
root n. 뿌리; 근원; 원인   personality n. 개성; 성격; 인물
conception n. 개념; 파악; 이해
examine v. 시험하다; 검사하다   shape v. 형성하다
raise v. 일으키다; 제기하다   efficiency n. 능률; 능력
estimate v. 어림잡다; 견적하다; 판단하다
consciousness n. 의식   account n. 설명; 근거
regard v. 고려, 관심   stupendous a. 엄청난; 굉장한

[Challenge 6]

문제 1

답 (1)

해설 본문은 '행복한 위엄'을 가로막는 가장 큰 장애물은 바로 '존경받으려는 욕망'이라고 말하고 있다. 이후 그로 말 미암아 발생하는 결과를 쭉 기술하고 있다. 고로 문제에서 요구하는 문제점의 가장 근본적인 원인은 첫 번째 문장에서 드러나는 '존경받으려는 욕망'에 해당한다.

해석 행복하고 기분 좋은 위엄을 성취하는 데 방해하는 가장 주된 문제점은 칭찬받으려는 소망에서 발생하는데, 이러한 소망은 대부분의 여성들이 타고 태어나는 성향이다. 이것은 자신의 위대한 강점과 유용성에 방해가 되는데, 이는 진정한 독립심을 앗아가고, 타인 대신 자신만을 생각하게 만들기 때문이다. 이것은 이들(여성들)이 허황되며 자의식이 강하게 만들며, 남자와 여자 친구 간의 행복하고 진정한 동료의식의 형성을 불가능하게 만드는 일종의 속박이다.

어 휘
chief a. 최고의; 주요한   acquire v. 획득하다; 얻다
cheerful a. 기운찬; 즐거운   dignity n. 존엄; 위엄
desire n. 욕구, 바람   admire v. 존경하다; 감복하다
tendency n. 경향, 풍조, 버릇
majority n. 대부분; 과반수; 다수
stand in the way of ~을 훼방놓다
usefulness n. 유용; 편리   bondage n. 구속[속박]
vain a. 헛된, 공허한, 허영심이 많은
self-conscious a. 자의식이 강한
render v. 만들다, 주다, 양도하다; 포기하다

[Challenge 7]

문제 1

답 (2)

해설 본문은 석회가 어떤 식으로 작용하는지 그 근본적인 성격을 규정하기 쉽지 않다는 점과 그 이유를 처음부터 끝까지 일관성 있게 전개하고 있다. 글 전개 방법은 나열이다.

본문분석

> 1) Despite the fact of the long-established and almost universal use of lime, it can scarcely be said that we as yet clearly understand the exact nature of its action. Much light, however, has been thrown of late years on the subject by the great advance which has been made in our knowledge of agricultural chemistry. 2) Nevertheless, there are many points connected with the action of lime on the soil which are still obscure. 3) Perhaps one reason for the conflicting ideas prevalent with regard to the value of this substance in agriculture is to be found in the fact that it acts in such a number of different ways, and that the nature of the changes it gives rise to in the soil is most complicated. The experience of agriculturists with lime in one part of the country often seems contradictory to the experience of those in other parts of the country. Its action on different soils is very dissimilar. 4) For these

> reasons, therefore, the discussion of the value of lime as a manure is by no means an easy one.

1) 중심 소재인 석회(lime)를 소개하면서 석회가 어떤 식으로 작용하는지의 성격을 규정하기 어렵다는 이야기를 배경으로 제시하고 있다.
2) 'Nevertheless' 이후 글의 주제를 이끌어 낼 수 있는 주제문이 등장한다: '석회를 정의하기 힘든 이유'
3) 구체적인 뒷받침 문장이 이어진다.
4) 글을 요약하고 있다.

문제 2

답 (1)

해설 빈칸이 들어간 문장과 앞에 전개된 내용이 서로 대조를 이루고 있다. 빈칸 문제 중 접속사를 고르는 것은 전체 문맥을 생각하면서 대부분 바로 앞 문장과 빈칸이 들어간 문장의 관계를 파악해 접근하는 유형이다.

문제 3

답 (4)

해설 세부 내용 확인 문제이다. 본문에 언급된 내용을 바탕으로 답을 이끌어 낸다.

> 'Its action on different soils is very dissimilar.'

해석 석회가 오랫동안 거의 모든 곳에 사용되고 있다는 사실에도 불구하고, 우리는 아직 이것이 어떻게 작용하는지에 대한 정확한 특성을 분명하게 이해하고 있다고 전혀 말할 수 없다. 그러나 농업 분야의 화학에 대한 우리 지식이 이루어낸 엄청난 업적에 의해 최근에 석회에 대한 많은 것이 밝혀지고 있다. 그러나 석회의 토양에 대한 작용과 관련된 많은 점들은 여전히 불분명하다. 아마도 농업 분야에서 이 물질(석회)의 가치와 관련해서 상충하는 견해들이 존재하는 이유 중 하나는 이것이 수없이 많은 다양한 방식으로 작용하는 점과 이것이 토양에 일으키는 변화의 특성이 아주 복잡하기 때문일 것이다. 어떤 지역 농업가들이 경험하는 석회는 다른 지역의 농업가들이 경험한 것과 상반된 것처럼 보이는 경우가 종종 있다. 다양한 토양에 미치는 이것의 영향력도 아주 다르다. 그러므로 이러한 이유에서 퇴비로서 석회의 가치에 대한 논의는 전혀 쉬운 것이 아니다.

어 휘

- **established** *a.* 확실한; 기정의, 설립된
- **use** *n.* 사용, 용도, 습관 **lime** *n.* 석회
- **advance** *n.* 진전, 진보; 승급 **agricultural** *a.* 농업의
- **chemistry** *n.* 화학; 화학작용 **connect** *v.* 연결하다; 접속하다
- **obscure** *a.* 분명치 않은; 불확실한
- **conflicting** *a.* (의견 등이) 상반하는
- **prevalent** *a.* 보급된; 널리 행해지는
- **with regard to** ~에 관해
- **substance** *n.* 물질; 실질, 요지
- **omplicated** *a.* 복잡한, 까다로운
- **contradictory** *a.* 모순된; 양립하지 않은
- **dissimilar** *a.* 닮지 않은; 다른
- **manure** *n.* 거름, 비료 **by no means** 절대 ~이 아닌

[Challenge 8]

본문은 나열(Listing)을 이용해 글이 전개되고 있다. 본문을 근거로 환경 대책에 대한 각 방법에 대한 특성을 장단점을 중심으로 기록해 보자.

	특성
Method 1	
Method 2	
Method 3	

문제 1

답 (4)

해설 탄소세금제(emission tax)에서 첫 번째 방법인 탄소 배출 거래제와 달리 정부가 pollution credit의 양을 정하고 분배하는 위치에 있지 않기에 부패의 기회가 줄어든다는 것은 옳은 설명이다. 보기 항 (2)와 같이 정부 재정의 보완책으로 탄소세금제를 활용할 수 있다. 보기 항 (3)도 탄소 배출 거래제를 다루는 초반부에 언급이 되어 있다. 보기 항 (4)에서 'safety valve'는 탄소 배출 거래제와 탄소세금제를 모두 보완하여 나온 제도이다.

문제 2

답 (1)

해설 때로 빈칸 문제는 전체 지문의 주제를 고려하면서 문맥상 적절한 표현을 골라야 하는 경우도 있지만, 본문과 같이 빈칸이 주어진 문장만으로 해결이 되는 경우도 있다. 여러 경우의 수를 생각하여 접근해야 한다.

1) 앞에서 전개된 내용을 바탕으로 답을 이끌어 내는 경우 (결론적 내용에 해당하는 경우가 많다)
2) 뒤의 부연 진술을 확인한 후 빈칸의 답을 이끌어 내는 경우 (일반 진술 후 구체적 진술의 경우)
3) 전체 문맥과 함께 앞뒤를 모두 파악해야 하는 경우
4) 빈칸이 들어간 문장만으로 해결이 가능한 경우

본문의 경우 'that' 이하의 내용을 부정적인 결과로 파악할 수 있기에 '단점'의 의미인 보기 항 (1)이 가장 적절하다. 보기 항 (2)를 조심한다.

문제 3

답 (4)

해설 보기 항 (1)은 'cap-and-trade system'에 대한 내용이다. 보기 항 (2)의 경우, '정부는 탄소량을 규제할 수 있는 능력이 있는 동시에 가격에 대한 조정 능력을 함께 갖추고 있다.'는 틀린 표현이다. 보기 항 (3)의 경우 본문의 내용을 정확히 파악하지 못하는 경우 무슨 말인지 알 수가 없다. 우선 세 번째 옵션인 '안전 장치'는 앞에서 설명한 두 제도를 보완한 것을 말한다. 즉, 시장의 불확실성에 대비하여 정부가 '가격에 상한선'을 설정하는 것을 말하는데 보기 항 (3)의 경우 그런 불확실성이 cap-and-trade보다 더 보장이 안 된다는 말은 틀린 표현이다. 보기 항 (4)는 바로 뒤따르는 내용에서 확인할 수 있다.

해석 탄소배출의 한계와 허용치에 대한 상호무역제도(emission cap-and-permit trading system)는 전반적인 배출량을 정하고, 다양한 가격을 허용하는 양적 도구이다. 미래의 공급과 수요 상황의 불확실성(시장의 휘발성)이 고정된 수의 오염할당분과 더불어 오염할당분의 차기 가격에 대한 불확실성을 조성한다. 따라서 산업은 이러한 불확실한 시장의 조건에 적응하는 비용을 감수해야 한다. 그러므로 불확실한 시장이란 부담은 통제 기관이라기보다는 산업이 짊어지는데, 일반적으로 이것이 더욱 효율적이다. 그러나 불확실한 시장의 조건 아래서 통제 기관이 한계치를 수정하는 능력은 "승자와 패자"를 골라내는 능력으로 전이되어 부패의 가능성을 제기한다. 대조적으로 탄소배출세는 경제활동에 따라 탄소배출의 양을 조절하도록 허용하는 반면 가격을 고정시키기 때문에 가격 도구라 한다. 탄소배출세의 주된 단점은 환경적 결과(예를 들어, 배출량에 대한 한계)가 보장되지 않는다는 점이다. 한편, 세금은 산업에서 자본을 제거하면서 유용한 경제 활동을 억압할 가능성이 있지만, 반대로 오염을 일으키는 주범은 세금의 양만큼 이윤을 예측할 수 있기에 미래의 불확실성에 대해 그만큼 대비를 할 필요가 없게 된다. 불확실한 시장의 부담은 산업 자체라기보단 세금을 부과하는 통제 기관이 짊어지게 되고, 이는 일반적으로 덜 효율적이다. 장점이라면 일정한 세율과 불확실한 시장 조건 아래 세금을 매기는 기관은 "승자와 패자"를 고르는 입장에 놓이지 않게 된다. "안전밸브"라고 알려진 세 번째 선택사항은 바로 가격과 양을 혼합한 도구이다. 이 제도는 근본적으로 배출량의 한계를 설정하고, 허용치를 교역하게 하는 제도이지만, 최대(또는 최소) 허용 가격에 제약을 둔다. 탄소를 배출하는 단체는 시장에서 허용치를 구입할 것인지 정부로부터 정해진 기준 가격(trigger price)에 허용치를 구입할 것인지 선택권을 가진다. 이 제도는 때로 정부에 새로운 정보가 드러나면서 제도를 조정할 수 있다는 유동성을 제공함으로써 (앞에서 언급한) 두 제도가 가지는 단점을 보완하는 방법으로 추천된다. 기준 가격을 적당히 높게 설정하거나 허용치의 수를 적절히 낮춤으로써 안전밸브는 순수한 양 또는 가격 메커니즘을 따라가는 데 사용될 수 있다는 점을 보였다

| 참고 사항 |

탄소베출제의 단순 모형은 다음과 같다.

Controlling Agency (Credits=Permits : 탄소허용치)

	도시 A	도시 B	도시 C
베정량	10 Credits	8 Credits	6 Credits
소비량	8 Credits	9 Credits	10 Credits

각 단체에게 탄소 허용치를 제공하는 통제 기관(Controlling Agency)을 일반적으로 정부라고 가정할 때, 도시 A, B, C에 여러 가지 조건(전년 탄소 배출량, 산업화 정도, 환경 관련 기술 개발 여부, 자금 상황 등)을 감안하여 탄소 배출량의 상한선을 각각 배정해 준다. 각 도시는 부여받은 탄소량에 대해 올해 더 많은 탄소량을 배출할지 아니면 탄소량을 줄일지 결정하게 된다. 탄소량을 조금 늘려서라도 생산을 늘리려는 도시(도시 B와 도시 C)의 경우 추가로 발생한 탄소량만큼 다른 도시에서 사오게 된다(때로는 정부에서 일정한 금액으로 판매 — 이는 곧 세금의 형태로 수입이 됨). 도시 A와 같이 배급받은 탄소량보다 더 적게 사용했을 경우, 남은 탄소를 다른 도시에 판매할 수 있게 된다. 이 경우 수익이 발생하여 도시 A는 환경 친화 정책으로 정부의 보조금뿐 아니라 탄소 허용량 판매 수익이라는 득을 얻게 된다. 이러한 모형에서 각 도시는 내년도 탄소 배출량을 최대한 줄여 정부의 보조금 및 남은 탄소 판매로 이득을 보려고 할 것인데, 이러한 과정에서 자연스레 탄소량을 줄여 환경을 보전하는 효과까지 얻게 된다. 이렇듯 자유 시장경제 안에서 이루어지는 탄소의 수요와 공급으로 발생하는 경제적 이득뿐 아니라 환경 보전의 결과를 이끌어 내려는 시도가 탄소 배출제의 기본 안이다.

어휘

quantity *n.* 양   overall *a.* 전부의; 종합의
vary *v.* ~에 변화를 주다[가하다], 다양하게 하다
couple *v.* 연결하다, 협력하다
bear *v.* (의무·책임을) 지다, 떠맡다; (비용을) 부담하다
volatile *a.* (가격·가치 등이) 심하게[끊임없이] 변동하는
translate *v.* ① 번역하다 ② (다른 형식으로) 옮기다, 고치다
corruption *n.* 타락, 퇴폐; 부패(행위)   guarantee *v.* 보증하다
suppress *v.* ① 억압하다; (반란 등을) 가라앉히다, 진압하다 ② 억누르다
conversely *ad.* 역으로   hedge *v.* ~에 예방책을 세우다
cap *v.* (가격 등의) 상한을 정하다
marketplace *n.* 시장, 장터; 상업의 중심지
trigger price 트리거 가격, 지표 가격 (덤핑 조사의 계기가 되는 가격)
fundamental *a.* 기초의, 기본의, 근본적인, 중요[주요]한, 필수의
flexibility *n.* 구부리기 쉬움, 유연성; 융통성, 신축성; (빛의) 굴절률
mimic *v.* 흉내를 내다; 흉내를 내며 조롱하다; 모방하다; 모사하다

[Challenge 9]

문제 1

답 (2)

해설 본문은 주로 콜레라의 치료 방법 중 'liquids'를 통한 방법을 소개하고 있다.

해석 대부분의 경우 콜레라는 경구 수분 보충 요법으로 성공적으로 치료할 수 있는데, 이것은 아주 효과적이고, 안전하며 투여가 쉽다. 쌀로 만든 용액은 효능이 높은 관계로 포도당으로 만든 용액보다 더 선호된다. 심각한 탈수 현상이 발생하는 경우, 정맥에 수분을 바로 주입할 필요가 있다. 링거 유산액은 아주 선호되는 용액이다. 설사가 멈출 때까지 아주 많은 양을 계속해서 바꿔줄 필요가 있다. 사람 몸무게의 10%를 물로 처음 2~4시간 동안 계속 주어야 한다. 만약 시중에서 파는 경구용 수액제가 너무 비싸거나 구하기 쉽지 않은 경우, 직접 만들 수 있다. 끓인 물 1리터, 소금 한 작은술, 설탕 여덟 작은술, 칼슘과 맛을 높이기 위해 으깬 바나나를 추가하면 된다.

어휘

cholera n. 콜레라 **treat** v. 치료하다
rehydration n. ① (요업공학) 재수화 ② (식품공학) 복원
prefer v. ~을 택하다
dehydration n. 탈수, 건조 ; [의학]탈수증
intravenous a. 정맥(내)의, 정맥주사(의)
diarrhea n. [의학]설사
subside v. 잠잠해지다, (비바람·소동 따위가) 진정되다
fluid n. ① 유동체, 유체(~ substance) ② 액체; (동물·식물의) 분비액
recipe n. (약제 등의) 처방(전) (기호 R); (요리의) 조리법
mash v. (음식을 부드럽게) 으깨다

[Challenge 10]

문제 1

답 (3)

해설 본문은 특정 현상에 대해 일반적으로 알려진 두 가지 답변 중 글쓴이가 옳다고 생각하는 견해를 제시한 후, 이에 대한 뒷받침 문장을 전개하고 있다.

문제 2

답 (3)

해설 문제에서 제시된 'occasions'란 바로 앞 문장에서 다음의 밑줄 친 부분을 가리킨다. 'I must enter my most decided protest against making it a practice to inhale through the mouth.' 즉, 입을 통해서 숨을 쉬는 때를 언급하는 것인데, 이를 가장 잘 드러내는 보기는 가수가 깊은 숨을 쉬지 않고 반호흡을 하는 (3)이 가장 적절하다. 호흡과 관련된 보기를 고르는 단순한 문제로 파악할 수도 있다.

문제 3

답 (3)

해설 dust and other impurities'에서 콧구멍을 통과하면서 정화 작용이 일어남을 확인할 수 있으며, 아래의 본문에서 콧구멍을 통과하면서 직접적으로 찬 공기가 소리 기관에 닿지 않고, 따뜻해진 후 거치는 것을 알 수 있다.

> its temperature is not materially altered ... The consequence is that the throat and voice-box, when heated by singing or talking, or by hot rooms, are often exposed to cold, raw, and foggy winter air, and serious derangements of the respiratory organs are the natural consequence.

해석 호흡을 입을 통해서 해야 하는가 코를 통해서 해야 하는가라는 질문에 대하여, 나는 입을 통해서 들이마신다는 것에 철저하게 반대하는 바이다. 물론 이것이 불가피할 때가 있는 경우도 있다. 그러나 '완전히 들이마시는' 또는 '온전히 들이마시는' 것은 순간에 일어나는 것이 아니다. 시간이 걸리고 점차적으로 꾸준히, 그리고 전혀 방해가 없이 이루어져야 한다. 이러한 행위는 항상 코를 통해서만 이루어진다. 입은 본래 숨 쉬는 용도가 아닌 반면, 코는 특히 이러한 목적을 위해 놀랍도록 적응되어 있다. 이러한 (코의) 통로를 통해 폐가 잘 부풀고 재빠르게 채워질 뿐 아니라, 이것은 매우 정교하게 고안되어 있어서 "인공호흡기" 역할도 동시에 하여, 공기가 발음 기관의 더욱 섬세한 부분에 닿기 전에 정화하고 따뜻하게 해준다. 반면, 입을 통해서 숨을 들이마시게 되면, 공기가 후두로 바로 운반이 되는데, 이때 먼지 또는 다른 불순물이 함께 들어오고, 들어오는 공기 온도가 현저하게 바뀌지 않는다(그렇기에 아주 섬세한 발음 기관에 따뜻하지 않은 공기가 손상을 줄 수 있음). 결론은 목과 후두가 노래를 해서, 말을 해서, 아니면 방이 더워서 열을 받으면 종종 차갑고, 으슬으슬하고, 안개 서린 겨울 공기에 노출되어 호흡 기관의 심각한 장애가 자연스런 결과로 발생한다는 것이다. 게다가, 이러한 해로운 숨쉬기 습관에 일단 물리게(걸리게) 되면, 우리는 곧 입을 벌리고 자며, 목이 건조하게 되어 결국 많은 질병의 씨앗을 뿌리게 된다.

어휘

inspiration n. 숨을 들이쉼 **nostril** n. 콧구멍
protest n. 이의제기, 항의
make[enter, lodge] a protest with a person against
에게 ~에 대해 항의하다, 이의를 신청하다
inhale v. 숨을 들이쉬다 **occasion** n. 때
unavoidable a. 피할 수 없는 **complete** a. 온전한
inflation n. 팽창 **moment** n. 0
gradually ad. 점진적으로 **steadily** ad. 지속적으로
interruption n. 방해 **admirably** ad. 감3탄할 만하게

Day 3

adapt *v.* 적응하다   lung *n.* 폐   fill *v.* 채우다
channel *n.* 경로, 수단   cunningly *ad.* 교묘하게
devise *v.* 고안해 내다   respirator *n.* 인공호흡기
delicate *a.* 섬세한   vocal *a.* 음성의
organ *n.* (생물의) 기관   voice-box *n.* 후두(喉頭)
dust *n.* 먼지   impurity *n.* 불순물   temperature *n.* 온도
materially *ad.* 현저하게   alter *v.* 바꾸다
expose *v.* 노출하다   raw *a.* 날것의   foggy *a.* 안개 낀
derangement *n.* 착란, 혼란
respiratory *a.* 호흡의   pernicious *a.* 유독한
contract *v.* (병에) 걸리다   parch *v.* 바싹 마르게 하다
seed *n.* 씨앗   disorder *n.* (신체 기능의) 장애

Day 4

[Challenge 1]

문제 1

답 (4)

해설 본문은 미괄식 구성의 전형적 패턴을 따르고 있다. 개별적 사항을 일반화하는 마지막 문장의 'these'를 확인한다.

> 1) Making a study schedule is one important step in becoming a successful student in college. Students should schedule one hour of study time for every one hour of class time. At exam time, more study time may be necessary. 2) Also, students must study in an appropriate place. It is important to study in a quiet place away from the distraction of other people and such things as the television and the radio. Students should find a comfortable place with plenty of space for all the necessary study supplies. 3) Then, students need to study the information in small amounts. It is a good idea to learn the required concepts slowly and thoroughly instead of trying to learn everything on the evening before the exam. 4) Students who want to be successful in college should remember these three helpful study strategies.

1) 구체적 진술 1: Make a study schedule
2) 구체적 진술 2: Study in a appropriate place
3) 구체적 진술 3: Study information in small amounts
4) 글의 결론: 성공적인 대학생이 되기 위해 위의 3가지 학습 전략을 기억해야 한다.

해설 습 계획을 짜는 것은 성공적인 대학생이 되는 첫 번째 중요한 단계이다. 학생은 매 시간의 수업에 맞는 학습 시간을 짜야 한다. 시험 기간에는 더 많은 시간이 필요할지도 모른다. 또한 학생은 적절한 장소에서 공부해야 한다. 다른 사람이나 TV 그리고 라디오와 같은 것에 방해를 받지 않는 조용한 장소에서 공부하는 것은 중요하다. 학생은 모든 필요한 학용품을 놓을 수 있는 여유 있는 공간이 제공되는 편안한 장소를 찾아야 한다. 그리고 학생은 적은 양으로 나누어 정보를 공부할 필요가 있다. 시험 전날 저녁에 전부 익히려 하기보다는 필요한 개념을 천천히 철저하게 익히는 게 좋다. 대학생활을 성공적으로 보내려는 학생은 이런 유용한 세 가지 학습 전략을 기억해야만 한다.

어휘

successful *a.* 성공한, 성공적인
necessary *a.* 필요한, 필연적인
appropriate *a.* 적절한   distraction *n.* 집중을 방해하는 것
comfortable *a.* 편한, 쾌적한   plenty *n.* 풍부한 양
supply *n.* 필수품   concept *n.* 개념
thoroughly *ad.* 대단히, 완전히, 철저하게
strategy *n.* 전략

[Challenge 2]

문제 1

답 (3)

해설 본문은 현재 농가에서 낭비되고 있는 수력에 관한 글로, 그 효용성을 강조하면서 수력 이용을 촉구하는 내용이다. 현재 농가가 지닌 문제점을 지적하고 이에 대한 대안을 제시한 후 그 타당한 이유가 제시되는 글의 패턴을 파악한다.

문제 2

답 (1)

해설 본문에서 현재 물이 낭비되고 있다고 말하고 있다. 'Since water-power is running to waste on tens of thousands of our farms throughout the country.' 보기 항 (1)은 잘못된 표현이다.

해설 평범한 농부가 얻을 수 있는 수단 내 현대 설비로 인해 전기 생산은 나름의 독특한 편성과 함께 수차나 가솔린(또는 다른 형태의 내연기관) 엔진 또는 일반적인 풍차와 같이 믿을 만한 동력원이 갖추어진다면 자동화가 된다. 수차는 후미진 발전소에서 발전기로 쓰이기에 이상적인 주된 동력이다. 수력은 전국의 수많은 농가에서 낭비되고 있기에, 여기에 많은 관심이 필요하다. 농장의 목초지에 물을 댈 수 있는 작고 무시될 만한 작은 시내도 위험하고, 불편한 기름 램프를 대신해서 깨끗하고, 시원하며 안전한 빛을 농가에 공급할 만큼의 충분한 힘을 가지고 있다. 25~50마력의 동력을 발생시킬 수 있는 작은 시내는 농부에게 (사실상 초기 설치 비용 외의 비용이 없이) 빛뿐만 아니라 탈곡과 같은 훨씬 많은 노동이 들어가는 농가의 작업조차 할 수 있는 힘을 제공해 준다. 게다가 빨래, 다리미질 그리고 요리뿐 아니라 동시에 추운 겨울에 집을 따뜻하게 보존하는 능력까지 제공해 준다. 1마력이 못 되는 에너지로 농장을 밝히고, 5마력이 못 되는 에너지로 불빛과 작은 동력을 제공하고 고된 부엌일을 덜어주는 것이다.

어휘

appliance *n.* 설비, 장치, 기기
generation *n.* (전기, 열 등의) 발생
electricity *n.* 전기; 전류   unique *a.* 유일무이한
convenience *n.* 편리, 편의; 형편이 좋음
automatic *a.* 자동의   provided *conj.* (만약) ~라면
dependable *a.* 신뢰할 수 있는   source *n.* 근원, 출처
internal *a.* 내부의; 국내의   combustion *n.* 연소; 산화
windmill *n.* 풍차   ideal *a.* 이상적인
prime *a.* 첫째의; 가장 중요한; 기초적인
isolated *a.* 격리된   attention *n.* 주의, 관심
tiny *a.* 작은; 조그마한   brook *n.* 시내
pasture *n.* 목장; 목초지   farmstead *n.* 농장
inconvenient *a.* 불편한, 형편이 나쁜
capable *a.* 유능한; 능력이 있는   horsepower *n.* 마력
operation *n.* 작용, 효력, 조작, 운영
thresh *v.* 탈곡[타작]하다   ironing *n.* 다림질
provide *v.* 제공하다; 주다   drudgery *n.* 단조롭고 힘든 일

[Challenge 3]

문제 1
답 (2)
해설 본문에서 상업 운임의 중요성을 언급하고 있지만, 그렇다고 이것이 시민의 권리를 억누를 만큼 중요하다고 말하는 것은 논리적 비약이다. 보기 항 (2)는 틀린 표현이다.

문제 2
답 (2)
해설 삽입구를 고르는 문제이다. 보기 항에서 알 수 있듯이, 'if not'으로 시작하는 양보구문의 삽입인데, 바로 뒤에 이어지는 진술보다 더 중요하고 근본적인 의미를 지닌 표현이 와야 한다. 고로, 'comfort, growth, prosperity, happiness'보다 더 근본적이고 중요한 표현을 전달하는 보기 항은 (2)이다.

문제 3
답 (1)
해설 앞에서 전개된 내용을 요약/정리하는 내용이 뒤따르고 있다.
해석 미국의 상업은 미국 존재 자체는 아니라 하더라도 적어도 미국의 안락, 성장, 번영 그리고 행복을 위해 필수적이다. 미국 국민의 소질, 성격 그리고 습관은 아주 상업적이다. 이들의 도시는 이 상업을 기초로 형성되었고 존재하고 있다. 우리의 농업, 어업, 예술 그리고 제조는 모두 이 상업과 관련이 되어 있으며 거기에 의존한다. 간단히 말해, 상업은 이 나라가 현재의 나라가 되도록 만든 장본인이며, 이것을 파괴하거나 무시하는 경우 사람들이 빈곤과 고통에 휩싸이게 된다. 상당히 많은 수의 사람들이 직접적으로 오로지 선박으로 생계를 유지한다. 다른 시민의 권리와 마찬가지로 상업과 바다 운임의 권리 보전을 위해 사회는 믿음의 서약을 한다. 이런 관점에서, 내가 만약 우리가 상업을 보호하고 이 둘을 보전하기 위한 유일하고도 확실한 방법으로 우리나라가 적절한 방어 자세를 취하게 하기 위해 분발해야 한다고 말하지 않는다면, 나는 아마도 의무 불이행의 책임을 져야 할 것이다.

어휘

commerce *n.* 상업, 통상; 무역; 거래
essential *a.* 근본적인, 본질적인; 가장 중요한
comfort *n.* 위로, 위안, 안락   prosperity *n.* 번영; 번창; 부유
genius *n.* 풍조, 특질
commercial *a.* 상업의, 영리적인; 돈벌이 위주인
agriculture *n.* 농업, 농학
manufactures *n.* (대량 생산) 제품
connect *v.* 잇다; 연결[접속]하다   poverty *n.* 가난, 빈곤, 결핍
distress *n.* 고통, 고충   solely *ad.* 혼자서, 단독으로, 오로지
pledge *n.* 맹세하다, 서약하다   preservation *n.* 보존, 저장
affair *n.* 일, 요건, 업무
guilty *a.* 유죄의; 죄를 범한; 떳떳하지 못한
forbear *v.* 억제하다; 삼가다; 멀리하다
recommend *v.* 추천하다, 권고하다
exertion *n.* 노력, 전력, 분발   protect *v.* 보호하다, 지키다
suitable *a.* 적당한, 상당한, 어울리는
posture *n.* 자세, 태도   defense *n.* 방위, 방어, 변명
preserve *v.* 보존[유지하다]; 보호하다

[Challenge 4]

문제 1
답 (2)
해설 본문의 핵심어는 바로 'female friendship'이다. 여성(암컷) 간의 우정은 여성(암컷) 자신을 보호하고, 오래 존속하게 하는 자연이 선사한 하나의 방어 체계임을 설명하고 있다.

문제 2
답 (3)
해설 드라마의 주인공 Hannah를 통해서 여자끼리의 정이 인간에게도 해당됨을 알 수 있다. 덜 사회적인 사람(이는 동물) 우정을 통해 더 사교적인 사람이 된다는 내용은 없다. 보기 (3)은 옳은 진술이다('female chacma baboons with strong sororal bonds have lower levels of stress hormones'를 참고). 본문 마지막 부분을 보면, 우정의 깊이 또한 중요한 역할을 한다는 점을 파악할 수 있다.

문제 3

답 (4)

해설 빈칸이 들어간 문맥을 보면, 아프리카 코끼리, 쥐 그리고 원숭이 등이 서로 상호 호혜적인 우정을 맺는다고 나와 있는데, 이러한 요소는 삶의 기본적인 단위이며 이를 통해 많은 이득을 얻었다고 언급하고 있다. 순접 추가의 〈not only A but also B〉는 A = B이므로 답에 들어갈 표현은 A 부분의 내용과 같은 맥락이 되어야 한다. 고로, 동물들이 애당초(in the first place) 동료와 우정을 맺었던 이유를 설명해 준다는 내용이 전개되어야 하므로 이를 가장 잘 드러내는 보기는 'going herd(무리를 짓다)'이다.

문제 4

답 (2)

해설 본문 마지막 부분에서 적은 숫자지만 친밀한 친구관계를 유지하는 것이 폭넓지만 얇은 관계의 우정을 형성하는 경우보다 덜 스트레스를 받는다는 내용이 전개되므로 이를 자연스럽게 받을 수 있는 내용은 보기 (2)에 해당한다.

해석 HBO의 새로운 히트 시리즈 "Girls"의 놀라울 정도로 침울한 20대 중반의 여주인공 한나를 처음 만났을 때, 그녀에게는 Penway Park의 볼링 레인보다 그녀를 치는 스트라이크가 더 많은 듯 보인다. 그녀의 부모님은 그녀의 월 용돈을 줄였다. 그녀의 문학 잡지 사장은 그녀를 무보수 인턴에서 정규직으로 돌리길 꺼린다. 그녀는 뉴욕시에 산다. 그녀는 영문학을 전공했다.

그러나 이런 모든 투석(볼링의 핀처럼 나를 강타하는 부정적 요소)과 위험 요소를 상쇄하는 강력한 방어 체계가 있으니, 바로 여자 친구들이다. 한나에게는 탄탄한 유대 관계를 맺고 있는 세 명의 여자 친구가 있는데, 한 명은 단짝 친구이고, 두 명은 그다음으로 친한 친구들이다. 이 여자 친구들 중 어느 누구도 빌려서 생활하는 아파트에서 여분의 방도 없이 살면서 물질적 지원을 많이 해주지 못하지만, 이들은 서로 감정적으로 지렛대 역할을 해준다. 그녀의 명목상(작품 이름과 같은)의 인물들이 모두 남자들과 데이트를 한다지만, 여자끼리의 우정이야말로 "이 프로그램의 진정한 로맨스"라고 할 수 있다.

도시의 정글과 마찬가지로, 자연의 정글 또한 마찬가지다. 연구가들은 최근 암컷끼리의 우정이 자연에서 선호하는, 이야기를 풀어내는 도구 중 하나라는 많은 증거를 모았다. 아프리카 코끼리와 협간의 쥐, 케냐의 파란 원숭이 그리고 뉴질랜드 야생말의 암컷 사이에 오가는 친밀하고 오래 지속되는 상호 호혜적인 관계는 사회생활의 기본적인 단위로 밝혀졌는데, 이는 기존 구성원들의 유대를 높여줄 뿐 아니라 왜 동물의 조상들이 애당초 굳이 떼를 지어 살게 되었는지를 설명해 주는 요소이다.

과학자들은 암컷 원숭이가 한 쌍이 서로 쾌락적인 애착 상태로 가는 과정을 지켜보는 관측 단계에서 양측이 고른 파트너를 향한 잘 다듬어진 우정이 갖는 이점을 수치화하는 단계로 이동하고 있다. 과학자들은 자매처럼 강력한 유대관계를 가진 암컷 차크마개코원숭이들이 그렇지 않은 동료보다 스트레스 호르몬 수치가 낮고, 상당히 더 오래 살며, 새끼들을 잘 키워 독립을 더 잘 시킨다는 것을 발견했다.

마찬가지로, 암컷 친구가 있는 야생 암말의 경우 사회적 유대가 결여된 암말보다 수컷 말들에게 괴롭힘을 당하는 경우가 덜하고 새끼들이 더 오래 살았다. 보금자리 파트너로 친구를 선택할 수 있도록 허용된 암컷 쥐들은, 좋아하지 않는 쥐와 짚단을 함께 쓰도록 강요된 암컷들보다 새끼를 더 많이 가졌다. 연구원들은 수적으로는 적지만 현실적으로 털 손질을 해주는 친구가 있는 암컷 원숭이가, 사교망이 넓지만 관계가 깊지 못한 암컷보다 스트레스 호르몬인 코티솔 분비가 들쭉날쭉한 경향이 덜하다는 것을 알아냈다.

어 휘

mopey a. 침울한
stipend n. 수당, 급료
sling n. 투석기, 새총, 일격
tight-knit a. (계획이) 빈틈없는, (조직이) 긴밀한
confederate n. 동맹자, 일당, 한패
runners-up n. 차선자
tourniquet n. 지혈기
titular character (소설 등의) 주제 인물
hedonic n. 쾌락의   foal n. (말·나귀 따위의) 새끼
well-groomed a. 단정한
sororal a. 자매의
mare n. 암말   pup n. 강아지, 새끼

[Challenge 5]

문제 1

답 (4)

해설 보기 항 (1)은 두 번째 문단 첫 번째 문장에서 발견할 수 있다. 보기 항 (2)의 경우 첫 번째 문단 초반부에서 확인할 수 있으며, 보기 항 (3)은 아래 본문에 명시되어 있다.

> Indeed, it has been said that Rome had influenced Christianity quite as much as Christianity did Rome.

또한, 아래 보기에서 기독교도 이교도를 박해했음을 알 수 있다.

In the same manner that the early emperors had ordered the persecution of Christianity, so the later ones ordered the persecution of heathendom, nor had the Church grown civilized or Christian enough to oppose this method of conversion

문제 2

답 (3)

해설 문장 삽입 문제는 대명사, 정관사, it 그리고 접속사 등을 활용하면 접근이 용이하다. 해석 자체로 접근하기보다는 단서를 찾는 연습을 한다. 본문 (c)의 내용을 보게 되면, 'They'가 나오는데 이를 받을 수 있는 구체적인 대상이 앞에 드러나 있지 않다. 제시된 문장의 'The legal-minded Romans'가 이를 받고 있음을 알 수 있다.

문제 3

답 (3)

해설 밑줄 친 부분에서 이교도들은 자신의 종교를 위해 순교할 만큼 열정적이지 않음을 파악할 수 있다. 즉, 종교를 지키기 위해 목숨을 내놓지는 않았기 때문에, 많은 사람이 죽을 일이 없었다는 것을 알 수 있다.

해석 이 황폐하고 험난한 시대를 지나면서 인류를 유지하고 인류의 진보를 도왔던 영향력 중에서 가장 중요한 영향력에 대한 이야기가 아직 남았다. 그것은 바로 기독교, 현재 로마 가톨릭 교회라는 구체적인 형태를 갖추고 있는 그 기독교였다. 고대 제국에 의해 그 정복자에게 부여된 모든 제도 중에서 가장 강력한 것은 바로 이 교회였다. 게다가, 로마는 기독교가 로마에 미친 영향력만큼 기독교에 영향을 꽤나 미쳤다고 여겨진다. 법률적 성향을 지닌 로마 사람들은 확고한 조직, 성직, 위계를 세우는 것과 관련된 정확한 이론과 신조를 전개할 것을 주장했다. 이들은 단지 개인적인 신념과 충동쯤이었던 것에 조직적 법의 중요성을 부여했다. 그래서 교회는 견고하고 강하게 성장했다.

초기 황제들이 기독교 박해를 명령했던 것과 마찬가지로 후대 황제들도 이교도 박해를 명했는데, 교회도 이러한 방법의 개종을 반대할 만큼 문명화되거나 기독교적이진 못했다. 그러나 모든 당사자(기독교든 이교도든)에게 다행히도, 이교도는 순교를 주장할 만큼 충분히 열정적인 면이 부족했으며 그래서 인간이 궁극적으로 가장 순수한 종교에조차 부여한 이 박해의 정신은 여전히 숨어있었다(겉으로 드러나지 않았다. 다시 말해 기독교가 로마로부터 받은 엄청난 참담함이 이교도들에게는 일어나지 않았다는 뜻).

어휘

wandering *a.* 헤매는; 방랑하는
desolate *a.* 황폐한; 황량한; 쓸쓸한
sustain *v.* 지탱하다, 지속시키다
humanity *n.* 인류; 인간성; 인간애
onward *ad.* 앞으로; 전방에 **definite** *a.* 뚜렷한; 명확한
bequeath *v.* (후세에) 전하다; 남기다
ancient *a.* 옛날의; 고대의 **empire** *n.* 제국; 통치
conqueror *n.* 정복자; 승리자 **belief** *n.* 확신, 신뢰, 신앙
impulse *n.* (갑작스러운) 충동 **persecution** *n.* 박해
heathendom *n.* 이교도 **civilize** *v.* 문명화하다; 교화하다
oppose *v.* 반대하다; 대항하다
conversion *n.* 개종, 전향; 전환, 개조
scarce *a.* 부족한; 결핍; 적은 **sufficiently** *ad.* 충분히
enthusiastic *a.* 열심인; 열정적인
insist *v.* 우기다; 주장하다; 고집하다
martyrdom *n.* 순교 **spirit** *n.* 정신; 영
impart *v.* 나누어 주다; 전하다 **latent** *a.* 숨어 있는; 잠재적인

[Challenge 6]

문제 1

답 (3)

해설 본문은 토머스 페인이라는 사람이 어떤 인물인지 구체적으로 묘사하는 글이다. 글을 읽으면서 주인공의 특징이 나오는 부분은 표시를 해 둘 필요가 있다. 토머스 페인은 본문 초반에서 알 수 있듯이, 알다가도 모를 인물로 묘사되고 있다. 고로, 보기 항 (1)은 적절한 표현이다. 같은 맥락에서 보기 항 (2)도 본문 전반에 깔린 내용이다. 하지만 보기 항 (3)의 경우, 토머스 페인은 무엇보다 이성과 논리를 강조한 사람이라고 했다. 'When he believed something, he was incapable of hiding such belief or even tempering it.'에서 보기 항 (4)도 옳다는 것을 알 수 있다.

문제 2

답 (2)

해설 본문에서 토머스 페인은 남의 사랑과 증오를 다 받은 인물이며, 어떤 상황에서도 그가 옳다고 생각하는 점은 남의 마음을 상하게 하더라도 전한다고 했다. 고로, 이러한 맥락에서 그가 가지고 있지 않은 성격이란 바로 '무관심'이라고 볼 수 있다. 보기 항 (1)을 고르지 말아야 한다. 본문에서 그가 부정적으로 묘사되는 부분도 있지만, 많은 사람에게 사랑과 존경을 받은 측면도 있음을 간과해선 안 된다.

해석 토머스 페인에 대해서 우리는 아주 많이 알면서도 동시에 그에 대해서 거의 모르는 점은 참 이상하다. 모든 친구만큼이나 그는 적을 두고 있었다. 그는 아주 사랑을 받는 동시에 격렬히 미움을 받았으며, 칭찬과 중상, 조롱과 존경을 받았다. 그가 일으키지 못한 유일한 감정이란 바로 무관심이었다. 그는 격하기 쉬운 성격에 화를 잘 내고 숨김없이 말하는 사람이었다. 그가 어떤 것을 믿었을 때, 그는 이 믿음을 숨길 수 없었으며, 이것을 조절조차 할 수 없었다. 그는

이성과 논리를 숭상했으며, 다른 이가 이러한 특성이 없으면 경멸했다. 그는 스스로 그가 다른 이에게 일으킨 동일한 강도로 사랑하고 증오했다.

어휘

curious *a.* 별난; 진기한
violently *ad.* 격렬하게; 맹렬하게
praise *v.* 칭찬하다; 찬양하다
slander *v.* 중상하다; 비방하다
mock *v.* 조롱하다 **revere** *v.* 존경하다; 숭배하다
emotion *n.* 감정
provoke *v.* 일으키다; 성나게 하다; 유발시키다
volatile *a.* 변덕스러운 **outspoken** *a.* 거침없이 말하는
hide *v.* 숨기다; 잠복하다; 비밀로 하다
temper *v.* 부드럽게 하다; 진정시키다; 담금질하다
worship *v.* 열렬히 숭배하다 **reason** *n.* 이성
logic *n.* 논리; 논법 **despise** *v.* 경멸하다
absence *n.* 부재; 결석 **quality** *n.* 특성, 특징
intensity *n.* 강도, 세기; 격렬함

attach *v.* 붙이다, 첨가시키다 **literal** *a.* 문자의, 글자 그대로의
assertion *n.* 단언, 주장 **inanimate** *a.* 무생물의
imaginative *a.* 상상의, 가공의
latitude *n.* (사상, 견해 등의) 허용 정도
conceivably *ad.* 상상할 수 있게
humorous *a.* 유머러스한, 익살스러운
significant *a.* 중요한 **extent** *n.* 넓이, 정도, 범위
possess *v.* 소유하다, 가지고 있다
purchase *v.* (노력하여) 얻다
in relation to ~에 관하여(관련하여)
represent *v.* 묘사하다, 나타나다, 그리다

[Challenge 7]

문제 1

답 (1)

해설 아래의 본문에서 답을 이끌어 낼 수 있다.

> to achieve this effect, the cartoonist must picture the table as having human features

해석 그러면 물질과 정신 사이의 이런 논리적 관계란 무엇인가? 이 질문은 예를 들어 만화가가 특정한 탁자가 화가 났거나 고통을 느낀다는 것을 어떻게 보여주는가를 고찰함으로써 최선의 답변을 내릴 수 있다. 자, 위에서 언급한 바와 같이, 특정한 생명력이 없는 물체가 화를 내거나 고통을 느낀다는 주장을 문자 그대로 적용한다는 것은 불가능하다. 그러나 분명 특정한 목적을 위해 어떤 상상의 폭을 허용할 경우 만화가는 자신의 상상력으로 탁자가 화를 내고 있다는 것을 유머 있게 묘사할 수 있다. 그러나 이 관계에서 중요한 것은, 이러한 효과를 거두려면 만화가가 탁자를 인간의 특성이 있는 모습으로 그려야 한다는 것, 다시 말해서 그려진 탁자가 자연스러운 인간의 화난 표정을 짓고 있어야 그것이 우리에게 화난 모습으로 보이게 될 것이라는 점이다. 즉, 탁자와의 관계에서 노여움이라는 개념은 그 탁자가 인간과 같은 어떤 모습으로 그려질 때만 얻을 수 있다.

어휘

logical *a.* 논리적인 **connection** *n.* 연결, 관계
physical *a.* 물리적인 **mental** *a.* 마음의, 정신의
cartoonist *n.* 만화가 **indicate** *v.* 가리키다, 지적하다

[Challenge 8]

문제 1

답 (2)

해설 글의 도입부에 문장 단위의 빈칸이 주어진 경우 일반 진술에 해당하는 주제문 또는 중심 내용을 압축적으로 반영한 문장인 경우가 많다. 이후 전개되는 구체적 진술을 바탕으로 빈칸의 내용을 이끌어 내야 한다. 본문은 루퍼트 머독이 운영하는 회사가 개인의 휴대폰을 통해 개인정보를 수집했다는 스캔들에 관한 내용이다. 카메라를 통해 개인의 사생활을 '지켜보던' 1984년의 소설과 달리 휴대폰을 통해 '귀로 들으며' 감시하는 내용이다. 고로 보기 (2)가 가장 적절한 답안이 된다.

문제 2

답 (4)

해설 'He stressed egalitarianism, while warning about the dangers of concentrated power in government as well as corporations.' 부분에서 보기 (4)의 내용을 추론할 수 있다. 보기 (1)과 같이 본문에서 영국 정부가 현재의 상황을 수수방관하고 있다는 내용은 없다. 보기 (2)와 같이 개인정보를 수집한 머독이 이에 대한 비난과 혐의를 용케 비켜나갈 수 있다는 내용도 없다. 오히려, 'Revelations that Rupert Murdoch's News International Corp. for years has conducted massive hacking into British cell phone information are truly shocking.'의 내용을 통해 그가 곧 정당한 법적 처벌을 받을 것이란 추론이 더 적절하다. 본문 마지막에서 보는 바와 같이 기업으로부터 개인정보를 전적으로 보호한다는 것은 쉬운 일이 아니라는 말 ("guarding individual freedom, including privacy, from intrusive power structures inevitably is a challenge")은 언급이 되어 있지만, 그렇다고 보기 (3)과 같이 '거의 불가능하다'고 보는 것은 논리적 비약이다.

해석 "빅 브라더가 당신을 지켜보고 있다"는 영국의 작가 조지 오웰의 고전 "1984"에서 핵심적인 문구였다. 이제 우리는 빅 브라더가 (몰래) 듣고 있는 것도 알게 되었다. 루퍼

트 머독의 News International Corp.이 수년간 영국의 휴대전화 번호 정보를 대량으로 해킹했다는 발표는 실로 충격적이다. 알려진 대상에는 살해된 어린 여자아이와 작전 중 사망한 군인 가족들의 전화 내용이 포함되어 있다. 영국의 정당들로서는 보기 드물게도 의회에 모여 이 회사를 비난했다. 스캔들에 포함된 내용 중 경찰이 뇌물을 받았다는 것도 있다. 영국에서 머독의 정치적 영향력은 엄청나다. 정치권 인사들은 (자신들을) 난처하게 할 수도 혹은 지지해 줄 수도 있는 그가 가진 힘을 두려워하며, 그의 호의를 얻기 위해 노력해왔다. 오웰은 20세기의 위대한 작가 중 한 명으로 열렬한 사회주의자였다. 그러나 다른 좌파와 달리, 그는 노동자 계층과 개인적으로 연관이 있었는데, 이는 그가 노동자 중의 한 명이었기 때문이었다. 그는 평등주의를 강조하는 동시에 정부뿐 아니라 기업에 집중된 권력의 위험성을 경고했다. 머독과 관련된 정보 누출 스캔들은 특히나 복잡한 양상을 보이기에, 미디어 제국 전체를 흔들 수도 있다. 그러나 불가피하게 권리를 침해하는 권력 조직으로부터 사생활을 비롯하여 개인의 자유를 보호하기란 쉬운 일이 아니다.

어휘

punch-line *n.* (농담·연설·광고·우스갯소리 등의) 급소가 되는 문구
in action 작전 중에   **allegation** *n.* 진술, 증거 없는 주장
payoff *n.* 뇌물   **across the spectrum** 전반에 걸쳐
egalitarianism *n.* 인류 평등주의   **bring down** 붕괴시키다

[Challenge 9]

문제 1

답 (1)

해설 본문은 퉁구스 창조 신화를 다루는 내용이다.

문제 2

답 (3)

해설 Buga와 Buninka가 처음 만났을 때 다툰 내용은 누가 세상을 처음 만들었는지에 관한 것이다. Buga가 처음 땅을 드러내고, 내려갔을 때 이미 Buninka가 존재하고 있었다. Buga는 사람의 몸 각 부분에 맞는 다양한 재료를 활용했다. 고로, 보기 항 (3)은 옳은 표현이다. 보기 항 (4)는 함정이다. 본문에서 모든 죽은 자가 다 Buninka에게 가는 것이 아니라, 'the evil join Buninka in hell'에서 알 수 있듯이 죽은 자 중 악한 이만 그에게 가도록 Buninka에게 허용을 했다.

문제 3

답 (2)

해설 (a)는 Buga, (b)는 Buninka를 가리킨다는 것을 목적어 자리의 대상을 통해 쉽게 파악할 수 있다. 그러므로 보기 (c)의 대상이 누구를 가리키는지 알 경우 보기 (d)의 내용은 파악할 필요가 없다. 'Buga agreed he would bow to Buninka's powers'에서 he는 Buga를 가리킨다. 그러므로 답은 (2)이다.

해석 퉁구스족 창조 신화에 따르면 과거의 한때 모든 곳은 물만이 존재했다. 가장 중요한 신인 Buga는 이 물에 맞서 불을 발산했다. 긴 투쟁 끝에 대부분 물은 없어지고 땅이 출현했다. 그런 다음 Buga는 빛을 창조하고 이것을 어둠과 구별했으며, 새로 창조한 땅으로 내려갔다. 거기서 그는 Buninka라는 악마와 직면했으며, 누가 세상을 창조했는지에 대해 논쟁이 일어났다. Buninka는 악했고 Buga의 창조를 훼손하려고 했다. 그는 Buga의 12줄 수금을 끊어버렸고, Buga는 너무 화가 나 Buninka에게 바다 한가운데서 전나무를 만들어 자라게 한 후 꿈쩍 않고 서 있게 하라고 요구했다. Buga는 Buninka가 만약 그렇게 할 수 있다면 그의 힘에 복종할 것이며, 만약 실패하면 Buga 자신도 그와 같은 도전을 하겠다고 했다. 만약 Buga가 성공한다면, Buninka는 Buga가 가장 강력한 창조주라는 것을 그에게 인정해야만 한다. Buninka는 도전에 응했으며 바다에서 전나무가 솟아오를 것을 명령했다. 그 나무는 자랐지만, 약하고 앞뒤로 움직였다. Buga는 그런 다음 두 번째 나무를 만들었지만, 이것은 번성하고 위엄 있는 나무로 자랐다. Buninka는 Buga의 위대한 힘을 어쩔 수 없이 인정했으며, 경의를 표했다. Buga가 Buninka의 머리에 손을 얹자 그의 머리는 철로 변했다. 이것이 Buninka에게 큰 고통을 주었기에, 그는 Buga에게 풀어달라고 요구했으며, Buga는 이를 불쌍히 여겼다. Buninka는 그런 다음 지구를 떠돌 수 있었다. Buga는 인간을 만들기 위해서 물질을 모았다. 동쪽에서 그는 철을 모았으며, 남쪽에서는 불, 서쪽에서는 물 그리고 북쪽에는 흙을 모았다. 흙에서 그는 살과 뼈를 만들고, 철에서 심장, 물에서 피를 만들고, 불로 이들에게 생명력을 불어넣었다. 이렇게 그는 남자와 여자 두 존재를 만들었다. Buninka는 인간에게 어떠한 상해를 가하는 것도 엄격히 금지되었지만, 이들이 수가 증가하면서 그는 반은 자신의 것으로 주장하길 원했다. Buga는 그에게 어떠한 살아 있는 사람을 주는 것도 거부했다. 그러나 Buninka는 악한 남녀가 죽은 뒤에는 가지는 것이 허용되었고, Buga는 자신에게 덕이 있는 자만을 속하게 했다. 그리고 죽음 후, 악한 이는 Buninka와 지옥에서 만난다. 그곳은 지구의 중심으로 이들은 거기서 벌을 받는다.

어휘

creation *n.* 창조(물)   **myth** *n.* 신화
central *a.* 중심의   **deity** *n.* 신
issue *v.* 나타나다; 공표하다   **consume** *v.* 소비하다, 소모하다
emerge *v.* 나오다, 나타나다
separate *v.* 갈라서 떼어놓다, 분리하다
darkness *n.* 암흑; 무지   **descend** *v.* 내려가다, 내려오다
newly *ad.* 최근, 새로이   **confront** *v.* 직면하다, 대면하다
dispute *v.* 논쟁하다, 논하다
spiteful *a.* 원한을 품은, 심술궂은

string *v.* 현을 매다, 실을 꿰다   **lyre** *n.* 수금
fir-tree *n.* 전나무   **bow** *v.* 굴복하다, 항복하다
concede *v.* 인정하다, 시인하다
creator *n.* 창조자   **bob** *v.* 갑자기 움직이다
fro *ad.* 저 쪽으로   **thrive** *v.* 번창하다, 번성하다
stately *a.* 당당한, 위엄 있는   **homage** *n.* 존경
relent *v.* 누그러지다, 측은하게 생각하다
gather *v.* 모으다   **flesh** *n.* 살   **bone** *n.* 뼈
blood *n.* 피   **vitality** *n.* 생명력, 활기
vicious *a.* 사악한, 악의 있는   **virtuous** *a.* 덕이 높은, 정숙한

[Challenge 10]

문제 1

답 (4)

해설 본문 마지막 부분에서 John Jay가 처음부터 'radical'하지 않았다는 점을 파악할 수 있다.

문제 2

답 (4)

해설 본문은 John Jay의 헌법 초안 작성을 둘러싼 분분한 의견에 대해 글쓴이가 견해를 드러낸 것이다. 전체적으로 '정치적' 성격이 드러난다는 것을 알 수 있다.

문제 3

답 (1)

해설 빈칸이 들어간 진술 앞쪽의 내용은 다음과 같다.

> Too much and too little credit has been given Jay for his part in the work.

즉, 앞에서 전개된 견해에 대한 상반된 글이 이후 전개되는데, 첫 번째 'too much credit'에 대한 진술이 나오고 다음 'too little credit'에 대한 내용이 나오고 있다. 고로, 이 둘을 연결하는 접속사는 대조를 드러내는 보기 항 (1)이 가장 적절하다.

문제 4

답 (1)

해설 비유적으로 쓰인 표현이다. 우선 잔칫집에 초대된 정치인을 말하고 있으며, 이후 전개되는 내용으로 보아 '주정부의 법과 관습'은 독립된 주의 실정에 맞는 '개정법'을 선택하는 난항을 묘사하고 있다. 고로, 어떤 '음식(dish)'을 선택할지 모른다는 내용은 어떤 '법과 관습'을 선택할지 모른다는 것의 비유적 표현이다.

해석 John Jay가 시골로 은둔하여 헌법의 초안을 작성하기 시작한 것은 바로 1777년 초봄이었다. 그의 이런 은둔은 Cowper가 다음과 같은 상황에 한탄한 것을 회상케 한다.

"거친 광야의 오두막
후미진 곳의 경계 없는 인접한 곳
압제와 속임수 성공과 실패의 전쟁 소문은
더 이상 나에게 다다르지 않으리"

이 작업에서 Jay가 한 일에 대해 너무나 지나친 공로와 함께 너무나 적은 공로가 주어졌다. 한 작가는 그가 "거의 탐험하지 않은 영역을 개척해 들어갔다"고 말한다. 반면에 John Adams는 Jefferson에게 Jay의 '모델과 초석'은 Virginia의 George Wythe에게 쓴 자신의 편지 내용이라고 썼다. 어느 것도 사실이 아니다. 이 영역은 이미 누군가 다녀갔으며, John Adams의 편지는 주지사가 모든 관직을 임명할 때 Council of Appointment의 동의를 얻어 선출하는 것을 제외하곤 이미 기존에 없었던 어떠한 제안도 포함하고 있지 않았다. 국민이 주지사를 선출하게 하도록 하는 그의 계획은 나중에 나오게 된다. Jay는 "우리가 알다시피 구성할 정부가 있으며, 하나님은 이것이 무엇과 같을지 알고 계신다. 잔칫집 손님처럼 우리의 정치인들은 잔칫집 손님처럼 어떤 음식을 선택할까 하는 것에 대해 당황하고 결정을 내리기 힘들어한다."라고 했다. 그러나 Jay는 분명 기존의 집 요리(영국의 법과 관습)를 선호했지만, 그가 얼마나 쉽게 주정부의 법과 관습을 독립 주의 요구에 따라 개작했는지 주목하는 것은 참 흥미롭다.

어휘

withdraw *v.* 물러나다   **draft** *v.* 초안을 작성하다
constitution *n.* 헌법   **retirement** *n.* 은퇴
recall *v.* 생각나게 하다   **lodge** *n.* 오두막집
wilderness *n.* 야생   **boundless** *a.* 경계 없는
contiguity *n.* 접촉   **shade** *n.* 그늘   **rumour** *n.* 소문
oppression *n.* 압박   **deceit** *n.* 속임
credit *n.* 공적을 인정하기   **eunexplored** *a.* 탐험되지 않은
model *n.* 모형   **foundation** *n.* 토대, 기초
existence *n.* 존재   **election** *n.* 선거
consent *n.* 동의, 승인   **governor** *n.* 주지사
elect *v.* 선출하다   **resemble** *v.* 닮다   **guest** *n.* 손님
feast *n.* 축제   **perplexed** *a.* 복잡한
undetermined *a.* 미결정의   **prefer** *v.* ~을 (…보다) 좋아하다
note *v.* 주목하다   **adapt** *v.* 개작하다, 적응시키다
provincial *a.* 지방의   **independent State** 독립 주

Day 5

[Challenge 1]

문제 1

답 (1)

해설 본문은 교육이 어떠한 목적을 지니고 있어야 하는지 정의를 내리는 글이다.

문제 2

답 (4)

해설 빈칸이 들어간 문장 앞뒤를 파악한다.

> Considered in this light, the school is ____(a)____, since we continue throughout our lives to acquire experience.

since 이후 전개되는 내용을 근거로 빈칸에 들어간 표현을 추론할 수 있다. 'continue throughout our lives'에서 알 수 있듯이, 학교라는 공간은 인간의 학습이 일어나는 특정 시점의 한 장소이다. 교육이 학교에서만 끝나는 것이 아니라는 점을 생각하여 보기 항을 고른다.

해석 아이는 자신의 능력을 사용하는 데 미성숙하기에, 아이가 충분히 발달할 수 있도록 교육하는 것이 교육의 첫 번째 임무다. 이런 교육에는 신체적, 정신적, 도덕적인 것이 있다. 아이는 무지하기에, 아이에게 지금까지의 인간의 경험을 전수하는 것이 교육의 일이다. 이것은 당연히 (properly) 가르치는 일이다. 이런 측면에서 생각해 보면 학교는 교육 기관 중 하나일 뿐인데, 이는 우리가 일생 동안 경험을 통한 습득을 계속하기 때문이다. 그러기에 교육의 첫 번째 목적은 학생에게 학문을 사랑할 수 있도록 격려하고, 독립적으로 공부할 수 있는 습관을 형성하고 이상을 갖도록 하는 것이다. 이 두 가지, 즉 능력의 배양과 경험의 전수가 선생의 몫이 된다. 모든 조직과 통솔은 이 두 측면의 목적의 보조일 뿐이다. 추구해야 할 목적은 삶을 유용하고 행복하게 만드는 데 필요하고 개인이 삶의 모든 행로로부터 학문을 계속 이어갈 수 있도록 하는 그런 자원을 갖춘 완전히 성장한 신체적, 지적 그리고 도덕적 성인이다.

어휘

immature *a.* 미숙한, 미완성의
capacity *n.* 수용할 수 있는 능력(크기); 능력; 자격
development *n.* 발달, 발육; 성장; 개발
communicate *v.* 전달하다; 통보하다
properly *ad.* 당연히; 똑바로; 올바르게
acquire *v.* 손에 넣다; 획득하다
stimulate *v.* 자극하다; 격려하다
pupil *n.* 학생, 제자   ideal *n.* 이상, 극치, 전형
independent *a.* 독립한; 자주의
cultivation *n.* 배양, 양성   transmission *n.* 전달, 전송
subsidiary *a.* 보조의; 부차적인   manhood *n.* 인격; 남자임
resource *n.* 자원, 물자, 수단
enable *v.* ~할 힘을 주다; 가능성을 주다

[Challenge 2]

문제 1

답 (2)

해설 본문에서 부정적으로 묘사되는 사람이 두 명 나온다. 두 번째 사람에 대한 묘사가 시작되는 곳은 (b)이다.

문제 2

답 (2)

해설 본문에서 묘사되는 주인공은 다음과 같은 생각을 하고 있다.

> all the time he shirks his work, and considers he is justified in trying to deceive his employer on the ground of the insufficiency of his wages

고로 보기 항 (2)는 틀린 표현이다.

문제 3

답 (3)

해설 자신의 과욕으로 건강을 잃고는 돈으로 그것을 고친 후 다시 과욕을 일삼는 사람이다. 즉, 자신의 건강을 해하는 근본적인 원인이 과욕에 있음에도 그것을 인식하지 못하고 건강을 바라는 사람이다.

해석 정말 비참할 정도로 가난한 사람이 있다. 그는 자신의 환경과 집의 안락이 향상되어야 한다고 극도로 근심하면서도 항상 자신의 일은 기피하고, 자기 임금이 불충분하다는 이유로 자신의 고용주를 속이려 하는 것이 정당하다고 생각한다. 이런 사람은 진정한 재산의 근간이 되는 이러한 원리의 단순한 기초도 이해하지 못하며, 자기 불행에서 빠져나오기에 부적절할 뿐 아니라 실질적으로 나태하고, 기만적이

며 남자답지 못한 생각에 머물러 있고 행함으로서 훨씬 더 깊은 비참함에 자신을 끌어들이고 있는 것이다. 과욕(과식)의 결과로 고통스럽고 잘 낫지 않는 질병의 희생자인 부자가 있다. 그는 이 병에서 벗어나기 위해 많은 돈을 줄 용의가 있지만 자신의 그런 과욕의 욕망은 희생하려 하지 않는다. 그는 풍부하고 진귀한 음식을 위한 자신의 취향을 만족시키려 하는 동시에 자신의 건강도 가지려 한다. 이러한 사람은 건강을 지키기 적절하지 않은데, 이는 그가 건강한 삶의 첫 번째 원칙을 배우지 않았기 때문이다.

어 휘

- **wretchedly** *ad.* 지독하게 **extremely** *ad.* 극단으로, 아주
- **anxious** *a.* 걱정하여, 염려하여 **surroundings** *n.* 주위, 환경
- **shirk** *v.* 회피하다; 기피하다 **justify** *v.* 정당화하다; 옳다고 하다
- **deceive** *v.* 속이다; 기만하다; 현혹시키다
- **insufficiency** *n.* 불충분; 부족
- **wage** *n.* 임금, 급료; 보상 **rudiments** *n.* 기본, 기초
- **prosperity** *n.* 번영, 번창; 부유 **unfitted** *a.* 부적당한; 적임이 아닌
- **wretchedness** *n.* 가엾음, 불쌍함
- **attract** *v.* 끌어들이다 **dwell** *v.* (마음에) 남아있다
- **indolent** *a.* 나태한; 게으른
- **deceptive** *a.* 사람을 현혹시키는; 거짓의; 사기의
- **unmanly** *a.* 계집애 같은; 겁 많은 **victim** *n.* 희생자
- **persistent** *a.* 끊임없이 반복되는
- **gluttony** *n.* 대식; 폭식 **sum** *n.* 총계, 총액
- **get rid of** ~을 제거하다
- **gluttonous** *a.* 많이 먹는; 탐욕스러운 **desire** *n.* 욕구, 욕망
- **gratify** *v.* 만족시키다; 충족시키다

[Challenge 3]

문제 1

답 (2)

해설 문은 근접학에 대해서 개괄적으로 다루고 있다. 주제를 고를 때 주의할 것은 부분적인 내용, 다시 말해 보기 항(1)과 같은 내용을 주제로 선정해서는 안 된다는 점이다.

문제 2

답 (1)

해설 보기 항 (1)은 적절한 예가 아니다. 본문에서 정의하는 primary territory는 'someone has exclusive use of it'이다. 즉, 특정 인물만이 사용할 수 있는 권한으로 집을 예로 들 수 있다. 주어진 예는 표를 사면 누구나 사용할 수 있는 국립 주차장을 예로 들고 있는 잘못된 예이다.

문제 3

답 (1)

해설 내 것이라고 생각하는 자리에 다른 이가 앉으면, 자신의 영역을 침범 당했다고 생각한다는 내용이다.

해석 근접학이란 사람들이 자신을 둘러싸고 있는 물리적 공간을 어떻게 사용하고 인식하는지를 연구하는 학문이다. 특정 메시지를 보내고 받는 사람 사이의 공간은 이 메시지를 해석하는 방식에 영향을 미친다. 공간의 인식과 사용은 문화와 문화 내 다른 환경에 따라 상당히 다르다. 비언어적 의사소통 공간은 4가지의 주요 항목으로 나눌 수 있다. 사적, 사회적, 개인적 그리고 공공의 공간으로 볼 수 있다. 의사소통하는 사람들 사이의 거리는 또한 성별과 지위 그리고 사회적 역할에 따라 영향을 받기도 한다. 근접학은 1950년대와 60년대 Edward T. Hall이 처음 발전시킨 것이다. Hall의 연구는 동물이 자신의 영역을 어떤 식으로 증명하는지에 관한 이전의 연구에 영감을 받은 것이다. 영역이란 용어는 근접학에서 개인적 공간과 관련된 인간의 행위를 설명하는 데 여전히 사용이 된다. Hargie & Dickson은 이러한 영역을 4가지로 구분했다.

1. 주된 영역: 이것은 이 영역에 대한 독점적 사용을 가진 사람과 관련된 영역을 나타낸다. 예를 들면, 표 없이는 사람들이 입장할 수 없는 국립공원이 있다.

2. 부차적 영역: 이전의 형태와는 달리 점유권이 존재하지 않지만, 사람들은 여전히 이 특정한 공간에 일종의 소유권을 가지고 있다고 느낀다. 예를 들어, 어떤 사람이 매일 기차에서 동일한 좌석에 앉는데, 만약 누군가 거기에 앉으면 권리를 침해당했다고 생각한다.

3. 공공 영역: 이것은 모든 이에게 열린 공간이지만 단지 정해진 시간에만 허용되는 구역을 말한다. 주차장이나 도서관의 자리를 예로 들 수 있겠다. 비록 사람들은 이 장소에 대해 제한된 권리만을 갖고 있음에도, 그 정도를 넘는 경우가 종종 있다. 예로 들자면, 사람들은 누군가 그 공간을 차지하기 위해 기다림에도 불구하고 주차장을 떠나는 데 더 오랜 시간을 끈다.

4. 상호 공간: 이것은 상호작용을 하는 다른 이에 의해서 만들어진 공간이다. 예를 들자면, 한 무리가 보도 위에서 서로 이야기를 할 때, 다른 사람들은 이것을 방해하기보다는, 이 무리 주변을 돌아서 걸어간다.

어 휘

- **proxemics** *n.* 근접학
- **perceive** *v.* 지각하다; 눈치를 채다; 이해하다
- **sender** *n.* 발송인 **receiver** *n.* 수령인
- **interpret** *v.* 뜻을 이해하다; 해석하다
- **perception** *n.* 지각; 인식 **vary** *v.* 서로 다르다; 가지각색이다
- **nonverbal** *a.* 말을 쓰지 않는; 비언어적인
- **intimate** *a.* 친밀한; 사적인, 은밀한 **status** *n.* 상태; 지위
- **inspire** *v.* 고무시키다; 초래하다
- **demonstrate** *v.* 증명하다; 설명하다
- **territoriality** *n.* 영토권; 세력권 **term** *n.* 기간; 임기; 조건
- **territory** *n.* 영토; 영역 **primary** *a.* 첫째의; 최초의

refer *v.* 가리키다; 언급하다
exclusive *a.* 배타적인, 독점적인; 유일한
occupancy *n.* 점유; 점령   ownership *n.* 소유권
aggrieve *v.* (권리 등을) 침범하다
available *a.* 이용 가능한; 유효한
exceed *v.* 넘다; 초과하다   interaction *n.* 상호작용
footpath *n.* 보행자용의 작은 길
disturb *v.* 방해하다; 어지럽히다; 불안하게 하다

[Challenge 4]

문제 1

답 (3)

해설 본문은 기술 교사가 기술 철학이란 학문을 공부해야 하는 이유를 밝히는 글이다. 일반 진술에서 구체적 진술로 전개되는 전형적인 두괄식의 글이다. 일반적으로 첫 번째 문장 또는 글의 전반부에서 중심 소재와 주제 설정이 가능한 주제 문이 등장한다.

본문분석

> Let us consider what those who teach about technology could gain from the philosophy of technology. 1) There are at least four reasons for technology educators to get acquainted with this discipline. ① The philosophy of technology can be a source of inspiration for determining the content of a curriculum, ② it can yield insights into how to construct teaching and learning situations, ③ it can provide a conceptual basis and proper understanding of technology which can help technology educators respond to unforeseen situations while teaching about technology, ④ it can help to position the teaching of technology among other subjects, and it can help identify the research agenda for educational research in technology education.

1) 주제문이다: 기술 철학이 기술을 가르치는 사람에게 필요 한 4가지 이유

2) 뒷받침 문장으로 앞에서 언급한 4가지 이유를 밝히고 있다.

① 이유 1   ② 이유 2   ③ 이유 3   ④ 이유 4

해설 기술을 가르치는 사람이 기술 철학에서 무엇을 얻을 수 있는지 생각해 보자. 기술 교육가들이 이 학문에 정통해 야 하는 적어도 네 가지 이유가 있다. 기술 철학은 특정 교과의 내용을 결정하는 데 영감을 주는 소스로 작용할 수 있 으며, 교수와 학습 상황을 어떻게 구성할지에 대한 통찰력 을 제공할 수 있으며, 기술을 가르치는 동안 뜻밖의 상황에 대처하는 데 도움을 줄 수 있는 기술에 대한 개념적 기반과 적절한 해석을 제공할 수 있다. 또한, 이것을 통해 다른 과 목 사이에 기술 교육의 입지를 설정하는 데 도움이 되며, 동 시에 기술 교육의 교육적 연구를 위한 연구 의제를 찾는 데 도움을 준다.

어 휘

be[get, become] acquainted with ~을 알다, 정통하다
inspiration *n.* 영감(靈感)
content *n.* (책, 프로그램 등의) 내용, 주제
yield *v.* 생기게 하다, 산출(産出)하다(produce); (이익 따위를) 가 져오다
insight *n.* 통찰, 간파; 통찰력
conceptual *a.* 개념상의
subject *n.* 학과, 학문   identify *v.* 찾다; 확인하다
agenda *n.* 안건, 의사일정, 의제 (본디 *agendum*의 복수꼴; 보통 단수 취급)

[Challenge 5]

문제 1

답 (1)

해설 본문은 신경 단위인 뉴런에 관한 개괄적인 설명이다. 부분 적인 내용을 주제로 선정하지 않도록 주의한다.

문제 2

답 (2)

해설 첫 번째 문장에서 뉴런은 특정 종류의 세포라고 표현하고 있다.

해석 뉴런은 특별한 종류의 세포로 대부분 동물의 몸에서 발견된다(정확히 말하자면 모든 진정후생동물 – 해면과 몇 몇 다른 아주 단순한 동물만이 여기서 제외된다). 뉴런을 정 의하는 특징은 전기적 흥분성과 시냅스(신경 세포의 자극 전달부)의 존재인데, 시냅스는 다른 세포에 신호를 전달하 는 데 사용되는 복잡한 막질의 연결부이다. 생체 구조와 신 진대사를 지원하는 신경교세포를 포함해 신체의 뉴런이 함 께 신경조직을 형성한다. 척추동물에서 대부분 뉴런은 중추 신경조직에 속하지만, 어떤 것은 주변의 신경구에 있으며, 많은 감각 뉴런의 경우 망막과 달팽이관과 같은 감각 기관 에 위치한다.

어 휘

neuron *n.* 뉴런   precise *a.* 정밀한; 정확한
exclude *v.* 제외[베제]하다
sponge *n.* (해면) 동물   feature *n.* 특징, 특성
define *v.* 규정하다; 정의를 말하다
electrical *a.* 전기의; 전기와 같은   excitability *n.* 흥분성
presence *n.* 존재; 현존; 출석   synapse *n.* 시냅스
membrane *n.* 얇은 막   junction *n.* 연결 지점

transmit *v.* 보내다; 전도하다 signal *n.* 신호; 전조, 징후
glial *a.* 신경교의 structural *a.* 구조상의
metabolic *a.* 신진[물질]대사의 support *n.* 지지; 원조
constitute *v.* 구성하다; 조직하다; 제정하다
vertebrate *n.* 척추동물 reside *v.* 살다; 존재하다; 거주하다
peripheral *a.* 주위의, 주변의
ganglia *n.* (ganglion의 복수) 신경절, 신경구
sensory *a.* 지각의; 감각의 situate *v.* 놓다; 위치를 정하다
retina *n.* (눈의) 망막 cochlea *n.* 달팽이관

influential *a.* 영향을 미치는
performance *n.* (의식 등의) 거행
underlie *v.* ① ~의 밑에 있다[가로놓이다] ② 《비유적》~의 기초가 되다, ~의 근저에 있다
efficacy *n.* 효험, 효력, 유효

[Challenge 6]

문제 1

답 (1)

해설 공자가 정부의 위계 조직에 반대했다는 내용은 본문에 없다. 오히려 윗사람이 덕을 갖추었을 때 아랫사람이 자연히 존경을 표한다는 내용과 통치하는 자와 통치받는 자의 설정으로 보아 위계 질서가 존재함을 추론할 수 있다.

해석 공자의 경우 뛰어난 통치력을 특징짓는 것은 바로 '덕'을 갖추는 것이었다. 물적인 힘에 의존하지 않고, 추종자가 따르도록 이끌어 내는 일종의 도덕적 능력으로 인식된 이러한 '덕'은 또한 통치자가 자신을 어지럽히지 않고, 충성스럽고 효율적인 대리인을 믿음으로써 국가의 질서를 잘 유지할 수 있도록 해주었다. 공자는 주장하길 "덕으로 통치하는 자는 마치 북극성과 같다. 북극성은 자신의 자리를 지키는 동시에 다른 덜 중요한 별들이 이 별을 중심으로 경의를 표한다." (논어 2.1) 이러한 왕의 '덕'을 유지하고 배양하는 방법은 의식(고대 중국의 귀족 정치의 삶을 밝히고, 강조하는 의식)의 실천과 제정을 통해서 가능했다. 영향력 있는 한 연구에서 Herbert Fingarette는 다양한 의식의 실천은 올바르고 진지하게 이루어질 경우 통치자의 목적을 성취하는 데 있어 왕의 '덕'의 효율성의 근간이 되는 '마법과 같은' 특징을 지닌다고 주장한다.

어 휘

Confucius *n.* 공자
characterize *v.* ① ~의 특색을 이루다, 특징지우다; ~의 성격을 나타내다 ② ~의 특성을 기술[묘사]하다
rulership *n.* 통치자의 지위 conceive *v.* (~을) (…로) 여기다
recourse *n.* 의지, 의뢰
enable *v.* ~에게 힘[능력]을 주다, ~에게 권한[자격]을 주다
deputy *n.* 대리인; 대리역, 부관; 대표자
govern *v.* (국가·국민 등을) 통치하다, 다스리다(rule)
analogy *n.* 유사, 비슷함, 비유
cultivate *v.* (재능·품성·습관 따위를) 신장하다, 계발[연마]하다; 수련하다
enactment *n.* (법률의) 제정; 법규, 조례, 법령
punctuate *v.* ① 구두점을 찍다 ② (말 따위에) 힘을 주다, 강조하다

[Challenge 7]

문제 1

답 (3)

해설 본문은 어린아이들을 대상으로 한 광고 및 일반 광고가 아이들에게 악영향을 미치기에 아이들이 TV를 보는 시간대에 광고를 금해야 한다고 주장하는 내용이다.

문제 2

답 (1)

해설 보기 항 (1)의 경우 첫 번째 문장에 명시되어 있다. (2)의 경우 'used to'(과거의 습관)가 아니라 현재도 금지하고 있다. (3)의 경우 미국에서 이러한 금지법을 통과시키려는 제안이 일어나고 있음이 본문에 드러나 있다 ("recommending that advertising targeting children under the age of eight be restricted"). (4)와 같이 'the main culprit'이라고 말할 근거는 본문에 없다.

문제 3

답 (2)

해설 구체적 내용 확인 문제이다. "preference for a product has been shown to occur with as little as a single commercial exposure and strengthened with repeated exposures."를 참조한다.

문제 4

답 (3)

해설 속사를 넣는 문제이다. 앞 문장과 뒤에 이어지는 문장과의 관계를 밝혀야 한다. 광고가 아이의 상품 선호도에 영향을 미친다는 내용과 함께 이러한 선호도가 다른 악영향을 불러온다는 추가적 부연이 이어지고 있다. 고로, 보기 항 (3)이 가장 적절하다.

해석 1991년 이래 스웨덴은 아이가 보는 최고 시청률 시간대에 방영되는 모든 광고를 금하고 있는데, 이는 10살 이하 아이들은 광고와 실제 프로그램 사이의 차이를 구별할 능력이 없으며, 12세까지 광고의 목적을 이해하지 못한다는 결과를 반영한 것이다. 미국의 APA에서 낸 연구는 8세 이하의 아이는 TV로 방영되는 광고의 내용을 비판적으로 이해할 수 있는 능력이 없으며, 광고의 메시지를 옳고, 정확하며, 치우침이 없는 온전한 것으로 받아들이는 경향이 있다는 점을 보였다. 오늘날 어린아이들이 비만에 허덕이는 증상으로 증명되었듯이 이러한 광고는 건강하지 못한 식습관

으로 이어질 수 있다. 이러한 이유에서 APA 대책 위원회는 8살 이하의 아이들을 대상으로 하는 광고는 법적으로 금지되어야 한다고 권고하고 있다.

"아이들이 광고를 회상하는 것과 상품 선호도에 대한 연구를 통해 광고는 일반적으로 어린 소비자가 자신들의 상품을 사도록 실질적으로 만든다는 것을 볼 수 있다. 연구 결과 아이들은 이 TV 광고에 노출된 내용을 떠올리며, 상품에 대한 선호도는 한 번 노출만으로도 발생하며, 반복적인 노출을 통해 강화된다는 점이 나타났다. 게다가, 이러한 상품 선호도는 아이들의 상품 구매 요청에 영향을 미치는데, 이것은 부모의 구매 결정에 영향을 미치고, 부모가 이러한 요청을 거부할 때 부모와 아이 간의 마찰을 조장한다. 어린이 시청자에게 위험한 주로 어른을 대상으로 한 특정 광고 캠페인에 관한 우려가 있다. 예를 들어, 맥주 광고는 일반적으로 스포츠 경기를 내보내는 동안 방영되는데, 수없이 많은 아이들이 이것을 보면서, 9~10세 정도의 어린 아이들이 이러한 브랜드에 익숙해지는 동시에 음주에 대한 좀 더 긍정적인 태도를 갖도록 조장한다. 또 다른 아주 민감한 내용의 부분은 영화와 비디오 게임과 같이 폭력적인 미디어 제품의 광고이다. 이러한 광고는 어린 아이의 폭력적인 행위의 가능성을 높이고, 아이들의 실제 세계의 폭력에 대한 감각을 떨어뜨리는 과격한 미디어 문화에 일조한다.

본문분석

1) Sweden, since 1991 has banned all advertising during children's prime time due to findings that children under 10 are incapable of telling the difference between a commercial and a program, and cannot understand the purpose of a commercial until the age of 12.

2) In the US, research from the American Psychological Association (APA) shows that children under the age of eight are unable to critically comprehend televised advertising messages and are prone to accept advertiser messages as truthful, accurate and unbiased. This can lead to unhealthy eating habits as evidenced by today's youth obesity epidemic. For these reasons, a task force of the American Psychological Association (APA) is recommending that ① <u>advertising targeting children under the age of eight be restricted.</u>

3) The research on children's commercial recall and product preferences confirms that advertising does typically get young consumersto buy their products. Findings show that children recall content from the ads to which they've been exposed and preference for a product has been shown to occur with as little as a single commercial exposure and strengthened with repeated exposures. ____(a)____ , these product preferences can affect children's product purchase requests, which can put pressure on parents' purchasing decisions and instigate parent-child conflicts when parents deny their children's requests. There are concerns regarding certain commercial campaigns primarily targeting adults that pose risks for child-viewers. For example, beer ads are commonly shown during sports events and seen by millions of children, creating both brand familiarity and more positive attitudes toward drinking in children as young as 9-10 years of age. Another area of sensitive advertising content involves commercials for violent media products such as motion pictures and video games. Such ads contribute to a violent media culture which increases the likelihood of youngsters' aggressive behavior and desensitizes children to real-world violence.

1) 어린아이들이 시청하는 황금 시간대 광고를 금한 스웨덴의 예(바람직한 사례로)를 들면서

2) 관점을 미국으로 옮긴 후 현재 미국의 경우, 앞선 사례와 마찬가지로 광고에 대한 아이들의 비판적 수용력 결여로 적절한 조치가 이루어져야 한다고 주장하고 있다.
   ① 글쓴이의 궁극적 주장이다: 주제문.

3) 아이들에게 미치는 광고의 악영향을 구체적 연구 결과와 사례(나쁜 식사습관, 음주 그리고 폭력)를 들면서 주장의 근거를 확보하고 있다.

본문은 '현상(아이들 시간대 방영되는 광고) – 문제점 지적 – 대안(글쓴이의 궁극적 주장 – 주장에 대한 부연근거 확보(연구 결과))'의 패턴으로 전개되고 있음을 파악한다.

어 휘

ban *v.* 금(지)하다
incapable *a.* ~할 힘이 없는, ~을 할 수 없는
commercial *n.* (TV, 라디오의) 광고
comprehend *v.* (완전히) 이해하다, 파악하다, 깨닫다
be prone to ~하기 쉽다, ~의 경향이 있다; ~에 걸리기 쉽다
unbiased *a.* 선입관[편견]이 없는, 공평한
obesity *n.* 비만, 비대   **preference** *n.* 선호

confirm *v.* 확실히 하다, 확증하다, ~이 옳음[정확함]을 증명하다
exposed *a.* 드러난, (위험 따위에) 노출된
strengthen *v.* 강하게[튼튼하게] 하다, 강화하다
put pressure on ~에게 압력을 가하다
instigate *v.* 부추기다, 선동하다(incite
familiarity *n.* 익숙함; 친근감
likelihood *n.* 있음직한 일(probability), 정말 같음; 가능성
aggressive *a.* ① 침략적인, 공세의 ② 진취적[적극적]인
desensitize *v.* ~에 대해 둔감하게 만들다

[Challenge 8]

문제 1

답 (3)

해설 주인공과 함께 영국의 위대한 시인 Wordsworth와 Coleridge가 겪은 일화이다. 목줄을 말에서 빼내지 못하면서 겪게 된 당황스러운 상황을 묘사하고 있는데, 본문 마지막에서 위대한 두 시인은 한 여종이 말의 목줄을 빼내는 것을 보고 놀라움과 함께 색다른 지식을 얻었다고 말하고 있다. 이러한 이야기를 반영하는 보기 항은 (3)이다. 보기 항 (2)는 대상이 잘못 설정되어 있다. 일반적으로 이야기체의 글에서는 구체적인 사건을 중심으로 주인공들이 어떤 식으로 반응하는지를 주시하도록 한다.

문제 2

답 (2)

해설 ⓐ는 말에서 목줄을 빼내지 못하는 상황에서 세 남자가 당황해하는 것을 나타낸다.

문제 3

답 (2)

해설 본문에 명시되어 있는 Mr. Coleridge의 분석을 확인해서 답을 골라야 한다.

> the horse's head must have grown since the collar was put on

해석 나는 말을 끌고 마구간으로 갔는데, 이전에 겪어보지 못했던 당황스러운 상황이 벌어졌다. 나는 별 어려움 없이 마구를 걷어냈는데, 여러 번 힘들게 시도해도 목줄은 제거할 수가 없었다. 절망감에 나는 조수를 불렀는데, 도움의 손길이 곧 다가왔다. Wordsworth 씨는 자신의 재능을 드러냈다. 그러나 여러 번 시도해도 실패를 하자, 그는 실행하기 불가능한 것으로 간주하고 이것을 성취하는 것을 포기했다. Coleridge 씨가 시도를 했는데, 그의 전임자와 마찬가지로 그다지 다루는 솜씨가 좋지 않았다. 왜냐하면, 거의 교살 직전까지 그 불쌍한 말의 목을 뒤튼 데다가 눈에도 큰 위험이 있게 되자, 그는 이 소용이 없는 일을 포기하고, 목줄을 끼운 다음 말의 머리가 너무 커진 것이 틀림없다고 말했다. 왜냐하면, 그는 "이렇게 큰 머리가 이렇게 작은 목줄을 통과하는 것은 사실 불가능하기 때문에!"라고 말했다. 바로 그 순간, 한 여종이 가까이 와 이런 당황스러운 상황의 원인을 이해하고, "아! 주인님," 그녀가 말했다. "일을 잘못 처리하고 계세요. 이렇게 하셔야 해요." 그러면서 그녀가 목줄을 완전히 위아래로 바꾸고는, 순간 그것을 빼냈는데, 창피함과 놀라움에 각자 우리가 아직 알지 못한 세상의 높은 지식이 있다는 색다른 만족감을 얻었다.

어 휘

stable *n.* 마구간 perplexity *n.* 당혹; 혼란
harness *n.* 마구 strenuous *a.* 정력적인; 열심인
despair *n.* 절망; 자포자기 assistance *n.* 원조, 도움
ingenuity *n.* 기발한 재주; 교묘 relinquish *v.* 포기[양도]하다
impracticable *a.* 실행하기 어려운
groom *v.* (말을) 손질하다, 돌보다
predecessor *n.* 전임자, 선배 twist *v.* 뒤틀다; 얽히게 하다
strangulation *n.* 목 조름; 질식
pronounce *v.* 말하다; 선언하다
downright *a.* 명백한; 솔직한; 노골적인
impossibility *n.* 불가능 narrow *a.* 폭이 좁은, 답답한
collar *n.* 목에 대는 마구 servant *n.* 고용인; 하인 공무원
consternation *n.* 놀람; 당황 slip off 벗다
humiliation *n.* 굴욕 wonderment *n.* 놀라움, 경탄, 경이
attain *v.* 이루다; 달성하다

[Challenge 9]

문제 1

답 (3)

해설 진정한 단짝이란 어떤 것인지 정의내리는 지문이다. 단짝이 아닌 경우를 예로 들면서 단짝의 정의를 더욱 두드러지게 설명하고 있다. 이런 글쓰기 방법은 대조를 통해서 특정 대상을 강조하는 방법으로, 예를 들어 사과의 특징을 설명하는 글은 독자가 알고 있을 특정 과일과 비교/대조했을 때 더욱 쉽게 이해할 수 있다.

문제 2

답 (4)

해설 본문에서 사람은 자신과 함께 있는 사람에 의해서 평가될 수 있다고는 했지만, 반드시 그렇게 평가를 받아야 한다고 말하는 것은 옳지 못하다.

문제 3

답 (1)

해설 친구를 통해서 내가 평가되기에, 내가 좋게 평가될 수 있도록 해 주는 그런 친구를 사귀라는 말이다. 고로, 보기 항 (1)이 가장 적절한 표현이다.

문제 4

답 (1)

해설 본문의 (b)는 '언질을 주다'라는 의미로 쓰이고 있다. '약속하다'의 의미가 아님을 기억할 것. give you the heads up은 '미리 알려주다'의 의미이다.

해석 유유상종이란 말이 있다. 사람은 친구를 통해서 알 수 있다. 그러므로 너의 친구가 너 자신이 올바른 사람이란 것을 보이는 그런 친구가 되어야 하는 것이 중요하다. 특별히 사귀기 힘든 사람이 아니라면 아이는 친구가 꽤 있을 것이고, 다시 말해 그가 알고 친하게 지내는 단짝이 있을 것이다. 그러나 이것을 넘어 그는 아마도 특정한 한 명의 친구가 있을 터인데, 이 단짝은 그의 모든 계획을 공유하고, 그의 삶의 모든 것에 대해 자세히 이야기하며, 종종 어떤 장난도 함께 하는 친구이다. 서로 도움을 주는 단짝은 거의 같은 나이 때이다. 나이가 많은 이와 어린 사람 사이에 우정이 있지만 이들은 정확히 말해 단짝은 아니다. 이런 종류의 우정은 만약 나이 많은 이가 올바르게 이끌면 아주 유용하지만, 만약 나이 많은 이가 둘 중 약하거나 더욱이 만약 사악한 마음에 이끌린 사람이면 이러한 아는 사이는 아이에게 일어날 수 있는 최악의 상황 중 하나이다. 아이는 나이 많은 이에 의존하면 그의 모든 나쁜 습관을 배우기에, 너무나 쉽게 영향을 받는 미성년자는 완전한 불행에 닥치게 된다. 무언가 나쁜 것을 하도록 권하는 사람이나 탈선의 길에 들어섰을 때 당신을 보고도 충고하지 않는 자는 친구라는 이름을 부여할 가치가 없는 이임을 명심하라. 같은 나이의 단짝은 전혀 이와 다른 사람이다. 종종 이들은 서로 전혀 다른 성향과 취향의 사람인데 이러한 차이점에 의해 서로 이끌린다. 아주 활달한 친구가 아주 조용하고 명상적인 친구와 함께 단짝이 되는 경우가 흔하다. 한 사람은 생각하는 자이고, 또 한 사람은 행동하는 자이다. 이러한 우정은 평생 지속되기도 하지만, 일반적으로 어린 시절에 주로 잘 지낸다.

어휘

flock v. 모이다   sort n. 종류, 성질, 품질
disagreeable a. 불유쾌한; 마음에 들지 않는
fair a. 꽤 많은; 상당한   fellow n. 동무, 친구
ssociate v. 어울리다, 사귀다
particular a. 특별한; 특유의; 독특한   chum n. 단짝; 짝
share v. (생각, 경험 등을) 공유하다
scheme n. 계획; 기획; 설계   mischief n. 장난, 나쁜 짓
elder a. 손위의, 연장의   aright ad. 바르게; 정확히
viciously ad. 사악하게   incline v. 기울다; 마음에 내키다
acquaintance n. 면식; 아는 사람   hang v. 매달다; 걸다
pupil n. 학생   utterly ad. 아주, 전혀, 완전히
grief n. 슬픔; 비통

worthy a. ~을 받을 만한   counsel v. 충고하다
season n. 시기, 시절, 한창 때   tack n. 방침, 방식
article n. 사람   disposition n. 성질, 기질
taste n. 기호, 취향   unfrequently ad. 흔하게 않게
meditative a. 묵상의; 숙고의   boyhood n. 소년기

[Challenge 10]

문제 1

답 (3)

해설 아이를 키우는 부부를 통해 남자와 여자는 특정 상황에 전혀 다르게 반응한다는 점을 대조의 글 전개 방식을 통해 전달하고 있다.

해석 자녀를 둔 사람들이 전부 정신을 팔거나 패션 감각을 잃게 되는지는 확인할 수 없다. 예를 들면, 내 남편의 경우 자신의 셔츠에 단추 채우는 것을 깜박한다거나 서로 다른 색깔의 신발을 신은 적이 없다. 따라서 이에 대한 답은 우리 여자들이 성격상 선천적으로 다르다는 사실에 있는 게 틀림없다. 남자들은 아이들이 졸졸 따라다니며 빽빽 울어대도 완벽하게 옷을 갖춰 입고 만족스럽게 서둘러 직장에 나갈 수 있다. 하지만 동정심 많은 우리 여자들은 아이들을 육아보호소에 맡겨놓고 가는 이상의 뭔가를 해주고 싶어 한다. 아이가 왜 우는지를 알아내서 이를 어떻게든 좋은 상황으로 만들려고 한다. 콧물 닦아 주고, 안아주고, 달래주다 보면 우리는 때로 집에 잠가두고 나온 자동차 키와 같은 작은 물건들을 깜빡 잊게 되고 만다.

어휘

ascertain v. 알아내다, 확인하다
scoot off to ~로 급히 나가다

Day 6

[Challenge 1]

문제 1

답 (4)

해설 보기 항 (1)은 글쓴이(작가)가 가르치는 일을 지겹다고 생각하는 사람에게 전달해 주려는 궁극적인 내용이다. 보기 항 (2)는 본문에서 가르치는 일이 지겹다고 생각하는 사람에 해당한다. "Others love the work: they hover around the schoolroom as long as they can, and never cease to think, and seldom to talk, of their delightful labors."에서 보기 항 (3)을 추론할 수 있다. 보기 항 (4)에서 작가는 어떤 상황에서는 가르치는 것이 아주 힘들고 에너지가 많이 드는 것으로 생각한다고 했지만, "I shall attempt to accomplish, is to show my readers⋯ how it happens that it is, in any case, so pleasant."에서 알 수 있듯이 가르치는 일은 정말 즐거운 것이며, 이렇게 바꿀 수 있다고 주장하고 있다.

문제 2

답 (3)

해설 바로 이어지는 본문 내용은 가르치는 일에 대해 극명하게 대조되는 견해를 진술하고 있다. 단순한 원리이긴 하나, 첫 번째 문장에서 빈칸이 나오면 대부분 바로 뒤에 이어지는 구체적 진술을 바탕으로 답을 이끌어 낼 수 있는 경우가 많다. 이 관계는 일반 진술과 구체적 진술의 관계로 뒤에 전개된 뒷받침 문장을 통해 앞의 주제문을 이끌어내는 원리와 같은 방식이다.

해석 가장 두드러진 상반된 견해는 가르치는 일의 즐거움에 관한 것으로 아는 사람들 사이에 널리 퍼져 있다. 어떤 교사는 단지 강요에 의해서 매일의 업무를 수행한다. 이들은 이 일을 견딜 수 없는 고된 일이라 여긴다. (반면) 어떤 이는 이 일을 아주 좋아한다. 이들은 할 수 있는 한 학교 교실에 붙어 있으며, 자신의 이런 즐거운 일을 생각하고 말하는 것을 좀처럼 멈추지 않는다. 불행히도, 전자에 해당하는 사람이 많으며, 이 책에서 내가 성취하려고 하는 첫 번째 목표는 나의 독자들, 특히나 가르치는 일을 지치고 열이 없는 고된 일로 간주하는 데 너무 익숙해진 사람에게 그것이 어떤 상황에서 어떻게 일어나든 얼마나 즐거운 일인지 보여주는 것이다. 인간의 마음은 근본적으로 같다. 나에게 지겹고 재미없는 일은 동일한 상황에 동일한 방법으로 추구한다면 다른 이에게도 동일하다. 그리고 만약 이 가르치는 일이 즐겁고, 활력이 되고 흥미롭게 된다면 모두에게도 그러할 수 있다.

어휘

singular *a.* 두드러진; 보통이 아닌　opinion *n.* 의견; 견해
prevail *v.* 만연하다; 이기다
community *n.* 사회, 공동체; 단체　in regard to ~에 대하여
leasantness *n.* 호감, 기분 좋음　daily *a.* 매일의, 일상의
task *n.* 일; 임무; 고된 일　compulsion *n.* 강요; 강제
intolerable *a.* 견딜[참을] 수 없는
drudgery *n.* 고된 일; 단조로운 일
hover *v.* 맴돌다, 서성이다　cease *v.* 그만두다; 멈추다
look upon ~ as …을 ~로 여기다　weary *a.* 지치게 하는
heartless *a.* 무정한; 냉혹한　toil *n.* 힘든 일; 수고, 노고
tedious *a.* 지루한; 싫증나는, 장황한
joyless *a.* 즐겁지 않은; 쓸쓸한
animating *a.* 생기를 주는; 고무적인

[Challenge 2]

문제 1

답 (4)

해설 본문 후반부의 내용을 확인해 보자.

> To love, to marry, to rear a family, is by no means an entire statement of the obligations and privileges of women.

모든 여인이 가정을 꾸리는 것이 아니라는 근거로 가족을 돌보는 것은 여성이 해야 하는 의무이자 권리의 전부가 아니라고 말하고 있다.

문제 2

답 (3)

해설 마지막 문장에 근거가 숨어 있다.

> because no woman always has lover, husband, or children; many fail to have all of them in succession; and a few never have either of them.

글쓴이는 어떤 여성의 경우 남자친구, 남편 또는 아이를 다 가질 수 없거나 아예 없는 경우가 있다는 점을 근거로 삼고 있다.

해석 여성의 특별한 사명은 종종 아내와 어머니로서의 역할이라고 여겨진다. 그렇다면 남자가 남편이 되고 아버지가 되는 것은 특별한 사명이 아닌가? 만약 여성이 남편의 행복과 가치를 더하는 것으로 여겨진다면, 남자 또한 자신의 부인의 행복과 가치를 더하는 것으로 여겨져야 한다. 이 둘 모두 아이를 보호하고 교육시켜야 할 의무가 있다. 그리고 자기 발전과 사회의 공공 이익을 위한 다른 의무 또한 이들 모두에게 공통적으로 해당한다. 그러므로 여성의 특정한 일이라는 것이 남자의 협조자라는 주장은 여성이 남성보다 더 법적으로 도덕적으로 굴복해야 한다는 것을 의미하는 것이 아니다. 왜냐하면 한 여성의 고귀한 의무는 다른 인간과 마찬가지로 하나님의 자녀로서 자신의 본성을 완성해 나감으로써 이 땅에서 자신의 개인적 운명을 실천하는 것이기 때문이다. 사랑에 빠져 결혼하고 가정을 돌보는 것이 여성의 의무와 권리의 전체 내용이 아닌 것이다. 왜냐하면 모든 여성이 반드시 사랑하는 사람, 남편 또는 아이가 있는 것이 아니기 때문이다. 많은 이가 연속으로 이 모든 것을 가지지 못하며, 어떤 이는 이것 중 하나도 가지지 못하는 경우도 있다.

어휘

peculiar *a*. 독특한, 고유의; 기묘한   mission *n*. 임무; 직무
be bound to ~하게 되어 있다
private *a*. 사적인; 개인에 속하는
improvement *n*. 개량; 개선; 진보
in common 공동으로   assertion *n*. 단언, 주장
distinctive *a*. 독특한; 구별이 되는
imply *v*. 함축하다; 의미하다
legally *ad*. 법률상으로; 합법적으로
morally *ad*. 도덕상으로   subservient *a*. 비굴한, 굴종하는
supreme *a*. 최고의; 최상의   nature *n*. 본성; 천성
fulfil *v*. 이행하다; 완수하다; 성취하다
personal *a*. 개인의, 본인 스스로의
by no means 절대 ~이 아닌   statement *n*. 성명; 진술
obligation *n*. 의무; 책임   privilege *n*. 특권; 특전
succession *n*. 연속; 연속물; 상속(권)

[Challenge 3]

문제 1

답 (3)

해설 "About the nature of the relationship between them he is not so clear."에서 보기 (3)이 옳음을 알 수 있다. 나머지는 모두 본문과 일치하지 않는다.

문제 2

답 (4)

해설 "at the end of the work he speaks as if the state were merely ancillary to the moral life of the individual" 부분에서 국가는 단지 개인의 도덕적 삶에 부수적인 것으로 간주되고 있다.

문제 3

답 (2)

해설 put up with에서 with가 관계대명사 앞으로 전치된 형태다.

해설 완벽한 정치학은 편의상 윤리학과 정치학으로 불릴 수 있는 두 부분으로 나뉜다. 아리스토텔레스의 윤리학은 물론 사회적이고 그의 정치학은 윤리적이다. 그는 '윤리학'에서 개인은 본질적으로 사회의 일원이라는 사실을 잊지 않으며, '정치학'에서는 국가의 안녕은 시민의 행복한 삶 속에서만 존재한다는 사실을 잊지 않는다. 그럼에도 그는 이 두 과제 사이에 차이가 존재한다는 사실을 의심하지 않는다. 이들 사이의 관계의 본질에 관해 그는 분명한 태도를 보이지 않는다. '윤리학'의 초두에서 그는 국가의 이익을 개인의 이익보다 '더 크고 더 완벽한' 것으로 묘사하며 후자는 전자를 달성할 수 없다면 그냥 감수해야 할 어떤 것 정도로 치부한다. 그러나 개인의 삶의 가치에 대한 그의 의식은 논의를 진행하면서 성장하는 것처럼 보이며, 저술의 종장에 가서는 국가가 인간의 욕망이 이성에 굴복하게 만들 때 필요한 강제 요소를 제공해주는 부속품에 지나지 않는 듯이 말한다.

어휘

science *n*. 학(學)   for convenience 편의상
enquiry *n*. 연구, 과제   at the outset of ~의 초기에
ancillary *a*. 부수적인, 종속적인
subservient *a*. 공헌이 되는, 복종하는

[Challenge 4]

문제 1

답 (2)

해설 본문은 위대한 사회학자 막스 베버를 훌륭한 선생으로 묘사하는 글이다.

문제 2

답 (4)

해설 본문 마지막에서 막스 베버의 교수 방법론이 소개되고 있다.

> There is a direct simplicity in his manner and method. "I am here to call your attention to things. I say humbly of myself I am not one to solve their needs. I can help. I have a greater experience."

즉, 학생이 스스로 문제를 풀어갈 수 있도록 돕는 조력자의 성격으로 자신을 포함한 교사를 정의하고 있다.

문제 3

답 (1)

해설 본문에서 sap은 '원기, 활기, 열정'의 뜻으로 쓰이고 있다. 주의할 것은 sap은 동사로 '활기를 없애다'의 뜻으로 쓰이기도 한다는 점이다.

문제 4

답 (3)

해설 (1) dig one's heels in은 '자기 입장을 고수하다', (2) take a different path는 '다른 길을 선택하다'의 의미이다. (3) blaze a trail은 '새로운 길을 개척하다'의 뜻이다.

문제 5

답 (3)

해설 빈칸이 들어간 인용구 내에서 해답을 이끌어 낼 수 있다.

> "I go a little further, I give you myself. Teaching is more than imparting knowledge. It is a kind of _____(c)_____."

막스는 교육이란 자신이 경험한 노하우가 담긴 '자신'을 주는 것이라 정의하고 있다. 이와 같은 맥락에서 빈칸에 알맞은 말은 자신의 생명과 같은 피를 주는 행위인 '수혈'로 볼 수 있다.

해석 "이곳을 떠나, 예술을 사랑한다면, 겸손함을 지녀라. 나는 여러분 모두가 탐구의 삶을 살기 바란다." 자신을 보고 있는 원형으로 앉은 학생들의 얼굴이 교차하는 둥근 모닥불 빛에 밝혀진 그의 찬란한 얼굴은 바로 자신의 수업, 자기 자신의 풍부한 철학을 반영하는 것이다. 그의 탐구는 여전히 결실을 맺고, 그의 눈은 예리하며, 그의 예술과 인간의 언어는 과거의 진정한 보물의 원기를 가득 담고 있는 동시에 그의 손은 여전히 새로운 일에 착수한다.

지난 5년간 두 번이나 그는 가르침을 주기 위해 Long Island에 있는 자신의 고향과 작업실을 떠났다. 많은 가르침을 주기 위해, "나는 좀 더 멀리 간다. 나는 나 자신을 준다. 가르침은 지식을 주입하는 것 이상이다. 이것은 일종의 영적인 수혈이다." 그의 영감은 "네가 인생에서 가질 수 있는 가장 위대한 동반자 - 바로 열정 - 그것이 바로 예술이다"라는 말에 드러나 있듯 의문시되는 것을 주류로 이끌어 올리는 확실한 능력을 지니고 있다.

막스 베버는 자신을 잘 표현할 수 있는 선생이다. 최고 경지에 놓인 학문에 대한 그의 정확한 (faithful) 연구의 권위는 그가 구사하는 짧은 문장을 통해 울려 퍼진다. 그가 슬라이드를 보여주면서, 하나의 흥미로운 내용에서 다른 것으로 열의가 넘치게 넘어갈 때, 그는 "이것은 나의 오페라이다. 나는 여기에 내 작은 주머니가 있다는 걸 아는 것처럼 이런 연구에 대해서 잘 알고 있다."라고 말한다. 그는 자신의 셔츠를 만진다. "여러분은 이런 것들을 공부해야 한다. 이 세상에서 숨어 공부하는 이런 아름다운 순간"이라고 말한다. 그의 태도와 방법에는 단도직입적인 단순함이 있다. "나는 사물에 대한 여러분의 주의를 환기시키고자 여기에 있는 것이다. 나 자신에 대해 겸허히 말하자면 나는 여러분의 필요를 해결해 주는 사람은 아니다. 내가 도울 수는 있다. 나에게는 많은 경험이 있으니까."

어휘

- **surround** *v.* 에워싸다; 둘러싸다
- **reverence** *n.* 숭배; 존경
- **illumine** *v.* 환하게 만들다; (~에 불을) 비추다
- **bonfire** *n.* 모닥불   **radiance** *n.* 광휘
- **interlace** *v.* 섞어 짜다; 엮다   **lift** *v.* 들어 올리다
- **echo** *v.* (의견 등에) 반향을 보이다
- **philosophy** *n.* 철학; 지식에 대한 애(愛)
- **fruitful** *a.* 열매가 많이 열리는; 결실이 풍성한
- **keen** *a.* 날카로운; 예리한; 예민한; 열심인
- **fullness** *n.* 충만; 충실   **treasure** *n.* 보배; 소중한 것
- **abundantly** *ad.* 풍부하게
- **articulate** *a.* (생각을) 명확히 표현하는
- **dart** *v.* 휙 던지다; 쏘다   **exuberantly** *ad.* 열의가 넘치게
- **simplicity** *n.* 단순; 간소; 순박함
- **humbly** *ad.* 겸손하게; 천한 신분으로

[Challenge 5]

문제 1

답 (1)

해설 바닐라(꼬투리)의 부족으로 아이스크림 가격 상승이 불가피하게 되었다는 내용이다. "The stocks in the world are being run down, and we are getting to a point now where we are likely to see the price suddenly shoot upwards"를 참조한다.

문제 2

답 (1)

해설 앞뒤 문맥으로 보아 지금까지 현 아이스크림의 가격이 유지된 것은 제조사들이 희생을 감수했기 때문으로 볼 수 있다. 빈칸에 들어갈 표현은 'take the hit(희생을 감수하다)'가 가장 적절하다.

해석 아이스크림 가격이 곧 상승할 것이라고 London Daily Telegraph는 보도했다. 문제가 무엇인가? 분명한 것은, 인도에서 멕시코까지 전 세계에서 생산이 줄어들었는데, 이는 전 세계의 아이스크림 소비자들에게는 좋지 않아 보인다. 바닐라의 가격은 이미 킬로당 25달러에서 거의 40

달러로 상승했다. 하지만 지금까지 아이스크림 생산자들이 희생을 감수하고 있는 것이다. Mintec 시장 분석가인 Nick Peksa는 이것이 전면적으로 아이스크림에 영향을 미칠 것으로 생각하고 있다. 그는 "세계의 바닐라 저장고가 줄어들고 있으며, 현재 가격이 급격하게 치솟는 상황에 이르고 있다. 킬로당 아이스크림 생산에 있어 가장 비싼 성분이기에 일부 생산자들은 추가 비용을 감내하지 못할 가능성이 크다. 약 10%까지 아이스크림 가격을 올릴 것으로 보인다"라고 설명했다.

어휘

grim *a.* 냉혹한, 모진 **across the board** 전면적으로
shoot upwards 상승하다

[Challenge 6]

문제 1

답 (4)

해설 보기 항목 (1)에서 'the majority of'라는 표현을 쓸 근거가 없다. 오바마의 예를 통해서 알 수 있듯이, 글쓴이는 트위터가 정치적 견해를 형성하는 데 큰 영향력을 보인다고 생각하고 있다. (3)에서 오바마가 처음에 온라인 네트워킹을 사용하는 것을 꺼렸다고 했는데, 그런 점은 본문에서 발견할 수 없다. 보기 항목 (4)는 두 번째 문단 첫 번째 문장에 잘 드러나 있다.

문제 2

답 (1)

해설 본문은 소셜 네트워킹이 점차 그 영향력이 커가고 있다는 내용을 다루고 있다. 오바마 대통령의 구체적 예를 통해 소셜 네트워킹이 정치 의견 수렴에 어떻게 잘 활용되는지를 보여주는 동시에 이러한 점을 간과한 매케인의 패배를 대조적으로 드러내면서 소셜 네트워킹이 정치적 토론장으로 효과가 있으며, 또한 앞으로 사라지지 않을 것이라고 강조하고 있다. 고로 그 영향력이 점차 높아질 것을 예측한다는 점에서 소셜 네트워킹을 사용하라는 제안인 보기 항목 (1)이 가장 적절하다.

해설 트위터의 영향력은 상대적이긴 하지만 정치 전문가와 기자들이 자신의 관점을 권력이 높은 정치인과 수다를 통해 나누면서 그들의 마음속에 성공적으로 자리를 잡았다. 오바마 대통령은 페이스북, 마이스페이스 그리고 트위터를 이용해 사회 연결망의 고위층을 성공적으로 이용했으며, 이것의 도움으로 대통령직을 손에 넣었다. 그는 거대한 팔로잉(following)을 모을 수 있었으며, 이들 대부분은 오늘날까지 여전히 그 수가 늘고 있다. 그는 이러한 토론장을 활용하여 자신의 의안을 진척시키고, 정치적 메시지를 공유했다. 그가 이러한 토론장을 통해 거둔 성과는 엄청난 것이었기 때문에, 다른 정치인들도 이것에 주목하고 자신의 목적에 맞게 사용하고 있다.

오바마의 완강한 정치적 상대였던 매케인은 오바마만큼 온라인 표를 찾아 확보하려고 노력하지 않았던 인물이었던 것 같다. 그가 만약 소셜 미디어를 받아들였다면 그 기회를 더 높일 수 있었겠는가? 어느 누구도 이러한 온라인상의 사회에서 네트워킹을 많이 한다는 것이 도움을 주었을지 또는 기회에 나쁜 영향을 미쳤는지에 대해 확실히 말할 순 없다. 그러나 한 가지 분명한 사실이 있는데, 그것은 바로 소셜 네트워킹은 상당한 효과가 있으며, 사라지지 않으리라는 것이다. 제안을 하자면 바로 소셜 네트워킹 기차에 오르라는 것이다.

어휘

albeit *conj.* 비록 ~일지라도(although)
pundit *n.* 박식한 사람, 전문가
maneuver *v.* (사람·물건을) 교묘하게 유도하다, (사람을) 계략적으로 이끌다; 교묘한 방법으로 (결과를) 이끌어내다
stratosphere *n.* (물가의) 최고가, 최고 수준; (계급·등급 등의) 최상층
cinch *v.* 《미국》(말의) 뱃대끈을 죄다;《미국 구어》꽉 쥐다;《속어》확인하다; (확실히) 손에 넣다; 보증하다
presidency *n.* 대통령의 직[지위, 임기]
platform *n.* 의견 발표 기회
staunch *a.* (사람·주장 따위가) 신조에 철두철미한, 완고한, 충실한
opponent *n.* 상대; 반대자 **reluctant** *a.* 마음 내키지 않는
embrace *v.* ① 얼싸안다, 껴안다(hug), 포옹하다 ② (기꺼이) 맞이하다, 환영하다

[Challenge 7]

문제 1

답 (3)

해설 'Principle of noncompetition'은 본문에서 자신의 이해관계에 해를 끼칠 것 같은 경쟁을 기득권자들이 서로 경쟁을 멀리하는 성향을 묘사하는 말이다. 고로 보기 항목 (1)은 바람직하지 못하다. 보기 항목 (2)의 경우, 돈과 선거에서 선출될 가능성의 관계는 반비례가 아니라 정비례이다. '(only access to money from investors makes a real campaign possible)'. 보기 항목 (3)은 옳다. 보기 항목 (4)는 본문에 제시된 'principle of noncompetition across investor blocs'에 위배된다.

해석 해석 국회의원이 선거에서 이기려면 돈이 필요하다. 토머스 퍼거슨은 이것을 "선거 비용 조건"이라고 부르면서, 미국의 정치 역학 관계 이론의 핵심으로 삼는다. 퍼거슨의 이론에서 주목할 만한 것은 두 가지의 추가적인 견해이다. 그 첫 번째는 금전적 이해 집단 간의 경쟁은 의제에 대한 접근 문제를 해결하지 못하는 경향이 있다는 주장이다. 퍼거슨은 이것을 "투자자 연합 간 비경쟁 원칙"이라고 부르면서, "주요 투자자들이 공통으로 가지는 중요한 이해관계에 영향을 미치는 모든 문제의 경우, 어떠한 정당 경쟁도 일어나지 않는다."라고 지적한다. 두 번째, 퍼거슨은 제일 비싼 값을

부른 사람이라 하여 쉽게 당선되는 것은 아니지만, 투자자들의 돈에 접근하는 길만이 현실적인 선거 운동을 할 수 있게 해준다고 주장한다. 국회의원은 당선되려면 돈이 필요하므로, 금전적 이해집단이 지지하지 않는 견해를 취할 수는 없다. 비록 그러한 견해가 중위 투표자의 정리에서 말하는 "정보를 완전히 갖춘 유권자"층에서는 승리한다 하더라도, 유권자는 재원을 모을 거래 비용을 극복할 수 없으므로, 제시된 선택을 받아들일 수밖에 없다.

어 휘

- **representative** *n.* ① 대표자, 대행자, 대리인 ② 대의원; (R-)《미국》하원 의원
- **dynamics** *n.* ① (물리학) 역학 ② (원)동력, 힘, 활력, 정신 역학
- **competition** *n.* 경쟁, 겨루기
- **bloc** *n.* (정치상·경제상의) 블록, …권(圈)
- **bidder** *n.* 값을 부르는 사람, 입찰[경매]자
- **theorem** *n.* ① 일반 원리, 법칙 ② (수학·논리학) 정리(定理)
- **transaction** *n.* (업무) 처리, 취급 (of); 거래
- **pool** *v.* 공동 계산으로 하다; 공동 출자[부담]하다
- **resources** *n.* (보통 pl.) 자원; 물자; 재원(~ of money)

[Challenge 8]

문제 1

답 (2)

해설 본문의 내용을 간략히 요약하면 다음과 같다. 고대 윤리학은 도덕 철학인 동시에 해야 할 의무로 이는 외적인 환경과는 별개로 어떠한 상황에서 반드시 해야 할 것을 의미한다는 내용이다. 보기 항목 (2)에서 독일인은 의무론을 설명하기 위한 새로운 단어를 고안해야 했다고 말하는데, 사실 이런 용어가 이미 존재하고 있었다는 것을 본문에서 알 수 있다. 일반적으로 내용일치 문제(유추도 어디까지나 본문의 내용을 바탕으로 하기에 여기 포함시키도록 한다)의 경우 글의 요지와 관련해서도 나오지만, 이렇게 괄호 안의 추가적인 내용도 보기 항목으로 활용되므로 꼼꼼히 읽어야 한다.

해석 고대 윤리학은 일반적으로 도덕적 철학을 의미했는데, 이는 또한 해야 할 의무의 이론이라 불렸다. 뒤에, 이 이름을 도덕 철학의 일부분, 말하자면 현상(외계)의 법(독일어의 경우 적절한 용어는 Tugendlehre로 볼 수 있음)에 영향 받지 않는 해야 할 의무의 원칙으로 한정하는 것이 바람직하다는 것을 알았다. 게다가 일반 의무론의 체계는 현상의 법을 처리할 수 있는 법률과 그렇지 못한 윤리학으로 나뉘며, 우리는 이러한 구분을 여전히 고수한다.

어 휘

- **ethics** *n.* 윤리학
- **ancient** *a.* 고대의; 옛날의
- **signify** *v.* 의미하다; 뜻하다; 묘사하다
- **doctrine** *n.* 교의; 교리; 주의
- **subsequently** *ad.* 그 후, 뒤에
- **advisable** *a.* 권할 만한; 바람직한
- **confine** *v.* 제한하다; 한하다
- **namely** *ad.* 즉, 다시 말하면
- **subject** *a.* ~의 권한 아래 있는
- **external** *a.* 외부의; 표면의; 대외적인
- **suitable** *a.* 적당한; 어울리는
- **deontology** *n.* 의무론, 도의론
- **jurisprudence** *n.* 법학; 이론; 법률학

[Challenge 9]

문제 1

답 (1)

해설 본문은 유대 마을의 다양한 측면의 이야기를 다루고 있다. 중간에 나오는 부분적인 이야기에 집착하게 되면, 전체를 다룰 수 있는 주제를 고를 수 없게 된다. 첫 번째 문장을 통해 주제를 설정하고, 이후 문장은 이 주제에 대한 뒷받침 내용(대조/묘사)으로 전개되고 있다.

문제 2

답 (4)

해설 복도처럼 생긴 길 양쪽에 늘어선 집을 생각한 후, 양쪽 지붕이 서로 연결되어 덮고 있다면 도로가 어떤 모습으로 보일지 생각해 본다.

문제 3

답 (3)

해설 본문의 다음 사항을 확인한다.

> Those inhabited by the more opulent are kept tolerably neat, and are adorned with rich and curious furniture; but they are, for the most part, exceedingly dirty.

보기 항목 (3)에 쓰인 'flawlessly immaculate'와 같은 극단적인 표현은 내용일치 문제에서 함정으로 자주 등장한다. 즉, '깨끗함'과 관련된 단어가 본문에 언급되었기에 이와 관련하여 오답을 유도하고 있다.

해석 유대인 마을은 무어인의 마을과는 상당히 다른 독특한 점이 있다. 그러나 그 차이점은 아주 적다. 거리는 마찬가지로 좁고 지저분하며, 집은 외부의 창문이 없다. 지붕은 또한 꽤 평평한 편이다. 유일한 차이점이란 거리가 각 방면의 집에서 뻗어져 나온 지붕으로 덮여 있어 지하 통로의 모습을 갖추고 있다는 점이다. 지붕에서 집 사이의 의사소통이 정규적으로 이루어지는데, 이것은 기분전환의 아주 인

기 있는 장소이다. 어떤 여성들은 이 평평한 지붕 위를 제외하곤 바람을 쐬는 경우가 거의 없다. 간단히 말해, 유대인이 되었건 무어인이 되었건 두 거주민 모두 이 지붕 위에서 춤추고, 노래하고 모든 종류의 유희를 즐긴다. (무어인과 마찬가지로) 유대인의 집의 방은 길고, 좁으며 천장이 높아 복도를 연상시킨다. 대부분의 집은 여러 가정이 함께 사는데, 일반적으로 대가족이다. 좀 더 부유한 사람들이 거주하는 집의 경우 견딜 만하게 깔끔하게 유지되어 있으며, 값비싼 진귀한 가구로 장식이 되어 있다. 그러나 대부분의 집이 지나칠 정도로 더럽다. 그리고 이들이 고기를 튀길 때 사용하는 엄청난 양의 마늘과 기름에서 나는 냄새는 후각이 완전히 없어지지 않은 사람이(즉, 후각의 기능이 약간만 있는 사람이라면) 질식사 할 만큼 심하다. 이들의 입맛은 이들이 사용하는 기름과 관련해 아주 세련되어 고급스러운 맛의 이유로 다른 어떤 것보다 우리의 램프 오일을 선호한다.

어휘

distinct *a.* 뚜렷이 다른   variation *n.* 변화[차이]
be covered with ~으로 덮여있다
extend *v.* 더 길게[넓게] 만들다
recreation *n.* 레크리에이션, 오락   inhabitant *n.* 주민
amusement *n.* 오락, 놀이   lofty *a.* 아주 높은, 우뚝한
gallery *n.* 미술관, 화랑; 수평 갱도
occupy *v.* 차지하다, 사용하다   opulent *a.* 호화스러운, 부유한
tolerably *ad.* 참을 수 있을 만큼, 견딜만하게
neat *a.* 정돈된, 단정한   adorn *v.* 꾸미다, 장식하다
curious *a.* 별난, 특이한   exhalation *n.* 발산, 증발
garlic *n.* 마늘   suffocate *v.* 질식사하다; 질식하게 하다
divest *v.* 박탈하다, 빼앗다
exquisitely *ad.* 아주 아름답게, 절묘하게
refine *v.* 정제[제련]하다; 세련되게 하다

[Challenge 10]

문제 1

답 (1)

해설 본문은 John Gilpin이란 시가 어떻게 해서 쓰이게 되었는지 그 유래를 다루는 내용이다. 일반적으로 이런 글의 유형은 크게 다음과 같은 두 가지로 구분된다.

1) 구체적 현상을 제시한 후 그 현상의 기원을 찾아가는 경우 (시간적으로 현재에서 과거로 넘어간다).

2) 과거의 구체적인 상황을 전개하고, 이로 인해 특정한 현상, 물건 등이 발생하게 되었다는 내용으로 전개(시간적으로 과거에서 현재로 넘어간다).

문제 2

답 (4)

해설 Cowper가 우울증에서 빠져나오도록 도운 것은 John Gilpin의 이야기이고, 이 사건을 바탕으로 시를 쓴 것이다.

문제 3

답 (3)

해설 한바탕 웃음이란 뜻으로 쓰이고 있다.

해설 어느 오후 Cowper의 교양 있는 친구인 Austen 부인이 그의 작은 저녁 사교 모임에 참여했을 때, 우연히 그녀는 그가 큰 실망에 잠긴 것을 목격했다. 이러한 경우에 그녀는 즉시 그러한 상황에서 빠져나올 수 있도록 그녀의 쾌활한 힘의 모든 원천을 쓰는 것이 습관이었다. 그녀는 그에게 John Gilpin의 이야기(어린 시절부터 그녀의 기억 속에 소중히 간직되어 온)를 들려주면서, 눈앞의 (일시적인) 우울한 때를 없애보려고 했다. 이 이야기가 Cowper의 일시적 기분(fancy)에 미친 영향은 마법과 같은 분위기를 자아냈다. 그는 다음 날 그녀에게 그녀가 들려준 이야기를 회상하면서 얻게 된 포복절도할 웃음이 밤새도록 그를 잠 못 이루게 했으며, 이것을 이야기로 썼다고 했다. 그래서 John Gilpin이란 즐거운 시가 생기게 되었다.

어휘

accomplished *a.* 교양 있는; 숙달된
observe *v.* 관찰하다   sink into ~에 빠져들다
dejection *n.* 실의, 낙담   custom *n.* 습관
resource *n.* 자원, 원천   sprightly *ad.* 쾌활한, 활기 넘치는
immediate *a.* 즉각적인, 당면한
relief *n.* 안도, 안심, 경감   treasure *v.* 소중하게 간수하다
dissipate *v.* ~을 쫓아버리다, 일소하다
gloom *n.* 우울, 침울   fancy *n.* 망상, 환상
enchantment *n.* 황홀감, 매력
convulsion *n.* (웃음 등의) 심한 발작   recollection *n.* 기억

Day 7

[Challenge 1]

문제 1

답 (1)

해설 'There is no place in the world for idle people.' 근면함에 관한 글이다. 중간에 나오는 저축에 관한 내용에 휩쓸려 제재를 검소함으로 잡아서는 안 된다. 전체적인 내용은 '마이클의 근면한, 지칠 줄 모르는 성실함'임을 파악한다.

문제 2

답 (1)

해설 문항의 첫 번째 문장과 마지막 문장을 잘 살펴보면서, 이 야기의 흐름을 따라 답을 선정하도록 한다. 본문의 곳곳에 힌트가 있는데, 예를 들어 (a)는 (b) 다음에 올 가능성이 크다. (a)의 다음 표현을 보자. 'By this time he had got two children, and the eldest was old enough to learn to read.'의 밑줄 친 부분보다 (b)의 'Michael had been a sailor in his youth, but when he married'의 내용이 앞서야 하기 때문이다. 이렇듯 문장 배열 문제는 '대명사, 접속사, 관사 그리고 시간적 순서에 따라 발생하는 행위 등'을 고려하여 정답에 접근한다.

해석 "세상에는 누구나 뭔가를 할 만큼 충분한 일이 있다. 게으른 사람에게 알맞은 장소란 없다." 이것은 바구니 제조업자인 나이 든 마이클이 그의 자녀들에게 말하곤 했던 것이다. 그리고 아이들이 자라면서 이러한 훌륭한 교훈을 감사할 만큼의 충분한 이유를 찾게 되었다.

마이클은 젊었을 때 뱃사람이었지만, 결혼을 하면서 시골의 한 장소에 정착해 바구니 만드는 일을 시작했다. 처음에 그는 바구니 만들 작대를 살 충분한 돈이 거의 없었지만, 열심히 일해서 그는 곧 돈과 신용도 함께 얻게 되었다. 마을의 어떤 이도 마이클보다 일찍 일어나지 못했으며, 대부분의 사람들이 잠자리에 들 때 그는 일을 끝마쳤.

일주일에 그가 벌 수 있는 돈의 액수는 적었지만, 그는 항상 얼마간을 저축했는데, 단돈 1페니가 생겨도 그랬게 했다. 매달 그는 저축을 했으며, 처음 6년간 25파운드를 저축했다.

이 시기에 그는 두 아이를 얻었고 큰애는 글을 읽을 만큼 컸다. 딸애는 마이클이 일을 하는 옆에서 책을 읽으며 앉아 있곤 했으며, 그는 아이가 도움이 필요하면 가르쳐주었다. 그러는 동안에 그의 부인은 집에서 다른 일을 하고 있거나 근처에 사는 농부들과 함께 일하고 있었다.

마이클은 이제 소와 돼지 두 마리를 샀으며, 이것으로 인해 어느 정도의 이윤을 냈다. 6년 안에 그는 그가 살고 있던 오두막집을 샀다. 이후 12년 즉, 결혼하고 24년 후 그는 작은 농장을 임대했다. 이 시기에 그는 7명의 아이를 얻었다. 그가 오두막집을 더 크게 지으면서 이들 모두는 집에서 함께 살면서 그를 도왔다. 손위 사내 아이들은 농장에서 일했고 여자 아이들은 엄마의 보호 아래 소에서 우유를 짜고 버터를 만들고 닭을 키웠다.

마이클의 경우 비록 부유했지만 과거의 일을 유지하면서 오랜 습관(부지런한 습관)을 계속 이어갔다. 그가 살던 장소를 내가 떠나기 전에 마지막으로 그를 보았을 때, 그는 일하면서 큰애들에게 글을 가르쳤던 것처럼 막내에게 글 읽는 방법을 가르쳐주고 있었다. 나는 종종 마이클의 말을 기억한다. "세상에 게으른 사람의 자리란 없다."

어 휘

proper *a.* 적당한, 알맞은
idle *a.* 게으름뱅이의; 한가한, 무익한; 쓸데없는
lesson *n.* 교훈 sailor *n.* 뱃사람 settle *v.* 자리 잡다
rod *n.* 장대; 지팡이   credit *n.* 신용; 영예; 공적
sum *n.* 액수; 총계   penny *n.* 페니
savings *n.* 저축, 절약된 금액   cottage *n.* 시골집; 작은집
care *n.* 걱정, 관심; 돌봄   poultry *n.* 가금류

[Challenge 2]

문제 1

답 (1)

해설 주어진 문장에서 'the time'을 구체적으로 받을 수 있는 상황이 앞에 전개됨을 활용한다.

문제 2

답 (3)

해설 pecuniary는 '금전상의'라는 뜻으로 돈과 관련된 표현이다.

문제 3

답 (4)

해설 문에서 돈은 지극히 부정적인 것으로 묘사되고 있다. 또한 본문은 정직함을 찬양하는 글이므로 보기 항목 (4)는 본문의 맥락과 일치하지 않는다.

해석 모든 행동과 태도에서 엄격한 정직이 너를 인도하도록 해라. 아무리 사소한 정도라도 이 정직의 원칙(명령)에서 벗어나지 말도록 해라. 이 길을 가는 데 너를 유혹하는 강력한 꿈이 있을 것이다. 득을 위한 욕구 - 탐욕의 목소리 - 는 종종 이익을 위해 정직을 어겨도 된다고 속삭인다. 정직의 명령이 중단되고 약간의 부정직함이 큰 이익이 되는 것처럼 보이는 때가 있다. 이 매혹의 노래를 믿지 마라. 이때가 바로 속아서 심각하게 해를 받을 수 있는 가장 위험한 때이다. 비록 정직함을 고수함으로 인해 실질적으로 손해를 보는 때가 있기도 하지만, 조금도 위축되지 마라. 정직을 엄격하게 따름으로 인해 언제든 금전상의 관점에서 무슨 손해를 보더라도, 정직하다는 명성을 쌓고 지키면, 장기적으로 100배를 보상받게 된다. 단순히 금전상의 관점에서 바라보던 공동체는 자신의 거래에서 정직하지 못한(사기꾼이라 알려진) 사람보다 정직의 명성을 쌓은 사람에게 더 빨리 격려와 후원, 일을 주게 될 것이다. 젊은이와 관련된 모든 고려사항, 종교, 도덕 그리고 금전적인 면에서 삶의 초기에 이들이 지속적인 지표로서 흔들리지 않는 정직과 성실의 법칙을 세울 수 있도록 이들을 격려하는 일에 협력하라. 모든 가능한 관점과 상상할 수 있는 모든 조건의 상황에서 "정직이 최상의 방책이다."라는 말은 언제나 진실임을 잊지 말도록 하라.

어 휘

rigid *a.* 엄격한, 융통성 없는
tempt *v.* 유혹하다, 부추기다　swerve *v.* 방향을 바꾸다
dictate *n.* (따라야 하는) 명령, 규칙
trivial *a.* 사소한, 하찮은　allurement *n.* 매혹, 유혹
entice *v.* 유도[유인]하다　appetite *n.* 식욕, 욕구
avarice *n.* 탐욕　whisper *v.* 속삭이다, 소곤거리다
violate *v.* 위반하다, 어기다
adhere *v.* 들러붙다, 부착되다
shrink *v.* 움츠러들다　pecuniary *a.* 금전의
submission *n.* 항복, 굴복
preserve *v.* 지키다, 보호하다, 보존하다
ntegrity *n.* 진실성, 완전한 상태
community *n.* 주민, 지역사회
countenance *n.* 찬성, 격려
patronage *n.* 후원, 지원　reputation *n.* 평판, 명성
fraudulent *a.* 사기를 치는　urge *v.* 충고하다, 설득하다
outset *n.* 착수, 시초
unswerving *a.* 약해지지 않는, 변함없는
constant *a.* 끊임없는, 거듭되는
conceivable *a.* 상상할 수 있는

[Challenge 3]

문제 1

답 (2)

해설 재미있는 일화가 소개되고 있다. 본문에서 책 가게 점원이 짧은 설교를 달라고 하자 Sterne의 설교를 준 것으로 보아 그의 설교는 아주 간결하다는 것을 추론해 낼 수 있다.

해석 Sterne의 설교는 일반적으로 아주 짧은데, 이런 상황으로 인해 Bath에 있는 Bull's 도서관에서 다음과 같은 농담이 생겼다. 한 하인이 주인의 명을 받고 Smallridge의 설교 중 하나를 구입하려 왔는데, 그때 실수로 그는 짧은 종교 설교를 달라고 청했다. 책 가게 점원이 그가 요구한 것에 대해 뭐라고 답해야 할지 쩔쩔매고 있는데, 거기 있던 한 신사가 "그에게 Sterne의 설교를 주면 됩니다."라고 제안했다고 한다.

어 휘

sermon *n.* 설교; 잔소리　circumstance *n.* 상황; 환경
give rise to ~이 생기게 하다　footman *n.* 종복; 하인; 마부
purchase *v.* 사다; 구입하다　puzzled *a.* 어리둥절해하는
present *a.* 출석한

[Challenge 4]

문제 1

답 (3)

해설 에스키모 예술의 특징을 설명하는 글이다.

문제 2

답 (2)

해설 "The more we look at these carvings, the more life we perceive hidden within them."에서 보기 (2)의 내용을 파악할 수 있다.

해석 고금의 가장 훌륭한 에스키모 조각품들은 언어와 시간이라는 엄청난 장벽을 뛰어넘어 (지금의) 우리와 직접적으로 소통할 강력한 능력을 보유하고 있는 것 같다. 이러한 조각품들을 보면 볼수록 우리는 그 이면에 감춰진 더욱 큰 생명력을 느끼게 된다. 우리는 동물, 인간과 신비한 세계의 미묘한 생존 형태를 발견하게 된다. 이들 조각품들은 얼어붙은 땅의 차가운 조각상이 아니다. 대신 이 조각상들은 그들을 둘러싼 삶의 기쁨과 공포, 황량함을 잘 인식하고 있는 활기찬 사람들의 열정적 감정을 우리에게 보여주고 있다. 에스키모 조각가들은 꿈에 감동한 사람들이다. 외부인들과 새롭게 관계를 맺으면서도 그들은 여전히 자신들만의 신비한 이미지에 관심을 둔다.

어휘

- **carving** *n.* 조각(술)
- **barrier** *n.* 장벽, 장애(물), 울타리
- **subtle** *a.* 미묘한, 포착하기 힘든, 난해한, 예민한, 명민한
- **reveal** *v.* 드러내다
- **vital** *a.* 생기가 넘치는
- **tranquility** *n.* 평정, 평온, 평안, 침착

[Challenge 5]

문제 1

답 (2)

해설 본문은 미국의 젊은이에게 '소유의 관점에서 수단과 방법을 동원해서라도 성공(ambition of property)을 이루어야 한다.'라는 잘못된 야망을 바로잡아 주기 위해 쓴 글이다. 두 번째 문단을 통해 구체적인 이야기를 통해서 글쓴이가 생각하는 미국의 젊은이에게 심어주고 싶은 진정한 야망을 드러내고 있다.

문제 2

답 (2)

해설 뒤에 이어지는 진술을 바탕으로 밑줄 친 표현의 의미를 파악한다. 1번 문제와 같은 맥락에서 소유와 관련된 그릇된 욕망 하나만을 추구하는 잘못된 가치관을 심어주는 것을 가리킨다.

문제 3

답 (1)

해설 본문에서 burn은 '마음속에 강한 인상을 주다, 새기다'의 뜻으로 쓰이고 있다.

해석 우리 미국인의 삶의 가장 큰 단점은 우리가 영웅을 숭배하는 사람들이라는 점이 아니라 우리가 단지 한 종류의 영웅만을 숭배한다는 점이다. 우리는 단지 한 종류의 성취만을 인식한다. 우리는 단지 하나의 천재만을 바라본다. 두 세대 동안 우리의 젊은이들은 가치 있는 야망이라 여기는 것은 단지 하나밖에 없다고 믿게 이끌어졌다. 바로 소유의 야망이다. 어떠한 희생을 치르더라도 성공을 한다는 것이 우리 소년과 소녀 앞에 드높여진 이상이다. 그리고 오늘날 우리는 이러한 왜곡되고 부정한 삶의 관점의 결과(보상물)를 거두어들이고 있는 것이다.

나는 최근에 성 바오로와 미니애폴리스에서 오랫동안 살아온 어떤 사람을 만났다. 그 지역은 알다시피 북유럽 이민자와 그 후손들이 많이 사는 곳이다. 이 남자는 나에게 자신은 노르웨이 사람들의 높은 이상주의에 특히나 감명을 받았다고 했다. 그는 사업을 통해서 노동자와 하녀 등의 낮은 계층이라 불리는 노르웨이 이민자들과 만나게 되었는데, 그는 이 젊은 남녀에게 다음과 같은 동일한 질문을 했다. "당신 나라에서 가장 위대한 사람은 누구인지 말해 주세요. 당신 나라의 젊은이들이 영감을 얻기 위해 바라보는 사람은 누구입니까? 아이들이 따라하고 모방하며 존경하는 사람은 누구입니까?"라고 물었다. 그는 이 질문에 거의 같은 대답을 받았다고 말한다. 이들 노동자와 하녀의 마음에조차 새겨져 있는 노르웨이의 위대한 이름은 딱 네 명이다. Ole Bull, Bjornson, Ibsen, Nansen. 반복해서 그는 같은 질문을 던졌는데, 반복해서 그는 같은 대답을 들었다. Ole Bull, Bjornson, Ibsen, Nansen은 각각 위대한 음악가, 위대한 소설가, 위대한 극작가, 위대한 과학자였다.

어휘

- **grave** *a.* 중대한, 예사롭지 않은   **defect** *n.* 결점, 결함
- **worshiper** *n.* 숭배자   **sort** *n.* 종류, 성질, 분류
- **genius** *n.* 천재; 비상한 재주   **generation** *n.* 세대, 대
- **property** *n.* 재산; 소유(권)   **ideal** *n.* 이상, 극치
- **hold up** 떠받치다, 지연시키다
- **reap** *v.* 거두다, 획득하다   **reward** *n.* 보수; 응보
- **distort** *v.* 찡그리다, 비틀다   **unjust** *a.* 부정한
- **neighborhood** *n.* 근처   **section** *n.* 구역, 지구
- **people** *v.* 사람을 살게 하다, ~에 살다
- **immigrant** *n.* 이주자, 이민   **descendant** *n.* 자손, 후예
- **idealism** *n.* 이상주의   **in contact with** ~에 접촉하여
- **workingman** *n.* 노동자, 장인   **servant** *n.* 사용인, 고용인
- **inspiration** *n.* 고취, 고무   **imitate** *v.* 모방하다, 흉내 내다
- **emulate** *v.* 모방하다   **admire** *v.* 존경하다; 찬탄하다
- **novelist** *n.* 소설가, 작가   **dramatist** *n.* 극작가

[Challenge 6]

문제 1

답 (4)

해설 동물 실험과 유아 관찰을 통해서 밝혀진 바는 무엇인가? 전두 피질과 대상 영속성 사이에 관련성이 있다는 것이다. 일반적으로 실험을 통해서 밝혀낸 사실이 글의 요지이며, 여기서 글의 주제를 이끌어낼 수 있다.

* 실험과 조사가 들어간 지문은 다음과 같은 점을 유의한다.

> 1) 실험의 목적/의도 = 글의 주제이자 제목
> 2) 실험의 결과 = 글의 요지(요지에서 글의 주제를 이끌어 낼 수 있다

해석 영장류 동물의 실험을 통해서 원숭이는 보이지 않는 대상의 이동을 추적할 수 있고, 눈에 보이지 않는 사물의 이동은 전두엽 피질에 나타나며, 전두 피질의 발달은 대상 영속성의 개념 습득과 관련이 있다는 것을 볼 수 있다. 인간 유아에게서 나타나는 다양한 증거가 이와 일치한다. 예를 들어, 전두 피질의 시냅스 형성은 유아기에 최고치에 이르며, 유아에서 뇌 영상 자료를 모으기 위해서 적외선 분광기

를 사용한 최근 실험에서 전두 피질의 활동은 물체 영속성의 작업이 성공적으로 이루어졌다는 것과 관련성이 있다는 것을 드러낸다.

어 휘

primate *n.* 영장류　　track *v.* 추적하다
displacement *n.* 전위; 이동
invisible *a.* 눈에 보이지 않는; 확실치 않는
target *n.* 과녁, 표적, 목표물
represent *v.* 보여주다, 나타내다
prefrontal *a.* 전두엽의　　cortex *n.* 외피
frontal *a.* 앞(쪽)의; 정면의　　acquisition *n.* 획득, 습득
permanence *n.* 영구, 영속(성)
infant *n.* 유아 *a.* 유아용의
be consistent with ~와 일치하다
formation *n.* 형성, 구성, 조직　　synapse *n.* 시냅스
peak *v.* 최고조까지 오르다　　infancy *n.* 유년기, 초기
infrared *a.* 적외선의　　spectroscopy *n.* 분광학
neuroimaging *n.* 뇌 영상　　activity *n.* 활성도, 활성
completion *n.* 성취, 완성　　object *n.* 대상, 목적, 목표
permanence *n.* 영구, 영속성

[Challenge 7]

문제 1

답 (3)

해설 현 정부에 대해 글을 쓰는 작가의 어려움을 기술하고 있다. 글의 초반부에서 일반 역사가와의 대조를 통해 이런 작가의 어려움을 설명한 후 계속해서 뒷받침 내용이 전개되고 있다.

문제 2

답 (2)

해설 본문에서 여러 번 언급된 원인이다.

> the object is in constant change, what he sees is changing daily, these are changing too, what he illustrates are altered in one way, and his sources of illustration are altered probably in a different way

일반적으로 이런 문제는 글에서 궁극적으로 전달하려는 요지와 관련이 되는데, 이는 전달하고자 하는 중요 내용을 글쓴이가 여러 번 반복해서 강조하려 하기 때문이다. 본문에서 자주 반복되는 단어, 표현은 글쓴이가 강조하는 내용임을 기억하자.

해석 실질적으로 (현재) 운영되고 있으며, 권력 안에 있는 국가 조직 즉 현재 존속하고 있는 국가에 대해서 글을 쓰려는 작가의 길을 방해하는 큰 어려움이 있다. 이 어려움은 그 대상이 항상 변한다는 것이다. 역사 작가는 이러한 어려움을 느낄 필요가 없다. 그는 단지 과거를 다룰 뿐이다. 그는 그 국가가 그가 시작하는 연도에는 여차여차한 방식으로 일했고, 그가 끝내는 연도에는 어떤 면에서 여차여차한 점이 다르다고 분명히 말할 수 있다. 그는 정해진 한 시점에서 시작해서 또한 정해진 다른 한 시점에서 끝낸다. 그러나 자신 앞에 있는 것을 쓰고자 하는 동시대 작가는 당황스럽다. 그가 보는 것은 매일 변하고 있기 때문이다. 그는 어떤 시점에 서 있는 그대로를 써야만 하는데, 그렇지 않으면 그는 자신의 진술에서 실제로는 같은 시대에 일어날 수 없는 일을 나란히 놓게 될 것이다(즉, 일어난 사건에 대한 기록을 하는 듯하나 현재도 그 사건은 일어나기에 이 기록은 정확히 일치하지 않는다는 뜻). 더 큰 어려움은 작가는 당대의 정부를 다루면서 그것을 가장 중요한 당대의 다른 정부와 비교하기 마련인데 이것들도 변하고 있기는 마찬가지이기 때문이다. 그가 설명하려는 것은 어떤 방식으로든 변경되며 그가 활용한 설명의 출처는 어쩌면 또 다른 방식으로 변경될 수도 있다.

어 휘

constitution *n.* 헌법
contemporary *a.* 동시대의; 현대의
puzzle *v.* 갈피를 못잡게 하다, 당황케 하다
perplex *v.* 갈피를 못잡게 하다; 복잡하게 하다
daily *ad.* 매일, 날마다
contemporaneous *a.* 동시의; 같은 시기의
illustration *n.* 삽화; 도해, 설명; 해설
alter *v.* 바꾸다; 고치다

[Challenge 8]

문제 1

답 (2)

해설 본문은 Essay on the History of Civil Society를 통해 드러난 아담 퍼거슨이 바라보는 사회 사상에 대한 설명이다. 좀 더 자세히 보면, 첫 번째 문단은 퍼거슨의 'theory of citizenship'이고, 두 번째 문단은 'human history'를 바라보는 관점 그리고 마지막 문단은 진보 사상(Idea of Progress)에 대한 견해이다.

문제 2

답 (2)

해설 밑줄 친 내용은 수많은 개인이 자신의 이익만을 추구하는 행위를 통해서도 'coherent and even effective'한 결과를 이끌어낼 수 있다는 퍼거슨의 믿음을 드러낸다. 즉, 의도하지 않은 결과를 각 개인의 이득 추구에서 이끌어 낼 수 있다는 의미이다. 이러한 의미를 가장 잘 전달하는 보기 항은 (2)이다.

문제 3

답 (3)

해설 앞뒤 전개된 내용의 관계를 밝혀 가장 적절한 연결사를 고르도록 한다. 빈칸 앞은 개인의 이익 추구에 따른 상업적 성장이 긍정적인 결과(a self-sustaining progress)를 가져온다이고, 이후 이러한 상업적 성장은 오히려 로마 시대와 비슷한 붕괴를 가져올 수 있다는 모순적 상황을 전개하고 있다. 즉, 하나의 대상의 두 가지 상반된 모순을 전개하는 내용이므로 보기 항 (3)의 '역설적으로'라는 표현이 가장 적절하다.

해석 Essay on the History of Civil Society에서 퍼거슨은 고전 작가와 현대 여행 문학을 인용하여 시민과 공동체 덕목을 저버린 것에 대한 비판의 시선으로 현대 상업 사회를 분석한다. 퍼거슨의 시민 이론의 핵심 주제는 충돌, 놀이, 정치 참여 그리고 군사적 용맹이다. 그는 다른 사람의 입장에 자신을 놓아보는 노력을 강조하면서, "공감"은 "인류의 특징"으로서 "인간 본성의 부수적 속성"이라고 한다. 다른 스코틀랜드 지식인과 마찬가지로 그의 친구인 아담 스미스와 데이비드 흄과 같이 그는 자생적 질서를 강조한다. 다시 말해 일관성 있고 효과적이기까지 한 결과는 때로 수많은 개인의 통제되지 않은 행위의 결과에서 발생한다.

퍼거슨은 인간이 속한 자연 역사와 사회 역사 두 층의 합성으로 역사를 보았다. 자연 역사는 하나님이 창조한 것이다. 그리고 진화하는 인간에 의해서 창조되기도 한다. 사회 역사는 이러한 자연 역사의 진화에 따라 인간에 의해서 만들어지고, 이러한 요소로 인해 사회 역사는 경우에 따라 후퇴를 경험한다. 그리고 일반적으로 인간은 하나님에게 힘을 받아 사회 역사의 진화를 추구한다. 인간은 자신만을 위해 사는 것이 아니라 하나님의 섭리를 위해서 존재한다. 그는 이상적인 남성의 특성으로 중세 기사도의 여러 측면을 강조했다. 영국의 신사와 젊은 남자들은 남을 기쁘게 하고 싶다는 욕망과 같은, 매우 여성적인 것으로 여기는 그런 예의 바람을 베풀고 내면적인 덕과 정중함이 배어 나오는 조금은 깊이 있는 인품으로 그 '여자들'을 대하라는 충고를 받았다. 퍼거슨은 진보 사상을 이끈 주도적인 주창자였다. 그는 개인의 사리 추구를 통한 상업 사회의 성장이 곧 자립적인 진보를 촉진할 수 있다고 믿었다. 그러나 역설적으로 퍼거슨은 또한 이러한 상업적 성장이 덕의 추락을 조장하고 고로 궁극적으로 로마의 멸망과 비슷한 붕괴로 이끈다고 보았다. 퍼거슨은 독실한 장로교 교인으로, 진보와 인간의 자유의지를 명령하는 하나님의 섭리의 문맥 안에서 두 발전을 놓음으로써 이런 눈에 보이는 모순을 해결했다. 퍼거슨의 경우, 인간이 행위를 통해 얻은 지식 또는 이러한 행위가 일시적인 퇴보의 결과를 가져온다 하더라도, 이러한 지식은 궁극적으로 손에 넣기 쉽지 않은 완벽성을 향한 진보적이며, 점근적인 성장의 내재적 일부분을 형성한다고 보았다.

어휘

draw on ① (장갑·양말 따위를) 끼다, 신다 ② ~을 꾀어 들이다; (~하도록) 격려하다 (to do); (기대감 따위가) ~에게 행동을 계속하게 하다; (일을) 일으키다, 야기하다
classical *a.* (문학·예술에서) 고전적인, 정통파의
critique *n.* (문예 작품 따위의) 비평, 비판; 평론, 비판문
abandonment *n.* 포기, 유기; 자포자기, 방종
communal *a.* 공동의
conflict *n.* (무력에 의한 비교적 장기간의) 싸움, 다툼, 투쟁, 전투; 분쟁
valor *n.* (특히 싸움터에서의) 용기, 강용
put oneself in[into] a person's shoes ~의 입장이 되어 생각하다
appurtenance *n.* (보통 pl.) 부속물, 종속물
species *n.* ① (공통된 특성을 가진) 종류 ② 인종
intellectual *n.* 지식인, 인텔리; 지식 계급
spontaneous *a.* 자발적인, 자진해서 하는, 임의의
coherent *a.* (의론 등이) 시종일관된, 이치가 닿는
-tiered *a.* 층을 이루고 있는, 계단식으로 된
synthesis *n.* 종합, 통합, 조립
progressive *a.* ① (부단히) 전진하는 ② 진보주의의 ③ 점진적인; 누진적인
setback *n.* ① (진행 따위의) 방해, 정지; 좌절, 차질 ② 역류, 역 수(逆水)
empower *v.* ~에게 권력[권한]을 주다(authorize), ~에게 능력[자격]을 주다; (~을) 할 수 있게 하다(enable)
providential *a.* 섭리의, 신의 뜻에 의한
medieval *a.* 중세(풍)의   **chivalry** *n.* 기사도, 기사도적 정신
dispense *v.* 분배하다, 나누어 주다; 베풀다
feminine *a.* 여자의, 여성[부인]의
promote *v.* 진전[진척]시키다, 조장[증진]하다, 장려하다
foster *v.* 육성[촉진, 조장]하다
retrogression *n.* 쇠퇴, 퇴행, 역행   **asymptotic** *a.* 점근선의

[Challenge 9]

문제 1

답 (3)

해설 멸망 앞에 서 있는 로마를 암울하게 묘사하고 있는 글이다.

문제 2

답 (1)

해설 문제 1에서도 말했듯이, 멸망 앞에 놓인 비참한 로마를 그리는 글로 본문에서 부정적인 어감의 표현이 넘쳐나고 있음을 확인할 수 있다.

문제 3

답 (4)

해설 보기 항 (4)는 반의어로 구성되어 있다.

해석 로마는 절정을 지나 1,400년의 어두운 골짜기를 바라보며 서 있었다. 로마의 뒤에는 Caesar, Sallust, Cicero, Catullus, Vergil 그리고 Horace의 무덤이 놓여 있다. 로마 앞에는 광기와 학대의 세기가 놓여 있고, 로마의 주변에는 구역질나는 수많은 사치, 약탈로 가득한 집, 어리석음으로 가득한 입 그리고 불만족한 영혼들로 가득했다. 로마의 위에는 미스터리와 침묵만이 있을 뿐이고, 로마의 행렬에는 로마가 아예 태어나지 않았더라면 인간에게 더 좋지 않았을까 하는 철학자가 있으며, 인생을 불행으로 간주하고 멸망만을 유일한 행복으로 간주했다. 시인들은 '농담과 사소한 것' 이상 노래하는 것이 없으며, 단지 어설픈 외설로 가득한 이익만을 추구한다. 곧 이들은 매춘부의 덕, 도둑의 성실함, 살인자의 부드러움 그리고 억압의 정의를 찬양하기까지 할 것이다. 몹시 싫은 자기 모순의 종류만이 대상을 이끈다. 여자 같은 남자, 남자 같은 여자, 기분 좋은 냉소, 믿음이 없는 사제, 신용이 없는 부자, 신을 높이는 동시에 경멸하며, 민중을 증오하면서 동시에 민중의 피를 빨아 먹으며 사는 귀족이 있을 뿐이다. 여기엔 권력을 경멸하는 듯 꾸며대는 동시에 그것을 얻으려는 공화주의 제국과 황제의 비참한 장관이 있을 뿐이다.

어휘

- grave n. 무덤; 분묘
- madness n. 광기; 정신착란; 열기
- tread down 억누르다, 짓밟다
- multitude n. 다수; 군중; 군집
- spoil v. 강탈, 약탈
- folly n. 어리석음, 우둔
- discontent n. 불만; 불평
- philosopher n. 철학자
- deem v. 생각하다; 간주하다
- extinction n. 사멸; 전멸
- pleasantry n. 기분 좋음; 익살
- trifle n. 하찮은 것; 소량
- obscenity n. 외설; 음란
- virtue n. 미덕; 선행; 덕
- harlot n. 매춘부; 창부
- integrity n. 성실; 정직
- tenderness n. 유연함, 부드러움
- oppression n. 압박; 억압
- caravan n. (사막을 건너는) 대상
- abhorrent a. 몹시 싫은; 지겨운
- effeminate a. 여자 같은
- masculine a. 남성의; 남자다운
- cheerful a. 기분 좋은; 마음을 밝게 하는
- cynic n. 냉소하는 사람
- infidel n. 신을 믿지 않는; 이교도의
- priest n. 성직자; 목사
- patrician n. 귀족
- honor v. 예우하다; 예배하다
- despise v. 경멸하다; 멸시하다
- populace n. 민중; 대중; 시민
- spectacle n. 광경; 미관; 장관
- republican a. 공화 정체의
- empire n. 제국
- disdain v. 경멸하다; 멸시하다

[Challenge 10]

문제 1

답 (4)

해설 보기 항 (4)만이 본문에서 근거를 찾을 수 있다. 보기 항 (1)은 본문 초반에 언급된 바로 보아 종교적 관점에서만 기술되었다는 표현은 옳지 못하다. 보기 항 (2)에서 지구가 Gaia에 의해서 창조되었다고 했는데, 본문에 Gaia와 지구와의 구체적 관계에 대한 언급은 없다. 보기 항 (3)에서 과학자들은 최근 Gaia라는 이론을 어느 정도 받아들이고 있지만 이교도 신과의 관련성으로 기피하는 경향을 보인다고 했다. 고로, 보기 항 (4)는 옳은 진술이다.

문제 2

답 (3)

해설 'the semantics and the use of metaphor'에서 알 수 있듯이 과학자들이 Gaia 이론을 반대하는 것은 그것이 과학적 신빙성에 의한 것이 아니라 '그것이 가지는 의미와 비유적 사용' 때문이라고 말하고 있다. 즉, Gaia라는 단어가 가지는 이교도적 신의 의미로 인한 것임을 알 수 있다.

해석 Lovelock은 Gaia: A New Look at Life on Earth(1979년에 처음 출판된 Gaia에 대한 초기 책)에 대한 대중의 반응에 경악했다. "나는 이것이 종교서적으로 간주될지 전혀 생각하지 못했다."라고 그는 1988년 신판(follow-up)인 The Ages of Gaia에서 속내를 드러냈다. "지금도 들어오지만 3분의 2가량 받은 편지는 종교적 신념의 맥락에서 해석된 Gaia의 의미에 관한 것이다." Gaia 이론과 지구의 날의 역사를 접목한 것을 통해 일부에서는 고대 이교도 신을 뻔뻔히 찬양하는 것에 뿌리를 둔 것으로 매년 이것을 준수하는 행위를 비난하는 데까지 이르지만, 그렇다고 일부에서 종교적 연관을 갖는다는 사실을 부인할 순 없다. 이러한 연관성으로 인해 많은 과학자들은 Lovelock의 이론을 심각하게 받아들이는 것을 거부했다. 그러나 결국 그는 이들의 반대는 "Gaia의 과학성 때문이 아니라 그 의미와 은유적 사용 때문"이라는 점을 알게 되었다. "신 다원주의 생물학자들은 창조론자, 정통주의자 그리고 선민사상을 옹호하는 사람들의 비판을 받아넘기는 데 나름의 어려운 시기를 거쳤다." 그는 한 비평가가 그에게 말한 것을 설명했다. "Gaia는 다음과 같은 잘못된 이론 중 단지 또 다른 것처럼 보였다. 즉, 대지의 어머니에 대한 뉴에이지적 종교 신념은 그에게 교회의 저주였다." Gaia의 2000년도 판인 Gaia: A New Look at Life on Earth에서 Lovelock은 "이제 대부분 과학자들이 Gaia 이론을 받아들이는 것처럼 보이며, 이것을 자신의 연구에 적용하는 듯하다. 그러나 이들은 여전히 Gaia라는 이름을 거부하고 Earth system Science 또는 Geophysiology라는 대칭을 선호한다."라고 썼다.

어휘

inkling *n.* 암시
condemn *v.* 비난하다, 힐난하다, 나무라다
unabashed *a.* 얼굴을 붉히지 않는, 뻔뻔스러운; 겁내지 않는, 태연한
pagan *a.* 이교(도)의; 우상 숭배의; 무종교의
semantics *n.* (*pl.*) 의미론; 어의론
metaphor *n.* 은유(隱喩), 암유(暗喩)
biologist *n.* 생물학자
fend off 받아넘기다, 피하다
recount *v.* 자세히 얘기하다; 차례대로 얘기하다; 하나하나 열거하다
anathema *n.* ① 교회의 저주, 아나테마; (가톨릭 교회에서의) 파 문(破門)
② (일반적) 저주; 증오

Day 8

[Challenge 1]

문제 1

답 (3)

해설 본문은 창조적 사고를 위해 필요한 요소를 나열(Listing)의 전개 방법을 이용하여 설명하고 있다. 주제문이 생략된 구체적 진술만으로 구성된 글로 주제가 숨어있는(latent) 형태이다. 이런 경우 독자는 구체적 진술을 바탕으로 일반 진술인 주제문을 이끌어 내는 동시에 주제를 설정할 수 있어야 한다.

문제 2

답 (1)

해설 '중요하지 않은 것은 모두 옆에 두고'라는 뜻으로 쓰인 것은 보기 항 (1)이다.

문제 3

답 (4)

해설 본문에서 언급되지 않은 사항은 'Fast decision-making'이다.

해석 그래서 창조적인 사고의 성공적인 첫 번째 열쇠는 바로 분명함이다. 당신이 정확히 무엇을 얻고자 하는지, 현재 정확히 어떠한 문제에 직면했는지를 명확히 하는 데 도움이 되는 궁금증들에 대해 철저히 생각하고 논의하고 질문할 시간을 가져라. 분명치 않은 사고는 분명치 않은 답변을 가지고 오는 것과 마찬가지로 분명한 사고는 분명한 답변을 이끌어 낸다. 두 번째 핵심은 바로 집중이다. 다른 모든 것을 뒤로 하고, 모든 정신의 힘을 하나의 문제를 풀거나, 하나의 특정한 장애를 극복하거나 또는 하나의 중요한 목적을 성취하려는 것에 초점을 맞추는 데 집중하라. 정신의 흐트러짐 없이 하나의 문제에 집중하는 능력은 뛰어난 사고를 하는 사람의 가장 큰 특징이다. 세 번째 핵심은 바로 열린 마음이다. 일반적인 사람들은 그가 있는 곳에서 원하는 곳으로 가게 되는 사고방식에 고정되는 경향이 있다. 그러나 창조적으로 사고하는 사람은 매우 융통성이 있고, 문제에 접근하는 여러 다양한 방식에 있어서도 개방적인 경향이 있다. 일반 사람들은 성급히 결론에 도달하는 경향이 있고 특정한 목적을 성취하는 데 단지 하나의 방법만이 있다고 단정한다. 반면 뛰어난 사상가는 더 인내심이 있으며 어떤 결정을 내리기 전에 다양한 옵션을 고려한다.

어휘

key *n.* 비결, 열쇠   clarity *n.* 명료함, 맑음
clarify *v.* 분명[명료]하게 하다, 해명하다
fuzzy *a.* 희미한, 분명하지 않은
concentration *n.* 집중, 전념
diversion *n.* (방향, 주의 등을) 전환, 기분 전환
distraction *n.* 정신이 흐트러짐, 산만
hallmark *n.* 특징, 특성   superior *a.* 상급의, 우수한
fixed *a.* 고정된, 일정한   flexible *a.* 융통성이 있는
tendency *n.* 경향, 풍조, 추세
conclusion *n.* 결말, 종결, 결론   option *n.* 선택할 수 있는 것

[Challenge 2]

문제 1

답 (4)

해설 본문은 '정당의 강령'과 같은 Coffee Party(커피 당)의 성명(Statement)에 해당한다.

문제 2

답 (1)

해설 첫 번째 빈칸은 바로 앞에 전개된 내용에서 힌트를 얻을 수 있다. 커피 당은 특정 단체에 속하지 않고 회원들 간의 원칙과 사실에 입각해서 입장을 표명한다고 했으니, 보기 항 모두가 우선될 가능성이 크다. 두 번째 빈칸은 바로 부사구의 표현인 'By seeking and spreading accurate information'에서 보기 항 (1)이 가장 적절한 것을 알 수 있다. (c)의 경우 자신들이 지지하는 지도자를 방해하는 사람은 당연히 책임을 묻는다는 의미로 'hold accountable'이 맞는 표현이다. 마지막으로 (d)의 경우 주어인 'the influence of money, and the politics of fear and exclusion'은 부정적인 영향을 미치는 요소이므로 국민을 위한 정부에 방해가 되는 것임을 알 수 있다. 또한 'in the way of'와 짝을 이루는 것은 'stand'이다.

해석 우리는 공정하고, 포용적인 사회를 만들기 위해 열심히 일하는 미국인들입니다. 우리 구성원들은 우리나라의 도시, 마을, 이웃에서 발견되는 생각, 배경 그리고 환경의 다양성을 드러냅니다. 우리는 민주주의를 강화하기 위해 공동의 기반과 집단적인 행위를 추구하는 미국인을 위한 만남의 장소입니다. 우리는 모든 정당과 명칭에서 독립됨을 주장합니다. 맞습니다. 우리는 어느 당에도 속하지 않습니다. 그러나 이것이 우리가 어떠한 입장도 취하지 않는다는 것을 의미하진 않습니다. 커피 당 구성원들은 당과의 관련성에 기

반해서가 아닌 원칙과 사실에 근거해 입장을 취한다는 의미입니다. 정확한 정보를 추구하고 퍼뜨리면서 우리는 정확한 정보를 기반으로 한 결정을 바탕으로 조치를 취하고 정치에 참여합니다. 커피 당은 모든 연령, 인종, 신체적 능력 그리고 성향의 남녀가 존중하는 마음으로 정직한 생각의 교환을 위해 함께 모일 수 있는 장소를 제공합니다. 우리는 함께 이야기 나누고 배움으로 우리 나라가 직면한 문제를 해결할 수 있는 조치를 취할 수 있습니다. 국가의 목적과 함께 우리는 각자의 구성원에 의해 선출된 지역의 계획을 추구할 수 있도록 전국의 커피 당의 집회(chapters)를 장려합니다. 유권자와 민중 지원자로서 우리는 연방 정부가 우리의 적이 아니라 우리 집단 의지의 표현임을 인정합니다. 우리는 확실한 해결책을 향해 일하는 지도자를 지지하고 동시에 이들을 방해하는 사람들에게 책임을 물을 것임을 서약합니다. 커피 당은 돈의 영향력과 두려움과 배제의 정치는 '국민의, 국민에 의한, 국민을 위한' 정부에 방해가 된다고 믿습니다.

어휘

inclusive *a.* 포용적인, 차별이 없는; 포괄적인
represent *v.* 대표하다; 나타내다
label *n.* (사람·단체·사상 등의 특색을 나타내는) 호칭
partisan *n.* 한 동아리, 도당, 일당
chapter *n.* (조합·협회 등의) 지부, 분회
grassroots *n.* (정치 운동 등의) 기반, 기초; 일반 대중
will *n.* 의지   **pledge** *v.* 서약[약속]하다
obstruct *v.* ① (길 따위를) 막다; 차단하다 ② (일의 진행·행동 따위를) 방해하다(hinder)
exclusion *n.* 제외, 배제, 배척; 거절, 축출

[Challenge 3]

문제 1

답 (3)

해설 원인에 대한 철저한 분석 이전에 행해야 할 가장 근본적인 단계는 자료 수집이다.

문제 2

답 (3)

해설 보기 항 (2)와 (3)은 본문의 내용을 떠나 서로 의미적으로 상충된다는 것을 알 수 있다. 때로 보기 항만으로도 어느 정도 대략의 답을 구할 수 있는 문제가 나온다. 보기 항들 간에 모순된 내용을 전달하는 것은 따로 표시를 해 두고 본문을 대조하며 확인한다. 보기 항 (3)에 대한 내용은 없다.

해석 Mazengarb 위원회는 청소년 비행 문제에 대한 장기적인 연구가 있어야 한다고 의견을 제시한다. 사실 현 위원회는 여러 목격자들로부터 이러한 제안에 대한 증언을 들었으며, 우리는 이런 점을 듣게 된 것에 크게 감명을 받았다.

만약 누군가 특정 문제에 대한 해결책을 강구하려 하면, 이 문제 자체에 대한 철저한 분석이 근본적 필수조건임은 두말하면 잔소리다. 우선 사실을 알아보는 것이다. 이런 해악의 본질과 그 정도가 무엇인지 알아야 한다. 이것의 원인과 사건에 대한 많은 자료를 확보해야 한다. 이러한 물증을 가지고 있으면 유용한 치료 방법을 찾는 유리한 고지를 점령하게 된다. 사실을 찾는 이 작업은 길고도 고된 일일 수 있다. 이것을 폭넓은 지식과 경험을 가진 전문가에게 맡길 필요가 있다. 이 보고서의 초반에 언급된 부서 간 위원회의 설치로 이미 시작된 셈이다. 우리는 정부가 이 특별 제안을 호의적으로 고려해주기를 강력히 권하며, 이것이 실시될 수 있는 방법과 수단이 발견되기를 희망한다. 우리는 이 제안이 이 문제에 대한 접근을 하는 데 아주 중요하다고 생각하며, 정부에 의해서 고려되어야 한다고 생각한다.

어휘

long-term *a.* 장기적인   **delinquency** *n.* (청소년) 비행
witness *n.* 증언, 목격자   **remedy** *n.* 치료, 의료, 구제책
thorough *a.* 철저한, 충분한   **diagnosis** *n.* 진단(법)
fundamental *a.* 기초의, 근본의   **prerequisite** *n.* 필수조건
extent *n.* 넓이, 크기, 정도, 범위   **incidence** *n.* 범위, 발생률
material *n.* 재료, 소재   **position** *n.* 지위, 위치
arduous *a.* 힘든, 곤란한   **entrust** *v.* 맡기다, 기탁하다
expert *n.* 숙련자, 전문가   **recommend** *v.* 추천하다
favourable *a.* 호의적인

[Challenge 4]

문제 1

답 (2)

해설 'some painters like Whistler, Sargent, and Mary Cassatt belong to the English or French school, but they are the exceptions. Almost all U.S. artists have developed on their own.' 부분에서 알 수 있듯이 언급된 예술가들은 영국이나 프랑스 학파에 속한다고 하면서 이들은 예외적일 뿐이라고 했다. 여기서 예외라는 말은 대부분의 미국 예술가들은 유럽의 영향을 받지 않았지만, 이들은 영향을 받았다는 의미다.

문제 2

답 (1)

해설 the Old World는 본문에서 유럽을 가리킨다.

해석 미국의 그림은 다른 것과 구별되는 나름의 독특한 풍미가 있다. 사실 Whistler, Sargent, Mary Cassatt와 같은 일부 화가들이 영국 또는 프랑스 학파에 속하지만 이들은 예외이다. 거의 모든 미국의 예술가들은 나름의 방식을 발전시켰다. 이들은 스스로 깨친 예술가들로 자신의 재능을

어느 정도 완성했다. 어쩔 수 없는 필요에 의해 유럽을 방문한 화가들은 이미 (예술적으로) 성숙한 상태였다. 이들에게 유럽 (Old World)은 자신들이 이미 가지고 있는 기존의 스타일을 수정하기보다는 자신의 기법을 향상시키는 데 도움을 주었다. Grant Wood와 같은 예술가의 경우 유럽 여행은 자신의 국적인 뿌리에 대한 인식을 고무시켰으며, 자신이 속한 진정한 장소는 자신의 나라와 자기 자신의 환경이라는 점을 확신했다.

어 휘

singular *a.* 독특한, 유독한   flavor *n.* 맛, 풍미
exception *n.* 예외 (상황)   self-taught *a.* 독학의
the Old World 유럽   existing *a.* 기존의

[Challenge 5]

문제 1

답 (1)

해설 본문은 시간의 흐름(chronical flow)에 따라 생물학 무기에 관한 역사적 배경, 발전 과정 그리고 현재 어떤 상황에 놓여 있는지를 간략하게 기록하고 있다. 고로 생물학 무기에 관한 간략한 역사를 살펴보는 내용이므로 보기 항 (1)이 가장 적절하다.

문제 2

답 (2)

해설 시간의 흐름에 따른 기술 방법이다. '고대 → 현대'로 넘어가면서 생물학 무기에 관한 내용을 다룬다는 점을 감안하면 쉽게 답을 구할 수 있다.

해석 (a) 때때로 인간은 서로를 죽이기 위한 새로운 수단을 위해 지구상의 모든 실행 가능한 선택 사항에 몰두한다. 인간들은 산림을 훼손하고, 자연을 약탈하며, 살육을 위한 인간 욕망에 불을 붙이기 위해 종교, 철학, 과학 그리고 예술을 유용했다. 그런 과정 중에 우리는 자연의 가장 가공할 만한 바이러스, 박테리아 그리고 균이란 적까지 무기화했다. (c) 생물학 무기의 사용은 고대시대까지 거슬러 올라간다. 기원전 1,500년까지 거슬러 올라가 소아시아의 히타이트는 접촉 전염의 가공할 힘을 인식했으며, 적군의 땅에 역병에 걸린 환자를 보냈다. 군대 또한 오래 전부터 생물학 무기의 힘을 알고 있었기에, 포위된 성에 죽은 시체를 투척하거나 적의 우물을 감염 균으로 오염시켰다. 어떤 역사학자는 모세가 이집트에 대해 내린 성경의 전염병 재앙이 화가 난 신의 저주라기보다는 생물학 전쟁의 집중된 전략이었을 가능성이 크다는 주장을 했다. (d) 이런 인류 초기 이래, 의료과학 분야의 발달 덕분에 해로운 병원균과, 면역체계가 병원균을 다루는 방식에 대한 이해도가 대단히 높아졌다. 그러나 이런 의학의 발달은 백신과 치료법 개발을 가져온 동시에, 인류에 가장 파괴적인 생물학 요소를 지나치게 무기화하는 상황을 만들어냈다. (b) 20세기 초반에는 독일과 일본 두 나라뿐 아니라 미국, 영국 그리고 러시아와 같은 나라에서 잇따른 생물학 무기 프로그램의 발달로 탄저병이 생물학 무기로 사용되었다. 오늘날 생물학 무기는 1972년 생물학 무기 조약과 제네바 협약에 따라 법으로 금지되어 있다. 그러나 수많은 나라에서 축적된 생물학 무기를 없애고, 확산 연구를 멈추었지만, 여전히 그 위협은 남아있다.

어 휘

viable *a.* ① (계획 따위가) 실행 가능한, 실용적인 ② 살아갈 수 있 는, 생명력 있는
level *v.* 완전히 파괴해 버리다   plunder *v.* ~로부터 약탈[수탈]하다
divert *v.* 전용[유용]하다
bloodshed *n.* 유혈(의 참사), 살해; 학살
formidable *a.* ① 무서운, 만만찮은, 얕잡을 수 없는 ② 매우 어려 운, 감당할 수 없는
fungal *a.* 균에 의하여 생긴   anthrax *n.* 탄저(炭疽)(병)
subsequent *a.* 뒤의, 차후의; 다음의, 계속해서 일어나는
stockpile *n.* 비축[축적](량), (자재 따위의) 재고
proliferation *n.* 증식; (핵병기 따위의) 확산
catapult *v.* ~로 쏘다, 발사하다, 발진시키다
besiege *v.* ~을 포위 공격하다; ~을 에워싸다
biblical *a.* (또는 B-) 성경의   vengeful *a.* 복수심에 불타는
vastly *ad.* 엄청나게, 대단히
vaccination *n.* 종두(種痘); 백신 주사

[Challenge 6]

문제 1

답 (3)

해설 특정 악에 반하는 대중의 감정을 일으키는 것이 중요하다는 본문 초반의 내용과 이후 Clarkson, Wilberforce 등을 위시해서 식민지 내 노예 차별 제도를 없애는 노력에서도 대중의 감정을 일깨우는 것의 중요성을 드러내고 있다 (the effort was to enlighten and direct public sentiment in a community in order to lead them to rectify an evil existing among THEMSELVES).

문제 2

답 (1)

해설 문제에서 요구하는 사항은 본문에서 제시된 'the evil(노예 무역과 노예 제도)'을 제거하는 구체적인 방법이 아닌 것을 고르라는 것인데, (1)에 나와 있는 대중적 감정(국민의 여론)을 일으키는 것은 문제에서 요구하는 방법으로 인해 나타나는 결과이다.

즉, 'the evil'를 제거하기 위해선 국민적 여론을 형성해야 하는데, 그것을 하기 위한 구체적인 방법에 대한 기술이 나머지 보기에 해당한다.

해석 우선 이 사회에서 행위의 주된 법칙은 주로 과거의 경험에서 비롯된 잘못된 연역적 결과에 전적으로 기초한다. 경험에서 본 바와 같이, 특정한 도덕적 악이 한 사회에 존재할 때, 이러한 행위에 반하는 국민적 감정을 깨우려는 노력과, 개인적 영향력의 행사와 본보기의 이행을 적절하게 조화시키는 일이 종종 이러한 악을 개선하는 경향을 보였다. 게다가 무절제한 행위와 관련해 객관적 사실의 수집, 대중 설교자들의 수고, 그리고 출판물의 배포는 이러한 악을 줄이는 데 큰 영향을 미쳤다. 영국의 노예무역과 노예제도와 관련해서도 그러하다. 영국은 자국의 무역을 규제하고, 자국의 지배 아래 있는 모든 노예에게 자유를 줄 수 있는 힘을 지녔다. 그러나 이들은 이 문제에 관해 그들이 지고 있는 의무에는 전혀 마음을 쓰지 않았다. Clarkson, Wilberforce 그리고 그들의 보좌인들은 국민의 감정을 일으키고 영향을 미칠 수 있는 운영체제를 시작했으며, 이들은 노예무역의 억압과 영국의 식민지 내 노예제도의 점진적 폐지에 성공했다. 이 두 경우 모두에서, 그들 자신 안에 존재하는 악을 개선하도록 스스로를 이끌기 위해서, 비록 주체는 그 사회의 일부분이지만, 완전히 그들의 영향 하에 있는 그 사회 속에는 대중의 감정을 일깨우고 지도하는 노력이 있었다.

어휘

deduction *n.* 연역법, 연역　　**moral** *a.* 도덕상의; 윤리상의
awaken *v.* 일으키다; 자각시키다; (감정 따위를) 불러일으키다
sentiment *n.* (감정 섞인) 의견, 감정; 정서
combination *n.* 결합, 연결
rectify *v.* 바로잡다; 고치다; 수정하다
respect *n.* 대목, 사항
intemperance *n.* 방종; 무절제, 과격; 난폭
distribution *n.* 분배; 배급; 베풂
diminish *v.* 줄이다, 감소하다
reference *n.* (~와의) 관계, 관련
slavery *n.* 노예제도; 노예; 고역
possess *v.* 소유하다; 점유하다
regulate *v.* 규제하다; 규정하다
dominion *n.* 지배권; 지배, 통치
unmindful *a.* 신경 안 쓰는; 무관심한
commence *v.* 시작되다[하다]　　**secure** *v.* 지키다; 확보하다
suppression *n.* 진압; 억제　　**gradual** *a.* 점진적인
abolition *n.* 폐지　　**colony** *n.* 식민지; 식민지 이민단
enlighten *v.* 이해시키다; 깨우치다　　**portion** *n.* 부분, 몫

[Challenge 7]

문제 1

답 (2)

해설 숫자 처리는 아주 기본적인 단계의 컴퓨터에 해당하는 것이고, 가상주행 시뮬레이터는 숫자 처리를 창조적인 방법으로 활용한 예라고 볼 수 있다. 보기 (2)는 컴퓨터에 관한 내용을 다루는 전반부에서 쉽게 찾을 수 있다.

문제 2

답 (3)

해설 중심 소재인 computer와 brain의 비교임을 감안하면 쉽게 답을 고를 수 있다.

해석 컴퓨터는 원래 그냥 수치를 계산하는 기계였지만 현재는 이런 숫자 처리 기능이 수천 가지 상상의 방식으로 활용되어 비디오 게임과 워드 프로세서와 같은 새로운 가상 기계가 만들어지게 되었다. 이런 기계들에서 (컴퓨터의) 기본적인 숫자 처리 기능은 거의 눈에 보이지 않으며, 이런 새로운 힘은 마술처럼 보이기까지 한다. 마찬가지로 우리의 뇌는 언어 처리를 위해서 만들어진 것이 아니지만(최근에 발견된 아주 주변적인 기관을 제외하곤) 현재 성인의 뇌에서 발생하는 활동의 상당 부분 – 아마도 대부분 – 은 일종의 언어 처리 활동, 즉 발화와 이해 그리고 일련의 방식으로 언어적 항목을 열거하고 재배열하는 것과도 관계되어 있다. 그리고 이런 활동들은 정말 마술처럼 보이는 방식으로 기저를 이루는 하드웨어 기능을 증폭하고 변형시킨다.

어휘

number-cruncher *n.* 숫자 처리기
harness *v.* (하천·폭포·바람 등 자연력을 동력으로) 이용하다
peripheral *a.* 주변의　　**rehearsal** *n.* 예행연습, 열거
take place 일어나다, 발생하다　　**rearrangement** *n.* 재배열
underlying *a.* 밑에 있는; 기초가 되는, 근원적인, 제 1의
surrogate *n.* 대리(물)

[Challenge 8]

문제 1

답 (1)

해설 본문에서 제시되는 구체적 두 사례를 통해 전달하려는 내용은 자전거와 자동차의 예기치 못한 충돌 사건을 기록하는 블랙박스 역할의 카메라이다. 보기 (1)이 가장 적절한 제목에 해당한다.

문제 2

답 (4)

해설 본문만으로 (4)와 같은 내용을 추론하는 것은 논리적 비약이다. 상식선에선 어느 정도 옳다고 볼 수 있으나 본문에 드러나

문제 3

답 (2)

해설 본문에서 언급되고 있는 카메라는 사고가 난 후 이를 기록하는 비행기의 블랙박스와 같은 역할을 하고 있다.

해석 지난 몇 년 간 인기를 끌기 시작한 이 새로운 카메라는 스키, 서핑 및 그 밖의 스포츠를 즐기는 동안 비디오와 사진을 찍는 용도로 만들어졌다. 마찬가지로, 많은 자전거 이용자들도 이 카메라를 사용해 자신들이 자전거 타는 모습을 기념으로 남긴다. GoPro와 Contour는 인기 있는 모델을 제작한다. GoPro에 따르면 자전거 소매상을 통한 판매가 지난해 같은 시기와 비교했을 때 올해 지금까지 거의 두 배로 증가했다고 한다. 지금껏 찍힌 자전거 충돌 비디오 중 가장 두드러지는 것은 4월에 찍힌 것으로, 버클리 언덕을 오르던 두 명의 브라질인 자전거 운전자를 접은 색 자동차가 쳐서 넘어뜨리고 달아난 것이었다. 버클리 경찰에 따르면, 자전거를 탄 사람 중 어느 누구도 심각하게 다치진 않았다고 한다. 이 충돌 장면을 찍은 비디오는 유튜브에서 362,000번 이상 시청되었다. 버클리 경찰은 자동차의 번호판을 인식하고, 나중에 등록된 차량의 남자를 찾아냈다. 이들은 그가 자동차의 운전자를 은폐하기 위해 자신의 차를 도난 당했다고 거짓 신고한 것으로 보고 여전히 이 사건을 조사하고 있다고 경찰 대변인인 Andrew Greenwood 소장은 말했다.

최근 한 금요일 저녁 워싱턴 도심지의 거리가 집으로 향하는 자동차로 붐빌 때, Wilder 씨는 이마에 카메라를 둘러메고 자전거를 타고 있었는데, 마치 머리에 램프를 쓴 동굴 탐험가 같았다.

그는 주차된 자동차와 도로의 차 사이를 서둘러 지나가고 있었는데, 이따금씩 자신과 지나가는 자동차 사이의 공간이 1피트 정도도 되지 않을 때도 있었다. Wilder 씨가 지난 8월에 워싱턴에서 있었던 자신의 충돌 장면을 찍은 이 비디오는 처음에 자신을 친 운전자를 찾는 데 그리 큰 도움을 줄 것이라 보이진 않았다. 그러나 National Geographic의 사진 담당부서에서 일하던 Wilder 씨는 이 비디오를 장면마다 검토하다가 자신이 바닥에 누워있을 때 포착된 차량의 번호판이 선명하게 찍힌 사진 한 장을 찾아냈다. Columbia 지구 법무 장관은 운전자 John W. Diehl을 사고 현장을 떠난 혐의로 고소했다. 이 지역 중범죄를 담당하는 연방 경찰 또한 이 사건을 현재 검토 중이다. Diehl 씨의 변호사 Adam R. Hunter는 진술을 거부했다. 법무장관 대변인에 따르면 Diehl 씨는 무죄를 주장했다고 한다. Wilder 씨는 "대부분 자전거 운전자들이 카메라를 사용하지 않기에, Diehl 씨가 뺑소니를 쳐도 괜찮다고 생각했을 것이다"라고 말했다.

어 휘

catch on 인기를 끌다
knock someone down and speed off 뺑소니를 치다
cover up 은폐하다   be jammed with ~로 붐비다
spelunker n. 동굴탐험가   frame by frame 장면마다

[Challenge 9]

문제 1

답 (3)

해설 첫 번째 문단은 'Limited Opportunities to Learn'에 관한 내용이고, 두 번째 문단은 'Limited Access to Institutional and Other Resources'에 관한 내용인데, 두 번째 문단이 (c)에서 시작된다. 각 문단별 단락별 주제를 파악하는 데 주력해야 한다.

문제 2

답 (2)

해설 전체적으로 소수 민족 학생의 학업 성취도가 취약하게 된 요인을 설명하고 있다.

문제 3

답 (3)

해설 보기 (3)의 경우 본문 마지막에 언급된 내용과 관련된다. 본문은 건강과 교육 성취의 관계를 살펴보고 있는 것이지 그것이 생명에 영향을 주는지에 관한 내용을 다루고 있진 않다.

문제 4

답 (2)

해설 앞에서 전개된 내용과 같은 맥락에서 추가적인 정보가 이어지고 있다.

해석 학교에서 누가 엄격한 교과 교육을 받는가에 관한 문헌을 검토한 결과, 표준화 시험의 결과를 바탕으로 소수 인종과 민족 출신, 특히나 저소득층 출신들이 "낮은 능력"으로 판명되고 낮은 코스 또는 학력부족 수업에 배정되는 경우가 수치상 불균형적으로 많은 것으로 보인다. 대조적으로 유럽 출신의 특히나 수입이 높은 집안의 사람들은 "재능이 있고, 능력 있는" 학생으로 간주되는 경향이 커 좀 더 높은 상급반의 프로그램에 배치된다. 코스 등록 자체가 학생이 받게 되는 수업의 수준과 이들이 노출된 교과 과정과 교습의 질을 결정짓기에, 이것이 의미하는 것은 평균적으로 소수 학생들은 상대적인 다수에 해당하는 학생들보다 높은 질의 교과 과정에 참여할 가능성이 더 낮다는 것이다. 높은 수준의 내용을 배울 기회가 상실된 것으로 인해 낮은 학업 성적의 결과가 나온다.

잘 갖추어진 도서관, 멘토링, 튜터링, 질 좋은 수업, 엄격한 교과 과정, 카운슬러—학생 그리고 선생님과 학생의 비율이 낮은 점, 작은 교실 사이즈, 방과 후 실습 그리고 컴퓨터와 다른 기술 기자재는 높은 수준의 학업 성취도를 가능하게 하는 선행 조건으로 여겨지는 교육에 있어서 핵심적인 자원의 예이다. 불행히도, 특정 소수 단체(혹은, 라틴계와 인디언 미국인 등), 특히 수입이 낮은 가정 출신의 수적 불균형을 이루는 학생들은 이러한 자원에 대한 제한적 접근만이 허용되는 학교에 다닐 가능성이 커 학업적으로 잘할 수 있는 기회가 줄어들게 된다. 게다가, 이런 학생들 다수는 경제적으로 어려운 사회에서 살고 있는데, 거기서 이들은 열악한 건강 상태와 영양실조를 겪으며, 이러한 요소가 이들이 교육적으로 더 취약한 상황에 놓이게 한다.

어 휘

review v. 검토하다 literature n. (특정 분야의) 문헌
access n. 접근권 rigorous a. 준엄한
curricular a. 교육과정의 standardize v. 표준화하다
disproportionate a. 불균형의 racial a. 인종상의
ethnic a. 민족의 minority n. 소수
low-income a. 저임금의 background n. 배경
assign v. 배정하다 low-track n. 낮은 코스
remedial a. 보충적인 in contrast 대조적으로
descent n. 가계, 혈통 talented a. 재능 있는
enrich v. 질적으로 향상시키다 accelerate v. 가속하다
track n. 과정 enrollment n. 등록
curriculum n. 교육과정 instruction n. 교수, 교육
expose v. 노출하다 minority a. 소수 민족의
average n. 평균 majority n. 다수
peer n. 동료
engage in high-caliber curricula 우수한 교육과정에 참여하다
diminish v. 차츰 사라지다 material n. 내용; 자료
academic a. 학업의 equip v. 갖추다
mentoring n. 조언하는 일 tutoring n. 가르치는 일
counselor n. 상담자 ratio n. 비율
extracurricular experience 비교과 과정에서의 경험
key a. 가장 중요한, 핵심적인 view v. 여기다, 생각하다
precondition n. 전제 조건 enable v. 가능하게 하다
Latino n. 미국에서 살아가는 라틴인
Native Americans n. 미국 원주민
minimize v. 최소화하다 academically ad. 학문적으로
distress a. (경제적으로) 곤궁에 처한
community n. 사회, 공동체 inadequate a. 불충분한
nutrition n. 영양분

[Challenge 10]

문제 1

답 (3)

해설 본문 첫 번째 문장과 전체적인 문맥에서 돈은 정치적 영향력이 있다는 점을 파악할 수 있다.

해석 퍼거슨의 주된 이론에 따르면 직장과 공동체 내 부를 바탕으로 한 신분의 차이는 일이 벌어지는 정치와 사회 환경에서 권력의 차이로 확장된다는 것이다. 고로 어떤 원천이든 부의 축적은 특권의 영속성에 대한 요구를 이끌어낸다. 부는 또한 정부 정책에 대한 불균형적 영향력을 낳는다 (afford). 돈을 가진 사람은 다른 부자와 이익을 공유하고 자신의 권력을 사용하여 이러한 이익이 보호될 수 있도록 보장할 수 있는 필요성을 인식한다.

어 휘

accumulation n. ① 집적, 축적, 누적 ② 축적[퇴적]물, 모인 돈
perpetuation n. 영속시킴, 불후케 함
disproportionate a. 불균형의, 어울리지 않는 (to)

Day 9

[Challenge 1]

문제 1

답 (2)

해설 특정 질병에 관한 특징을 기술하고 있다.

문제 2

답 (3)

해설 다음 본문에서 보기 항 (3)은 틀린 진술임을 알 수 있다.

> while the closest scrutiny, and the most rigorous medical tests, fail to establish any material distinction between the state of the sufferer and what we conceive of absolute death.

문제 3

답 (3)

해설 (c)는 본문에서 말하는 병을 말하고, 나머지는 이로 인해 발생하는 증상과 관련된 표현이다.

해석 몇 년 동안 나는 정확한 이름이 없어서 의사들이 강경증이라고 부르기로 한 특이한 병에 시달리고 있었다. 비록 이 병의 직접적인 요인과 병리적 선행요소, 심지어 실질적인 진단조차 여전히 미스터리이지만, 이 병의 분명한 특징은 충분히 잘 알려져 있다. 이것의 증상은 아주 다양한 것처럼 보인다. 때로 환자는 하루 종일, 또는 그보다 짧은 시간 동안 아주 무기력하게 누워 있기만 한다. 그는 감각이 없으며 외적인 움직임도 없다. 그러나 심장박동은 여전히 희미하게나마 인식할 수 있게 뛰고 있다. 약간의 온기는 남아 있으며, 뺨의 중간에 아직 색이 남아 있으며, 거울을 입에 가져다 대면, 활동이 없고 일정하지 않은 심폐활동의 떨림을 감지할 수 있다. 그런 다음 이런 혼수상태의 기간이 몇 주간, 심지어 몇 달간 지속된다. 아무리 자세히 정확한 의학 테스트를 한다 해도, 환자의 상태와 우리가 절대적 죽음이라 인식하는 것과의 실질적인 구분을 할 수가 없다. 아주 일반적으로 순전히 이전부터 이 병을 앓아왔다는 그의 친구들의 지식과, 막연한 의심이 드는 것, 그리고 무엇보다 부패가 거의 보이지 않는다는 점에 의해서만 섣부른 매장을 면할 수 있다. (즉, 매장하지 않는 이유는 그의 몸이 부패하지 않기 때문이다). 이 병의 악화는 다행히도 아주 점진적으로 일어난다. 그 첫 번째 발병은 분명히 있다는 것은 알지만 모호하다. 발작은 점차적으로 더욱 뚜렷해지며, 이전보다 매번 더 오랜 기간 동안 지속된다. 매장을 할 주된 확신이 바로 여기서 생긴다. 첫 번째 발작증상이, 가끔 발견되는 극심한 형태를 보이는 불행한 사람들은 거의 다 불가피하게 생매장 된다.

어 휘

subject a. 받기 쉬운, 종속하기 쉬운
singular a. 이상한; 보기 드문   *disorder* n. 장애
physician n. 의사   *term* v. …을 (~라고) 부르다
catalepsy n. 강경증(몸이 갑자기 뻣뻣해지면서 순간적으로 감각 이 없어지는 상태)
default n. 불이행, 태만   *definitive* a. 결정적인, 최후의
predispose v. 미리 (~의) 경향을 주다; (병에) 걸리기 쉽게 하다
diagnosis n. 진단(법); 원인 분석
mysterious a. 신비한, 불가사의한
variation n. 변화, 변동   *chiefly* ad. 주로, 대개
exaggerate v. 과장하다, 과대하다
lethargy n. 혼수(상태)   *senseless* a. 무감각의
externally ad. 외부에, 표면적으로
motionless a. 움직이지 않는, 정지한
pulsation n. 맥박, 고동   *faintly* ad. 희미하게, 어렴풋이
perceptible a. 인지할 수 있는   *trace* n. 기미, 기색
warmth n. 따뜻함, 온기   *linger* v. 오래 머무르다, 남다
application n. 적용   *detect* v. 발견하다, 간파하다
orpid a. 움직이지 않는, 무감각한, 둔한
unequal a. 고르지 않은, 불규칙한
vacillate v. 흔들리다, 진동하다
duration n. 지속 기간, 지속   *trance* n. 몽환의 경지, 최면 상태
scrutiny n. (면밀한) 조사   *rigorous* a. 준엄한, 가혹한
medical a. 의학의, 의술의   *material* a. 중요한, 필수의
sufferer n. 환자; 피해자
conceive v. 마음에 품다, 상상하다, 생각하다
absolute a. 절대의, 순수한, 확실한
premature a. 조숙한, 시기상조의
interment n. 매장   *solely* ad. 오로지, 오직
consequent a. 결과로서 일어나는
decay n. 부패, 부식   *advance* n. (병세의) 진행, 진전
malady n. 병, 질병   *gradual* a. 단계적인, 점차적인
manifestation n. 표현, 표시, 명시
unequivocal a. 모호하지 않은, 명료한
successively ad. 잇따라, 계속해서
distinctive a. 독특한, 구별이 분명한
endure v. 견디다, 인내하다   *preceding* a. 이전의, 전술한

principal *a.* 주요한   security *n.* 안전, 보안, 방위
inevitably *ad.* 불가피하게, 필연적으로
consign *v.* (좋지 않은 상황에) 처하게 되다
tomb *n.* 무덤

[Challenge 2]

문제 1

답 (1)

해설 본문은 논쟁을 좋아하는 프랭클린이 소크라테스 대화법을 알게 되면서 일어나는 일화를 이야기하고 있다.

문제 2

답 (3)

해설 보기 항 (3)의 경우 프랭클린은 소크라테스의 대화법을 알게 되자마자 매혹되었다고 본문에 나와 있다(the Socratic method of argumentation at once secured his approval and admiration). 보기 항 (3)의 다음 본문에서 추론해 낼 수 있다.

> before long he became satisfied of the folly of these disputations, in which each party struggles, <u>not for truth, but for victory</u>.

즉, 소크라테스는 진리 도달을 위한 수단으로 자신의 대화법을 사용한 반면 프랭클린은 나중에 이것을 승리를 위한 도구로 만족했다고 기술하고 있다.

문제 3

답 (2)

해설 바로 이어지는 부연설명에서 답변을 이끌어 낼 수 있다.

> each party struggles, not for truth, but <u>for victory</u>. It is simply an exercise of ＿＿(a)＿＿, in which the man who has the most <u>skill and muscle</u> discomfits his antagonist.

즉, 진리 추구의 대화법을 단순히 승리를 위한 기술과 힘의 싸움으로 변질된 지적 논쟁으로 비유하고 있다. 이러한 측면을 가장 잘 반영하는 보기 항은 (2)이다.

해설 프랭클린은 본성적으로 논쟁을 좋아하는 성향을 지녔다. 그는 예리한 지력으로 동료들과의 논쟁에서 적어도 자신의 판단으로 반드시 승리할 것이라 확신했다. 그러나 그가 누리는 데 익숙했던 그런 것과는 너무 다른 소크라테스식 논쟁법은 단번에 그의 인정과 감탄을 자아냈다. 소크라테스는 노골적인 반박 또는 독단적인 주장으로 상대를 공격하는 무례함에 죄책감을 느끼지 않았다. 결코 기대를 어기지 않은 공손함과 모든 이들로부터 존경받는 겸손한 행동으로, 그는 자신의 동료 논쟁 상대를 일련의 연속적 질문으로 그가 주장하는 관점에 동의하게 만들었다. 프랭클린은 즉시 이 새로이 발견한 기술을 실행하기 시작했다. 그는 놀라울 정도로 성공적이었으며, 가장 친근하고, 사랑받는 동료 중 한 명이 되었다. 그러나 오래지 않아 그는 이 논박의 어리석은 측면에 안주하고 마는데, 바로 각 당사자가 진리를 위해서가 아니라 승리를 위해서 논쟁을 한 것이었다. 이것은 단순히 가장 노련한 기술과 근육을 가진 자가 그의 상대를 좌절시키는 그런 지적 검투사의 행위였을 뿐이다. 제퍼슨은 그의 조카에게 논쟁을 피하라고 경고했다. 그는 "나는 평생 서로 논쟁하여 헤어지지 않는 사람을 못 봤다. 각자 이전보다 더욱 자기 자신만의 견해가 옳음을 확신할 뿐이다."라고 말했다.

어 휘

disputatious *a.* 논쟁을 좋아하는
keen *a.* 날카로운, 예리한   intellect *n.* 지력, 이성
associate *n.* (사업, 직장) 동료   socratic *a.* 소크라테스의
accustom *v.* 익숙케 하다   indulge *v.* 만족시키다, 충족시키다
secure *v.* 얻어 내다   approval *n.* 승인, 인가, 재가
admiration *n.* 감탄, 칭찬   guilty *a.* 유죄의, 떳떳하지 못한
discourtesy *n.* 무례, 버릇없음   assail *v.* 습격하다, 공격하다
contradiction *n.* 반박   positive *a.* 확신하는, 단정적인
assertion *n.* 단언, 주장   politeness *n.* 공손, 예의바름
modesty *n.* 겸손, 조심성, 정숙
demeanor *n.* 태도, 품행, 행실   regard *n.* 존경, 높은 평가
disputant *n.* 논쟁자, 논객   assent *v.* 동의하다, 찬성하다
advocate *v.* 지지[옹호]하다
commence *v.* 시작하다, 개시하다
agreeable *a.* 기분이 좋은, 유쾌한
beloved *a.* 인기 많은   folly *n.* 어리석음, 우둔
disputation *n.* 논쟁, 논의   exercise *n.* 행위, 행동
gladiator *n.* 검투사   discomfit *v.* 깨뜨리다, 좌절시키다
antagonist *n.* 적수, 적대자
convince *v.* 납득시키다, 깨닫게 하다
correctness *n.* 옳음, 정당

[Challenge 3]

문제 1

답 (4)

해설 본문은 여성이 낙태 후 겪게 되는 현상을 권위 있는 단체의 말을 인용하고, 구체적인 예를 곁들어 자세하게 설명하고 있다.

문제 2

답 (2)

해설 보기 항 (2)는 'The American Psychiatric Association has identified abortion as one of the stressor events that can trigger post-traumatic stress disorder (PTSD).'에서 알 수 있듯이 옳은 설명이다. 또한 본문에서 'post-abortion syndrome is a form of PTSD'라고 명시하는 동시에 낙태는 실질적으로 한 생명을 죽인다는 점에서 전쟁과 유사점이 있다는 것을 본문에서 유추할 수 있다. 보기 항 (3)의 경우 대부분의 낙태를 경험한 여성이 죄책감과 수치심을 느끼긴 했지만, 모든 여성이 비슷한 감성적인 증상을 보인 것은 아니다. 보기 항 (4)의 경우 'abortion-on-demand'의 경우 'self-destruct mode'가 거의 발생하지 않는다고 했는데 본문에 이런 내용은 명시되어 있지 않다. 또한 이것이 언급된 부분을 보게 되면, 낙태를 한 여성에게 자주 발생한다는 의미로 'Frequently'가 쓰이고 있다.

문제 3

답 (3)

해설 바로 뒤에 이어지는 내용을 확인한다.

> the memory _____ (a) _____ her. She heard this little voice in her head: "Abortion, abortion; you're a terrible, awful person."

일종의 환영의 목소리가 나타나 그녀를 괴롭힌다는 것을 알 수 있다. 이런 표현에 가장 적절한 단어는 'haunt'이다.

해석 낙태를 한 후, 많은 여성들은 임신과 아기에 대한 스트레스와 책임감을 회피한 것에 안도감을 느끼지만, 낙태는 결국 수백만의 여성에게 심각한 정서적인 피해를 입힌다. 미국 정신학회에선 낙태가 PTSD(외상후 스트레스 장애)를 유발할 수 있는 스트레스의 요인이 되는 사건 중 하나로 인정했다. 우리 대부분은 PTSD를 전쟁의 결과로 고통 받는 베트남 용사와 연관 짓는다. 그러나 낙태 후 증상도 낙태를 경험한 여성에게 영향을 미치는 일종의 PTSD이다. 아이의 죽음은 한 사람이 인생에서 경험할 수 있는 가장 큰 스트레스가 발생하는 순간 중 하나이다. 낙태 후 증상은 손실의 일부인 고통과 슬픔을 느끼도록 스스로를 내버려두지 않고, 슬퍼하지 않은 정서적 스트레스이다. 정서적으로 건강하기 위해서 우리 모두는 손실을 겪으면서 슬퍼해야 한다. 그러나 만약 내가 속한 사회가 그 안에서 내가 슬퍼할 것이 전혀 없다고 말한다면 어떻게 하겠는가? 만약 여성이 자신의 아기를 위해 슬퍼해야 할 필요성을 인식하지 못하거나 그녀가 그런 일이 일어나기를 거부할 경우, 이 감성적인 고통은 다른 곳으로 가게 된다. 종종 한 여성이 낙태를 한 후, 그녀는 한 CPC 상담사가 묘사한 '자기 파괴 모드'로 들어가게 된다. 다시 임신을 하고, 다른 남자와 관계를 맺고, 자신을 벌하며, 일반적으로 심각한 우울증이 취할 수 있는 여러 합병증들을 보인다. 낙태 후 증후군을 경험하는 여성은 일반적으로 혼란스럽고, 엄청난 죄책감을 느낀다. 한 연구 보도에 따르면 낙태를 한 92%의 여성이 죄책감을 느꼈다고 했다. 현재 낙태 후 치료 단체에 속한 한 여성은 낙태를 한 후 이 기억이 자신을 괴롭혔다고 진술했다. 그녀는 자신의 머릿속에서 '낙태, 낙태, 너는 끔찍한 사람이야'라는 작은 소리를 계속 들었다고 했다. 많은 여성에게 죄책감은 그녀와 자신의 아이를 해치도록 한 의사와 상담사, 그녀에게 낙태를 강요한 남편이나 남자친구 혹은 부모님, 임신을 하고 낙태를 한 자신에 대한 심각한 노여움을 통해 나타난다.

어 휘

abortion *n.* 낙태   pregnancy *n.* 임신
trigger *v.* (일련의 사건·반응 등을) 일으키다, 촉발시키다
post-traumatic stress disorder *n.* 외상 후 스트레스 장애 (큰 정신적 충격 때문에 겪게 되는 의학적 증상)
grieve *v.* 슬프게 하다, 비탄에 젖게 하다

[Challenge 4]

문제 1

답 (1)

해설 고용주와 피고용인의 근본적인 차이점에 관한 이야기다.

해석 근면과 절약은 서로 밀접한 관련이 있다. 경제 연구에 따르면 고용주의 95%는 이들이 체계적으로 돈을 저축했기 때문에 고용주라는 것을 분명히 보여주고 있다. 젊었을 때부터 돈을 체계적으로 모은 사람은 자동적으로 고용주가 된다. 수천의 직원을 둔 사람이든 작은 시골 가게의 두세 사람의 직원을 둔 사람이건 모두 고용주인 것이다. 이 동일한 연구에 따르면 95%의 임금 노동자는 이들이 버는 즉시 돈을 습관적으로 썼기에 임금 노동자가 되었다고 말하고 있다. 이들은 필연적으로 임금 노동자로 남는 것이다. 이것은 어떠한 노동 지도자도 부인할 수 없는 너무나 중요한 사실이다. 이 점은 고용주도 그의 임금 노동자와 같은 동네에서 같은 임금을 받고 시작한 사람이라는 점을 고려할 때 특히나 눈에 띄는 사실이다. 고용주는 근본적으로 근면하고 검소했으며, 임금 노동자로 남은 사람은 그렇지 않았다.

어 휘

thrift *n.* 검약; 검소   ally *v.* 동맹[결연, 제휴]하다
systematically *ad.* 체계적으로; 조직적으로
automatically *ad.* 자동적으로, 무의식적으로
clerk *n.* 사무관; 점원   wage *n.* 임금; 급료
of necessity 필연적으로   labour *n.* 근로; 애씀
disprove *v.* 반증을 들다; 그릇됨을 밝히다
significant *a.* 중대한; 함축성 있는
striking *a.* 현저한; 두드러진
industrious *a.* 부지런한; 근면한

[Challenge 5]

문제 1

답 (4)

해설 본문은 점심을 싸 오는 학생보다 학교 점심 프로그램에 참여한 학생이 더 건강하다는 내용을 골자로 학교 무료 급식을 옹호하는 글이다.

해석 무상급식 자격에 대한 논란이 있지만, 학생들은 언제나 점심을 학교에 싸 가지고 갈 수 있다, 그렇지 않은가? 전국의 학교 식당에서 내가 본 것은 이것이 아니다. USDA가 가장 최근에 실시한 학교 음식에 관한 전반적인 연구에서 62%의 학생들은 급식을 선택했고, 약 10%만이 조사하는 당일 집에서 도시락을 싸 가지고 왔다. 다른 아이들은? 어떤 아이는 점심을 먹지 않았다(4%의 초등학생과 8%의 고등학생). 또 다른 아이들은 학교 식당에서 먹고 싶은 음식을 메뉴에서 골라 사 먹었으며, 어떤 아이들은 학교 밖에서 음식을 구매하는가 하면, 어떤 아이들은 자판기 또는 학교 가게에서 음식을 사먹었다. 아이들이 나름대로 선택한 음식은 연방정부의 'reimbursable' 음식이라고 알려진 영양 지침을 만족하는 학교 음식보다 일반적으로 건강에 좋은 것이 아니었다. 최근의 한 영양 평가에 따르면, 학교 급식에 참여한 고등학생은 참여하지 않은 학생보다 비타민 A, B12, 칼슘, 칼륨과 그리고 다른 영양분을 상당히 더 많이 소비했다. 다른 연구에서도 공립학교 점심 프로그램에 참여하는 아이들이 그렇지 않은 아이들보다 더 많은 우유를 섭취했고, 반면 스낵과 당분 그리고 단 음료의 섭취는 적었다. 일부 어떤 가정에서는 정성껏 싼 도시락을 보내기도 하지만, 아이들은 대부분 단 음료와 과자 봉지가 든 점심을 학교에 가지고 오는 경우가 허다했다.

어 휘

eligibility *n.* 자격; 적임, 적격성
problematic *a.* 문제의, 문제가 되는; 미심쩍은, 불확실한
comprehensive *a.* 포괄적인; 범위가 넓은
survey *v.* 조사하다, 검사[사정]하다
elementary *a.* 초등교육[학교]의
a la carte *a.* 좋아하는 요리의(메뉴에 관한 단어로 각 코스가 각각 분리되어 가격을 지불하는 방식)
nutrition *n.* 영양; 영양 공급
reimbursable *a.* 변제할 수 있는; 배상할 수 있는
assessment *n.* 평가   **potassium** *n.* 《화학》칼륨, 포타슘
household *n.* 가족, 세대; 한 집안

[Challenge 6]

문제 1

답 (2)

해설 보기 항 (1)은 'The spread of e-mail and easy access to e-mail-harvesting software significantly lowered the cost of sending scam letters by using the Internet.' (2)의 경우 다음 내용을 통해 옳지 않음을 파악할 수 있다. 'Several unemployed university students first used this scam as a means of manipulating business visitors interested in shady deals in the Nigerian oil sector' 참고. (3)과 (4)는 본문 마지막 부분에 잘 명시되어 있다.

문제 2

답 (2)

해설 앞뒤 문맥을 보면, 전통적인 조직범죄와는 다르다고 언급하고 있다. 보기 항 (1)은 앞뒤 문맥이 아닌 단순히 '다양한 방법'이란 말뭉치에 익숙해서 나온 답일 가능성이 크다.

해석 선금 사기란 일종의 신용 사기로, 상당한 수익을 벌어들일 수 있다는 희망에 일정한 돈을 선불하도록 목표 대상을 꾀는 것이다. 이런 다양한 종류의 사기 중에는 Nigerian Letter(소위 419 사기, 나이지리아 사기, 나이지리아 은행 사기 또는 나이지리아 돈 제안으로 불리기도 함), 러시아/우크라이나 사기와 마찬가지로 겁은 돈 사기인 Spanish Prisoner(전자보다 덜 대중적이지만 널리 퍼져 있음)가 있다. 소위 러시아와 나이지리아 사기는 전통적인 조직범죄와는 전적으로 다른 것을 대표한다. 그러므로 그들은 다양한 전혀(altogether) 다른 종류의 접근방식을 사용하는 경향이 있다. 비록 Spanish Prisoner와 같이 좀 더 오래된 사기와 비슷하긴 하지만, 현대 419 사기는 석유산업을 기반으로 한 나이지리아 경제가 추락하면서 1980년대 초반에 시작되었다. 무직 상태의 대학생들이 처음에는 나이지리아 석유산업 분야의 불법 거래에 관심을 보이는 사업가들을 속이는 수단으로 신용 사기를 치다가 서구 사업가들을 표적으로 삼은 이후에는 더 다양한 사람들에게 손을 뻗었다. 1990년대 초반에서 중반까지의 사기꾼들은 회사를 범행 대상으로 하여 편지, 팩스 또는 텔렉스를 통해 사기성 메시지를 보냈다. 이메일의 보급과 이메일을 수집하는 소프트웨어에 대한 용이한 접근은 인터넷 사용을 통한 사기성 편지의 전송 비용을 상당히 낮추었다. 2000년대에 419 사기는 아프리카, 아시아, 동유럽 지역에서, 그리고 더 최근에는 북미와 서유럽(주로 영국과 네덜란드) 그리고 호주 등지에서 비슷한 모방 사건을 일으켰다.

어 휘

advance-fee fraud *n.* 선금 사기
confidence *n.* 신용; 신뢰; 자신, 확신

gain n. 이익, 이득   variation n. 변화; 변동; 변이
scam n. 사기   stand for 나타내다; 뜻하다; 대표하다
dissimilar a. 닮지 않은   breed n. 종류; 품종
approach n. (문제 등의) 접근법
originate v. 시작하다; 유래하다; 생기다
decline v. 기울다; 쇠하다; 쇠퇴하다
manipulate v. 교묘하게 조종하다
shady a. 의심스러운   sector n. 분야; 영역; 방면
population n. 인구; 주민   via prep. ~을 경유하여; 거쳐
elex n. 텔렉스   access n. 접근; 면접; 출입
harvest v. 수확하다   spur v. 자극하다
imitation n. 모방; 모조품; 흉내

지막 후자를 개인이 소유할 수 있는 공식적인 교육 증명서와 무형의 가치 복합체와, 행실에서 나오는 문화 양식에 대한 지식으로 정의했다. 부르디외가 제시한 핵심인 견해는 자본 형태는 대체 가능하다는 점인데, 다시 말해 이들은 서로 각자를 위해 교환이 가능하고 실질적으로 각자의 발전을 위해 서로의 교환을 요구한다. 예를 들어 어느 정도의 중요성을 지니는 사회 자본은 개인이 다른 이와 관계를 형성할 수 있도록 가능하게 하는 어느 정도의 물질적 자원의 투자와 어느 정도의 문화적 지식의 습득이 없이는 거의 얻을 수 없다.

어휘

controversy n. 논쟁, 논란   social capital 사회적 자본
application n. 적용, 응용   unit n. 단위; 구성
original a. 최초의; 독창적인   theoretical a. 이론적인
concept n. 개념, 구상   sociologist n. 사회학자
center v. 집중시키다   accrue v. 누적되다; 저절로 생기다
virtue n. 장점, 가치   treatment n. 취급, 대우
instrumental a. 도움이 되는, 유익한
intentionally ad. 계획적으로, 고의로
brilliant a. 찬란하게 빛나는; 훌륭한
interaction n. 상호 작용   define v. 규정짓다, 정의를 내리다
formal a. 정식의, 공식적인   credential n. 자격 증명서
intangible a. 만질 수 없는, 파악하기 어려운
complex n. 복합체   demeanor n. 태도; 품행
insight n. 통찰, 이해   trade v. 교환하다

[Challenge 7]

문제 1

답 (1)

해설 보기 항 (2)는 지적 자본(intellectual capital)에 관한 내용이고, (3)과 (4)는 사회 자본(social capital)에 관한 내용이다. 보기 항 (1)이 문화 자본에 대한 설명으로 본문 'the formal educational credentials that an individual possesses and the more intangible complex of values and knowledge of cultural forms in his or her demeanor.'에서 알 수 있다.

문제 2

답 (1)

해설 'that is'는 앞의 내용을 재진술하는 것이므로 뒤의 내용과 일치하는 단어를 찾아 넣는다.

문제 3

답 (4)

해설 'for example'로 보아 앞쪽에 일반 진술이 드러나 있어야 한다. 제시문의 내용을 먼저 파악하고, 이후 이것이 무엇에 관한 구체적인 예인지를 생각해 본다. 본문 마지막을 확인한다.

해석 사회 자본을 둘러싼 많은 부분의 논란은 다른 종류의 문제에 대한 이것의 적용과, 또 다양한 분석 단위를 포함하는 이론 안에서 이것을 사용하는 것과 관련이 있다. 이 개념을 처음 이론적으로 발달시킨 프랑스의 사회학자 부르디외와 미국의 사회학자 콜먼은 분석의 단위로서 개인 또는 작은 단체에 주안점을 두었다. 어느 정도의 상당한 편차가 있지만 두 학자 모두 다른 이와의 유대로 인해 개인 또는 가족에게 쌓이는 득에 초점을 두었다. 부르디외가 이 개념을 다루는 것은 특히나 유용한데, 사람들은 의도적으로 나중에 이들이 얻게 될 이익을 위해 관계를 형성한다고 했다. 기지 넘치는 몇몇 페이지를 보면, 그 프랑스의 사회학자는 경제 자본, 사회 자본 그리고 문화 자본의 관계를 다루었는데, 마

[Challenge 8]

문제 1

답 (4)

해설 (a)는 북한이 최근 남한의 한 섬인 연평도에 포격을 했다는 글의 배경을 설명하고 있다. 이러한 배경 속에서 일본이 느끼는 위협과 그에 따른 입장이 이후 본문 끝까지 전개되고 있다.

문제 2

답 (4)

해설 최근 발생한 북한의 연평도 공격에 대한 일본의 입장이 드러난 글이다. 불안한 동북아시아의 정세에 따른 국방비 예산을 확보해야 한다는 주장의 내용이 드러나 있다. 이러한 일본의 입장을 가장 잘 전달하는 내용을 제목으로 선정해야 한다.

문제 3

답 (2)

해설 보기 항 (2)에 북한이 일본인을 유괴한 것은 북한의 스파이로 만들기 위해서였다고 본문에 언급되어 있다.

해석 지난 달 북한은 연평도를 공격한 후, 남한의 한 군사기지를 타격해 4명의 사상자를 발생시키면서 동아시아의 긴장감을 극도로 고조시켰다. 남한은 그 당시 군사훈련을 실행하고 있었다고 말했지만, 시험 사격은 북한을 조준한 것이 아니라고 주장했다. "우리 일본은 북한의 연평도 포 공격에 대해 아주 강한 위기감을 가지고 있다"고 국방부 부장관인 하지메 히로타는 말했다. "이것은 우리 일본이 참을 수 없는 행위이다. 일본을 포함한 동북아의 다른 나라들은 이 행위를 아주 큰 위협으로 보고 있다." 히로타는 이 공격으로 일본이 남한 및 미국과 더 강력한 유대를 형성하는 것을 보게 될 것이며, 중요한 것은 더 이상의 공격 확대를 피하는 것이라고 말했다. "우리는 북한이 앞으로의 상황에 어떻게 대처할지 알 수가 없다"고 그는 말했다. 일본은 평양의 핵과 미사일 프로그램에 대해 강경한 입장을 오래 동안 취해오고 있으며, 1970년대와 80년대 일본 국민을 유괴하여 북한의 스파이로 훈련시키려 했던 것은 여전히 국민들 사이에서 격한 감정을 일으키는 요소이다. 일본은 남한 및 미국과 밀접한 협력을 약속했으며, 유엔 안보리에서 이 사안을 어떻게 다룰지에 대해 이들과 논의할 것이라고 말했다. 일본은 또한 아시아의 점차 불안해지는 정세에 맞추어 국방 예산을 증가해야 한다고 히로타는 주장했다. 북한이 연평도를 공격한 1주일 후, 북한은 자신의 핵 프로그램에 진전을 이루었다고 선언했다. 일본이 맺은 중국과 러시아의 유대도 오래 지속된 영토 분쟁에 따른 분노로 인해 아직 불안한 상태이다. "나의 개인적 견해로는 일본이 국방 예산을 늘려야 한다는 점은 인정하지만 동시에 일본이 선진국 중에서 현재 재정조건이 가장 열악하다"라고 런던을 기반으로 하는 연구소인 IISS의 Manama Dialogue 회의에서 그는 말했다. "일본을 둘러싼 아시아의 환경은 불안이 고조된 상태이며, 고로 한 국가로서 우리는 필요한 예산을 확보할 의지를 가져야만 한다."

어휘

tension *n.* (정치·사회적인) 긴장 관계
shell *v.* 포격하다(bombard), 폭격하다
conduct *v.* 실시하다 **artillery** *n.* 포, 대포
parliamentary *a.* 의회의 **threat** *n.* 으름, 위협, 협박
forge *v.* 구축하다
escalation *n.* (수·양·금액의) 점증, (규모·범위·강도의) 단계 적 확대; (전쟁 규모의) 에스컬레이션
stance *n.* 입장, 태도 **kidnapping** *n.* 유괴, 납치
pledge *v.* 서약[약속]하다 **fiscal** *a.* 국고의; 재정(상)의, 회계의

[Challenge 9]

문제 1

답 (3)
해설 보기 항 (3)은 본문의 다음 부분과 일치하지 않는다.

> The idea is probably that, assuming the necessary capability, a man's reluctance to govern affords a good guarantee that he will govern well and efficiently

즉, 통치할 능력이 있지만 그가 의도적으로 통치할 욕심을 부리지 않는다는 의미로 해석할 수 있다. 오히려 이럴 때 국가를 효율적으로 통치할 수 있다는 내용이다.

해설 플라톤은 그의 저서인 "공화국" 어디선가 통치할 욕망을 지니고 있지 않은 자가 국가를 경영하면 일이 잘 풀린다고 말한다. 아마도 이 생각은 필요한 능력을 갖췄음에도 통치하려는 한 남자의 내키지 않는 마음이 오히려 그가 더 잘 효율적으로 통치할 것이라는 보장을 해준다는 의미일 것이다. 반면, 통치하려는 욕망을 가진 자는 쉽게 자신의 힘을 악용하여 폭군이 되거나, 통치하려는 욕망에 의해 그가 통치해야 할 국민에게 의지해야 하는 의외의 상황에 빠지게 되어 그의 정부는 실질적으로 환상이 되어 버린다는 뜻일 것이다.

어휘

state *n.* 국가, 정부 **assuming** *conj.* 가령 ~라면
capability *n.* 할 수 있음, 가능성
reluctance *n.* 마음이 내키지 않음
guarantee *n.* 보장(하는 것) **desirous** *a.* 열망하는
tyrant *n.* 폭군, 압제자
unforeseen *a.* 생각하지 않은, 뜻하지 않은, 우연의
situation *n.* 정세, 형세 **rule** *v.* 통치하다
illusion *n.* 환영, 환각

[Challenge 10]

문제 1

답 (4)
해설 (1)의 경우 본문에서 최근 CO2의 증가는 개발도상국(특히, 중국과 인도)의 후발 산업개발로 인한 것이라 언급했으므로, 한동안 지속될 것을 오히려 예상할 수 있으며(본문 마지막 참조), 보기 항 같은 내용은 언급이 없다. (2)의 경우 'emerging economies had a strong economic performance despite the financial crisis, and recorded substantial increases in CO2 emissions'에서 옳지 않다는 것을 알 수 있다. (3)에서 'carbon intensity'는 The poor improvements in carbon intensity에서 알 수 있듯이 향상되지 않았다.

문제 2

답 (3)

해설 접속사가 들어갈 빈칸이다. 빈칸이 들어간 문장과 앞 문장과의 관계를 밝힌다. 앞에 언급된 사항의 구체적 예를 제시하는 문장이다. 고로 보기 항 (3)이 가장 적절하다.

해석 전 세계 이산화탄소 – 지구 온난화의 주범 – 배출량이 좀처럼 줄어들 기미가 보이지 않는 데다 2010년에는 최고치에 도달할 것으로 영국의 Exeter 대학이 이끈 연구에서 드러났다. 이 연구는 또한 영국의 East Anglia 대학과 다른 글로벌 기관과 공동 연구한 것으로, GCP가 제공하는 연간 탄소 예산 업데이트의 일환이다. Nature Geoscience지의 12월 21일에 발표된 한 논문에서 저자들은 작년 세계를 강타한 대형 금융 위기에도 불구하고, 2009년 화석 연료를 태운 것에서 발생한 세계 이산화탄소 배출량은 2008년 수치보다 1.3%밖에 적지 않다는 점을 발견했다. 이것은 일 년 전 예상한 하락치의 반절도 되지 않는 수치이다. 전 세계 금융 위기는 서구 경제에 심각한 여파를 미쳐, 이산화탄소 배출의 상당한 감소를 이끌었다. 예를 들어, 영국의 이산화탄소 배출량은 2008년보다 2009년에 8.6% 더 낮았다. 미국, 일본, 프랑스, 독일 그리고 다른 대부분의 산업국에도 비슷한 수치가 적용된다. 그러나 개발도상국의 경제의 경우 금융 위기에도 불구하고 두드러진 경제 실적을 올려, 엄청난 양의 이산화탄소 배출량을 기록했다 (예를 들어, 중국의 경우 8%, 인도의 경우 6.2%). 연구를 이끄는 저자인 Pierre Friedlingstein 교수는 "2009년 이산화탄소 감소는 1년 전 예상 수치에 반도 되질 못한다. 이것은 세계 GDP의 감소가 기대한 것보다 적어서이며, GDP 단위당 방출되는 이산화탄소 양인 세계 GDP의 탄소 집약도가 2009년보다 단지 0.7만큼 향상되었을 뿐인데 이는 매년 1.7%라는 장기적인 평균보다 아래를 훨씬 밑도는 수치이다. 탄소 집약도가 이처럼 저조하게 상향된 점은 상대적으로 높은 탄소 집약도와 탄소 의존도가 증가하는 개발도상국에 의해서 생산된 화석 연료에 의해 발생한 이산화탄소의 증가량으로 인한 것이다. 이 연구는 만약 경제 성장이 예상대로 진행된다면, 세계 화석 연료 배출량은 2010년에 3%보다 더 증가하여, 2000년에서 2008년까지 관측된 높은 탄소 배출 증가 비율에 도달하게 될 것으로 내다보고 있다.

어휘

abate *v.* 줄다; (기세·격렬함이) 약해지다, 누그러지다
emission *n.* ① (빛·열·향기 따위의) 방사, 발산 ② 배기방출
fossil *n.* 화석   drop *n.* (가격 따위의) 하락
emerging economies 신흥경제국, 개발도상국
performance *n.* 성적, 성과
substantial *a.* (양·정도 따위가) 상당한, 꽤 많은
intensity *n.* (물리학) 강도; 농도
reliance *n.* 의존, 의지

Day 10

[Challenge 1]

문제 1

답 (1)

해설 'Observatory'는 스트리퍼가 공연을 하는 이색적인 클럽을 말한다.

문제 2

답 (2)

해설 'the lion's share'라는 것은 '아주 많은 몫'을 말한다. 즉, 정부가 수입의 많은 몫을 챙겨간다는 의미이다.

문제 3

답 (4)

해설 'make-believe'는 '가짜, 가공의'라는 뜻이다.

해석 'Observatory'는 가장 정평 있는 레크리에이션 장소와 같았다. 크고 소란스러우며, 정부가 일반적으로 엄청난 이득을 취해가는 자유로운 가격에 정찰제가 아닌 음식과 음료 그리고 오락물을 판매하는 곳이었다. 이곳의 테마(angle)는 별자리로 꾸며져 있었다. 천장은 천천히 회전하는 별 무리로 푸른색의 희미한 빛이 감돌고, 스트리퍼는 모조품 우주복을 입고 공연을 시작했다. 우주 정복의 여러 단계를 그린 꽤 멋진 벽화가 있었다. Lancaster는 그중 하나에 흐뭇해했다.

어휘

- **observatory** *n.* 천문대; 전망대
- **approved** *a.* 정평 있는, 공인된
- **recreation** *n.* 휴양, 오락; 기분전환
- **raucous** *a.* 목이 쉰; 귀에 거슬리는; 무질서하고 혼란한
- **uncontrollable** *a.* 지배할 수 없는; 억제할 수 없는
- **share** *n.* 몫; 배당된 몫; 할당
- **astronomy** *n.* 천문학
- **haze** *n.* 아지랑이; 안개; 탁함
- **glitter** *n.* 반짝임; 빛남
- **wheel** *v.* 선회하다
- **constellation** *n.* 별자리
- **spacesuit** *n.* 우주복
- **mural** *n.* 벽; 벽화
- **depict** *v.* 그리다; 묘사하다

[Challenge 2]

문제 1

답 (2)

해설 스타벅스 커피가 전 세계 곳곳에 퍼져 있다는 내용이 이어지는 것으로 보아 스타벅스 사장은 일시적 유행이 아니라 트렌드를 볼 줄 아는 사람이었음을 추론할 수 있다.

문제 2

답 (3)

해설 'The first company that can correctly identify a new trend has a competitive edge — an advantage — over other companies.'에서 보기 (3)을 추론할 수 있다. 보기 (1)의 경우 본문 마지막과 연관된 내용인데, 환경 문제에 대한 관심이 트렌드인 것은 옳으나, 본문에서 언급하고 있는 수영복은 일시적 유행에 해당하며, 이에 돈을 투자한 사람을 부정적으로 기술하는 내용에서 보기 (4)는 틀린 진술임을 알 수 있다. 보기 (2)에서 스타벅스 사장은 트렌드를 볼 줄 아는 인물로 묘사되고 있다.

해석 때로 일시적 유행과 트렌드의 차이를 알아채는(구별하는) 것은 쉽지 않다. 일시적 유행은 아주 짧은 시간 지속되며 그다지 중요하지 않은 반면, 트렌드는 훨씬 더 오래 지속된다. 최근 트렌드의 한 예로 건강에 대한 관심을 들 수 있는데, 일시적인 많은 유행이 이러한 트렌드에서 나온다. 에어로빅 운동, 콜레스테롤 관리와 같은 것들이 그것이다. 트렌드 스파팅(경향 포착)이란 초기 단계에서 트렌드를 판별해내는 능력이라고 할 수 있는데, 사업에서는 극히 중요한 능력이다. 새로운 트렌드를 정확하게 판별해내는 첫 번째 기업은 다른 기업들에 비해 경쟁력, 즉 이점을 갖게 된다. 스타벅스 커피 체인점을 차린 사람은 품질과 다양성이 갖춰진 커피에 대한 사람들의 관심, 바로 그 트렌드를 알아차릴 수 있었다. 오늘날, 사람들은 쇼핑센터나 공항, 슈퍼마켓 등 어디서나 스타벅스 제품을 구매한다. 그러나 대중문화가 항상 새롭게 발달하는 상황에서 일시적 유행과 트렌드를 구별하는 것은 어렵다. 녹색평화운동 수영복에 돈을 투자한 사람들은 아마도 자신의 결정을 후회하고 있을지도 모른다. 분명, 이들은 일시적 유행을 트렌드로 착각한 것이다.

어휘

- **fad** *n.* 일시적 유행
- **competitive edge** 경쟁상의 우위성
- **mistake A for B** A를 B로 착각하다

Day 10

[Challenge 3]

문제 1

답 (1)

해설 첫 번째 문단은 주인공이 어린 시절 수학에 관심이 있고, 성장해서 바다로 항해를 떠나면서 선원들에게 항해를 가르쳤다는 이야기를 다루고, 두 번째 문단에서 Prince 선장과 선원 사이의 구체적 사례를 언급하는 내용이다. 그러므로 (b)에서 문단을 나누는 것이 가장 적절하다.

문제 2

답 (4)

해설 보기 항 (2)의 경우 본문에서 선원들에게 수학을 가르치는 그의 능력으로 추론해 낼 수 있다. 보기 항 (4)의 경우 본문에서 추론할 수 없다.

문제 3

답 (2)

해설 밑줄 친 부분의 직역은 '긴 실타래를 풀다'로, 우리말로 '장광설을 늘어놓다'라는 의미이다. 일반적으로 선원들이 서로 만나 이야기를 나눌 때 일상적인 대화를 나눌 터인데, 본문에서 주인공으로 인해 수학에 관한 문제를 푸는 모습이 이후 전개되고 있다.

해석 Nathaniel Bowditch는 Laplace의 "Me'canique Ce'leste"의 번역자로, 어린 시절부터 수학 공부에 두각을 나타냈다. 1788년 그가 고작 15살이 되는 해에 그는 직접 1790년도 달력을 만들었는데, 여기에는 달력에 보통 있는 모든 목록, 일식의 계산 그리고 다른 현상들, 심지어 날씨에 보통 있는 일반적인 예측까지도 포함되어 있었다. Bowditch는 바다에서 자랐으며(바다와 인연을 맺고 자랐으며), 초기 항해 때 자신의 주위에 있는 평범한 선원들에게 항해술을 가르쳤다. 그와 자주 항해를 한 Prince 선장은 이야기하길 어느 날 배의 화물 관리인이 그에게 말했다고 한다. "선장님, 와보세요. 긴 배의 갑판 아래 바람을 피해 선원들이 하는 이야기를 들어봐요." 그래서 이들은 앞으로 나아가 보았는데, 선장은 선원들이 자신들의 장광설을 늘어놓는 대신 진지하게 책, 석판, 연필을 가지고 탄젠트, 시컨트, 고도, 높이 그리고 굴절에 관한 고상한 내용을 이야기하는 것을 보고 놀랐다. 특히 이들 중 두 명이 아주 열정적으로 논쟁을 벌이고 있었는데, 둘 중 한 명이 다른 이에게 "야 Jack! 너 답으로 뭘 냈어?" 하고 소리쳤고, "나는 사인이야." 라고 답했다. 그러자 다른 선원이 "아니야, 너 틀렸어. 그거 코사인이야."라고 답했다.

어휘

mathematical *a.* 수리적인
almanack *n.* 책력
calculation *n.* 계산; 숙고
eclipse *n.* (해·달의) 식, 소멸
phenomena *n.* 현상, 사상, 사건(phenomenon의 복수)
customary *a.* 습관적인, 재래의
prediction *n.* 예언하기, 예보
breed *v.* 기르다, 길러내다
voyage *n.* 항해, 항행
navigation *n.* 운항, 항해
relate *v.* 이야기하다, 말하다
supercargo *n.* 화물 관리인   vessel *n.* 배
lee *n.* 바람을 받지 않는 쪽
spin *v.* (이야기를) 만들어내다
yarn *n.* 실, 털실   earnestly *ad.* 열심히, 진심으로
engage *v.* ~에 관여시키다   slate *n.* 석판
tangt *n.* 탄젠트   secant *n.* 시컨트
altitude *n.* 높이, 고도
dip *n.* 하강(도), 경사도   refraction *n.* 굴절(작용)
zealously *ad.* 열광적으로, 열심히
sine *n.* 사인   cosine *n.* 코사인

[Challenge 4]

문제 1

답 (1)

해설 본문은 인종차별 제도가 철폐된 이후(the post-apartheid era) 아동의 권리를 보장하는 새로운 법이 헌법에 반영되었다는 내용을 골자로 하고 있다. 보장의 구체적인 항목으로 'Section 28 of South Africa's Bill of Rights'와 'the Basic Conditions of Employment Act, the Domestic Violence Act, the Child Justice Act and the Sexual Offences Act'를 언급한 후, 2005년 아동 법령안과 수정안을 다시 추가적으로 제시한 후 부연 설명이 이어지고 있다.

해석 1995년 7월 16일 아동 권리에 관한 협약을 비준한 후, 새로운 남아프리카의 입안자(헌법)는 자국의 헌법에 이러한 실천적 가르침을 포함시켰다. 남아프리카의 권리 장전의 28조항은 법 제도 안에서 아이는 주체성, 기본적 국가 서비스, 교육 그리고 보호를 받을 권리가 있다는 점을 보장한다. 아파르트헤이트 시대 이후에 도입된 아동의 권리를 보호하는 다른 주된 법에는 기본적 고용 조건에 관한 법령, 가정 내 폭력에 관련된 법령, 아동 공정법과 성범죄 관련 법령이 포함된다. 아동 권리 체제에 가장 포괄적인 추가는 바로 2005년의 아동 법령 수정안으로 권리 장전의 조항을 강화하고 부모와 보호자의 책임감을 구체화한 것이다. 주목할 만한 조항을 살펴보면 가장인 16세 이상의 청소년이 국가 보조금을 받을 수 있는 권리와 HIV 테스트와 치료를 받을 수 있는 권리가 포함된 젊은 사람들의 건강 보험에 대한 좀 더 폭넓은 권리가 포함된다.

어휘

- **ratify** v. 비준하다; 실증하다
- **convention** n. 협약; 합의
- **architect** n. 설계자[건설자]
- **embed** v. 끼워 넣다
- **precept** n. 교훈, 가르침; 격언
- **constitution** n. 헌법
- **bill** n. 법안; 의안
- **identity** n. 정체성
- **legislation** n. 입법; 법률 제정
- **introduce** v. 안으로 들이다; 도입하다
- **apartheid** n. 인종 차별 정책
- **era** n. 기원; 연대; 시기
- **employment** n. 사용; 고용
- **act** n. 법령, 조례
- **domestic** a. 가정의; 국내의
- **comprehensive** a. 포괄적인; 범위가 넓은
- **framework** n. 체제, 체계
- **amendment** n. 변경; 개선; 수정안
- **reinforce** v. 강화하다, 보강하다
- **provision** n. 예비, 규정, 조항
- **detail** v. 상세히 열거하다[알리다]
- **guardian** n. 보호자; 관리인
- **access** n. 접근
- **grant** n. (정부나 단체에서 주는) 보조금
- **consent** n. 동의, 허가

[Challenge 5]

문제 1

답 (2)

해설 본문은 중국 정부에 반대하는 Liu Xiaobo에게 노벨상을 주기로 한 결정에 분노한 중국 정부가 노벨상 웹사이트를 차단했다는 내용을 중심으로 전개되고 있다.

문제 2

답 (3)

해설 현재 노벨상 웹사이트는 차단된 상태다. 고로 중국 과학자들이 이 사이트에 방문하기 원한다면, 이 방화벽을 뚫어야 하는데, 본문에서 이것을 중국의 만리장성에 비유하여 설명하고 있다. 고로 이러한 방화벽(Wall)을 뚫는 방법은 이것을 타고 넘어가는 것으로 비유할 수 있다.

해석 중국의 과학자들이 노벨상 공식 웹사이트를 방문하기를 원한다면 '방화 대장성'을 타는 법을 배워야 할지도 모르겠다. 중국 내 이 사이트의 URL을 브라우저의 주소창에 넣을 경우 "연결이 리셋되었습니다"라는 문장과 함께 공백만이 나올 뿐이다. 이런 차단은 노르웨이 노벨상 위원회가 중국 정부에 반대하는 Liu Xiaobo에게 평화상을 수여하려는 결정에 대한 조치이다. 중국 정부는 현재 감옥에 있는 Liu와 그의 가족이 오늘 아침 일찍 열린 식에서 상을 받지 못하도록 여행을 허용하지 않았다. 이러한 '단순하고 잔인한 차단'은 '목에 음식이 걸릴까 봐 음식을 거부하는 것'과 마찬가지라고 베이징의 Tsinghua 대학 생물학 교수인 Yan Ning이 자신의 ScienceNet.cn 블로그에서 애통해했다. Yan은 지난달 이 사이트가 더 이상 접근이 되지 않는다는 것을 발견하기 전까지 자신의 학생들을 위한 읽기 자료를 위해 강의를 다운로드하기 위해 정기적으로 이 노벨 사이트에 방문했다고 말한다.

어휘

- **yield** v. (결과를) 산출(産出)하다(produce)
- **reset** v. (기기 등의 숫자, 시간 등을) 다시 맞추다
- **dissident** n. 반체제 인사
- **simplistic** a. 극단적으로 단순[평이, 간이]화한
- **crude** a. 막된, 상스러운
- **lockade** n. (출입) 봉쇄(선)
- **kin** a. 같은 종류의, 유사한
- **choking** n. 숨이 막힘
- **lament** v. 슬퍼하다, 비탄하다; 애도하다, 애석해 하다

[Challenge 6]

문제 1

답 (2)

해설 본문에서 Julian Assange는 현재 스웨덴이 아니라 영국에 구류되어 있다고 했다.

문제 2

답 (2)

해설 밑줄 친 뒤에 전개되는 내용을 보면 좀 더 그 의미가 명확해진다. 즉, 인터넷을 통제하려는 억압적 정부를 통해 얻은 교훈은 무엇인가? 'The Internet is an extremely open system with very low barriers to access and use,' said Vint Cerf, Google's vice president. 'The ease of moving digital information around makes it very difficult to suppress once it is accessible.'에서 알 수 있듯이, 인터넷은 통제가 거의 불가능한 사이버 공간임을 알 수 있다.

문제 3

답 (3)

해설 첫 번째 빈칸 앞뒤 문장의 관계는 인과이다. 두 번째 빈칸은 두 대상의 대조되는 상황을 연결하고 있으므로 'By contrast'가 가장 적절하다.

해석 지난 며칠간 비밀폭로 사이트인 위키리크스는 그것의 존재를 위협하는 것처럼 보이는 일련의 공격을 받았다. 주된 웹 주소가 중단되고, PayPal(인터넷 금융결제 시스템) 계좌는 동결되었으며, 인터넷 서버는 중단되었다. 결과는: 위키리크스는 적어도 온라인에 정보를 유출하는 능력을 보았을 때, 현재 이전 어느 때보다 더 강하다. 인터넷 호스트 하나를 사용하지 못하도록 막으면, 위키리크스는 간단히 다른 호스트로 넘어간다. 반면, 위키리크스를 '흉내 내는' 웹사이트 — 위키리크스의 주요한 콘텐츠 페이지들을 효과적으로 모방한 — 는 지난주 몇 십 개에서 일요일 200개가 넘었다. 수요일 오전에는 이러한 사이트의 수가 천 개를 넘었다.

동시에 위키리크스를 지지하는 세력들은 위키리크스와 연루될까 두려워서 이 회사와 관계를 끊은 인터넷 회사에 보복 공격을 하면서 반격을 감행한 듯 보였다. 수요일 해커들은 재빠르게 마스터카드와 비자 사이트에 대한 접근을 차단했는데, 이는 이 두 회사가 위키리크스에 기부하는 것을 멈췄다고 발표했기 때문이었다. 위키리크스의 장기적인 생존은 성범죄 혐의와 관련되어 스웨덴으로 가능한 본국 송환을 기다리면서 동시에 영국에 구류 중인 위키리크스의 주요 창시자인 줄리언 어산지를 포함한 수없이 많은 알려지지 않은 사람들에게 달려 있다. 그러나 그 웹사이트가 반복되는 좌절에도 되살아나는 것은 인터넷을 통제하려는 시도를 한 더 억압적인 정부에 의해 이미 얻은 교훈을 더욱 강조하고 있다. "인터넷은 접속하고 사용하는 데 거의 장벽이 없는 극도로 개방된 시스템이다."라고 Vint Cerf, 구글의 부사장이 말했다. "디지털 정보 이동의 용이성 때문에 일단 접속이 가능하면 억압한다는 것은 거의 불가능하다." 게다가 민감한 미국의 외교 전보의 유출에 대한 전 세계의 분노에도 불구하고, 어산지가 운영하는 이 웹사이트는 수요일 교만하게도 그대로 남아 있었다. 지난주 내내 반복되는 익명의 사이버 공격이나, 자금과 웹 소스에 대한 접근을 끊으려는 수차례 시도에도 불구하고, 해를 입은 증거가 거의 없는 상황에서 국무부의 정보는 계속해서 공개되고 있었다. 대조적으로 위키리크스를 차단한 회사는 오히려 한동안 몇 시간 동안 접속을 못 하도록 한 사이버 공격으로 공공연히 몸살을 앓았다. '현직 해커들'의 한 단체는 마스터카드와 비자를 일명 '보복 작전'의 일환으로 지목한 반면, 익명의 공격자들이 최근 Paypal을 공격했는데, 이 회사는 서비스 조건을 어겼다고 인용하면서 위키리크스와의 관계를 끊었다.

어휘

blow *n.* 강타(hit), 구타; 급습
deactivate *v.* 활동력을 잃게 하다
freeze *v.* (외국 자산 따위를) 동결하다, (은행 예금 따위를) 봉쇄하 다; (물가·임금 따위를) 동결하다, 고정시키다
boot *n.* (the ~)《속어》해고   clone *n.* 《컴퓨터》복제품
surpass *v.* ~을 능가하다, 뛰어나다; ~을 넘다[초월하다]
offensive *n.* 공격 태세   stage *v.* ~을 꾀하다, 조직하다
retaliatory *a.* 보복적인   donation *n.* 증여, 기증, 기부
extradition *n.* (국제 간의) 도망범 인도, 망명자 소환
allegation *n.* 증거 없는 주장, 혐의
underscore *v.* 의미상 강조하다
suppress *v.* 억압하다   uproar *n.* 소란, 소동; 소음
defiantly *ad.* 반항적으로, 도전적으로
steady *a.* ① 고정된, 확고한, 흔들리지 않는 ② 안정된; 견고한
leak *v.* 새게 하다; (비밀 등을) 누설하다, 흘리다
anonymous *a.* 익명의; 변명[가명]의
render *v.* ~로 만들다, ~이 되게 하다
assailant *n.* 공격자; 가해자; 적

[Challenge 7]

문제 1

답 (4)

해설 유교주의는 윗사람과 아랫사람을 근본적으로 구별하여 각자의 자리에서 충성을 다할 것을 요구하고 있다. 즉, 이러한 사상은 사람들 사이에 근본적인 평등보다는 계급 의식을 강화하여 계급 차별을 형성하는 데 용이하게 쓰일 수 있다.

해석 유교는 중국에서 가장 영향력 있는 종교였다. 이것은 공자에 의해 창설되었다. 유교는 기원전 202년에 한 왕조의 설립부터 1911년 황제 시대가 끝날 때까지 계속 국교였다. 유교의 가르침은 2,000년 넘게 국가 공직 시험의 과목이었다. 유교는 사람들이 사회의 조화를 유지하기 위해 자신의 위치를 받아들여야 한다고 주장했다. 이것은 근본적으로 윗사람과 아랫사람 간의 5가지 중요한 관계를 명시하고 있다. 아랫사람은 윗사람에게 온전한 충성과 복종을 맹세해야 하며, 윗사람은 아랫사람에게 자비와 동정을 베풀어야 한다. 효는 공자가 강조한 가장 중요한 자질 중 하나였다.

어휘

Confucianism *n.* 유교   state religion 국가 종교
from the establishment of ~의 설립 이래
Han Dynasty 한 왕조   imperial epoch 황제 시대
confucian teachings 유교의 가르침(또는 공자의 가르침)
civil service examinations 공직 시험
maintain *v.* 주장하다   embrace *v.* 받아들이다
station in life 삶의 (각자의) 위치
intrinsical *a.* 내재적인   superior *a.* 우월한 (- inferior)
benevolent *a.* 호혜적인   compassionate *a.* 측은히 여기는
filial piety *n.* 효   quality *n.* (사람의) 자질

[Challenge 8]

문제 1

답 (2)

해설 빈칸을 기준으로 앞에서는 숙련공에 대해서 자신의 의견을 전달할 수단을 제공한다는 개념을 말하고 있고, 이후 단지 이러한 숙련공만이 아닌 비숙련공에게도 자신의 의견을 전달할 수단을 제공하려는 시도인 'the Reform Act of 1867'이 다루어지고 있다. 고로 빈칸에 들어갈 내용은 순접 강조의 'but'이 들어가야 한다.

문제 2

답 (2)

해설 바로 뒤에 이어지는 내용을 통해서 추론할 수 있다. 새로운 개정으로 인해 숙련공이 아닌 비숙련공에게도 투표권을 줌으로써 더 많은 이에게 정치적 권리를 행사할 수 있는 기회를 제공

되지만, 사실 점원과 같은 일반인들은 임금이 적기에 일을 많이 해야 하고 이로 인해 교육을 받을 시간이 없다고 말하고 있다. 고로 보기 항 (2)가 가장 적절한 답안이 된다.

문제 3

답 (1)

해설 본문에서 거친 일을 한다는 이야기는 있지만 이것으로 인해 몸이 허약해져서 지적 활동에 방해가 되었다는 내용은 없다.

해석 현재 직면한 문제는 이런 독특한 기존의 제도가 얼마나 존속할 수 있느냐와 이것이 얼마나 크게 수정될 것인가이다. 이 기존의 제도가 완전히 바뀌거나 더 나은 상황을 위해 바뀔 수 있다는 생각을 즉시 제쳐두어야 함을 유감스럽게 생각한다. 새로운 유권자 계층이 기존의 유권자보다 복잡한 문제에 관해 건실한 의견을 더 잘 형성할 수 있다고 기대하지 않는다. 국가적인 사안에 대하여 탁월한 견해를 제시할 수 있는 의사가 반영되지 않는 숙련공 계층이 있었고, 그들의 의사를 표현할 수단이 있어야 한다는 견해가 실제로 있었다. 우리는 이들에게 이러한 수단을 제공하기 위한 정교한 계획을 짜곤 했다. 그러나 1867년 개혁안은 단순히 숙련공에만 머물지 않았다. 이 개혁안 덕분에 비숙련공에게도 선거권이 주어졌다. 물론 어느 누구도 특별한 기술도 없고, 단지 집이 있다는 이유로 자격이 있다는 일반 노동자가 많은 지적 문제를 판단할 수 있다고 주장하진 않는다. 한 사무실의 심부름꾼이 점원보다 더 지적이지 않으며, 교육을 더 잘 받기는커녕 (교육 수준이) 더 떨어진다. 그러나 이 심부름꾼은 아마도 새롭게 선거권이 부여된 계층의 가장 훌륭한 예일 것이다. 평범한 사람은 고된 노동을 통해 매우 적은 임금을 벌 수 있을 뿐이다. 이들은 자신을 위한 시간을 할애할 수 없는데, 이는 이들이 종일 노동을 하기 때문이다. 이들의 어린 시절 교육은 너무 부족했기 때문에 대부분의 경우 이들이 시간이 있다 하더라도 이것을 좋은 의도로 사용할 수 있을지는 의심스럽다.

어휘

- grave *a.* 중대한, 중요한
- peculiar *a.* 특유한, 독특한
- voter *n.* 투표자, 유권자
- unrepresented *a.* 대표 예시되지 않는
- artisan *n.* 장인
- superior *a.* 우수한, 우월한
- frame *v.* (계획·체제·법규)의 틀을 잡다, (특정한 방식으로) 표현 하다
- elaborate *a.* 정교한, 정성을 들인
- enfranchise *v.* 선거권을 주다
- contend *v.* 주장하다; 겨루다
- rate *v.* 평가하다; 등급을 매기다
- messenger *n.* 전달자
- specimen *n.* 견본, 샘플
- scanty *a.* 얼마 안 되는, 빈약한
- coarse *a.* 거친, 굵은
- whole day 종일
- dubious *a.* 의심하는, 미심쩍은

[Challenge 9]

문제 1

답 (1)

해설 노인에게 한 Harry의 행위가 어떤 측면을 강조하는 것인지 생각해 본다.

문제 2

답 (3)

해설 노인의 아들은 군 복무 중 병으로 고국으로 돌아와 현재는 병원에서 치료를 받고 있다. 아래 본문과 비교해 본다.

> His son was a soldier, and had been in the West Indies for some years; but he caught the yellow fever, and was sent home sick.

해석 Rachel Jenkins라는 이름의 가난한 여인이 있었는데, 그녀는 다른 집과 어느 정도 거리가 있는 매우 작은 오두막에 살았다. 그녀는 과부이며 아주 가난했지만 깨끗하고 주의 깊은 여인이었다. 그래서 그녀의 오두막은 항상 보기에 깔끔하고 안락한 느낌을 주었다. 그녀는 대부분의 시간을 실을 짜는 데 보내곤 했다. 그녀에게는 한 아들이 있었는데, 이름은 Harry였다. 그는 12살로 주위에 사는 사람들에게 팔던 테이프와 실, 핀과 바늘 그리고 그런 류의 여러 물건으로 가득 찬 바구니를 들고 다니곤 했다. 그는 아침에 나가 저녁에 들어오곤 했다. 그리고 어머니는 아이가 집에 돌아올 때면 항상 기뻐했을 것이다. 어느 저녁, 그가 집에 오는 길에 어머니의 집에서 한 반 마일 떨어진 지점에서 그는 길가에 앉아 있는 한 노인을 보았는데, 그는 아주 피곤해 마치 더 이상 걸을 수 없는 것처럼 보였다. 그의 머리는 백발이 성성했으며, 얼굴과 손은 야위고 주름이 많았다. Harry는 그에게 친절한 말투로 "피곤해 보이세요, 어르신. 걸어갈 길이 먼가요?"라고 물었다. 그 노인은 옆 동네까지 걸어가야 하는데 아직 12마일이나 더 남았다고 말했다. 그러나 너무 피곤해서 그가 그날 밤에 도착할 수 없을 거라고 했다. 이것을 듣고, Harry는 "저희 집에 가시면 좋겠는데, 어머니가 집에서 주무셔도 좋아하실 거예요."라고 말했다. 그 노인은 그에게 감사하곤 함께 길을 가겠다고 했다. 그리고 그는 Harry의 어깨에 자신의 팔을 올리고 집으로 향해 천천히 걸어갔다. Harry의 어머니는 문밖에서 이들을 마중했다. Harry가 어떻게 노인을 만났는지 자초지종을 말하자 그녀는 노인을 만나서 반갑다며 차를 좀 마시게 안으로 들어오라고 말했다. 차를 마시고 난 후 노인은 Sarah Jenkins에게 자신의 아들을 보러 가는 중이라고 말했다. 아들은 그가 가려는 마을의 병원에 몸져누워 있다고 말했다. 그의 아들은 군인으로 수년 동안 서인도 제도에 있었는데, 황열병에 걸려 아픈 채 집으로 보내졌다. 다음 날 노인은 길을 떠나면서 Sarah Jenkins와 Harry를 축복했는데, 이는 이들을 위해 감사와 기도 외에는 보답할 것이 없는 그에게 선행을 베풀어주었기 때문이었다.

Day 10

어 휘

cottage *n.* (시골 등의) 작은 집   distance *n.* 거리
neatness *n.* 단정함, 깔끔함   spinning *n.* 방적, 실잣기
thread *n.* 바느질   pin *n.* 핀
way-side *n.* 길가   wrinkle *v.* 주름이 지다
yellow fever *n.* 황열병   bless *v.* 복을 빌다

어 휘

unconsciously *ad.* 무의식중에
modify *v.* 수정하다   speech *n.* 말
conform *v.* 따르다, 순응하다
linguist *n.* 어학자   accommodation *n.* 적응, 순응
ethnographer *n.* 민속학자   socialization *n.* 사회화
acquire *v.* 손에 넣다   infant *n.* 유아
reinforce *v.* 강화하다   adaptation *n.* 적응
language-minority speaker 소수만 쓰는 언어를 사용하는 사람
nonverbal cues 바디랭귀지
exaggerate *v.* 과장하다

[Challenge 10]

문제 1

답 (3)

해설 본문은 accommodation에 관한 개괄적인 글이다. subtopic이 갈리는 지점은 accommodation에 대한 추가적인 새로운 정보를 전달하는 'also'가 들어 있는 (다)이다. 문화인류학과 언어학에서 자주 나오는 개념이므로 'accommodation'과 함께 'speech act'에 대해서 보충 공부를 반드시 해 두길 권한다.

문제 2

답 (2)

해설 보기 항 (1)에서 'in general'이라고 표현했는데 그런 일반화를 본문에서 이끌어 낼 수 없다(두 번째 문단 참조). 본문의 'especially when emphasizing differences in status by age, gender, and experience'로 보아 보기 항 (2)는 옳은 설명이다. 보기 항 (3)의 경우 nonverbal cues에 대한 언급이 있지만 상황에 따라 정도의 차이가 있지 일상 대화에서 nonverbal cues가 안 쓰이는 것은 아니다. 보기 항 (4)에서 새로운 공동체를 형성하는 데 accommodation이 중요한 개념으로 작용한다고 했는데, 그런 사항은 알 수 없다.

해석 대화를 나눌 때, 사람들은 다른 사람의 말투에 일치하도록 자신의 언어를 무의식적으로 바꾸곤 한다. 이런 종류의 조정을 언어학자는 '적응'이라 부른다. 언어 사회화(언어 사용을 위해 필요한 규칙을 습득하는 것)에 관심이 있는 문화 인류학자들은 이문화 간의 언어 사용 연구에 있어 '적응'이 얼마나 중요한 역할을 하는지 설명한다. 모든 사회의 유아, 어린이 그리고 청소년은 어른과 자신의 또래들이 하는 말을 모방하면서 말한다. 게다가 다양한 문화적 개념을 강화(특히 나이, 성 그리고 경험에 따른 지위의 차이를 강조할 때)하는 데 언어가 사용되는 방법의 차이는 적어도 부분적으로 언어와 화자 말투를 따라하며 습득된다. 적응은 또한 규모가 더 큰 단체의 언어와 다른 언어를 구사하는 새로운 구성원을 위해 언어 공동체 전체가 행하는 적응을 가리키기도 한다. 이런 종류의 적응은 일반적으로 소수 언어 화자가 존재하는 접촉 상황에서 일어난다. 종종 규모가 큰 언어 공동체 구성원은 새로운 구성원과 의사소통을 형성하기 위한 방법으로 더 많은 비언어적 단서(과장된 손, 팔 그리고 얼굴 표정)를 사용한다.

Day 11

[Challenge 1]

문제 1

답 (2)

해설 본문은 겉보기에 혼란스럽게 보이는 마음이 실상 자연의 모든 다른 것과 마찬가지로 법칙을 따름을 다루고 있다. 'laws that govern the association of ideas'에서 알 수 있듯이 '생각의 연상 법칙'에 관한 내용을 다루고 있다. 보기 항 (3)의 내용은 이 글 이후에 전개될 내용으로 적합한 주제이다.

문제 2

답 (4)

해설 'Yet mental processes are as law-abiding as anything else in Nature.'에서 알 수 있듯이 정신 작용인 마음은 일정한 법칙을 따르고 있다고 본문에서 말하고 있다.

해석 만약 세상에서 완전히 혼돈스럽게 보이는 어떤 것이 있다면, 이것은 바로 마음이 하나의 주제에 관해서 생각하다가 다른 주제로 넘어가는 방식일 것이다. 마음이 뉴욕에서 샌프란시스코, 샌프란시스코에서 도쿄 그리고 전 세계를 확 지나가는 데 필요한 시간은 찰나이다. 그러나 정신 활동은 자연의 다른 모든 것과 마찬가지로 법칙을 따르고 있다. 이것이 사실이기에 만약 처음 유아기 감각으로부터 얻은 과거의 경험을 세세히 알고, 현재 생각하는 바를 또한 안다면, 당신의 생각 속 만화경 화면에 어떤 생각이 다음에 나타날지 수학적으로 정확하게 예측할 수 있다. 이것은 생각의 연상을 관장하는 법칙에 의해서 가능하다. 이러한 법칙은 본질적으로 판단과 생각이 구분되고 저장되는 방법과 그것들이 의식적으로 기억되는 순서가 어떠한 다른 판단과 생각이 가장 습관적으로, 최근에, 근접하게 그리고 생생하게 연관되어 있는지에 달려 있다는 것이다.

어휘

utterly *ad.* 아주, 완전히   chaotic *a.* 혼돈된; 무질서한
wander *v.* 헤매다; 빗나가다
flash *v.* 번쩍이다; 빛나다; 번개처럼 스치다
law-abiding *a.* 법을 준수하는   detail *n.* 세부; 상세
infantile *a.* 유아의; 아이다운   sensation *n.* 감각; 마음
mathematical *a.* 수학의; 수리적인
certainty *n.* 확실성; 확실
kaleidoscopic *a.* 만화경 같은; 변화무쌍한
association *n.* 연관; 연상   substance *n.* 물질; 실질; 요지
classify *v.* 분류하다   store *v.* 저축하다; 저장하다
consciousness *n.* 의식   habitually *ad.* 습관적으로
vividly *ad.* 생생하게; 선명하게

[Challenge 2]

문제 1

답 (1)

해설 일반적으로 영어권 글은 첫 번째 문장에서 전체 글의 흐름을 파악할 수 있다. 본문의 첫 번째 문장을 확인해 보자.

> Some may think there is danger of setting too high a standard of action.

우선 첫 번째 문장이 'Some may think...'로 시작하는 것으로 보아 만약 일반 통념 비판의 글이면 이후 글쓴이의 주장이 드러나기 전 'but'과 같은 역접의 접속사가 등장한다. 또한 첫 번째 문장의 내용을 볼 경우, 어떤 사람들은 행위의 기준(목표)을 높이 잡는 것을 위험한 것으로 본다고 말하고 있는데, 이후 글쓴이는 이와 반대의 주장을 할 가능성이 크다. 본문에서 'however' 이후 완벽한 모델 상(높은 이상)을 제시할수록 아이는 더욱 나아진다고 주장하고 있다. 고로 주제는 보기 항 (1)이 된다.

문제 2

답 (1)

해설 아이는 무엇이든 자신 앞에 제시되는 것을 모방할 수 있다고 했다. 고로 글의 주제가 높은 이상 추구라는 점에서 가능한 모든 것을 추구해야 한다는 내용이 빈칸에 와야 한다.

해석 어떤 이는 행위 기준을 너무 높이 잡으면 위험하다고 생각할지 모른다. 아이는 상대적으로 완벽한 사람을 모방하기보단 열등한 대상을 가짐으로 훨씬 더 빨리 글쓰기를 배운다고 선생님들이 주장하는 것을 들은 적이 있는데, 이들은 '너무 완벽한 대상을 부여하게 되면 학생은 쉽게 기가 꺾이기 때문이다. 그러나 만약 그 자신보다 (그 대상이) 조금 앞선다면, 그는 그가 곧 그것과 동일하게 될 것이라는 신념에서 용기를 가지게 된다.'라고 말한다. 그러나 나는 이것이 그렇지 않다는 것을 확신한다. 아이에게 더욱 완벽한 대상을 제시하면 할수록 더 좋다. 왜냐하면 이것은 세상의 이치로 아이가 이것을 모방하는 것이 가능하기 때문이다. 그리고 인간이 해온 것이 무엇이든지 간에 모든 아이들이 닮아가도록 이성적으로 기대되는 원칙상 절대 가능한 것들은 인간이 할 수 있다는 것이다. 그렇기에 인간의 행위에서 일반적으로 무엇이든 가능한 것은 목표로 삼아야 한다. 나는 자

신의 창조물 앞에 완벽한 행위의 기준을 제시하고 이것에 부응하도록 만드는 것이 하나님의 섭리의 일부라는 걸 증명하겠다.

어휘

- standard *n.* 표준; 기준; 규격
- contend *v.* 주장하다   inferior *a.* 떨어지는, 열등한
- imitate *v.* 모방하다; 흉내를 내다
- comparatively *ad.* 비교적, 상대적으로
- pupil *n.* 학생   discourage *v.* 용기를 잃게 하다; 단념시키다
- equal *v.* ~과 동등한 일을 해내다   convinced *a.* 확신하는
- aspire *v.* 열망하다; 포부를 갖다   conduct *n.* 행위; 행동; 지도
- divine *a.* 신의; 신성한   rational *a.* 이성이 있는; 이성적인
- creature *n.* 창조물; 피조물
- come up to (특정 지점·위치까지) 오다[닿다], (요구되는 수준에) 미치다[이르다]

[Challenge 3]

문제 1

답 (3)

해설 언어는 나름의 문법적 체제를 가지고 있기에 일관성 있는 문장을 형성할 수 있다. 보기 항 (1)은 틀리며, 보기 항 (2)에서 syntax와 grammar는 같은 단어이다. 보기 항 (4)에서 문장에 의미를 부여하는 것이 coherence라고 했는데, 논리적 구조를 부여하는 것이 coherence이며 촘스키의 예에서 알 수 있듯이 coherence를 갖추고 있다 하더라도 의미를 전달하지 못하는 문장을 만들어 낼 수 있다.

문제 2

답 (2)

해설 촘스키가 제시한 문장은 실용적인 측면에서 실질적으로 특정한 의미를 전달하지 못한다. 하지만 이 문장은 문법적 요소(각 자리에 맞는 품사가 적절히 쓰이고 있음)를 갖추고 있기에 coherent하다. 아래 문장에 잘 드러나 있다.

> through grammatical organization language has coherence

해설 논리적 또는 일관성 있는 형태로 단어를 일직선으로 정렬(문장)하는 것이 바로 문법이다. 통어법이라고 불리는 문법에 대한 이해는 언어학자에게 아주 중요한데, 이는 문법적 조직을 통해서 언어는 일관성을 갖추게 되기 때문이다. 일관성이란 음성적인 의미를 형성하기 위해 각 품사를 논리적으로 결합한 것을 말한다. 예를 들어 다음의 문장을 생각해 보자. "우리는 연을 가지고 나가 하루 종일 날렸다." 영어 화자의 경우 이러한 단어를 인식할 수 있는 형태로 정렬(명사구의 '연'과 동사구의 '우리는 가지고 나갔다'와 '날렸다')을 합함으로 청자는 이 문장의 전반적 의미를 알 수 있게 된다. 만약 말의 순서가 무작위로 된다면, 이 문장은 일관성을 잃게 된다. "(Day and all we flew them out took kites the" — 이 문장을 말로 표현했을 때 의미 전달을 이루지 못한다). 그러므로 문법은 논리적 구조로서 문장을 함께 뭉쳐주는 접착제와 같다. 언어학자인 노암 촘스키는 그의 유명한 문장을 통해 통일성의 개념을 잘 설명했다. "무색의 녹색 개념은 극도로 화가 나서 잔다." 비록 이 문장은 모순점을 포함하고 있어 실질적인 의미를 거의 전달하지 못하지만, 이 문장은 여전히 일관성을 갖추고 있는데, 이는 다양한 품사가 논리적 순서대로 잘 정렬이 되어 있기 때문이다.

어휘

- linear *a.* 직선의; 1차의; 직선 모양의
- arrangement *n.* 정렬, 배치   coherent *a.* 시종 일관된
- grammar *n.* 문법 (= syntax)   linguist *n.* 언어학자
- organization *n.* 조직, 구성   bind *v.* 묶다
- randomize *v.* 무작위로 추출하다
- illustrate *v.* 설명하다, 예증하다
- furious *a.* 성난, 사납게 몰아치는, 맹렬한
- sequential *a.* 순차적인, 잇따라 일어나는

[Challenge 4]

문제 1

답 (1)

해설 첫 번째 문장에서 알 수 있듯이 본문은 '사상과 믿음의 불일치'에 관한 내용이다.

문제 2

답 (3)

해설 아래 본문의 내용에서 답의 근거를 찾을 수 있다.

> this wide possibility of contradiction is particularly to be recognized <u>when the differing ideas or beliefs have arisen not within the same individual mind but in different minds,</u> and are therefore colored by personal or partisan interest and warped by idiosyncrasy of mental constitution.

문제 3

답 (2)

해설 첫 번째 문장에서 제시하고 있는 'contradictions among ideas and beliefs'에 대한 구체적인 설명이 이어지고 있다.

해설 내가 가정하기를 사상과 믿음 사이의 모순들은 우리가 소위 논리적 비양립성이라 부르는 특정한 것 외에도 정도와 형태에 있어서 다양하다고 여겨진다. 예를 들어, 하나의 인식은 다른 인식과 외형적으로 불일치하거나 또는 음조

적으로 불협할 수 있다. 객관적인 증거로 뒷받침되지 않는 단순한 믿음은 다른 단순한 믿음과 감정적으로 모순될 수 있는데, 이는 하나의 판단이 논리적으로 다른 판단과 대립되는 것과 마찬가지 상황이다. 그리고 이런 폭넓은 모순의 가능성은 서로 다른 생각이나 믿음이, 의견이 같은 개인의 마음속에서가 아닌 의견이 다른 개인의 마음속에서 발생했을 때 특히 인식된다. 그래서 개인이나 당파의 이익에 영향을 받고 사고방식의 차이로 인해 왜곡된다. 우리가 현재 관심을 가지고 있는 사상과 믿음의, 아니 그들 사이의 모순은 단순한 논리적 논쟁보다 더욱 광범위하고 다양하다. 이들은 또한 확정적이지도, 정확하지도 않다. 이것들은 문화 충돌이다. 그리고 그 안에서 단지 특정한 사상이나 태고의 믿음이라는 것과는 거리가 먼 서로 상반되는 힘이 사실상 사상, 믿음, 선입견, 동정, 반감 그리고 개인적 관심사의 다소 당황스러울 정도인 복합물을 이룬다.

어 휘

- **contradiction** n. 모순; 반박
- **mode** n. 양식; 방식
- **besides** prep. ~외에
- **specific** a. 특정한
- **logical** a. 논리적인; 필연의
- **incompatibility** n. 양립하지 않음; 불화합성
- **perception** n. 지각(작용), 인식
- **pictorially** ad. 그림을 넣어
- **inconsistent** n. 모순되는, 불일치하는
- **tonically** ad. 음조적으로
- **discordant** a. 조화하지 않은; 불협화음의
- **mere** a. 단순한, 단지 ~에 불과한
- **objective** a. 객관적인; 편견이 없는
- **antagonistic** a. 대립하는; 반대하는
- **irreconcilable** a. 대립하는; 모순된
- **possibility** n. 가능성; 실현성
- **partisan** a. 당파심이 강한
- **warp** v. 휘게 하다; 뒤틀다; 왜곡하다
- **idiosyncrasy** n. (개인의) 특질, 특이성
- **constitution** n. 구성, 조직, 조성
- **concern** v. 관계하다, 관심을 갖다; 염려하다
- **extensive** a. 광대한, 넓은
- **duel** n. 결투; 싸움; 투쟁
- **definite** a. 뚜렷한, 명확한
- **precise** a. 정밀[정확]한
- **conflict** n. 충돌, 투쟁, 전투
- **pristine** a. 원래의, 옛날의
- **bewilder** v. 어리둥절케 하다
- **prejudice** n. 편견, 선입관
- **sympathy** n. 동정, 호의, 헤아림
- **antipathy** n. 반감, 혐오

[Challenge 5]

문제 1

답 (2)

해설 본문은 초기 증기기관을 발견했다고 여겨지는 사람에 대한 이야기를 시간의 순서에 따라 인물을 하나씩 열거하며 구체적 설명이 따르는 구조를 취하고 있다.

문제 2

답 (2)

해설 보기 항 (2)는 본문의 다음 부분과 일치하지 않는다.

> though evidence is found that such devices as were described by Hero were sometimes used for trivial purposes.

문제 3

답 (1)

해설 빈칸이 들어간 문장의 종속절과 주절의 내용이 서로 대조를 이루고 있다. 양보의 'while'을 쓰는 것이 가장 적절하다.

해석 Hero는 그가 언급한 어떠한 장치를 유용한 목적에 응용하는 것에 대한 제안을 하지 않는다. Hero가 살던 시대에서 16세기 후반과 17세기 초까지 Hero가 언급한 그러한 장치가 때로 사소한 목적에 사용되었다는 증거는 있지만, 그 이상의 어떤 기록도 존재하지 않는다. 다음 공헌자인 Edward Somerset은 분명 최초의 실용적인 증기기관을 만든 정도는 아니더라도 그것을 제안한 공로를 인정받을 만하다. 1663년 런던에서 출판된 "Century of Scantlings and Inventions"에서 그는 직접적인 증기 압력에 의해 두 개의 용기에서 물에 힘을 가함으로 물을 올리는 것뿐 아니라 한쪽 끝은 레버, 다른 한 쪽은 펌프를 작동하게 하는 일종의 상호 피스톤을 마음에 구상한 것을 보이는 장치를 기술하고 있다. 그의 설명은 다소 애매하고 구체적 그림도 존재하지 않기에 위에서 언급된 이중 작용 외에 그의 장치에 독특한 창의적인 특징이 있는지 없는지는 말하기가 어렵다. 그가 언급한 장치가 실제로 만들어졌는지에 대한 직접적인 믿을 만한 기록도 남아 있지 않지만, 많은 사람은 그가 실제로 피스톤을 포함한 증기기관을 만들고 운행했다고 주장한다. 1675년 Samuel Moreland 경은 '물을 끌어 올리는 강력한 특정 장비'를 선보인 것으로 인해 찰스 2세에 의해 훈장을 받았다. 비록 이 장치의 설계에 대한 어떠한 기록도 보이지 않지만, 1822년에 출판된 수학 사전에 Moreland가 최초로 증기 기관을 설명했다고 인정하고 있으며, 이 주제에 대해 그가 쓴 보고서가 여전히 대영박물관에 보존되어 있다.

어 휘

- **application** n. 적용, 응용
- **device** n. 장치; 고안, 계획
- **trivial** a. 하찮은, 대단치 않은, 평범한
- **contributor** n. 공헌한 사람, 기부자

apparently *ad.* 명백히, 외견상으로
credit *n.* 신용, 영예   steam engine *n.* 증기 기관
have in mind ~을 염두에 두다[생각하다]
receiver *n.* 용기, 저장소   direct *a.* 똑바른, 직접의
pressure *n.* 압력, 압축   reciprocate *v.* 왕복 운동을 하다
piston *n.* 피스톤
actuate *v.* (동력원이 기계를) 움직이다; (장치 등을) 발동하다[시키다]
lever *n.* 지레   operate *v.* 작동하다, 움직이다
pump *n.* 펌프   obscure *a.* 애매한, 분명하지 않은
extant *a.* (문서 따위가) 현존하는, 잔존하는
distinctly *ad.* 뚜렷하게; 별개로   novel *a.* 새로운, 신기한
feature *n.* 특징, 특색   aside from ~을 제외하고, ~이외에
authentic *a.* 확실한, 근거 있는, 진짜의
construct *v.* 세우다, 꾸미다, 구성하다
decorate *v.* 훈장을 주다
demonstration *n.* 증명, 논증, 증거; 실물 선전
treatise *n.* 논문, 보고서   preserve *v.* 보존하다, 유지하다

[Challenge 6]

문제 1

답 (3)

해설 서로 다른 관점에서 해결점을 찾기 쉽지 않은 노예 제도에 관한 내용이다. 어떤 이는 성경에서 노예 제도를 인정한다고 주장하는 반면, 어떤 이는 전혀 그렇지 않다는 등 노예 제도에 관해 상충하는 다양한 관점을 드러내고 있다.

문제 2

답 (4)

해설 본문에서 노예 제도를 둘러싸고 성경에서 바라보는 노예 제도의 관점은 사람마다 다르게 해석되고 있다. 고로, 성경에 노예 제도에 대한 하나의 해석만이 존재한다고 규정할 수 없다.

문제 3

답 (1)

해설 본문에서 'ghost'는 전국에 퍼져 있는 노예 제도를 말한다.

> Wherever we go, north or south, east or west, at the fireside, in the factory, the rail-car or the steamboat, in the state legislatures or the national Congress, this "ghost that will not down" obtrudes itself.

어디를 가도 이 'ghost(= slavery)'가 불쑥 머리를 내민다고 말하고 있다.

문제 4

답 (4)

해설 (d)는 가목적어이고, 나머지는 모두 노예 제도를 지칭한 것이다.

문제 5

답 (1)

해설 express는 형용사로 '명백한, 분명한, 겉으로 드러나는'이란 뜻이다.

해석 다른 어떤 주제보다 현재 국가적 관심사로 여겨질 수 있는 것이 있다면, 이것은 노예 제도의 문제이다. 동서남북, 집안 난롯가, 공장, 철도 또는 기선, 주(州)의회 또는 국회 어디를 가나 이 '사라지지 않는 유령'은 불쑥 튀어나온다. 이 갈등은 언론, 설교, 포럼 같은 것을 포함하며 정당에 의한 타협과, 이도저도 아닌 애매한 태도에 대한 종교단체의 필사적인 노력에도 불구하고, 노예 제도는 심화되고 있을 뿐이다. 그러나 다른 국가 중대사와 비교했을 때, 이것(노예 제도)의 독특한 특징은 양당이 공격과 방어를 위한 공통의 무기로 성경에서 그 근본적인 주장을 이끌어 온다는 것이다. 한편에선 미국에 존재하는 이 노예 제도는 도덕적 악이 아니라고 주장한다. 이는 부모와 자식, 남편과 부인 그리고 사회의 다른 관계만큼 무구하고 합법적인 관계라는 것이다. 그리고 수익의 목적으로 인간을 사고, 팔고 소유하는 권리는 하나님의 명확한 허락으로 주어졌고, 예수와 그의 열두 제자들에 의해서 인정된 것이다. 이 권리는 황금률에 기반을 하고 있다. 켄터키 주 Bacon 대학의 Shannon 박사는 "나는 성경에 대한 심각한 무지, 아니면 기독교인이라 공언하는 사람들이 표현하는 파렴치와 신성모독의 극치(sublimity) 중 어느 것이 가장 무책임한 행동인지 좀처럼 모르겠다. 그리고 나는 하나님의 책은 노예 소유에 대한 어떠한 제재도 하지 않았음을 단호히 확언한다."라고 말한다. 이러한 모든 주장은 당연히 다음과 같이 요약할 수 있다. "노예 제도는 가부장제에 의해서 실행되고, 모세의 율법에서 하나님으로부터 허락받고 합법임을 인정받았고, 예수와 그의 열두 제자들이 부인하지 않았기에, 이것은 옳았다. 만약 옳다면 여전히 그러하다. 그러므로 남부 노예 제도는 옳은 것이다." 반면, 노예를 재산시하는 제도는 성경의 어디에도 정당화되었거나 용인되어 있지 않고, 성경의 정신이나 가르침 모두에 완전 정반대라는 주장도 있다.

어 휘

slavery *n.* 노예 제도; 노예
fireside *n.* 난롯가   steamboat *n.* 기선
legislature *n.* 입법부; 입법기관   Congress *n.* 의회; 국회
obtrude *v.* 불쑥 내밀다, 끼어들다
strife *n.* 투쟁; 다툼; 싸움   pulpit *n.* 설교단
forum *n.* 토론회   compromise *n.* 타협, 양보
desperate *a.* 필사적인
non-committal *a.* 의견을 밝히지 않은, 어정쩡한

distinctive *a.* 독특한, 특이한   **feature** *n.* 특징
compare *v.* 비교하다; 대조하다 (with)
principal *a.* 주요한; 중요한   **argument** *n.* 논의, 논증, 논거
armory *n.* 병기고   **lawful** *a.* 합법의, 적당한, 타당한
permission *n.* 허가; 면허; 인가
sanction *v.* 허가하다; 제재를 가하다   **apostle** *n.* 사자, 사도
unaccountable *a.* 책임질 필요 없는
profound *a.* 깊은, 밑바닥의, 뜻 깊은, 심원한
sublimity *n.* 장엄, 숭고, 고상
impudence *n.* 철면피; 뻔뻔스러움
infidelity *n.* 신을 믿지 않음; 불신앙
manifest *v.* 나타내다, 드러내 보이다
profess *v.* 공헌하다; 명하다   **affirm** *v.* 확인하다, 단언하다
affirmation *n.* 단언, 주장   **fairly** *ad.* 꽤
sum *v.* 요약하다   **patriarch** *n.* (가정의) 가장; 족장
denounce *v.* 공공연히 비난하다
contend *v.* 주장하다   **chattel** *n.* 동산; 소지품
warrant *v.* 정당화하다

[Challenge 7]

문제 1

답 (1)

해설 다원주의의 구체적 내용으로 우수한 점을 살피기 전에 다원주의가 무엇인지를 정의하는 글이다. 글의 주제가 드러나는 다음 문장을 확인하자.

> It is obviously useless to discuss any theory until we are agreed as to what that theory is. The question, therefore, What is Darwinism? must take precedence of all discussion of its merits.

해설 온 세계와 과학계 그리고 종교계 모두를 혼란에 빠뜨린 저자의 실제 견해에 관하여 엄청난 혼란과 다양한 의견들이 퍼지고 있다. 만약 어떤 사람이 '나는 다원주의자입니다'라고 말하면, 많은 사람들은 그가 자기 자신을 사실상 무신론자로 인정했다고 생각한다. 반면 다른 사람들은 그가 한 가지 건전한 진화론의 형태를 받아들였다고 생각한다. 이것은 아주 치명적인 악이다. 우리가 그 이론이 무엇인지에 관하여 동의하기 전까지는 어떤 이론에 대해 논의하는 것은 분명히 소용없는 짓이다. 그러므로 "다원주의란 무엇인가?" 하는 질문은 이것이 가진 장점에 대한 모든 논쟁 이전에 선행되어야 한다. 경험을 통해 알 수 있는 가장 중요한 (big) 사실은 우주가 존재한다는 것이다. 인간의 마음을 가장 무겁게 누르는 거대한 문제는 이것의 존재를 설명하는 것이다. 이것의 기원은 무엇인가? 우리가 주위에서 목격하는 변화는 어떠한 원인에 의한 것인가? 우리는 우주의 일부분이기에 이러한 질문은 우리에 관한 것이다. 인간의 기원, 본성 그리고 운명은 무엇인가? Huxley 교수는 "인간에 대한 문제 중의 문제 — 다른 모든 문제의 기저에 있고 다른 어떤 것보다 흥미로운 문제 — 는 인간이 자연에서 차지하는 위치와 우주 만물과의 관계를 확인하는 것이다. 우리 인간이 어디서 왔으며, 자연에 가하는 인간의 힘과 우리에게 가하는 자연의 힘의 한계는 무엇이고, 우리는 어떤 목적을 향해 나아가고 있는지가 항상 새롭게 제시되는 문제이며 세상에 태어나는 모든 사람에게 끊임없는 관심과 함께 주어진다."고 말하는데 일리가 있다. 다윈은 이러한 질문에 답변하려는 일에 착수한다. 그는 모든 살아 있는 인간이 깊은 관심을 보이는 문제의 해결책을 제안한다. 그러므로 다원주의란 적어도 지구상의 생명체에 관한 한 우주의 한 이론이다.

어휘

confusion *n.* 혼동; 혼란; 당황   **diversity** *n.* 다양성
avow *v.* 공언하다; 인정하다; 자백하다
virtually *ad.* 사실상; 실질적으로   **atheist** *n.* 무신론자
adopt *v.* 채용[채택]하다; 적용하다
precedence *n.* 선행; 우위   **account for** ~을 설명하다
origin *n.* 기원; 발달; 태생   **witness** *v.* 목격하다
concern *v.* ~에 관계하다   **destiny** *n.* 운명; 숙명; 운
mankind *n.* 인류; 인간; 사람
underlie *v.* 기초가 되다, 근거하다
ascertainment *n.* 확인   **occupy** *v.* 차지하다; 점령하다
present *v.* 제시하다, 내놓다
undiminished *a.* (힘 따위가) 줄지 않는; 쇠퇴하지 않는
undertake *v.* 시작하다, 착수하다
propose *v.* 제안하다   **solution** *n.* 해결; 해명
organism *n.* 유기체; 생물체

[Challenge 8]

문제 1

답 (3)

해설 여러 번 반복하지만 영어권 글은 첫 번째 문장을 놓쳐서는 안 된다. 글 전체의 나침반 역할을 하는 주제를 제시하는 동시에 본문에서 구체적으로 어떤 내용이 다루어질지 예측할 수 있다. 아래 첫 번째 문장을 보고 대략 본문의 내용을 예측해 보자.

> Negotiators from different cultures may tend to view the purpose of a negotiation differently.

문화권에 따라 협상은 서로 다른 목적을 가진다고 했으므로, 이후 서로 다른 문화권의 소개와 함께 각각의 문화권에서 협상이 어떻게 해석되는지 살펴보는 구체적 예가 전개될 가능성이 크다.

문제 2

답 (1)

해설 주절의 내용으로 보아, 앞의 부사절은 계약의 중요성을 어느 정도는 인정한다는 내용인 보기 (1)이 가장 적절하다.

문제 3

답 (4)

해설 (4)에서 서로 문화가 다른 협상가들의 계약이 거의 모든 경우 교착상태에 빠진다고 했는데, 본문에 이런 확률의 내용을 다루는 점은 없다. 협상에 대해 바라보는 관점이 다른 점을 인식해 그에 대한 적절한 이해가 바탕이 되어야 한다고 주장하는 내용이다.

해석 서로 다른 문화권의 협상가는 특정 협상에 대한 목적을 다르게 보는 경향이 있을 수 있다. 어떤 문화의 협상가들의 경우, 비즈니스 협상의 목적은 무엇보다 당사자 간의 계약을 체결하는 것이나, 다른 문화의 경우 협상의 목적은 계약 체결이라기보다 두 당사자 간의 관계를 형성하는 것이라고 생각한다. 비록 서면상의 계약이 서로의 관계를 나타내는 것이라 해도, 계약의 본질은 바로 그 관계 자체이다. 예를 들어 The Global Negotiator에서 자세히 보고된 바와 같이 내가 12개국의 400명이 넘는 사람들을 대상으로 행한 조사에서 나는 스페인 응답자의 74%가 협상의 목적은 계약이라고 주장한 반면, 인도인 중역 간부의 33%만이 비슷한 견해를 내놓았다는 것을 알아냈다. 접근 방법의 차이를 통해 협상의 목적은 종종 관계의 형성이라고 말하는 특정 아시아 협상가가 왜 협상 준비에 더 많은 시간과 노력을 기울이고, 그 반면 북미 사람들은 종종 거래 성사의 첫 번째 단계를 서둘러 처리하려고 하는지의 이유를 설명해 주기도 한다. 협상의 준비 단계에서 당사자들이 서로를 철저하게 알아가려는 것은 좋은 사업 관계를 유지하는 데 아주 중요한 기반이 된다. 이것은 목적이 단지 계약일 경우에는 덜 중요하게 보일 수 있다. 그러므로 상대방이 당신의 협상의 목적을 어떻게 바라보는지가 아주 중요하다.

어휘

negotiator *n.* 협상[교섭]자; 거래인
view *v.* (~라고) 여기다, 생각하다   foremost *a.* 맨 먼저의, 최초의
contract *n.* 계약   party *n.* (계약 등의) 당사자
creation *n.* 창조(물), 창작
essence *n.* 본질, 진수, 정수   survey *n.* (설문) 조사
respondent *n.* 응답자   executive *n.* 중역
approach *n.* 접근법, 처리 방법
explain *v.* 분명[명백]하게 하다, 설명하다
preliminaries *n.* 예비 행위   rush *v.* 돌진하다, 달려들다
thoroughly *ad.* 철저하게, 충분하게
crucial *a.* 결정적인, 중대한   foundation *n.* 기초, 토대, 근거
counterpart *n.* 짝의 한쪽, 상대물, 대응자

[Challenge 9]

문제 1

답 (3)

해설 빨간색과 관련된 동양과 아프리카의 전통을 소개하는 글이다.

문제 2

답 (2)

해설 이후에 전개되는 내용은 앞에서 전개된 긍정적인 면과는 대조적으로 부정적인 측면의 빨간색을 드러내므로 보기 항 (2)가 가장 적절하다.

문제 3

답 (4)

해설 본문에서 알 수 있듯이, 색상은 나라와 문화에 따라 다르게 해석되고 있다. 이는 색깔이 그 자체로 절대적인 내재적 의미를 전달하는 것이 아니라 상대적으로 해석되는 것임을 알 수 있다. 고로 보기 항 (4)는 옳다.

해석 중국에서 적색은 불과 남쪽(일반적인 남쪽과 특히 남중국)을 상징한다. 이 색은 용기, 충성, 명예, 성공, 운, 다산, 행복, 열정 그리고 여름과 관련되는 대부분 긍정적인 의미가 내포되어 있다. 중국의 문화 전통에서 적색은 결혼(신부가 전통적으로 빨간색 드레스를 입는다)과 연관이 있으며, 또한 빨간 종이는 희사금이나 다른 물건들을 싸는 데 사용된다. 만다린으로 쓰인 특별한 빨간색 봉투는 새해 세뱃돈으로 사용된다. 좀 더 부정적인 측면에선 부고는 전통적으로 빨간색 잉크로 쓰며, 누군가의 이름을 빨간색으로 쓰는 행위는 자신의 삶에서 그 사람을 없앤다는 의미를 전달하거나 이들이 죽었다는 것을 뜻한다. 빨간색은 또한 여성과 남성(각각 음과 양)과 모두 관련이 있다.

일본에서 빨간색은 영웅을 나타내는 전통적인 색상이다. 인도 아대륙에서 빨간색은 신부의 전통적인 옷 색상이며, 종종 미디어에서 결혼한 여성의 상징적인 색으로 사용된다. 이 색은 순결과 이것이 열과 다산의 의미로 연결되면서 결혼 관계의 성욕과 관련이 된다. 이것은 또한 부와 아름다움 그리고 여신인 Lakshmi의 색상이기도 하다.

중앙 아프리카에서 Ndembu의 용사들은 의식을 할 때 빨간색으로 자신을 문지른다. 이들의 문화는 빨간색을 생명과 건강의 상징으로 보기에, 아픈 사람도 빨간색으로 몸을 칠한다. 대부분의 중앙아프리카 문화와 마찬가지로, Ndembu족은 빨간색을 흑색보다는 좋지만 흰색만큼은 좋지 않은 애매한 색으로 본다. 그러나 아프리카의 다른 지역에서 빨간색은 슬픔의 색으로 죽음을 상징한다. 아프리카의 많은 지역에서 빨간색이 죽음과 관련이 되기에 적십자는 그 대륙의 여러 지역에서 녹색과 흰색으로 (상징) 색을 바꾸었다.

어 휘

- **connotation** *n.* 함축, 언외지의(言外之意)
- **fertility** *n.* ① (토지가) 기름짐, 비옥 ② 다산(多産), 풍부
- **associate with** ~과 관련시켜 생각하다
- **wrap** *v.* 감싸다, 싸다; 포장하다   **Mandarin** *n.* 표준 중국어
- **monetary** *a.* 화폐의, 통화의; 금전(상)의; 금융의, 재정(상)의
- **obituary** *n.* (약력을 붙여 신문에 싣는) 사망 기사, 사망 광고
- **yin and yang** 음과 양
- **heroic** *a.* 영웅적인, 씩씩한, 용감한; 대담한
- **bridal** *a.* 새색시의, 신부의; 혼례의
- **purity** *n.* ① 청정, 순수 ② 깨끗함, 청결, 맑음
- **ambivalent** *a.* 양면 가치의; 상반되는 감정[태도, 의미]를 가진; 유동적인

[Challenge 10]

문제 1
답 (1)

해설 본문 첫 번째 문장에서 알 수 있듯이, 쿤이 설정한 과학 발달의 모형을 제시하고 있다. 본문에 이러한 과학 발달의 모형을 설명하기 위해 '정상 과학'과 '혁명적 과학'을 언급한 후 각각의 특성, 특히 정상 과학을 퍼즐에 비유하면서 설명하고 있다.

문제 2
답 (1)

해설 보기 항 (1)은 'scientific revolutions involve a revision to existing scientific belief or practice'로 보아 옳지 않다. 전체적으로 과학적 혁명의 개념 자체가 기존의 과학으로 풀 수 없는 현상에 대한 해결책을 제시하는 새로운 과학이라는 점을 감안하면 쉽게 접근이 가능하다. 또한 주의할 것은 새로운 패러다임에 의해 형성된 이러한 과학적 혁명이라 해서 과학 현상에 대한 모든 답변을 가지고 있다는 점도 틀린 진술임을 기억해야 한다(본문 마지막 참조).

문제 3
답 (3)

해설 바로 앞 문장에서 근거를 찾을 수 있다. 즉, 퍼즐을 푸는 사람은 어느 정도 '익숙함을 가지고' 푼다고 했으므로 보기 항 (3)이 가장 적절하다.

문제 4
답 (1)

해설 바로 앞에서 전개된 내용을 바탕으로 빈칸에 들어갈 말을 이끌어내야 한다. 앞에서 이전 정상 과학에서 설명할 수 있는 현상이 혁명적 과학에선 오히려 설명되지 않는 것도 있다고 말하고 있으므로, 이를 가장 잘 드러내는 표현은 'Kuhn-loss'가 된다. 쿤의 이론 자체가 대실패라고 표현한 보기 항 (2)는 부분적인 잘못을 전체로 확대 해석하고 있다는 점에서 오답이다.

해석 쿤에 따르면, 특정 과학의 발달은 고정된(획일적) 것이 아니라 '정상'과 '혁명'의 단계를 반복하는 것이다. 혁명적 단계는 단순히 가속화되는 진보의 시기가 아니라 정상 과학과는 질적으로 다른 것이다. 정상 과학은 적어도 겉으로 보기에 과학 진보의 평범한 누계적 형태를 닮았다. 쿤은 정상 과학을 '퍼즐 풀기'로 묘사한다. 이 용어가 정상 과학이 극적이지 않다는 것을 암시하지만, 이것의 주된 목적은 낱말 퍼즐 또는 체스 퍼즐이나 조각 퍼즐을 하는 사람과 같이, 퍼즐을 푸는 사람은 이 퍼즐을 풀 상당한 기회가 있을 거라고 기대하는 점과 그렇게 하는 것은 자신의 능력에 주로 달려 있으며, 퍼즐 자체와 해결 방법이 높은 유사성을 보인다는 내용을 전달하는 것이다. 퍼즐을 푸는 사람은 전혀 새로운 영역으로 들어가는 것이 아니다. 왜냐하면, 퍼즐과 해결책은 익숙하고 상대적으로 간단하기 때문에, 정상 과학은 점점 늘어가는 퍼즐 풀이법을 계속 쌓아갈 것을 기대한다.

하지만 혁명적 과학은 누계적이지 않은데, 쿤에 따르면 이는 과학적 혁명은 기존의 과학적 신념 또는 관행에 수정을 요구하기 때문이다. 이전 단계의 모든 정상 과학의 성취가 혁명을 통해 보존되지 않으며, 이후 과학은 이전 과학의 기간에 성공적으로 설명되었던 것으로 간주되던 현상을 설명하지 못할 수도 있다. 이러한 과학 혁명의 특성은 '쿤로스'라고 알려졌다.

어 휘

- **uniform** *a.* 획일적인, 한결같은
- **alternate** *v.* 교체[교대]시키다
- **qualitatively** *ad.* 질적으로   **resemble** *v.* ~와 닮다
- **familiarity** *n.* 익숙함; 친근함   **territory** *n.* 영역, 구역
- **straightforward** *a.* (일이) 간단한
- **preceding** *a.* (보통 the ~) 이전의; 바로 전의; 전술한

Day 12

[Challenge 1]

문제 1

답 (2)

해설 본문은 현재 중국 경제에 대해서 인플레이션으로 인한 경기 침체의 우려가 높아지는 상황이 그다지 근심할 수준이 아니며, 두 가지 이유를 통해 근거를 제시하는 글이다.

문제 2

답 (2)

해설 국내 부동산 시장의 거품과 인플레를 지칭하는 표현이다.

해석 현재 가장 크게 성장하고 있는 시장에 대한 물음표는 단연 중국이다. 중국 경제는 세계의 주된 성장 엔진 중 하나이며, 중국의 성장은 이번 연도에 거의 11%까지 치솟았다.

그러나 경제 관측자들 사이에서 중국 정부가 급격한 경제성장의 둔화 없이는, 풍요로운 세계 경제에 나쁜 영향을 끼칠 수 있는 물가 상승을 감당할 수 없을 것이라는 우려가 증폭되고 있다. 뉴욕 타임스를 살펴보자.

그러나 점차적으로 많은 경제학자들이 현재 중국 — 세계 금융위기 동안 세계에서 가장 빠르게 성장하는 경제 강대국인 — 은 치솟는 물가, 증가하는 정부 부재와 부동산 거품으로 인해 내년에는 성장이 둔화될 수 있다고 우려하고 있다.

두 평가 기관인 Moody's와 Fitch Ratings는 말하길 중국은 여전히 성장을 위한 균형이 잘 잡혀 있다. 그러나 이들은 또한 최근 중국 은행 제도에 숨겨진 위험에 대해서 경고했다. Fitch 사는 심지어 부동산 시장과 관련이 있는 대출 상환의 불이행으로 인한 또 다른 한파가 불어닥칠 가능성조차 암시했다.

약 10%대의 연간 성장률을 보이고 있는 중국의 급격한 경기 침체는 전 세계 경제에 심각한 타격을 미치는데, 이는 천연 자원에 대한 중국의 엄청난 수요가 아시아와 남미의 성장을 뒷받침하는 데 큰 역할을 하고 있기 때문이다.

그리고 중국이 미국 재무부 부채에 대한 주요 재권 보유국이며, 최근 미국의 주요한 투자지인 점을 고려할 때, 중국의 경기 침체는 미국 회사에 큰 타격을 미치게 된다.

그리고 여러 가지가 있다. 정말 걱정할 만한 원인이 있는가? 글쎄, 걱정할 만한 원인은 항상 있었다. 그러나 나는 두 가지 이유에서, 다른 국가들의 경우에서보다 중국 내 파열음에 대해 덜 걱정하는 바이다. 우선 중국의 부동산 시장이 일촉즉발의 혼란 상황을 겪고 있는 정도에 대해 과장하기가 쉽다.

일부 해안 지역의 경우 수입과 임대에 관한 소비자 물가지수가 분명 경제 혼란의 위험 영역에 있는 것은 맞지만, 다른 곳의 주택 시장은 2007년에 비해 그리 비싸지 않거나 수입에 대해 상대적으로 더욱 가격 절충이 가능해졌다. 또 다른 이유는 중국 정부가 부정적인 충격에 대해 자국 경제를 완충할 수 있는 재정 능력과 정치적 능력을 소유하고 있다는 점이다. 중국 경제가 내년에 불안정한 경제적 충격을 겪는 것을 예상해 볼 수도 있지만, 중국은 대부분의 국가보다 이것을 잘 대처할 수 있는 자세를 취하고 있다.

어 휘

emerging *a.* 최근 만들어진[생겨난]
principal *a.* 주요한; 제1의; 중요한
roar *v.* ① (큰 짐승 등이) 으르렁거리다, (크고 깊은 소리로) 울리다 ② 고함치다, 함성을 지르다 ③ 폭소를 터뜨리다
slowdown *n.* 속력을 늦춤, 감속;《미국》(공장의) 조업 단축; 경 기 후퇴
pillar *n.* ① 기둥; 표주(標柱), 기념주; 대각(臺脚) ②《비유적》(국 가·활동의) 대들보
stall *v.* ~을 막다른 궁지에 빠뜨리다   **mount** *v.* 증가하다
credit ratings agency 신용평가회사
poise *v.* ① 균형을 잡히게 하다, 평형이 되게 하다 ② (어떤 자세를) 취하다, (어떤 상태·위치를) 유지하다 ③ (~의) 준비를 하다, (~할) 각오를 하다
hint *v.* 넌지시 말하다, 암시하다
voracious *a.* ① 게걸스레 먹는, 대식(大食)하는, 폭식하는 ② 탐욕스러운, 물릴 줄 모르는
prop up 지지하다
holder *n.* (권리·관직·토지·기록 등의) 소유[보유]자; (어음 따 위의) 소지인
overstate *v.* 허풍을 떨다, 과장하다
affordable *a.* 줄 수 있는; 입수 가능한, (값이) 알맞은
destabilize *v.* (체제·국가·정부 등을) 불안정하게 만들다
handle *v.* 취급하다, 처리하다; (문제를) 논하다

[Challenge 2]

문제 1

답 (1)

해설 "The poets' concern was with certain events of the past, not with their relationship to other events, past or present, and in the case of Homer, not even with the consequences or dates of those events."와 이후 진술을 통해서 (2), (3), (4)에 대한 내용을 이끌어 낼 수 있다. 보기 (1)의

경우 'They knew all about these epic figures: their names, their genealogies, and their exploits.'와 호머의 일리아드와 같은 이야기에서 이끌어 낼 수 있다.

문제 2

답 (1)

해설 언제 어떤 일이 일어났는지에 대한 정확한 시간을 기록하지 않고, 단순히 '먼 과거'라고 표현하고 있다는 점에서 'historically imprecise'가 가장 적절하다.

해석 한때 영웅과 여걸의 시대가 있었다는 것을 의심하는 그리스 사람들은 거의 없었다. 이들은 이 서사적 영웅들에 대한 모든 것 즉, 이들의 이름, 계보, 업적 등을 알고 있었다. 호머는 이들에 관한 가장 권위 있는 정보원이긴 하지만 결코 유일한 사람이라고 할 순 없었다.

안타깝게도 호머나 그 밖의 초기 그리스 시인들은 우리가 이해하는 것만큼 역사에 관한 흥미가 조금도 없었다. 이 시인들의 관심사는 과거의 특정 사건들에 관한 것이었고, 다른 사건들 및 과거 혹은 현재와의 관계가 어떤지는 관심 밖이었다.

호머의 경우 이러한 사건들의 결과나 이 사건들이 언제 발생했는지 그 날짜조차 관심이 없었다. 트로이 전쟁의 결과, 트로이의 몰락과 파괴, 그리고 그리스 승리의 성과는 전쟁을 연구하는 역사가에게는 아주 중요했을 것이다. 하지만, 일리아드를 지은 시인인 호머는 이 모든 것에 무관심했다. 그는 "아주 먼 옛날"이라는 말 외에는 트로이 전쟁이 언제 있었는지에 관한 암시를 전혀 주지 않는다.

어 휘

heroine *n.* 여장부
epic *a.* 서사의, 영웅이야기의
by no means 결코 ~아니다
have the slightest interest in ~에 조금도 관심이 없다
consequence *n.* 결과, 여파
be indifferent to ~에 무관심하다

[Challenge 3]

문제 1

답 (4)

해설 밑줄 친 사람들의 주장은 행위를 통한 학습을 강조하는 사람들로서 실제 생활의 경험을 교육의 기본으로 삼는다. 즉, 이들은 문학을 이와는 동떨어진 것으로 열심히 공부하기보단 직접 나가 스스로 뭔가를 행함으로써 교육이 발생한다고 믿는 사람들이다. 그러므로 (D)가 가장 적절하다.

문제 2

답 (3)

해설 문의 주장은 두 번째 문단에서 문제 제기로 시작하는 부분에서 발견할 수 있다. 즉, 문학은 삶에서 '삶을 재창조'하면 현재의 삶을 새로운 관점에서 조명해 주는 기능이 있다고 말하고 있다. 그러므로 첫 번째 본문과의 연장선에서 문학의 이런 기능은 중요하면서 학교 교과목에 반드시 포함시켜야 한다는 것이 글쓴이의 주장인 것이다. 단순히 문학의 중요한 기능에 대한 글이 아님을 주의해야 한다.

해석 지나치게 엄격하고 세세히 구별되어 규격화된 커리큘럼에 불만스러운 몇몇 교육철학자들은 유일한 학습의 원천으로 '생활 체험'을 지지하는 입장에 크게 흔들리고 있다. 그들은 단지 '해보는 것'을 통해 학습이 일어날 수 있다고 주장한다. 이를 두고 "과목이 아니라, 아이를 가르쳐라"는 말을 서슴없이 하면서도 그들은 그것의 불합리함을 보지 못하고 학습 방법을 개진하는 수단으로 엄격한 공부의 목표만을 주장한다. 이러한 접근 방식을 지지하는 사람들 모두가 명작 연구를 모조리 배제하는 것은 아니지만, 위대한 문학작품을 차츰 하위에 두는 것에서 증거로 나타나듯이 이러한 철학의 영향이 공교육 커리큘럼에서 느껴지고 있다. 그러면, 왜 문학을 가르치는가? 단지 삶 자체가 우리의 선생님이 되어 준다면, 왜 문학작품을 읽는가? 아리스토텔레스는 예술가는 삶으로부터 삶을 재창조함으로써 인간이 처한 상황을 보여 준다고 주장한다. 위대한 작가는 의식적이든 무의식적이든 우리 자신과 우리가 살고 있는 세상에 대한 우리의 이해를 넓힘으로써 인간이 처한 상황을 아주 효과적으로 보여준다. 그래서 문학의 기능, 즉 우리 자신의 삶의 영역을 확장하는 것은 그 자체로 매우 중요하다. 만일 그렇다면, 우리가 해야 하는 일은 분리시키기보다는 문학은 삶을 밝게 비추는 삶의 그런 부분이라고 우리를 반대하는 사람들을 납득시키는 것이다.

어 휘

rigid *a.* 굳은 완고한 엄격한
overrefined *a.* 지나치게 세세히 구별된 아주 세련된
espousal *n.* (주의, 학설의) 옹호, 지지
spout *vt.* 내뿜다, 분출하다 막힘없이 말하다
absurdity *n.* 불합리, 어리석음
rigorous *a.* 준엄한, 가혹한, 엄격한
adherent *n.* 지지자, 신봉자
eliminate *vt.* 제거하다, 베제하다 무시하다
evidence *vt.* 증언하다 명시하다
subordination *n.* 예속시킴, 하위, 종속
reveal *vt.* 드러내다, 누설하다, 폭로하다 나타내다
tellingly *ad.* 유효하게, 재미있게
extend *vt.* (손, 발을) 뻗다 (선, 거리, 기한, 범위를) 연장하다, 확 대하다
function *n.* 기능, 역할

Day 12

sphere *n.* 구(球), (활동) 영역, (세력) 범위
convince *vt.* ~에게 납득시키다
dissenter *n.* 반대자, 불찬성자
illumine *vt.* 조명하다, 밝게 비추다(=illuminate)
plead *vt.* 변호하다
retention *n.* 보존 유지

[Challenge 4]

문제 1

답 (2)

해설 제목은 글의 주제를 반영하는 표현이어야 한다. 주제는 일반적으로 문두에서 찾을 수 있는데, 첫 번째 문장에서 보는 바와 같이 국제통화기금과 유럽연합으로부터 구제 금융을 받은 아일랜드가 과학 분야의 예산안을 높였다는 이야기를 중심으로 글이 전개되고 있다. 이후 이번 예산 증감은 기초과학 분야가 아닌 '상용화 연구'에 대한 예산 증가라는 우려가 나왔다는 이야기는 있지만, 글의 주된 요지에 해당하는 내용은 아니다.

문제 2

답 (2)

해설 바로 앞에서 전개된 내용과 같이 현재 아일랜드 정부는 국제기금과 유럽연합의 금융구제로 정부 재정 삭감에 노력을 기울이고 있다. 이러한 현상을 가장 잘 드러내는 표현은 '허리를 졸라매는 즉, 긴축재정'을 뜻하는 보기 항 (2)가 가장 적절하다.

해석 아일랜드 정부는 최근의 금융구제 이후 160억 유로를 삭감하도록 강요받았음에도 2011년 연구 자금 지원을 12.5%까지 늘렸다. 어제 아일랜드의 하원인 Dáil에서 4표 차로 통과된 예산안은 국제통화기금과 유럽연합이 지난달 1,850억 유로에 해당하는 구제금융 패키지를 제공하기로 선언한 다음에 나온 것이다. 이번 조치에는 세금 인상, 국가 공무원 수를 줄이는 특별한 목적, 사회복지기금과 최저임금 삭감, 그리고 전직 공무원에게 지급하는 연금 수당 삭감 등이 포함되어 있다. 그러나 이런 긴축재정 와중에 아일랜드는 자국의 과학과 연구비를 유지하기로 결정했을 뿐만 아니라 8분의 1 수준까지 상향하기로 결정했다. 과학기술부 장관이면서 동시에 재무부 장관의 동생인 Conor Lenihan은 "첨단 과학 창업과 집중적인 상용화 연구에 대한 예산은 최근 3년 동안 처음 인상된 것이다"라고 말했다. '상용화 연구'에 대한 이런 강조는 아일랜드의 연구 투자 자산이 더욱 집중적으로 적용되면서 기초 과학에 대한 재정은 난관에 봉착할 것이라고 몇몇 과학자들을 우려케 했다. 이들은 또한 내각 개편 이후 3월에 발표된 정책 변화에 대해 우려했다. 이러한 조치는 HEA(고등교육청) — 아일랜드에서 과학에 재정 지원을 하는 주 공립 단체 중 하나 — 가 운영하는 수익성 좋은 연구 프로그램에 대한 통제권을 Lenihan 장관의 새로운 부서로 넘겨주었다. 반면 아일랜드의 다른 주요 자금 지원 단체인 아일랜드의 과학재단(SFI)은 아직은 건재하며, 2011년 예산을 일정 부분 증액했다. 이 단체는 사람들에게 자금을 지원하는 반면 고등교육청은 기반시설에 자금을 지원하는 경향을 보인다. 현재는 폐지된 과학연구 협회의 전 총무인 Dáil Leech는 "지난 2년 동안 가중된 결과는 투자자들의, 연구 예산 중 30% 이상의 삭감으로 대부분 SIF에서 발생했다"라고 했다. SIF는 아일랜드에서 과학을 지원하는 주요한 공공기관이다.

어휘

bailout *n.* (특히 재정적인) 긴급 원조
rescue *n.* 구출, 구조   welfare *n.* 복지, 후생
pension *n.* G) 연금, 양로 연금, 부조금 @ (학자·예술가 등에게 주는) 장려금
innovation *n.* 혁신, 일신   cabinet *n.* (보통 the C-) 내각
reshuffle *n.* (내각의) 개조
lucrative *a.* 유리한, 수지맞는, 돈이 벌리는
infrastructure *n.* (수도·전기·학교·에너지 공급·폐기물 처리 등 사회의) 기간 시설, 산업 기반, 사회적 생산 기반
defunct *a.* 죽은; 소멸한; 현존하지 않는
cumulative *a.* 축적적[점증적, 누가적(累加的)]인, 누적하는

[Challenge 5]

문제 1

답 (1)

해설 고대 도시의 특성을 기술하는 글이다. 현대의 계획도시에 비해 규칙성이 없다는 것이 가장 큰 특징이다.

문제 2

답 (4)

해설 보기 항 (4)에서 이성적이라고 해서 반드시 큰 도시를 건설할 것이라는 점은 본문에 드러나 있지 않다.

해석 게다가 또한 이 고대 도시는 처음에 기껏해야 부락에 불과하던 것에서부터 시간이 흘러 큰 도시가 되었는데, 일반적으로 전문 건축가가 넓은 공터에 자유롭게 계획한, 규칙적으로 건설된 도시와 비교했을 때 그리 잘 짜여 있지 않았다. 그래서 과거 여러 건축물들이 미적 측면에서 후대의 건축물과 종종 그 어깨를 나란히 하거나 능가하기도 하지만 이것들을 무작위로 병치시켜 보면, 여기저기 큰 것 작은 것, 그래서 결과적으로 거리가 삐뚤어지고 규칙성이 없어 누구나 이성에 이끌린 인간의 의지라기보단 우연에 의해서 이러한 정렬에 이르렀다고 쉽게 단언하게 될 것이다.

어휘

- ancient *a.* 옛날의; 고대의   regularity *n.* 규칙적임
- construct *v.* 조립하다; 세우다; 건설하다
- professional *a.* 직업의; 전문직의
- architect *n.* 건축가; 설계사   plain *n.* 평원, 평지
- surpass *v.* ~보다 낫다, 능가하다, 뛰어나다
- observe *v.* 관찰하다, 주시하다
- indiscriminate *a.* 무차별의; 닥치는 대로의
- juxtaposition *n.* 나란히 놓기, 병렬
- consequent *a.* 결과로서 일어나는; 필연상의
- crookedness *n.* 꼬부라짐, 뒤틀림
- irregularity *n.* 불규칙   dispose *v.* ~의 경향을 갖게 하다
- allege *v.* 단언하다; 주장하다   arrangement *n.* 배열; 정리

[Challenge 6]

문제 1

답 (1)

해설 Glass는 자신의 고전 음악 창작에 대중 음악적 요소를 활용하였는데, 'Popular elements do not appear out of place in Glass's classical music' 부분에서 알 수 있듯이, 이러한 요소가 전혀 어색하게 들리지 않았다고 했다. 즉, 고전 음악 요소 내에서 대중 음악 스타일을 잘 표현했다고 볼 수 있다. 보기 (1)과 같이 두 장르의 수준 높은 통합으로 한 장르처럼 들린다는 내용은 본문과 일치하지 않는다.

해석 1960년대 미국에서 동면 상태였던 접근방식인, 클래식 음악 작곡에 대중 음악 요소를 활용하는 관행이 다시 살아나면서, 작곡가 Philip Glass는 대중 음악을 모방하지 않으면서도 그 기풍을 받아들였다. Glass는 락 가수인 David Bowie와 Brian Eno의 음악을 두 개의 교향곡에 바탕으로 깔았지만 이들 교향곡은 그만의 독특한 음색을 드러낸다. 대중 음악적 요소는 Glass의 클래식 음악에서 전혀 어색하게 들리지 않는데, 이는 초기부터 특정 하모니와 리듬을 락 음악과 공유해 온 덕분이다. 그러나 이러한 대중적 요소를 사용했다고 해서 Glass가 대중 음악 작곡가가 된 것은 아니다. 그의 음악은 고전 음악을 듣는 사람을 끌어들이기 위해 포장된 대중 음악의 변형이 아니다. 오히려 고전이라기보다는 락에 흠뻑 젖은 청중을 위한 고급 예술에 해당한다.

어휘

- hibernation *n.* 동면, 잠식
- embrace *v.* 포용하다
- ethos *n.* 사회사조, 풍조
- out of place 부적절한
- steeped in ~에 푹 빠진

[Challenge 7]

문제 1

답 (4)

해설 본문에서 이탈리아가 그리스 철학 서적을 해석한 주된 국가라고 볼 근거는 없다.

해석 현대 과학은 르네상스를 그 시작점으로 삼으며, 이 시기는 영적/지적 부활의 놀라운 시기로 천 년간의 무지와 미신의 지배에 마침표를 찍는다. 인간은 다시 한 번 교리에 홀리지 않은 채 자연으로 눈을 돌렸다. 이들은 콘스탄티노플을 터키가 차지한 후 이탈리아에 도착한 믿을 만한 각색본에서 직접 번역된 그리스 고전 철학의 놀라운 사실들을 재발견했다. 고대 이오니아인들의 물질주의적 세계관과 원자론자들은 과학을 올바른 길로 이끌었다.

어휘

- renaissance *n.* 문예부흥; 르네상스
- marvelous *a.* 놀라운
- spiritual *a.* 정신의; 정신적인; 영적인
- intellectual *a.* 지적인; 지능적인   rebirth *n.* 재생; 갱생
- reign *n.* 지배; 통치   ignorance *n.* 무지, 무학
- superstition *n.* 미신; 미신적 관습
- humanity *n.* 인류; 인간애   dogma *n.* 교의; 교리
- classical *a.* 고전적인; 고전(시대의)
- Greek philosophy *n.* 그리스 철학
- reliable *a.* 믿을 수 있는; 믿음직한   version *n.* -판, 형태
- Constantinople *n.* 콘스탄티노플(이스탄불(터키의 도시)의 옛 이름)
- materialist *n.* 유물론자   outlook *n.* 관점, 세계관
- atomist *n.* 원자론자

[Challenge 8]

문제 1

답 (2)

해설 본문은 소의 나이를 측정하는 방법에 관한 내용이다.

문제 2

답 (4)

해설 'At two years of age a circle of thicker matter begins to form on the animal's horns, which becomes clearly defined at three years of age, when another circle begins to form, and an additional circle every year thereafter'의 내용을 보면, 암소의 경우 2년 차에 형성된 원이 3년 차에 아주 명확한 윤곽이 드러나며, 이때 추가적인 원이 형성되기 시작하므로 3살 때 최대로 눈에 보이는 원의 수는 2개이다. 따라서, 4살 때 최대로 보이는 원의 수는 3개가 되어야 한다.

문제 3

답 (1)

해설 'The rings on a bull's horns do not show themselves until he is five years old'에서 알 수 있듯이, 황소의 경우 5살이 되어야 나이테가 나타난다고 했으므로 4살 때에는 아무것도 보이지 않는다.

해석 암소의 뿔은 그 소의 나이를 정확히 나타내는 것으로 알려져 있지만, 항상 그렇지만은 않다. 그러나 일반적인 목적에서 다음과 같은 방법은 거의 옳다고 볼 수 있다. 2살 때 원형의 두꺼운 물질이 암소의 뿔 위에 형성되기 시작하는데, 이것은 3살 때 아주 분명해지며, 다시 이때 다른 원이 형성되기 시작하고 이후 매년 추가적으로 하나씩 늘어난다. 황소 뿔의 원은 5살이 되기 전까지 보이지 않는다. 그래서 황소의 경우 원 개수에 5를 더해야 한다. 원형이 분명하거나 두드러지지 않을 경우 이를 적용할 수 없다. 게다가 부도덕한 거래인들은 때로 나이 든 소의 원 몇 개를 줄로 잘라 없앤다.

어휘

horn *n.* 뿔
furnish *v.* ① (필요한 물건을) 공급하다, 제공하다, 주다 ② ~에 (필수품, 특히 가구를) 비치하다, 갖추다, 설비하다
indication *n.* 지시, 지적; 표시; 암시
define *v.* ~의 윤곽을 뚜렷이 보이다
additional *a.* 부가의[적], 추가의
distinct *a.* ① 별개의, 다른, 독특한(individual) ② 뚜렷한, 명백한
file off 떼어내다, 잘라내다

[Challenge 9]

문제 1

답 (1)

해설 유교와 도교의 쇠퇴가 불교의 확산을 도왔다는 내용도 다루고 있지만, 본문은 "유교와 도교의 쇠퇴와 배경"을 주된 내용으로 다루고 있다.

문제 2

답 (4)

해설 불교의 수용과 전파가 한 왕조 이후 가속화되었던 이유는 그동안 백성이 겪는 문제를 해결해 왔던 유교의 쇠락과 도교에 대한 국민의 외면이다. 빈칸 앞에서 유교를 신봉하던 관료의 부패와 함께 같은 맥락에서 도교를 다루고 있으므로 보기 항 (4)가 가장 적절하다.

해석 불교의 수용과 전파는 유교와 도교의 쇠퇴에 의해 더욱 가속화되었다. 한 왕조는 유교를 근간으로 한 정부를 세웠다. 한 왕조는 이전 왕조에서 파괴된 유교 경전을 복원하고 유교 연구를 장려했다. 그리고 공자를 국가적 숭배의 대상으로 세웠다(유교를 국교로 천명했다). 법과 질서는 모두 공자가 주창했던 이상과 원칙을 바탕에 두었다.

한 왕조 시대의 부와 권력의 엄청난 증대는 통치자와 관료의 성품에 있어서 점진적으로 타락으로 이어졌다. 유교가 제시하던 규율은 더 이상 지도자를 존중하지 않는 국민에게 무거운 짐일 뿐이었다. 유교는 삶의 문제에 대한 온전한 해결책으로서 그 영향력을 잃었다. 동시에 도교는 무지하고 이기적인 승려의 무리를 옹호하는 무의미하고 미신적인 의식이 되었다. 동해에 존재한다고 여겨졌던 불명의 섬으로 불노장생의 약을 찾으러 갔다 실패한 초기 도교의 신비주의자들의 높은 종교적 이상은 외면당했다.

어휘

introduction *n.* 도입, 입문
spread *n.* 보급, 전파   **buddhism** *n.* 불교
hasten *v.* 서두르다; 재촉하다
decline *n.* 쇠퇴, 악화
confucianism *n.* 유교   **taoism** *n.* 도교
Han dynasty *n.* 한 왕조
stablish 확립하다, 설립하다
reproduce *v.* 재생하다, 복원하다
classic *n.* 고전 문학, 고전 강의
previous *a.* 앞의, 이전의
worship *n.* 예배, 숭배   **regulation** *n.* 규정, 규칙, 조례
advocate *v.* 옹호하다   **wealth** *n.* 부, 재산
gradual *a.* 단계적인, 점차적인
deterioration *n.* 황폐
official *n.* 관리, 관료
burdensome *a.* 무거운 짐이 되는, 번거로운
cease *v.* 그만두다, 그치다   **hold** *n.* 지배력, 영향력
complete *a.* 완전한; 완벽한; 전부의
veritable *a.* 진실의, 틀림없는   **jumble** *n.* 뒤범벅, 혼란
superstitious *a.* 미신적인, 미신에 의한
rite *n.* 의례; 의식   **serve** *v.* (~으로) 쓸모 있다
horde *n.* 큰 무리
ignorant *a.* 무지한, 무학의
selfish *a.* 이기주의의, 이기적인
priest *n.* 성직자; 목사, 승려   **mystic** *n.* 신비론자
search *n.* 수색   **elixir** *n.* (만병통치) 영약
fruitless *a.* 결실이 없는; 효과 없는; 무익한
isle *n.* 섬   **immortal** *a.* 죽지 않은, 불후의

[Challenge 10]

문제 1

답 (4)

해설 본문은 건강보험료를 제대로 내지 않으면서 혜택을 보는 사람에 대한 지적이므로 보기 (4)가 제목으로 가장 적절하다.

문제 2

답 (2)

해설 부유한 사람들이 자신의 이름을 회사 장부에 올리는 이유는 바로 임금에 따라 보험료가 산정되기 때문이다.

해석 건강보험제도에 무임승차하는 부유한 자영업자들의 문제는 이미 잘 알려져 있다. 자신의 상당한 개인적 부에 상응하는 보험료를 내지 않기 위해서, 이들은 자신의 이름을 회사 임금 장부에 올리고 종업원으로 등록한다. 이런 관행을 억제하기 위해 국민건강보험공단은 월별 급여 외에 소득이 있는 피고용인에게 추가적인 보험금을 부과하기 시작했다. 최근 한 보도에 따르면 "무임승차"의 문제는 단지 돈이 많은 자영업자에게만 해당하는 것이 아니라 임금이 낮은 (그러나 부유한) 사람들 사이에서도 심각하다고 말한다. 이 보고서에 따르면, 약 5백만 명의 임금 노동자들이 자신을 자영업자 또는 피부양자로 등록해 보험료를 줄이거나 전혀 내지 않고 있다고 한다. 자영업자의 보험료가 수입뿐 아니라 부동산과 자동차와 같은 자산에 기반을 두고 산정되기에 재산이 적은 고용인은 자신을 자영업자로 제시하면 보험료를 낮출 수 있게 된다.

어 휘

affluent *a.* 부유한
free ride 무임승차; 힘들이지 않고 얻은 이익, 공짜
commensurate with ~와 비례하는, 상응한
payroll *n.* 임금 대장, 종업원 명부
curb *v.* 억제하다
premium *n.* 보험료

Day 13

[Challenge 1]

문제 1

답 (2)

해설 본문에 소개된 시스템은 얼굴 전체를 스캔하지 않는다고 했기에 보기 항 (1)은 바른 내용이 아니다. 보기 항 (3)에서 두 사람은 문화인류학이 아닌 인지과학(cognitive science)과 관련된 분야의 사람이다. 본문의 'there is great variety in expression across both individuals and cultures' 부분과 보기 항 (4)의 'facial expressions are fairly fixed in number across cultures' 부분은 일치하지 않는다.

해석 어떤 악마가 인간의 마음에 숨어 있을지 누가 알겠는가? Prabir Bhattacharya와 그의 컴퓨터는 알지도 모른다. 그와 Concordia의 대학원생인 Abu Sayeed Sohail은 인간의 얼굴 표정을 감지하고 구분하는 컴퓨터 이미지 처리 시스템을 개발하고 있다. 이 시스템의 목적은 개인 사진을 찍고 분석하는 것이다. 만약 누군가 군중 중 아무나의 사진을 찍어 아주 빠르게 이 사진을 처리하면, 문제가 있는 사람을 인식할 가능성이 있다. 얼굴 표정은 사실 얼굴 전체와 관련된 것이 아니라 눈, 코, 입 근처 피부 밑 근육들의 특정한 배열과 관련이 있다. Bhattacharya와 Sohail의 시스템은 얼굴의 15개 주요 지점을 측정하고, 그런 다음 이 측정치와 거기에 일치하는 얼굴 표정과 대조한다. 비록 개인과 문화마다 표정이 다양하지만, 이 둘은 비교적 보편적인 7가지 기본 표정을 밝혀냈다.

어 휘

lurk v. 숨어있다   process v. 처리하다
detect v. 발견하다   classify v. 분류하다
facial a. 얼굴의, 앞면의
random a. 무작위의, 닥치는 대로 하는
crowd n. 군중, 인파(throng)   potential n. 가능성, 잠재
identify v. 확인하다, 알아보다   problematic a. 문제가 있는
entire a. 전체의, 온   specific a. 구체적인, 특정한
muscle n. 근육, 힘, 근력   measure v. 측정하다, 재다
identifiable a. 인식 가능한, 알아볼 수 있는
variety n. 여러 가지, 갖가지, 각양각색, 다양성
universal a. 일반적인, 보편적인

[Challenge 2]

문제 1

답 (3)

해설 보기 항 (4)의 오답을 피해야 한다. 당연히 제시된 문장의 재진술을 나타내는 in other words를 사용하는 것이 맞지만 (d)와 혼동할 여지가 있다. 이때 활용할 수 있는 것은 바로 in fact이다. in fact는 앞에서 진술된 내용을 더욱 자세히 부연하는 기능을 한다. 만약 보기 항 (4)의 자리에 제시문을 넣을 경우, 더 세부적인 사실이 먼저 나오게 되는 오류를 범하게 된다. 제시된 문장에서 뇌와 몸의 크기 사이의 관계를 다루고 있으므로 본문에서도 두 대상이 등장하는 곳을 찾아야 한다.

| 참고사항 |

글의 초반부에서 but(however)이 보일 경우 다음과 같은 두 가지 형태의 글일 가능성이 크다.

1) 일반 통념 비판

2) 앞에서 진술된 내용에 대한 상반된 주장 전개

어느 글에나 해당되는 중요한 것으로 but(however) 바로 뒤에 전개되는 내용이 글쓴이가 주장하는 요지에 해당한다는 점이다. 당연히 뒷받침 문장이 이어진다.

```
주장A _____.
    but ___ 주제문(주장 A와 반대되는 내용의 전개) __.
        뒷받침 문장
```

해석 나는 거대한 몸집을 가진 "stegosaurus"의 납작하고 작은 머리가, 상대적으로 머리가 무거운 우리의 주관적인 입장에서 작은 두뇌를 가지고 있다는 것을 부인하고 싶지 않다. 그러나 나는 우리가 이 짐승에게서 더 많은 것을 기대해서는 안 된다고 말하고 싶다. 우선 거대한 동물은 같은 종의 작은 동물에 비해 상대적으로 작은 뇌를 가지고 있다. 같은 종의 동물 사이에서는(예를 들자면 모든 파충류와, 모든 포유류) 뇌의 크기와 몸의 크기의 비율은 눈에 띄게 규칙적이다. 우리가 쥐에서 코끼리로 또는 작은 도마뱀에서 코모도 용으로 즉, 작은 동물에서 큰 동물로 이동하면서, 뇌의 크기는 증가하지만, 몸이 커지는 속도만큼 그렇게 빠르지는 않다. 다시 말해, 몸은 뇌보다 빠르게 성장하고, 거대한 동물은 몸의 무게에 비해 뇌의 무게의 비율이 낮다. 사실 뇌는 몸보다 약 3분의 2만큼밖에 빨리 자라지 않는다. 거대한 동

물이 같은 종의 작은 동물보다 항상 더 어리석다고 믿을 만한 이유가 없기에, 거대한 동물이 상대적으로 작은 뇌를 가지고 있어도 작은 동물만큼 잘할 수 있기에 작은 뇌가 필요하다고 결론을 지어야 한다. 만약 이러한 관계를 인식하지 않으면, 특히 공룡과 같은 거대한 동물의 정신 능력을 과소평가하게 될 가능성이 크다.

어휘

flatten *v.* 평평하게 하다   **minuscule** *a.* 아주 작은; 하잘것없는
top-subjective *a.* 상부가 무거운
perspective *n.* 전망; 시각, 견지
assert *v.* ① 단언하다, 역설하다; 강력히 주장하다 ② (권리 따위를) 주장[옹호]하다; (~ oneself) 제 주장을 세우다
beast *n.* 짐승   **correlation** *n.* 상호 관계
kindred *a.* ① 혈연의, 친척 관계의 ② 유사한, 같은 성질의
reptile *n.* 파충류의 동물   **conclude** *v.* ~에 결말을 짓다
underestimate *v.* 실제보다 낮게[적게] 어림하다

[Challenge 3]

문제 1

답 (2)

해설 본문의 첫 번째 문장과 마지막 문장에 글쓴이의 견해가 드러난다.

문제 2

답 (3)

해설 본문의 요지는 '의료보험보다 사람이 살고 일하는 환경이 한 나라의 건강 상태를 결정짓는다'는 내용이다. 이러한 견해로 보아 글쓴이는 외적인 사회 결정 요인(social determinant)을 아주 중요시 여기는 것을 알 수 있다. 의료 보험에 대한 글쓴이의 견해는 마지막 문장에 활용된 비교급에서 알 수 있듯이, 의료 보험은 부차적인 요소이지 결정적 요인은 아니라고 말하고 있다. 'while crucial to individual survival'에서도 알 수 있듯이, 보기 (4)와 같이 의료 보험 자체를 부정적으로 보아 없애는 것을 글쓴이의 주장으로 보는 것은 논리적 비약이다.

해석 Elizabeth H. Bradley와 Lauren Taylor는 '건강의 사회적 결정 요인'이란 말을 언급하진 않았지만, 어떤 나라에서든, 어떤 집단의 건강 상태는 사람들이 살고 일하는 환경이 결정짓는다는 심오한 진리를 잘 드러낸다. 이와 함께 직감에 반하는 진리가 도출된다. 우선, 건강 보험은 개인의 생존에 필수적이기는 하지만 기껏해야 국민 건강에 최소한의 공헌만을 할 뿐이다. 둘째, 대부분의 사회·경제 정책은 사실상 보건 정책이라 할 수 있는데, 이는 이러한 정책이 사회 결정 요인에 영향을 미치기 때문이다. 완벽한 미국의 건강 보험 제도조차도 (현재의 우리 제도는 고사하고) 그 자체로는 건강이 심각할 정도로 편재된 현상을 고칠 수 없다. 나의 동료들과 내가 1960년대 미시시피의 델타에 있던 최초의 지역 보건센터에서 일할 때, 우리 의사들은 많은 생명을 구하고, 이들의 엄청난 고통을 경감시켰다. 우리는 농장의 무너지는 오두막을 고치고, 위생 변소를 지었다. 지독한 빈곤과 실업과 영양실조에 직면해, 우리는 주민들로 하여금 수십 톤의 채소를 재배하는 협동 농장을 만들고, 직업과 교육의 길을 열어주었다. 이러한 개입이 생명을 살리고, 고통을 줄이며 우리가 대상으로 삼은 주민들의 건강을 향상시키는 데 우리의 의과적 치료보다 훨씬 더 나은 성과를 냈다.

어휘

counterintuitive *a.* 직감에 반하는
determinant *n.* 결정자, 결정 요소
abysmal *a.* 심연의, 끝없이 깊은
shack *n.* 오두막, 낡아빠진 집

[Challenge 4]

문제 1

답 (3)

해설 본문 마지막에서 확인할 수 있듯이, 미국이 아닌 한국 교육이 창의성 부족과 지나친 사교육 조장으로 국민의 지속적인 비판을 받고 있다고 지적하고 있다. 보기 항 (3)은 잘못된 진술이다.

해석 미국 대통령 오바마는 화요일 미국의 아이들이 극심한 국제 경쟁의 시대에서 살아남도록 돕기 위해 보충 수업과 방과 후 교육 활동을 받아들이는 데 한국을 살펴보도록 미국에 요구했다. 그는 우리의 아이들이 매년 한국의 아이들보다 한 달 이상 적게 학교에서 보낸다고 말했다. "이것은 21세기 경제를 위해 우리 아이들을 준비시키는 방법이 아니다."라며 오바마는 최근 수십 년간의 최악의 불경기에 대처하기 위한 경기 부양책인 7천 8백 7십 억 달러 중, 4백 10억 달러를 할당한 미국의 교육 체제의 전면적인 개혁의 필요성을 강조하면서 이렇게 말했다. "우리는 미국 아이들이 일과가 끝나고 집에서 땅을 갈아야 했던, 농부들의 나라였을 때 계획된 수업 일정을 더 이상 허용할 수는 없다."고 그는 말했다. 오바마 미 대통령은 미국인들이 "여름 활동이 되었든지, 이를 원하는 아이들을 위한 보충 수업을 통해서든지 방과 후 교육 활동을 확대할 뿐만 아니라, 더 많은 시간을 포함하는 수업 시수에 대해서 다시 생각해보기"를 요구했다. 오바마의 이런 언급은 한국의 교육 체제가 창의성이 부족하고, 사교육에 지나친 의존을 보이는 이유로 국민의 지속적인 비판을 받고 있는 상황에서 많은 한국 사람들에게 충격으로 다가왔다.

어휘

call for ~을 요구하다, ~을 필요로 하다
adopt *v.* (의견·방침·조치 따위를) 채용[채택]하다, 골라잡다
keen *a.* (경쟁·고통·식욕 따위가) 격렬한

remark *n.* 소견, 비평, 단평   sweeping *a.* 전면적인, 철저한
earmark *v.* (자금 따위를 특정한 용도에) 책정하다
recession *n.* (일시적인) 경기 후퇴(slump)
plow *v.* (쟁기·괭이로) 갈다(till); 갈아 일구다
private tutoring [교육학] 과외공부

[Challenge 5]

문제 1

답 (1)

해설 문은 중독이 정신 건강, 즉 성격에 미치는 영향력을 설명하는 글이다. 요약하자면, '마약 – 뇌의 화학물질에 영향 – 뇌의 특정한 구조 변화에 영향 – 급격한 성격의 변화'로 설명하고 있다. 따라서 보기 항 (1)이 가장 적절하다.

문제 2

답 (1)

해설 극단적 표현이 들어간 보기 항 (1)과 같은 내용은 본문에 명시되어 있지 않는 한 정답이 아닐 가능성이 크다. 본문에서 헤로인이 니코틴보다 더 유해한 중독 물질이긴 하나 그것이 가장 해롭다는 말을 하진 않았다.

해석 중독은 어떤 물질을 얼마나 사용하느냐에 따라 달라질 수는 있지만 다양한 방식으로 한 개인의 성격과 행동에 영향을 미친다. 어떤 물질은 다른 물질보다 정신 건강에 더 큰 영향을 미치는데, 예를 들자면, 헤로인은 니코틴보다 더 강하며, 뇌에 더 큰 영향을 미친다. 추가적으로 우리 모두는 각자 심리적 구성에 있어서 구별이 되는데, 이것은 어떤 두 사람도 같은 방식으로 영향을 받지 않는다는 것을 의미한다. 따라서 동일한 물질을 사용하더라도 어떤 사람은 다른 사람보다 더 큰 피해를 입게 되는데, 이는 주로 뇌의 화학물질로 인한 것이다. 그렇다면 이러한 중독이 한 사람의 정신 건강과 행위에 어떻게 작용하는가? 가장 눈에 띄는 증상은 이들이 전혀 다른 성격을 드러내는 방식으로 행동한다는 점이다. 말수가 적어지거나 아니면 의도적으로 공격적이게 된다. 자해하거나, 거짓말, 사기 또는 절도를 범한다. 또는 가족과 친구보다 자신의 중독의 필요성을 더욱 우위에 두게 된다. 다른 예로, 편집증, 불면증, 자존감 상실 또는 자신과 타인에 대한 불신이 있다. 반면 이들은 오직 자신의 요구만 중요하고, 다른 이들의 요구는 중요하지 않듯 교만하고 무례하게 행동할지도 모른다. 중독이 점차 심해지면, 가족과 친구들을 기피하고, 오히려 자신이 모르는 사람과 시간을 보낸다. 뇌의 화학물질은 중독에 의해서 영향을 받는데, 예를 들면, 메트암페타민(crystal meth; 신종 마약), 암페타민(각성제), 마리화나(cannabis), 엑스터시를 복용한다거나 지나친 음주가 있다. 이러한 것들은 한 사람의 뇌의 특정한 구조를 변형시키는 영향력을 가지고 있어 그 사람의 성격에도 급격한 영향을 미친다.

어휘

addiction *n.* 중독, 탐닉   substance *n.* 물질(material); 물체
heroin *n.* 헤로인(모르핀제; 진정제·마약)
psychological *a.* 심리(상)의, 심리학적인; 정신적인
secretive *a.* 숨기는, 말을 잘 하지 않는
paranoia *n.* [정신의학]편집병(偏執病)
self-esteem *n.* 자존; 자부(심), 자만(심)
arrogant *a.* 거드럭거리는, 거만[오만]한
uncaring *a.* 부주의한, 멍한
worsen *v.* 악화하다, 악화시키다
withdraw *v.* 물러나다, 떠나다
personality *n.* 성격, 인격; 인물

[Challenge 6]

문제 1

답 (1)

해설 막스 웨버는 청교도 정신과 자본주의 정신의 발달과의 관계를 중요시 여긴 것을 다음의 본문에서 확인할 수 있다.

> connection that Max Weber drew between Protestantism and the development of the spirit of modern capitalism

문제 2

답 (2)

해설 본문에서 Jere Cohen은 막스 웨버가 주장한 청교도와 자본주의 정신 사이의 관계성에 문제를 제기한 것을 볼 수 있다. 보기 항 (3)은 막스 웨버가 아닌 Jere Cohen의 주장이다.

해석 AJS에 실린 Jere Cohen의 글인 "르네상스 시대 이탈리아에 존재한 합리적 자본주의"는 막스 웨버가 청교도주의와 현대 자본주의 정신의 발달 사이에 이끌어 낸 열띤 논쟁의 연관성에 아주 중요한 새로운 이의를 제기한다. Cohen의 주장은 어떤 특정하지 않은 일반적인 의미에서 자본주의가 청교도주의보다 더 오래된 것이라는 것을 주장하는 것이 아니라 "웨버의 관점에서 현대 자본주의는 종교 개혁 이전의 가톨릭 국가에 이미 존재하고 있었다"는 것을 보여주기 위함이다. 이런 도전은 "자본주의" 또는 "합리주의"라는 사상의 개념적 분석과 재작업에 기초하기보다는 종교개혁 이전의 이탈리아의 역사적 연구에서 가져온 방대한 자료의 전개에 기초한다.

어휘

article *n.* 기사; 글
rational *a.* 이성적인; 합리적인
capitalism *n.* 자본주의
Renaissance *n.* 르네상스
modern *a.* 현대의; 근대의
intention *n.* 의향; 의지; 목적
nspecified *a.* 명시되지 않은
Protestantism *n.* (개)신교
conceptual *a.* 개념상의
notion *n.* 관념; 개념; 생각
rationality *n.* 합리성
deployment *n.* 전개; 배치
mass *n.* (양이) 많은
data *n.* 자료; 데이터
historical *a.* 역사(상)의

[Challenge 7]

문제 1

답 (4)

해설 본문은 부르디외가 주장한 허비투스에 관한 내용이다. 보기 항 (4)와 같이 내재화된 허비투스와 분리된다는 내용도 없거니와 한번 내재화된 허비투스를 버린다는 개념도 본문과 일치하지 않는다. 이는 본문에서 허비투스를 내재화된 생산양식으로 보고 무의식적으로 규칙적인 행동, 문화 등을 다시 재생산하는 특징을 기술하고 있기 때문이다.

문제 2

답 (4)

해설 접속사를 넣는 문제이다. 앞에서 전개된 내용과 빈칸이 들어간 내용과의 관계를 살펴보자.

> In Bourdieu's writings there are countless definitions and formulations of the term. ___(a)___ most simply put, habitus is an internalized structure or set of structures

빈칸 앞에는 부르디외 글에서 이 용어(허비투스)에 관한 끝없는 정의를 내리고 있다고 한 후, 그중 간략한 하나의 개념만을 제시하고 있다. 여기서 주목할 것은 '끝없는 정의'와 '간략한 하나의 개념'의 대조이다. 이를 우리말로 풀어쓰자면, '허비투스의 개념은 부르디외가 자신의 글에서 끝없이 다양한 정의를 내리지만, 간단히 말해서(하나로 요약하자면)...'이다. 보기 항 (4)가 정답이다.

문제 3

답 (1)

해설 본문은 부르디외가 주장한 허비투스에 대한 간략한 정의를 내리는 글이다.

해석 'Habitus'는 부르디외의 전체 언어 개념의 요체로, 적어도 이로 인해 유명하다. 부르디외의 글에는 이 용어에 대한 정의와 표현들이 수없이 많이 나온다. 그러나 아주 간단히 말해 'habitus'란 한 개인이 자기가 속한 세상 내에서 어떻게 행동하고 반응할지를 결정짓는 내재화된 구조(기존의 외적 구조에서 얻어지는)로 Thompson이 표현한 것처럼 '어떠한 "규칙"에 의해서 의식적으로 조정되거나 지켜지는 것 없이 규칙적으로 발생하는 행위, 인식 그리고 태도를 만들어 내도록' 작용한다. Outline of a Theory of Practice 에서 부르디외는 'habitus'를 사회 세상의 좀 더 폭넓은 객관적인 구조와의 관계 밖에서 발생하는 '지속적이고, 전위 가능한 성향'을 가진 생성 체제로 정의한다. 생각하고, 느끼고, 행동하는 지속적인 성향과 구조화된 경향의 내적 집합체로서 'habitus'는 개인의 행위에 조직성, 통일성과 일관성을 제공하는 기능의 '지휘자 없는 조정'의 특성을 지닌다.

어휘

arguably *ad.* 거의 틀림없이, 논란의 여지가 있지만
lynchpin *n.* 핵심이 되는 인물[것]
entire *a.* 전체의
corpus *n.* 언어 자료; 말뭉치
internalize *v.* 내면화하다
external *a.* 외부의
phrase *n.* 표현
perception *n.* 인식
co-ordinate *v.* 조정하다; 편성하다
durable *a.* 오래 견디는
proclivity *n.* 경향
systematicity *n.* 체계성, 조직성
coherence *n.* 결합
consistency *n.* 일관성

[Challenge 8]

문제 1

답 (3)

해설 독점 판매상들은 더 많은 사람들이 경기와 돈을 챙길 수 있다는 점을 고려해 경기 연기를 주장한 것이다.

해석 Jeffrey T. Kuhner는 너무나 논란이 많고 눈으로 인해 취소된 NFL 게임을 다른 시간대로 연기하는 것에 대한 실질적인 조종자들, 즉 NFL 변호사와 특권 판매자를 간과하는 듯하다. 변호사들은 경기에 오다가 사고가 발생한 사람들이 소송을 걸 수 있다는 위험성을 검토한다. 그렇게 함으로 이들은 오히려 자신이 속한 단체 자체의 목적에 독이 된다. 특권 판매상들은 줄어든 좌석 수와 그로 인한 판매 부진을 바라보면서, 이 경기에 더 많은 사람들을 불러들일 수 있는 시간대로 연기하는 것을 로비 활동을 통해 강력히 주장할 것이다.

어휘

overlook *v.* 간과하다
postpone *v.* 연기하다(put off), 미루다
NFL 미국 프로 미식축구 연맹(National Football League)
concession *n.* (주로 정부에 의한) 허가, 면허, 특허, 이권(利權), 특권
examine *v.* 검토하다, 조사[심사]하다
lawsuit *n.* 소송
poison *v.* 나쁜 영향을 주다
lobby *v.* (의회 로비에서 의원에게) 압력을 가하다, 로비 운동하다; (의안을) 억지로 통과시키다
postponement *n.* 연기, 유예

Day 13

[Challenge 9]

문제 1

답 (2)

해설 첫 번째 문단은 다양한 부패가 있음을 설명하는 내용이고, 두 번째 문단은 구체적 예를 들어 정부 부패를 다루고 있다.

문제 2

답 (1)

해설 본문에서 언급된 정치 부패를 잠시 살펴보면 다음과 같다.

* buying votes → frame-up ballot
* obtaining financial support by giving rewards only accessible by governments → Illegal fund- raising
* to the elimination of people standing in the way of those in power → A purge of dissident members

본문에서 제시된 내용과 같은 맥락을 이루지 못하는 보기 항은 (1)에 해당한다.

해석 부패는 하나의 절대적인 상태가 아니다. 이것은 노골적인 독재자에 의해서 행해진 폭력 행위에서부터, 왜곡된 법과 완벽한 도덕 사회에서 비열한 짓으로 간주하는 행위에 눈감은 것에 이르기까지 다양하다. 정치 부패는 정부에 의해서만 접근 가능한 대가를 제공함으로써 표를 사거나 재정 지원을 얻는 것에서부터, 정적의 제거에까지 이르는 모든 것을 의미할 수 있다.

1993년 다양한 정부의 계층을 포함하는 심각한 부패가 있다는 주장이 호주, 볼리비아, 브라질, 불가리아, 프랑스, 아이티, 인도, 이탈리아, 일본, 말레이시아, 파라과이, 남아프리카, 스페인 그리고 미국과 같은 다양한 나라에서 표면화되었다. 브라질에서 이 주장은 대통령 사퇴와 탄핵을 위한 잇따른 조치를 야기했다. 이탈리아에서는 정치 지도자가 사퇴를 하고, 전 총리를 포함한 정치인과 이탈리아 마피아 간의 관계에 의혹이 제기되면서 중요한 청문회가 시작되었다. 일본의 경우, 총리는 불신임을 받고 해임되었다.

어 휘

corruption *n.* 부패, 타락
range *v.* (범위가 ~에서 …에) 이르다   violence *n.* 폭력
perpetrate *v.* 행하다   outright *a.* 노골적인
dictator *n.* 독재자   blind eye *n.* 눈 감아주기
turn to ~로 되다   offensive *a.* 불쾌한
financial *a.* 재무상의   reward *n.* 대가
accessible *a.* 접근 가능한   elimination *n.* 제거
allegation *n.* 주장
surface *v.* (숨어있던 것이) 드러나다, 표면화하다
diverse *a.* 가지각색의   resignation *n.* 사임
subsequent *a.* 차후의   impeachment *n.* 탄핵
resign *v.* 사임하다   judicial *a.* 사법상의
inquiry *n.* 조사, 취조   instigate *v.* 실시하게 하다
allege *v.* 혐의를 주장하다   former *a.* 이전의
prime minister *n.* 총리   discredit *v.* 신임을 떨어뜨리다
remove *v.* 해임하다

[Challenge 10]

문제 1

답 (2)

해설 본문의 중반부에 나오는 실화는 첫 번째 문장에서 제시된 주제를 뒷받침하는 구체적 예가 된다. 이야기 속에서 'making'과 'manufacturing'의 차이점이 어떻게 드러나는지 주의하면서 읽어야 한다.

문제 2

답 (1)

해설 앞에서 Mr. Maudslay는 해군 위원회의 요청을 받아들이기를 꺼려했지만, 이후 시험 삼아 시도하는 모습이 나오므로 'however'를 넣는 것이 가장 적절하다.

문제 3

답 (3)

해설 'manufacture'라는 말은 대량 생산을 하는 경우에만 적용하는 단어라고 본문 맨 첫 부분에 설명이 되어 있다. 'manufactured'가 아니라 'made'로 하는 것이 적절하다.

문제 4

답 (4)

해설 (4)에서 도구(장비)로 인해 비용이 하락한 것은 맞지만, 더 많은 도구를 만들어 비용을 더 떨어뜨렸다는 내용은 없다.

해석 'making'과 'manufacturing'이란 단어 사이에는 상당한 차이점이 존재한다. 전자는 적은 양을 만드는 것을 지칭하는 반면, 후자는 아주 많은 양의 개별 물건을 만드는 것을 지칭한다. 이 둘의 차이점은 도구와 기계 수출(Export of Tools and Machinery)에 관해 하원으로 구성된 위원회 앞으로 제출된 증거자료에 잘 드러나 있다. 이 사안에서 Maudslay는 그가 해군 위원회에 의해서 선박용 물탱크를 만들어 달라는 요청을 받았는데, 그는 이것이 자신의 일과는 좀 벗어나는 것이 아닌가 하는 생각이 들어서, 이것을 하기가 좀 꺼려졌다. 그러나 그는 시험 삼아 하나를 만드는 것에 착수했다. 대못이 들어갈 구멍을 프레스를 이용해서 손으로 펀치를 내고, 각 물탱크에 필요한 1,680개의 구멍은 7실링이 들었다. 아주 많은 양이 필요한 해군 위원회는 그가 여러 달 동안에 일주일에 40개의 물탱크를 공급해 줄 것을 제안했다. 엄청난 주문으로 인해 대량 생산을 시작하고 이 특별한 일을 위한 도구를 만드는 것이 그럴 만큼의 가치가 있게 되었다. 그래서 Maudslay는 만약 위원회가 그에게 물탱크 2,000개를 주문하면, 일주일에 80개씩 제공하겠다고 제

안했다. 주문을 받고 그는 도구를 만들고, 이것을 이용해서 각 물통에 필요한 대못 구멍을 뚫는 비용을 7실링에서 9펜스까지 내렸다. 그는 6개월간 일주일에 98개의 물탱크를 공급했으며, 각 물탱크에 책정된 가격은 17파운드에서 15파운드로 내렸다.

어 휘

considerable *a.* 상당한, 중요한
manufacture *v.* 생산하다   refer *v.* 의미하다
individual *a.* 개개의   illustrate *v.* 설명하다
state *v.* 말하다, 진술하다
unwilling *a.* 내키지 않는, 마지못해하는
undertake *v.* 떠맡다   trial *n.* 시도
punch *n.* 구멍 뚫는 기구 *v.* (뾰족한 것으로) 구멍을 뚫다
press *n.* 압축기   magnitude *n.* 크기
commence *v.* 시작하다   express *a.* 특별한; 신속한
rate *n.* 비율   expense *n.* 비용, 지출
reduce *v.* 축소하다   charge *v.* 부과하다

Day 14

[Challenge 1]

문제 1

답 (2)

해설 본문에 제시되는 실험을 정확히 파악하도록 한다. 12마리의 야생 까마귀를 잡았을 때 쓴 마스크와 먹이를 줄 때 쓴 마스크가 달랐다. 각각의 마스크를 보여주었을 때 뇌의 활동 영역이 달랐다는 점에서 까마귀는 시각적 인식과 함께 과거에 대한 기억을 활용해서 두려움의 대상을 인식할 수 있다는 것을 추론할 수 있다.

해석 까마귀는 얼굴을 잊지 않는다. 특히 자신들이 두려워하는 얼굴은 더욱 그러하다. 이제, 새의 뇌 활동 이미지를 통해 이들이 익숙한 얼굴을 볼 때 신경학적으로 어떤 반응을 보이는지가 밝혀졌다. 워싱턴 대학의 연구원들은 동일한 마스크를 쓰고 12마리의 야생 까마귀를 잡았다. 이들 과학자들은 한 달간 새 우리에 까마귀를 가두는 다른 '보호자' 가면을 쓰고 먹이를 주었다. 얼마 후 이 팀은 새에게 두 개의 다른 마스크를 쓴 인간들을 보여주면서 양자 단층촬영 장치를 이용하여 까마귀 뇌의 활동을 관측했다. 과학자들이 새를 잡을 때 썼던 '위협을 가하는' 마스크는 두려움과 관련된 뇌의 영역을 활성화시켰다. 반면 먹이를 줄 때 썼던 보호자 가면은 보상과 동기부여와 관련된 또 다른 영역을 활성화시켰다.

어 휘

don v. (옷·모자 따위를) 걸치다, 입다, 쓰다
associated with ~와 관련된

[Challenge 2]

문제 1

답 (4)

해설 본문에서 기술이 불필요한 사치를 조장한다는 내용은 드러나 있지 않다.

문제 2

답 (1)

해설 (a)를 제외한 모두는 현재의 성공을 위한 '밑거름'인 원인에 해당하는 사항이다. (a)는 앞의 것에 의해 이루어진 문명의 이기의 정도를 나타낸 말이다.

해석 거의 모든 계층의 사회가 소모하는 이 엄청난 양의 문명의 이기를 형성하는 데 사용된 도구와 기계의 고안을 이렇게 다양하고 완벽하게 이끌어 온 것보다 우리나라를 더욱 다른 나라와 구별되게 하는 단일의 사건은 아마도 존재하지 않을 것이다. 엄청난 양의 인내를 필요로 하는 생각과 반복되는 실험 그리고 천재들의 행복한 노력에 의해 우리의 제품이 만들어지고 현재의 최고의 상태까지 이르게 된 것은 거의 상상할 수조차 없는 일이다(그만큼 비교할 수 없이 위대한 것임). 우리가 살고 있는 방을 둘러보거나, 대도시의 번잡한 도시를 장식한 모든 문명의 이기와 인간이 원하는 사치품을 전한 가게를 둘러보면, 우리는 역사에서 지금의 우월성의 길로 점진적으로 이르게 한 일련의 실패를 발견하게 된다. 그리고 우리는 심지어 그것들 중 가장 하찮은 것을 만드는 기술에 있어서도 그 단순함에 감탄하게 되거나 또는 예상치 못한 결과에 의해 관심을 집중하게 되는 과정을 발견하게 된다.

어 휘

distinguish v. 구별하다
remarkably ad. 두드러지게, 현저하게, 몹시, 매우
extent n. 정도, 크기   perfection n. 완벽, 완성
contrivance n. 고안, 발명
consume v. 소모하다, 먹다, 소비하다
community n. 주민, 주민 사회, 공동체
exertion n. 노력, 행사, 분투   genius n. 천재성, 천재
manufacture n. 제조, 생산   excellence n. 뛰어남, 탁월함
inhabit v. 살다, 거주하다
storehouse n. 창고, 정보, 지식 등의 보고
luxury n. 호화스러움, 사치   deck v. 꾸미다, 장식하다
crowded a. 붐비는, 가득 찬   a series of 일련의
notice v. 알아차리다, 인지하다
insignificant a. 중요하지 않은
process n. 과정, 절차   calculate v. (~하도록) 만들어져 있다
admiration n. 감탄, 존경   simplicity n. 간단함, 평이함
rivet v. 고정시키다

[Challenge 3]

문제 1

답 (2)

해설 본문은 대공황 시절 모래 먼지 폭풍이 농부에게 미친 영향을 기술하는 글이다. (1)은 지나치게 포괄적이며, (3)의 경우 본문에 드러나는 인과적 현상을 제대로 설명해 주지 못한다. 보기 (4)도 적절하지 못하다.

해석 이전의 불황에서 농부들은 통상 공황의 심각한 피해를 받지 않았는데, 이는 적어도 먹을 양식은 스스로 구할 수 있었기 때문이다. 불행히도, 대공황 때에는 가뭄과 모래 먼지 폭풍이 대초원 지대를 강타했다. 수년간의 과도한 방목과 가뭄의 영향이 겹치면서 목초지가 사라져갔다. 표토가 바람에 노출되면서 강한 바람이 느슨한 모래를 수마일 휘몰아 날려버렸다. 모래 먼지 폭풍이 가는 길에 서 있는 모든 것을 파괴하면서, 농부들은 수확물을 얻지 못하는 상태가 되었다. 소작농의 경우 특히 심각한 피해를 받았다. 모래 먼지 폭풍이 닥치기 이전에도, 트랙터의 발명은 농사를 짓는 인력의 필요성을 급격하게 감소시켰다. 이러한 소작농들의 경우 씨앗을 사기 위해 돈을 빌려, 곡식을 거두면 이를 통해 돈을 갚는 식으로 대개 이미 빚을 지고 있는 상태였다. 모래 먼지 폭풍이 곡식에 피해를 입히게 되자, 소작농들은 자신과 가족을 먹여 살릴 수 없을 뿐 아니라 빚을 갚을 수도 없게 되었다. 그러자 은행은 이 소농장들에 대한 담보권을 행사하고, 농부의 가족들은 집도 없이 실직 상태가 되고 말았다.

어휘
depression *n.* 불황
horrendous *a.* 무서운, 끔찍한
topsoil *n.* 표토
foreclose *n.* 담보권을 실행하다

[Challenge 4]

문제 1

답 (3)

해설 본문은 문명이란 질서를 기반으로 세워진다고 말하고 있다. 본문 중반 이후 현대 문명의 위기라 할 수 있는 문제점으로 질서를 바로잡는 권위의 원칙이 심각하게 무너졌다(the principle of authority has been dangerously impaired)고 말하고 있다. 보기 항 (3)은 본문에서 발견할 수 있는 내용이 아니다.

문제 2

답 (4)

해설 문명의 기초가 되는 질서가 붕괴된 현재의 위험성을 제기한 후 글쓴이는 이러한 사회를 유지하기 위해 어떤 제안을 할지 생각해 본다. 글쓴이가 강조하는 사회란 바로 질서이다.

해석 내가 이해하기에 문명은 거의 질서와 같은 의미이다. 재산 분배, 가족 관계, 상속법 등과 같은 문제에 관해 우리가 얼마나 다른 견해를 가지든 간에, 내가 생각하기에 대부분의 우리는, 질서 없이는 우리가 생각하는 문명도 존재할 수 없다고 생각할 것이다. 인간은 미래를 내다볼 수 없기에 미래에 대한 걱정은 무익한 것이며 존재할 수 있는 최상의 세계에서 모든 것은 최상을 위한 것이라 낙관론자는 주장하

지만 최근 몇 년간 권위의 원칙이 위험할 정도로 손상을 입었다는 불편한 의심이 발생했으며, 이 사회를 유지하기 원한다면 사회가 재조직되어야 한다는 것은 분명하다.

어휘
civilization *n.* 문명; 문화
apprehend *v.* 염려하다; 이해하다
synonymous *a.* 동의어[유의어]의
distribution *n.* 분배; 배분, 분포
property *n.* 재산; 자산
domestic *a.* 가정의; 국내의
inheritance *n.* 상속, 유산
optimist *n.* 낙천주의자
contend *v.* 주장하다
foresee *v.* 예견하다; 미리 알다
futile *a.* 쓸데없는; 무익한
inevitably *ad.* 불가피하게; 필연적으로
recent *a.* 근래의; 최근의
suspicion *n.* 혐의, 의심
authority *n.* 권위; 권력
dangerously *ad.* 위험하게; 위태롭게
impair *v.* 해치다; 손상하다
cohere *v.* 밀착하다, 응집하다, 한데 모이다

[Challenge 5]

문제 1

답 (4)

해설 헌법에 국민 주권주의가 명시되어 있음에도 과거에는 소수 정치인들이 국민의 분노를 두려워한 나머지 투표권을 제한했는데, 이러한 투표권을 행사할 수 있는 조건을 열거하고 있다.

문제 2

답 (3)

해설 본문 마지막을 보면, 빚이 없는 100파운드 가치의 자유 부동산 소유자는 상원의원을 뽑을 투표권이 있는 것이지 상원의원석에 출마할 수 있다는 의미는 아니다.

문제 3

답 (1)

해설 헌법의 첫 조항을 말하는데, 'This'가 가리키는 대상을 찾도록 한다.

해석 주 의회의 구성원을 뽑는 사람들의 자격 조건은 참정권을 크게 제한했다. 이론적으로 모든 애국자는 국민의 자유권을 믿었으며, 헌법의 첫 번째 조항에서 "무슨 명목에 의해서든 국민으로부터 유래하거나 주어지지 않은 어떠한 권위도 국민에게 행사될 수 없다."라고 선언하고 있다. 이 굉장한 첫 번째 조항은 국민 주권을 보장하는 것이다. 그러나

실질적으로 헌법을 제정한 사람들은 왕의 폭정만큼이나 민중의 분노를 두려워했기에 소수에게 이 권한을 제한하는 것이 현명하다고 생각했다. 시가 20파운드의 자유 보유 부동산을 소유하거나 연 40실링의 전셋집을 보유한 성인 남자 시민은 하원의원 선출을 할 수 있으며, 빚이 없는 시가 100파운드의 자유부동산 소유자는 상원의원을 선출할 수 있었다.

어휘

qualification *n.* 자격, 권한, 조건 vote *v.* 투표하다
legislature *n.* 입법부, 입법기관
suffrage *n.* 투표(권); 참정권
theoretically *ad.* 이론적[성]으로 patriot *n.* 애국자
liberty *n.* 자유   article *n.* 조항, 조목
Constitution *n.* 헌법 declare *v.* 선언하다; 발표하다
authority *n.* 권위, 권력, 권한 pretence *n.* 구실, 핑계, 명목
derive *v.* 끌어내다; 기원을 찾다 (from)
grant *v.* 주다, 수여하다 exordium *n.* 첫머리, 서두
popular *a.* 대중의 sovereignty *n.* 주권, 종주권
practice *n.* 실행, 실천 passion *n.* 열정, 열애
multitude *n.* 다수, 군중, 군집
tyranny *n.* 포악, 폭정 deem *v.* ~으로 생각하다, 간주하다
possess *v.* 소유하다, 가지고 있다
freehold *n.* (부동산, 관직 따위의) 자유 보유(권)
rent *v.* 임대하다 tenement *n.* 집; 건물
yearly *a.* 매년의, 연1회의 shilling *n.* 실링(영국의 화폐 단위)
assemblyman *n.* 의원 debt *n.* 빚, 부채
senator *n.* 원로원 의원; (미국) 상원 의원

[Challenge 6]

문제 1

답 (4)

해설 본문을 읽고, 주제를 찾기 힘들 경우 문제에 주어진 보기 항의 내용을 바탕으로 본문과 비교하면서 답에 접근할 수 있다. 본문은 물에 살기 위해 물고기가 어떻게 자신의 몸을 적응했는지(물고기의 발달에 물이 미친 영향)를 다루는 내용이다. 보기 (1)의 경우 물고기와 온혈 동물의 비교라는 내용인데 본문과는 거리가 멀다. 보기 (2)의 경우 바닷물과 민물의 환경이 다르다는 내용인데, 이도 본문과 거리가 멀다. 보기 (3)도 본문과 무관한 주제에 해당한다. 본문의 내용이 정확히 파악이 되지 않아 답을 고르기 힘들 경우 문제의 보기 항을 함께 읽으면서 보기 항이 주제일 경우 본문과 같은 내용이 다뤄질지 생각해 보도록 한다.

해석 물속에서 사는 한 가지 이점은 물이 손쉽게 체중을 지탱해준다는 점이다. 따라서 물속에 사는 물고기는 대부분 무중력 상태에 있게 된다. 이러한 무중력 상태는 다시 말하면 두 가지를 의미한다. 첫째, 물고기는 약한 중력 상태에서 단순한 뼈 구조를 가지고도 잘 살아갈 수 있으며, 둘째, 물고기의 크기를 제약하는 요인이 실질적으로 제거된다는 것이다. 그러나 물속에서 사는 것에 한 가지 근본적으로 어려운 점이 있다. 물고기가 물속에서 이동하기 위해서는 실제로 물을 옆으로 밀어내야 한다. 대부분의 물고기는 뱀과 같은 동작으로 앞뒤로 흔들면서 이 일을 할 수 있다. 그다음, 물은 물고기의 좁아지는 측면을 따라 뒤로 흐르면서 꼬리 부분에서 좁아지는데, (이러한 과정이) 물고기가 전방으로 나아가는 데 도움을 준다. 납작하고 모난 형상은 물속에서 움직임을 어렵게 만들 뿐이다. 이런 이유로 물고기는 이와 같은 특수성에 대처할 수 있도록 멋지게 적응된 기본적인 형상을 가지고 있다.

어휘

in turn 이번에는, 또한
shove *v.* 밀고 나아가다, 밀어 제치다
wiggle *v.* (뒤)흔들다
close in 포위하다, 좁아지다

[Challenge 7]

문제 1

답 (4)

해설 글의 도입부에서 춤과 관련된 글임을 파악할 수 있고, however 이후 동물과 달리 인간은 상징적 표현으로 춤을 사용한다고 강조하면서 이러한 점을 드러내는 초기 인류가 행한 춤의 종류를 기술하고 있다. 본문은 상징적 표현인 춤과 그 형태에 관한 글이다. 이러한 점을 가장 잘 드러내는 제목은 보기 (4)이다.

문제 2

답 (1)

해설 'it is possible that dance developed along with the evolution of our species.'에서 보기 (1)를 추론할 수 있다.

해석 사람들이 언제 춤을 추기 시작했는지는 알려지지 않았다. 하지만, 춤은 우리 인류의 진화와 함께 발전했을 것이다. 많은 동물은 인간의 구애 및 놀이와 비슷한 환경에서 춤과 같은 움직임을 구사한다. 그러나 이와 같은 의식에는 인간의 춤에 존재하는 의식적인 상징의 사용이 빠져 있다. 이런 종류의 춤에 관한 정보를 얻기 위해 오늘날 우리가 참고할 수 있는 여러 원시 집단들이 있다. 예를 들면, 호주 원주민과 여러 아프리카 부족들 중에 재주가 있는 사람들은 다

양한 춤을 보여준다. 그들의 춤이 외부인에게는 때로 단순하게 보일 수 있지만 대개 그렇지 않다. 보통 이 춤은 고도로 세련된 종교적 또는 철학적 관념이 수반된 복잡한 의식의 일부를 구성한다.

어 휘

along with ~와 함께
courtship n. 구애, 구혼
aborigine n. 오스트레일리아 원주민

[Challenge 8]

문제 1

답 (3)

해설 미국 영사에게 도움을 받은 것은 West Point가 아니라 그가 반정부 그리스에 가담했을 때 있었던 일이다.

문제 2

답 (3)

해설 다음 본문에서 확인할 수 있다.

> the birth of a son to his adopted father, by a second marriage, an event which cut off his expectations as an heir

해석 영국에서 고전 교육을 받은 후, 그는 고국으로 돌아와 버지니아 대학에 입학한 후, 화려한 정규 과정을 마친 후 최종 학기에 반에서 수석으로 졸업하게 되었다. 그 후 그는 그리스 반정부 시위에 철없이 가담했다가, 시위가 성 피터스버그에서 끝나고, 거기서 여권이 없는 관계로 어려움에 처해진다. 이 상황에서 그는 미국의 영사의 도움으로 집에 돌아가게 된다. 그는 이제 West Point에 있는 군 사관학교에 들어가고, 거기서 그의 양아버지가 재혼을 통해 아들을 낳았다는 소식이 전해지자 퇴학 처분을 받는다. 이 사건으로 인해 그는 상속자로서 유산이 끊기게 된다. 유언장에 자신의 이름이 거론되지 않은 Allan의 죽음은 곧 이러한 측면에서 모든 의혹을 사라지게 했으며, 즉시 그는 경제적 후원을 얻기 위해서 글을 쓰기로 결심했다.

어 휘

classical a. 고전적인, 정통파의
extravagant a. 사치스러운   follow v. 좇다, 계속하다
reformation n. 개혁, 개정, 개심
extremity n. 끝, 말단, 파멸   graduate v. 졸업하다 (from)
honor n. (대학 등의) 우등   boyish a. 아이 같은, 유치한
join v. 결합하다, 합류하다   fortune n. 운, 재산
insurgent a. 모반하는, 폭동을 일으키는 n. 폭도, 반란자
passport n. 여권
rescue v. 구조하다, 보호하다, (법적으로) 탈환하다

consul n. 영사   military academy n. 군사학교
dismissal n. 면직, 해고, 퇴학
adopt v. 양자로 삼다, 채용하다; 채택하다
marriage n. 결혼(식)   cut off 떼어 버리다, 삭제하다
expectation n. 예상, 기대, 희망
heir n. 상속인, 후계자   mention v. 말하다, 언급하다
relieve v. (곤궁 등에서) 해방시키다, 구제하다
regard n. (~에 대한) 관심, 고려   commit v. (~에) 전념하다
authorship n. 저작자임, 원작자
support n. 부양; 경제적 후원자; 원조자

[Challenge 9]

문제 1

답 (4)

해설 보기 항 (4)와 관련하여 아래 본문을 확인해 보자.

> Modern Europeans believe that tobacco was introduced from America in the time of Queen Isabella and Queen Elizabeth.

즉, 본문에선 현대 유럽인들이 담배가 미국에서 도입된 것으로 생각하고 있다고 기술하고 있다.

문제 2

답 (3)

해설 relate는 '전하다, 이야기하다'의 뜻으로 쓰이고 있다.

문제 3

답 (2)

해설 손을 씻는 행위는 마치 종교적 의무와 유사한 널리 받아들여진 국가적 습관이라고 했으므로 "사회적 의무"가 정답으로 가장 적절하다. 사회적으로 존중되고, 준수되는 일반적인 문화적 관행이다.

해석 아즈텍 사람들 사이에서, 결혼한 여자는 남편에게 극진하고 정중한 대우를 받았다. 여성들은 고대 그리스와 마찬가지로 하녀와 음악가가 들려주는 발라드와 사랑 이야기를 들으면서 방적과 자수를 놓는 일을 했다. 연회나 다른 사교 모임에서 여성은 남성과 동등한 몫을 지녔다. 때로 이러한 잔치는 사치스러운 준비를 하고, 수많은 하인을 대동하여 성대하게 열리곤 했다. 고대와 현대의 멕시코인들은 항상 열정적으로 꽃을 좋아했으며, 대부분의 경우, 홀과 뜰만이 온갖 빛깔의 달콤한 향기를 내는 꽃으로 온통 뒤덮여 (strewed) 장식되어 있을 뿐 아니라 방마다 향기가 스며 있었다. 하객은 앉으면서 자신들 앞에 놓여 있는 물병과 냅킨을 발견할 수 있었는데, 이는 식사 전후에 손을 씻는 것이 거의 종교적 의무에 가까운 국가적 습관이기 때문이었다. 현대 유럽인들은 담배가 이사벨라와 엘리자베스 여왕 때 미국에서 도입된 것으로 생각하지만, 이 시기 이전에 아즈텍

사람들은 연회에서 회중에게 '향기로운 궐련'을 지인에게 제공했는데, 이것은 "파이프 안에 향기로운 물질을 섞거나, 거북이 껍질 또는 은 튜브에 넣은 담배의 형태로 제공되었다." 식후 연초는 '낮잠'에 들기 위한 당연한 준비 과정이었다. 현대 멕시코의 후손과 같이 아즈텍 여인들도 멕시코인들이 '담배'라 부르는 것을 향유했는지는 알려져 있지 않다.

어휘

respectfully *ad.* 공손하게　feminine *a.* 여성의
occupation *n.* 직업　spin *v.* ~을 잣다[방적하다]
embroidery *n.* 자수(법)
ballad *n.* 발라드　relate *v.* 이야기하다
maiden *n.* 처녀, 아가씨　banquet *n.* 성대한 연회
social *a.* 사교적인　entertainment *n.* 오락, 여흥, 접대
share *n.* 몫　festivity *n.* 축제 행사
costly *a.* 많은 비용이 드는　preparation *n.* 준비, 대비
numerous *a.* 수많은　attendant *n.* 종업원, 하인
passionately *ad.* 열렬히, 격렬하게
fond *a.* 좋아하는, 애정을 느끼는
strew *v.* 흩다, 흩뿌리다　adorn *v.* 꾸미다, 장식하다
profusion *n.* 다량, 풍성함　blossom *n.* 꽃
hue *n.* 빛깔, 색조　odor *n.* 냄새　perfume *n.* 향수, 향기
scent *v.* 향기가 나다　ewer *n.* 큰 물병(단지)
cotton *n.* 목화, 면직물　habit *n.* 버릇, 습관
religious *a.* 종교의, 신앙심이 깊은, 독실한
obligation *n.* 의무　fragrant *a.* 향기로운, 향긋한
weed *n.* 궐련, 담배　aromatic *a.* 향이 좋은
substance *n.* 물질, 실체, 본질
insert *v.* 삽입하다, 끼워 넣다
tortoise-shell *n.* 거북이 껍질
preliminary *a.* 예비의 *n.* 예비 행위　siesta *n.* 낮잠
nap *n.* 낮잠　descendant *n.* 자손, 후예
appreciate *v.* 진가를 알아보다(인정하다); 감상하다, 음미하다
tobacco *n.* 담배

[Challenge 10]

문제 1

답 (2)

해설 학교 내 건강 검진이 반드시 필요함을 다루는 글이다.

문제 2

답 (3)

해설 본문 마지막 부분에서 건강 검진 제도를 시행한 이래 긍정적인 결과가 현저하게 나타났다고 말하면서, 이러한 결과를 통해서 부모와 교사가 이 제도의 유용성을 인식하게 되었다고 말하고 있다.

문제 3

답 (1)

문제 4

답 (3)

해설 보기 항 (3)은 본문에서 말하는 건강 검진의 결과와는 정반대의 현상이다.

해석 건강 진단(medical inspection)은 교육자와 의사가 함께 손을 잡고 펼치는 학교 생활의 연장으로, 학생 한 명 한 명이 국가에서 제공하는 무상 교육을 최대한 활용할 수 있도록 건강하고 활력이 넘치는 환경을 보장하기 위한 것이다. 이것의 목적은 학교 아이들에게 더 건강한 환경을 제공하고 질병으로부터 (이들을) 보호하며, 이들이 더 건강하고, 행복하며 더 진취적이게 만드는 것이다. 이것은 아이의 신체적 상태와 정신적 상태 사이의 밀접한 관련성과, 교육이 결과적으로 건강한 환경에 의존한다는 인식에 기반을 둔 것이다. 건강 검진 운동이 여전히 미국에서 그 초기 단계에 머물러 있던 때에 클리블랜드에서 건강 검진의 가치가 인정되었다. 다른 곳과 마찬가지로 여기서 학교 아이들의 신체적 건강을 지키는 것에 대한 중대한 필요성에 대한 이러한 갑작스러운 인식은 현대 도시 환경에서 의무 교육 자체가 의무적 질병이 된다는 것을 발견한 것에서 나왔다. 자체적인 보호를 위해서 이 주는 모든 어린이가 학교에 다녀야 한다고 선포했으며, 가난하거나 부자거나 똑똑하건 좀 우둔하건 건강하든 아프든 모두 모아 강력하고 차별이 없는 의무 교육 기관을 운영하고 있다. 이 목적은 이러한 아이들이 건강한 정신을 소유하는 것을 보장하는 데 있다. 바로 과거에 학교 교육을 통해 건강하지 않은 신체를 가지도록 하는 눈에 보이지 않는 결과가 조성이 되었다는 것이다. 건강 검진은 이러한 환경을 개선하려고 고안되었다. 이것의 목적은 바로 예방과 치료이다. 이것이 설립된 이래, 건강 검진의 긍정적인 결과가 현저했다. 전염병은 미리 예방되고 차단되었다. 아이들의 청결이 눈에 띄도록 향상되었다. 교사와 학부모는 새로운 제도 아래 아이들이 위험하고 실제적인 전염병이 만연한 시대에, 학교에서 계속적으로 공부하는 것이 안전하다는 것을 알게 된 것이다.

어휘

medical *a.* 의학의, 의술의　inspection *n.* 검사, 조사
extension *n.* 연장, 늘임, 확대　educator *n.* 교육자
physician *n.* 의사　insure *v.* 보증하다
vitality *n.* 생명력, 활력　enable *v.* ~을 할 수 있게 하다
take advantage of ~을 이용하다
safeguard *v.* 보호하다　render *v.* (어떤 상태가 되게) 만들다
vigorous *a.* 활발한　recognition *n.* 인지, 인식
intimate *a.* 친밀한, 친한; 심오한, 본질적인
consequent *a.* 결과로서 일어나는
movement *n.* 운동　infancy *n.* 유년기, 초기
imperative *a.* 명령적인, 강제적인, 절박한

necessity *n.* 필요(성); 필수품
welfare *n.* 복지, 후생   discovery *n.* 발견(물)
compulsory *a.* 강제된, 의무적인, 필수의
protection *n.* 보호   decree *v.* 포고하다
attend *v.* (~에) 다니다; 참석하다
indiscriminating *a.* 무차별의, 닥치는 대로의
agency *n.* 정부 기관, ~청
gather *v.* 모으다, 모이다   bright *a.* 머리가 좋은
dull *a.* 둔한   sound *a.* 건전한
unforeseen *a.* 생각하지 않은, 뜻하지 않은
device *n.* 장치   remedy *v.* 치료하다, 고치다
prevention *n.* 방지, 예방   cure *n.* 치료
establishment *n.* 설립, 창립   evident *a.* 분명한, 명백한
epidemic *n.* 유행병, 전염병   check *v.* 저지하다
improvement *n.* 개량, 개선
note *n.* 각서, 메모, 주의, 주목 *v.* 주의하다, 주목하다
cleanliness *n.* 청결(함)   neatness *n.* 깔끔함
threatened *a.* 위험에 직면한

Day 15

[Challenge 1]

문제 1

답 (4)

해설 본문은 문화 상대주의 관점에서 몸짓과 행위를 이해해야 한다고 주장하고 있다. 보기 항 (4)와 같이 사람들이 태어날 때부터 다른 이의 행위를 과장해서 해석한다는 내용을 유추할 근거는 본문에 없다.

문제 2

답 (2)

해설 앞에서 설명한 내용에 대한 구체적인 예가 제시되고 있다.

문제 3

답 (2)

해설 다른 사람에 대해 판단을 내린다는 의미이다.

해석 몸짓 및 몸의 움직임을 이용하여 최대한의 효과를 낼 수 있게 하는 방법이 있다. 특정한 몸짓을 사용할 경우, 그 몸짓을 사용할 때 이것이 적절한지를 정확히 하기 위해 그것이 사용되는 문맥을 철저히 고려해야 한다. 어떤 몸짓 표현은 공통되는 반면, 문화와 관습에 따라 다른 표현으로 나타나기도 한다. 우리는 우리와 다른 문화권의 사람들이 어떤 특정 몸짓에 대해 우리가 의도한 것과는 전혀 다른 것으로 받아들일 수 있다는 것을 명심해야 한다. 그리고 어떤 문화도 다른 문화보다 더 옳거나 틀리다고 주장해선 안 된다. 때로는 이러한 점으로 인해 몸짓이 어떤 의미에서 틀린 것이기 때문이 아니라 단순히 서로의 오해를 불러올 수 있다는 여지에서 우리가 이런 몸짓을 피하는 게 적절할 수 있다. 예를 들어, 다리를 꼬는 여성은 그 과정에서 허벅지 공간을 드러낼 수 있기에, 이들이 의도하지 않은 메시지를 드러내기도 한다. 몸짓은 또한 우리가 숨기기를 선호하는 또는 그런 것이 더 이점이 되는 감정이나 느낌을 보는 이에게 유출해 주기도 한다.

우리가 어떤 사람에 대해 판단을 내리기 전에, 그 사람이 명확한 행위를 보이는지를 확인하는 것이 중요하다. 큰소리로 시끄럽게 말하는 사람이 사려 깊은 사람일 수도 있으며, 말이 없는 사람은 너무 피곤한 단순한 이유로 대화를 듣지 않을 수도 있다. 우리는 항상 하나 이상의 표현, 하나 이상의 단서를 찾도록 해야 한다. 행위를 해석하되, 확대 해석은 피하도록 할 필요가 있다.

어휘

gesture *n.* 몸짓　movement *n.* 움직임; 운동
context *n.* 전후관계; 문맥　appropriate *a.* 적절한
universal *a.* 보편적인　convention *n.* 관습, 관례
dictate *v.* 지시하다　bear in mind 명심하다
radically *ad.* 철저히　intend *v.* 의도하다, 작정하다
serve *v.* (~하는 데) 도움이 되다
misinterpretation *n.* 오해; 오역
cross *v.* 교차시키다　reveal *v.* 드러내다, 누설하다
expanse *n.* 광활한 공간　thigh *n.* 넓적다리
convey *v.* (말, 태도 등이) 전달하다
message *n.* 전하는 말, 전언
observer *n.* 관찰자　leakage *n.* 샘; 누출
emotion *n.* 감동, 감격　prefer *v.* 선호하다
advantage *n.* 유리, 이익, 우세
conceal *v.* 숨기다, 비밀로 하다
verdict *n.* 판단, 결론　crucial *a.* 결정적인, 중대한
display *v.* 보이다, 나타내다
unequivocal *a.* 모호하지 않은, 명백한
boisterous *a.* 시끄러운
considerate *a.* 사려깊은, 인정이 많은
symptom *n.* 징후, 조짐, 전조
interpret *v.* 해석하다; 통역하다

[Challenge 2]

문제 1

답 (2)

해설 Alfred Wegener가 죽은 후 자신의 대륙 이동설에 대한 더 많은 지지 이론이 나타나 그가 주장했던 대륙 이동설의 메커니즘이 바로 convection currents임이 밝혀진 내용을 다루고 있다. 즉, Alfred Wegener 이후 더 많은 증거가 제기되어 그의 대륙 이동설이 일반적으로 옳다고 받아들여진다는 내용이다. 본문의 중간 부분에 주제를 설정할 수 있는 내용이 드러나 있다. "These ideas were rejected by geologists of the time, but after Wegener's death more research was done into one of his hypotheses that the mantle undergoes thermal convection."

문제 2

답 (2)

해설 우선 땅 밑의 아주 뜨거운 마그마가 상승한 후, 표면과 가

까워지면서 식은 후, 굳었다가 다시 가라앉고(무게로 인해), 그런 다음 다시 가열된 후 상승하는 반복을 거치게 되면서 대류가 일어난다.

해석 Alfred Wegener가 자신의 대륙 이동설을 뒷받침하기 위해 제시한 놀라운 증거에도 불구하고, 그에게는 어떻게 대륙이 실질적으로 이동할 수 있는지를 설명하는 유기적인 논리가 부족했다. 이것에 관한 정보는 Wegener 사후에야 비로소 드러났다. Wegener는 원래 대륙은 지구의 자전에 의해 발생하는 원심력(centrifugal forces) 또는 태양과 달에 의해 발생하는 중력의 결과로 대양저(ocean floor)를 통해 천천히 나아간다고 믿었다. 이러한 생각은 그 당시의 지질학자들에 의해 배척당했지만, Wegener가 죽은 후, 맨틀이 열에 의한 대류(convection)를 겪는다는 그의 가설에 더 많은 연구가 이루어졌다. 이러한 대류의 흐름은 맨틀의 아주 깊은 곳에 존재하는, 엄청나게 뜨거운 마그마가 상승한 후 식었다가 가라앉고, 다시 열을 받아 상승하는 사이클을 반복하면서 발생한다. Arthur Holmes는 열대류 흐름은 컨베이어 벨트와 같으며, 위쪽으로 솟아오르는 압력은 대륙을 쪼개고 이렇게 갈라진 대륙을 반대 방향으로 밀어낼 수 있다고 주장했다. 이 이론은 그 당시 거의 관심을 불러일으키지 못했지만, 현재 대류 흐름은 대륙 이동을 일으키는 유기적인 원인으로 받아들여지고 있다.

어휘

in support of ~을 지지[옹호]하여   drift *n.* 이동, 표류
hypothesis *n.* 가설, 추정, 추측
lack *n.* 부족, 결핍 *v.* ~이 부족하다
mechanism *n.* 방법, 메커니즘
plow *n.* 쟁기, 경작 *v.* 갈다, 경작하다, (토지가) 경작에 적합하다
floor *n.* (동굴 등의) 밑바닥; 바다 바닥, 해상(海床)
centrifugal force *n.* 원심력   rotation *n.* 회전, 자전
gravitational *a.* 중력의   mantle *n.* (지구의) 맨틀
undergo *v.* 겪다   thermal *a.* 열의
convection current *n.* 대류   upwelling *n.* 용승
pressure *n.* 압력   opposite *a.* 반대쪽의

[Challenge 3]

문제 1

답 (3)

해설 본문은 초기 미국 헌법에 들어 있지 않던 권리장전이 어떠한 배경과 과정을 거쳐 미국 헌법과 주 헌법에 적용되게 되었는지에 관한 내용을 다루고 있다. 즉, '미국 권리장전'에 관한 내용을 다루고 있다.

문제 2

답 (3)

해설 본문에서 미국인들은 심리적 이유로 권리장전이 헌법에 기술되길 원했으며, 초기 헌법 제정자들은 이러한 권리장전을 당연한 것으로 여겼기에 굳이 기술할 필요가 없다고 여겼다. 미국의 권리장전이 영국의 권리장전으로부터 직접적인 영향을 받았는가는 본문에서 알 수가 없다.

해석 미국 헌법 입안자들은 헌법 문서에 권리장전을 포함시키지 않았다. 이 누락의 이유는 기본권에 무관심해서가 아니라, 헌법이 언론의 자유나 집회결사의 자유와 같은 사항들에 대해서 구체적으로 권한을 인정하지 않았다고 해서 그러한 권한이 존재하지 않는다고 할 수는 없기 때문이었다. 이러한 주장은 논리적으로는 그럴 듯하지만, 심리적으로는 그렇지 않다. 왜냐하면 대체로 미국인들은 자기들의 권리를 구체적으로 헌법에 포함시키기를 원했기 때문이다. 초대 의회가 출범한 지 얼마 후 제임스 매디슨은 개헌으로서 장문의 권리장전을 상정시켰다. 이 중 12개 조항이 의회에서 통과되었으며, 그중에서도 불과 10개 조항만이 각 주에서 비준되었는데 이 조항들은 1791년 12월 15일 헌법의 일부가 되어 소위 권리장전으로 알려지게 되었다. 이 조항들의 대부분은 정부에 대한 제약이며, 중앙정부가 해서는 안 되는 사항들이다. 그러나 결국에는 일반적 의미에서 주 정부들에게도 적용되는 것으로 해석되었다. 거의 모든 주가 주 헌법의 일부 혹은 그 수정 조항으로서 권리장전을 갖고 있으므로 미 국민은 어디에 있건 누구나 그 같은 권리장전에 의해 지방, 주, 중앙을 막론하고 정부가 저지를지 모를 횡포로부터 보호된다고 말해도 과언이 아니다.

어휘

framer *n.* (헌법) 제정자   constitution *n.* 헌법
bill *n.* 법안   document *n.* 문서, 서류; 기록
indifference *n.* 무관심, 냉담 무차별
fundamental *a.* 기초의, 기본의
specifically *ad.* 특유하게, 특수하게   grant *v.* 주다, 수여하다
assembly *n.* 집회; (주 의회의) 하원   set forth 발표하다
congress *n.* 의회   introduce *v.* (법안을) 제출하다
amendment *n.* 변경, 개선; (법안) 수정안
ratify *v.* 비준[재가] 하다   interpret *v.* 해석하다, 통역하다
protection *n.* 보호, 후안, 두둔

[Challenge 4]

문제 1

답 (3)

해설 보기 항 (3)의 경우 글 전반에 걸쳐 미국이 테러리스트에 대한 보복적 전쟁을 빌미로 군사 원조를 확대하고 있음을 확인할 수 있다. 보기 항 (1)은 미국이 군사 원조에 대한 제약을 적극적으로 철폐하려는 모습을 확인할 수 있으므로 옳지 않고, 보기 항 (2)의 경우 본문 마지막 쪽에 기자의 질문에 침묵하는 모습을 볼 수 있으므로 옳지 않다. 보기 항 (4)의 'sit on the fence'는

갈팡질팡하는 미국의 모습을 묘사하고 있는데, 본문에서 대테러 군사 원조 확대에 대한 미국의 입장은 'aggressive'하다고 볼 수 있다.

문제 2

답 (3)

문제 3

답 (4)

해설 앞에서 전개된 'The relentless assault on [U.S.] military aid restrictions'와 'win blanket exemptions for aid distributed as part of the 'war on terror''로 보아 '철회하다'의 4번 항이 가장 적절하다.

해석 9/11 공격 직후 시작된 미국의 군사 원조 제약에 대한 무자비한 공격은 계속해서 줄지 않고 있다. 이번 봄 부시 행정부는 기존의 대부분 제약과 보고 요구 조항을 철회하는 내용의 미국 국방부 예산안(FY2002)의 보조 충당 예산을 포함함으로써 '테러와의 전쟁'의 일부분으로 배분될 원조를 위한 전면적인(blanket) 면제 혜택을 얻어내려 다시 시도했다. 부시 행정부의 두 번째 시도는 더 성공적이었다. 국방부의 두 핵심적인 자금 할당액 — 테러와의 전쟁에서 수행할 미 작전을 지원하는 국가들에게 돈을 배상하기 위한 삼억 구천만 달러와 '특정 1급 작전'을 위한 일억 이천만 달러 — 이 이제 '다른 어떤 법안에도 불구하고' 전해질 수 있게 되었다. 이것이 의미하는 것은 이러한 어마어마한 군사 원조 비용에 대한 어떠한 일반적인 규제도 없다는 것이다.

'1급 작전'에 관한 조항은 특히 문제가 되는데, 이는 '다른 상황에선 법으로 허용되지 않는 프로젝트'를 허용하는 것으로, 다른 말로 연막 작전을 말한다. 보조금의 설명이 불투명 뿐 아니라 한 국방부 위원회 직원에게 정보를 좀 더 얻으려는 시도는 수포로 돌아갔다. 그는 모든 정보가 '일급'이라는 명목 하에 의도된 자금 사용처, 외국 원조 제한의 적절성, 보고 요구 조항에 대한 질문에 대한 답변을 거부했다. 즉, 이러한 원조에 대해 국민은 조사할 길이 없으며, 국회는 이것을 그저 묵인하고 있다.

어휘

assault n. 습격, 공격   unabated a. 약해지지 않는
exemption n. (의무 등의) 면제
supplemental a. 보충의, 추가[부록]의
appropriation n. (의회가 승인한) 지출금, 예산 (금액)
allocation n. 할당, 배당, 배치
reimburse v. (빚 따위를) 갚다, 상환하다
notwithstanding prep. ~에도 불구하고(in spite of)
rovision n. (법률) 규정, 조항
covert a. 숨은; (위협·눈짓 등) 암암리의, 은밀한
opaque a. 불투명한, 분명치 않은

committee n. 위원회, (집합적) 위원
applicability n. 적응성, 응용(가능)성; 적절함
scrutiny n. (면밀한) 음미[조사], 자세히 보는 일

[Challenge 5]

문제 1

답 (1)

해설 마르크스의 오래된 인용구의 내용은 '능력에 따라 일하고, 필요에 따라 분배한다.'의 의미로 이는 다시 말해, 능력에 따른 분배의 자본주의 법칙이 아닌, 능력과 관련 없이 필요하면 가진 자의 돈을 빼앗아 필요한 자에게 준다는 사회주의 성격을 말하는 것이다. 본문에서 글쓴이는 이런 민주당의 입장을 비판하고 있다.

해석 민주당은 부동산세에 대한 확실한 강령이 부족하다 — 열심히 일하라, 절약하고, 투자하라 그러면 사후에 정부가 절반을 가져갈 것이다. 만일 그들이 정부가 그들 돈의 절반을 가져간다는 사실을 알고 있다면, 어느 누가 노력하기로 마음먹고, 새로운 사업을 시작하려 하겠는가? 열심히 일하고 위험을 감수한다는 것이 그리 만만치는 않다. 민주당은 이 세상의 Joe Kennedy와 달리 아이들이 부를 축적하지 못한다는 것을 깨닫지 못한다. 자신의 삶을 바쳐 얻은 것의 반을 빼앗는다는 것은 삶을 송두리째 산산조각 낼 수도 있다. 이 모든 과정은 "능력에 따라 일하고 필요에 따라 분배한다."는 오랜 마르크스 슬로건의 냄새가 난다.

어휘

Democrat n. 민주당
Uncle Sam n. 미국 정부(때때로 흰 수염에 높은 중절모를 쓴 키 큰 남자로 묘사된다.)
accumulating a. 축적되는, 늘어나는
rip v. 찢다, 해어지게 하다   smack of ~의 김새가 보이다

[Challenge 6]

문제 1

답 (4)

해설 주인공이 사업을 성공하게 된 것은 자본 때문이 아니다. 본문에도 언급되었듯이 그는 새로운 사업을 할 때 돈이 한 푼도 없었다. 다음 본문의 내용을 확인하자.

> I had a spotless character, enjoyed good credit, and possessed a thorough knowledge of my business; advantages which I easily persuaded myself would enable me to succeed without the actual possession of capital.

문제 2

답 (3)

해설 선대를 말한다.

문제 3

답 (2)

해설 돈이 한 푼도 없다는 의미이다.

문제 4

답 (2)

해설 본문 마지막 두 문장을 확인하면 보기 항 (2)가 옳지 않다는 것을 알 수 있다.

> had I been prudent enough to confine myself strictly to this branch of the business, I would now, without doubt, have been a wealthy and successful merchant.
>
> The year 1857 opened auspiciously, and I continued to prosper almost to the end of it, when a storm swept over the commercial world, which involved hundreds of firms in bankruptcy and ruin.

즉, 1857년 말부터 경기가 악화하면서 많은 기업이 도산했다고 말하고 있으며, 앞에서 자신이 지금 하고 있는 이 일에만 몰두했더라면 지금쯤 아주 큰 부자가 되었을 것이라고 말하는 것으로 보아, 주인공은 장사가 잘 되면서 확장을 하다 경기 부진으로 어려움을 겪게 되었다는 사실을 추론할 수 있다.

해석 1856년 초에 나는 북쪽의 한 도시에서 상인으로 모든 비용을 내가 들여 (on my own account) 사업을 시작했다. 이 시기 이전에 나는 동업을 했는데, 성공적이지 못했지만 내가 새로운 사업을 할 목적으로 친구들이 나에게 선대를 해준 작은 자본금으로 채권자에게 돈을 모두 지불했다. 그래서 내가 사업을 시작할 때, 나는 말 그대로 땡전 한 푼 없었다. 그러나 나는 성격에 오점이 없었고, 신용이 좋았으며, 내 사업에 대한 철저한 지식을 가지고 있었다. 나는 이러한 장점들이 나를 실질적인 자본 없이도 성공할 수 있게 해 줄 것이라고 확신했다. 나의 사업 인맥은 세계 각지에 걸쳐 있었으며, 일반적으로 외국 상인의 가장 최고 계층에 해당되었다. 나는 보통 편지로 주문을 받았는데, 때로는 확보할 수 없을 것 같은 집에는 외상거래 계좌를 터주었다. 그러나 상품이 목적지에 도착하기 오래 전에 송금을 받는 경우가 많았다. (give open credits: 외상거래 계좌를 트다) 이 장사는 신용이며, 이것의 성공을 위해 인격과 지위 모두가 필요했다. 그리고 내가 이 사업 분야에만 철저하게 한정시킬 만큼 신중했더라면, 지금 나는 의심 없이 부유하고 성공적인 상인이 되었을 것이다. 사업을 시작한 첫 해 후반에 나의 원부에는 만족스러운 예금 잔고가 들어 있었다. 1857년은 순조롭게 시작되었고, 나는 그해 말까지 계속 번창했는데, 바로 그때 금융계에 폭풍이 몰아치면서 수백 개의 회사가 도산하고 망했다.

어 휘

commence v. 시작되다[하다]
engage v. 종사하다, 관여하다
unsuccessful a. 성공하지 못한   partnership n. 동업자임
creditor n. 채권자   capital n. 자본
for the purpose of ~의 목적으로
literally ad. 글자 그대로
shilling n. 실링(영국에서 1971년까지 사용되던 주화)
spotless a. 티끌 하나 없는   scatter v. 뿌리다, 흩어지다
remittance n. 송금액   merchandise n. 물품, 상품
prudent a. 신중한
ledger n. (은행·사업체 등에서 거래 내역을 적은) 원장
auspiciously ad. 순조롭게; 길조로

[Challenge 7]

문제 1

답 (2)

해설 'In addition to depleting resources'에서 알 수 있듯이, 고갈되고 있는 자원의 이야기와 관련된 보기 항을 골라야 한다. 보기 항 (2)가 가장 적절하다.

문제 2

답 (2)

해설 지문은 '인구 과잉으로 발생하는 문제점'을 나열을 통한 병렬 구조로 전개하고 있다.

문제 3

답 (3)

해설 본문에서 개발도상국의 경우 경제 문제가 환경 문제보다 우선시되는 경향이 있다고 말했다. ('Developing nations often promote industries that pollute to compete economically.') 보기 항 (3)은 본문 마지막에 명시되어 있다. 본문 (4)의 경우 본문에서 그 근거를 찾을 수 없으며, 본문의 구체적 명시가 없이 핵가족이 대가족보다 집 안사(事)를 처리하는 데 더 효율적이라고 단적으로 말할 순 없다.

해석 자원 고갈과 더불어 인구 과잉은 환경 문제를 증가시키고 있다. 오염은 인구 과잉에 의해 그 정도가 심해지는 환경 문제이다. 더 많은 사람들이 더 많은 차를 몰고, 더 많은 전기를 사용하고, 더 많은 쓰레기를 버리고, 그리고 더 많은 나무를 베기 때문에 우리가 겪는 환경 문제는 엄청나게 증가했다. 지구는 오염을 많이 일으키는 사람들이 적을 때는

이를 수월하게 감당할 수 있다. 그러나 우리와 같이 더 많은 이들이 오염을 일으키면, 엄청난 문제가 발생한다. 오염은 개발도상국에서 극대화된다. 인구가 크게 증가한 나라들이 부유하게 됨에 따라, 오염도 그들의 부와 함께 증가한다. 개발도상국은 경제적으로 경쟁력을 갖추기 위해 오염을 발생시키는 산업이라도 장려한다. 이러한 산업들은 성장을 촉진시키기 위해 엄격하게 규제를 하지 않는 편이다.

지구에 환경적인 부담을 주는 문제 외에도, 인구 과잉은 오늘날의 사회에 수많은 사회 문제를 발생시킨다. 이러한 예 중 하나는 최근 오하이오 대학에서 보여준 연구에서 잘 드러나는데, 가족의 규모가 클수록 아이들은 학교에서 더 적응을 못하고 나쁘게 행동했다. "미국 사회학 학회의 10월분에 실린 이 연구는 가족의 규모가 증가하면서, 부모는 아이들과 학교에 대한 대화가 줄고, 교육적 기대가 적으며, 대학 등록금을 덜 저축하는 동시에 교육 여건에 대한 준비를 덜 하게 된다는 사실을 발견했다."

개인의 정치적 힘도 인구가 증가하면서 줄어든다. 인구가 증가하면, 미국 연방과 주 의회의 각 대표 (상원도 마찬가지로)는 더 폭넓은 인구를 대변해야 한다. 이러한 문제는 국회의원의 수가 늘어나면서 처음 제기되었다. 그러나 미국 하원의원 수가 435명에 다다랐을 때, 그 수만 해도 상상할 수 없을 정도였으며, 따라서 국회의원의 수에 제한을 가하게 되었다. 링컨 시절에, 한 의회구에 주민 수는 약 185,000명이었다. 오늘날에는 각 선거구에 약 600,000명이 있다. 유일한 대안은 국회의원의 수를 늘리는 것이지만, 이것은 국회의 효율성을 저하시킬 뿐이다.

어휘

- **deplete** v. (세력·자원 따위를) 고갈[소모]시키다
- **magnitude** n. (길이·규모·수량) 크기, 양
- **overpopulation** n. 인구 과잉   **sustain** v. 견디다, 지탱하다
- **pollute** v. 오염시키다   **massive** a. 거대한, 대단한
- **developing nations** 개발도상국
- **promote** v. 도모하다, 조장하다 **compete** v. 경쟁하다
- **regulate** v. 규제하다
- **stimulate** v. 자극하다, (경기 성장을) 부추기다
- **strain** n. 부담, 중압(감); 압력, 압박
- **describe** v. 묘사하다, 설명하다
- **education expectations** 교육 기대
- **US representatives** 미국 하원 (cf. senators 상원의원)
- **alternative** n. 대안   **efficiency** n. 효율성

[Challenge 8]

문제 1

답 (4)

해설 첫 번째 문장 '(our basic grammar skills are regressing)'에서 알 수 있듯이, 인터넷 채팅 문화로 인해 영어의 철자에 부정적인 영향을 미치는 현상과 그에 대한 인터넷 사용자들의 반응을 짚어보는 내용이 본문의 골자이다. 이런 점을 가장 잘 반영하는 내용은 보기 항 (4)이다.

문제 2

답 (2)

문제 3

답 (4)

해설 빈칸 앞의 인용구를 보면, 정확한 철자 표기의 중요성을 강조하는 듯하지만 'but'으로 내용의 전환을 이루고 있다. 이 점을 감안하여 문맥상 가장 적절한 표현을 골라야 한다. 즉, 무시할 수 없는 인터넷 영향력으로 인해 많은 이들이 대안적 철자를 쓴다면 사용자에 맞는 새로운 문법(철자법)이 필요하다는 내용이 나와야 한다. 고로 보기 항 (4)가 가장 적절하다.

해석 우리가 초고속 정보를 마음대로 사용할 수 있을지는 모르지만, 우리의 기본적인 문법 지식은 퇴보하고 있다. 영어 철자학회에서 최근 발표된 연구에 따르면, 웹사이트는 영어라는 언어를 완전히 바꾸었을 뿐 아니라 철자를 잘못 쓰는 문화로 바꾸어버렸다. "인터넷에서 다양한 종류의 철자 사용이, 오타 교정이나 철자 법칙에 따를 필요가 없다는 일반적인 인식이 팽배한 인터넷 채팅방과 소셜 네트워크 사이트에서 빠르게 타이핑하는 사람들에 의해서 증가하고 있다"고 보고서는 말하면서 문법에 대한 우리의 태도가 점차 관대해지고 있다는 것을 드러냈다. 그러나 혼란스러운 말로 웹의 실질적인 위험 요소는 속기인가? 만약 정확한 문법 사용이 잘못된 방향으로 계속된다면, 아이들은 먼저 배우려는 것은 고사하고 틀린 것을 고치려 하지 않게 된다.

급성장하는 인터넷 세대에 초점을 둔 이 보고서는 18세와 24세 사이의 5명 중 한 명은 사전이나 맞춤법 검사 프로그램의 도움 없이는 중요한 이메일을 쓸 자신이 없다고 전하고 있는데, 이런 무서운 통계는 이들을 컴퓨터 이전의 시대를 기억하지 못하는 사람 중 빙산의 일각으로 보고 있다. 연구에 참여한 사람들 중 거의 3분의 1이 인터넷 채팅에서 혼란스러운 대안적 철자 (alt=alternative)를 '전적으로 받아들일 수 없는' 것으로 보는 반면, 다른 3분의 2는 이 단어들이 사전에 포함되는 것을 지지한다는 의견을 나타냈다. "정확한 철자 사용은 아주 중요하지만, 최근의 조사에서 볼 수 있듯이 인터넷의 전례 없는 영향력과 규모는 새로운 사회 관행을 일으켰으며, 철자 또한 그 변화의 한 요소일 뿐이라고 결론지을 수 있다"고 영어 철자학회의 의장인 Jack Bovill이 보고서에서 전했다. 아마도 문법에도 컴퓨터의 재부팅 기능을 사용해야 할지 모르겠다.

어 휘

- **disposal** *n.* 처분, 처리; 베치, 배열(配列)
- **grammar** *n.* 문법
- **regress** *v.* 되돌아가다; 역행하다; 퇴보하다
- **release** *v.* 공개[발표, 발매]하다
- **reveal** *v.* (숨겨졌던 것을) 드러내다; 알리다
- **alter** *v.* (모양·성질 등을) 바꾸다, 변경하다
- **misspeller** *n.* 철자를 잘못 쓰는 사람
- **variant** *a.* 다른, 상이한, 가지가지의
- **typo** *n.* (*pl.* ~s)《구어》인쇄[식자]공
- **commonplace** *n.* 흔히 있는 일
- **shorthand** *n.* 약칭
- **irrelevancy** *n.* 부적절; 무관함
- **burgeon** *v.* (급격히) 성장[발전]하다 (into)
- **stat** *n.* 통계(학)
- **alt-spelling** *n.* 철자가 바뀐 말
- **rebel** *a.* 모반한, 반역의, 반도의; 반역적[반항적]인
- **unprecedented** *a.* 선례[전례]가 없는, 미증유의, 새로운

[Challenge 9]

문제 1
답 (2)
해설 황소를 만난 한 소녀의 용감하고 재치 있는 일화에 관한 이야기이다.

문제 2
답 (2)
해설 빈칸 문제의 경우 전체적 문맥을 감안하면서, 앞뒤의 문맥을 반드시 확인해야 한다. 본문의 내용을 살펴보자.

> as it is the nature of these animals to attack persons ____(a)____, her life would be in great danger if she attempted to run, and would be inevitably lost if she chanced to fall

빈칸에 앞에서 황소의 본성이 ___하기에 공격한다고 했다. 그리고 뒤에 만약 여성이 달리려고 시도한다면 큰 위험에 처한다고 말하고 있으므로, 보기 항 (2)가 가장 적절하다.

문제 3
답 (4)
해설 앞에서도 그녀가 직접 실천하는 것에서 알 수 있듯이 ("Accordingly, turning her face towards the animal with the firmest aspect she could assume, she fixed her eyes steadily upon his.") 사자를 지속적으로 바라봄으로 통제할 수 있다는 내용의 (4)가 가장 적절하다.

문제 4
답 (3)
해설 (e)의 경우 황소의 격정적인 감정의 상태를 나타내고, 나머지는 모두 B양이 보인 차분하고 지혜로운 처사와 관련이 있다.

문제 5
답 (1)
해설 보기 항 (1)이 본문의 B양이 보인 행동과 같은 행동이다.

해석 B양은 한 번은 다른 젊은 여인과 들판을 지나 함께 걷고 있었는데, 그때 마침 황소가 잔뜩 성난 채로 이들에게 달려들었다. 그녀의 친구가 계단 (stile)으로 달려가려 하자 B양이 막아서며 그녀가 스스로를 지킬 만큼 계단에 빨리 갈 수 없고, 이런 동물들은 도망가는 사람을 공격하는 성향이 있어서 도망치려 하면 아주 위험하며, 만약 넘어지기라도 하면 반드시 목숨을 잃을 수 있다고 말했다. 그러나 만약 그 계단으로 슬며시 움직이면, 서로 거리를 둠으로 황소의 관심을 돌릴 수 있게 된다고 했다. 따라서 최대한 안정적인 자세로 그 동물을 향해 얼굴을 돌려 그에게서 눈을 떼지 않았다. 여행자들에 따르면, 사자도 사람이 지속적으로 바라보면 통제할 수 있다고 한다. 그러나 사자를 등지는 순간 사자는 그를 자신의 먹이로 삼아 달려든다는 것이다. B양은 이 동물들의 특성을 잘 알고 있던 터라, 서두르지 않고 침착하게 자신과 친구의 안전에 이를 적용했다. 침착한 자세로, 그녀는 황소의 질주 (career)를 저지했다. 그러나 그 황소는 통제되는 것에 울부짖고 발과 뿔로 땅을 헤집어가며 극심한 분노를 보였다. 그가 그렇게 땅바닥에 자신의 분노를 분출하는 동안, 그녀는 그에게서 눈을 떼지 않고 조심스럽게 몇 발짝 뒤로 물러났다. 그 황소는 그녀가 물러서는 것을 보자, 그녀가 멈출 때까지 전진했다. 그리곤 그 또한 다가서다 멈추었고, 다시 미친 듯이 날뛰었다. 그래서 이런 과정을 반복하면서, 그녀는 마침내 그 계단에 도착할 수 있었으며, 거기서 그녀는 스스로를 지킬 수 있었다. 그리고 어린 여자에게서 좀처럼 보이지 않는 침착한 마음으로 그녀는 자신뿐만 아니라 자신의 목숨이 위태로운 상태에서 그녀의 친구 또한 구해냈다. 이후 언젠가 이 황소는 자신의 주인을 들이받았다.

어 휘

- **in company with** ~와 함께
- **malevolence** *n.* 악의, 나쁜 마음
- **stile** *n.* 밟고 넘는 계단
- **inevitably** *ad.* 필연적으로, 불가피하게도
- **spring upon** ~에게 달려들다
- **indignation** *n.* 분개, 분함
- **roar** *v.* 으르렁거리다
- **tear** *v.* 찢다, 뜯다
- **horn** *n.* 뿔
- **vent** *v.* (분통을) 터뜨리다
- **turf** *n.* 잔디
- **retreat** *v.* 후퇴하다
- **renew** *v.* 재개하다, 갱신하다
- **frantic** *a.* 정신없이 서두르는, 제정신이 아닌
- **afterwards** *ad.* 나중에, 그 뒤에
- **gore** *v.* 뿔[엄니]로 들이받다
- **master** *n.* 주인

[Challenge 10]

문제 1

답 (3)

해설 본문에서 등장하는 실험의 결과는 무엇인가? 궁극적으로 multitasking을 할 경우 dopamine이 방출되는데, 이것이 사람들에게 일을 더 효율적으로 많이 처리했다는 착각을 일으킨다는 내용이다. 결국, multitasking은 한 사람이 일을 하나씩 처리한 경우보다 더 오류가 많고 비효율적이라고 말하고 있다. 내용 일치 문제의 경우 본문에 등장하는 부분적인 내용을 보기 항으로 구성하는 경우도 있지만, 글에서 중심적으로 전달하고자 하는 요지를 중심으로 보기 항이 구성된다는 점을 잊지 말아야 한다.

문제 2

답 (1)

해설 뇌가 multitasking을 하는 사람에게 일종의 'false' 신호를 보내는 내용이 바로 뒤에 이어진다. 이를 가장 잘 반영한 보기 항은 (1)에 해당한다.

해석 일터가 어떻게 비효율성을 조장하는지 그 예를 하나 드리겠습니다. 만약 당신이 일주일 당 50~60시간 일을 지속적으로 하고, 더욱 중요한 것은 우리를 다른 사람과 이어주는 전자기기에 끊임없이 구속될 때 우리는 건강한 인간관계에 필요한 감성적 측면을 가지기가 아주 어렵게 되어 삶의 건강한 관점을 유지할 수가 없습니다. 새로운 뇌 실험에서 우리가 인지적 과부하 상태일 때, 도파민과 다른 뇌 화학물질이 방출되는데 이것은 우리에게 헛된 자신감을 심어준다는 사실이 발견되었습니다. 그래서 우리는 한꺼번에 여러 일을 하는 것이 더욱 생산적이고 효과적이라고 생각하는 환상에 빠지게 됩니다. 제가 알고 있는 다중 작업에 관한 모든 연구에서 일부 집단의 사람들은 여러 가지 일을 맡게 되고, 다음과 같은 말을 듣습니다. "당신은 여러 가지 일을 한꺼번에 할 수 있습니다. 하고 싶은 대로 하세요." 다른 집단의 경우 동일한 작업을 순서대로 완수하라는 지시를 받는데, 작업 하나가 끝나면 다음 작업을 시작하는 식입니다. 모든 실험에서 목격한 바로 선형으로 (순서대로) 작업을 한 집단이 동시에 여러 일을 한 사람보다 실수도 적으면서, 더 빠르게 모든 작업을 수행한 것으로 확인되었습니다. 그러나 다중 작업자들이 인터뷰를 할 때, 이들은 자신들이 순차적으로 일한 사람들보다 더 잘했다고 확신을 가집니다. 이는 과중한 일을 다루도록 하는 일종의 뇌의 장난입니다. "만약 내가 너에게 특정 도파민을 준다면, 너는 이만큼의 스트레스를 감당할 수 있는 자신감을 느끼게 될 거야"라고 뇌가 말하는 것입니다. 문제는 도파민이 우리가 정작 어리석은 짓을 하고 있을 때, 우리가 스스로를 똑똑하게 느끼게 만든다는 것입니다. 그런 이유에서 스트레스를 받는 상황에서 내린 결정은 항상 위험한 것입니다.

어휘

foster *v.* 조장하다 **ineffectiveness** *n.* 비효율
keep a perspective on ~에 관한 관점을 견지하다
healthy *a.* 건강한
tethered to ~에 매여 있는, 구속되어 있는
keep someone connected to ~에 계속 연결되어 있게 하다
cognitive *a.* 인지의   **overload** *n.* 과부하
multitasking *n.* 다중 작업   **be aware of** ~을 인식하다
be given 주어지다   **in consecutive order** 순서대로
linearly *ad.* 직선으로, 순서대로
outperform *v.* ~보다 실력·기량이 우세하다, 뛰어나다

Day 16

[Challenge 1]

문제 1

답 (4)

해설 앞에서 '생물학적 통제, 즉 유전공학을 통해 새로운 질병 치료가 가능한 새로운 시대'라고 말하고 있다. 따라서 보기 항 (4)가 가장 적절하다.

문제 2

답 (1)

해설 앞뒤 문장의 내용이 대조를 이루고 있다.

문제 3

답 (4)

해설 cloning의 대표적 예가 돌리에 해당한다. 보기 항 (1)은 본문과 전혀 다른 내용이다. 보기 항 (2)는 'Although there were several others (lambs that were not only cloned but genetically modified as well), Dolly became the best known.'으로 보아 틀린 진술이다. 보기 항 (3)은 'a clone may share the donor's genetic make-up, every individual is, well, individual — the unique product of genetic, environmental and experiential inputs.'에서 틀린 진술임을 알 수 있다. 보기 항 (4)의 내용은 본문 후반부 내용의 전제이다.

문제 4

답 (4)

해설 글쓴이의 견해가 드러나는 본문 마지막을 참고하여 답을 고르도록 한다. 'I say, let's have a rational plan backed up by statistical evidence that something has an effect; but once we get to a certain point, let's proceed with that 'something' to a clinical trial.' 역접 'But' 이후 글쓴이의 주장이 담긴 견해가 드러난다. 마지막에서 알 수 있듯이, 어느 정도 시기가 지나고 나면 임상실험을 바로 실천하자는 의도가 잘 드러나 있다. 따라서 보기 항 (4)가 가장 적절하다.

해석 우리는 Ian Wilmut 경이 스스로 생물학적으로 불가능한 것이 있다는 개념이 구시대의 유물이라고 믿는 "생물학적 통제의 시대"라고 부른 새로운 시대에 살고 있다. 1996년 Wilmut은 어른의 체세포에서 첫 번째 포유동물 복제에 성공했다. 비록 여러 다른 복제 동물이 있었지만 (복제된 것뿐 아니라 유전적으로 변형된 양), 돌리가 가장 잘 알려지게 되었다. 그녀는 전혀 다른 어른의 체세포가 완벽한 유전체를 포함하고 있다는 것을 증명했다. 물론 가장 큰 흥미를 자아낸 것은 바로 인간 복제의 개념이었다. 그러나 지금은 분명 복제물이 유전자를 기증한 사람의 유전적 기질을 공유하지만, 모든 개인이 나름의 독특한 개성 — 유전, 환경 그리고 실험적으로 투입된 정보에 따른 독특한 부산물 — 을 지닌다는 것을 이해하고 있다. 복제는 우리가 가장 두려워하는 병과 죽음에 대한 그다지 좋은 방지책 (hedge)은 아닐 것이다. 그럼에도 유전공학, 염색체 제조, 줄기세포 주입 그리고 게놈 분석이란 주제를 모두 섞을 때, 거의 모든 것이 가능한 것처럼 보인다. 물론, 모든 것이 아직 가능하진 않다. 가장 가능성이 높은 줄기세포를 기반으로 한 재생 의약품조차, 아직 충족시켜야 하는 수많은 단기 연구 대상을 필요로 하는 장기적인 목표이다. 여기에는 생물학적 관점에서 세포가 치료를 위해 어떻게 작용하는지와 환자에게 이것이 어떻게 작용하는 것인지에 대한 이해가 아직 과제로 남아 있다. LA의 CSRMI 소장인 Clive Svendsen은 "사용할 수 있는 가장 정밀한 과학을 적용해야만 할 뿐 아니라 접근 방법에 있어서도 실용적이어야 한다."라고 말한다. "우리가 환자를 치료하기 전 이것에 관한 모든 것을 알 필요가 있다"고 말하는 사람들이 있는 반면, "나는 난 개의치 않아. 그 줄기세포를 넣어. 지금 환자가 죽어가고 있잖아"라고 말하는 사람들도 있다. 나는 '통계적 자료로 뒷받침할 수 있는 합리적인 계획을 가지고 뭔가 효과를 얻을 수 있도록 하자'고 주장하는 바이다. 그러나 우리가 일단 일정 수준에 달했을 때, 우리는 그 '무언가'를 임상실험을 통해 진전시켜야 한다고 생각한다.

어휘

differentiate v. 구별짓다, 구별[차별]하다, 식별하다
duplicate n. (동일물의) 2통 중 하나; (그림·사진 따위의) 복제
spawn v. 대량 생산하다   **intrigue** n. 흥미로움
hedge n. (손실·위험 따위에 대한) 방지책 (against)
chromosome n. [생물]염색체
stemcell n. [해부학·물리]줄기 세포
perspective n. 관점, 시각   **pragmatic** a. 실용적인
rigorous a. 철저한, 엄격한

Day 16

[Challenge 2]

문제 1

답 (2)

해설 보기 항 (2)에서 작가가 다른 인용 없이 스스로의 번역에만 의존했다는 것은 본문과 일치하지 않는다.

해석 여기에 실린 토착 이집트 문학의 견본은 무덤, 파피루스 사본, 그리고 다른 유적지에서 가져온 것이며, 거의 예외 없이 각각의 견본은 그 자체로 완전하다. 대부분의 원문 번역은 이집트 학자들이 영어, 프랑스어, 독일어 그리고 이탈리아어로 번역한 학술지에 이미 나타나 있지만 어떤 것은 처음 영어로 그 모습을 드러낸다. 나는 일일이 내가 한 번역과 원문을 대조했으며, 최근에 나온 정확한 텍스트 판 덕분에 지금까지 난해했던 많은 지문을 분명히 해석할 수 있게 되었다. 이집트어와 영어의 관용어 사이의 차이점이 허용하는 한에서 문자 그대로 번역을 한 것이지만, 영어에서 연결된 의미를 갖도록 원래의 작품에서 관사를 넣거나 종종 어순을 바꿔야 했다. 이 때문에 이집트 작가들이 즐겨 쓰는, 종종 극적 효과를 위해 사용했던 짧고 일관성 없는 문장들을 없애야만 했다. 너무 간략한 표현들은 부연했으며, 알려지지 않은 다수의 표현에 대한 의미는 어림짐작으로 했음을 밝힌다.

어 휘

specimen *n.* 견본, 표본   herein *ad.* 여기서, 여기에서
papyri *n.* 파피루스   Egyptologist *n.* 이집트 학자
collate *v.* (여러 출처에서 정보를) 수집, 분석하다; (종이나 페이지 를) 순서대로 모으다
hitherto *ad.* 지금까지, 그때까지
extraordinarily *ad.* 이례적으로, 유별나게, 엄청나게
paraphrase *v.* 다른 말로 바꾸어 표현하다

[Challenge 3]

문제 1

답 (2)

해설 구체적 사실 확인 문제이다. 아래의 본문에서 답을 얻을 수 있다.

> This right springs from the great truth that government is established for the benefit of the governed.

문제 2

답 (1)

해설 미국인들은 영국의 통치를 받을 때부터 이 청원권이란 개념에 아주 익숙해 있다고 했다. 그리고는 새로운 정부를 구성해 헌법을 작성할 때, 이 청원권을 포함시키지 않았는데, 이는 당연히 이러한 권리가 위험에 처할 것이라는 생각조차 하지 않았을 것을 예측할 수 있기에 보기 (4)보단 (1)이 좀 더 적절한 표현이 된다. '위협을 안 받을 것이라 생각하고'의 의미는 위협이 도사리고 있는지 고려한 후 그렇지 않을 거라 생각했다는 의미이다.

문제 3

답 (3)

해설 본문에서 미국의 새로운 정부는 이러한 권리 (청원권)가 너무 익숙해 당연히 여겼기에 이 조항을 헌법에 넣지 않았다고 본문에 나와 있다.

> So accustomed were the Americans to the exercise of this right, even during their subjection to the British crown, that, on the formation of the Federal Constitution, the Convention, not conceiving that it could be endangered, made no provision for its security.

즉, 청원권을 너무나 당연한 것으로 여겼기에 헌법에 포함시키지 않았다.

해석 청원권은 바로 그 시민 정부의 제도에 의해 확립되었으며, 태고부터 우리 영국 조상들의 의문의 여지가 없는 권리 중의 하나로 인식되어 왔다. 이 권리는 정부가 국민의 이익을 위해서 세워진 것이라는 위대한 진리에서 기인한다. 그리고 국민은 이 권리를 통해 자신의 통치자에게 요구와 불만을 드러내는 수단으로 작용한다. 영국 왕실의 지배하에 있을 때조차 미국인은 이 권리의 행사에 너무나 익숙했기 때문에 연방 헌법을 세울 때, 의회 (the Convention)는 이것이 위협을 받을 것을 인식하지 못하고 이것의 보장에 대한 어떠한 조항도 만들지 않았다. 그러나 새로운 정부 아래 구성된 바로 첫 번째 국회에서 이 누락된 부분이 개정되었다. 이 권리는 특정 다수당에게 골칫거리로 판명되어 이를 억압하려는 특정 다수당에게는 골칫거리일 수 있다고 간주되었다. 이에 따라 수정안이 제출되어 채택되었다. 이것에 의해 "폐해를 없애고자 국민이 평화롭게 집회를 열고 정부에 탄원을 낼 수 있는 권리"를 제한하는 법을 국회가 만들지 못하도록 하는 것이다.

어 휘

petition *n.* 청원(서), 탄원(서)   institution *n.* 제도, 관례, 관습
immemorial *a.* 태고의
unquestionable *a.* 의심할 바 없는, 논의할 바 없는
spring from ~로부터 기인하다, 나오다
acquaint *v.* 숙지시키다, 정통하다   want *n.* 필요, 욕구
grievance *n.* 불만, 불평
accustom *v.* 익숙케 하다, 습관들이게 하다
subjection *n.* 종속, 복종
convention *n.* 집회, 대회, 대표자 회의
provision *n.* (법률 등의) 조항, 규정   faction *n.* 도당, 당파

amendment *n.* (법령의) 수정안
abridge *v.* (권리, 권한 등을) 삭감하다
redress *n.* 배상; 구제(책)

[Challenge 4]

문제 1

답 (3)

해설 본문은 법원에 증거물로 제시할 수 있는 기준이 무엇에 의해 결정되는지를 다루는 내용이다. 본문에서 'Gossip may be fine in the office or at school, but it's a different matter in the courtroom'의 'but' 이후 본격적인 글의 화제가 등장한다. 즉, 법정에서 증거로 허용되는 기준에 관한 글로 1975년에 국회법을 통과한 'The Federal Rules of Evidence'를 따른다고 설명되어 있다.

문제 2

답 (3)

해설 'gossip'에 관한 이야기를 다루는 첫 번째 문장과 달리 법원에선 특정 법칙에 따라 증거를 구별한다는 내용이 시작하는 (c)가 정답이다. 'but' 이후 '법원에서 다뤄지는 증거'로 화제가 전환된다는 점을 확인한다.

문제 3

답 (1)

해설 앞에서 전개한 '전화기 게임'에서 알 수 있듯이, 구두로 전달된 말이나 소위 '풍문'은 전달 과정에서 내용이 바뀌는 경우가 많기에 '믿을 만한 정보'가 되지 못한다. 따라서 보기 항 (1)이 가장 적절하다.

해설 가십이나 스캔들 정보를 전달하는 가장 일반적인 형태 중 하나는 바로 "그가 또는 그녀가 말했다"의 방법이다. 물론 이러한 행위의 위험성은 신뢰성을 잃을 가능성이 크다는 것이다 (공신력이 떨어질 수 있다는 점이다). 특정 이야기를 전달하는 사람은 실제 이야기가 일어날 때 그 자리에 없었던 사람이다. 보통 이야기는 친구들 사이에서 떠돌다가 결국 사실은 온데간데없어지고 만다. 이것은 '전화기 게임'과 아주 흡사하다. 둘러앉은 참가자 중 한 사람이 옆 사람에게 한 문장을 전달한다. 이야기를 들은 사람은 동일한 문장을 바로 옆 사람에게 전달하고, 이 말이 마지막으로 원래 처음 말한 사람에게 돌아올 때까지 계속 옆으로 전달된다. 이 게임의 핵심은 원래 문장과 마지막 문장을 비교하는 것이다. 두 문장은 상당히 다를 가능성이 아주 크다. 이 놀이를 해 보았다면, 구어의 민감한 특징과 또 낭설이 얼마나 믿을 수 없는지 이해하게 될 것이다. 이런 가십은 사무실이나 학교에서는 괜찮을지 모르지만, 재판 중에서는 전혀 다른 문제이다. 변호사가 어떤 것의 진실 또는 거짓에 대해 판사 또는 배심원을 확신시킬 필요가 있다면, 이들은 종종 자신의 주장을 뒷받침할 증거를 제공한다. 어떤 것이든 증거

로 간주될 수 있지만, 법원이 재판 중에 특정 진술이나 사물을 고려하게 될지를 실질적으로 결정하는 것은 일련의 법칙에 따른다. 미국에서, 연방 증거 법칙은 1965년 수석 재판관인 Earl Warren이 만들고, 1975년에 국회에서 법으로 인정된 것으로 법원에서 증거로 인정되는 것과 아닌 것을 자세히 설명하고 있다. 비록 주마다 증거에 관해서는 자체적으로 약간씩 법칙이 다르지만, 일반적으로 연방 정부의 지침을 따른다.

어휘

relay *v.* (정보, 뉴스 등을 받아서) 전달하다
gossip *n.* 잡담(chatter), 한담, 세상 이야기; 남의 소문 이야기; 험담
potential *n.* 가능성
unreliability *n.* 신뢰할 수 없음, 의지할 수 없음
unfold *v.* (어떤 내용이 서서히) 펼쳐지다[밝혀지다]
mangle *v.* 망쳐버리다, 결딴내다
whisper *v.* ~에게 작은 소리로 속삭이다. 살그머니 이야기를 퍼뜨리다
compare *v.* 비교하다, 대조하다 (with), 비유하다, 비기다 (to)
falsity *n.* 허위(성), 기만성; 불신; 거짓말; 잘못
contemplate *v.* 찬찬히 보다, 잘 생각하다, 심사숙고하다
lay out (세밀하게) 계획[설계, 기획]하다
admissible *a.* 참가(입장, 입회, 입학)할 자격이 있는; (지위에) 취임할 자격이 있는

[Challenge 5]

문제 1

답 (3)

해설 보기 항 (3)의 경우 다음 본문에서 옳다는 것을 알 수 있다.

> As long as self-interest is restrained by competition, society benefits from lower prices and greater choices.

문제 2

답 (1)

해설 제시된 빈칸을 중심으로 앞뒤의 내용을 잘 파악하여 가장 적절한 표현을 골라야 한다.

> In the Soviet Union, the Communist Party still rules, but the extraordinary social and economic chaos gripping the country suggests that ___(a)___. In the West, many commentators acclaim the triumph of capitalism over communism.

빈칸 앞에서 전개된 내용은 소련의 공산당이 여전히 통치는 하지만 사회/경제적 혼란이 심각하다는 이야기를 하고 있다. 바로 뒤에 이어지는 내용은 서양에선 많은 이들이 이것을 공산주의에

대한 자본주의의 승리로 주장한다는 내용이다. 따라서 빈칸에 들어갈 단어는 'the extraordinary social and economic chaos gripping the country'로 인해 일어날 수 있는 가장 적절한 결과를 제시하면 된다. 이를 가장 잘 반영한 보기 항은 (1)이다.

문제 3

답 (4)

해설 보기 항 (4)에서 자본주의는 경제 제도를 부패시킬 수 있다고 했는데, 부패시키는 주체는 자본주의가 아니라 자본가이다 (capitalists could corrupt the system). 자본주의 자체가 경제 제도이다.

해석 공산주의 체제는 1989년 말에 동유럽에서 갑작스레 예상 밖으로 무너졌다. 소련은 공산당이 여전히 통치하고 있지만, 이 나라의 발을 묶는 엄청난 사회 경제적 혼돈은 이 정당이 얼마 지속되지 않을 것을 보여준다. 서구 사회에서 많은 평론가들은 공산주의에 대한 자본주의의 승리라며 쾌재를 부른다. 그러나 자본주의의 성공과 존속이 소련의 공산주의 실패와 몰락에 의해서 보장되는 것은 아니다. 자본주의는 사유 재산을 보호하고 경쟁 시장에서 자유 무역을 인정하는 법적 제도이다. 개인은 자신의 이익을 추구하는 데 자유롭다. 개인의 이익이 경쟁에 의해서 제한되는 한, 사회는 더 낮은 가격과 폭넓은 선택의 이점을 갖는다. 자기 이익 추구의 이런 강력한 힘은 협작과 부패로 빠지는 경향이 있다는 문제점이 있다. 다시 말해, 자본가는 권력을 추구하고 자신들의 입맛대로 시장을 조작하여 사회에 손해를 끼친다는 것이다.

자본주의의 학문적 아버지는 바로 아담 스미스다. 그는 200여 년 전에 경쟁 시장이 "보이지 않는 손"과 같이 개인의 이익을 공익을 위한 힘으로 바꾼다고 간주했다. 스미스는 자본과 노동의 최적의 분배를 보장함으로써 경쟁이 어떻게 생산성과 사회복지를 최대화하는지를 설명했다. 그러나 항상 실용주의자였던 그는 자본가가 이 제도를 부패시킬 수 있다고 생각했다. "동일한 업종의 사람들은 잠시 유희를 위해서라도 좀처럼 서로 만나지 않는다. 이들의 대화는 대중에 반하는 음모나 또는 가격 향상을 위한 책략으로 끝난다."

어 휘

collapse *v.* 붕괴하다　grip *v.* 사로잡다
commentator *n.* 해설자　acclaim *v.* 칭송하다, 환호를 보내다
triumph *n.* 업적, 대성공　survival *n.* 생존; 유물
guarantee *v.* 보장[약속]하다
demise *n.* 종말, 죽음, 사망　legal *a.* 합법적인
competitive *a.* 경쟁하는, 경쟁력 있는
competition *n.* 경쟁, 대회　collusion *n.* 공모, 결탁
corruption *n.* 부패　detriment *n.* 손상

public good *n.* 공익　optimal *a.* 최선의, 최상의
allocation *n.* 할당, 배당　pragmatist *n.* 실용주의자
merriment *n.* 유쾌하게 떠들썩함　diversion *n.* 오락, 기분전환
conspiracy *n.* 음모, 모의　contrivance *n.* 계략, 수단

[Challenge 6]

문제 1

답 (1)

해설 유대인의 속담인 "직업을 가지도록 기르지 않으려면 교수대에 보내라"는 직업을 갖는 것의 중요성을 강조한 말이다.

문제 2

답 (4)

해설 다음 본문에서 보기 항 (4)는 옳지 않다는 것을 알 수 있다.

> Both men and women, in fashionable life, are apt to regard all labor — not only manual, but mental — as mere drudgery.

해설 모든 젊은 여성은 특정 직업 또는 소명을 가져야 한다. 유대인들은 옛날에 자신의 자식들 중 누구든 직업을 가지도록 기르지 않으려면 교수대에 보내도록 기른다는 속담을 가지고 있을 정도였다. 그리고 이슬람교도와 이교도들 또한 이와 같은 속담을 가지고 있다. 그러나 애석하게도 이에 반하는 심리가 만연해 있는 것이 현실이다. 상류층 사람들은 육체 노동뿐 아니라 모든 정신 노동을 그저 힘든 일로만 간주하려는 경향이 있다. 이들은 아마도 마지못해 일할 것이다. 이들이 하려고 해서 하는 경우는 거의 없다. 또는 적어도 이러한 생각 (노동을 고된 일로 간주하는 것)은 이들이 부지런해야만 하는 일을 시작할 때 느끼는 감정처럼 보인다. 고백하건대 어떤 이는 결국 일하는 행위에 너무나 익숙해져서 습관처럼 아니면 이것을 관두는 날에는 이들이 자신의 본성적인 나태함을 없애거나 자신의 현재의 근면한 습관을 형성하려고 했을 때만큼이나 비참하게 될 것이기에 이 일을 계속한다고 한다.

어 휘

avocation *n.* 취미, 부업　calling *n.* 소명
gallows *n.* 교수대　mohammedan *n.* 이슬람교
pagan *n.* 이교도　maxim *n.* 격언, 금언
reverse *n.* 역, 반대　be apt to ~하는 경향이 있다
manual *a.* 손으로 하는, 육체노동의
drudgery *n.* 힘들고 단조로운 일　labor *n.* 노동, 수고
discontinuance *n.* 정지, 중지, 단절
render *v.* (어떤 상태가 되게) 만들다
miserable *a.* 비참한　indolence *n.* 게으름, 나태

[Challenge 7]

문제 1

답 (3)

해설 두 번째 문단에서 볼 수 있듯이, 경제에 대한 미국 개입의 성격이 변했다는 것을 알 수 있다. 보기 항 (4)의 경우 경기 부양책보다는 복지정책에 미국 정부가 더 치중했다고 말하는데, 내용의 진위 여부를 떠나 본문에서 이 같은 정보를 알 수 없다. 유추 문제라 하더라도 본문에 제시된 사실 (text-based facts)만을 바탕으로 이끌어 낼 수 있는 정보여야 한다.

문제 2

답 (3)

해설 우선 빈칸이 들어간 문장에서 이끌어 낼 수 있는 정보는 빈칸의 단어가 부정적인 어감을 가지고 있어야 한다는 점이다. "As the sometimes _____ approach to regulation demonstrates, Americans often disagree about the appropriate role of government in the economy." 그리고 첫 번째 문단에서 보다시피, 미국은 자유방임의 자본주의적 성격 (belief in 'free enterprise')을 지니고 있는 동시에 정부의 적극적 개입을 또한 요구하는 '상반된' 성격을 가지고 있음을 이끌어 낼 수 있다.

해석 그러나 미국인들의 '자유기업'에 대한 확신이 정부의 주요한 역할을 배제하진 않았다. 미국인들은 이따금 시장 세력에 도전할 만큼 강력한 지배력을 키워나갈 것처럼 보이는 기업이 나타나면 정부가 나서서 그 기업을 해체하거나 규제해주길 바란다. 또한 민간 경제가 간과할 수 있는 문제, 이를테면 교육이나 환경 보호와 같은 문제들은 정부가 관여해주기를 원한다. 그리고 시장 원리를 옹호하기는 하지만 때로는 새로운 산업을 육성하고 자국 기업을 경쟁에서 보호해주는 일에도 정부가 나서주길 원한다.

이처럼 미국인들이 규제에 대해 일관적이지 않은 생각을 갖고 있는 것처럼, 경제에서도 정부의 역할에 대해 상반된 견해를 가진다. 대체로, 1930년대부터 1970년대까지 정부는 비대해졌고 더 적극적으로 경제 문제에 개입했다. 하지만 1960년대와 1970년대 들어 경제 불황은 미국인들에게 사회 경제 문제를 해결하는 정부 능력에 대해 회의감을 심어주었다. 노인들을 위해 각각 퇴직 소득과 건강보험을 제공하는 사회보장제도와 의료보험을 포함하는 주요 사회제도는 재심 기간에도 유지되었다. 그러나 1980년대 들어 연방 정부의 성장 속도는 상당히 느려졌다.

어휘

preclude *v.* 제외하다, 방해하다, 막다; 못하게[불가능하게] 하다
defy *v.* ~에 도전하다, (권위 등에) 반항하다[(법률 따위를) 무시하다
address *v.* (문제를) 역점을 두어 다루다

advocacy *n.* 옹호, 지지; 고취
nurture *v.* 육성[양성]하다
intervene *v.* 개입하다, 간섭하다 (in)

[Challenge 8]

문제 1

답 (2)

해설 공산당 선언 초안의 진정한 저작자가 누구인지를 밝히는 글이다.

문제 2

답 (2)

해설 보기 (2)에서 엥겔스가 공산당 선언 작성을 완성할 수 있었다고 했지만, "From Engels's drafts Marx was able to write The Communist Manifesto, where he combined more of his ideas along with Engels's drafts and work, The Condition of the Working Class in England."에서 알 수 있듯이 공산당 선언을 쓴 것은 마르크스이며, 책의 표지에는 엥겔스와 공동 저작이었음을 밝히고 있을 뿐이다. (1)의 경우 글의 초반에 공산당 선언의 초안은 문답식으로 되어 있다고 언급되어 있다. 보기 (3)과 (4)는 본문에 모두 언급되어 있다.

해석 프리드리히 엥겔스는 공산당 선언으로 이어지는 초안을 작성한 사람으로 종종 여겨진다. 1847년 7월 엥겔스는 공산주의자 연맹에 선출이 되는데, 거기서 그는 공산당 문답집을 작성하는 일을 맡게 된다. 이것이 바로 공산당 신앙고백의 초안 (Draft of a Communist Confession of Faith)이 된다. 이 초안은 거의 20여 개의 질문으로 구성되어 있으며, 이 질문들은 그 당시 엥겔스와 칼 마르크스가 가졌던 사상을 표출하는 데 도움을 주었다. 1847년 10월에 엥겔스는 공산당 원칙 (The Principles of Communism)이라는 타이틀의 공산주의자 연맹을 위한 두 번째 초안을 작성한다. 이 글은 1914년까지 출판이 되지 않았지만 공산당 선언의 기초가 되었다. 엥겔스의 이 초안으로부터, 마르크스는 한때 공산주의자 동맹에게서 의뢰 받은 공산당 선언 (The Communist Manifesto)을 작성할 수 있게 되는데, 거기서 그는 자신의 이론에 엥겔스의 초안과 '영국 노동자계급의 상태' (The Condition of the Working Class in England)라는 글을 합친다. 표제지에는 '영속한 공동 저작'과 함께 엥겔스와 칼 마르크스의 이름이 둘 다 보이지만, 1883년의 독일 판 공산당 선언의 서문에서 엥겔스는 공산당 선언은 "본질적으로 마르크스의 업적"이며, "기본적인 사상은 온전히 마르크스의 것이다"라고 말했다. 엥겔스는 마르크스 사후에 다음과 같이 썼다. "나는 마르크스와 작업하기 이전과 그와 협업한 40년간 이 이론의 초석을 놓는 데 일정 부분 독자적인 지분을 갖고 있지만 주된 기본 원칙의

대부분은 마르크스가 제안한 것임을 부인할 수 없다. 마르크스는 천재였다. 그와 다른 우리는 기껏해야 재능이 있을 뿐이었다. 그가 없었다면, 이 이론은 지금의 모습과 전혀 달랐을 것이다. 그러므로 이 책이 그의 이름을 취하는 것은 당연한 것이다."

어휘
credit *v.* ~을 ~로 여기다: (공적 등을) (남에게) 돌리다
draft *n.* 초안
preface *n.* 서문
collaboration *n.* 공동 연구, 협력
catechism *n.* 교리 문답, 문답식 교과서

[Challenge 9]

문제 1

답 (1)

해설 본문 초반에 제시되고 있듯이, '적정 가격'에 대한 스콜라 학파의 견해가 잘못 해석되었다고 하면서 이에 대한 바른 견해를 제시하고 있다. 본문에 제시된 스콜라 학파의 견해를 잠시 살펴보면 적정 '가격'에 대한 상당히 현대적 관점을 취하고 있다는 것을 볼 수 있다 (To the contrary, de Roover showed, for the Scholastics the just price was the market price, the price arrived at by the interaction of buyers and sellers on the market) 또한 바로 이어지는 표현에서도 알 수 있듯이 당시 국가가 책정한 가격은 공정하다고 여겨졌지만 이에 대해서도 스콜라 학파는 의구심을 드러냈다.

문제 2

답 (4)

해설 De Roover의 주장은 스콜라 학파가 정의로운 가격을 고정된 가치나 국가가 결정하는 가치가 아니라 구매자와 판매자의 상호 작용에 의해 결정되는 시장 가격으로 이해했다는 것이다. 그러므로, 이러한 해석은 중세 경제 사상을 현대 시장 이론, 특히 수요와 공급과 관련된 이론과 같은 맥락에서 중세 경제 개념과 현대 경제 개념 사이의 차이보다는 연속성으로 봐야 한다는 견해이다. 이와 같은 맥락의 내용은 (4)이다.

문제 3

답 (2)

해설 빈칸이 들어간 문장을 확인해 보자.

> Scholastics, in those rare instances when they mentioned the guilds at all, chided them for their (a)_____ behavior.

비판을 하는 주체가 스콜라 학파이다. 또한 빈칸의 행위의 주체가 길드라는 점을 감안할 때 스콜라 학파는 이들의 '독점적' 행위를 비판했음을 추론할 수 있다. 이런 문제의 경우 다음과 같은 방법을 사용하면 풀이 시간을 줄일 수 있다. 'chide A for B'의 표현은 'A가 한 B의 행위를 나무라다'의 뜻인데 일반적으로 B는 부정적인 행위가 와야 함을 알 수 있다. 따라서 빈칸에 들어갈 단어가 부정적 어감을 전달하기 때문에 보기 항 (1)과 (4) 같은 긍정적 의미의 표현은 들어가기 힘들다.

해석 Raymond de Roover는 주목받지 못한 인물들에 관해 학술지에 혁신적인 논문을 연달아 써내면서 Schumpeter의 연구를 확장했다. de Roover는 후기 중세와 초기 현대 경제사상 특히나 적정 가격이라는 주제에 있어 이들이 받아들인 견해에 거대한 획을 그었다. de Roover의 연구 이전에 "적정 가격"이란 스콜라 개념은 어처구니없을 정도로 잘못 이해되어 왔다. 스콜라 학파는 특정한 객관적 기준이 제품의 "적정 가격"을 결정하는 데 도움을 줄 수 있다고 믿었던 것으로 여겨졌다. 대조적으로 de Roover는 스콜라 학파의 적정 가격이란 시장의 가격이며, 이 시장의 가격은 시장에서 생산자와 구매자 사이의 상호 작용에 의해서 결정된 것이라고 주장했다. (이 진술은 특정 조건에 영향을 받는다. 만약 국가가 가격을 책정하면, 국가가 책정한 가격은 적정한 것으로 여겨진다. 그러나 여기에서도 일부 스콜라 학자들은 비시장 가격과 국가가 적정 가격을 객관적으로 확인하고 책정하는 능력에 대해 의구심을 가졌다.) 이 분야의 이전 연구는 de Roover가 보인 바와 같이 스콜라 학파와 교회법 학자들의 더 폭넓은 합의를 훼손시키면서, 상대적으로 중요하지 않은 Heinrich von Langenstein의 특이한 관점을 지나치게 강조했다. 신학자들이 공권력에 의한 "적정 가격" 형성을 장려하고 생산자와 소비자 모두에게 공정성을 증진하는 수단으로 길드 체제를 권장하는 19세기와 20세기 낭만파와 조합주의자들이 지지한 중세 경제사상의 관점은 de Roover의 재평가를 극복하지 못했다 (비판받았다는 뜻). 후자의 경우 이들이 길드를 조금이라도 언급한 드문 상황에서 스콜라 학파는 이들의 독점적 행위를 이유로 이들을 비난했다고 나타난다. Roover는 "나는 이들이 길드 제도를 선호했다는 점을 이들의 어떤 문헌에서도 발견한 적이 없다"고 말했는데, "이러한 점이 종종 기독교 사회의 이상적인 조직처럼 묘사되어 있고, 현대 산업주의의 폐해에 대한 만병통치약으로 추천된다."

어휘
pathbreaking *a.* 혁신적인   article *n.* 기사, 논설, 논문

journal *n.* 정기 간행물   puncture *v.* 구멍을 뚫다
substantial *a.* 상당한   medieval *a.* 중세의
grotesquely *ad.* 터무니없게   Scholastic *n.* 스콜라 학자
statement *n.* 성명, 진술   be subject to ~의 지배를 받다
proviso *n.* 단서   skeptical *a.* 의심이 많은, 회의적인
idiosyncratic *a.* 색다른; 특유한
unimportant *a.* 중요하지 않은
at the expense of ~을 잃어가며   consensus *n.* 일치, 합의
canonist *n.* 교회법 학자   medieval *a.* 중세풍의, 중세의
Romantic *n.* 낭만파   corporatist *n.* 협동 조합주의자
theologian *n.* 신학자   guild *n.* 길드(중세의 상인조합)
vehicle *n.* 매개물, 매체   evaluation *n.* 평가
evidence *n.* 증거; 흔적   treatise *n.* 논문, 전문 서적
panacea *n.* 만병통치약

[Challenge 10]

문제 1

답 (2)

해설 그레고리의 열정적인 설교로 인해 아르메니아인들이 개종함으로써 아르메니아 문학에 끼친 영향을 추론해야 한다. 바로 뒤에 이어지는 표현으로 보아 교회는 이와 관련된 것이 아무것도 없다고 말하고 있다.

문제 2

답 (1)

해설 stamp out은 "뿌리를 뽑다, 소탕하다"의 뜻이다.

문제 3

답 (3)

해설 본문에서 그레고리는 아르메니아 문학을 없애려고 한 장본인이다. 이런 사람이 통치하는 시대에 아르메니아 문학의 영웅이 찬사를 받았을 것이란 말은 옳지 않다.

문제 4

답 (1)

해설 말 그대로 본문에 나오는 아르메니아 이교도 문학이 모두 없어진 것이 아니란 뜻이다.

문제 5

답 (4)

해설 아르메니아 문학을 없애려고 한 그레고리는 아르메니아인을 모두 개종하려는 교회의 입장이며, 교회 역사 편찬자들도 같은 입장이다. 그런데, 오히려 이러한 교회 역사 편찬자들로 인해 아르메니아 문학이 계속 지속되었다 (we owe the fragments we possess of early Armenian poetry to these same ecclesiastical critics)고 말하고 있으므로 보기 항 (4)가 가장 적절하다.

해석 아르메니아 선지자 그레고리의 열정적인 설교의 영향 아래서 전 아르메니아 국민의 개종으로 대부분의 원시 아르메니아 문학작품 — 신화적 전설과 시인이 노래한 영웅의 행위를 담은 가곡 — 이 모두 사라졌다는 것에는 의심할 여지가 없다. 교회는 이것을 전혀 보존하고 있지 않다. 그레고리는 이교도 신전을 파괴했을 뿐 아니라 이교도 문학 — 국가적 영웅과 신의 행적을 기리는 시와 기록된 전통 — 도 모두 근절하려 했다. 만약 인류의 낭만적 정신이 이들의 설화와 민담에 애정을 가지고 매진하지 않았더라면 그도 성공했을 것이다 (아르메니아 문학을 모두 없애지는 못했다는 뜻). 이 시대를 언급하는 교회 역사가들은 아주 묘하게도 이들의 종교적 우월성에도 불구하고, 아르메니아인들이 12세기까지 이들의 이교도 민요를 계속해서 노래했다고 말한다. 초기 아르메니아 시의 단편들을 우리가 소유하게 된 것은 아이러니하게도 이와 같은 종교 비평가들 때문이다. 이러한 단편 작품들은 대중적인 시로 마음을 흔드는 강렬한 비유적 묘사들로 가득해, 주로 왕족의 결혼이나 종교 축제를 축하하는 데 쓰이거나, 죽은 자를 위한 진혼곡이나 관습 민요에도 쓰였다.

어휘

passionate *a.* 욕정을 느끼는; 격정적인, 열정적인, 열렬한
preaching *n.* 설교   mythological *a.* (고대) 신화의
chant *n.* 구호; 성가
deed *n.* (보통 아주 좋거나 아주 나쁜) 행위
pagan *n.* 이교도   stamp out 근절하다
cling *v.* 꼭 붙잡다, 매달리다, 달라붙다, 애착을 갖다
fondly *a.* 애정을 듬뿍 담고
folk-lore *n.* 민속, 전통 문화   ecclesiastical *a.* 기독교의
historiographer *n.* 사료 편찬 위원, 수사가(修史家), 역사가
quaintly *ad.* 색다르게, 예스럽게
poesy *n.* (집합적으로) 시 (= poetry)
dirge *n.* (장례식 때 부르는) 만가, 장송곡

Day 17

[Challenge 1]

문제 1

답 (1)

해설 본문은 주로 부모로서 아이를 어떻게 다뤄야 하는지에 관한 내용을 다루고 있다.

문제 2

답 (4)

해설 빈칸을 중심으로 앞뒤 내용의 관계를 파악해야 한다.

> It is true that temptation and forgetfulness may lead some of the young occasionally to grasp the lamp, even after they are told better; but the consequent ___(a)___ generally restores them to their reason.

빈칸 앞의 내용은 아이들이 새로운 것을 만지고 싶은 유혹과 부모님이 한 말을 잊어버리는 경향으로 인해 또다시 위험한 것을 잡으려 한다는 점이다. 이후 'but'이 등장하고 있으므로, 앞에서 전개된 내용과 대조를 이루어야 한다. 또한 'consequent'라는 단어는 앞에서 일어난 사건 이후에 발생하는 것을 나타낸다. 고로 앞에서 등불을 잡은 후 겪게 되는 고통으로 인해 다시 이성적인 판단을 한다는 이야기가 전개되고 있다.

문제 3

답 (4)

해설 본문에서 아이가 등불을 만지려는 행위는 호기심에서 그러는 것이지, 그로 인해 발생하는 고통을 즐기기 위해서가 아니다.

해석 아이는 불을 밝히는 램프를 잡으려 애쓴다. 그런 반면 부모는 아이가 그것을 못하도록 만류하려 애쓴다. 기어코 아이는 그것을 잡고, 그 고통을 결과로 맞본다. 그러나 마침내 부모가 아이를 적절하게 다룬다면, 아이는 고통을 피하기 위해서는 부모의 충고를 받아들여 지시를 따라야 함을 배운다. 적어도 이것이 이성적으로 잘 관리했을 때 자연스레 발생하는 결과이다. 그리고 부모의 충고를 구하는 습관은 일단 형성되면 쉽게 사라지지 않는다. 잘 타이른 이후에도 어린이들이 유혹과 망각으로 인해 때때로 램프를 잡는 것이 사실이다. 그러나 그 결과로 발생하는 고통을 느끼고 나면 보통은 자신의 이성을 다시 따르게 된다. 자식이 부모를 의지하고 신뢰하는 습관이 깨지는 경우는 부모가 충고하는 것을 등한시하거나 거부할 때이며, 오랫동안 아이에게 거의 또는 전혀 관심을 표하지 않을 때 발생하는 것이다. 사실 아무리 잘 보살피지 않았다 하여도 이렇게 터놓고 얘기를 한다든지, 질문을 한다든지, 조언을 구하는 성향을 어느 정도 초기에 습득하지 못하는 아이는 거의 없다.

어 휘

grasp *v.* 붙잡다, 움켜잡다 indication *n.* 지시, 지적
counsel *n.* 의논, 협의, 조언
eradicate *v.* 뿌리째 뽑다; 근절하다; 박멸하다
temptation *n.* 유혹(물)
forgetfulness *n.* 잘 잊어버림, 부주의
consequent *a.* 결과로서 일어나는, 필연의
filial *a.* 자식(으로)의 reliance *n.* 믿음, 의지, 신뢰
confide *v.* (비밀 따위를) 털어놓다, 신뢰하다
inquire *v.* 묻다; 문의하다
disposition *n.* 성질; 기질

[Challenge 2]

문제 1

답 (2)

해설 본문은 번영의 근본적인 요소가 무엇인지를 주장하는 글이다.

문제 2

답 (1)

해설 (a) 이후에 전개되는 내용은 제시문에 대한 뒷받침 문장에 해당한다.

해석 신념과 통찰력은 한 나라의 부에서 오는 것이 아니다. 오히려 부를 만들어 내는 것이 신념과 통찰력이다. 한 나라의 부는 그 자원에 의존하는 것이 아니다. 자원이 어느 정도 필수적이며 아주 가치가 있는 것은 사실이다. 그러나 오늘날에는 자원이 풍부한 나라가 부의 측면에서 가장 가난한 나라이다. 미국과 같은 나라를 생각해 볼 때조차, 이러한 원칙이 그대로 적용된다. 석탄, 철 그리고 구리는 이 나라에 수천 년간 매장되어 있었다. 그러나 고작 최근 50년이 되어서야 이것들이 사용되었다. 수력은 오늘날에조차 전혀 이용되지 않은 채로 존재한다. 전 세계를 한번 보라. 원료의 증가는 없다. 천 년 전에 오늘날 우리가 가진 것보다 더 많은 원료가 존재했지만, 그 당시 땅에서 이 석탄을 캐내고, 수력을 이용하고 철도를 세우고 다른 가치 있는 일을 할 통찰력

과 신념을 가진 사람이 없었다. 그렇기에 나는 번영의 핵심은 바로 신념이라고 말하는 바이다.

어 휘

faith *n.* 신념, 신앙   **vision** *n.* 시력; 시각, 선견; 통찰력
raw material *n.* 원재료
essential *a.* 근본적인, 필수의, 본질적인
exist *v.* 존재하다, 현존하다
absolutely *ad.* 절대적으로, 참말로   **harness** *v.* 이용하다
build *v.* 세우다, 조립하다   **railroad** *n.* 철도(선로)
fundamental *n.* 핵심, 기본 원칙   **prosperity** *n.* 번영; 번창

[Challenge 3]

문제 1
답 (1)
해설 'bum on seat'는 원래 극장에서 돈만 모으는 수단으로 별로 중요하게 여기지 않는 관객을 뜻하는데, 여기선 부정적으로 묘사되는 돈 많은 기업 지도층을 일컫고 있다. 모르는 표현이 나왔을 경우 당황하지 말고, 앞뒤 문맥을 확인하고 보기 항목 중 가장 거리가 먼 것을 하나씩 먼저 제거하는 소거법을 활용한다.

문제 2
답 (3)
해설 권력은 행사하고 그에 대한 책임은 묻지 않는 행태를 기술하고 있는 내용으로 보기 (3)이 가장 적절하다.

문제 3
답 (1)
해설 "This confuses power with efficiency. Just because a person can make big changes does not mean they are 'clever', such power comes with the position"부분과 "those in power" 즉, 권력을 가진 사람은 긍정 또는 부정의 큰 변화를 일으킬 수 있음을 파악할 수 있다.

문제 4
답 (1)
해설 (가)는 일반인을 가리키고, 나머지는 모두 기업 지도층(중역)을 지칭한다.

문제 5
답 (2)
해설 제시된 문장에서 추가 부연을 나타내는 'in fact'를 확인할 수 있다. 즉, 지도층의 성공과 관련된 내용의 부연이므로 (d) 자리에 들어가는 것이 가장 적절하다.

해설 기업 지도층의 가장 매력 없는 면의 하나는 자신들이 '특별한' 사람, 어쩌면 일반인들보다 '더 낫다고' 생각하는 많은 기업 중역들의 망상이다. 이것은 권력과 효율성을 혼동하는 것이다. 한 사람이 큰 변화를 일구어 낸다는 것이 곧 이들은 '현명함'을 의미하는 것이 아닌 것처럼 이러한 권력은 (단지) 지위에서 나오는 것이다. 이것은 'bum on seat'의 내재적 특성이 아니다. ('bum on seat'은 극장에서 돈을 모으는 수단으로 별로 중요하게 여기지 않는 관객을 뜻하는데, 여기선 돈 많은 기업 지도층을 일컫고 있음) 그러나 오늘날의 자기중심적 사고의 사회에서는 기업 합병은 그러나 CEO 자신을 더욱 성공하도록 만들어 주는 것으로 여겨지는데, 이는 아마도 이들이 뜻하지 않게 더 많은 자산과 사람을 '소유하게' 되기 때문일 것이다. 그러나 명령(edict)을 통해 거대한 변화를 일구어 내는 이런 능력은 그런 변화가 대개 회사의 '순이익'과 관련이 없는 사회 영역에 거대한 파괴적 작용을 이끌어 내기도 한다는 사실을 숨기는 것이다. 이상하게도 이런 부정적인 전반적 변화에 대한 책임감을 이들 중역들이 주장한 적은 절대 없다. 자본주의적 가치 체계는 사실 기독교의 7가지 죄악 중 5가지 즉, 자만심, 시기, 욕심, 탐욕, 욕정을 긍정적인 사회적 가치로 변형시켜 이것들을 모든 경제 기업에 필수적인 동기로 다루었다. 반면, 사랑과 겸손으로 시작하는 기본 덕목은 '사업에는 좋지 않은' 것으로 거부되었다.

이러한 중역실(boardroom)의 의도된, 편협된 목적이 변화를 선동한다고 생각해 보더라도, 역사를 돌아볼 때 이 땅에서 실패란 성공보다 훨씬 더 흔한 것임을 알 수 있다. 게다가 대부분의 성공은 재계의 조치에 따르기 마련인 것들(예를 들면, 시장의 호기로 발생하는 주가 상승)이라, 이런 우발적 요소가 힘을 보태주지 않으면 상황은 금방 뒤집어지게 된다. 더욱이 이런 과대망상 때문에 '사장'은 그 회사의 다른 구성원들로부터 전문적 조언을 듣지 못하게 된다. 이런 거만한 행위의 부작용으로 사실상 많은 회사들이 실패를 맛보게 된다. 이는 이들 스스로 자신을 '신이 인류에게 주신 선물'이라고 생각하는 것과는 거리가 멀고, 오히려 현실적으로 지구상에서 가장 무지하고, 편협하며 상상력이 없는 사람들이기 때문이다.

어 휘

appealing *a.* 매력적인
delusion *n.* 망상
intrinsic *a.* 내재적인
ego-tripping *a.* 자기중심적인, 방자한 행동의
edict *n.* 칙령, 포고; 명령
bottom-line *n.* 순이익, 최종결과, 사실의 핵심(쟁점)
avarice *n.* 탐욕
lust *n.* 욕망, 관능적인 욕구
cardinal *a.* 주요한, 기본적인

Day 17

[Challenge 4]

문제 1

답 (1)

해설 첫 번째 문장이 주제문이고, 이후 구체적 예시를 통해 뒷받침 문장을 제시하고 있다.

문제 2

답 (4)

해설 주제문에서 알 수 있듯이, 유전공학이 위험한 알레르기를 발생시킬 수 있다는 부정적 관점을 드러내고 있다.

해석 유전자 변형 농산물은 이전에는 그 음식에 있지 않았던 알려진 또는 알려지지 않은 알레르기를 유발할 수 있다. 예를 들자면, 브라질 땅콩에서 추출한 유전자가 포함된 유전 조작 콩이 콩 알레르기가 있는 사람의 혈청에 알레르기 반응을 일으킬 수 있다는 것이 발견되었다. 과학자들이 이 특정한 경우에 발생하는 위험 요소를 발견할 수 있었던 이유는 콩 알레르기가 아주 일반적이며, 알레르기 반응을 일으키는 개인 혈청에 대해 적절한 실험을 할 수 있었기 때문이었다. 다른 알레르기 반응을 확인하는 실험은 훨씬 어렵다. 유전공학으로 인해 익숙한 음식에서 인간이 먹는 음식 중 기존에 없었던 물질이 나오게 되면 어떤 이가 이것에 알레르기 반응을 보일지 파악하는 것이 불가능해진다.

어 휘

genetic engineering 유전자 공학
allergen n. 알레르겐(알레르기를 일으키는 물질)
soybean n. 콩   nut n. 견과(호두·개암·텝 따위)
serum n. [생물]혈청; [의학]혈청; 유장(乳漿), 림프액
fatal a. 치명적인   proper a. 적당한, 타당한
potential n. 가능성   substance n. 물질
previously ad. 전에(는), 본래는, 사전에, 먼저, 미리

[Challenge 5]

문제 1

답 (2)

해설 역접의 'however'로 보아 앞에서 무엇인가 알 수 없는 정보가 나와야 하고, 주어진 문장 뒤에서는 이에 대한 뒷받침 문장이 진술되어야 한다. 고로, 청동기 시기에 아일랜드가 고립되지 않고 대륙과 연결되어 있다는 증거가 구체적으로 전개되는 곳은 바로 (b)이다.

참고 1. 제시문은 'However'를 동반한 주제문으로 볼 수 있다. 고로 이후 전개된 내용은 이에 대한 증거로 구체적 예가 등장하는 뒷받침 문장에 해당한다.

참조 2. 본문은 두 문단으로 나눌 수 있는데, 첫 번째 문단은 아일랜드가 청동기 시대에 대륙과 소통했다는 내용으로 구성되고, 두 번째 문단 'The Bronze-Age people...'로 시작되는 문장은 청동기 시대 사람들의 생활상의 특징을 드러내는 내용으로 구성된다.

문제 2

답 (1)

해설 보기 항 (4)는 고르지 말아야 한다. Gold Rush는 새로 발견된 금 매장지로 한몫 보려는 사람들이 갑자기 몰려드는 현상을 가리키는 말이다. 금이 많이 매장된 장소와 비유되는 곳은 황금의 도시 El Dorado에 해당한다.

해석 John Abercromby는 아일랜드 내 화장된 봉분에서 출토된 음식을 담는 토기 목록을 제공하고 있는데, 여기에 1912년에 County Dublin의 Crumlin 채석장에서 발견된 초기 형태의 음식 토기를 추가해야 한다. 그러나 앞으로 행할 발굴을 통해 현재 답변을 제공하지 못하거나 또는 단지 불확실한 답변만을 제공하는 수많은 질문들을 알아내야 하는 것이 (숙제로) 남아 있다. 그러나 이것만은 분명하다. 청동기 시대에 아일랜드는 고립되어 있던 것이 아니라 대륙과 직접적인 교류를 하며 자리를 잡았다. 스칸디나비아의 영향력은 New Grange 부족의 거대한 고분에서 찾을 수 있다. 그리고 이베리아의 영향력은 후기 형태의 청동기에서 발견할 수 있다. 청동기 시대의 아일랜드는 일종의 서양의 El Dorado라고 할 수 있었는데, 이는 금이 풍부하였기 때문이다. 아일랜드의 금장식은 대륙과 스칸디나비아 모두에서 발견된다. 반면 스칸디나비아의 호박이 아일랜드에서 발견되기도 한다. 청동기 사람들은 천을 짜는 데 능했다. 때로는 정교하게 짠 말머리 장식이 사용되었다. 손으로 도기를 만드는 기술은 아주 높이 평가될 정도였다. 청동 면도기가 발견된 수로 판단해보건대, 면도가 아주 흔했던 것이 틀림없다.

어 휘

vessel n. 용기(容器), 그릇
cremate v. 불태워 재로 만들다, 소각하다; 화장하다
burial n. 매장, 장례식   quarry n. 채석장
excavation n. 발굴(물), 출토품
doubtful a. 의심(의혹)을 품고 있는, 확신을 못 하는
detect v. (나쁜 짓 따위를) 발견하다, 간파하다, ~임을 발견하다
amber n. 호박   weave v. (직물·바구니 따위를) 짜다, 뜨다
ornament n. 꾸밈, 장식; 장식품
pottery n. 도기, 오지그릇   razor n. 면도칼

[Challenge 6]

문제 1

답 (4)

해설 본문은 현재 주택 시장을 아주 암울하게 묘사하고 있다. 'foreclosure'는 주택 시장의 위기로 인해서 발생하는 현상(결

과)이다. 작가의 집 주위에 집이 많지 않은 것이 아니라 내놓은 빈집이 많은 것이다. 본문 내용의 전체적인 분위기를 아주 잘 드러내는 것은 보기 항목 (4)이다.

문제 2

답 (4)

해설 본문에서 말하는 'superrich oligarchs'는 세금을 면제받은 권력자를 지칭한다. 글쓴이는 이들이 절대 자비를 들여 이런 빈집을 사 경제 회복에 조금이라도 도움을 줄 그런 애국심이 없다고 비꼬고 있다.

해석 나는 자동차를 타고 동네를 지날 때마다 거의 다 죽어가는 주택 시장의 흔적을 본다. 4분의 1도 못 되는 거리 안에 팔려고 내놓은 집이 4채나 되는 것을 볼 수 있다. (우리 구역으로 더 거슬러 들어가서 다 세지는 못했어요..) 그리고 이들 집은 몇 개월째 시장에 나와 있다. 이상한 것은 우리 동네의 집들은 압류 때문에 어려움을 겪는 지역에 있는 게 아니라는 점이다. 이들 집 중 3채는 여러 가지 이유로 이사를 해야 했던 사람들이 소유하고 있다. 그중 하나는 8개월 전에 죽은 노인의 집이다. 집을 팔 수가 없는데, 이는 사는 사람이 없기 때문이다. 정말이지, 이것이 경제에 큰 타격을 주고 있다. 내 생각은 이렇다. 최근에 세금 면제를 받은 정말 부자인 소수 권력자들이 자신의 재산을 나누어, 이런 집들을 살 것이라고 생각하나? 있죠요, 그냥 애국적인 태도만 취하는 것뿐이네요. 나라와 모두를 사랑한다니.

어 휘

moribund *a.* 빈사의, 죽어가는; 소멸해가는; 활동 휴지(休止) 상태 의, 정체한

subdivision *n.* 재분, 잘게 나눔, 세분; [미국](토지의) 분필(分筆), 구획[대지]분할

odd *a.* ① 기수[홀수]의 ② 기묘한, 이상한, 뜻밖의; 묘한

plague *v.* 역병[재앙 따위]에 걸리게 하다, 고통당하다

foreclosures *n.* [금융](빌려 간 돈에 대한) 담보권 행사, 압류

tremendous *a.* 무서운, 굉장한, 무시무시한;《구어》거대한; 굉장 한 양의

patriotic *a.* 애국적인, 애국의, 우국의

[Challenge 7]

문제 1

답 (2)

해설 특정 현상과 잠재된 단점을 기술하는 설명문이다.

문제 2

답 (4)

해설 'minority firms risk expanding too fast and overextending themselves financially, since most are small concerns and, unlike large businesses, they often need to make substantial investments in new plants, staff, equipment, and the like in order to perform work subcontracted to them.'에서 보기 (4)에 대한 답변을 이끌어 낼 수 있다.

문제 3

답 (3)

해설 'they lack access to the sizable orders and subcontracts that are generated by large companies'에서 보기 (3)이 답임을 알 수 있다.

문제 4

답 (3)

해설 'a minority enterprise that secures the business of one large corporate customer often runs the danger of becoming — and remaining — dependent.'에서 소수민족 회사가 대기업에 의존해 고객을 확보할 경우 발생하는 위험성을 지적하고 있으므로, 보기 (3)과 같이 대기업 의존성을 피할 수 있는 고객 기반을 확장해야 함을 알 수 있다.

해석 최근 미국 내 소수민족이 운영하는 기업들은 새롭고 중대한 위험뿐 아니라 전례 없는 호기를 누리고 있다. 인권 운동가들은 오랫동안 흑인, 히스패닉 그리고 다른 소수민족들이 자신만의 기업을 세우는 데 어려움을 겪은 주된 이유 중 하나는 바로 대기업에 의해 창출되는 상당한 양의 주문과 하청을 따낼 수 없기 때문이라고 주장해 왔다. 이제 국회는 50만 달러 이상의 정부 계약을 따낸 기업들이 소수민족이 운영하는 하청업체를 찾는 데 온 힘을 다할 것을 법에 따라 요구하고 있다. 실제로 몇몇 정부 기관과 지방 기관들은 소수민족 기업에 공공사업 계약을 일부 분배하는 데 구체적인 비율 목표를 세우기까지 했다. 기업의 반응은 상당했던 것으로 보인다. 1977년에 수집한 수치에 따르면, 소수민족 기업과의 계약은 1972년의 7,700만 달러에서 1977년에 11억 달러까지 상승했다. 1980년대 초에 소수민족 기업과의 계약 예상 통계를 보면 향후 10년간 연속해서 연간 530억이 넘는 것으로 추정된다.

소수민족 기업들로서는 전망이 밝지만, 이렇게 후원이 늘어나는 것이 이들에게 위험 요소가 되기도 한다. 우선, 소수민족 기업들은 지나치게 빨리 확장해 자금을 과도하게 지출할 위험이 있다. 이는 소수민족 기업들 대부분이 작은 회사(concerns)이기 때문에, 대기업과 달리 자신들에게 하청된 일을 처리하기 위해서 종종 새로운 공장, 직원, 장비 등에 상당한 투자를 할 필요가 있기 때문이다. 이후 어떠한 이유에서 하청이 줄어들 경우, 이런 기업들은 고정비용을 감당하지 못할 가능성이 있다. 두 번째 위험 요소는 백인 소유의 회사가 소수민족이 소유한 회사와 합작 투자의 형태를 통해 높은 할당을 챙기려고 할 수도 있다는 점이다. 물론, 많은 경우 합작 투자에 대한 합법적 이유도 존재한다. 분명히 백인과 소수민족 기업들은 하나의 팀을 이루어 혼자서는 얻을 수 없는 사업을 얻어내기도 한다. 그러나 인권단체와 소

소수민족 사업주들은 소수민족 기업들이 합법적 합작 투자의 온전한 파트너로 받아들여지기보다는 백인 기업의 입김으로 '최전선'에 세워지는 경우가 많다고 국회에 불만을 제기하고 있다. 세 번째는 한 대기업에 의존해 고객을 확보한 소수민족 기업의 경우 의존적이 되거나 계속 그런 관계를 유지해야 하는 위험이 있다. 최상의 상황에서도 더 크고 더 기반이 튼튼한 회사와의 치열한 경쟁으로 작은 회사들은 자신들의 고객 기반을 늘리기가 쉽지 않다.

어휘

minority-owned *a.* 소수민족이 운영하는
unprecedented *a.* 전례가 없는
award A to B B에게 A를 주다
apportion *v.* 할당하다, 분배하다
letup *n.* 감소, 중지
crippling *a.* 큰 손해를 주는
legitimate *a.* 합법의, 정당한
backing *n.* 지지, 후원

[Challenge 8]

문제 1

답 (2)

해설 바로 이어지는 내용인 'make the understanding of chemical reactions as dull and as dogmatic an affair as the reading of Virgil's Aeneid' 부분을 통해 과학 교육을 반대하는, 즉 'The pioneers of the teaching of science'와는 대조적인 인물임을 알 수 있다.

문제 2

답 (4)

해설 작가는 현 과학 교육에 대해 상당히 부정적인 관점을 취하면서 두 번째 문단 전반에 걸쳐 그 문제점을 지적하고 있다. 'As to the learning of scientific method, the whole thing is palpably a farce.' 부분에서 과학에 대한 그의 관점을 파악할 수 있다.

문제 3

답 (2)

해설 두 번째 문단 중반 이후에 나오는 과학 교육의 문제점을 파악하도록 한다. 보기 (2)에 대한 내용은 본문과 일치하지 않는다.

문제 4

답 (2)

해설 문제점으로 지적하는 부분에 해당하는 내용은 'teaches him how to think logically and inductively by studying scientific method'이다.

문제 5

답 (3)

해설 점성학은 과학이 아니라 미신에 기반을 둔다. 앞뒤 문맥을 통해 과학과 대치되는 개념임을 파악한 후 답을 고르도록 한다.

해석 과학 교육의 선구자들은 과학을 교육에 도입함으로써 인습, 인위성 그리고 회고적 사고라는 고전 연구의 특징을 제거할 수 있을 것이라 생각했지만, 이들은 상당히 실망하고 말았다. 마찬가지로 당시 인문주의자들은 고전 작가에 대한 연구가 중세 스콜라 철학의 진부한 현학과 미신을 당장 없애줄 거라 생각했다. 이 둘의 맞수였던 전문직 교사들은 화학 작용을 Virgil의 Aeneid를 읽는 것처럼 지루하고 독단적으로 이해하도록 만들어버렸다.

과학을 교육에 활용하자는 주된 주장은 이것이 아이에게 우리가 사는 실제 우주에 대한 것을 가르치고, 아이가 과학적 발견의 결과에 익숙해지도록 하며, 동시에 과학적 방법을 연구함으로써 논리적이고 귀납적으로 사고할 수 있는 방법을 가르친다는 것이다. 이들 목적 중 첫 번째는 어느 정도 제한적인 성공을 거두었지만 두 번째 부분에 있어서는 실질적으로 전혀 그렇지 못했다. 중등학교나 공립학교 교육 과정을 통과한 지역사회의 특권층 사람들은 백년 전의 기초적인 물리나 화학에 대해서는 어느 정도 알 수 있겠지만, 영리한 소년이 학교 수업 시간 외에 무선에 관해 흥미를 갖거나 과학 쪽으로 취미가 있어 알아낸 사실 이상으로 아는 게 거의 없을 거라는 것이다. 과학적 방법의 학습에 관해서는 전반적으로 눈에 보일 정도로 우스꽝스럽다. 실제로, 아이들은 과학적 방법을 익히지 못하고 있을 뿐 아니라 그와는 정반대로, 말하자면 말이 되든 안 되든 들은 대로만 믿고 질문을 받았을 때 들은 대로 읊어대야 하는 것이다. 교육받은 사람들이 인종 이론과 같은 위협적인 내용은 말할 것도 없고, 심령술이나 점성술과 같은 말도 안 되는 것에 반응하는 것을 보게 되면, 영국 또는 독일의 50년간의 과학적 방법에 대한 교육은 어떤 식으로든 가시적인 성과를 전혀 내지 못했다는 것을 보여준다. 과학적 방법을 배우는 유일한 길은 개인적으로 오랜 세월 고된 경험을 통해 익히는 방법뿐이다. 그리고 교육 제도나 사회 제도가 이런 것이 가능하도록 바뀌지 않는 한, 우리가 기대할 수 있는 최상은 과학 기술을 어느 정도 익힐 수 있는 소수와 이를 활용하고 개발할 수 있는 그보다 더 소수의 사람들을 배출하는 것일 뿐이다.

어휘

conventionality *n.* 인습
artificiality *n.* 인위성

backward-lookingness *n.* 회고적 사고
classical studies 고전학문 **humanist** *n.* 인문주의자
banish *v.* 추방하다, 내쫓다 **dull** *a.* 지루한, 활기 없는
pedantry *n.* 아는 체함, 현학; 규칙·학설·선례 따위에 얽매임
scholasticism *n.* 스콜라 철학; 전통 존중, 학풍 고집
dogmatic *a.* 독단적인, 교리의
acquaint *v.* ~에게 숙지시키다
quackery *n.* 엉터리없는 말, 말도 안 되는 것
alter *v.* 바꾸다, 변경하다

어휘
inevitably *ad.* 필연적으로, 불가피하게 **bishop** *n.* 주교, 비숍
quotation *n.* 인용(문) **be apt to** ~하는 경향이 있다
aphorism *n.* 경구 **revelation** *n.* 폭로, 드러냄, 계시
widespread *a.* 광범위한, 널리 퍼진 **involve** *v.* 관련시키다
respected *a.* 훌륭한, 소문난 **centre** *n.* 중심, 중앙

[Challenge 9]

문제 1
답 (4)
해설 본문은 역사적, 철학적 사례를 활용하여 권력, 특히 절대 권력이 어떻게 부패로 이어지는 경향이 있는지 주로 다루고 있으므로 이를 가장 잘 반영한 제목은 (4)이다.

문제 2
답 (4)
해설 본문에서 정치 권력이 특정 제도 안에서만 부패의 성향을 보인다고 말하는 부분은 없다.

해석 이것은 필연적으로 부패의(부패하는) 특징이 있는가? 1887년 영국의 역사가 Lord Acton은 Mandell Creighton 주교에게 쓴 편지에서 세계에서 가장 많이 인용되는 말 중 하나가 되는 문장을 쓴다. '권력은 부패하는 경향이 있으며, 절대 권력은 절대적으로 부패한다.' 권력과 부패의 연관성은 오래전부터 인식되어왔다. Chatham의 백작인 William Pitt는 1770년 상원(the House of Lords)에서 한 연설에서 다음과 같이 말했다. '무한의 권력은 이것을 소유한 사람의 마음을 부패시키는 경향이 있다.'
그리스 철학자 플라톤은 기원전 4세기에 공화국이 추구하는 정책에서 개인적 이득을 얻으려 하지 않는 정치인만이 통치를 할 자격이 있다고 주장했다. 이것은 또한 권력을 취하려는 사람은 이것을 할 자격이 가장 적은 사람일 가능성이 아주 크다는 경구에서도 인식된다.
현대에도 부패한 정치 지도자들의 수많은 예가 있다. 동독의 Erich Honecker, 중앙아프리카 공화국의 Jean-Bedel Bokassa, 그리고 전 소련의 스탈린 등 더 많은 예가 있다. 세계의 자유 민주주의는 상대적으로 덜 발달된 정치에서 발견되는 이런 종류의 부패에 면역이 되어 있다고 여겨졌지만, 이탈리아에서 가장 촉망받는 정치인들 중 몇몇이 연루된 이탈리아 전역의 마피아의 부패에 대한 폭로는 이 문제를 다시 한번 유럽인의 생활의 중심에 드러나게 하는 계기가 된다.

[Challenge 10]

문제 1
답 (4)
해설 비유법 중 '행동, 개념, 물체' 등을 그와 유사한 성질을 지닌 다른 말로 대체하는 것을 은유라고 한다. 본문에서 등장하는 '배물방개붙이 애벌레'를 대체하는 말로 robbers를 사용하고 있다. 보기 (5)의 직유의 경우, 비슷한 성질이나 모양을 가진 두 사물을 '같이, 같은, 처럼, 듯이, 양(as, like와 같은)' 등의 말로 직접적으로 연관 지어야 한다.

문제 2
답 (3)
해설 배물방개붙이 애벌레는 상대적으로 몸집이 작지만 먹이를 잡는 데 있어서는 그 교묘함이 다른 어느 육지 동물보다 더 훌륭하다고 찬사하고 있다.

해석 연못 세계와 수족관에는 일부 끔찍한 약탈자들이 있는데, 우리 눈앞에서 벌어지는 치열한 생존 경쟁의 잔인함을 목격하게 될 수도 있다. 만약 수족관에 물고기를 섞어서 넣는다면, 곧 새로 들어온 물고기들 사이에서 이런 충돌의 예를 볼 수 있는데, 거기에는 배물방개붙이(Dytiscus) 유충도 있을 것이다. 이들의 상대적인 몸집을 고려할 때, 이 동물이 자신의 먹이를 죽이기 위해 사용하는 탐심과 교묘함은 호랑이, 사자, 늑대와 같은 악명 높은 약탈자들의 방법조차 무색케 한다. 배물방개붙이 유충과 비교했을 때 이들은 모두 양과 같다.

어휘
aquarium *n.* 수족관
embittered *a.* 비참한
considering *prep.* ~을 고려할 때
eclipse *v.* ~의 명성·중요성 따위를 가리다, 무색하게 하다, 능가하다

Day 18

[Challenge 1]

문제 1

답 (1)

해설 식물의 광합성에 관한 글이다.

문제 2

답 (1)

해설 본문을 통해 단백질은 서로 뭉쳐 덩어리를 형성한다는 것을 파악할 수 있다. 광합성의 첫 번째 단계에서는 빛을 사용하나 두 번째 단계에서는 사용하지 않는다고 했다. 산소와 수소 이온은 광합성 과정에서 발생한다. 탄수화물은 두 번째 과정에서 형성된다고 세 번째 문단 마지막 부분에서 언급되어 있다.

문제 3

답 (3)

해설 부연을 이끄는 콜론을 활용한다. 바로 이어지는 내용(after the first one has been pushed, each protein transfers energy to each member along down the line)으로 보아 '도미노'가 가장 적절한 비유이다. 식물에게 일광욕은 생명이다. 사실, 식물은 태양에 자신을 최대한 노출하는 동시에 (사는 데) 필수적인 물의 손실을 예방하기 위한 온갖 방식을 발달시켰다. 일부 조류와 박테리아와 함께 식물도 광합성을 하는데, 이는 태양 에너지를 사용하여 생체합성물을 합성하는 과정이다. 광합성을 하는 유기체는 이산화탄소와 물을 사용하여 이런 합성물을 만들어내는데, 이들이 방출하는 부산물이 바로 산소와 탄수화물이다.

식물은 우리(인간)가 숨 쉴 수 있는 산소를 제공한다. 이제 이런 짤막한 정보를 알았으니, 왜 환경 운동가들이 열대우림, 습지대, 자연 서식지가 급속하게 파괴되고 있는 것에 기겁을 하는지 좀 더 잘 이해할 수 있을 것이다. 지구상에 식물의 수가 적으면 적을수록, 숨 쉬기와 같은 중요한 것을 위한 산소가 덜 생성되는 것이다.

광합성은 두 가지 과정으로 나뉜다. 첫 번째 과정에는 빛이 필요하고 두 번째 과정에서는 빛이 필요하지 않다. 광합성의 첫 번째 단계에서 엽록체(chloroplast)라 불리는 세포 단백질 색소는 빛에 반응하여 높은 에너지 상태에 이른다. 그런 다음 엽록체는 이 에너지를 전자를 통해 다른 단백질 복합체로 전달한다. 이 단백질 덩어리를 전자전달계(electron ransport chain)라고 한다.

이 단백질 복합체는 도미노와 같이 작용한다. 첫 번째 단백질이 에너지를 받으면, 각각의 단백질은 이 에너지를 일렬로 늘어선 각 단백질에게 전달한다. 이 과정에서 물이 분해되고, 산소와 수소 이온을 발산한다. 전자전달계에서 나온 전자는 이들 수소 이온 및 NADP+와 결합하여 ATP와 축소된 단위의 NADP+를 형성한다. 이 에너지 저장 형태인 ATP와 NADPH를 사용하여 두 번째 광합성 단계에서 이산화탄소를 전환시켜 탄수화물을 만든다. 식물은 그런 다음 이 탄수화물을 분해하여 생존에 필요한 에너지로 사용하게 되는 것이다.

어 휘

algae *n.* 조류
Photosynthesis *n.* 광합성
carbohydrate *n.* 탄수화물
tidbit *n.* 작은 조각
freak out 기겁하다
chloroplast *n.* 엽록체

[Challenge 2]

문제 1

답 (2)

해설 실험으로 밝혀진 사실이 글의 요지에 해당한다. 특정 음식을 먹는 행위를 반복적으로 상상하면 그 음식에 대한 식욕이 떨어진다는 것이 실험의 결과이다. 고로 보기 항 (2)가 정답이다.

해석 특정 음식물 섭취는 보통 이후 습관적으로 이를 섭취했을 때 그 양이 줄어들며, 이는 음식에 대한 반응과 이것을 먹으려는 동기가 줄어드는 것을 의미한다. 우리는 특정 음식에 대한 습관적인 섭취가 이러한 음식 섭취를 상상하는 것만으로도 발생하는 사실을 밝혀냈다. 다섯 번의 실험을 통해 특정 음식(치즈와 같은)을 먹는 것을 여러 번 반복적으로 상상한 사람들은, 그 음식을 덜 상상한 사람이나 다른 음식(사탕 같은)을 먹는 것을 상상한 사람 또는 그 음식을 상상하지 않은 사람보다 그 음식을 덜 섭취했다. 그 음식을 덜 먹고 싶어서였지 맛이 떨어지기 때문이 아니었기에 이들은 그렇게 행동했다. 이러한 결과가 나타내는 것은 심적 표상 자체만으로도 특정 자극에 대한 습관이 생길 수 있다는 점이다.

어휘

- subsequent *a.* 뒤의, 차후의; 다음의
- intake *n.* 섭취
- habituation *n.* 습관화
- responsiveness *n.* 민감성
- motivation *n.* 자극, 유도; (심리학) (행동의) 동기 부여; 하고 싶은 기분, 열의, 욕구
- merely *ad.* 단지, 그저, 다만; 전혀
- repeatedly *ad.* 되풀이하여, 몇 번이고
- palatable *a.* (음식 등이) 입에 맞는, 맛난, 풍미 좋은
- representation *n.* 표시, 표현, 묘사
- stimulus *n.* 자극; 격려, 고무

[Challenge 3]

문제 1

답 (3)

해설 첫 번째 문장이 주제문이다. 즉, '정치 부패의 공통된 특징'을 나열하고 있다.

문제 2

답 (1)

해설 (2)는 'glass ceiling', (3)은 'affirmative action'에 관한 내용이다. (4)는 'political correctness'이다. 'granting favours to win votes'의 의미를 가장 잘 반영하고 있는 보기는 (1)이다.

문제 3

답 (4)

해설 부대 상황의 'with'가 이끄는 내용을 활용한다.

> It is an _____(b)_____ process, with one favour demanding another and one shady deal leading to the next.

거짓된(부정한) 호의로 둔갑한 거래가 다시 다른 거짓된 거래를 불러일으킨다고 하고 있다. 고로 빈칸에 들어갈 단어는 우선 부정적 어감을 전달해야 한다. 'shady'와 '거짓된 호의'를 가장 잘 드러내는 표현은 'insidious'이다.

해석 전 세계적인 정치 부패를 분석한 결과 공통적 요소를 나타내고 있다. 우선, 많은 경우, 개인, 정부 또는 정당이 장기간 권력을 지속적으로 유지하고 있었다. 둘째는 첫 번째 요소에서 파생되는 것으로, 공무 수행이 아닌 권력이 정치적 삶의 주된 목표가 되었다. 셋째, 주된 목적인 정권을 이양하지 않음에 따라 실질적으로 이러한 목적에 부합한다면, 어떠한 행위도 받아들여진다. 다시 말해서, 도덕이나 정직은 권력 유지에 있어 두 번째로 중요한 요소이다. 필연적으로, 득표를 위해 특례(favors)를 베풀거나(이권 유도형 정치), 자신의 정당의 정치 자금을 획득하려는 의도에서 특례(favors)를 베푸는 정치인이 여기에 해당한다. 이것은 한 번

의 호의가 다른 호의를 요구하고, 하나의 불법 거래가 또 다른 불법 거래에 이르는 잠식 과정인 것이다.

어휘

- analysis *n.* 분석
- regime *n.* 정권, 제도, 체제
- party *n.* 정당
- continuously *ad.* 계속해서, 연속적으로
- retention *n.* 보유, 유지
- virtually *ad.* 사실상, 거의
- acceptable *a.* 용인되는, 받아들여지는
- further *v.* 발전시키다, 조성하다
- probity *n.* 정직성
- inevitably *ad.* 필연적이다시피
- involve *v.* 연루시키다; 포함하다
- grant *v.* 주다, 수여하다
- favour *n.* 호의, 지지
- vote *n.* 표, 득표
- obtain *v.* 얻다, 획득하다
- shady *a.* 떳떳하지 못한, 수상한

[Challenge 4]

문제 1

답 (2)

해설 본문은 특정 현상(정치 부패)에 대한 문제점 인식 및 거기에 대한 대안을 제시하는 글이다.

문제 2

답 (3)

해설 다음 본문의 내용을 가장 잘 반영한 보기 항을 골라야 한다.

> There are probably few politicians whose hands are absolutely clean.

아주 기본적인 사항이지만 답은 언제나 본문에 기초한다는 것을 절대 잊으면 안 된다. 항상 근거를 찾는 연습을 꾸준히 해야 한다.

문제 3

답 (4)

해설 해석이 조금 까다로울 수 있다. 가정법이 들어간 문장인데, if가 생략되고 should가 앞으로 나온 형태이다.

> there is always an effective opposition ready to take over should the party in power ___(b)___,

현 여당이 어떤 경우에 처해졌을 때 능력 있는 야당이 권력을 떠맡을지 생각하면 된다.

해석 그래서 인간의 본성이 그러하다는 점에서 Acton 경이 옳았던 것으로 보인다. 이러한 증거는 누구나 세계 전역에

걸쳐 찾아볼 수 있다. 아마도 티끌 하나 없이 손이 깨끗한 정치인은 거의 없을 것이다. 여기에 해답은 있는가? 분명 간단하고 즉각적인 답안은 없다.

대부분의 나라에서 이것은 장기간에 걸친 고된 과정일 것이다. 만약 권력을 가진 정당이 흔들린다면 유능한 반대당이 항상 권력을 차지하기 위해 벼르고 있기에 다수당의 정치 이론은 좀 더 현실적이어야 한다. 정부는 대중의 감시에 개방적이어야 하며, 정치 자금에 대한 정당들의 책임감이 여기에 포함이 되어야 한다. 그러나 무엇보다 정치인에 대한 대중의 존경이 회복되어야 한다. 이것은 정치인 스스로 자신이 이윤 추구를 위해서가 아니라 공무 수행을 위해 선출되었다고 인식하고 있음을 행동으로 보임으로써 이루어질 수 있다.

어휘

politician *n.* 정치인 instant *a.* 즉각적인, 순간의
long-haul *a.* 장거리의 multiparty *a.* 여러 정당의
scrutiny *n.* 정밀 조사, 철저한 검토 include *v.* 포함하다
accountability *n.* 책임, 의무 restore *v.* 회복시키다
demonstrate *v.* 입증[실증]하다 deed *n.* 행위[행동]
elect *v.* 선출하다, 선택하다
serve *v.* (사람, 국가 등을 위해) 일[봉사]하다

[Challenge 5]

문제 1

답 (2)

해설 지시 대상을 정확히 파악해야 한다. 본문에 학자와 이론이 많이 등장하고 있어 혼동되기 쉽다. 정리하면 다음과 같다.

Stalin – Socialism in One Country
Trotsky – Permanent Revolution = a variety of Menshevism
Lenin – Proletariat Revolution

본문에서 Stalin이 반대한 이 이론은 Trotsky의 영속 혁명 (Permanent Revolution)이다.

해석 '일국 사회주의' 이론은 이 이론에 반대하여 Stalin이 생각한 것으로, 소련이 국제적 마르크스주의의 발전에 의존하는 것에 반대하는 것이다. 이 주제에 관한 그의 첫 번째 시나리오 '시월 혁명과 러시아 공산당 전술'에서 그는 영속 혁명이라는 Trotsky의 이론이 Lenin의 프롤레타리아 혁명과는 상반되며, 나아가 'Trotsky의 이 이론이 단지 멘셰비키 정책의 변형일 뿐이다'라고까지 주장하는 의견을 분명히 드러냈다. 게다가, '일국 사회주의' 이론은 Trotsky의 이론과 정반대의 입장에서 만들어졌다. Trotsky는, 그가 종종 인용하는 '일국 사회주의 이론은 영속 혁명 이론에 일관되게 반대하는 유일한 이론이다'라는 것을 선언하는 이 부분만큼은 인정했다.

어휘

socialism *n.* 사회주의 conceive *v.* 마음에 품다, 생각해 내다
response *n.* 응답, 대응 foster *v.* 기르다, 양육하다
international *a.* 국제상의 tactics *n.* 용병, 전술
run counter to ~에 거스르다, ~에 반대하는 행동을 취하다
roletariat *a.* 프롤레타리아의 *n.* 프롤레타리아
Menshevism *n.* 멘셰비키주의[사상] quote *v.* 인용하다

[Challenge 6]

문제 1

답 (4)

해설 (d)를 중심으로 앞뒤의 내용을 확인해 보자.

> The baby blues may last only a few hours or as long as one to two weeks after delivery. (d) The baby blues alway require treatment from a health-care provider.

(d) 문장 앞뒤의 내용을 보면, 산후 우울증은 (짧게는) 몇 시간 또는 1, 2주 지속되며 다른 어머니들과 대화를 통해서 상태를 호전시킬 수 있다고 했으므로 보기 (c)와 같이 '항상 의료진의 진료가 필요하다'는 내용은 본문의 맥락과는 어긋난다.

해석 소위 '산후 우울증'이라고 불리는 현상은 출산 후 바로 며칠 안에 많은 여성에게 발생하는 현상이다. 엄마가 된 사람은 갑작스러운 감정의 기복을 겪는데, 아주 기뻤다가 다시 아주 슬프거나 화를 낸다. 산모는 아무런 이유 없이 안절부절 못하고, 짜증을 내며, 불안해 하거나, 걱정하고, 외로워하거나, 슬퍼한다. 산후 우울증은 출산 후 몇 시간 또는 1~2주까지만 지속된다. 산후 우울증은 의료진의 진료가 항상 필요하다. 종종 새로운 엄마들을 위한 단체에 가입하거나 다른 엄마들과 이야기를 나누는 것도 도움이 된다.

어휘

so called 소위 childbirth *n.* 출산
mood *n.* 기분, 마음가짐 swing *n.* 변화, 변동
impatient *a.* 안절부절 못하는 irritable *a.* 성미가 급한, 성마른
restless *a.* 침착하지 못한, 들떠있는
anxious *a.* 걱정스러운, 불만스러운 as long as ~하는 한
delivery *n.* 출산 health-care provider *n.* 의료인
support *n.* 지지; 도움

[Challenge 7]

문제 1

답 (4)

해설 동기에 관한 언급은 본문에 없다. 아래 본문을 확인해 보자.

> True greatness in a man is gauged by what he accomplished in life, and the impress he left upon his fellow-men.

문제 2

답 (3)

해설 아래 문장에 밑줄 친 부분의 내용을 확인해 보자.

> They are too often swayed by emotions, and their intellectual powers, which ____(a)____ might exert a controlling influence, are thus weakened, and often result in failure.

즉, (a)의 앞과 뒤의 내용이 서로 대조를 이루고 있다. 고로 부사 자리에 올 수 있으면서 대조를 드러내는 표현은 otherwise이다.

해석 진정한 정치란 교묘한 기술이다. 시, 음악, 그림, 조각 그리고 건축도 기쁨과 쾌감, 영감을 주지만, 생각과 행동이 위대한 정치가와 외교관 그리고 지도자는 모든 계층과 종교를 아우르는 감탄을 자아낸다. 논리적 사고, 호소력 그리고 재치는 반드시 관심과 존경을 이끌어내기 마련이다. 항상 그러하였으며, 앞으로도 의문의 여지없이 그럴 것이다. 그러나 수없이 많은 매우 유능하고 우수한 사람도 평정심과 산출 능력이 부족하다. 이들은 너무 쉽게 감정에 휘말리고, 통제력을 행사해야 할 이들의 지적 능력은 약화되고 종종 실패로 나타난다. 한 사람의 진정한 위대함이란 그가 삶에서 성취한 것과 그가 그의 동료들에게 끼친 영향으로 평가된다. 이것은 하나의 행위 또는 많은 행위들로 구성되는 것이 아니라 오히려 그가 살았던 시대에 끼친 영향과 그가 대중으로부터 사라진 다음 이것이 얼마나 오래 지속되는가로 이루어진다.

어 휘

- statesmanship *n.* 정치적 수완
- masterful *a.* 능수능란한
- sculpture *n.* 조각
- architecture *n.* 건축(술)
- thrill *v.* 황홀하게 하다
- statesman *n.* 정치인
- convince *v.* 납득시키다, 확인시키다
- tactfulness *n.* 재치
- unquestionably *ad.* 의심할 바 없이
- brilliant *a.* 뛰어난, 우수한, 훌륭한
- calculation *n.* 계산; 타산; 추정, 예상
- sway *v.* 흔들리다, 동요하다
- exert *v.* 발휘하다, 쓰다
- A result in B A가 B를 초래하다
- failure *n.* 실패
- greatness *n.* 큼, 위대함
- gauge *v.* 평가[판단]하다
- fellow *n.* 동무, 친구
- endure *v.* 견디다, 인내하다; 지속되다
- throng *n.* 군중, 다수

[Challenge 8]

문제 1

답 (4)

해설 다음 본문의 내용을 보면 보기 항 (4)는 옳지 않음을 알 수 있다.

> there would be <u>no new U.S. offshore drilling permits</u> issued until a federal investigation into the oil spill is completed May 28.

문제 2

답 (3)

해설 현재 가장 시급한 것은 석유가 유출되는 부위를 돔으로 막는 것이다.

해석 석유회사 BP의 관계자는 수중에서 정유가 새는 것을 막도록 고안된 큰 폐쇄로가 현재 멕시코 만의 목표 지점에 떠 있다고 말한다. 이 관계자가 말하길 이 장치가 멕시코 만 수심 1,500미터에 위치한 유출이 발생한 유정 가까이 낮게 가라앉고 있다고 한다. 이들은 금요일이 끝나갈 즈음이 되면 주된 유출부 위에 정확히 돔을 위치시킬 것으로 내다보고 있다. 이 관계자는 이런 종류의 장치는 이 깊이에서 한 번도 사용해 본 적이 없어서 이들은 이것이 효과가 있을 것인지는 장담하지 못한다고 말한다. 그러나 상황이 잘 풀리면 이들은 이 돔이 다음 주 즈음 멕시코 만 표면의 보트에 연료를 공급할 준비가 될 것으로 기대하고 있다. 피해를 입은 유정은 2주 전에 유정 굴착 장치가 폭발하면서 가라앉은 이후 매일 수천 리터를 방류하고 있다. 원유는 목요일 루이지애나 남부 해안 근처의 보초도(堡應島)까지 이르렀는데, 그곳은 다양한 종류의 민감한 동물의 서식지이다. 미 내무부 장관인 Ken Salazar는 목요일 기자회견에서 이번 원유 유출 사건에 대한 연방 조사가 5월 28일에 끝나기 전까지 새로운 미 해변 굴착은 허용되지 않을 것이라 말했다. 그는 또한 BP와 그 제휴업체가 "아주 중대한 실수"를 했으며 회사의 "생명이 위태롭다"고 말했다. Salazar는 이것에 대해 자세히 더 언급하진 않았다. 유출을 막으려는 BP의 다른 노력으로, 회사는 석유 저장고에서 새는 것을 펌프로 끌어 올려 담을 구조정을 파고 있다. 그러나 BP는 석유를 담을 공간이 준비되려면 약 3개월이 걸릴 것이라고 전했다.

어 휘

- containment *n.* 방지, 견제
- dome *n.* 반구형의 덮개
- gulf *n.* 만
- leak *v.* (액체, 기체가) 새다
- chamber *n.* 방, -실
- cap *n.* 뚜껑 *v.* (~으로) 덮다

underwater *a.* 물속의
suspend *v.* ~속에 떠 있다; 중지하다, 정지하다
funnel *v.* 좁은 통로로 흐르게 하다   rig *n.* (석유 등의) 굴착 장치
explode *v.* 폭발시키다, 파열시키다
coast *n.* 연안, 해안   fragile *a.* 망가지기 쉬운, 허약한, 덧없는
habitat *n.* 서식지   offshore *a.* 앞바다의, 연안의
federal *a.* 연방제의   elaborate *v.* 자세히 말하다
contain *v.* 내포하다, 포함하다   pump *v.* 펌프로 퍼올리다
reservoir *n.* 저장소, 저수지

어휘
licentiousness *n.* 음탕, 음란, 방탕
unbind *v.* 묶은 것을 풀다; 속박을 풀다, 석방하다
burdensome *a.* 부담스러운, 힘든
virtuous *a.* 도덕적인, 고결한
discard *v.* 버리다
moderation *n.* 적당함, 온건, 절제
harass *v.* 괴롭히다
spare *v.* 인정을 베풀다
neither A nor B A분 아니라 B도 역시 아니다(양자부정)
common people *n.* 일반 사람들
sentence *n.* 형벌, 선고
exasperate *v.* 몹시 화나게 하다
unseasonable *a.* 계절적으로 볼 때 이상한
threaten *v.* 위협하다   scarcity *n.* 부족, 결핍
urge *v.* 강력히 권고하다, 설득하려고 하다
force *n.* 물리적, 폭력, 힘
approve *v.* 승인하다   cruelty *n.* 잔인성, 포악함
cruel *a.* 잔인한   rejoice *v.* 크게[대단히] 기뻐하다
gladiator *n.* 검투사

[Challenge 9]

문제 1

답 (2)

해설 폭군으로서의 카이사르를 다루는 내용이다.

문제 2

답 (1)

해설 통제 불능의 상황을 묘사하는 단어이다.

문제 3

답 (4)

해설 제시된 문장이 들어갈 본문의 앞뒤에 지시대명사, 관사, 접속사가 있는지 확인해야 한다. 우선 제시문의 내용을 보면, Honoratus가 끈질기게 그(카이사르)를 말리지 않았더라면, 한 명도 남김없이 다 죽였을 것이라고 말하고 있다. (e) 뒤의 내용을 살펴보자.

> This circumstance was also a proof of the cruelty of his nature

즉, 이 문장 바로 앞에는 카이사르의 잔인한 성격을 드러내는 구체적 상황(circumstance)이 전개되어야 함을 알 수 있다.

해석 방탕함이 극심해지자 카이사르는 모든 덕망 있는 충신들의 부담이 되기 시작했다. 그리고 그는 절제를 잃고 동로마의 모든 지역을 착취했고, 국민의 존중을 받은 사람이건 다른 도시의 지배층이건 인정을 베풀지 않았으며, 일반 국민들은 말할 것도 없었다. 마침내 그는 단 하나의 판결로 모든 안티옥의 주요 인사를 사형에 처하라고 명령했다. 도시는 식량 부족으로 위협받는 적절하지 못한 시기에 시장 가격을 낮추도록 명령을 내린 탓에 이들은 감정이 격화되어 그에게 반대하고, 그가 허용하는 정도를 넘어서 강력하게 반대했다 (urge). 만약 Honoratus가 그 당시 동쪽의 백작으로서 끈질기게 지속적으로 그를 말리지 않았더라면 그는 마지막 한 사람까지 전부 죽였을 것이다. 이러한 상황은 또한 그의 잔인한 천성의 증거였는데, 그는 잔인한 경기를 즐겼으며, 원형 경기장(arena; 로마의 옛 경기장)에서 종종 금지되었던 옛날 검투사가 한 명을 죽이는 전투를 보면서 어떤 위대한 성취를 이루듯 기뻐하곤 했다.

[Challenge 10]

문제 1

답 (2)

해설 본문은 직관적 지식과 논리적 지식의 차이점에 대해 논의하면서 직관적 지식이 일상적이고 실용적인 상황에서 어떻게 선호되고 인정되는지를 주로 다루고 있다.

문제 2

답 (2)

해설 앞에서 직관적 지식이 실제 생활에서 유용하게 쓰이는 다양한 예를 들고 있다. 반면 빈칸 이후에는 이러한 상황과는 달리 직관이 이론과 철학의 영역에서 인정받지 못한다고 하고 있으므로, 역접의 'but'으로 연결하는 것이 가장 자연스럽다.

해석 인간의 지식에는 두 가지 형태가 있다. 직관적 지식과 논리적 지식이다. 일상의 삶에서는 직관적 지식이 지속적으로 설득력을 얻는다. 특정 진실을 표현한다는 것은 불가능하다고 여겨진다. 다시 말해 이것은 삼단논법으로 증명할 수 없다. 바로 직관적으로 알아야 하는 것이다. 정치인은 실제적인 상황에서의 분명한 지식을 갖추지 못한 추상적인 논객에게서 허점을 발견한다. 교사는 최우선적으로 학생에게 직관 능력을 계발할 필요성을 강조한다. 예술 작품을 판단하는 비평가는 이론과 추상을 구분하고, 직접적인 직관으로 이를 판단하는 것을 명예로운 일이라고 생각한다. 실리적인 사람은 이성보다 직관에 기대 살아간다고 주장한다. 그러나 일상에서 직관적 지식에 내려지는 충분한 평가가 이론과

철학의 영역에서는 그에 동등한 적절한 평가를 얻지는 못한다.

어휘

intuitive *a.* 직각적[직관적]인; 직관적으로 얻은
demonstrable *a.* 논증[증명, 명시]할 수 있는; 명백한
syllogism *n.* 삼단 논법
pedagogue *n.* 교사, 교육자
abstraction *n.* 추상 (작용); 추상 개념
profess *v.* 공언하다, 명언하다
adequate *a.* (어떤 목적에) 어울리는, 적당한

Day 19

[Challenge 1]

문제 1

답 (2)

해설 본문은 첫 번째 문단에서 주제를 드러내고 이후 앞에서 설정한 주제를 뒷받침하는 내용으로 전개되는 전형적인 두괄식 지문이다.

문제 2

답 (2)

해설 본문 도입부에 언급한 바와 같이 위의 지문은 'fact, opinion, belief, prejudice'를 차례대로 설명하고 있기에 마지막 문장 다음 문단에서 전개될 내용은 'prejudice'에 관한 내용이 나오면 된다.

문제 3

답 (2)

해설 문제 2에서 설명한 바와 같이 본문은 세 가지 주장 즉, 'fact, opinion, belief'를 차례로 기술하고 있다. 'fact'에 관한 설명이 첫 번째 문단을 이루고, 'opinion'에 관한 내용이 두 번째 문단, 마지막으로 'belief'에 관한 내용이 마지막 세 번째 문단을 이룬다. 'belief'에 관한 내용이 시작되는 곳은 (나)이다.

해석 개인의 신념을 형성함에 있어 우리는 종종 우리의 가치나 느낌, 취향, 그리고 과거의 경험이라는 여과기를 통해 실질적 증거를 해석하곤 한다. 따라서 우리가 말하고 글을 작성하면서 만들어내는 대부분의 문장은 사실, 의견, 믿음, 그리고 편견들에 대한 주장이다. 주장의 유용성이나 타당성은 그 주장의 본질이 다음 중 어디에 속하느냐에 따라 개선되거나 약화될 수 있다. 사실(Fact)은 검증할 수 있다. 우리는 증거를 연구함으로써 그것이 진실인지 확인할 수 있다. 여기에는 숫자, 날짜, 증언 등이 포함된다. 사실의 진실성은 측정기나 기록, 혹은 기억이 옳다고 가정하면 논외의 것이 된다. 사실은 주장을 함에 있어 결정적 근거를 제공한다. 그러나 사실은 우리가 그것을 문맥 속에서 결론을 내리고 의미를 부여하지 않는다면 그 자체로는 의미가 없다. 의견(Opinion)은 사실(Fact)에 기반을 둔, 사실적 증거로부터 타당한 결론을 내리기 위한 정직한 시도이다. (예를 들어, 우리는 수많은 사람이 적절한 의료 혜택을 받지 못한다는 것을 알고 있고, 그래서 당신은 수십억 달러가 들더라도 국가가 국민 건강 보험을 설립해야 한다고 의견을 제시할 수 있다.) 의견은 증거가 어떻게 해석되느냐에 따라 변할 수 있다. 의견은, 그 자체로는 설득력이 부족하다. 당신은 독자로 하여금 당신의 논거가 무엇이며, 어떻게 그런 의견에 도달했는지 알게 해야 한다. 의견과 달리, 믿음(belief, 신념, 소신)은 문화적 혹은 개인적인 (종교적) 믿음(faith), 도덕성, 혹은 가치에 기반을 둔 신념이다. "사형은 합법적인 살인이다"와 같은 문장은 관점의 표현이라는 점에서 "의견"이라고 불리지만, 그것은 사실(fact)이나 다른 증거에 기반을 둔 것이 아니다. 이런 믿음은 이성적이거나 논리적인 방법으로는 반박할 수 있거나 심지어 논쟁이 가능한 것이 아니다. 믿음(belief)은 논쟁이 불가능하기 때문에 논제로서의 역할은 하지 못한다. (물론, 청중이 그런 믿음을 공유하고 있음을 당신이 알 경우에는 이런 감성적인 주장이 유용할 수 있다.)

어휘

conviction n. 신념, 확신   interpret v. 해석하다, 통역하다
factual a. 사실의, 실제의   filter v. 거르다; 여과하다
assertion n. 단언, 주장
acceptability n. 수용성; 용인 가능성
verifiable a. 입증할 수 있는, 증언할 수 있는
argument n. 논의; 논증   crucial a. 결정적인, 중대한
conclusion n. 결말; 종결
institute v. 만들다, 설치하다, 제정하다
health insurance 건강보험
changeable a. 변화하기 쉬운; 변덕스러운
convince v. 납득시키다, 설득하다
capital punishment n. 사형
legalize v. 법률상 정당하다고 인정하다
murder n. 살인   viewpoint n. 견해; 견지
disprove v. 반증을 들다, 논박하다
inarguable a. 논쟁의 여지가 없는
thesis n. 논제; 주제

[Challenge 2]

문제 1

답 (1)

해설 첫 번째 문장이 주제문이다. '인간은 지구의 표면의 산물이다'라는 요지 이후 지구 표면이 인간에게 어떤 것을 제공하여 인간을 '기르는'지를 설명하며 이를 뒷받침하고 있다. 부분적인 내용이나 글의 전체적 구조를 파악하지 못하면 오답을 고를 수 있으니 주의해야 한다.

문제 2

답 (1)

해설 보기 항 (1)에 대한 내용은 지문에서 여러 번 확인된다. 예를 들면, 'On the mountains she has given him leg muscles of iron to climb the slope; along the coast she has left these weak and flabby, but given him instead vigorous development of chest and arm to handle his paddle or oar.'에서 알 수 있듯이 인간은 자신보다 더욱 강한 대상에 대해 특정 능력을 통해 이를 극복할 수 있음을 알 수 있다.

문제 3

답 (4)

해설 보기 항 (1), (2), (3)은 모두 지구를 나타내는 말이고, 보기 항 (4)는 인간의 삶의 고역을 나타내는 말이다.

해석 인간은 지구 표면의 산물이다. 이것이 의미하는 것은 단지 그가 지구의 자손 또는 지구의 티끌 중의 하나라는 의미가 아니라 지구가 인간을 어머니처럼 돌보고, 먹이고, 일거리를 제공하며, 그의 사고를 결정하고, 그의 몸을 단련하는 (긍정적) 역경에 부딪히게 하고, 지혜를 갈고닦게 하며, 항해 또는 관개의 문제를 제시하는 동시에 이 모든 것에 대한 해결책에 힌트를 속삭여 준다는 의미이다. 지구는 인간의 뼈와 조직, 마음과 영혼에 깃들어 있다. 지구는 산 위의 경사면을 오를 수 있는 강력한 다리 근육을 주었으며, 해안을 따라서는 그에게 연약함을 남겨두었지만, 그 대신 그에게 가슴과 팔 근육의 원기 왕성한 발달로 노와 발판을 다룰 수 있도록 해 주었다. 강이 흐르는 계곡에서 지구는 그에게 기름진 토양을 주고, 틀에 박힌 평온하고 힘든 업무로 그의 생각과 야망을 제한하고, 그의 시야를 자신의 생활 영역으로 좁혔다. 바람이 휩쓰는 고원 위에 끊임없이 펼쳐지는 평원과, 어떠한 물의 흔적도 없는 사막과 같은 이곳에서 그는 자신의 양떼와 함께 이리저리 목초지와 오아시스를 떠돌고, 수많은 삶의 역경을 맞지만 고된 일을 피해, 풀을 뜯는 양떼를 바라보는 것은 삶을 관조할 수 있는 여유를 제공해 준다.

어 휘

mother *v.* (어머니처럼) 보살피다   confront *v.* 직면하게 만들다
wit *n.* 재치, 기지   navigation *n.* 항해, 운항
irrigation *n.* 관개   at the same time 동시에
flabby *a.* 축 늘어진, 무기력한
paddle *n.* 노, 주걱   oar *n.* 노
circumscribe *v.* 제한(억제)하다   dull *a.* 따분한; 침체된
cramped *a.* 비좁은   plateau *n.* 고원
boundless *a.* 끝이 없는   tract *n.* 지역, 지대
roam *v.* 돌아다니다, 배회하다
drudgery *n.* 힘들고 단조로운 일   grazing *n.* 방목지, 목초지

[Challenge 3]

문제 1

답 (1)

해설 (b) 흑사병에 주의해야 한다. 이 글은 흑사병의 이야기가 아니라 그것과 관련성이 있는 특이한 병리적 현상인 'St. John's Dance'에 관한 글이다.

문제 2

답 (3)

해설 관계대명사 'which' 이후의 부연 설명을 잘 보면, 이것이 구체적인 병의 발병과 증상에 관련된 단어라는 것을 알 수 있다.

문제 3

답 (1)

문제 4

답 (2)

해설 'It did not remain confined to particular localities, but was propagated by the sight of the sufferers' 참고.

해석 흑사병의 여파가 아직 가시지 않았으며, 수백의 희생자의 무덤이 재 닫히지도 않았을 때, 독일에서 이상한 환상이 생겨났는데, 이것은 많은 사람의 마음을 홀리고, 우리 본성의 신성함 대신 소름 돋는 미신의 마력 영역으로 몸과 영혼을 몰아넣었다. 이것은 가장 이상한 형태로 인간의 몸을 진노하게 하고 2세기가 넘도록 현대인에게 경악을 불러일으킨 경련(convulsion)이었는데, 이 시기 이후에 이 사건은 다시 발생한 적이 없었다. 이것은 St. John 또는 St. Vitus의 춤이라 불렸는데, 술을 마시고 떠들어대는 모양 때문에 얻은 이름으로 이런 난폭한 춤을 추면서, 비명을 지르고 분에 못 이겨 거품을 무는 귀신 들린 사람의 모습이었다. 이것은 특정 지역에 한정되지 않고 독일 전역과 북서쪽에 이르는 주변 국가에 악마의 전염병같이 병에 걸린 사람의 모습을 보는 것으로 퍼지게 되었는데, 이웃 나라들은 이미 그 당시에 유행하는 소문에 의해 이것을 받아들일 준비를 하고 있었다(전염에 대한 대비를 하고 있었다).

어 휘

subside *v.* 가라앉다, 진정되다   grave *n.* 무덤, 묘
divinity *n.* 신성   hellish *a.* 지옥의, 지옥과 같은
extraordinary *a.* 대단한, 이상한
infuriate *v.* 격노케 하다   frame *n.* 뼈대, 구조
reappear *v.* 다시 나타나다, 다시 등장하다
on account of ~때문에   whilst *conj.* ~하는 동안에
propagate *v.* 번식시키다; (병을) 만연시키다
sufferer *n.* 괴로워하는 사람

demoniacal a. 악마의, 악마 같은
epidemic n. 유행병, 전염병 **reception** n. 받아들임, 응접
prevailing a. 우세한, 주요한, 널리 보급된

[Challenge 4]

문제 1

답 (3)

해설 보기 항 (3)은 'Adorno saw that capitalism had not become more precarious or close to collapse, as Marx had predicted.'로 보아 틀린 표현이다.

문제 2

답 (2)

해설 괄호 안의 내용을 보면, 겉으로는 개개인의 특성에 맞는 미디어와 음악 상품으로 보이나 결국은 'distinctive'하지 않다고 말하고 있다. 고로 보기 항 (2)가 가장 적절하다. pseudoindividualization(가짜 개성화).

해석 아도르노는 자본주의가 사람들에게 수동적으로 안주하고 정치적으로 무관심하게 만들기 위해 '문화 산업(진정한 예술과는 정반대되는)'이라는 상품을 제공했다고 주장했다. 아도르노는 자본주의가 이미 마르크스가 예측했듯이, 더 위험해지거나 붕괴하지는 않을 것이라고 주장했다. 오히려, 이것은 겉보기에 견고해진 것처럼 보였다. 마르크스가 경제학에 초점을 둔 반면, 아도르노는 현 상태를 유지하기 위해 (자본주의가 취한) 문화의 역할을 강조했다. 대중 문화는 국민의 소극적 안주를 조장하면서, 자본주의 타도에 대해 무관심을 보이는 원인으로 나타났다. 아도르노는 문화 산업이, 사람들이 실질적으로 사회생활에 의문을 제기하게 만드는 좀 더 '진지하고' 비판적인 형태의 예술을 대체해 저급하고, 세련되지 못하며, 감성적인 상품만을 찍어낸다고 주장했다. 이런 문화 산업이 사람들 내 잘못된 욕구를 양산해 낸다. 이러한 욕구를 자본주의가 만들어내 만족시키며, 사람들의 진정한 욕구 즉, 자유, 인간의 가능성과 창조성의 온전한 표현, 순수한 창조적 행복을 대체하는 것이다. 상품 물신성(마케팅, 광고 그리고 미디어 산업에 의해 조장되는)은 사회관계와 문화 경험이 돈의 관점에서 객관화되는 것을 의미한다. 우리는 어떤 것이 값이 얼마나 나가느냐에 따라 기뻐한다. 대중 미디어와 음악 상품의 특징은 획일화(이것들은 기본적으로 흔해 빠진 데다 비슷한 것이다)와 가짜 개성화(부수적인 차이점이 이것들을 서로 독특하게 보이게 만들지만 실질적으로 그렇지 않다)이다. 문화 산업의 상품은 감성적이거나 겉으로는 감동적인 것 같지만, 아도르노는 이것을 카타르시스라고 본다 — 우리는 슬픈 영화나 노래에서 위로를 구하고 약간의 눈물을 흘린 후 다시 회복되는 듯 느낀다. 현대에 적용했을 때 가장 분명하게 귀결되는 이 주장은 바로 TV가 사람들이 서로 이야기하는 것을 막고, 삶의 억압을 의문시하지 못하게 만든다는 점이다. 대신 사람들은 일어나 직장(만약 직업이 있다면)에 갔다 집에 온 후 바로 TV를 켠 뒤, TV에 나오는 아무런 의미 없는 이야기를 잠자리에 들 때까지 (무비판적으로) 흡수하고 또 다시 이러한 일상의 순환 주기를 반복한다.

| 참고 사항 |

Commodity fetishism과 관련된 간략한 설명

소외의 개념은 마르크스의 후기의 저작들보다 초기의 저작들에서 큰 중요성을 띠고 있다. 그러나 후기 저작인 『자본론』 (Capital)에서 상품의 물신성(commodity fetishism)의 개념은 소외에 대한 마르크스의 관심이 확장된 것이다. 상품이란 사용가치와 교환가치를 가지고 있는 재화와 서비스(goods and services)를 말한다. 그러므로 상품의 개념은 시장의 개념과 밀접한 연관을 가지고 있다. 시장에서 상품 교환은 물건 간의 관계를 만들어 낸다. 이것은 사람 간의 관계를 만들어 내는 선물 교환과 대립을 이룬다.(commodity exchange creates a relationship between things, as opposed to gift exchange which creates a relationship between people) 상품의 물신성이란 상품 생산의 사회적 성격이 시장경제에서 위장되거나 숨겨지는 경향을 말한다. 시장에서 모든 상품들은 교환가치를 내재적으로 가지고 있는 듯이 나타난다. 이것은 가치란 인간의 노동 과정에 의해서 만들어진다는 사실을 위장하고 있는 것이다.(in the market, each commodity appears to possess an intrinsic exchange value, disguising the fact that value is created by the process of human labour)

어휘

argue v. 주장하다   **passively** ad. 수동적으로
apathetic a. 냉담한; 무관심한   **precarious** a. 불확실한
entrench v. 참호로 에워싸다[지키다]; 확고하게 하다
status quo n. 현재의 상황
overthrow v. 뒤집어엎다, 타도하다   **debased** a. (질) 떨어진
sentimental a. (이성을 떠나) 감정적인
fetishism n. 주물(呪物)[물신] 숭배   **formulaic** a. 정형화된
incidental a. 부수적인
restore v. (이전의 감정으로) 회복시키다

[Challenge 5]

문제 1

답 (4)

해설 첫 번째 문단의 첫 문장과 마지막 문장에서 주제를 파악할 수 있다.

① it may not be idle to suggest some possible errors

that should be avoided when we are thinking of rural society. — 시골 사회를 생각할 때 발생할 수 있는 피해야 할 실수

② Let us consider some of these possible sources of misconception. — 시골에 대한 그릇된 생각을 가지게 된 원인을 고려해 보자. 이를 통해 보기 항목 (4)가 답임을 알 수 있다.

문제 2

답 (1)

해설 주제에서 알 수 있듯이, 시골에 대한 잘못된 인식을 가지게 되는 여러 가지 요인을 검토하는 글이다. 시골에 대한 또 다른 잘못된 인식의 요소가 다루어질 것을 알 수 있다.

문제 3

답 (3)

해설 '무익한'이란 의미로 쓰이고 있다.

문제 4

답 (4)

해설 빈칸 문제는 언제나 전체 문맥을 고려하면서 빈칸이 들어간 문장과 앞뒤의 문장을 비교하며 접근해야 한다. 본문을 살펴보자.

> He forgets that he is one of a thousand in the city, and does not represent average city life. He fails to compare _____(a)_____, manifestly the only fair basis for comparison.

우선 본문에서 제시된 문장 바로 뒤에 나오는 문장의 첫 단어가 'or'이기에 화제가 바뀐다는 전제하에 빈칸이 들어간 문장과 바로 앞 문장과의 관계만 살펴보도록 한다. 빈칸 바로 앞 문장의 내용은 '그'가 자신은 단지 도시의 천 명 중 한 명에 불과하며 도시를 대표할 수 없다는 사실을 망각한다고 했다. 그렇다면 이러한 상황에서 그가 할 수 있는 실수는 무엇인지 생각 한다.

해설 농가 문제에 대한 사람들의 분명한 태도 변화를 고려할 때, 우리가 농촌 사회에 대해서 생각할 때 피해야 할 예상되는 실수들을 제시하는 것이 무익하진 않을 것이다. 이 학생은 의심할 여지없이 잘못된 견해에 반하여 이 문제에 접근할 것이다. 학생 자신은 아마도 신중히 자신의 견해를 세웠을 것이다. 일반적으로 도시인이 시골 출신일 경우, 한 세대 전 자신의 조상의 집을 떠올릴 것이고, 그렇지 않을 경우에는 여름 휴가나 간간이 갔던 내륙 출장에서 느낀 자신의 의견에 기대기 쉽다. 또는 그는 Shore Acres와 Old Homestead(오래된 농장 건물)의 그림을 머릿속에 그리기도 할 것이다. 어떤 경우든 이러한 이미지는 잘못될 가능성이 있으며, 결과적으로 현재의 상황에 대한 이 사람의 견해는 전적으로 부적절하게 된다. 이러한 잘못된 생각을 일으키는 몇 가지 원인에 대해서 고려해 보자.

우선 최고의 도시 환경과 전반적인 시골의 삶을 비교하는 것 자체가 잘못된 것이다. (그러나) 종종 이렇게 비교된다. 관측자는 일반적으로 교육, 문화, 여가를 향유하고, 여행 경험이 있으며, 정도의 차는 있어도 부를 갖추고 있다. 그가 아는 사람이란 거의 대부분 비슷한 능력, 학문, 성취를 지닌 사람들이다. 그는 자신과 그의 친구가 기대했던 환경과 어느 정도 일치하는 시골 환경을 찾지 못했을 때, 즉시 시골에서는 자신이 얻을 것이 전혀 없으며, 도시만이 인간의 더 높은 욕구를 충족하기에 적합하다고 결론을 내린다. 그는 자신이 그 도시에서 천 명 중 한 명에 불과하며 평균적인 도시의 삶을 대표하는 것이 아니라는 사실을 잊는다. 그는 비교를 위한 유일하게 공정한 기준인 평균적인 시골 조건과 평균적인 도시 조건을 비교하지 못한다. 또는 그 이상으로 더 가슴 아픈 실수를 할 수도 있다. 그는 각자 최악의 시골 조건과 최고의 도시 조건을 정반대로 설정할지도 모른다. 만약 계속해서 그가 농촌마다 궁전, 큰 도서관, 멋진 설교자, 극장 그리고 급격한 변화를 찾으려 한다면, 분명 그는 공평하게 시골의 빈민가와 도시의 빈민가를 견주어 보아야 한다. 도시의 생활은 극단에 치닫는다. 농촌의 삶은 다재로움에도 불구하고 더 단조롭다. 시골에는 부, 사치 그리고 편안함이 없다. 그렇지만 극단적 빈곤, 극악한 범죄, 형용할 수 없는 추잡함, 그리고 도덕적 부패 또한 없다. 농부들은 근본적으로 중산층이며 이러한 사실을 고려하지 않는 비교는 공정하지 않은 것이다.

어휘

idle a. 게으름뱅이의, 한가한, 태만한, 무익한
doubtless ad. 의심할 바 없이, 거의 틀림없이
misconception n. 오해, 그릇된 생각
thoughtfully ad. 생각이 깊게, 신중히
improbable a. 있을 법하지 않는
faulty a. 과실이 있는, 불안전한
appreciation n. 평가, 판단, 이해, 감상
inadequate a. 부적당한, 부적절한
acquaintance n. 지식, 면식, 아는 사람
err v. 정도에서 벗어나다, 헤매다, 실수하다
grievously ad. 슬프게도; 몹시   **slum** n. 빈민가
reek v. 연기를 내다, 김을 내다
unutterable a. 말로 표현할 수 없는, 철저한
filth n. 오물, 더러움   **sewage** n. 하수 오물
middle class n. 중산계층

Day 19

[Challenge 6]

문제 1

답 (2)

해설 미국의 식민지 정착 시절 독일인들의 이주에 관한 글이다.

문제 2

답 (2)

해설 혈통을 나타내는 단어를 고르면 된다. 'extraction'에 혈통이란 의미가 있다. 예) an American of Korean extraction 한국계 미국인

문제 3

답 (3)

해설 (d)는 라인강이 있는 독일을 지칭하는 것이고, 나머지는 모두 펜실베이니아를 지칭한다.

문제 4

답 (3)

해설 'In fact'에는 다음과 같은 두 가지 용법이 있다.

1. 사실은[실은](방금 한 말에 대해 자세한 내용을 덧붙일 때 씀)

예) I used to live in France; in fact, not far from where you're going.
전 예전에 프랑스에 살았어요. 사실은 당신이 가려고 하는 곳에서 멀지 않은 곳이에요.

2. 사실은[실제로는](특히 방금 한 말에 반대되는 내용을 강조할 때 씀)

예) I thought the work would be difficult. In actual fact, it's very easy.
나는 그 일이 힘들 거라고 생각했어. 실제로는 아주 쉬워.

해석 수치상의 중요도에 따르면 식민지 이주자들 중에서 그 수가 세 번째로 많은 것은 독일인이었다. 처음부터 독일인들은 식민지 기록에 등장했다. 첫 번째 제임스타운(Jamestown) 식민지의 수많은 예술가와 목수들은 독일인 혈통이었다. New Motherland의 유명한 주지사인 피터 미누이트(Peter Minuit)는 라인강(the Rhine)의 베젤(Wesel) 출신 독일인이었으며, 뉴욕주 행정부에 대항해 민중 봉기를 이끈 인물인 야콥 라이슬러(Jacob Leisler)도 프랑크푸르트(Frankfort-on-Main) 출신의 독일인이었다. 대대적인 독일인들의 이주는 펜실베이니아주의 건설과 함께 시작되었다. 펜실베이니아는 땅을 경작할 소작농을 찾고자 했는데, 라인강의 나라에서 농부를 끌어들이는 데 특히 더 노력했다. Frankfort Company라고 알려진 큰 협회는 펜실베이니아로부터 2만 에이커 이상의 땅을 사들이고, 1684년에 독일 이주민의 분포를 위해 저먼타운(Germantown)에 사무실을 설립했다. 기존의 뉴욕에서는 라인벡(Rhinebeck-on-the-Hudson)도 독일인의 분포를 위한 비슷한 기관으로 활동했다. 메인에서 조지아까지 독일 농부에 대한 유인책이 제시되었으며, 당시 거의 모든 식민지에서 독일인의 정착을 확인할 수 있었다. 사실 독일인의 이주가 너무 광범위하게 이루어져 독일 제후들은 너무 많은 백성을 잃는 것에 두려움을 느꼈으며, 영국은 자신의 해외 식민지로 외국인이 유입되는 것을 걱정했다. 그러나 어떤 것도 이러한 이동을 멈출 수는 없었다. 식민지 시기의 마지막 즈음에 독일인의 수는 20만 명 이상까지 치솟았다.

어 휘

colonist *n.* 식민지 주민　**artisan** *n.* 장인, 기능 보유자
carpenter *n.* 목수　**uprising** *n.* 봉기, 반란, 폭동
provincial *a.* 주의, 지방의　**peasant** *n.* 소작농
association *n.* 협회　**acre** *n.* 에이커
establish *v.* 설립하다, 수립하다　**center** *n.* 중심지, 센터
inducement *n.* 유인책[장려책]　**settlement** *n.* 정착(지)
frighten *v.* 겁먹게[놀라게] 만들다　**loss** *n.* 분실, 손실
alarm *v.* 불안하게 만들다　**influx** *n.* 밀어닥침
dominion *n.* 영토, 영지
colonial period *n.* 식민지 기간

[Challenge 7]

문제 1

답 (4)

해설 보기 항 (4)는 유물론을 나타내는 것으로 관념론과는 거리가 먼 개념이다. 나머지는 모두 본문에 언급된 내용이다.

문제 2

답 (3)

해설 '본성을 문밖으로 몰아내면, 본성이 창문으로 들어온다.'라고 했는데, 이는 인간 본성을 제거하게 되면 역사적 고찰이 쉽지 않다는 이야기다.

해석 독일의 위대한 관념론자인 셸링(Schelling)과 헤겔(Hegel)은 인간 본성을 불완전한 것으로 이해하는 관점을 취했다. 헤겔은 자신의 '역사 철학'에서 최상의 국가 조직을 추구하는 유토피아적 부르주아를 비웃는다. 독일의 관념론은 역사를 법에 종속하는 과정으로 인식했으며, 인간 본성 밖에서 역사 운동의 원동력을 찾았다. 이것은 진리를 향한 위대한 진보였다. 그러나 관념론자들은 절대적 개념인 '세계 정신'에서 원동력을 찾았다.

그리고 이들의 절대적 개념은 '인간의 사고 과정'의 추상적 개념에 지나지 않았으므로, 이들은 유물론자들의 옛 사랑인 인간의 본성을 다시 도입했다. 이때 이들은 독일 사상가들의 존경을 받을 만한 엄격한 사회에 가치 있는 옷을 입혔다. 본성을 문밖으로 몰아내면, 본성이 창문으로 들어온다. 독일의 관념론자에 의해 사회 과학이 이루어낸 위대한 공로에도 불구하고, 이 학문 분야의 근본적인 문제(인간의 본성)는

프랑스 유물론의 시대만큼이나 독일의 관념론 시대에서도 해결되지 않았다.

어 휘

idealistic *a.* 이상주의적인　　**philosopher** *n.* 철학자
insufficiency *n.* 불충분, 부족
bourgeoisie *n.* 중산 계급; 자본가 계급
in search of ~을 찾아서　　**motive-power** *n.* 동력원
historical *a.* 역사의　　**speculation** *n.* 사색, 숙고
reintroduce *v.* 재도입하다, 다시 제출하다
materialist *n.* 유물론자　　**robe** *n.* 관복, 예복
austere *a.* 엄격한, 준엄한

[Challenge 8]

문제 1

답 (3)

해설 공자가 이 책을 썼을 것이라 여겨진다고 했지, 썼다고 하진 않았다. '(be) attributed to'라는 표현을 정확히 알고 있어야 한다.

문제 2

답 (1)

해설 본문의 순수 학문은 존재론(ontology)이 아니라 우주론(cosmology)을 다루고 있다.

해석 고대 중국 우주철학에 따르면, 역경(변화에 관한 책)은 약 4,000년 전에 기록된 것으로, 이때 분리되지 않던 우주(텅 빈 공간으로 상징되는)가 이동하여, 빛 즉 양이 만들어지고, 운행이 멈추었을 때, 어두움 즉 음이 생겨났다. 양과 음(서로 얽혀 있는 흰색과 검은색의 구획으로 구성된 원으로 상징됨)은 이러한 극단의 근본적 힘 사이의 지속적인 상호작용을 통해 현재 인간이 인식하는 우주 내의 힘, 변화 그리고 조화를 만들어낸다. 역경에 관한 위대한 주석(Great Commentary)의 서론은 공자가 쓴 것으로 여겨지는데, 우리는 다음과 같은 내용을 발견할 수 있다. "하늘은 높고, 땅은 낮다. 고로 창조주와 피조물이 결정되었다. 낮고 높음의 차이로 열등하고 우등한 공간이 생겨난다. 운동과 정지에는 분명한 법칙이 존재한다. 이것에 따라 고정되고 영향을 받기 쉬운 선이 구별된다. 창조자의 방식은 남성을 이끌어내고, 피조물의 방식은 여성을 이끌어낸다." 양과 음의 내재적 상극 관계는 음/양으로 시작해서 고/저, 창조/피조, 불변/변화, 움직임/쉼 그리고 남성/여성의 구분뿐만 아니라 태양과 달, 날씨, 인간의 몸 그리고 신(모두 양)과 혼(모두 음) 사이의 구분까지 인간사의 다양한 영역의 관계로 확장된다.

어 휘

metaphysics *n.* 형이상학　　**I Ching** *n.* 역경(易經)
differentiate *v.* 구별하다, 구분 짓다　　**interplay** *n.* 상호 작용
bipolar *a.* 극단의
interwind *v.* 한데 감다, 얽히다, 얽히게 하다
segment *n.* 부분, 한 조각　　**commentary** *n.* 해설, 비판, 논의
attribute *v.* ~의 탓으로 돌리다　　**Confucius** *n.* 공자
correspondence *n.* 관련성
underlying *a.* 근본적인, 근원적인　　**polarity** *n.* 양극성, 극성

[Challenge 9]

문제 1

답 (4)

해설 본문 마지막 수사의문에서 보기 항목 (4)가 틀리다는 것을 알 수 있다. 부를 축적하려는 사람조차 자기희생이 필요하다고 하면서, 하물며 강하고 균형이 잡힌 삶을 실현하려는 사람은 어떻겠는가라고 묻고 있다.

해석 인간은 자신의 환경을 개선하려고 애를 쓰지만 정작 자기 자신은 개선하려고 하지 않는다. 그래서 이들은 제자리를 벗어나지 못한다. 스스로의 시련에서 물러서지 않은 사람은 자신의 마음 위에 세운 목표를 성취하는 데 절대 실패할 수 없다. 이것은 천국뿐만이 아니라 이 세상에서도 마찬가지다. 부를 축적하는 것만이 유일한 목적인 사람조차 자신의 목적을 성취하기 전에 엄청난 개인적인 희생을 감수할 준비를 해야 한다. 그런데 강하고 균형이 잡힌 삶을 실현하려는 사람은 얼마나 더 그러하겠는가?

어 휘

bound *a.* 묶인; 속박된
shrink *v.* 줄어들다, 오그라지다
crucifixion *n.* 십자가에 매달아 죽이는 것
earthly *a.* 세속적인　　**heavenly** *a.* 천국의, 하늘의
sole *a.* 유일한, 단 하나의

[Challenge 10]

문제 1

답 (3)

해설 본문은 알렉산더의 성품을 기술하는 글이다.

문제 2

답 (1)

해설 다음 본문의 내용을 살펴보자.

> At the same time, he was calm, collected, and considerate in emergencies requiring caution, and thoughtful and ____(a)____ in respect to the bearings and consequences of his acts.

빈칸에 들어갈 단어의 의미에 직접적으로 영향을 미치는 요소는

'in respect to'가 이끄는 구이다. 우선, 빈칸의 단어는 현재 알렉산더의 좋은 성품에 관한 이야기가 열거되고 있기에 긍정적인 어감을 전달하는 단어일 수밖에 없다. 예를 들어 보기 항 (3)과 같이 부정적인 어감의 표현은 들어갈 수 없다. 보기 항 (4)도 사람의 성품을 드러내기에 적합하지 않다. 'in respect to'가 이끄는 내용과 앞의 진술을 종합해 보면, "그는 조심성 있고, 생각이 깊으며, 스스로의 행동에 대한 결과에 선견지명이 있었다."라고 종합하는 것이 가장 적절하다. 이는 현재의 그의 행동이 어떤 결과를 가져올지 항상 고려했다는 점에서 유추할 수 있다.

문제 3

답 (1)

해설 글쓴이는 전체적으로 알렉산더를 옹호하면서 그의 성품을 찬양하는 방식으로 글을 쓰고 있다. 앞에서 기술된 그의 성품에 대한 행동과는 달리, 그가 이러한 성품을 불행히도 모두 전쟁에 쏟았다고 말하고 있다. 그러면서도 그를 옹호하는 입장에서 이에 대한 부연 진술을 전개하고 있다. 보기 항에서 이런 맥락에 가장 적절한 표현은 바로 앞에 전개된 내용에 대한 추가 부연을 이끄는 'in fact'가 가장 적절하다.

해석 알렉산더의 성공 비결은 바로 그의 성격에 있었다. 그는 정신적인 매력과 개성적인 매력을 두루 지녔는데, 이러한 매력은 어느 시대건 그것을 발산하는 사람에게 영향을 받는 모든 이들에게 신비함과 무한한 주도권을 제공해준다. 알렉산더는 아주 놀랄 정도로 이러한 특성을 지닌 것으로 묘사된다. 그는 실제 인상이 아주 좋았으며, 태도도 매력적이었다. 그는 활동적이고 체력도 좋았으며, 모든 일에 임함에 있어 열정과 열의로 가득했다. 동시에 그는 조용하고 침착하며, 치밀함이 요구되는 긴급한 상황에서도 아주 신중했고, 자신의 행동이 가져올 결과에 대해 선견지명이 있었다. 그는 강한 애착을 보였으며, 자신에게 보인 친절에 감사할 줄 알았다. 어떤 식으로든 그와 관련된 모든 사람의 감정에 대해 사려 깊고, 친구에게는 신의가 있으며, 적에게도 아량을 베풀었다. 한마디로, 그는 고귀한 성품을 지녔다. 하지만 불행히도 그는 자신의 이런 모든 에너지를 정복과 전쟁에 쏟았다. 사실, 그는 위대한 인격과 정신적 힘을 이것 외에 다른 곳에 행사할 그런 영역이 거의 없었던 시대에 살았다. 그는 위대한 열정을 가지고 자신의 일에 착수했으며, 그가 놓인 위치는 그에게 그 안에서 거대한 영향력을 행사할 기회를 제공해 주었다.

어 휘

unbounded *a.* 무한한, 끝없는
ascendency *n.* 지배력을 행사할 수 있는 지위, 지도권
prepossessing *a.* 매력적인
active *a.* 활동적인, 적극적인
athletic *a.* 탄탄한   ardor *n.* 열정, 정열
enthusiasm *n.* 열광, 열정   bearing *n.* 관련, 영향; 태도
consequence *n.* 결과; 중요함

form *v.* 형성하다
attachment *n.* 애착, 믿음, 지지   foe *n.* 적
noble *a.* 고결한, 고귀한
prodigious *a.* 엄청난, 굉장한

Day 20

[Challenge 1]

문제 1

답 (3)

해설 본문은 산불 예방의 중요성과 이를 위해 실용적인 순찰 기관 설치를 주장하는 글이다.

문제 2

답 (2)

해설 아래 본문과 보기 항 (2)를 비교해 보자.

> Theodore Roosevelt says: "I hold as first among the tasks before the states and the nation in their respective shares in forest conservation the organization of efficient fire patrols and the enactment of good fire laws on the part of the states."

일반적으로 내용 일치 문제에서 'only, never, always' 등과 같은 강조 부사가 보일 경우, 본문에서 직접 언급되었는지 반드시 살펴보아야 한다.

문제 3

답 (1)

해설 예방의 중요성에 관련 속담은 다음과 같다.

Forewarned is forearmed. = It is easy to be wise after the event. (일이 벌어진 후에 깨우치는 것은 쉽다.) = Don't close the barn door after the horse has been stolen. (소 잃고 외양간 고치지 말라.)

해석 러나 더 나은 국민 정서가 필요한 것처럼, 법을 집행하고 실제 발생하는 산불을 막을 수 있는 실질적인 기구가 있어야 한다. 도시가 체계적인 소방 부서에 의해 가장 잘 보호되듯이, 산림도 이 일을 하는 전문가에 의해만 효과적으로 보호될 수 있다. 대부분의 산불을 예방하는 사람은 화재가 발생한 후 따라가는 사람이 아니라, 이를 항상 찾아다니는 사람이다. 루스벨트 대통령은 "나는 산림 보존을 위해 각자의 몫을 담당하는 모든 주와 국가 앞에 부여받은 일들 중에서 효율적인 산불 정찰대의 조직과 모든 주에서의 적절한 산불 법의 제정을 우선시하겠다." 고 말했다. 국립보전위원회는 "자신의 국경 안에서 발생하는 산림 화재가 심각한 피해를 미치는 각 주, 즉 산림을 포함하는 모든 주는 산림 화재를 진압하기 위해 법령집에 관련법만 필요한 것이 아니라 화재에 대비해 실제로 산을 순찰하는 효과적인 인력이 필요하다." 고 보고하고 있다. 통제가 힘든 상황에서 여러 건의 화재 재난이 발생한다는 것은 공공연한 사실이다. 일반적으로 이러한 화재는 아주 사소한 것에서 발생하는데, 겉으로는 분명 눈에 띄지 않아 무해한 것으로 보이지만 나중에 바람과 더운 날씨 때문에 불길이 거세지는 것이다. 나중에 거진 불을 진압하는 것보다 초기 단계에서 이를 끄는 것이 훨씬 비용이 적고, 이미 거진 불(화재)은 큰 피해가 발생하기 전까지 성공적으로 진압하지 못하는 경우가 많다. 그리고 만약 진압이 요구된다면, 능력 있는 전문가가 이를 이끄는 것이 가장 중요하다. 순간순간이 중요하며 잘못된 판단으로 인한 피해는 어마어마하다. 대부분 서부의 주에는 이미 건기 동안 개간을 위한 화기 사용을 규제하는 법안이 있다. 고생하지 않고 안전하게 이를 성취하기 위해서는 소방 감독관이 인가를 내도록 하고 필요하면 이를 돕도록 해야 한다.

어휘

safeguard *v.* 보호하다   **task** *n.* 일, 임무, 작업
respective *a.* 각각의, 각기의
enactment *n.* (법률의) 제정, 법규, 조례
squarely *ad.* 똑바로; 정확하게
statute *n.* 법령; 규정   **innocent** *a.* 무해성의; 결백한
incipient *a.* 시초의, 발단의, 초기의
competent *a.* 적임의, 유능한, 적당한
warden *n.* 관리자, 감독자   **burning** *n.* 연소, 화재

[Challenge 2]

문제 1

답 (4)

해설 본문에서 모든 행위는 그것이 의도적이든 일시적인 행위였든 한 사람의 생각의 뿌리에서 나온 것이라 말하고 있다. 아래 본문을 참조해 보자.

> so every act of a man springs from the hidden seeds of thought, and could not have appeared without them. This applies equally to those acts called "spontaneous" and "unpremeditated" as to those, which are deliberately executed.

즉, 모든 행위는 바로 그 사람의 생각에서 일어난다고 말하고

이러한 원리가 그것이 일시적으로, 무의식에서 나온 행동이건 아니면 의도적으로 행한 것이건 모든 것에 적용된다고 말하고 있다. 하지만 보기 항 (4)와 같이 일시적인 행위가 무조건 나쁜 결과를 가져온다는 이야기는 본문에 없다.

문제 2

답 (2)

해설 (b)는 생각을 나타내는 비유적 표현이고, 나머지는 모두 행위를 나타낸다.

해석 "마음에 그리는 모습 그대로의 사람이 된다." 라는 경구는 한 사람의 전인격적인 면만을 포함할 뿐 아니라, 그 사람의 삶의 모든 상황까지 아우르는 뜻을 포함한다. 한 인간은 말 그대로 그 자신이 생각하는 바이며, 그의 성격은 그의 모든 생각의 총체인 것이다. 식물은 씨로부터 나오고, 씨가 없이는 자랄 수 없듯, 모든 사람의 행위는 사상이라는 숨은 씨에서 발생하고 이것이 없이는 발생할 수 없었을 것이다. 이것은 의도적으로 행해진 것과 '즉흥적'이고 '우발적'이라 불리는 행위에도 동일하게 적용된다. 행위는 사상이 꽃핀 것이며, 기쁨과 슬픔은 그것의 열매이다. 그러기에 인간은 자신이 경작한 것(자기 자신의 행위)의 달고 쓴 과일을 얻게 된다.

어휘

aphorism *n.* 격언, 경구   literally *ad.* 글자 뜻 그대로
spontaneous *a.* 자발적인, 자연의, 임의의
unpremeditated *a.* 미리 계획되지 않는, 고의적이지 않은
deliberately *ad.* 고의로, 일부러
execute *v.* 실행하다; 실시하다
blossom *n.* 꽃; 개화, 만발, (발육의) 초기; 전성기
garner *v.* 모으다, 축적하다   bitter *a.* 모진; 쓴
husbandry *n.* 농업, 경작

[Challenge 3]

문제 1

답 (3)

해설 본문에서 유교에 대한 관심이 증가하고 있는 곳은 아시아가 아니라 서양이다. 보기 항 (4)의 경우 본문 마지막에 유교로 인해 발생하는 도덕적 병폐가 언급되어 있다.

문제 2

답 (2)

해설 본문에서 전문가뿐 아니라 많은 서양인들이 자신들이 처한 문제를 해결하는 대안으로 유교를 생각하는 점은 언급되었으나, 이것이 유일한 해결책이라고 말하고 있진 않다.

문제 3

답 (2)

해설 문장 배열 문제의 경우 접속사, 대명사, 관사, 일련의 순서를 드러내는 동사 등을 활용하면 접근이 쉬워진다. 본문에서 활용할 수 있는 사항을 확인해 보자.

(a) At the same time, critics of Confucianism often flip this apparent strength into a moral failing: that it neglects individual rights and autonomy in favor of a life of relationship.

→ '동시에'라는 접속사구를 볼 수 있는데, 이는 앞에서 전개된 내용과 정반대의 내용을 전개할 때 쓸 수 있다. 뒤에 전개되는 내용은 유교의 도덕적 실패에 관한 내용이다.

(b) Moreover, the favored set of relationships is frequently criticized as patriarchal and oppressively hierarchical, reputedly stifling the self.

→ '게다가'는 앞에서 전개된 내용과 같은 맥락에서 추가적인 정보를 제공한다. 이후 유교의 부정적인 관점이 드러나기에, (c)가 아닌 (a) 뒤에 (b)가 온다는 것을 알 수 있다.

(c) By contrast, one of the strengths of Confucianism is frequently thought to lie in the way it conceives a fully human life in terms of relationship to others, structured by a set of duties to them that realize the self rather than constrain it.

→ '대조적'이란 표현인 'by contrast'는 앞에서 전개된 내용과 반대되는 내용을 전개한다. 이어지는 내용은 유교의 강점에 관한 이야기이다.

위에서 제시된 내용 앞에는 바로 서양 도덕성의 문제점을 언급하고 있다. 위의 내용상 (a)와 (c)가 나와야 하는데, 서로 대조를 이끄는 접속사구를 가지고 있으므로, 보기 항 (c)가 가장 먼저 나온다는 것을 알 수 있다.

문제 4

답 (3)

해설 문제에서 요구하는 사항은 유교에 대한 비판과 거리가 먼 것을 고르는 것이다. 보기 항 (3)은 유교의 장점에 관한 내용으로 본문에 언급되고 있다.

해석 특히나 유교에 관한 관심이 증가하는 궁극적인 이유는 철학자나 대학 교수뿐 아니라 점점 많은 서양인들이 유교가 실현 가능한 대안이 될 수도 있다는 생각에서 서양 도덕성의 핵심 주장에 반기를 들고 있기 때문이다. 어떤 반대 내용에 따르면 개인의 권리와 자율성에 부여된 서양 도덕성의 구심성은 개인이 다른 사람에게 가지는 책임감의 잘못된 이해를 가져왔다. 특히 미국의 경우가 이러한 면에서 가장 뚜렷한 사례로 제시된다. 세계에서 가장 풍요로운 나라이면서도, 가장 불평등한 나라로 국민의 건강과 교육과 같은 기본적인 것을 제공하는 데 실패한 나라이다. 이와 관련된 다른 반대 내용으로는, 서양의 도덕성은 다른 이에 대한 의무

를 수행하는 데 효과적이지 못한 논거를 제시하는데, 이는 이러한 의무의 실행이 올바르고 가치 있는 삶이라는 특정한 개념을 성취하는 데 어떻게 관련이 되어 있는지를 개인에게 보여주지 못하기 때문이다. MacIntyre는 이런 측면에서 가장 영향력 있는 비평가 중 한 명이다. 대조적으로 유교의 여러 강점 중 하나가 이것이 자신을 제약하는 것이 아니라 자기실현의 의무로 설정된 다른 이와의 관계적 측면에서 온전한 인간의 삶을 인식하는 방법이라고 여겨지는 경우가 종종 있다. 동시에 유교에 대한 비평가들은 종종 이런 분명한 강점을 도덕적 실패로 뒤집기도 한다. 유교는 관계를 중시하는 삶을 선호하기에 개인의 권리와 자율성을 무시한다는 것이다. 게다가, 바람직한 관계라는 것이 종종 가부장적이고 위계질서가 억압적이며, 자신을 억누르는 것으로 알려져 종종 비판을 받는다.

어휘

Confucianism *n.* 유교
viable *a.* 실행 가능한, 실용적인
autonomy *n.* 자치(권), 자율성
stunt *v.* 성장(발육)을 저지하다; 방해하다
preeminent *a.* 현저한; 탁월한   **specific** *a.* 특유한, 명확한
flip *v.* (홱) 뒤집(히)다
apparent *a.* 또렷한; 외견의
patriarchal *a.* 가부장제의, 가부장적인
oppressively *ad.* 압제적으로
hierarchical *a.* 계급에 따른
stifle *v.* 억누르다, 억압하다
conceive *v.* 마음에 품다, 착상하다, 고안하다
in terms of ~면에서
constrain *v.* 강제하다; 강요하다; 억압하다

[Challenge 4]

문제 1

답 (3)
해설 인지 심리학의 개념이 처음 출현하기 시작한 시점과 이후 어떤 식으로 발전해 왔는지 시간의 순서에 따라 설명하고 있다.

문제 2

답 (4)
해설 보기 항 (1)은 본문에 잠시 언급된 '경험주의'의 주장이며, 선택 (2)와 (3) 모두 '행동주의'에 해당하는 내용이다. 본 문제는 인지 심리학이란 것이 사람의 뇌 속의 소프트웨어 (software running on the computer that is the brain)와 같은 것을 다룬다는 본문의 내용에 비추어 보기 항 (4)를 고를 수 있도록 유도한 것이다.

문제 3

답 (3)
해설 George Miller가 등장하는 지문 마지막을 참조한다.

해설 인지 심리학은 가장 최근에 심리학 연구에 추가된 분야로 노암 촘스키가 1959년도에 좀 더 개괄적으로 행동주의와 경험주의를 비판하면서 시작된 "인지 혁명" 이후의 여파로 1950년대 후반과 1960년대 초반 이후 심리학 분야 안에서 독립적으로 발달하게 되었다. 계산심성론과 같은 인지 사고의 기원은 일찍이 17세기 데카르트까지 거슬러 올라가며, 1940년대와 50년대의 Alan Turing에 이른다. 인지 접근방법은 1958년 Donald Broadbent가 쓴 Perception and Communication에 의해 두드러지게 된다. 그 시기 이후, 이 분야의 주된 패러다임은 Broadbent가 제시한 정보 처리 인지 모델이 되었다. 이것은 정신 과정에 대한 사고와 추론의 한 방법으로, 뇌 속에 존재하는 컴퓨터에서 운영되는 소프트웨어와 같이 이것들을 그려내는 것이다. 이론은 데이터 입력, 표출, 계산 또는 처리 그리고 산출의 형태로 적용된다. 주된 정신 지식 표상의 체계로 언어에 적용된 인지 심리학은 나무와 네트워크의 심성 모형을 이용했다. 인공지능과 일반 심리학에 끼친 두드러진 공헌은 바로 의미망의 개념이다. 최초의 인지 심리학자 중 한 명인 George Miller는 영어의 의미망인 WordNet의 개발에 자신의 온 연구를 바친 사람으로 유명하다. 개발은 1985년에 시작되었고 현재는 많은 기계존재론의 기반이 되고 있다.

어휘

critique *n.* 평론   **behaviorism** *n.* 행동주의
empiricism *n.* 경험(실증)주의
computational *a.* 컴퓨터의, 컴퓨터를 사용한
trace *v.* 추적하다, 찾아내다   **proceed** *v.* 진행하다
approach *n.* 접근법   **prominence** *n.* 중요성, 명성
perception *n.* 지각, 자각, 통찰력
communication *n.* 의사소통, 연락
dominant *a.* 우세한, 지배적인   **paradigm** *n.* 전형적인 예
envision *v.* 마음속에 그리다[상상하다]
input *n.* 입력   **representation** *n.* 묘사, 표현
computation *n.* 계산   **exploit** *v.* 이용하다
network *n.* 망, 관계, 네트워크
singular *a.* 뛰어난, 두드러진; 단수형의
contribution *n.* 기여, 이바지
semantic *a.* 의미의, 의미론적인   **ontology** *n.* 존재론

[Challenge 5]

문제 1

답 (4)
해설 큰 정부는 효과가 없다는 것이 글의 요지이다. 보기 (1)

은 틀린 진술임을 알 수 있다. 미국의 적자재정 측면은 옳으나 'The nominal interest rate on 10-year bonds is a low 1.5 percent, and close to zero for shorter-maturity bonds.'로 보아 국채 이자율이 아주 낮다는 것을 파악할 수 있다. 'as if the federal government has been practicing austerity for the past few years' 부분에서 미국은 지난 몇 년간 계속해서 경기 부양책을 썼음을 알 수 있다.

문제 2

답 (3)

해설 글의 전반부에서도 언급했듯이, 정부 개입을 통해 경제 성장은 별 효과를 보지 못했다. 오바마 정부의 경우 ARRA를 통한 경기부양책(economy stimulus)을 썼으면 그 결과는 '희생(price)'만 있을 뿐이다. 정부가 돈을 쏟아부어도 제대로 경기는 돌아가지 않음을 알 수 있다.

문제 3

답 (3)

해설 본문 마지막 부분인 'It's time to admit the easy money, borrow-and-spend policies have failed and return to the limited-government principles that allow entrepreneurs to succeed.'에서 글쓴이는 궁극적으로 작은 정부를 지향함을 알 수 있다. 글의 요지를 이끄는 시그널인 'it's time to R(it's time that)'을 확인한다.

문제 4

답 (3)

해설 낮은 이자율은 저축 예금 또는 재무부 공채와 정부의 유가증권에 의존해서 생계를 꾸리는 사람에게 피해를 줄 것이다. 보기 (3)이 정답이다.

해설 세계 경제의 현 상황에서 경기를 부양할 수 있는 것은 아무것도 없다. 미국에서 일자리 창출은 하향세이고, 유럽연합은 악화하는 국가부재 위기를 3년째 겪고 있다. 대서양 양쪽의 어느 곳에서도 성장을 찾아볼 수 없다.

금리는 사실상 제로에 가까운 상황에 도달한 가운데, 통화정책 수단 가운데 사용 가능한 방법은 하나도 남지 않았다. 돈을 더 많이 찍는 것은 해답이 아니다. 클린턴 대통령 밑에서 백악관 경제수석을 지낸 래리 서머스 같은 케인스 지지자들은 이 점을 인정하고 경기부양용 돈을 더 많이 빌리는 것이 해결책이라고 주장한다. 그들의 주장을 들으면, 마치 연방정부가 지난 몇 년 동안 긴축정책을 추진해 온 것으로 착각하기 쉽다.

서머스는 민간기업들이 투자를 하여 경제에 시동을 거는 데 충분한 자금을 빌리지 않았다고 주장한다. 따라서 금리가 현저히 낮은 상태를 유지하고 있기 때문에 정부가 경제에 시동을 걸어야 한다는 것이다. 10년 만기 공채의 명목상 금리는 낮은 1.5%이며, 단기 공채의 금리는 제로에 가깝다.

미국은 이미 너무 많은 빚을 지고 있으므로 올해 정부 예산 적자는 1조 2,000억 달러가 될 것으로 예상된다. 이 액수는 오바마 대통령의 소위 경기부양 정책인 미 경기회복 및 재투자법(ARRA)에 따라 지출한 8,310억 달러보다 많다. 만약 대규모 지출론자들의 주장이 옳다면 이는 경제를 움직이도록 만들 수 있는 거액의 지출이지만, 미국의 연간 성장률은 고작 1.9%이며 일자리 증가율은 내려가고 있다.

단순히 싸다는 이유 때문에 정부가 돈을 더 많이 빌릴 경우 정부 재무의 증가가 경제를 다시 활성화시킬 것이라고 믿을 만한 이유가 거의 없다. 스탠퍼드 대학교의 경제학자 존 테일러가 추산하듯이, 오바마 행정부가 흥청망청으로 집행한 경기부양 예산 지출이 절정을 이루었을 때 ARRA는 국내총생산(GDP)의 0.21%에 도달했고, 연방 인프라 지출은 GDP의 0.05%였다. 그처럼 흥청망청으로 집행한 지출은 미국 경제를 부양시키지 못했으나 정부의 경기부양용 지출에는 대가가 따랐다.

국가재무는 현재 미국 GDP의 100%이며 2035년에는 180%로 폭발적인 팽창을 하리란 것이 미 의회 예산국의 예상이다. 부재 증가는 경제 성장에 장기적인 대가를 치르게 할 것이다. 이뿐만 아니라 제로금리의 유지는 저축한 사람들과 은퇴한 사람들 및 재무부 공채와 정부의 유가증권에 소득을 의존하는 사람들에게 손해를 끼친다.

정부 부문에는 생산성이 전혀 없다. 미국의 경제적 재앙을 해결하는 방법은 민간 부문에서 허용되는 것 말고 정부가 할 수 있는 것 가운데에서는 발견되지 않을 것이다. 기업의 성공을 가능케 하는 제한된 정부 원칙으로 돌아갈 때가 되었다.

어휘

stimulating *a.* 경기부양의
on the decline 추락하고 있는
monetary-policy 통화정책
print up 찍어내다
austerity *n.* 긴축(정책)
paltry *a.* 하찮은, 무가치한(petty)
woe *n.* 비애, 고통
entrepreneur *n.* 기업가

[Challenge 6]

문제 1

답 (4)

해설 글쓴이가 궁극적으로 주장하려는 내용이 드러나는 시점은 주제문인 'Social Darwinism did have some favorable effects.'이다. 이후 뒷받침 문장을 통해 자신의 견해를 드러내는 글이다. 고로 가장 적절한 주제는 보기 항 (4)가 된다. 도입부에 사회 진화론에 대한 일반적인 견해를 밝히고 있지만, 이는 글쓴이가 옹호하는 내용이 아닌 이와 다른 대조적 견해에 해당한다. 아래와 같은 구조를 취하고 있다.

도입부	사회 진화론에 대한 일반 통념
일반 진술	'But'이후 글쓴이의 주장(일반 통념에 반대되는 주장)
구체적 진술	뒷받침 진술

문제 2

답 (3)

해설 보기 항 (4)는 'He opposed direct and indiscriminate handouts to the poor'에서 알 수 있듯이 틀린 진술이다.

해석 모든 사회 진화론자들이 그렇게 극단적인 것은 아니며 사회 다원주의가 단지 식민지주의, 제국주의 그리고 다른 강제적인 착취('백인의 짐'은 또 다른 거의 전적으로 반대의 정당성을 말하다)만을 정당화하는 것은 아니다. 사실, 초기 사회 진화론자들은 이 이론을 자유방임적 자본주의의 논리적 확장으로 간주했었는데, 아마도 국가에서 운영하는 우생학 프로그램을 장려하기 위한 개념으로 사용한 것을 알았다면 경악했을 것이다. 비록 사회 다원주의의 도덕적 기반은 지금은 반대하는 것이 일반적이지만, 어느 정도 좋은 영향력을 미쳤다. 사회 다원주의의 신념은 가난한 자에게 터무니없을 정도의 원조를 막고, 대신 모든 계층의 사람들 중에서 가장 적합한 사람들이 사용할 수 있는 자원을 제공하고, 특정한 진짜 받을 만한 사람들을 선택해서 도움과 지원을 받도록 하는 것이다. Andrew Carnegie와 같은 주요 자본주의자들은 사회 다원주의와 박애정신을 합쳤다. 그는 자신의 어마어마한 재산을 이용해서 수백 개의 도서관과 대학교를 포함한 그 밖의 다른 공공기관을 설립했는데, 이것은 이러한 자원을 스스로 이용하려고 선택한 사람들을 위한 것이었다. 그는 가난한 사람들에 대한 직접적이고 무차별적인 기부를 반대했는데, 이는 이것이 자격이 있는 사람에게든, 없는 사람에게든 똑같이 혜택을 준다고 느꼈기 때문이다.

어휘

justification n. 정당하다고 규정함, 정당화
colonialism n. 식민주의 **imperialism** n. 제국주의
intrusive a. 강제하는; 침입하는
laissez-faire n. 자유방임주의
appall v. 오싹 소름이 끼치게 하다, 놀래게 하다
eugenics n. 우생학 **wanton** a. 터무니없는
handout n. (가난한 사람들에게) 거저 주는 것
walk of life n. 직업, 사회적 계급 **recipient** n. 수납자, 수령인
philanthropy n. 박애, 인자(仁慈), 자선
indiscriminate a. 무차별의, 닥치는 대로의

[Challenge 7]

문제 1

답 (1)

해설 'a typology of errors'에서 알 수 있듯이 에러의 유형을 구분하여 제시하고 있다.

문제 2

답 (3)

해설 제시문의 내용이 다소 어려울 경우 당황하는 경우가 있는데, 지시대명사 'this'가 가리키는 것이 무엇인지 뒤의 내용을 살펴보고 본문의 어디에 넣을 수 있을지 생각해 본다. Domain은 문맥적 상황이 있어야 이해할 수 있는 에러를 지칭하고, Extent의 경우 문장 내 추가, 생략, 대체 등을 통해 문장의 내용을 전달할 수 있도록 수정하는 것이다.

문제 3

답 (1)

해설 보기 항 (1)은 'happened'가 바른 표현인데, '~ed'를 생략한 'omissive'에 해당하는 에러인 반면 나머지는 모두 'additive'에 해당하는 오류이다.

해설 오류 분석가들은 조직적인 오류와 그렇지 않은 실수를 구별한다. 이들은 종종 오류를 유형화하려 한다. 오류는 누락, 추가, 대체 또는 어순과 관련된 기본적인 유형에 따라 구분된다. 이러한 에러는 (또한) 얼마나 확연한 오류인가에 따라 구분될 수 있다. '나는 화가 난'과 같은 명백한 오류는 문맥이 주어지지 않은 상황에서도 분명히 알 수 있지만, 걸으로 드러나지 않은 오류의 경우 문맥 안에서만 알 수 있다. 분석가가 검토하는 문맥의 범위인 도메인과 오류를 고치기 위해 반드시 바꾸어야 하는 말의 범위인 정도에 따른 구별은 이것과 아주 밀접한 관련이 있다. 오류는 또한 언어의 단계에 따라 구분할 수 있는데, 음성학적 오류, 어휘 오류, 의미상의 오류 등이 있다. 이러한 오류는 이것이 언어소통에 장애가 되는 정도에 따라 평가될 수 있다. 총체적 오류는 말 자체를 이해하기 어려운 반면에 부분적인 에러는 그렇지 않다. 위의 예 '나는 화가 난'의 경우는 의미가 분명하기에 부분적 오류이다.

어휘

distinguish v. 구별하다 **typology** n. 유형 분류 체계
classify v. 분류[구분]하다
omissive a. 게을리 하는, 태만한; 빠뜨리는
additive a. 추가하는; 부가적인 **substitutive** a. 대용이 되는
phonological a. 음운론의 **vocabulary** n. 어휘
lexical a. 어휘의 **syntactic** a. 구문론의
assess v. 재다, 평가하다 **degree** n. 정도
interfere v. 간섭하다, 방해하다
communication n. 의사소통, 연락

utterance *n.* 표현함, 입 밖에 냄   local *a.* 지역의
apparent *a.* 분명한, 명백한

[Challenge 8]

문제 1

답 (4)

해설 본문에서 말하는 계급의식을 조장하는 대상은 권력을 가진 기존의 대상이 아니라 개인의 사유, 이자 등을 반대하는 사회주의자들이다.

문제 2

답 (3)

해설 본문에서 사회주의의 성격으로 인구 증가를 통제한다는 이야기는 없다.

해석 사회주의의 궁극적인 목적은 통치적 기능으로서, 그리고 민중이 주도하는 정치 아래 모든 땅, 산업, 교통수단, 분배와 금융 및 집단적 경영을 공공의 선을 위해 국유화하는 것이다. 여기에는 개인의 이익, 임대와 이자의 폐지가 포함되며, 특히 인구의 증가 또는 집중으로 발생하는 가치의 증가에 의한 개인의 이익의 가능성을 배제한다. 대부분의 사회주의자들은 이러한 목적을 지속적인 단계에 따라 기존의 소유자에 대한 보상과 함께 점진적으로 달성하려 한다. 폭력적 소수 사회주의자들은 필요하면 유혈사태나 이들이 "expropriation(토지 몰수, 징수)"이라 부르는 압수로 한꺼번에(급격히; per saltum) 이것을 성취하려 한다. 모두가 똑같이 대다수를 차지하는 노동자 계층의 계급의식을 조장하거나 강조하고, 자신의 삶의 조건이 사회주의 정권 아래서 향상될 것이라고 주장함으로 자신들의 정치 선전을 행한다. 폭력을 일삼는 당파는 단지 계급의식뿐 아니라 계급 증오까지 선동한다.

어 휘

ultimate *a.* 최후의, 마지막의
nationalization *n.* 국유화, 국영
common good 공공의 선
abolition *n.* (법률, 습관 등의) 폐지, 철폐
private *a.* 사유의, 개인 소유의
successive *a.* 잇따른, 연속적인
compensation *n.* 배상, 보상
saltus *n.* 갑작스러운 변동, 격변
bloodshed *n.* 유혈 사태
confiscation *n.* 몰수, 압류
expropriation *n.* (토지 등의) 몰수

[Challenge 9]

문제 1

답 (1)

해설 첫 번째 문장과 인용구의 마지막 문장에서 요지를 찾을 수 있다.

해석 어떤 이들은 지능의 역할에 주목한다. 하나님은 인생사에서 가장 이성적인 설명이 가능한 존재이다. 종교적 진리와 인간의 마음은 비록 서로를 위해서 만들어지긴 했지만 조화를 이룬다. 신에 대한 사고가 이들에게 진정한 정신적 만족을 부여한다. 단테는 우리에게 말한다. "나의 심장의 삶, 바로 나의 내적 존재의 삶은 수없이 하나님의 발아래 닿는 달콤한 생각에 익숙한데, 다시 말해 나는 하늘에 계신 하나님의 왕국을 생각한다." 그리고 현대 영국의 사상가인 F.H. Bradley는 다음과 같이 쓴다. "우리는 모두 정도의 차이는 있지만 일상적인 현실의 영역 너머로 이끌린다고 생각한다. 어떤 이는 이쪽으로, 어떤 이는 다른 쪽으로 우리는 보이는 세상을 넘어선 것에 닿아 교감을 나눈다. 다양한 방법으로 우리는 우리를 지지하기도, 낮추기도, 책망하기도, 기쁘게도 하는 그런 높은 무언가를 발견한다. 그리고 다양한 사람들과 함께 우주를 이해하려는 지적 노력은 바로 신을 경험하는 주된 방법이다."

어 휘

prominence *n.* 두드러짐, 현저; 유명함
harmonize *v.* 조화시키다
communion *n.* (어떤 일을) 함께 함; 간담(懇談), 친교
chasten *v.* (신이 사람을) 징벌하다; (고생이 사람을) 단련하다; 잘못을 깨닫게 하다

[Challenge 10]

문제 1

답 (2)

해설 첫 번째 문단에서 드러나는 유대교에 관한 두 가지 주장이 옳지 못함을 반론하는 글이다.

문제 2

답 (3)

해설 본문은 유대인이 주장한 두 가지 측면을 반론하는 글이다. 첫 번째와 두 번째 유대인의 주장이 소개되는 그 경계가 바로 문단이 나눠지는 곳이다.

문제 3

답 (1)

해설 두 번째 문단의 내용은 행위는 완전한 규범의 문제가 아니라는 내용이다. 글의 통일성에 맞추어 나머지 문단의 내용은 모두 이를 뒷받침해야 한다. 빈칸이 들어간 문장을 살펴보자.

> but there was a whole class of actions described as 'matters given over to the heart,' delicate refinements of conduct which the law left _____ and were a concern exclusively of the feeling, the private judgment of the individual.

위 문장 구조를 보면, 콤마로 나열이 되어 있다. 다시 말해 A, B, C, and D라고 할 때, A, B, C, D는 모두 같은 의미를 전달하는 내용으로 구성되어 있다. 빈칸 앞에서 특정한 행위는 마음, 즉 감정에 의해서 해석되어야 한다고 말하면서, 바로 뒤에 이어지는 내용은 모두 'feeling'과 'private judgment'를 강조하는 내용이다. 따라서 빈칸에 들어갈 단어는 법이 관장할 수 없는 그런 행위를 나타내는 표현이 되어야 한다.

해석 유대교는 흔히 믿음이 자유로운 반면 행위에는 족쇄를 채운다고 말한다. 그러나 어느 쪽 주장도 엄밀히 말하면 사실이 아니다. 믿음은 온전히 자유롭지는 못하며 행위도 완전히 통제되지 않았다. '미슈나(Mishnah)'에서는 특정 계층의 불신자들은 앞으로 다가올 세상에 몫이 없다고 공언된다. 천국에서 제외된 이들 중엔 죽은 사람의 부활을 부인하는 사람도 있고, 율법, 즉 성서의 기원이 되는 신의 교리에 동의하기를 거부하는 사람도 있다. 따라서 믿음은 랍비식 체제에서 완벽하게 자유롭다고 말할 수 없다. 행위가 완전한 규범의 문제라는 주장도 마찬가지로 정확하지 않다. 인간은 율법이 요구하는 것 이상의 실천과 공덕의 실천으로 칭찬을 받을 뿐 아니라, 여러 랍비들이 진술한 실질적인 행위의 규칙에 중요한 차이가 있다. 그리고 '마음에 넘겨야 할 문제'로 설명되는 온갖 행동, 즉 법이 관장하지 않는 미묘한 행위의 개선이 있으며, 개인의 사적인 판단, 즉 오로지 감정에 관한 관심사가 있다.

어휘

Judaism *n.* 유대교
fetter *n.* 속박, 구속
assertion *n.* 주장, 행사
Mishnah *n.* 미슈나(Talmud의 제1부를 구성하는 유대교의 불성문 율집; A.D. 200년경의 편집)
portionless *a.* 배당이 없는
resurrection *n.* 그리스도 부활
doctrine *n.* 교리, 신조
Torah *n.* 유대교의 율법
scripture *n.* 성서, 성전
rabbinic *a.* 랍비식의
prescription *n.* 처방, 방안
supererogation *n.* 직무 이상으로 일하기; 적선, 공덕
divergence *n.* 분기; 일탈; 차이
refinement *n.* 개선, 개량

Day 21

[Challenge 1]

문제 1

답 (2)

해설 본문에서 궁극적으로 성공과 관련해 하고 싶은 말이 다음에서 잘 드러난다.

> Like all human affairs, success is partly a matter of predestination and partly of free will.

즉, 성공이란 한편으론 신의 축복에 의한 재능인 동시에 이러한 재능을 자신의 의미를 통해서 지속적으로 계발함으로써 얻어진다고 말하고 있다.

해석 나의 경우 내가 아는 일상사에서 성공의 분야를 언급하겠다. 그리고 나는 용어상의 모순으로 시작하겠다. 성공이란 신이 수혜자에게 내려주신 체질상의 기질이다. 그러나 동시에 당신이 요정이 가진 모든 재능을 가지고 있다 하더라도 완전히 실패할 수 있다. 인간은 자신의 신장을 1인치 늘릴 수는 없지만, 분별을 통해 그는 직립보행할 수 있다. 태어날 때 부여된 모든 재능은 단 하나의 저주로 모두 날아갈 수 있다. 인간의 다른 모든 일과 마찬가지로 성공이란 한편으로는 운명이며 다른 한편으로는 자유 의지이다. 천재적 재능을 만들어 낼 수는 없지만, 이 재능을 향상하거나 파괴할 수 있다. 그리고 대부분 사람들은 성공으로 바꿀 수 있는 장점을 지니고 있다. 그러나 이러한 귀중한 재능을 가진 사람은 이것을 계속 쌓아 확장해야 한다.

어휘

affair *n.* 일, 용건, 사건   temperament *n.* 기질, 성질
recipient *n.* 수납자, 수령자, 받는 사람
utterly *ad.* 아주, 전혀   stature *n.* 키, 신장; 성장, 발달
predestination *n.* 숙명, 운명   will *n.* 의지, 의도, 유언
hoard *v.* 저장하다, 축적하다

[Challenge 2]

문제 1

답 (1)

해설 본문의 내용은 와트가 실용적인 증기기관을 만들기 전 어린 시절 어떤 계기를 통해서 그가 나중에 이룰 큰 꿈을 실현하게 되는지를 다루고 있다. 현대의 모든 이기의 가장 기본적인 이 증기기관이 나오게 된 결정적 계기는 바로 주전자와 관련된 사건이다. 고로 보기 항 (1)이 이러한 관점을 포괄하는 주제가 될 수 있다.

문제 2

답 (3)

해설 다음의 본문과 보기 항 (3)을 비교해 보자.

> He was sure it could be made of great service to men. It was already used for driving engines, but the engines were not good, and it cost much money to work them. Watt thought they could be improved...

문제 3

답 (2)

해설 조건 부사절의 내용을 고르는 문제다. 주절의 내용을 보면, 증기가 다시 물로 변했다고 말했다. 당연히 이는 차가운 것에 닿아 온도가 떨어졌기 때문에 발생한 것임을 알 수 있다.

해석 James Watt라 불리는 스코틀랜드 아이가 있었다. 그는 그리 튼튼한 아이는 아니었기에 다른 아이들과 함께 달리거나 놀 수가 없었다. 그래서 집에서 혼자 놀아야 했다. 어느 휴일 오후에도 어린 James는 이런 식으로 혼자 놀고 있었다. 그는 접시를 들고 그 위에 끓는 주전자의 주둥이에서 나오는 스팀이 지나가게 했다. 그리고 지켜보다가 그는 이 접시 위에 작은 물방울이 맺히는 것을 보았다. 그는 이것이 아주 이상하다고 여기면서 왜 일어나는지 궁금해했다. 이는 그가 증기가 바로 열에 의해서 그 형태가 변한 물이라는 점과 이것이 다시 어떤 차가운 것에 닿으면 다시 물로 변한다는 사실을 몰랐기 때문이다. 그는 고모에게 이것을 설명해 달라고 물었는데, 그녀는 그에게 시간 낭비하지 말라는 소리만 해주었다. 만약 자기 조카가 나중에 어른이 되어서 하게 될 일을 볼 선견만 있었더라면 그녀는 절대 그가 시간을 낭비하는 것이라 생각하지 않았을 것이다. James Watt는 그 후로도, 증기와 그것의 놀라운 힘에 유년기 때만큼 관심을 가졌다. 그는 이것이 인간에게 큰 도움을 줄 것이라는 확신을 가졌다. 이것은 이미 엔진을 움직이는 데 사용되었지만, 엔진은 그리 성능이 좋지 않은데다, 이것을 움직이는 데 돈도 많이 들었다. Watt는 이것을 향상시킬 수 있다고 생각했지만, 이렇게 하는 방법을 알아내기까지 오랜 시간이 걸렸다. 종종 그는 마치 스팀에 의해 춤을 추는 듯한 주전자 뚜껑을 난로 옆에 앉아 바라보면서 많은 계획을 생

각했다. 그리고 마침내 묘안을 떠올렸다. 그의 계획 덕분에 엔진 작동이 크게 개선되었고, 이제 증기는 기차, 배, 제분소 그리고 공장을 돌리며, 우리의 가장 유용한 충신이 되었다.

어휘

amuse *v.* 즐겁게(미소 짓게) 하다
saucer *n.* 받침, 접시   **spout** *n.* (주전자 등의) 주둥이
foresee *v.* ~일 것이라고 생각하다, 예견하다
nephew *n.* 조카   **lid** *n.* 뚜껑
improvement *n.* 향상, 개선
servant *n.* 하인; 고용인, 종업원

[Challenge 3]

문제 1

답 (4)

해설 아이가 젖을 빠는 동안 발생하는 증상에 관한 기술이 첫 번째 단락이고, 두 번째 단락은 이에 대한 대책을 소개하는 것이다.

문제 2

답 (2)

해설 본문 마지막에 명시되어 있듯이, 위에 언급한 모든 증상의 원인인 아이가 젖 빠는 것을 중단해야 한다고 말하고 있다.

해석 첫 번째 증상은 아이가 빠는 행위를 하는 동안 등에서 뭔가 처지는(끌어당기는) 느낌이 생기고, 이후 명치에 가라앉고 빈 듯한 축 늘어진 느낌이 든다. 그런 다음에는 곧 식욕이 감퇴하고, 변비가 발생하며, 왼쪽에 고통이 따른다. 그런 다음 머리가 아픈데, 때로 아주 지끈지끈하고 귀에서 웡 하는 소리가 나며, 상당히 우울한 기분이 동반되면서 항상 어느 정도의 현기증이 난다. 이내 가슴에 통증이 오는데 숨이 가빠지며, 마른 기침이 나고 작은 움직임에도 심장이 두근거린다. 병이 진전되면서, 얼굴은 창백해지고, 몸은 쇠약해지고, 밤에 진땀을 흘리고, 엄청난 무기력과 함께 발목은 붓고 신경쇠약이 일어난다. 치료와 관련해 가장 유용하다고 말할 수 있는 것은 바로 이것이다. 약을 먹고, 기분 전환을 하고, 차가운 바다 목욕으로 우선 많은 것을 할 수 있지만, 그래도 가장 빠르고 효과적인 방법은 젖을 떼어 원인을 제거하는 것이다.

어휘

sensation *n.* 감각, 느낌   **suck** *v.* 입을 대어 빨다, 핥다
exhaust *v.* 다 써버리다, 고갈하다
appetite *n.* 식욕, 욕구   **costive** *a.* 변비의; 동작이 둔한
bowel *n.* 장, 창자, 내장   **throb** *v.* 가슴이 고동치다, 두근거리다
giddiness *n.* 어지러움, 현기증   **palpitation** *n.* 가슴이 두근거림, 떨림
exertion *n.* 노력, 분발   **profuse** *a.* 아낌없는, 후한, 풍부한
perspiration *n.* 발한(작용)
debility *n.* (육체적으로) 약함, 쇠약

ensue *v.* 계속해서 일어나다
in reference to ~에 관해서, 관련하여
wean *v.* 젖을 떼다

[Challenge 4]

문제 1

답 (1)

해설 본문에서 (1)에 대한 언급은 없으며, 이산화탄소의 양을 줄여 나무의 모공이 수축하지 못하게 만드는 것이 바람직한 방법이다.

해석 식물은 기후 시스템에 아주 복잡하고 다양한 영향을 미친다. 식물은 주위의 대기에서 이산화탄소를 취하지만, 이들은 또한 다른 영향을 미치기도 하는데, 예를 들어, 지표면에서 발생하는 수증기의 양을 변화시키기도 한다. 이러한 모든 요소를 고려하지 않고 기후 예측을 한다는 것은 불가능하다. 식물은 잎사귀의 작은 구멍을 통해 수분을 발산시키는 '증산'이라 불리는 작용을 하는데, 이것이 땀이 우리의 몸을 식히는 것과 같이 식물을 식혀 준다. 더운 날, 나무는 공기 중에 많은 수분을 방출하면서 주변을 시원하게 하는 자연 에어컨의 기능을 한다. 식물은 동일한 구멍을 통해 광합성을 위한 이산화탄소를 흡수한다. 그러나 이산화탄소의 농도가 높아지면, 나뭇잎의 구멍이 수축한다. 이 때문에 수분 방출이 적어지고, 냉각력이 약화된다. 온실가스로서 이산화탄소가 온도를 증가시키는 효과가 있다는 것은 오랫동안 알려진 사실이지만, 이산화탄소가 식물에게도 직접적인 영향을 주면서 지구를 따뜻하게 한다는 사실은 널리 인식되어 있지 않다.

어휘

evapotranspiration *n.* 증산 작용(토양면으로부터의 증발과 식물의 증산 작용에 의해 토양 중의 수분을 잃는 일)
diverse *a.* 다양한   **evaporation** *n.* 증발 (작용), (수분의) 발산
pore *n.* 털구멍; (식물에 나 있는) 기공(氣孔)
photosynthesis *n.* [생물]광합성(光合成)

[Challenge 5]

문제 1

답 (1)

해설 본문은 역청탄으로 원유를 만드는 회사들로 인해 캐나다의 산림과 숲이 파괴되고 있다는 내용으로, 글쓴이는 본문 마지막에서 이에 대한 미국의 적극적 환경보호 정책을 촉구하고 있다.

140

문제 2

답 (1)

해설 앞뒤 문맥을 보고 가장 적절한 내용을 선정해야 한다. 빈칸 앞쪽에서 'tar sands'를 원유로 바꾸는 것은 환경 친화적 기술 시대와는 전혀 다른 방향이며, 이후 다른 환경 친화적 대안을 통해 현 문제점을 해결해야 한다는 글쓴이의 요구가 드러나 있다. 고로 'tar sands'는 바람직하지 못하다는 내용이 들어가야 이후 이와 대조되는(instead) 환경 친화적 대안으로 자연스럽게 연결된다.

해석 캐나다의 석유 산업은 북부 수림대와 습지대 — 세계에서 마지막으로 남아있는 사람의 손이 닿지 않은 생태계 중 하나 — 를 미국의 석유 탱크로 바꾸고 있다. 앨버타의 북쪽 숲지대는 수많은 북미 명금과 물새의 산란지일 뿐 아니라 스라소니, 순록 그리고 회색곰을 포함한 다양한 종류의 동물 서식지이다. 석유 회사들은 석청이 소량 포함된 미사 매장층에 있는 역청탄을 재굴하기 위해 수십만 에이커의 야생 지역을 파헤치고 있다. 역청탄을 재굴 및 시추하고 석청을 원유로 바꾸는 행위는 엄청난 양의 에너지와 물을 사용하여 공기와 물에 심각한 오염을 발생시키며, 캐나다의 삼림과 습지대를 위험에 빠트리고 있다. 원주민의 경우 이 지역의 재굴 작업으로 인해 그 지역의 물 공급이 줄고, 유독한 물질에 노출이 증가한다. 무엇보다, 역청탄에서 합성 원유를 생산하는 과정에서 기존의 원유 생산보다 3배나 많은 온난화 오염 물질이 발생한다. 즉, 질 낮은 석유 원료를 얻기 위해 북쪽 지역의 역청탄을 재굴하려 몰려드는 현상은 방대한 야생 산림을 파괴하고 붕괴하게 될 것이다. 우리가 환경 친화적 에너지 미래를 받아들여야 할 때에, 역청탄은 전혀 잘못된 방향으로 우리를 이끄는 것이다. 미국은 대신 종합적인 석유 절약 계획을 시행하고, 연료 효율 기술, 하이브리드 자동차, 재생 가능한 에너지, 환경 친화적인 생물 연료를 늘려서 교통체계의 필요성을 충족시키는 올바른 성장 방안을 통해 석유 소비를 줄여야 한다.

어휘

- boreal *a.* 북쪽의; 북풍의; 한대(寒帶)의, 북방의
- intact *a.* 본래대로의, 손대지 않은
- diverse *a.* 다양한, 가지각색의   lynx *n.* 스라소니
- caribou *n.* 순록(북아메리카산)
- grizzly *a.* 회색의, 회색을 띤
- scrape *v.* 긁어 내다; (구멍 등을) 파다
- haven *n.* 안식처, 피난처   tar sand 역청사
- silty *n.* 침니(沈泥)(모래보다 곱고 진흙보다 거친 침적토(沈積土))
- bitumen *n.* 역청(歷靑), 아스팔트
- aboriginal *a.* 원주민의, 원래[토착]의
- synthetic *a.* 합성의, 인조의

[Challenge 6]

문제 1

답 (2)

해설 영어의 대부분의 글은 초반부에서 주제(무엇에 대한 글인지)를 밝히는 경우가 많다. 이런 글은 대부분 'General → Specific'으로 전개되는 것으로, 본문의 내용은 글쓴이가 처음에 설정한 주제에 대한 뒷받침 내용으로 통일성을 갖춘다. 본문은 음악에서 창의적 소질에 대한 평가 시도가 일고 있다는 내용으로 시작하며, 이후 예시를 통해 단계별로 측정하는 방법에 대한 구체적인 내용을 전개하고 있다. 보기 항 (2)가 가장 적절하다.

문제 2

답 (2)

해설 빈칸 앞에서 제시된 'divergent thinking(발산성 사고)'에서 힌트를 얻을 수 있다.

문제 3

답 (1)

해설 아이가 실질적으로 개구리를 이용하여 음악을 만들어 내는 것이 아니라 이러한 개구리의 '이미지'를 살려 만드는 것을 말한다. 그러므로 개구리를 직접적으로 이용한 보기 항 (2), (3), (4)는 오답이다.

해석 최근에서야 음악에서 창의적인 소질을 실질적으로 평가하려는 시도가 시작되었다. 대부분의 이런 시도는 6세에서 10세 사이의 어린아이들에게 초점이 맞추어 있으며, 게임과 같은 환경에서 음악과 관련된 과제를 행하면서 음악에서 발산적이고 수렴적인 사고력을 밝혀내려는 것이다. 예를 들자면, 내가 개발한 한 방법은 증폭된 목소리, 피아노와 둥근 스펀지 공 그리고 목공을 이용하여 아이들로 하여금 음악을 형상화하는 놀이에 참여하도록 하는 것이다. 이 작업은 아주 단순하게 시작한 후 발산성 사고라는 관점에서 좀 더 어려운 단계로 진행된다. 이 작업에는 옳고 그른 답이 존재하지 않는다.

이 평가 절차의 첫 번째는 아이가 사용하는 악기와 이것이 어떻게 배열되는지 친숙해지도록 고안된 단계이다. 아이들은 이 단계와 측정 전반에 걸쳐 '높음/낮음', '빠름/느림' 그리고 '소리가 큼/부드러움'이란 변수를 탐구한다. 아이들이 이러한 변수를 조작하는 방법은 다시 점수를 따기 위한 기본적인 요소 중 하나로 사용된다. 아이들은 물통에 담긴 빗물, 요술 엘리베이터 그리고 트럭의 소리의 이미지와 관련된 과제를 부여받는다.

중간 단계에서는 악기를 가지고 좀 더 어려운 활동을 하며, 악기를 따로따로 사용하여 음악을 만드는 것에 초점을 두도록 요구된다. 아이들은 타구봉과 목공을 가지고 일종의 음악적인 질문/답변의 대화에 들어가, 피아노 위의 둥근 공, 목소리 그리고 마이크를 가지고 노래를 만든다. 아이들은 '개구리' 음악의 개념(피아노 위에 공을 튕기고 굴려서)과 소나기 속에서 노래를 부르는 로봇의 개념(마이크를 통해 아이의 목소리로 만들어 냄)이 포함된 이미지를 사용한다.

이 절차의 마지막 단계에서 아이들은 주변에 배경이 덜 잡힌 작업 내에서 다양한 악기를 사용하도록 권장된다. 아이들은 시각 도구로서 그림을 사용하여 우주 이야기를 소리로 표현한다. 마지막으로 아이들이 악기를 전부 사용해서 처음, 중간, 끝이 있는 작곡을 하도록 시킨다.

이 측정과 이것과 같은 다른 측정을 통해 음악적 규칙뿐 아니라 음악적 창조성, 폭 그리고 유연성과 같은 요소에 관해 점수를 매길 수 있다. 이 활동에 실질적으로 관련된 아이의 비디오 또는 오디오 테이프를 분석한 것에 기초해서 측정 전략을 짠다. 평가 측정뿐 아니라 객관적 기준도 사용된다. 예를 들어, 음악적 폭은 창의적인 과제와 관련된 시간에 의해서 측정되고, 평가자들은 음의 높이, 박자 그리고 역동성을 어떻게 만들어 내는지를 관찰해 창의성을 평가한다.

어 휘

divergent *a.* 분기하는, 갈라지는; 발산의
convergent *a.* 한 점으로 향하는; 수렴(성)의
parameter *n.* 매개 요소, 한정 요소   **score** *v.* 점수를 매기다
singly *ad.* 하나씩, 따로따로   **mallet** *n.* 나무망치
microphone *n.* 마이크
syntax *n.* 구문(론)   **strategy** *n.* 용병학, 병법, 전략
be based on ~에 기초하다   **analysis** *n.* 분석, 분해
criteria *n.* 기준   **pitch** *n.* 음의 높이

[Challenge 7]

문제 1

답 (2)

해설 본문 첫 번째 문단에서 나타나는 바와 같이 동물과 구별되는 진정한 인간됨이란 무엇인지, 그 특성을 나열을 통해 살펴보는 글이다.

문제 2

답 (2)

해설 문장 배열의 문제는 언제나 문장 또는 문단의 첫 번째 문장을 잘 살펴보아야 한다.

(a) That degree of development which gives us the human mind is a clear distinction of race. The savage who can count a hundred is more human than the savage who can count ten.

→ 동물과 인간을 구별하는 특징 중 셀 수 있는 능력, 즉 수리인지 능력을 말하고 있다.

(b) Human life of any sort is dependent upon what Kropotkin calls "mutual aid," and human progress keeps step absolutely with that interchange of specialized services which makes society organic.

→ 인간 진보의 기반이 되는 상호 도움과 사회를 유기체가 되게 만드는 전문화된 서비스의 상호 교환 (인간의 사회성을 강조하는 문장이다)

(c) More prominent than either of these is the social nature of humanity.

→ 인간의 사회성을 처음 소개하는 문장이다. 고로 (c) → (b)가 되며, 앞에서 두 가지 특징 다음에 나오므로 앞쪽에 오지 않는다.

(d) Our human-ness is seen most clearly in three main lines.

→ 인간됨의 특징을 소개하려는 처음 문장에 해당한다.

고로, 위의 분석을 보면 나열할 문장을 모두 읽지 않아도 배열이 어느 정도 가능할 때가 있으므로 이러한 요소를 활용하는 것을 간과해선 안 된다.

해석 우리는 무생물체와 마찬가지로 무게, 불투명체 그리고 탄성 등의 특징을 가지고 있다. 분명 이러한 것은 인간적인 것(인간의 독특한 것)은 아니다. 우리는 다른 모든 생명체와 공통적인 특성 또한 가지고 있다. 예를 들면, 세포 구조, 세포 분열 그리고 영양분의 필요성이 그것이다. 이러한 것 역시 인간적인 것은 아니다. 우리는 고등 포유류와 공통되는 여러 다른 점이 있는데, 이러한 것은 우리에게만 있는 것이 아니다. 즉, 독특하게 '인간적인' 것은 아니다. 그럼 정작 인간적인 진정한 특성이란 무엇인가? 어떤 측면에서 인간이란 종이 다른 모든 종과 구별이 되는가?

우리의 인간다움이란 세 가지 측면에서 가장 뚜렷하게 발견된다. 이것은 기계적이고, 정신적이며, 사회적이다. 물건을 만들고 사용하는 우리의 능력은 근본적으로 인간적인 것이며, 우리만 신체 이외의 장비를 가지고 있다. 우리는 우리의 치아 외에 칼, 겁, 가위, 풀을 베는 기계를 사용한다. 우리의 손발톱 이외에 가래, 써레, 쟁기, 드릴, 준설기 등을 사용한다. 우리는 다재다능한 창조물로, 우리의 큰 두뇌 능력을 사용해서 다양하게 변형이 가능한 무기를 사용한다. 이것이 바로 우리의 주되고 중요한 차이점 중의 하나이다. 고대 야생 동물의 종은 단순히 뼈와 조개를 추적해서 알아내지만, 고대 인간의 종은 이들이 지은 건물, 도구 그리고 가정기구에 의해서 알 수 있다.

우리 인간의 마음에 부여한 발달의 정도가 바로 종을 뚜렷이 구분해주는 것이다. 100까지 셀 수 있는 야만인이 10가지 셀 수 있는 야만인보다 더 인간적이다.

이 둘보다 더 뚜렷한 특징이 바로 인간의 사회성이다. 우리 인간만이 유일하게 무리를 지어 사는 동물은 아니다. 개미나 흔히 보는 벌도 사회적 생명체이다. 그러나 이런 종류의 곤충들은 홀로 살아간다. 인간은 절대 그렇지 않다. 우리의 인간됨은 낮은 단계의 사회관계에서 시작해서 이 관계가 발달하면서 진보한다.

어떤 종류의 인간의 삶이든 Kropotkin이 말한 바와 같이 "상호 원조"에 의존하며 인간의 진보는 사회를 유기적으로 만드는 특성화된 서비스의 상호 교환과 절대적으로 나란히 나아간다. 개미가 자신의 먹이를 먹고 사는 것과 같이 소를 먹고 사는 유목민은 지능적으로 응용된 노동력으로 식량을 재배하는 농부보다 덜 인간적이다. 그리고 단순한 마을 시장에서 오늘날의 세계 무역에 이르는 무역과 상업의 확장 또한 인간다움의 확장인 것이다.

어 휘

in common with ~와 마찬가지로
inanimate *a.* 생명 없는, 무생물의
opacity *n.* 불투명   **resilience** *n.* 되=, 탄성
cellular *a.* 세포로 된, 세포질의
exclusively *ad.* 베타로, 독점적으로
distinctively *ad.* 독특하게, 특이하게
characteristic *a.* 특징, 특질   **species** *n.* 종
savage *n.* 야만인, 미개인   **interchange** *n.* 교환
specialize *v.* 전문으로 다루다   **organic** *a.* 유기적인
by no means 결코 ~이 아닌   **mow** *v.* 베다, 베어내다
claw *n.* 발톱   **spade** *n.* 가래, 삽
harrow *n.* 써레, 쇠토기   **plough** *n.* 쟁기
dredge *n.* 준설기   **protean** *a.* 변화무쌍한, 다양한
utensil *n.* 가정용품, 기구, 도구

[Challenge 8]

문제 1

답 (4)

해설 첫 번째 문단에서 다루고 있는 구체적 내용을 찾아내는 문제이다. 보기 항 (4)에 대한 언급은 없다. 쉬운 문제일수록 틀리지 말아야 한다.

문제 2

답 (2)

해설 밑줄 친 문장에서 'a special strength' 즉, '특별한 능력' 또는 '장점'에 주안점을 두어 생각해 본다.

문제 3

답 (2)

해설 고등 동물일수록 근친 교배에 더 민감하게 반응하기에 근친 교배의 횟수가 좀 더 하등한 동물보다 빨리 퇴화가 일어난다. 본문에 정확히 명시된 퇴화의 조건은 그 횟수와 관련이 있다는 것을 다음의 두 본문의 내용을 통해서 알 수 있다.

> After a certain number of generations however, degeneration apparently sets in."와 "successive generations of offspring of incestuous connection are not unknown; but, although statistics are lacking, it seems to be very often true that children of such unions are degenerate.

해석 동물의 번식에서 근친 교배는 그 종족의 향상을 위해 종종 사용이 되며, 많은 경우 눈에 보이는 해가 없이 수세대 동안 근친 교배의 예를 제시할 수 있다. 그러나 이러한 근친 교배를 위해 선택된 동물은 체질적으로 아주 건강해야 하며 병이 걸리지 않아야 하는 것이 일반적으로 알려져 있다. 그러나 특정 수의 세대가 지나면 퇴화가 분명히 자리를 잡는다. 근친 교배가 이루어지는 세대의 수는 종과 동물이 번식되는 목적에 따라 다르다. 소고기, 양고기 또는 돼지고기와 같은 고기가 주된 번식의 목적이 되는 경우 경주마의 번식과 같은 특정한 힘을 얻기 위한 번식의 경우보다 더 가까운 근친 교배가 가능하다.

그러나 인간의 경우 유전적 결합으로부터 그리 쉽게 자유롭지 못하다. 개인은 번식 목적을 위해 과학적으로 선택될 수 없다. 게다가, 인간의 몸은 하등 동물보다 더 섬세하게 구성되어 있고, 신경 조직은 더 많이 발달되어 있고, 세분화되어 있어, 인간의 퇴화는 근친 교배의 과정에서 더 빨리 자리를 잡는다. 낮은 동물과 같이 아주 가까운 근친 교배가 불가능하다고 가정하는 것은 이성적인 판단이다. 근친 결합이 건강한 자손을 낳은 경우도 잘 알려져 있지만, 근친의 자손이 대대로 이루어지는지는 알려져 있지 않다. 그러나 비록 통계치는 부족하지만, 이러한 결합으로 나온 자손들이 퇴화한다는 것은 사실인 경우가 많은 듯하다.

어 휘

inbreed *v.* 동종 번식하다   **resort** *v.* 의지하다; 신뢰하다
constitutionally *ad.* 체질적으로
mutton *n.* 양고기   **hereditary** *a.* 세습의; 유전상의
taint *n.* 오명, 오점   **degeneration** *n.* 퇴보; 악화
incestuous *a.* 근친상간의   **offspring** *n.* 자식; 자손
successive *a.* 잇따른; 계속되는
degenerate *v.* 나빠지다; 퇴보하다

[Challenge 9]

문제 1

답 (2)

해설 오스트리아 학파가 과학적 실험과 경제 모델링을 궁극적으로 반대하는 이유는 인간 행위의 불확실성 때문이다. 'altering their would-be actions'에서 인간 행위에 대한 불확실성을 알 수 있다. 밑줄 친 부분은 오스트리아 학파가 'testability in economics'가 불가능하다는 내용에 대한 근거로 제시되고 있다. 보기 항 (1)은 오히려 '현대 주류학파의 한계'로 기술되어야 하며, (3), (4)는 모두 이 학파와 반대의 내용을 전달하고 있다.

문제 2

답 (2)

해설 보기 항 (2)만이 오스트리아 학파와 관련된 주장이고, 나머지는 정부 개입과 시장 통제를 위한 모델링과 관련된 내용이다.

해석 오스트리아 경제학파의 원칙은 방법론적 개인주의 — 인간의 행위를 개인적 주체의 관점에서만 분석 — 를 엄격하게 고수하는 것을 주장한다. 이 경제학파는 또한 수학적 모델과 통계는 경제 이론을 분석하고 테스트하는 데 있어서 믿을 수 없는 수단이며, 인간 행동학이라 불리는 방법인 인간의 행위의 기본적인 원칙에서 논리적으로 경제 이론을 이끌어낼 것을 주장한다. 추가적으로 실험적 연구와 자연적 실험은 종종 주류 경제학에서 사용되지만, 오스트리아 경제학파는 경제학을 분석하는 것은 실질적으로 불가능하다고 본다. 이는 자신이 하려고 의도한 행위를 바꾸지 않으면서 실험실 환경에 놓일 수 없는 인간 주체에 의존하기 때문이다.

주류 경제학파는 일반적으로 현대 오스트리아 경제학파가 사용한 방법에 비판적이다. 특히 이 학파의 주된 방법은 선험적 '비—경험주의' 분석이며, 경제학에서 널리 행해지는 과학적 이론화의 관행과 다르다고 비판받아 왔다. 오스트리아 경제학파는 주로 인간 행위의 복잡성으로 인해 진화하는 시장에 대한 수학적 모델을 만드는 것은 극히 어려운 일이기에 경제에 자유방임적 태도를 취할 것을 주장한다. 이들은 경제 주체 간의 자발적인 계약적 합의 사항의 엄격한 집행을 주장하며, 상업 거래는 강제력이 최소한만 주어져야 한다고 주장한다. 특히 이들은 정부의 역할이 극히 제한적이어야 하며, 경제에 미치는 정부의 간섭을 가능한 한 최소화해야 한다고 주장한다.

어 휘

methodological *a.* 방법론의   **individualism** *n.* 개인주의
unreliable *a.* 신뢰할 수 없는   **means** *n.* 수단
praxeology *n.* 인간 행동학   **testability** *n.* 시험 가능성
a priori *a.* 선험적인   **empirical** *a.* 경험의
mathematical modeling 수학적 모델링
laissez faire *n.* 자유방임주의   **contractual** *a.* 계약상의
imposition *n.* (법률·세금 등의) 시행[도입]
coercive *a.* 강제적인
In particular 특별히   **argue for** ~에 관해 다투다
intervention *n.* 중재, 간섭

[Challenge 10]

문제 1

답 (3)

해설 보기 항 (1)은 "Walking is another example of the rapid exercise of volition with but little perception of each individual act of exercise."에서 힌트를 얻을 수 있다. (2)의 경우, "If a man goes down a lane by night he will stumble over many things which he would have avoided by day, although he would not have noticed them."에서 알 수 있다. 보기 항 (3)은 "Time was when walking was to each one of us a new and arduous task – as arduous as we should now find it to wheel a wheelbarrow on a tightrope."를 참조한다. 보기 항 (4)는 맨 마지막 문장을 참조.

해석 걷는 것은 각자가 행하는 행위에 대한 인식이 거의 없는 상황에서 순간적으로 의지를 행하는 또 다른 예에 해당한다. 우리가 길을 가다 장애물이 있으면 그것을 인식하지만, 우리가 인식했음에도 불구하고 우리가 인식한 것을 알아차리지 못하는 것은 당연지사이다. 이는 만약 한 사람이 밤에 길을 가다가, 그가 인식하지는 못했을 것이지만 낮에는 피했을 수많은 장애물을 보면 알 수 있다. 그러나 걷는 것이 마치 탄탄한 로프 위에서 외바퀴 수레를 끌 때 느끼는 힘겨움처럼 우리 각자에게 새롭고 힘든 때가 있었다. 반면, 현재 우리는 걸을 수 있는 능력을 확인하지 않고도 어느 정도 우리의 걸음을 생각할 수 있지만, 근육 동작 하나하나를 분명 고려하지 않고, 완전히 멈출 수는 없다.

어 휘

volition *n.* 의지; 결의
lane *n.* (산울타리, 벽 따위 사이의) 좁은 길
stumble *v.* 넘어지다; 비틀거리다 (over)
arduous *a.* 힘든, 어려운; 끈기 있는
wheelbarrow *n. v* 외바퀴 손수레

Day 22

[Challenge 1]

문제 1

답 (3)

해설 집에서 먹을 수 있는 좋은 물의 특성을 기술하는 글이다.

문제 2

답 (4)

해설 (d)를 제외한 나머지는 모두 물을 가리킨다. (d)는 it ~ that 강조구문의 it이다.

해석 가정용수 목적에 딱 맞는 순수한 물의 기준은 바로 그 부드러움에 있다. 이 특징은 비누로 손을 씻기만 해도 만지면 금방 알 수 있다. 좋은 물은 아주 투명하다. 약간 불투명한 것은 이물질이 들어 있음을 나타낸다. 물이 완벽하게 투명한지에 대한 판단을 하기 위해 일정량의 물을 아주 깊은 유리잔에 담는데, 이때 크면 클수록 좋으며, 그렇게 해야 수직으로 일정량의 액체를 내려다볼 수 있다. 그러면 당장 이 물을 눈과 빛 사이에 놓은 잔을 통해 바라보는 것보다 아주 약간의 탁한 정도도 훨씬 더 잘 발견할 수 있게 된다. 물은 완벽하게 색깔이 없어야 하며, 냄새도 없고 맛은 부드럽고 상쾌해야 한다. 다른 잔에 물을 부을 때 공기 방울이 나와야 한다. 끓을 때 부드럽게 진동해야 하고, 비누와 함께 일정한 유백색의 액체를 형성하는데, 몇 시간 지나서도 분리되지 않아야 한다. 일반 물이 그 맛과 함께 동물과 식물에 미치는 대부분의 순기능은 산소와 탄산가스 덕분이다.

어휘

opacity *v.* 불투명함   indicate *v.* 보여주다, 나타내다
extraneous *a.* 관련 없는   transparency *n.* 투명도
vessel *n.* 그릇, 용기, 통   perpendicularly *ad.* 수직적으로
muddiness *n.* 흐림   view *v.* 보다   devoid of ~이 없는
send out 보내다, 발송하다   air-bubble *n.* 기포
opaline *a.* 오팔 같은, 유광색이 나는

[Challenge 2]

문제 1

답 (2)

해설 여러 조건으로 인해 악화되는 시장에서 기업들이 이익을 얻기 위해 노력한다는 의미이다.

문제 2

답 (1)

해설 (1)는 디플레이션에 대한 대비책을 강구하는 공무원들에 대한 내용이다.

문제 3

답 (4)

해설 본문의 마지막 문장 참고. 디플레이션은 소비자들에게 이익을 가져다줄지 모르지만, 기업들에게는 그렇지 않다.

해석 경제 전반에 걸쳐 가격이 지속적으로 하락하는 현상인 디플레이션은 전반적으로 가격이 꾸준하게 오르는 상황에서는 그저 위협으로만 남아있다. 그러나 국가의 몇몇 주요 산업들에 있어 가격 하락은 현실이다. "많은 돈이 부족한 물건을 쫓아가는 대신에, 점점 많은 상품들이 얼마 안 되는 돈을 쫓아가고 있다"라고 조사관이 말했다. 미국 공무원들은 디플레이션이 일어날 것 같지 않다고 말하지만, 일단 디플레이션이 시작되면 멈추기 어렵기 때문에, 대비책들을 강구할 것을 고려하고 있다. 가격 결정력이 떨어지자, 경영자들은 생산량을 늘릴 때조차 가격을 낮출 수밖에 없었고, 결국 이것은 현재 경기 회복기의 일자리 감소로 이어졌다. 11월과 12월에 걸쳐 전국적으로 거의 이십만여 개의 일자리가 사라졌다. 그 주범은 많은 기업들이 이익을 취하며 팔 수 있는 것보다 더 많이 생산하고, 이용할 수 있는 것보다 더 많은 수용 능력을 갖추도록 만든 1990년의 경제 거품이었다. 그러나 중국과 같은 나라들로부터 값싼 물품 유입, 미국의 생산성 향상과 계속되던 탈규제화 추세 및 시장이 결정하는 가격 모두가 나름대로 역할을 담당했다. 수입이 막히자, 많은 기업들은 줄어드는 파이의 조각이라도 잡기 위해 가격을 더 하락시킴으로써 기업 문제를 악화시키고 있다. 오늘날의 주로 경제 약화에서 비롯된 가격 하락 파동은 소비자들에게는 계속해서 이익을 가져다주지만, 그 해악에 빠진 기업들에게 있어 가격 하락이 유익할 것은 거의 없다.

어휘

deflation *n.* 통화수축, 디플레이션
sustained *a.* 지속된, 일련의
mildly *ad.* 온순하게, 조심해서
chase *vt.* 쫓다, 손에 넣으려고 애쓰다
unlikely *a.* 가망 없는, 있음직하지 않은
preventive *a.* 예방의, 방지하는
culprit *n.* 죄인, 범죄자   surge *n.* 큰 파도, 굽이치는 파동
deregulation *n.* 규제 철폐   stagnant *a.* 불경기의, 부진한
revenue *n.* 소득, 세입   shrinking *a.* 위축되는

stem *vi.* 유래하다, 생기다
virtuous *a.* 덕이 높은, 고결한; 효험 있는
vise *n.* 악습, 악덕; 결함

[Challenge 3]

문제 1

답 (2)

해설 첫 번째 문장이 주제문이고, 이후 이를 뒷받침하는 문장이 전개되는 'General-Specific'의 전형이다. 첫 번째 문장에서 보다시피 본문은 '창조신화의 일반적 특징'을 다루고 있다.

문제 2

답 (2)

해설 본문에서 창조신화가 공통적인 요소를 가지고 있는 것은 맞지만, 서로 다른 문화권의 창조신화가 상호 영향을 미쳤다는 내용은 본문을 근거로 추론할 수 없다.

해설 모든 창조 신화에서 발견되는 몇 가지 특징이 있다. 이들 이야기에는 모두 줄거리나 등장인물이 신이나 인간의 형상을 한 인물 혹은 말을 하거나 쉽게 모습을 바꾸는 동물이 나온다. 이 이야기는 까마득하고 구체적이지 않은 과거를 배경으로 한다. 그리고 모든 창조신화는 이러한 창조신화를 공유하는 사회가 가지는 의미심장한 질문을 다루면서, 보편적 문맥에서 문화와 개인의 자기 정체성을 위한 이들의 핵심적인 세계관과 틀을 드러낸다. 일반적 주제에는 최초 혼돈 상태에서 세상의 만물이 어떻게 분류되었고, 모신과 부신이 어떻게 분리되었으며, 무한하고 영속하는 바다에서 땅이 어떻게 출현했는지 등이 있다.

어 휘

deity *n.* 신; 여신   figure *n.* 인물, 사람
dim *a.* 어둑한, 어스레한   nonspecific *a.* 특이하지 않은
motif *n.* 주제   fractionation *n.* 나눔, 분할
primordial *a.* 원시의, 최초의   infinite *a.* 무한한, 무수한
timeless *a.* 처음도 끝도 없는

[Challenge 4]

문제 1

답 (3)

해설 N. P. Willis가 Poe를 경제적으로 도왔다는 이야기와 그가 거절했다는 내용은 본문에 나오지 않는다.

문제 2

답 (4)

해설 가 Poe의 상황을 안타깝게 생각하고, 그의 건강이 악화된 것을 걱정한 것은 맞지만, 이러한 것이 그의 천재적인 재능을 앗아갈 것이라고 보진 않았다.

해석 Poe는 1809년 1월 19일에 보스턴에서 가난하게 태어나 1849년 10월 7일 볼티모어에서 고통스러운 환경 아래 죽는다. 그는 겨우 15년밖에 안 되는 문학 활동 기간 동안 단순히 생계만을 꾸리는 데에도 처절한 삶의 투쟁을 해야 했는데, 이러한 것이 그의 초기 전기 작가인 Griswold에 의해서 악의적으로 잘못 묘사되었다. 1845년에 처음 출간된 "The Raven"은 몇 달 안에 영어라는 언어가 쓰이는 곳에선 어디든 읽혀지고, 낭송되며, 패러디가 되었지만, 거의 굶어 죽어가는 상태였던 이 시인이 받은 거라고는 10달러가 전부였다! 1년도 안 되어 그의 동료 시인 N. P. Willis는 그 당시 뉴욕의 Fordham의 작은 오두막집의 아주 열악한 상황에서 살고 있는 소외된 작가와 그의 죽어가는 부인 그리고 그녀의 헌신적인 어머니를 대신해 천재를 찬양하는 사람들에게 감동적인 호소문을 발행했다. "여기 가장 훌륭한 학자이자 가장 창조적인 천재인 동시에 우리나라 문학계의 가장 근면한 사람 중 한 명이 있습니다. 그는 몸에 병을 얻어 일시적으로 노동을 할 수 없는 고로 자선 단체의 구호 대상이 되는 지경까지 전락했습니다. 천재적 재능과 사고 방식에 마땅한 섬세함으로 그가 되찾은 건강으로 다시 일을 시작함으로 그가 굴욕감을 느끼지 않을 정도의 독립심을 얻을 때까지 그가 도움이 보장되는 잠시 거쳐 갈 장소도 없으며, 그럴 듯한 은신처도 없습니다."

어 휘

subsistence *n.* 생존, 현존, 존재   malignantly *ad.* 악의 있게
misrepresent *v.* 잘못 전하다, 허위 진술하다
parody *v.* 서투르게 흉내를 내다
starve *v.* 굶주리다, 아사하다   on behalf of ~을 대표하여
devote *v.* (노력, 시간, 돈 따위를) 바치다
straiten *v.* 괴롭히다, 고생시키다   cottage *n.* 시골집, 작은 집
suspension *n.* 보류, 중지, 정지   delicacy *n.* 섬세함, 민감
resume *v.* 다시 시작하다, 되찾다   mortify *v.* 굴욕감을 주다

[Challenge 5]

문제 1

답 (4)

해설 흑사병이 유럽의 예술에 미친 영향을 기술한 글이다. 인과의 글 전개 방법이 잘 드러난 글이다.

해설 예술에 미친 피해는 회복할 수 없을 정도였다. 교회의 죽음으로 인해, 문자는 거의 사라졌으며, 교회 전체가 버림을 받았다. 조각도 바뀌었다. 관의 뚜껑에 시체의 그림이 그려졌다. 약 1400년경으로 추정되는 이러한 관 중에서 반은 사람의 몸이고 다른 반쪽은 조각난 의복의 시체를 드러냈다. 일부 조각들은 죽은 시체를 먹는 벌레와 달팽이를 새겨 넣었다. 그림 또한 흑사병에 영향을 받았다. 죽은 해골과 함께 사교 모임을 갖는 사람들을 포함한 그림이 아주 많았다.

이러한 그림은 세도 있는 사람들의 명령을 받고 만들어졌는데, 이것은 "죽음의 무도"라 불리었다. 예술가들은 기독교 종교관의 우상화된 것을 그리는 오랜 방식을 저버렸다. 이들은 자신을 둘러싼 죽음에 낙담해서 슬픈 사랑과 죽은 사람의 그림을 그리기 시작했다.

어 휘

irreparable *a.* 고칠[만회할, 돌이킬] 수 없는; 불치의
abandoned *a.* 버림받은; 자포자기한; 방탕한
coffin *n.* 관, 널   **corpse** *n.* (특히 사람의) 시체, 송장
shred *v.* 갈가리 찢다[찢기다]
munch *v.* 우적우적 먹다, 으드득으드득 깨물다
idolize *v.* 우상화하다; (우상을) 숭배하다

[Challenge 6]

문제 1

답 (3)

해설 세계 1차 대전을 통해서 글쓴이가 궁극적으로 전달하려는 사항과 관련지어 생각한다. 'Deliberately poor communication by all involved was at the crux of the problem.'및 'the diplomatic efforts of the British and Russian monarchs did not prevent conflict'에서 알 수 있듯이, 윗글은 의사소통(외교적 노력)의 부재를 전쟁의 가장 큰 주요 요인으로 파악하고 있다. 즉, 이 글은 바로 '외교술의 실패라는 의사소통의 부재'가 전쟁의 제1 원인임을 주된 내용으로 다루고 있다.

문제 2

답 (1)

해설 첫 번째 빈칸은 앞에서 언급된 문제점을 발생시키는 데 일조했던 또 다른 면을 설명하고, 두 번째 빈칸은 '영국, 독일, 러시아 모두 혈맹 관계의 귀족'임에도 불구하고 전쟁을 막지 못했으므로 이런 두 상황에 가장 적절한 답안은 (1)이다.

문제 3

답 (4)

해설 보기 항의 'them'은 앞에서 언급하고 있는 'they = Mistakes, blunders, poor communication, lies, distrust, tensions, the desire for recognition, revenge'이다. 즉, 이러한 것에 대한 적절한 통제가 없다면, 전쟁은 불가피한 결과가 된다.

해석 외교술이란 사실, 신의, 정보 그리고 원활한 의사소통에 달려있다. 이러한 모든 요소가 전쟁을 하겠다는 결심을 한 독일과 오스트리아에 의해 무시되었다. 독일의 외교단은 세르비아를 협박하는 오스트리아의 외교 문서의 내용을 있는 그대로 보지 않고 전쟁을 위한 실질적인 활동과 의도에 관한 연막 스크린을 걷어 던지기 위해 모든 것을 감행했다. 세르비아인 쪽에선 나름 러시아의 원조를 확신했으며, 자신들 진영에서 발생한 특정 활동에 대한 정보를 있는 그대로 받아들이지 않았다. 관련자 모두의 의도적인 이런 소통의 부재가 문제의 핵심이었다. 조치를 고려할 시간을 최소화하기 위해 가능한 한 늦게 최후통첩이 발표되었다. 국부적인 발칸 전쟁이 확대되는 것을 방지하기 위한 연합국의 외교적 조치는 무산되었다. 연합국들도 나름의 실수를 했다. 이들은 독일이 두 진영에서 전쟁을 위한 공격적인 작전계획을 가지고 있다는 점과 이것을 실행하기 위해 모든 준비가 되어 있다는 점을 전혀 몰랐다. 독일군은 영국이 프랑스와 벨기에를 원조하겠다고 나섰을 때 경악을 금치 못했는데, 영국이 벨기에에 대한 중립적 입장을 위반하는 것은 처벌받을 것이라는 점을 분명히 못박을 수 있음에도 불구하고 하지 않았다. 독일은 이것이 (영국이 프랑스와 벨기에를 도울 것이라는 점) 영국의 뻔한 반응일 것이라는 초기 영국의 외교 신호를 완전히 오해했다고 주장했다. 이 문제에 한몫을 한 것은 바로 독일의 장군들이 영국의 군대로부터 받은 위협을 무시했던 것인데, 이는 자신들의 군대였던 스팀롤러와 백만 군인과 비교했을 때, 영국 군대의 규모가 아주 작았기 때문이었다. 모순적으로 영국, 러시아 그리고 독일의 왕족 간의 혈연관계라는 점에도 불구하고, 영국과 러시아의 군주들의 외교적 노력이 제대로 이루어지지 않아 전쟁을 막지 못했다. 크고 잦은 실수, 진솔한 의사소통의 부재, 거짓말, 불신, 긴장, 인정받으려는 욕망, 복수 – 이 모든 것이 사실 인간의 조건을 구성하는 일부분이 아닌가? 이러한 힘은 국가, 이웃, 가족 그리고 개인에 영향을 미친다. 그리고 이들이 시작되는 것은 인간의 마음속이다. 이것들을 조절하지 못할 경우 궁극적으로 어떤 규모의 전쟁도 일어날 수 있다.

어 휘

diplomacy *n.* 외교; 외교술[수완]; 권모술수
crux *n.* 중요점, 핵심
steamroller *n.* 증기 롤러(도로 공사용)
blunder *n.* 큰 실수, 대(大)실책

[Challenge 7]

문제 1

답 (4)

해설 본문만으로 Buffon과 Huxley가 진화론의 여러 사상을 공유했다는 정보를 알 수는 없다.

문제 2

답 (1)

해설 다음 본문에서 답을 구할 수 있다.

> each possesses the power to adapt its organization to the changes of the outer world, and it is this power, put into action by the change of the universe, that has raised the simple zoophytes of the primitive world to continually higher stages of organization, and has introduced a countless variety of species into animate Nature.

보기 항 (1)의 adaptability가 답이다.

해설 Treviranus는 Huxley가 Lamarck와 나란히 평가한 인물로 Buffon의 이론을 주장한 사람으로 생물이 변이와 도태를 하는 데 있어 변화하는 환경의 영향력에 가장 큰 중요성을 부여한 인물이지만, 그는 또한 개인과 같은 종은 성장, 완성 그리고 소멸이라는 단계를 통과한다는 Goethian 적 사상을 전개했다. "따라서, 이것은 멸종을 일으키는 자연의 거대한 재앙으로만 볼 수 없다. 이것은 또한 존재 사이클의 완성으로, 이것에서 새로운 사이클이 다시 시작한다." Osborn 교수가 이러한 특성을 잘 설명한 문장을 인용해 보자. "모든 생명체에는 끊임없이 다양한 형태를 취할 수 있는 능력이 존재한다." 개개의 존재는 외부의 변화에 자신을 적응시킬 수 있는 능력을 소유하고 있으며, 원시 세계의 단순한 식충류가 지속적으로 높은 단계의 유기체로 진화하고, 다양한 종을 생물계(animate Nature)에 도입하는 것은 바로 이 우주의 변화에 의해서 실현되는 바로 이 힘(환경에 대한 적응)에 의해서이다.

어휘

eliminate v. 제거[베제]하다
catastrophe n. 대이변, 대실패, 참사, 재앙
organization n. 조직(화)   zoophyte n. 식충류
primitive a. 원시의, 원시적인
continually ad. 잇따라, 계속해서
introduce v. 소개하다, 안으로 끌어당기다
countless a. 셀 수 없는, 무한한   animate a. 살아 있는

[Challenge 8]

문제 1

답 (2)

해설 하나님은 공간에 속한 존재가 아니라고 본문에 언급되어 있다.

문제 2

답 (1)

해설 하나님이 편재한다는 개념을 자연 법칙을 따르는 인간이 이해하기 위해 필요한 것은 무엇인지 생각해야 한다. 자연 법칙을 따르는 공간적 개념에 영적인 측면을 부여해야 공간에 속한 인간이 그 범위를 초월한 하나님의 영적 편재를 그나마 이해할 수 있다. 아래 본문에서 그 힌트를 찾을 수 있다.

> That the Divine, that is, God, is not in space, although omnipresent and with every man in the world, and with every angel in heaven, and with every spirit under heaven, cannot be comprehended by a merely natural idea, but it can by a spiritual idea.

해설 신, 즉 하나님이 비록 어디에나 존재하고, 세상의 사람과, 하늘의 모든 천사와 그리고 하늘 아래 모든 영과 함께 존재하지만 사실 공간에 있지(속하지) 않다는 것은 단순히 자연적 개념으로 이해할 수 없으며, 이것은 영적인 개념으로 이해될 수 있는 것이다. 이것을 자연 개념으로 이해할 수 없는 이유는 자연 개념으로 봤을 때는 공간이 있기 때문이다. 세상에 존재하는 그런 것 밖에서 형성되신 분이시며, 눈에 보이는 세상의 모든 것에는 공간이 있다(즉, 자연 개념이란 말이다). 세상에서는 모든 것이 위대하건, 작건 공간의 성격을 가진다. 길고 넓고 높은 것도 공간의 성격을 지닌다. 간단히 말해 모든 수치, 모양 그리고 형태는 공간에 속한다. 이런 이유에서 신은 모든 곳에 계시기에 하나님이 공간에 있지 않다는 개념은 단순히 자연 개념으로 이해할 수 없다. 그러나 자연적 생각으로 인간은 신을 어떤 영적인 측면에서 받아들일 때에만 이것을 이해할 수 있다. 이런 이유에서 영적인 개념에 대해서 무엇인가를 먼저 논해야 하고, 그런 다음 생각을 논해야 한다. 영적인 개념은 공간에서는 어떤 것도 이끌어낼 수 없지만, 상태에서 그것이 가진 모든 것을 이끌어낸다. 상태는 사랑, 삶, 지혜, 애정, 기쁨 그로부터 발생하는 것에 입각한 것이다. 일반적으로 선과 진리에 바탕을 둔 것이다. 진정한 영적인 이러한 것들의 개념은 공간과 전혀 관계가 없다. 이것은 더 고상한 것이며 하늘이 땅을 내려다보듯 이것 아래 놓인 공간의 개념을 내려다본다.

어휘

omnipresent a. 동시에 어디든지 있는
spiritual idea 영적인 개념
in the world 속세에   therefrom ad. 그것으로부터
derive v. 끌어내다
predicate v. (특정 생각·원칙에) 근거를 두다
wisdom n. 지혜   affection n. 애정
truly ad. 진실로   look down upon ~을 낮춰보다

Day 22

[Challenge 9]

문제 1

답 (4)

해설 본문은 Van Helmont가 한 실험을 통해서 식물 성장의 핵심이 무엇인지를 알아내는 내용이다.

문제 2

답 (1)

해설 우선 본문 초반에 실험의 결과(all the products of vegetables were capable of being generated from water)가 제시된다. 이것에 대한 구체적인 실험이 소개되고 있다. 잊지 말아야 할 것은 근본적으로 물이 식물 성장의 핵심이라는 점이다. 빈칸의 내용을 확인해 보자.

> he pulled up his tree by the roots, shook all the earth off, the earth again, ____(a)____ weighed the earth and weighed the plant.

그는 뿌리를 뽑고, 흙을 털어냈다. 그는 뿌리를 뽑아 흙을 털고 무게를 측정했다. 이제 실험의 결과는 처음의 무게에서 나중의 무게를 빼면 계산할 수 있는데, 여기서 주의할 점은 흙을 뽑은 다음에 흙에 남아 있는 물의 중량을 함께 계산하면 안 되기에 이를 말려야 함을 추론할 수 있다.

문제 3

답 (3)

해설 힘의 결론 부분이다. 당연히 앞에서 이미 제시한 결과대로 실험을 통해서 밝힌 내용은 식물 성장의 주요인이 바로 물이라는 점이다.

해석 물 성장의 문제를 해결하려는 초기의 가장 중요한 시도 중 하나는 바로 17세기 초반에 번성한 연금술사 중 가장 유명한 사람 중 한 명인 Jean Baptiste Van Helmont에 의해서 이루어졌다. Van Helmont는 모든 야채의 생산은 물에서 만들어질 수 있다는 것을 결정적인 실험을 통해 증명했다. 이 고전적 실험의 구체적 내용은 다음과 같다.

"그는 특정한 무게(200 lb.)의 마른 토양을 취하고, 이 토양에 5 lb.의 무게가 나가는 버드나무를 심었다. 그리고 그는 깨끗한 빗물을 시간마다 조심스럽게 한 번씩 주고, 식물이 자라는 토양에 먼지나 흙이 못 들어가게 잘 보살폈다. 그는 5년 동안 계속 자라도록 했으며, 마지막 시기에, 실험이 충분히 오랫동안 실행되었다는 생각이 들어 그는 뿌리째 나무를 뽑고 흙을 털어내고 다시 흙을 말려 무게를 재고 식물의 무게를 쟀다. 그는 식물이 이제 169 lb. 3 온스가 나가는 반면, 토양의 무게는 이전의 무게인 거의 200 lb와 동일하다는 것을 알았다. 이것은 단지 2온스만 줄어든 무게였다." 그러므로 Van Helmont는 식물 영양물의 원천은 바로 물이라는 결론을 내렸다.

어휘

alchemist *n.* 연금술사   flourish *v.* 번성하다
willow *n.* 버드나무   weigh *v.* 무게를 달다
sufficiently *ad.* 충분하게   pull up *v.* 끌어올리다

[Challenge 10]

문제 1

답 (2)

해설 'Great Britain would not now carry upon her shoulders the responsibility of having during half a century supported the Turk against the Christian'에서 영국이란 것을 알 수 있다.

문제 2

답 (3)

해설 'backed the wrong horse'는 '질 말을 지지하다'라는 의미로 본문에서 정당성이 없는 Turk를 지지한 영국의 어리석음을 비유적으로 표현하는 말이다.

문제 3

답 (1)

해설 크림 전쟁의 원인을 논하고 있다.

문제 4

답 (3)

해설 터키가 정복한 국가에서 회유책을 썼다는 내용을 추론할 근거가 본문에 없다.

해석 이 전쟁은 과거 평화주의와 새로운 평화주의 모두를 정당화시킨다. 보편적 입장에서 크림 전쟁을 반대한 평화주의자들이 옳고 이들을 반대한 사람들은 틀렸다는 것이 증명되었다. 만약 대중의 의견이 이 평화주의자들의 원칙에 좀 더 많은 고려를 했다면, 이 나라는 "잘못된 말에 돈을 걸지" 않았을 것이며, 이 전쟁, 이 전쟁에 선행했던 두 전쟁 그리고 지난 60년간 발칸 반도가 전쟁의 장소가 되어 버린 것에 대한 수많은 증오를 피할 수 있었을지 모른다. 그리고 어떤 경우에서든 영국은 지금 자신의 어깨에 반세기 동안 기독교에 대항한 터키를 지지하는 것과 지금 일어난 것 — 유럽에서 터키의 통치의 붕괴 — 을 막기 위해 쓸데없는 노력을 해야 하는 책임감을 지니지 않았을 것이다.

이 전쟁의 근본적인 원인은 큰 의미에서건 좁은 의미에서건 경제적인 것에 있다. 우선 정복은 터키의 유일한 (돈을 버는) 일이었다. 터키는 정복한 사람들에게서 억지로 빼앗은 세금으로 살고, 이들을 생활의 수단으로 착취하기를 원했으며, 이러한 생각이 바로 터키의 실정의 주요 원인이었다. 그리고 큰 의미에서 이 전쟁의 목적이 경제적인 이유는 유럽의 경제발달의 주류에서 지리학적으로 멀리 떨어진 발칸 제국(the Balkans)은 유럽의 다른 지역에서 원시 종교와 인종

에 대한 증오를 줄이기 위한 목적에서 행해진 상호의존적인 사회생활과 무수한 교류가 그곳에서는 성장하지 못했기 때문이다.

어휘

pacifism *n.* 평화주의　abomination *n.* 혐오
peninsular *a.* 반도의　wring *v.* 짜다, 비틀다
misgovernment *n.* 실정, 악정
remote *a.* 외진, 외딴　geographically *ad.* 지리(학)적으로
drift *n.* 이동, 표류　interdependent *a.* 서로 돕는
innumerable *a.* 셀 수 없이 많은
attenuate *v.* 붉게 하다, 약화시키다

Day 23

[Challenge 1]

문제 1

답 (2)

해설 본문은 아기의 이가 날 때 느끼는 고통을 치료할 수 있는 다양한 방법을 주의점과 함께 소개하는 글이다.

문제 2

답 (1)

해설 이가 아플 때 바르는 젤의 역할에 관한 내용과 관련해서 빈칸이 주어졌다.

> Teething gels work as a _____ to dull the nerves in the gums so that the pain is less noticeable.

잇몸의 신경을 둔감하게 해 고통을 덜 느끼도록 만드는 것이므로 'numbing agent'가 가장 적절하다.

문제 3

답 (1)

해설 본문에서 아세트아미노펜과 이부프로펜은 하루에 세네 번 사용할 수 있다고 언급되어 있다. 또한 teething ring과 관련하여 본문에서는 부드러운 플라스틱으로 만들기 때문에 깨지기 쉽다고 했다. teething gel 자체는 감염 요소가 아니다.

문제 4

답 (2)

해설 본문의 내용을 확인해 보자.

> It should only be used a few times a day so that it does not ____(b)____ symptoms that are being experienced due to other medical conditions and not because of teething.

하루에 세네 번 정도만 사용하도록 권장된다. 이는 치통에 의해 발생하지 않는 증상과 다른 질병에 의한 증상까지 가려 그러한 통증을 인식하지 못하게 되는 상황이 벌어질 수 있기 때문이다.

해석 모든 부모가 아이의 고통을 치료하기 위해 마음 놓고 약을 사용하지는 않는다. 종종 잇몸이 붓고 아픈 것을 완화시켜주기 위해 아기의 잇몸에 약을 바른다. 이런 젤은 잇몸이 아프고 치통이 있을 때 성인들이 사용하는 치통 젤과 비슷하다. 그러나 아주 극소한 양이 투여된다. 치아 통증 완화 젤은 잇몸의 신경을 둔화시키는 마취제로 작용하여 고통이 덜 느껴지게 한다. 포장 상자의 사용 설명서를 잘 따라 정확한 양의 약을 투여하고 적절한 기술을 사용하여 감염의 위험을 줄이는 것이 중요하다. 약이 목을 마취하지 않도록 하는 것이 중요한데, 이는 이것이 정상적인 구역질 반응을 방해하거나 음식이 폐로 들어가게 만들 가능성이 있기 때문이다.

아세트아미노펜과 이부프로펜 역시 아이가 겪는 통증과 붓기를 치료하는 데 좋다. 그러나 6개월 이하의 아이에게 투여해서는 안 된다. 하루에 몇 번만 사용하도록 해 이것이 치아가 아니라 다른 질환에 의해서 발생하는 통증을 가리지 않게 해야 한다. 아스피린을 포함한 제품은 소아과 의사의 진단이 없이는 투여해서는 안 된다. 고리 물리개는 일반적으로 부드러운 플라스틱 도구로 아이가 물어 잇몸 조직에 자극을 줌으로 치아가 잇몸에서 성장해서 나오는 것을 촉진시키는 역할을 한다. 일부 고리 물리개는 잘 부서지거나 망가지기에 집안의 물건을 통해서도 다른 종류의 이가 나게 하는 도구를 만들 수 있다. 몇 분 동안 찬 물수건을 냉장실에 넣은 후 이것을 조심스럽게 잇몸에 대는 것도 효과적이다. 그러나 너무 지나치게 오래 아기의 잇몸에 대지는 말아야 한다.

어휘

gum *n.* 잇몸　administer *v.* (약을) 투여하다
in small doses (약을 복용할 때) 조금씩
dull *v.* 무디게 만들다
noticeable *a.* 알아차릴 수 있는, 느낄 수 있는
direction *n.* 지시; 사용법　medication *n.* 약
infection *n.* 전염, 감염　swelling *n.* 부기
symptom(s) *n.* 증상　pediatrician *n.* 소아과 의사
teething ring 이가 빨리 나도록 돕는 링
household item 집안 물건, 가정용품
washcloth *n.* 수건, 행주　effective *a.* 효과적인
for too long 지나치게 오래 동안
expose A to B A를 B에 노출시키다

[Challenge 2]

문제 1

답 (3)

해설 본문은 모든 인간의 번영의 근간은 바로 정직이라는 내용을 전달하고 있다. 주어진 문장의 내용은 책의 출판과 관련이 있으며, 결과적 용법의 'and'가 사용됨을 활용해야 한다. 책의 출판과 관련된 부분이면서, 제시된 문장의 원인으로 작용할 수 있

는 곳은 (c)가 된다. 'would'의 가정법을 활용할 수도 있다.

해석 정직은 지식의 어머니이다. 진실을 향한 소망은 모든 배움의 기본이며, 모든 경험의 가치 기준이며 모든 학문과 연구의 이유가 된다. 정직을 기반으로 삼지 않는다면, 우리의 교육 체계 전체가 무너질 것이다. 모든 신문과 정보 매체들은 엄청난 위기에 처할 것이다. 우리의 전 문명은 사람들이 정직하다는 가정에 기반을 둔다. 이 확신이 깨질 경우, 모든 구조가 무너진다. 그리고 진실을 가르치지 않는다면, 학교, 신문, 책 그리고 직업은 없는 편이 훨씬 낫기에 이것은 오히려 무너져야 한다. 자신을 겨눌 것이라면 전혀 총을 소유할 필요가 없다. 번영의 주춧돌은 바로 정직인 것이다.

어휘
- integrity n. 정직, 진실성
- investigation n. 조사
- entire a. 전체의
- civilization n. 문명
- assumption n. 가정
- confidence n. 확신, 자신; 신뢰
- shaken a. 흔들린
- structure n. 구조
- fall v. 떨어지다
- be better off (~하는 것이) 더 낫다
- profession n. 직업
- aim v. ~을 목표하다
- corner-stone n. 주춧돌

[Challenge 3]

문제 1
답 (1)
해설 첫 번째 문장에서 글의 방향을 이끌어 낼 수 있다. 즉, 젊은이들이 추구해야 할 것은 다름 아닌 좋은 성품이다. 그 토양 위에서만이 노동을 통한 아름다운 열매를 맺을 수 있다고 글쓴이는 조언하고 있다.

문제 2
답 (4)
해설 (d)를 제외한 나머지는 좋은 성품을 통해서 얻게 되는 득을 비유적으로 표현한 말이다.

문제 3
답 (2)
해설 본문은 끝까지 첫 번째 문장에서 언급한 좋은 성품을 가질 것을 조언하는 글이다. 본문 마지막에서 이런 '좋은 성품'이란 토양을 잘 갈고 닦으라고 말한다. 그 이유는 당연히 앞에서 언급한 모든 결실을 누리게 되기 때문이다. '좋은 성품'을 가장 잘 드러내는 표현은 보기 항 (2)의 'good reputation'이다.

문제 4
답 (2)
해설 위 글은 젊은이가 가장 먼저 추구해야 할 것이 좋은 성품이라고 말한 후 이에 대한 근거를 설득력 있게 본문에서 제시하고 있다. 즉, 이 글은 '젊은이에게 좋은 성품을 기르라'는 훈계적 글이다.

해석 젊은이가 추구해야 할 첫 번째는 좋은 성품을 확립하는 것이어야 한다. 미래에 대한 모든 계획, 기대 그리고 전망에서 이것이 그 주된 초석인 장엄한 출발점을 이루어야 한다. 이것이 앞으로 다가올 날의 번영과 행복의 모든 희망과 생각의 기반이어야 한다. 한 사람의 희망이 온전한 열매로 익기 위한 유일한 기반이다. 젊은 시절에 형성한 좋은 성품은 이것을 소유한 사람에게 풍부하고, 생산적인 도덕적 토양이 된다. 그 속에 심겨진 "생명의 나무"는 왕성한 성장력으로 싹을 트며 성장한다. 이런 토양에서 그 뿌리는 강하고 깊게 뿌리 내리며, 그것으로 인해 최상의 활력과 열매를 맺는다. 이것의 줄기는 웅대한 비율로 자라며, 넓게 퍼진 가지는 초록의 무성한 나뭇잎들에 덮여 '보기에 매우 좋으며' 때가 되면 가장 아름다운 꽃들이 온 가지를 붉게 물들일 것이다. 그리고 마침내 각각의 나뭇가지는 풍부한 황금빛 열매 아래로 구부러져 손에 떨어질 준비를 마친다. 삶의 시련과 무거운 어깨로 지쳐있을 때 고마운 그늘 아래 쉼과 평안을 누릴 수 있게 된다. 그리고 수고와 근심, 혹은 세월의 무게로 영혼이 지칠 때, 맛있는 열매를 따서 먹으며 원기를 회복하고 힘을 얻을 수 있다. 이러한 나무를 보고 싶은가? 기억할 것은 이 모든 것이 좋은 평판(성품)의 토양에서 자란다는 것이다! 이런 토양을 준비하도록 애써라.

어휘
- anticipation n. 기대; 예감
- mature v. 잘 익다, 숙성하다
- therein ad. 그 속에, 거기에
- spring forth 발생하다, 돌출하다
- vigorous a. 원기 왕성한, 활발한
- thence ad. 그렇기 때문에
- fruitfulness n. 비옥, 결실이 많음
- trunk n. 줄기, 나무의 몸통
- clothe v. 옷을 입히다
- luxuriant a. 번성한, 울창한
- foliage n. 잎
- blossom n. 꽃, 개화
- twig n. 잔가지
- at length 드디어
- repose n. 휴식, 휴양
- burden n. 무거운 짐
- pluck v. 뜯다, 잡아 뽑다
- weary v. 지치게 하다

[Challenge 4]

문제 1
답 (1)
해설 본문은 대상 영속성에 관한 내용이다.

문제 2
답 (1)
해설 빈칸 바로 앞에 있는 세미콜론을 활용한다. 세미콜론은 앞에서 전개된 내용에 대한 부차적 설명을 제공할 때 사용된다.

이 경우 앞에서 전개된 내용에 대한 적절한 관용구 또는 속담으로 앞의 내용에 대한 부가적 설명을 제공하고 있다. 아기가 태어난 지 얼마 안 되었을 때는 엄마가 앞에서 사라져도 울지 않는다고 했다. 이는 아이가 인식 자체를 못하기 때문이라고 본문에 언급이 되어 있다. 즉, 앞에 없으면, 마음에서도 멀어지는 현상과 같다.

문제 3

답 (3)

해설 대상 영속성과 분리 불안은 약 8개월로 거의 비슷한 시기에 형성된다는 것을 본문에서 알 수 있다.

해석 대상 영속성은 시각적 이미지를 계속 보유하고 이용하는 뇌의 능력을 가리킨다. 이 능력은 생후 8개월 정도에 발달한다. 이 능력은 아기의 재인 기억과는 구별된다. 예를 들어, 아기는 태어나서 3일째 되는 날 엄마를 알아볼 수 있으며 엄마를 바라보는 것을 좋아한다. 그러나 아기는 엄마가 없이 홀로 남겨져 있다고 해서 울지 않는다. "눈에서 멀어지면 마음에서도 멀어지는 현상." 8개월이 되었을 때, 아기는 엄마가 방에서 떠날 때 분리 불안 징후를 보이기 시작한다. 이것은 아이가 이제 자신이 잃어버린, 즉 엄마의 존재가 사라진 것을 인식할 수 있기 때문이다. 대상 영속성의 습득에 대한 다른 징후는 아이가 "peek—a—boo" 게임에 즐거워하는 점인데, 이는 아기가 엄마가 바로 앞의 시야에서 사라졌을 뿐 여전히 세상에 존재하고 가리고 있는 손이나 담요를 없애면 다시 엄마를 불러올 수 있다는 것을 알고 있다는 것을 여실히 드러내는 것이다.

어휘

utilize *v.* 활용하다, 이용하다
separation *n.* 분리, 구분
demonstrate *v.* 증명하다; 보여주다
graphically *ad.* 사실적으로, 생생하게
direct *a.* 직접적인
recall *v.* 다시 불러들이다
blanket *n.* 담요, 전체를 덮는 것

[Challenge 5]

문제 1

답 (1)

해설 본문은 헤론이라는 인물을 중심으로 스팀이 동력으로 과거에 사용되었다는 기록에 관한 내용이다.

문제 2

답 (3)

해설 아래 본문에서 보기 항 (3)은 틀리다는 것을 알 수 있다.

In a treatise of about that time entitled "Pneumatica", Hero, of Alexander, described not only existing devices of his predecessors and contemporaries but also an invention of his own which utilized the expansive force of steam for raising water above its natural level.

해석 증기의 팽창에 대한 인간의 최초의 지식과 사용의 시기가 알려져 있지 않지만, 이러한 지식이 기원전 150년 이전에 존재했다는 기록이 있다. 그 당시 "기체 역학(Pneumatica)"이라는 이름의 보고서에서, 알렉산드리아의 헤론은 그 선조와 동시대 사람이 고안한 기존의 장치뿐 아니라 자연 수위 이상으로 물을 올리기 위해 증기의 팽창력을 이용한 스스로 고안한 장치에 대한 설명을 하고 있다. 그는 증기가 힘의 동력으로 직접적으로 사용될 수 있는 3가지 방법을 분명하게 기술하고 있다. 증기의 탄성을 통해 물을 올리고, 팽창력을 이용해 무거운 짐을 올리며, 대기에 대한 반응에 의해 회전운동을 만들어 내는 것이 그것이다.

어휘

pneumatic *a.* 공기가 가득한; 공압의
predecessor *n.* 전임자   utilize *v.* 활용[이용]하다
expansive *a.* 팽창성 있는   elasticity *n.* 탄성, 탄력성
elevate *v.* (들어) 올리다   weight *n.* 무게, 체중
rotary *a.* 회전하는, 회전식의   motion *n.* 운동, 움직임
reaction *n.* 반응, 반작용   atmosphere *n.* 대기, 공기

[Challenge 6]

문제 1

답 (3)

해설 영어권의 글은 첫 번째 또는 두 번째 문장이 주제 문장일 가능성이 아주 크다. 다시 말해, 글의 주제를 선정할 때, 글의 초반을 집중해서 읽으면 답이 나올 가능성이 크며 주제가 선정되면 글을 읽기가 아주 수월한데, 이는 이후 이어지는 내용이 방금 설정한 주제에 대한 뒷받침 문장으로 이어지기에 예측하면서 글을 읽을 수 있기 때문이다. "Society exists through a process of transmission quite as much as biological life." 계승을 통한 사회의 존속을 다루는 내용이다.

문제 2

답 (3)

해설 보기 항 (3)은 본문에 정확히 명시되어 있다.

> The young of human beings compare so poorly in original efficiency with the young of many of the lower animals, that even the powers needed for physical sustentation have to be acquired under tuition.

문제 3

답 (3)

해설 해 문제에서 밑줄 친 부분의 구체적 내용을 물을 경우, 언제나 글 전체의 맥락 속에서 파악해야 한다. 단지 밑줄 친 부분의 단편적 지식으로 답했을 경우, 구체적으로 어떤 상황에 적용되는지 모르기 때문에 자기 생각의 함정에 빠질 수 있다.

해석 사회 또한 생물학적 생명과 마찬가지로 전송의 과정을 통해서 존재한다. 이 전송은 습관이나 생각과 감정이 이전 세대에서 다음 세대로 전달될 때 발생한다. 이런 이상과 희망, 기대, 기준, 의견 등을 기성세대가 다음 세대로 전달하지 않는다면 사회는 존속할 수 없다. 사회 구성원들이 계속적으로 존재한다면 그들은 아마도 새로 태어나는 구성원들을 가르칠 것이다. 그러나 이런 현상은 사회적 필요성보다는 개인적인 이해에 의해 행해지는 일이다.

만약 전염병이 한 번에 사회에서 모든 구성원의 목숨을 앗아간다면, 이 단체가 영원히 사라질 것은 분명하다. 동시에 사회를 구성하는 각 구성원의 죽음은 전염병이 이들을 한 번에 다 앗아간 것만큼 분명하다. 그러나 점차적인 나이의 차이가 바로 사상과 관습의 전달을 통해 지속적으로 사회 조직의 재편성을 가능하게 하는 것이다. 그러나 이러한 재생이 자동적으로 일어나는 것은 아니다. 성실하고 철저한 전송이 일어나도록 애를 쓰지 않는다면, 대부분의 문명 집단은 미개한 상태로 돌아가 야만적이 된다. 사실 젊은 인간은 너무 미성숙해서 이들이 다른 이의 인도나 도움이 없이 홀로 남겨진다면, 이들은 자신의 신체적 존속을 위해 필요한 기초적인 능력조차 얻을 수 없다. 어린 인간은 수많은 하등 동물들에 비해 효율성이 아주 떨어지기 때문에 신체적 생명 유지에 필요한 힘조차 다른 이의 도움을 통해서 얻을 수밖에 없다. 그렇다면 인간이 성취한 모든 다른 기술적, 예술적, 과학적 그리고 도덕적 업적과 관련해서 이러한 점이 훨씬 더 사실임은 말할 필요도 없다.

어휘

- **transmission** n. 전달, 전송
- **by means of** ~의 수단으로
- **communication** n. 전달, 통신, 교통
- **social need** 사회적 요구
- **plague** n. 역병, 재앙
- **carry off** 빼앗다, 획득하다
- **obvious** a. 명백한, 명료한
- **permanently** ad. 영구히
- **epidemic** n. 유행병, 전염병
- **reweave** v. 다시 짜다[엮다, 만들어 내다]
- **renewal** n. 새롭게 하기, 부활, 회복, 재생
- **automatic** a. 자동의, 자동적으로 따라오는
- **relapse** v. 거슬러 되돌아가다, 퇴보하다
- **barbarism** n. 야만, 미개, 포학
- **savagery** n. 야만, 미개
- **immature** a. 미숙한, 미성년의
- **rudimentary** a. 가장 기본적인
- **tuition** n. 수업, 교수, 수업료

[Challenge 7]

문제 1

답 (2)

해설 ferment = agitation, disquiet, unrest, commotion, tumult, turmoil, upheaval

문제 2

답 (3)

해설 본문에 'excess'라는 표현이 등장하나 보기 항과 같이 '신에 대한 지나친 관심'을 뜻하지는 않고 있다. 오히려 루터는 교회가 지나치게 세속화되는 것을 비판했다.

문제 3

답 (5)

해설 첫 번째 문단에서 두 번째 문단으로 넘어가는 내용에서 보기 (5)를 파악할 수 있다.

문제 4

답 (1)

해설 "The popes had once been great patrons of Renaissance arts and sciences"에서 교황이 르네상스 예술과 과학에 큰 후원자였다는 점에서 가톨릭의 목적과 르네상스 예술과 과학이 서로 충돌한다고 보지 않았음을 추론할 수 있다.

문제 5

답 (3)

해설 망원경이 마치 사람에게 치명타를 가한 것처럼 의인화하고 있다.

문제 6

답 (2)

해설 세 사상을 바탕으로 발전한 천동설의 경우 실질적으로 교회라는 외부적 요소에 의해 '정설'이라고 여겨졌다는 점과 코페르니쿠스가 망원경을 통해 지동설에 대한 과학적 근거를 제시했음에도 불구하고 재판을 받고, 가택연금된 사례를 통해 과학은 그 자체로는 중립적이지만 외부의 요소에 의해 왜곡될 수 있다는 점을 본문을 통해 파악할 수 있다. 보기 (2)가 정답이다.

해석 갈릴레오 갈릴레이는 1564년에 문화적 동요와 종교적

투쟁으로 인해 몸살을 앓던 유럽에서 태어났다. 종교와 세속적 지도자의 역할에 있어 강력한 힘을 발휘했던 로마 가톨릭 교회의 교황들은 당시의 세속적이고 퇴폐적인 정신에 노출되었으며, 이들의 개인적 부도덕성으로 인해 교황권의 명성이 역사적으로 최저에 이르게 된다. 1571년, 마틴 루터는 전직 수도사로서 지나치게 세속적이고, 정치적으로 부패했으며, 이교도적 요소로 기독교의 기본 정수를 흐린 이유로 가톨릭을 공격했다. 개혁을 바라는 그의 열정은 초기 "순결한" 기독교 개념에 호소하면서 청교도 개혁을 일으켰고, 유럽 기독교를 둘로 나누게 했다.

이에 대한 반응으로 로마 가톨릭은 전쟁을 위해 마음을 단단히 먹고, 종교개혁에 대한 반격을 시작하는데, 정통성과 참된 교회에 대한 충실함을 강조한 것이었다. 개혁에 대한 반격은 교회의 활기를 다시 불러일으키고, 어느 정도 과도함을 제거했다. 그러나 개혁에 대한 반격은 또한 고대 그리스와 로마의 고전 예술과 철학을 회복하고 재정비하려는 노력인 예술과 문학의 부흥 운동인 이탈리아의 르네상스가 쇠락하는 데 일조한다. 교황은 한때 르네상스 예술과 과학에 큰 후원자였으나 종교개혁에 대한 반격은 이러한 영역에 대한 교회의 세속적 관용에 종지부를 찍는다. 게다가 종교적 정통성에 새삼 중점을 두게 되자 새로 고개를 들던 과학 혁명과 곧 충돌하게 된다. 천문학을 연구하던 갈릴레오는 이런 충돌의 중심에 자신이 서 있음을 알게 된다.

갈릴레오 시대에 망원경 없이 연구를 하던 보수주의적 천문학자들은 고대의 자기중심주의 이론을 믿고 있었다. 이 천문론은 지구가 태양계의 중심에 있고, 태양과 다른 행성들이 (지구를 중심으로) 돈다고 믿는 것이었다. 사실, 일반 관측자에게는 태양이 아침에 뜨고 밤에 지기에 태양이 지구를 돌고 있는 게 말이 되는 것처럼 보였다. 아리스토텔레스와 로마의 천문학자 프톨레마이오스와 같은 고대의 권위 있는 사람들은 이러한 관점을 옹호했고, 이 개념은 또한 신의 창조물인 인간을 우주의 중심에 두는 가톨릭교회의 우주에 대한 관점과도 일치했다. 일반상식, 고대의 철학자 그리고 교회가 지지한 우주에 대한 지구 중심의 모델은 그 권위가 확고한 듯했다. 그러나 천동설은 공격을 받게 된다. 16세기 천문학자들은 무리하게 현대의 관측을 프톨레마이오스의 지구 중심 우주 모델 이론에 끼워 맞추려고 했다.

폴란드의 천문학자였던 니콜라스 코페르니쿠스는 천동설(지구 중심설)에 공공연히 의구심을 표명했으며, '지구를 포함한' 행성들이 태양을 돈다는 태양중심설을 제기했다. 태양계 배열을 수학적으로 좀 더 납득이 가게 하는 이 방식은 그 당시 얻을 수 있었던 데이터로는 천동설을 전적으로 버려야 함을 뒷받침할 수 없었기에 처음에는 그리 많은 지지자를 얻지 못했다. 하지만 16세기 말이 되면서, 요하네스 케플러와 같은 천문학자들 역시 코페르니쿠스의 이론을 받아들이기 시작했다.

궁극적으로 갈릴레오의 망원경은 천동설에 치명적인 타격을 주었다. 그러나 어떤 면에서 망원경은 갈릴레오 자신에게도 거의 치명적이었다. 신교라는 이단을 궁지에 몰아넣는 게 절실했던 가톨릭 교회는 자신들의 우주관에 대한 과학적인 공격을 받아들일 수 없었다. 피할 수 없는 시대의 압박으로 종교와 과학 간에 역사적 충돌이 시작되고, 이는 1633년 절정에 달하는데, 이때 교회는 갈릴레오를 재판에 넘기고, 갈릴레오 자신이 진술하고 출판했던 과학적 신념을 억지로 철회하게 했으며, 그를 평생 가택 연금 상태에 놓이게 했다.

어휘

ferment n. 동요, 소란   **decadent** a. 쇠퇴기에 접어든, 퇴폐적인
secular a. 세속적인   **papacy** n. 교황권, 교황의 직위
worldly a. 세속적인   **zeal** n. 열정
the Protestant Reformation 종교 개혁
steel oneself for[against] ~에 대해 맘을 모질게 먹다
fidelity n. 충성, 정절   **excess** n. 과도, 부절제
put an end to ~에 종지부를 찍다   **leniency** n. 관대함
egocentricity n. 이기주의, 자기중심주의
coincide with ~와 일치하다   **buttress** v. 지지하다, 보강하다
Ptolemaic a. 천동설의(=geocentric)
culminate v. 절정에 이르다
house arrest 가택 연금, 자택 구금

[Challenge 8]

문제 1

답 (3)

해설 문단이 두 개로 나눠진 지문이다. 문단이 두 개면 소주제도 두 개다. 전체 주제를 구성할 때는 이 두 문단을 포괄하는 주제를 선정해야 한다. 첫 번째 문단은 14세기에 아시아, 유럽 그리고 아프리카를 황폐하게 만든 흑사병에 관한 이야기인데, 간략한 특징과 기원 등 흑사병에 관한 전반적인 이야기를 하고 있다. 이런 관점을 가장 포괄적으로 잘 드러내는 보기 항은 (3)이다.

문제 2

답 (2)

해설 본문에서 흑사병에 의한 치사율이 상대적으로 낮다는 내용은 없다. 첫 번째 문단 마지막에 해당하는 다음 내용을 보면 치사율이 상당히 높았음을 알 수 있다.

> On account of these inflammatory boils, and from the black spots, indicative of a putrid decomposition, which appeared upon the skin, it was called in Germany and in the northern kingdoms of Europe the Black Death, and in Italy, la mortalega grande, the Great Mortality.

문제 3

답 (1)

해설 fford는 본문에서 '낳다, 제공하다'의 의미로 쓰이고 있다. 예) Reading affords pleasure. 독서는 즐거움을 낳는다. 예) The transaction afforded him a good profit. = The transaction afforded a good profit to him. 그 장사로 그는 한 몫 보았다.

해석 지금까지 중 가장 중요한 진척 중에 하나는 14세기의 엄청난 흑사병에 의해 제공된(발생된) 것으로, 이것은 아시아, 유럽 그리고 아프리카를 황폐하게 만들었으며, 이 지역의 사람들은 아직도 이 암울한 전설을 기억하고 있다. 이것은 동양에서 유래한 역병으로 다른 어떤 열병에서도 발생되지 않은 염증성 종기나 분비선 종양 등의 특징을 보인다. 이런 열에 의한 종기와 악취 나는 부패의 징조로서 피부에 나타나는 검은 색 점 때문에, 이것은 독일과 유럽의 북쪽 왕국에선 흑사병이라 불렸고, 이탈리아에선 대규모 떼죽음을 의미하는 la mortalega grande(Great Mortality)라고 불리었다.

이것의 증상과 그 과정에 관한 증언이 그리 많지는 않지만, 현대의 동일한 병의 징후와 이것들이 일치하는 점으로 봐서 이것만으로 이 병의 형태를 조명하는 데 충분하며, 이것들은 믿을 만한 가치가 있다. 아들인 Andronikus가 콘스탄티노플에서 이 역병에 걸려 죽은 황실 작가인 Kantakusenos는 그 병에 걸린 사람들이 넓적다리와 팔에 거대한 종기를 갖고 있고 이것이 터지면 아주 역겨운 물질을 내뿜는다는 것을 알았다. 림프선종은 동양의 전염병의 확실한 증상으로 알려지게 되었다. 왜냐하면 그가 얼굴과 팔 그리고 몸의 다른 부분에서 발생하는 작은 종기들을 역병에 의해서 생겨나는 것과 그렇지 않고 다른 병에 의해서 생겨나는 물집들을 완벽히 구분해 냈기 때문이다. 여러 경우 검은색 점은 몸 전체에 따로따로 나기도 하고, 한 덩어리로 합쳐서 나기도 했다.

어 휘

pestilence n. 악성 전염병
desolate v. 황폐하게 하다
inflammatory a. 염증성의   tumor n. 종양
gland n. (분비)선   febrile a. 열병성의
indicative a. ~을 나타내는
putrid a. 악취 나는   decomposition n. 부패
malady n. 질병   credence n. 신용
discharge n. 방출, 배출   infallible a. 절대 확실한
plainly ad. 명백히, 솔직하게   blister n. 물집
confluent a. 합류하는; 융합성의

[Challenge 9]

문제 1

답 (1)

해설 이 글은 도입부에서 'power'의 정의를 짧게 설명한 후, 'power'에는 5가지 종류가 있다고 밝히고 있다. 이를 주제(5가지 종류의 power)로 하여 본문에서 구체적으로 5가지 종류를 자세히 다루고 있다. 고로, 본문이 시작하는 (a)에서 두 번째 문단이 시작하는 것이 가장 적절하다.

문제 2

답 (1)

해설 빈칸이 들어간 부분의 내용은 reward power에 관한 설명인데, 앞에서 설명했던 coercive power와 마찬가지로 부모나 경찰이 동일하게 가지는 힘을 말한다. 빈칸에 앞에서 reward power에 대한 정의를 한 후 '마찬가지로' 부모는 'coercive power'뿐 아니라(as well) 'reward power'도 가진다는 내용으로 전개되는 것이 적절하다.

문제 3

답 (2)

해설 기 항 (1)은 본문에서 알 수 없는 사항이며, 일반적으로 힘(권력)이란 소수에서 다수로 전이되지 않으려는 특징을 가진다. 보기 항 (2)의 설명은 옳은 표현이다 (Expert power results from experience or education. Those individuals with more knowledge tend to have more power in situations where that knowledge is important). 이와 관련된 보기 항 (3)은 틀린 표현이다. 보기 항 (4)에 해당하는 'admiration or respect'는 referent power에 해당하는 내용이다.

해석 '힘'이란 것이 무엇인지 한번 자세히 살펴보자. 힘이란 일반적으로 한 사람에게 다른 사람보다 더 큰 영향력을 주는 특징을 지닌 것으로 간주된다. 이러한 특징은 지식일 수도 있고 경험일 수도 있으며, 직업의 지위 또는 돈일 수도 있다. 대부분의 사회 심리학자들에 따르면, 힘에는 강압, 보상, 합법, 전문 그리고 지시라는 다섯 종류가 있다.

강압적인 힘은 처벌을 의미한다. 예를 들어 부모는 아이에게 벌을 줄 수 있기 때문에 강압적인 힘을 가졌다고 볼 수 있다. 사장은 직원을 해고하거나 특정 직원에게 덜 만족스런 일을 부과할 수 있기에 강압적인 힘을 가지고 있다. 보상의 힘이란 이것과는 거의 반대에 해당한다. 이것은 보상하는 힘을 말한다. 이러한 의미에서 부모와 사장은 우리 삶의 다른 이와 마찬가지로 또한 이 같은 힘을 가지고 있다고 볼 수 있다. 합법적 힘이란 특정 권위에 의해서 허용된 힘을 가리키는데, 경찰관이 그 지역 또는 정부에 의해 가지는 힘 또는 교수가 학교의 규율에 따라 가지는 힘을 말한다. 전문적 힘이란 경험 또는 교육에 기인한다. 더 많은 지식을 가진 개인은 이러한 지식이 중요한 상황에서 더 큰 힘을 가지는 경향이 있다. 예를 들어, 의사는 배관공보다 의학과 관련된 긴

급한 상황에 더 큰 힘을 가지게 된다. 그러나 배관이 터지고 집에 홍수가 난 경우 의사는 결정을 내리는 사람이 아니다. 마지막으로 지시력이란 찬양 또는 존경을 지칭한다. 우리가 누군가를 그가 성취한 것, 태도 또는 다른 개인적인 특징으로 인해 존경할 때, 우리는 이들에게 우리에게 행사할 수 있는 더 큰 힘을 주는 경향이 있다. 당신이 우러러보는 '영웅' 또는 좋아하는 영화배우가 당신에게 뭔가를 부탁했다고 상상해 봐라. 우리는 그들에 대한 존경심에서 흔쾌히 따를 가능성이 아주 농후하다.

어 휘

attribute *n.* 특징　　influence *n.* 영향력
job title *n.* 직함　　coercive power 강압적인 힘
place child in time-out 벌로서 아이가 벽을 보게 하다
assign *v.* (일을) 맡기다　　pleasing *a.* 기분을 좋게 하는
(be) granted by ~에 의해 인정된
local government 지역 정부
A results from B A(결과)는 B(원인)로 인해 발생하다
(*cf.* A results in B) A(원인)는 B(결과)의 결과로 나타나다
plumber *n.* 배관공　　be flooded 물이 넘쳐 홍수가 나다
look up to ~을 우러러 보다　　comply *v.* 따르다

어 휘

episode *n.* 사건; 1회 방송분　　depression *n.* 우울증, 우울함
chronic *a.* 만성적인　　financial *a.* 금융의, 재정의
unwelcome *a.* 반갑지 않은
trigger *v.* 촉발하다
depressive *a.* 우울증의 *n.* 우울증 환자
psychological *a.* 심리학적인　　onset *n.* (불쾌한 일의) 시작
discrimination *n.* 차별, 식별
disproportionately *ad.* 불균형적으로
socioeconomically *ad.* 사회경제학적으로
counterpart *n.* 상대, 대응관계에 있는 것
immigrant *n.* 이민자　　vulnerable *a.* 취약한, 연약한
isolate *v.* 격리하다, 고립시키다

[Challenge 10]

문제 1

답 (3)

해설 본문은 '우울증의 원인'에 대한 글이다. 부분적인 내용이나 특이 사항을 주제로 설정하지 않도록 주의한다.

문제 2

답 (3)

해설 칸 이후에 나오는 구체적 부연 설명을 먼저 파악한다. 특정 단체가 다른 단체보다 우울증에 더 시달린다는 구체적인 예가 제시되어 있다.

해석 특정한 외부 사건이 우울증 증상을 유발하는 듯한 경우가 많다. 따라서 심각한 손해나, 만성질환, 곤란한 대인관계, 금전적 문제 또는 탐탁지 않은 삶의 변화와 같은 모든 것이 우울증 증상을 유발할 수 있다. 아주 종종, 유전적, 심리학적 그리고 환경적 요인이 복합적으로 우울증 유발과 관련된다. 우울증을 진전시키는 데 악영향을 미치는 스트레스 요인은 특정 그룹에 더욱 영향을 미치기도 한다. 예를 들어, 차별에 의한 영향을 종종 받는다고 느끼는 소수집단은 불균형적으로 묘사된다(즉 다른 그룹보다 훨씬 더 심각하게 묘사된다). 사회경제적으로 취약한 집단은 다른 기득권을 가지고 있는 집단에 비해 높은 우울증을 보인다. 미국의 이민자들은 우울증에 더 걸리기 쉬운데, 이는 특히나 언어적 고립으로 인해 더욱 그러하다.

Day 24

[Challenge 1]

문제 1

답 (3)

해설 as를 이용한 직유이다. 특정 대상, 현상을 설명할 때 독자가 익히 알고 있는 대상의 특성을 직접 비교함으로 이해를 돕는 수사법을 말한다.

> A good character cannot be inherited, <u>as</u> the estate of a father descends to his heirs.

문제 2

답 (4)

해설 본문에서 좋은 성품은 부모가 존경받는 성품을 가지고 있다 하더라도 근성과 수고를 통해서만 얻을 수 있다고 말하고 있다.

문제 3

답 (2)

해설 'standing and success'는 입신과 성공이란 뜻이다.

문제 4

답 (1)

해설 앞에서 언급된 비유적인 이야기를 활용해야 한다. 언덕 아래서 정상에 있기를 소망하는 것은 무용지물이다. 피와 땀을 통해 직접 언덕을 오를 때 그 정상에서 맛볼 수 있는 승리감을 누릴 수 있다. 고로 그가 해야 하는 행위는 자신의 소망하는 일을 위해 노력을 해야 한다는 의미를 전달하고 있는 보기 항 (1)이 가장 적절하다.

해석 좋은 성품은 아버지가 재산을 그의 자손에게 전할 수 있는 것처럼 그렇게 물려받을 수 있는 것은 아니다. 아무리 부모가 존경을 받고 훌륭한 사람이라 하더라도 그의 자식이 자신의 능력에 의해 그것을 받을 가치가 없는 한 부모의 이전 존경을 공유할 수가 없다. 염려스럽게도 너무나 많은 젊은이들이 자신의 입신과 인생의 성공을 위해 부모의 재산뿐 아니라 그들의 평판에도 기댄다. 이것은 견고한 기반이 아니다. 우리의 공화국에서 모든 개인은 자기 자신의 행위에 의해서 평가되는 것이지 그 사람의 연줄의 명성에 의해서 평가되는 것이 아니다. 젊은이가 존경받는 부모를 두고 있는 것은 여러 가지 측면에서 이득임은 의심할 여지가 없다. 그러나 만약 이들이 부모의 명성을 물려받을 거라면 이들은 그 부모가 행하는 덕을 실천해야만 한다.

좋은 성품은 금으로 살 수가 없다. 한 사람이 인도 제국의 모든 부를 다 가질 수 있을지 모르지만, 이것이 명성을 보장해 주진 못한다. 부로써 현명하고 훌륭하다는 평판을 살 수는 없다. 그 평판을 얻을 만한 장점이 없다면 말이다. 금의 광채로는 악하고 심술궂은 성향, 이기적인 마음, 부패한 마음 또는 악한 정욕과 성향을 감출 수 없는 것이다. 비록 아첨꾼들이 재물 때문에 부자들 앞에서 알랑거리거나 아첨하고 고개를 숙이지만, 사실 아첨꾼들은 속으로 부자들을 경멸하고 비난한다.

좋은 성품은 이것을 단순히 소망한다고 해서 얻을 수 있는 것이 아니다. 창조자는 현명하게 어떤 것을 원하는 욕망 자체가 그것을 보장해 주지 않도록 규정했다 (provide). 만약 그랬다면, 우리의 세상에는 곧 이상한 현상이 일어날 것이다. 의심할 여지없이 현재 그러한 상황보다 훨씬 좋아진다. 우리는 원하는 무엇이든 소망하는 특권을 가진다. 그러나 우리는 노동을 통해서 받을 가치가 있는 것만을 얻을 수 있는 것이다. 만약 언덕 아래서 정상에 있기를 소망하면서 하루 종일 서 있다면, 그의 이런 단순한 소망이 그를 거기에 데려다 주진 않는다. 그는 자신이 원하는 소망으로 인해 그것을 위한 적절한 노력을 하도록 만들어야 한다. 이것은 단지 참을성 있는 (persevering) 근성과 인내의 수고에 의해서만 가능하며, 한 번에 한 단계씩 나아가는 것에 만족해야 한다. 그렇게 함으로 그의 소망이 만족을 얻고 그는 결국 산마루에 오르게 된다.

어 휘

estate *n.* 토지, 재산, 유산
descend *v.* (조상에게서 자손으로) 전해지다
heir *n.* 상속인, 후계자
apprehend *v.* 염려(우려)하다; 붙잡다, 체포하다
republican *a.* 공화국의   **glitter** *n.* 반짝임, 빛남
crabbed *a.* 심술궂은, 까다로운
disposition *n.* 성질, 기질, 경향; 배열
vile *a.* 비열한, 야비한, 심한   **propensity** *n.* 경향, 성질
sycophantic *a.* 아첨하는, 중상적인
bow *v.* 고개를 숙이다, 절하다
obsequiously *ad.* 비굴하게
condemn *v.* 경멸하다, 업신여기다
hanger-on *n.* (무슨 이득을 노리고 유명인이나 중요한 행사의) 주 위를 어슬렁거리는 사람
persevering *a.* 참을성이 있는, 끈기 있는
brow *n.* 이마, 눈썹   **eminence** *n.* 언덕, 고지; 높음, 명성

[Challenge 2]

문제 1

답 (3)

해설 셰익스피어를 광적으로 좋아하는 아버지와 그를 기쁘게 해 주려는 아들이 벌이는 사건을 중심으로 글이 전개되고 있다. 아들이 아버지를 기쁘게 해 주려고 한 행동은 무엇인가?

문제 2

답 (3)

해설 본문에서 아버지가 아들에게 셰익스피어 작품을 조작하라고 부추기진 않았다. 아들이 아버지를 기쁘게 해 드릴 목적으로 몰래 한 일이다.

문제 3

답 (1)

해설 문맥상 '출처'를 나타내는 말이다.

문제 4

답 (4)

해설 주어진 빈칸이 들어간 문장은 인과의 분사구문이다.

> Having provided himself with the paper of the period and with ink prepared by a bookbinder, _____(b)_____.

아들이 만든 조작본은 당시의 종이와 제본업자가 준비한 잉크를 사용한 것이라 했다. 아버지는 또한 셰익스피어 작품이라면 너무나 좋아하기에, 이것이 정말 조작본이라는 점을 눈치채지 못했을 것을 추론할 수 있다.

문제 5

답 (2)

해설 '대단한 갈채'라는 의미로 쓰이고 있다. 문맥적 유추가 가능하니 본문 앞뒤를 잘 살펴보도록 한다.

해석 Samuel Ireland는 원래 Spitalfields에서 실크 상인이었는데, 문학 유물에 관한 그의 취향으로 인해 그 일을 위해 무역업을 버리고 여러 여행을 시작한다. 이 여행 중 한 곳은 Avon 강 답사로, 이것을 하는 동안 그는 열정적인 호기심으로 셰익스피어와 관련된 모든 장소를 탐험했다. 그는 16살짜리 아들과 동행했는데, 그에게 자신의 셰익스피어 광기의 일부를 심어주었다. 그 시인의 모든 유품에 아버지가 부여한 중요성과 그의 사본이라면 어떤 것이든 찾으려는 열정을 인식한 아들은 셰익스피어 시대의 언어와 방식으로 자신이 직접 몇몇 작품을 만들어 아버지를 기쁘게 하는 것이 그리 어렵지 않을 것이라 생각했다. 이러한 생각이 일정 기간 동안 그의 마음을 사로잡았으며, 1793년 그 당시 18살이었던 그는 셰익스피어의 서풍으로 쓰인 것으로 여겨지는 몇 개의 사본을 만드는데, 이것은 다른 많은 고(古)문서를 소유하고 있는 한 신사에게서 얻은 것이라 말했다. 아버지가 너무나 기뻐하는 모습을 본 그는 동일한 출처에서 온 것으로 기록된 다른 원문을 조작하게 된다. 이러한 성공에 담대해져, 그는 산문과 시 등 더 높은 단계의 작품에 과감히 뛰어든다. 마침내 그는 자신이 두 달의 기간에 쓴 Vortigern이라는 제목의 극 원본을 발견했다고 발표하게 이른다. 그 당시의 종이와 제본소에 의해서 준비된 잉크로 했기에, 사기라는 어떠한 의심도 들지 않았다. 이러한 것에 광적으로 빠진 아버지는 이런 소위 발견품이라는 것에 대단한 갈채를 보냈으며, 문학계와 모든 영국의 관심이 여기에 쏠렸다.

어휘

antiquity *n.* 오래됨; (고대) 유물
excursion *n.* 여행   ardent *a.* 열렬한, 열정적인
imbibe *v.* (술 등을) 마시다; 흡수하다, (사상 등을) 받아들이다
portion *n.* 한 조각, 일부, 몫   relic *n.* 유적, 유물
eagerness *n.* 열심, 열망   gratify *v.* 기쁘게 하다, 만족시키다
handwriting *n.* 손으로 씀, 육필   ecstasy *n.* 무아경, 황홀
fabrication *n.* 위조; 꾸며낸 것
embolden *v.* 담대하게 하다
venture *v.* 위험을 무릅쓰고 가다, 과감히 ~하다
prose *n.* 산문   verse *n.* 운문, 시
at length 드디어; 상세히   bookbinder *n.* 제본업자, 제본소
eclat *n.* 대단한 갈채

[Challenge 3]

문제 1

답 (1)

해설 본문은 self-image가 형성되는 단계를 설명하는 글이다. 첫 번째 문장의 'no self-image at birth'로 시작해서 중간 단계를 거쳐 'self-image'가 완성되는 보기 (1)의 내용이 가장 적절하다.

문제 2

답 (1)

해설 'a conscience, the sense of right and wrong'에서 보기 (A)의 내용을 파악할 수 있다.

해석 태어날 때 우리는 '자기 이미지'를 가지고 있지 않다. 우리는 주변의 빛과 소리가 뒤섞인 혼돈 속에서 어떤 것도 구분하지 못한다. 이런 '무차원'의 시기부터 시작하여 우리는 점차 주변 환경과 우리 자신을 구분하게 되고, 우리가 따로 떨어진 독립된 존재라는 걸 깨닫게 됨에 따라 정체성이 발달하게 된다. 그 다음으로, 우리는 선과 악을 구분하는 양심이 발달하게 된다. 더 나아가 우리가 타인과 함께 살아간다는 것을 깨닫게 되는 사회적 의식을 키우게 된다. 마지막

으로, 우리는 이 세상에서 우리가 지니는 가치에 대한 종합적 평가인 가치관을 발전시키게 된다. 이 모든 발전 과정의 총합은 자기 이미지라 불린다.

어휘

distinguish A from B A와 B를 구별하다
sense of identity 정체성
right and wrong 옳고 그름
estimation *n.* 평가

[Challenge 4]

문제 1

 (2)

해설 아래 본문을 통해서 Euclid는 기하학자(geometrician)라는 것을 알 수 있다.

> In order to study the principles of music and drawing, Galileo found it necessary to acquire some knowledge of geometry. His father seems to have foreseen the consequences of following this new pursuit, and though he did not prohibit him from reading Euclid

문제 2

답 (1)

해설 지시형용사 'this'를 이용해 'This employment of his hands'가 받는 것(antecedent)이 무엇인지 잘 생각해 본다.

문제 3

답 (2)

해설 본문의 단어는 '가난한'의 뜻이다. 'destitute'는 가난한 뜻을 전달하는 답이 될 수 있다. 그러나 1번의 'parsimonious' 라는 단어는 '인색한, 구두쇠'의 뜻이지, '가난한'의 뜻이 아니다. 'miserly'도 동일한 의미를 전달한다.

문제 4

답 (1)

문제 5

 (1)

해설 jealousy'를 '시기, 질투'로 해석했을 경우 문맥상 어색함을 먼저 파악해야 한다. 이 단어에 '경계, 조심'이란 뜻이 있다. 기본어휘 중에서 다의어는 독해에서 문맥상 어휘 문제로 나갈 수 있음을 기억하자.

해설 갈릴레오는 어린 시절을 다른 거의 모든 위대한 실험 철학자들처럼 도구와 기계를 만드는 데 보냈으며, 이러한 것은 대부분 자신과 자신의 학교 친구들을 기쁘게 하려는 의도였다. 그러나 그가 손으로 뭔가를 만드는 것이 그의 공부에 방해가 된 것은 아니었다. 아버지의 궁핍한 (straitened) 환경으로 그가 상당한 불이익을 안고 교육을 받기는 하였지만, 그는 고전 문학의 기본을 익혔으며, 그 시대의 모든 학문에 입문했다. 음악, 스케치와 그림은 그가 여가 시간에 주로 하는 것이었다. 그리고 그는 여러 악기, 특히 루트를 아주 잘 켜는 연주가로 인정될 만큼 이러한 예술에 능했으며, 그의 그림에 대한 지식은 당대의 가장 위대한 몇몇 예술가들로부터 큰 평가를 받았다.

갈릴레오는 화가가 되고 싶어 했다. 그러나 그의 아버지는 초기 천재적 재능의 분명한 징조를 알아보았으며 비록 감당할 재력이 절대 없었지만, 그는 갈릴레오가 의학 공부를 하도록 하기 위해 대학에 보내기로 결심한다. 그런 이유로 그는 Pisa 대학 예술학과 학생으로 1581년 11월 5일에 등록을 하고, 1567년부터 1592년까지 의과장을 지내는 유명한 식물학자 Andrew Cesalpino의 수하에서 의학 공부를 한다.

음악과 스케치의 원리를 공부하기 위해서 갈릴레오는 어느 정도의 기하학 지식의 필요성을 알게 된다. 그의 아버지는 이러한 새로운 직업 추구의 결과를 예측했던 것으로 보이며, 비록 그는 갈릴레오가 Pisa의 교수 중 한 명인 Ostilio Ricci의 지도 아래 유클리드를 읽는 것을 막지 않았지만, 그는 극도로 경계하며 진행 과정을 지켜본 후 이것이 그의 의학 공부를 방해해선 안 된다고 결심한다. 그러나 그리스 수학자의 증명은 갈릴레오의 열정적인 마음에 너무 매력적으로 보였다. 그의 온 관심은 그의 지력에 엄습하는 새로운 지식에 폭 빠져 있었다. 그리고 그의 열정을 저지하고 그의 생각을 전문적인 대상으로 이끌려는 그의 수많은 시도가 물거품이 되자 그의 아버지는 부모로서 가지는 통제를 포기하고 아들의 천재성을 최대한 발휘할 수 있는 여지를 허락했다.

어휘

chiefly *ad.* 주로; 흔히; 대개   **schoolfellow** *n.* 동창생; 학우
straiten *v.* 괴롭히다; 고생시키다   **proficiency** *n.* 숙달; 능숙함
reckon *v.* (~로) 여기다, 간주하다; 평가하다
lute *n.* 루트(현악기)   **botanist** *n.* 식물학자
geometry *n.* 기하학   **ardent** *a.* 열렬한; 불타는
be engrossed with ~에 몰두하다
burst *v.* 파열하다; 폭발하다; ~하고 싶어 참을 수 없다
fruitless *a.* 무익한; 효과 없는
ardour *n.* 열정   **oblige** *v.* 부득이 ~하게 하다
surrender *v.* 포기하다

[Challenge 5]

문제 1

답 (1)

해설 첫 번째 문장과 중간 'So complex…'로 시작하는 문장에서 주제문을 빼낼 수 있다. 즉, 인간이 밟고 자는 지리적 연구가 빠져서는 인간의 과학적 연구가 이루어질 수 없으며, 이것의 복잡성으로 인해 그에 대한 연구의 정당성이 제공된다고 말하고 있다.

문제 2

답 (2)

해설 빈칸 앞부분에서 제시한 학문은 'piecemeal and partial, limited'라고 말했기에 지리학에 대한 적절한 연구가 진행되지 않은 상태에서 만족스러운 답변을 얻는 것은 불가능하다는 보기항 (2)가 답이다.

해설 북극곰 또는 사막의 선인장을 그 서식지를 떠나 이해할 수 없는 것과 마찬가지로 인간을 그가 경작하는 땅 또는 그가 거니는 지역 또는 그가 교역하는 바다를 떠나 과학적으로 연구할 수 없다. (자신을 둘러싼) 환경과 인간의 관계는 고등 조직 식물이나 동물과 환경의 관계보다 무한대로 다양하고 복잡하다. 그 관계가 너무 복잡해서 타당하고 필요한 특별 연구 대상이 된다. 이들이 인류학, 민족학, 사회학 그리고 역사에서 받은 조사는 인종, 문화적 발달, 시대, 나라 또는 다양한 지리적 조건을 고려할 때 부분적이고 제한적이다. 역사가 사건의 원인을 설명하려는 한, 역사와 함께 모든 학문은 대부분 이 모든 것에 들어가 있는 지리적 요소를 철저하게 분석하지 않기에 이것이 가지고 있는 문제에 대한 만족스러운 해결책을 제공하지 못한다. 인간은 그가 "자연을 정복했다"는 것에 대해 큰소리치고, 자연은 인간에 대한 끊임없는 영향력에 대해 너무 조용해서, 인류 발달의 공식에서 지리적 요소는 무시되어왔다.

어휘

cactus *n.* 선인장　　infinitely *a.* 무한히, 한없이
numerous *a.* 다수의　　legitimate *a.* 타당한; 합법적인
anthropology *n.* 인류학　　ethnology *n.* 민족학
sociology *n.* 사회학　　piecemeal *a.* 조금씩의; 단편적인
epoch *n.* 시대　　geographic condition 지리학적 조건
ake into account ~을 고려하다
undertake to explain 설명하기로 하다
analyze *v.* 분석하다　　persistent *a.* 끊임없이 반복되는

[Challenge 6]

문제 1

답 (3)

해설 본문에서 필자는 전 인류에게 공통적인 문제의 해결을 위해서는 전 세계의 단합을 이끌어내야 하고, 그 방법은 자유 무역에 있다고 주장하고 있다.

문제 2

답 (4)

해설 조건절에서 at all이 쓰이면 그 의미는 '기왕 ~할 바엔'이다. (4)에서 they는 the world's problems를 지칭한다. 따라서 to solve는 수동형인 to be solved가 되어야 한다.

해설 현재 세계는 하나의 경제 단위이며 모든 집단이 그 밖의 다른 집단의 생산품에 접근할 수 있는 단계에 와 있다. 이것이 지닌 중요성은 아무리 강조해도 지나치지 않는다. 우리는 인류가 직면한 문제와 위험성이 전 세계적인 시대에 살고 있다. 핵전쟁, 화학 오염, 인구 과잉 그리고 온실 효과의 위험성은 세계적인 것이다. 어느 국가도 피할 수 없다. 이러한 문제들을 해결하려는 노력 역시 세계적이어야만 한다. 다른 국가들의 협력 없이는 어떤 국가도 단독으로 이것들 중 어느 하나라도 효과적으로 다룰 수 없다. 그러한 이유에서 이 모든 문제들에 대한 국제 회담이 계속 열리고 있다.

우리가 어떻게 경쟁, 의심, 증오 그리고 전쟁으로 얼룩진 역사를 지니고 수천 년간 분리되었던 국가들을 서로 협력하도록 설득할 수 있을까? 우리는 어떤 공통 관심사를 찾아내야만 한다. 언어, 종교, 문화 일반은 모두 분열을 낳는 것들이다. 과학은 통합적 요소이긴 하지만 과학에 전폭적으로 관심을 갖는 사람들은 거의 없다.

비즈니스가 남아 있다. 오늘날 자유 무역을 막는 것은 모두에게 손해를 끼친다. 세계 대부분에서 보호 무역주의의 위험성을 인식하고 있고, 일본과 그 밖의 곳에서 여전히 시행되는 보호 무역주의 형태들에 대한 반대가 일고 있다.

이미 대기업들은 다국적 기업이 되었고 세계적인 기준에서 생각하도록 요구된다. 민족주의나 애국심에서 나온 편협한 사고는 더 이상 이치에 맞지 않는다. 우리가 살아가려면 앞으로도 계속 이런 방향으로 나가야 하고, 무역을 촉진하여 계속해서 사업을 보다 국제화하려면 국제적인 사고를 증진시킬 필요가 있다. 이것은 세계적 문제들이 보다 해결되기 쉽도록 해 줄 것이다. 그 문제들이 해결될 수 있는 것이라면 말이다.

어휘

economic *a.* 경제의　　have access to 이용할 수 있다
overestimating *v.* 과대평가하다
worldwide *a.* 전 세계적인　　nuclear war 핵전쟁
chemical *a.* 화학의, 화학적인
예) There is a chemical lab in the school. 그 학교에는 화학 실험실이 있다.

greenhouse effect 온실 효과   nation *n.* 국가 (=country)
Efforts *n.* 노력, 수고   deal with 처리하다, 다루다
cooperate *v.* 합동하다, 협조하다   rivalry *n.* 경쟁의식
suspicion *n.* 혐의, 의혹   hatred *n.* 증오감
divisive *a.* 분열을 초래하는   in general 보통, 대개
overwhelming *a.* 압도적인, 강력한
interrupt *v.* 방해하다, 차단하다
예) I didn't mean to interrupt your phone call. 통화를 방해할 생각은 아니었습니다.

free international trade 자유국제무역
be aware of 조심해라   protectionism *n.* 보호무역주의
firms *n.* 회사   patriotism *n.* 애국심
make sense 이해가 되다, 이치에 맞다
facilitates trade 통상의 편의를 꾀하다
necessitate *v.* 필요하게 만들다

[Challenge 7]

문제 1

답 (5)

해설 제문을 이끄는 But의 기능을 In fact가 대신하고 있음을 파악한다. 'price-fixing is normal in all industrialized societies because the industrial system itself provides, as an effortless consequence of its own development, the price-fixing that it requires.'가 주제문이고 이후 이에 대한 뒷받침 진술이 이어지고 있다. 대기업에 의한 시장경제는 겉으로는 보이지 않는 손에 의한 가격 결정으로 보이나 실질적으로 기업의 이윤을 위해 몇몇 경쟁사가 맺는 '가격 담합'에 의해 돌아간다는 내용이다. 산업이 속한 경제가 자본주의가 되었건, 사회주의가 되었건 모든 산업은 '가격 담합'을 맺는다는 것이 요지다.

문제 2

답 (3)

해설 글쓴이는 대부분의 미국 경제학자들의 주장이 잘못되었다고 비판하고 이에 대한 근거를 제시하고 있다. 글쓴이의 태도로 보기 (3)이 가장 적절하다.

문제 3

답 (3)

해설 'A price that is determined by the seller or, for that matter, established by anyone other than the aggregate of consumers seems pernicious.'에서 알 수 있듯이 소비자가 아닌 다른 주체에 의해서 결정되기 때문에 'pernicious'라고 표현하고 있다. 보기 (3)이 정답이다. 참고로, 글쓴이는 이러한 견해가 옳지 못함을 근거와 함께 제시하고 있다.

문제 4

답 (2)

해설 'price-fixing is normal in all industrialized societies because the industrial system itself provides, as an effortless consequence of its own development, the price-fixing that it requires.'에서 알 수 있듯이 모든 산업화 사회에서 가격 담합을 하는 이유는 산업 제도의 발전의 당연한 결과로 필요하기 때문이라고 말하고 있다.

문제 5

답 (5)

해설 'These economies employ intentional price-fixing, usually in an overt fashion.'과 'Formal price-fixing by cartel and informal price-fixing by agreements covering the members of an industry are common-place'에서 답을 찾을 수 있다.

문제 6

답 (4)

해설 'Soviet firms have been given the power to fix prices.'에서 보기 (4)가 정답임을 알 수 있다.

문제 7

답 (2)

해설 In fact를 기준으로 글의 도입부에서 제시된 관점을 근거를 제시하며 비판하고 있다.

해설 미국의 대부분 경제학자들은 자유 시장의 마법에 매료되어 있는 듯하다. 결과적으로 자유 시장의 요구에 일치하지 않는 것은 어떤 것이든 좋거나 정상적으로 보이지 않는다. 판매자가 결정한 가격이거나, 이 점에 있어서 소비자 총체가 아닌 다른 것에 의해 결정되는 가격은 치명적인 것처럼 보인다. 따라서 가격 담합(판매자에 의한 가격 결정)을 "정상적"이고 가치 있는 경제적 기능을 지닌 것으로 생각하는 것에는 상당한 의지력이 필요하다. 사실(그러나), 가격 담합은 모든 산업화된 사회에서 정상적인 행위이다. 왜냐하면 산업 체계 자체가 점점 발전해감에 따라 당연한 결과로서 산업 체계가 요구하는 가격 담합을 제공하기 때문이다. 현대의 산업 계획은 큰 규모를 요구하고, 이에 대해 보상한다. 따라서 상대적으로 적은 수의 큰 회사가 동일한 소비자 단체를 놓고 경쟁을 벌이게 된다. 각각의 대기업은 자신의 필요를 고려하면서 행동하기에 경쟁사가 부과하는 것보다 더한 가격에 자사의 제품을 판매하는 것을 피한다는 점은 자유 시장 제도론의 옹호자들도 일반적으로 인정하는 것이다. 그러나 각각의 대기업은 또한 동일한 소비자를 놓고 경쟁하는 다른 대기업과 공통되는 필요성을 잘 고려하면서 행동해야 한다. 그러므로 각각의 회사는 지나친 가격 인하를 피하는데, 이는 가격 인하가 제품에 대한 안정적 수요에 대한 공동의 이해관계에 불리하게 작용하기 때문이다. 대부분

경제학자들은 가격 담합이 발생했을 때 이를 인지하지 못한다. 왜냐하면 대기업들 사이에서 뚜렷하게 드러나는 여러 합의에 의해 발생할 거라고 예상하기 때문이다. 사실은 그렇지가 않다.

게다가, 정부의 간섭 없이 자유시장이 운영되도록 허용하는 것이 가격을 구축하는 가장 효율적인 방법이라고 주장하는 경제학자들은 미국과 다른 비사회주의 국가의 경제를 고려하지 않았다. 이런 나라의 경제에서는 보통 공공연한 방식으로 의도적인 가격 담합을 한다. 기업연합(카르텔)이 주도하는 공식적인 가격 담합이나 특정 산업의 구성원들을 포함하는 합의에 의한 비공식 가격 담합은 일반적이다. 만약 자유 시장에 어떤 특별한 효율성이 존재하고, 가격 담합이 비효율적이었다면, 첫 번째를 피하고 두 번째를 활용한 나라들은 경제 발전에 상당한 고충을 겪었을 것이다. 이들이 그랬다는 증거는 없다.

사회주의 산업 또한 가격 통제라는 구조 안에서 작동한다. 1970년대 초 소련에서는 기업과 산업이 가격을 어느 정도 유연성 있게 조정할 수 있도록 하기 시작해서 좀 더 비공식적인 (경제) 발전적 면에서는 자본주의 제도와 일치하기도 했다. 미국의 경제학자들은 자유 시장으로의 복귀라고 이러한 변화를 칭찬했다. 그러나 소련의 기업들은 자본주의 회사만큼 거의 영향을 미치지 못하는 자유 시장에 의해 결정된 가격에 영향을 받지 않는다. 오히려 소련의 기업들은 가격을 정하는 권한을 부여받았다.

어 휘

be captivated by ~에 매료되다
spell n. 마력
accord with ~와 일치하다
aggregate n. 집계, 총계
price-fixing n. 가격협정
prejudicial a. 편파적인, 불리한
frame-work n. 구조, 체계

[Challenge 8]

문제 1

답 (3)

해설 돌로 만든 도구를 사용하던 동일한 사람들이 청동의 도입으로 가정환경과 문화가 어떤 식으로 변했는지를 본문에서 주로 다루고 있다. 집의 내면보다 외적인 변화가 많이 일어났음을 본문에서 알 수 있다. 보기 항 (3)이 가장 적절한 답안이다.

문제 2

답 (3)

해설 많은 작은 부락들이 전국에 퍼져있고, 집의 내부의 변화는 거의 볼 수 없다고 했다. 보기 항 (4)는 두 번째 문단에서 언급된 동굴에서 발견된 두 해골의 이야기인데, 두 번째 문단의 첫 번째 문장에서 알 수 있듯이 동굴은 위험한 시기에 잠시 은신처로서 활용되었을 뿐이다. (Caves were resorted to during this epoch only in times of danger).

문제 3

답 (3)

해설 동굴에서 발견된 두 해골에 관한 이야기인데, 이들이 왜 여기에서 죽게 되었는지 살펴보자.

> In some time of sudden danger workers in bronze fled hither with their stores, but owing to some cause were unable to escape the death from which they were fleeing, and their bodies ___(a)___ until the modern explorer made them a subject of scientific speculations.

위험한 상황에 직면한 이들은 저장품을 가지고 여기 동굴로 피신하였으나, 어떤 원인에 의해 죽음을 면하지 못하게 된 것이다. 그래서 이들의 시체는 현대 탐험가가 발견해 과학적 추정의 대상으로 삼기 전까지 발견되지 않았다.

해석 청동의 사용으로 가정 생활에서, 사람들의 문화에서 어떤 변화가 왔는지를 살펴보도록 하자. 우리가 먼저 생각할 것은 특정한 새로운 인종을 다루는 것이 아니라 신석기 시대의 말기에 유럽에 거주한 동일한 인종을 다룬다는 점이다. 돌로 만든 도구로 자연을 이겨낸 사람들은 무기와 효용성이 크게 향상된 도구를 소유하게 되었다. 결과적으로 그들은 문화의 진보를 이룰 수 있었다. 우리는 집안에서는 아주 큰 변화는 기대할 수 없다. 그러나 집이 훨씬 더 견고하게 잘 지어지긴 했다. 금속의 도구는 돌로 만든 가장 최상의 도구보다 훨씬 앞선 것은 분명하다. 금속 도끼, 칼, 톱 그리고 끌과 정에 도움으로 이들의 오두막은 크기와 모양이 크게 향상되었다. 이들은 여전히 호수 주변에 정착했지만, 청동기 시대의 집들은 훨씬 더 튼튼하게 (substantially) 지어졌으며, 호숫가보다 멀리 위치했다. 요새화된 장소가 여전히 많았다. 이 시대의 수천 개의 유적들이 아일랜드에서 발견되었다. 그러나 숲이 개간되고 야생 동물들은 사라지는 반면 사회는 더욱 정착되고 작은 마을들이 전국에 흩어져 증가했던 것으로 보인다.

이 시대에는 위험한 때를 대비해 동굴에 의지했다(때로 위험의 시기에 동굴을 사용했다는 뜻). 영국의 Heathbury Burn의 한 동굴에는 두 사람의 해골 일부가 있었는데, 이것들은 많은 청동 제품과 청동 도끼를 주조하는 주형의 주위에서 발견되었다. 이 이야기를 이해하는 것은 어렵지 않다. 갑작스러운 위험의 시기에 청동 작업자 둘이 비축품을 가지고 이곳으로 피신했을 것이며 어떤 이유에서인지 이들이 달아나던 것으로부터의 죽음을 피할 수 없었을 것이며, 이들의 시체는 현대 탐험가들이 발견해 과학 연구의 대상으로 삼기 이전까지 발견되지 않았다는 이야기다.

어휘

Neolithic *a.* 신석기 시대의   gouge *n.* 둥근끌
chisel *n.* 끌, 정   settlement *n.* 정착지
substantially *ad.* 상당히; 튼튼하게
shore *n.* 해변, 호숫가   hamlet *n.* 작은 마을, 부락
scatter *v.* 뿔뿔이 흩어버리다   resort *v.* (~에) 의지하다, 기대다
epoch *n.* 시대; 신기원   portion *n.* 한 조각, 부분, 일부
mould *n.* 형, 주형   ax *n.* 도끼
flee *v.* 달아나다, 도망가다   hither *ad.* 여기에
owing to ~때문에   speculation *n.* 사색, 숙고; 추측

어휘

contemplate *v.* 찬찬히 보다; 잘 생각하다; 심사숙고하다
connexion *n.* 연관성, 관련성
trace *v.* 추적하다; 출처를 조사하다   extrinsic *a.* 외적인
exert *v.* 발휘하다; 쓰다; 휘두르다   sentient *a.* 지각력이 있는
eminent *a.* 저명한; 탁월한, 뛰어난
preside *v.* 의장노릇을 하다; 관장하다
guide *v.* 인도하다, 이끌다
solemn *a.* 엄숙한, 근엄한

[Challenge 9]

문제 1

답 (1)

해설 본문 중간에 있는 'but'을 중심으로 앞에서는 지적 존재로서의 인간을 다루고, 뒤에서는 도덕적 존재로서의 인간을 다루고 있다.

문제 2

답 (4)

해설 빈칸에 들어갈 접속사 앞에서 다뤄지는 내용은 인간을 지적 존재로 간주하고 있다. 그러나 빈칸 바로 뒤에 이어지는 내용은 이와 상반되는 견해로 인간을 도덕적 존재로 상정하고 이야기를 이끌어 가고 있다.

해석 인간은 지적이고 도덕적 존재로 간주된다. 그의 지적 능력으로 그는 지식을 습득하고, 사실 간의 연관성을 관찰해 여기에서 이끌어 낸 결론을 추론해 낸다. 그러나 이러한 정신 작용은 아무리 높은 교양의 상태라도 외재적 종류의 진실만을 추구하게 되는데, 다시 말해 개인의 도덕적 상태라든가 다른 지각적 존재와의 관계성에 어떠한 영향도 미치지 못한다. 이러한 것들은 이기적이고, 자신의 욕구 이상의 것을 느끼지 못하거나 피상적인 순간들만을 즐기는 사람들에게서 뚜렷하게 나타난다. 그러나 우리가 인간을 도덕적 존재로 간주할 때, 우리의 관점에 새로운 관계의 지평이 열리고 이러한 관계는 더욱 중요한 의미를 지닌다. 우리는 그가 도덕적 정부의 훌륭한 체제에서 한 자리를 차지하고 거기서 중요한 위치를 가지고 고귀한 의무를 행하는 것을 본다. 우리는 만물의 체계를 다스리는 위대한 도덕적 주관자와 현재의 상황을 통해서 그를 준비하도록 의도된 미래의 존재 상태와 특별한 관계 속에 그가 놓여 있음을 발견한다. 우리는 그가 이러한 관계를 느낄 수 있는 적합한 사람이 되게 하는 능력과 그의 도덕적 수양 상태를 수행할 숭고한 책임감을 행하도록 의도된 원칙을 소유한 것을 발견한다.

[Challenge 10]

문제 1

답 (3)

해설 본문은 무한한 하나님과 유한한 인간의 통합을 주장하는 종교 자체를 거부하고 있다. 즉, 유한한 인간은 무한이라 상정된 하나님과 통합을 이루는 것 자체가 불가능하다고 말하면서 종교 자체를 부정하고 있다. 보기 항 (3)만이 가장 적절한 표현이다.

해석 종교는 인간이 종교를 통해 하나님과 통합되거나 의사소통을 한다고 말한다. 그런데 (또한) 하나님은 무한하다고 말하지 않는가? 만약 하나님이 무한하다면, 어찌 유한한 인간이 그와 함께 의사소통 또는 그 어떠한 관계를 맺을 수 있겠는가? 관계가 형성되지 않은 곳에는, 통합이나 일치 혹은 의무도 있을 수 없다. 만약 하나님과 인간 사이에 의무가 없다면, 인간을 위한 종교도 존재하지 않는다. 게다가 하나님이 유한하다고 말하는 그 순간부터 유한한 존재인 인간을 위한 모든 종교를 스스로 없애는 것이 된다. 무한이란 개념은 본보기, 원형 또는 대상이 없는 개념일 뿐이다.

어휘

infinite *a.* 무한한   finite *a.* 유한한
correspondence *n.* 관련성(유사함)   duty *n.* 의무
annihilate *v.* 절멸하다, 폐지하다
prototype *n.* 원형; 본, 표준

Day 25

[Challenge 1]

문제 1

답 (4)

해설 수족관에서 그가 일하면서 번 돈에 관한 내용은 없다. 50 paise or 1 rupee는 그가 용돈으로 받은 돈이다.

문제 2

답 (3)

해설 그가 정직함을 가지고 있다고 볼 수는 있지만, 본문에서 그가 그것으로 인해 큰돈을 벌었다는 내용은 없다.

해석 내가 학교를 막 졸업했을 때, 나는 세상물정 모르는 어린 아이였다는 걸 이해해야 한다. 나는 스스로 어디도 여행한 적이 없기에 기차표를 구입한 적도 없었다. 대다수의 또래처럼 나는 부모 또는 친척들과 여행을 했으며, 이들이 모든 결정을 내렸기 때문이다. 나는 돈을 다루는 방법에 대한 경험이 없었다(나의 지식은 간간히 용돈으로 받은 50 paise 또는 1 rupee를 쓰는 것에 한정되었다). 그래서 나는 더 멀리 넓게 여행하기로 목표를 정한 반면, 나의 부모님은 현명하게 내가 Goa 지역 내에서 혼자 지내는 방법을 배우는 것으로 시작하는 것이 좋겠다고 생각하셨다. 그리고 장마철이었기에 전국을 여행한다는 것은 훨씬 더 어려운 일이라고 부모님은 설명하셨다. 그래서 나는 마을에서 가장 가까운 도시인 Mapusa의 수족관 가게에서 일을 돕는 것으로 시작했다. 이 가게의 주인은 Ashok D'Cruz로 아버지의 대학 친구였다. 나는 Ashok에 대해 할 말이 있다. 그는 평범한 사업가가 아니었다. 물고기를 키우는 것이 그의 취미였다. 그는 물고기를 팔아 돈을 버는 것보다 물고기에 대해 고객과 이야기를 나누는 것에 훨씬 더 흥미를 가지고 있었다. 나는 그가 한 번도 자신의 물고기를 사라고 고객에게 강요하는 것을 본 적이 없다.

어 휘

raw *a.* 생것의, 가공하지 않은 rupee *n.* 루피(화폐단위)
proprietor *n.* 소유자; 경영자
college *n.* 칼리지(대학원을 두지 않고 교양학부만 가르치는 대학); 집합, 단체
stock *n.* 재고(품), 사들인 물건

[Challenge 2]

문제 1

답 (3)

해설 본문은 우리가 경험한 지식에 대한 회상과 관련해서 기억 속에 불러낼 수 없는 경험의 원인이 바로 현재의 우리와 관련성이 없기 때문이라고 말하고 있다. 즉 망각의 원인에 대한 글이다.

해석 기억이 분명 그 범위가 한정된 것처럼 보이는 것은 당연하다. 이것은 기억을 불러일으키려는 의지력이 한정되어 있기 때문이다. 그러나 우리가 특정 경험을 회상하려는 의지력이 없어서 이러한 경험을 정신적으로 따라가는 과정이 모두 우리에게 없어진 것은 아니다. 우리가 불러낼 수 없는 이러한 경험은 우리가 특별한 관심을 두는 것이 아니기에 이러한 경험이 발생할 때 우리가 무시하는 경험들이다. 이런 경험은 여전히 정신 속에 존재하지만, 이러한 경험을 불러일으킬 힘과 연관된 정신적 관련성이 의식 속에 발생하지 않을 뿐이다.

어 휘

decidedly *ad.* 확실히, 단호히
scope *n.* 범위, 영역
voluntary *a.* 자발적인, 임의의 *v.* 상기하다, 회상하다
recall *n.* 회상, 기억(능력)   deliberately *ad.* 신중히; 고의로
association *n.* 연합, 관련, 연관성
awaken *v.* 깨우다, 일으키다, 불러일으키다
consciousness *n.* 자각, 의식

[Challenge 3]

문제 1

답 (4)

해설 본문에서 아기의 언어 발달을 위해 부모가 언어 수업을 들어야 한다는 언급은 없다.

문제 2

답 (2)

해설 아기의 언어능력과 뇌의 연결고리를 연구하는 분야는 (뇌)인지과학이다.

문제 3

답 (1)

해설 본문에서 Campbell이 믿는 사실은 아기가 뱃속에 있을 때, 법과 관련된 이야기를 들려주면 법과 관련된 직업을 가진다는 뜻이 아니라, 아기는 이미 뱃속에서부터 언어 능력을 발달시킨다는 의미로 말하고 있다.

해석 아기가 아는 것이 의사, 연구자 그리고 부모들의 흥미를 끌고 있다. 뇌파와 그 밖의 지표들을 측정할 수 있는 기술의 발달로 연구자들이 발견한 것은 우리가 생각하는 것보다 아이는 더 많은 것을 알고 있다는 점이다. 아기들이 무엇을 알고 언제 이것을 아는가? 이러한 질문에 연구자들은 아기들의 뇌를 관찰함으로써 알아내려고 한다. 노스웨스턴 대학의 연구자들은 최근 아기가 말을 시작하기 훨씬 이전부터 아기들이 말을 인식하고 이것이 지시하는 것과 연관시킬 수 있다는 결론을 냈다. 4개월 반인 Finn은 말을 못 한다. 그러나 그는 어머니가 말하는 것에 분명히 반응한다. 노스웨스턴 대학의 연구와 다른 연구에 따르면 부모가 할 수 있는 최선의 것 중 하나는 아이에게 말을 하는 것이라고 나타난다. Covington Campbell은 아기가 태어나기도 전에 아기에게 말하기 시작했다. "나는 항상 Finn에게 말을 했어요. 내가 하는 일을 들려주는 식이었죠."라고 말했다. Campbell은 Finn을 가졌을 때 법대에 다니고 있었다. "전 법대의 마지막 학기를 보내고 있었습니다. 그래서 추측컨대 제 아이는 법률가가 될 것 같아요. 30년 후에 와서 확인해보세요. 왜냐하면 아이는 제가 법인 수업을 들을 동안 살아있었고, 수업을 들었거든요."라고 말했다. Kathy Hirsh-Pasek 교수는 필라델피아의 템플 대학에서 아동 언어 연구소 소장이다. "우리는 언어 발달의 가장 첫 번째 과정은 실질적으로 어머니 배 속에 있을 때 시작한다고 보는데, 왜냐하면 아기들이 엄마가 하는 말을 들을 수 있기 때문입니다."라고 말했다. 연구자들은 바로 이때가 아기들이 언어의 멜로디를 익히는 때라고 말한다.

어휘

fascinate v. 황홀케 하다, 매혹시키다
brain wave n. 뇌파
indicator n. 지표, 척도
monitor v. 감시하다, 조정하다
pregnant a. 임신한
semester n. (1년 2학기제의) 한 학기, 반 학년
litigator n. 소송자, 기소자
corporation n. 법인; 기업
womb n. 자궁
overhear v. 엿듣다, 도청하다

[Challenge 4]

문제 1

답 (2)

해설 본문에서 글쓴이가 독재의 경우 저항권을 주장하고 있다는 내용은 없다.

해석 내가 생각하는 이상적인 정치란 민주주의이다. 모든 이가 한 개인으로 존경받으며 어떤 사람도 우상화되지 않는다. 참으로 운명의 장난인 것은 나 자신이 나의 동료들로부터 엄청난 존경과 갈망의 대상이라는 점이다. 이러한 이유는 나의 미약한 능력을 가지고 끊임없는 노력을 통해서 얻어낸 몇 가지 생각을 이해할 수 있는, 많은 사람들은 성취할 수 없는 욕망일 것이다. 어떤 단체든 자신의 목적에 도달하려 한다면, 한 사람이 생각과 지도를 해야 하며 일반적으로 책임을 져야 한다는 것을 알고 있다. 그러나 이러한 지도받는 이(the led)는 강압적으로 이끌려선 안 되며, 이들은 자신의 지도자를 스스로 선택할 수 있어야 한다.

어휘

political a. 정치와 관련된, 정치적인   idolize v. 숭배하다
recipient n. (어떤 것을) 받는 사람, 수령인
excessive a. 지나친, 과도한   admiration n. 감탄, 존경
reverence n. 숭배   unattainable a. 도달 불가능한
feeble a. 아주 약한, (효과·의지 등이) 허약한, 미미한
ceaseless a. 끊임없는   bear v. (책임 등을) 떠맡다
coerce v. (협박하여) 강압하다

[Challenge 5]

문제 1

답 (2)

해설 '방침을 바꾼다'의 의미로 새로운 방침 즉, 원칙을 택한다는 뜻이다.

문제 2

답 (3)

해설 본문은 원칙에 의해서 움직이는 자와 자신만의 이익을 위해서 움직이는 대조되는 두 대상을 다루는 글이다.

문제 3

답 (3)

해설 자기중심적 사고가 너무 강해 스스로가 자기의 '적'임을 망각한다는 의미이다.

문제 4

답 (1)

해설 전체 문맥을 생각하면서 빈칸 앞뒤의 내용을 종합적으로 살펴야 한다.

> The man of principle looks upon these incidents as comparatively insignificant, and not to be weighed with loss of character, loss of Truth. To desert Truth is, to him, the only happening which ____(다)____.

원칙을 고수하는 사람은 'the loss of his wealth, his comforts, or his life'를 상대적으로 중요하지 않게 여긴다고 했다. 그러나 진실을 고수하는 사람에게 진실을 버린다는 것은 바로 그 자체가 재앙이라고 말할 수 있을 것이다.

해설 원칙이 아니라 자신에 의해서 지배되는 사람은 그의 이기적 평안이 위협을 받을 때 자신의 방침을 바꾼다(change one's front). 자기 자신의 이득을 옹호하고 보호하려는 성향이 깊어 그 목적에 도움이 되는 수단이라면 모두 합법적이라고 간주한다. 그는 적에게서 자신을 보호할 방법만 줄곧 구상하느라, 너무 자기중심이 되어 스스로가 자신의 적임을 인식하지 못한다. 이러한 사람의 일은 무너지게 마련인데, 이는 이것이 진실과 진정한 힘으로부터 단절되어 있기 때문이다. 자기 자신에 근거한 모든 노력은 멸망한다. 단지 무너지지 않은 원칙 위에 세워진 일만이 영속한다. 원칙 위에 세워진 사람은 어떤 상황에서도 동일하게 차분하고, 용감하며 침착하다. 시련의 시기가 닥쳐왔을 때, 그리고 자신의 안일과 진실 사이에서 선택해야 할 때 그는 자신의 안일을 포기하고 (진실에 대한) 자신의 소신을 지킨다. 고문과 죽음이 예상된다 하더라도, 그것이 그의 원칙을 바꾸거나 좌절시키지 못한다. 자신만을 위한 사람은 자신의 부, 안위 또는 생명의 상실을 그에게 발생할 수 있는 가장 최악의 재앙이라 여긴다. 원칙을 지키는 사람은 이러한 사건을 상대적으로 사소한 것으로 여기고 인격의 상실, 진리의 상실로 평가하지 않는다. (weigh = consider) 진실을 버리는 것만이 그에게 재앙이라 불릴 수 있는 유일한 사건이다.

어휘

threaten *v.* 협박하다, 위협하다   guard *v.* 지키다, 보호하다
lawful *a.* 합법의, 적법의   subserve *v.* 도움이 되다, 유용하다
scheme *v.* 계획하다, 꾸미다   self-centered *a.* 자기중심적인
perceive *v.* 지각하다, 감지하다
crumble *v.* 부서지다, 무너지다   divorce *v.* 이혼하다; 분리하다
indestructible *a.* 파괴할 수 없는, 불멸의
calm *a.* 조용한   dauntless *a.* 불굴의, 용감한
self-possessed *a.* 침착한   torture *n.* 고문, 심한 고통
calamity *n.* 재난, 참화   befall *v.* 일어나다, 생기다
look upon A as B A를 B로 여기다
incident *n.* 사건   comparatively *ad.* 비교적
insignificant *a.* 무의미한, 하찮은
weigh *v.* 무게를 달다; 평가하다   desert *v.* 버리다

[Challenge 6]

문제 1

답 (4)

해설 보기 항 (4)은 역사 비평가의 특징이다.

문제 2

답 (2)

해설 역사에 관한 이야기에서 자연과학의 이야기로 넘어간 부분이다. 이 점을 감안하여 빈칸이 들어간 문맥을 살펴보자.

> Treating the individual, sensuous, changing objects as mere unsubstantial appearances (phenomena), scientific investigation becomes a search for the universal laws which rule the ____(a)____ changes of events.

주어가 과학적 연구(scientific investigation)이며 보편적 지식을 추구한다고 했다. 이는 다른 말로, 시대별로 변화하는 특성을 지닌 현상이 아니라 시대를 불문하고 공통된 현상에 적용되는 법칙을 말한다. 고로 'timeless'가 가장 적절하다.

문제 3

답 (1)

해설 문제 2와 마찬가지로 자연 과학에 관한 내용이다.

> Out of this colorful world of the senses, science creates a system of abstract concepts, in which the true nature of things is conceived to exist — a world of colorless and soundless atoms, ____(b)____ all their earthly sensuous qualities.

즉, 과학은 추상적 개념의 체계를 구축한다고 했다. 즉, 외적 환경에 변하지 않는 모든 사물에 적용되는 근본적인 특성을 추구하는 것이기 때문에 각각이 가진 외적 특성은 모두 없애야 함을 알 수 있다. 또한 본문의 직접적인 힌트가 되는 부분이 바로 'colorless and soundless'이다.

문제 4

답 (2)

해설 밑줄 친 부분은 보편적 법칙이 세상의 다양한 법칙에 공통적으로 적용된다는 것을 말한다. 자연과학은 다양한 현상에서 공통점을 이끌어 내어 보편적 법칙을 만들어내는 것이라고 말한 점을 적용하면 된다.

해설 자연과학이 추상적인 것을 강조하는 반면, 역사는 구체적인 것을 강조하는 점은 이 두 학문 연구의 결과를 비교해보면 더욱 극명해진다. 역사 비평가들이 자신의 역사적

자료를 연구하는 데 사용하는 개념이 아무리 섬세하다 하더라도, 이 연구의 궁극적인 목적은 항상 수없이 많은 사건 중에서 과거에 일어난 특정한 한 사건의 생생한 묘사를 만들어내는 것이다. 그러나 역사가 우리에게 제공하는 것은 그들의 주관으로 가득한, 그들의 생생한 글 솜씨로 재탄생된 인간과 인간의 삶일 뿐이다. 그러므로, 과거의 사람들과 언어, 그들의 생활 방식과 믿음, 권력과 자유를 위한 이들의 투쟁은 모두 역사의 입을 통해서 우리에게 전해진다. 자연과학이 우리에게 제공해 주는 세상과 얼마나 다른 것인가! 이들이 처음 가지고 시작했던 내용이 아무리 구체적이라 해도, 이 학문의 목적은 바로 이론, 즉 결론적으로 변화의 수학적 법칙을 이끌어내는 것이다. 각각의 감각적이고 다변하는 사물들을 하나의 단순한 현상으로 취급하면서, 과학 탐구는 시대를 초월하는 사건 변화를 지배하는 보편적인 법칙을 찾는 것이다. 갖가지 감각이 넘쳐나는 이 세계에서 과학은 추상적인 개념 체계를 만들어내는데, 이 체계 내에서 사물의 진정한 본성, 즉 세상의 감각적 특성을 모두 뺀 무색과 무음의 원자로 구성된 세계가 존재하는 것으로 인식된다. 이것이 바로 사고가 인식에 대한 승리를 한 것이다. 변화에 흔들리지 않는 과학은 영원과 불변의 맛을 낸다. 엄밀한 의미의 그런 변화는 아니지만 변하지 않는 형태의 변화를 추구하는 것이 과학이다.

어 휘

natural science *n.* 자연과학
abstract *a.* 추상적인; 관념상의 *n.* 추상
concrete *a.* 구체적인
finespun *a.* 아주 가늘게 자아낸, 섬세한; 면밀한
individuality *n.* 개성; 개체   vivacity *n.* 쾌활함, 활발함
eventually *ad.* 최후에는, 드디어
mathematical formulation 수리공식
sensuous *a.* 감각적인; 오감에 의한
unsubstantial *a.* 실체가 없는, 견고하지 않은
colorful *a.* 색채가 풍부한, 다채로운
atom *n.* 원자, 미분자   earthly *a.* 이 세상의, 세속적인
anchor *n.* 닻, (마음을) 받쳐주는 것
eternal *a.* 무구한, 불멸의

[Challenge 7]

문제 1

답 (4)

해설 특정 정보를 독자에게 알려주는 내용의 글이다.

문제 2

답 (4)

해설 본문에서 뉴욕의 상층부 사람들은 'r'을 사용하는 경향을 보인다는 점은 맞으나, 뉴욕 사람들만이 'r'을 쓴다는 이야기는 없다.

문제 3

답 (2)

해설 앞에서 언급한 내용에 대한 구체적인 예가 뒤따르고 있다.

해설 회 언어학은 다양한 상황에서 적절하게 언어의 규칙을 사용하는 인간의 능력을 설명하는 연구이다. 예를 들어 어떤 상황에선 Ms.(결혼 안 한 여인 앞에), Mrs. (결혼한 부인), Mary 또는 박사 아니면 단순히 "당신"이라 특정 사람을 불러야 적절한 때가 있다. 용어, 액센트 또는 발음의 선택이 때론 더 많은 공감과 이해를 이끌어 내기도 한다. 예를 들어, 미국식 영어의 특정 방언에서 'r' 소리의 발음은 사회 계층과 관련이 있다. "fourth floor"와 같은 표현에서 어떤 사람은 'r'를 발음하는 반면 다른 이는 그렇지 않은데, 'r' 소리의 용례는 특정 사회경제적 영역 내에서 일관성이 있다는 주장이 있다. 뉴욕시에서 사용되는 영어에 관한 한 연구에 따르면, 중하층 계급에서 상위 계층으로 이동을 갈망하는 사람은 'r'를 발음하는 것에 특권을 부여한다. 때로 이들은 실제 상층 부류의 사람들보다 'r' 소리를 지나치게 강하게 하는 성향을 보이기도 한다.

어 휘

socio-linguistic studies *n.* 사회언어(학) 연구
appropriately *ad.* 적합하게, 적당하게
induce *v.* 유도하다; 초래하다
empathy *n.* 감정이입   dialect *n.* 방언; 사투리
be linked to ~와 연결되어 있다
consistent *a.* 일치하는, 일관성 있는
socioeconomic niche *n.* 사회경제적 분야
emulate *v.* 모방하다, 따라 하다

[Challenge 8]

문제 1

답 (2)

해설 본문은 오바마 대통령이 최근 공화당과 맺은 동의안에 대해 자신이 속한 민주당원에게 클린턴을 통해 설득하려는 내용이다. 초기 오바마 대통령의 계획과는 달리 중저소득층에게만 세금 혜택을 주는 것이 아니라 2년간 모든 이에게 해당하는 세금 혜택을 제시한 것('Obama's deal with Republicans entails new tax credits and tax cut extension for all income groups for two years.')에 민주당원들은 현재 분노한 상태이다. 즉, 본문은 '오바마가 공화당과 맺은 세금삭감안'에 대한 내용을 중심으로 전개되고 있다.

문제 2

답 (1)

해설 첫 번째 빈칸 – 민주당원들은 현재 대통령이 공화당과 맺은 협의안에 반대하고 있다. 'Democrats charge that the president caved in too quickly to Republican demands and that he should have stuck with his original argument to extend tax cuts only for lower-and middle-income groups.'에서 알 수 있다. 두 번째 빈칸 – 인과의 등위접속사 'and'를 이용한다. 앞의 내용을 보면 'House Democrats passed a resolution overwhelmingly rejecting the deal'이라고 했으므로 이후 전개되는 내용은 대통령과 자신의 당 사이에 '불화'가 증가한다는 내용이 들어가면 된다.

문제 3

답 (1)

해설 본문에서 오바마 대통령이 현재 의안을 통과시키려는 구체적인 목적이 드러나 있다. 'The payroll tax credit will actually create a fair number of jobs... to lower the unemployment rate' 참고.

해설 오바마 대통령은 많은 자유 민주당원들의 분노를 자아낸 공화당과의 세금 감면 협약의 장점을 내세우기 위해 긴급 기자회견에 전 대통령이자 민주당의 영향력 있는 인사인 빌 클린턴을 내세웠다. 클린턴은 "전체적인 관점에서 이 동의안은 가장 많은 미국인을 돕고, 경제 회복을 가속화하고 더 많은 직업을 창출할 기회를 극대화하는 동시에 다른 금융 붕괴 때 발생했던 경기 회복이 다시 침체 국면에 빠질 가능성을 최소화할 수 있다는 점에서 양당이 체결한 최고의 합의안이라고 본다"고 말했다. 근로소득공제는 "실질적으로 수없이 많은 직업을 창출할 것"이라고 그는 덧붙였다. "나는 이것이 실업률을 줄이고 우리가 계속 앞으로 나아갈 수 있도록 도울 것으로 여긴다." 오늘 브리핑을 하는 동안 아주 편안하게 보인 클린턴은 이전에 오바마 대통령의 의료 개혁 법안을 적극 지지했는데, 대통령을 지지하는 의안에 의심을 가진 자신의 민주당원들에게 압박을 주었다. 공화당과 맺은 오바마의 계약에는 2년간 모든 소득층에 적용되는 새로운 세금 공제와 세금 삭감 연장이 포함되어 있다. 또한 여기에는 유산에 대한 세금도 낮추는 부동산 세 조항도 포함이 되어 있다. 민주당원들은 대통령이 공화당의 요구에 너무 쉽게 굴복한 것이며 그는 중/저소득층에게만 세금 삭감을 확대한다는 원래의 주장을 계속 고수했어야 한다고 비난한다. 목요일 민주 하원에서 이 합의안을 전적으로 거부하는 결의안을 통과시키고, 대통령 자신이 속한 당 내 점차 커져가는 불화를 더욱 강화시켰다. 오늘 상원에서 Bernie Sanders 의원은 8시간 이상 이 원안에 대한 반대 주장을 펼쳤는데, 그는 대통령이 '나쁜 협상'을 한 것이라고 말했다. 오바마는 2011년에 미국의 중산층이 높은 세금 증가에 타격을 입지 않도록 하기 위해 어쩔 수 없이 협상안을 찾아야 했다고 주장한다. 백악관은 또한 약 9백만의 미국인을 돕는 것으로 보이는 여러 세금 공제와 실업수당을 확장한다는 것을 포함한 조치를 취했다.

어휘

heavyweight n. (학계·정계 따위의) 유력자, 중진, 영향력 있는 사람
impromptu a. 준비 없이 한, 즉석에서 한, 즉흥적으로 한
Democratic a. 《미국》민주당의 (cf. Republican 공화당)
bipartisan a. 두 정당(연립)의
economic recovery 경기 회복
slip back 다시 미끄러져 되돌아가다
financial collapse 재정 붕괴   tax credit 세금 면제
unemployment rate 실업률
stump for ~을 적극적으로 지지하다
inherited income 상속세
stick with ~을 계속 고수하다
cave in (~에) 항복하다   resolution n. 결의안
rail against ~에 (반대하여) 악담을 퍼붓다
unemployment benefits n. 실직 수당
slap v. (세금을) 징수하다

[Challenge 9]

문제 1

답 (5)

해설 본문은 노동시장의 문제로 드러나는 경제적 고난의 정도를 사회 통계 수치가 제대로 드러내지 못하고 있다는 것을 지적하는 글이다.

문제 2

답 (4)

해설 'The unemployment counts exclude the millions of fully employed workers whose wages are so low that their families remain in poverty.'에서 알 수 있듯이 실질적으로 빈곤을 겪는 사람은 직업이 없는 사람(사실 대부분 직업이 없는 사람은 글의 전반부에서 언급 했듯이 노인이나 장애인 또는 가족 내에서 경제적 책임을 질 필요가 없는 사람)이 아니라, 일을 하고 있지만 사실 임금이 낮아 빈곤 상태에 허덕이는 사람이다. 하지만 이들은 노동시장에서 '고용된' 사람에 포함되기에 노동시장 문제를 제대로 드러내지 못하고 있다고 지적하고 있다.

문제 3

답 (2)

해설 'Unemployment does not have the same dire consequences today as it did in the 1930's'에서 알 수 있듯이 현재의 실직이 과거보다 그리 심각한 영향을 미치는 것은 아니라고 언급하고 있다.

문제 4

답 (3)

해설 본문은 문제점이 현재의 사회 통계 수치가 노동시장의 문제를 제대로 반영하지 못한다는 점이다. 그러므로 이에 대한 해결책은 노동시장의 문제(2번 문제 참고)를 제대로 반영할 수 있는 적절한 사회 통계 지수의 개발이 될 수 있다.

문제 5

답 (2)

해설 문제에서 지적하고 있는 내용은 'Yet there are also many ways our social statistics underestimate the degree of labor-market-related hardship.' 이후 전개되고 있다. 보기 (2)가 정답임을 알 수 있다.

문제 6

답 (1)

해설 'income transfers in our country have always focused on the elderly, disabled, and dependent, neglecting the needs of the working poor'에서 보기 (1)이 정답임을 알 수 있다.

문제 7

답 (5)

해설 'Earnings and income data also overstate the dimensions of hardship. Among the millions with hourly earnings at or below the minimum wage level, the overwhelming majority are from multiple- earner, relatively affluent families.'에서 보기 (5)의 내용을 파악할 수 있다.

해석 노동시장 문제로 얼마나 많은 사람이 고통을 당하고 있는가? 이는 가장 중요하면서도 논쟁거리가 되는 사회 정책 문제 중 하나이다. 여러 가지로, 우리 사회의 사회 통계는 어려움의 정도를 과장하는 면이 있다. 오늘날의 실업은, 1930년대 당시 대부분 실업자들이 주된 수입원이고, 수입과 돈벌이가 대개 최저 생계수단에 가까우며, 노동시장에서 구직에 실패한 사람들을 위해 대응할 만한 어떤 사회적 제도가 마련되지 않았던 때와 비슷할 정도로 심각한 영향을 미치지는 않는다.

생활이 점차 풍족해지고, 돈 버는 사람이 한 사람 이상인 가정이 늘어나고, 실업자들 중에서 부차적인 소득을 올리는 사람이 증가하며, 사회복지 안전망이 향상되면서 실직 상태로 인한 영향력이 완화되었다. 소득 자료 또한 어려움의 범위를 과장하고 있다. 시간당 소득이 최저 임금 수준 정도거나 그 이하인 수백만 명의 사람 중 대부분은 복수의 소득자이고, 상대적으로 집이 풍족하게 사는 사람들이다.

빈곤 통계에 의해 계산된 이들 대부분은 노인 또는 장애인이거나, 노동 인구에 들어가지 않는 가족 부양 의무를 가진 사람들이다. 따라서 빈곤 통계는 노동시장의 "병리"를 정확히 드러내는 지수가 될 수 없다. 그러나 사회 통계가 노동 및 시장과 관련된 어려움의 정도를 과소평가하는 측면 또한 많다. 실업 총계에는 풀타임 노동자이지만 임금이 너무 낮아 가정이 빈곤 상태에서 벗어나지 못하는 수백만 사람들은 제외되고 있다.

낮은 임금과 반복되거나 장기화되는 실업은 상호작용하는 경우가 빈번하여 자기 부양 능력을 약화시킨다. 올해 특정 기간에 실직을 경험한 수는 다른 어느 달보다 실직 수가 몇 배에 달하기에, 비록 어떤 달에는 실직을 겪은 사람들이 소수에 불과하겠지만, 어쩔 수 없이 일을 하지 못하는 사람들의 수는 연간 평균 실업률과 비슷하거나 그보다 넘을 가능성이 있다.

월별 실업 통계에 계산되는 사람 중에 면면을 보면 풀타임 직업을 구할 능력이 없어서 파트타임 일을 하거나 일자리를 원하지만 노동력에서 제외된 사람들도 있다. 결국, 우리나라의 소득 이전(income transfer)은 노인과 장애인, 얹혀사는 사람에게 늘 초점을 맞추다 보니 가난한 노동자 계층의 필요는 무시하게 되었다. 그것은 현금과 현물 양도의 엄청난 확대가 반드시 노동시장에서 낙오된 사람들을 적절하게 보호해주는 것은 아니라는 것을 뜻한다.

어 휘

breadwinner *n.* 한 가정의 벌이를 하는 사람
countervail *v.* 상쇄하다, 무효로 하다, ~에 대항하다(against)
affluence *n.* 풍부함, 풍요
mitigate *v.* 누그러뜨리다, 완화하다
overstate *v.* 허풍을 떨다, 과장하다
overwhelming *a.* 압도적인, 저항할 수 없는
labor force 노동력
pathology *n.* 병리학; 병리
tally *n.* 기록, 수치

[Challenge 10]

문제 1

답 (1), (3)

해설 밑줄 친 (가)에서 정의되는 pun의 의미는 두 가지를 만족해야 한다. 하나는 특정 단어나 표현이 두 가지로 해석되어야 하고, 다른 하나는 문장 전체의 의미가 달라야 한다는 점이다. 아래의 설명과 같이 (1)의 patient와 (3)의 left가 이를 충족한다.

1. patient는 "인내하는"의 뜻과 "환자"라는 뜻을 모두 가지고 있다.

2. left는 "왼쪽"이란 뜻도 있지만, "남겨진"의 뜻으로 문맥상 생존의 의미로도 볼 수 있다.

해석 현재 미국에서는 많은 사람이 유교보다는 도교와 불교에 관심이 많습니다. 사실 대부분의 사람은 단지 공자를 "공자 가라사대"라고 하는 우스꽝스러운 동음이의어 말장난이나 농담으로만 알고 있습니다. 동음이의어 말장난은 단어로 하는 놀이입니다. 그건 보통 우습지요. 왜냐하면 하나의 단어에 두 가지의 뜻이 있어서 한마디의 격언이 완전히 다른 뜻의 말이 되기 때문입니다. 이 격언들을 공자에게 돌려보면, 문법은 보통 맞지 않을뿐더러 어떤 면에서는 그 격언이 마치 외국인이 말하는 것처럼 들리게 만듭니다. 공자는 이런 것들을 말하지 않았지만, 그런 농담의 일부는 이런 우스운 격언들도 한 현자로부터 비롯되었다는 것입니다. 예를 들면, 다음과 같은 격언을 보십시오. "공자 가라사대, 기찻길을 베고 자는 사람은 머리가 깨질 듯한 두통을 느끼며 잠에서 깰 것이다." (해석은 이렇게 했으나 문법적으로는 맞지 않는 문장임) 이 격언에서의 유머는 "머리가 깨질 듯한 두통"이라는 구절에서 비롯됩니다. 보통 이 구절은 무척 아픈 두통을 뜻하지요. 그렇지만 기차가 기찻길을 따라 온다면 그 사람의 머리는 두 쪽으로 갈라지고, 따라서 이것은 "머리가 깨지는 두통"이 되는 것입니다. 문법적으로 이 격언은 이렇게 써야 합니다. "공자 가라사대, 기찻길을 베고 자는 사람은 머리가 깨질 듯한 두통을 느끼며 잠에서 깰 것이다."

어 휘

Buddhism *n.* 불교   Taoism *n.* 도교
Confucianism *n.* 유교
splitting *a.* 뻐개지는 듯한, (두통 따위가) 심한; 귀청이 터질 것 같은

Day 26

[Challenge 1]

문제 1

답 (3)

해설 paraphrasing 문제다. 보기 항 (2)와 (3)을 혼동할 수 있지만, 밑줄 친 부분에서 나오는 '오늘날보다'라는 표현까지 잘 드러내는 표현은 (3)이다.

문제 2

답 (3)

해설 내용 일치 문제에서 오답을 유도할 때 빈번하게 사용하는 방법은 다음과 같다. 1) 부분과 전체(일반화) 2) 논리적 비약 3) 과장 그리고 4) 극단적 표현(only, always, never 등) 등이 있다. 보기 항 (3)에서 'There has never been any one…'이란 극단적 표현이 쓰이고 있다. 본문에 이런 표현이 명시되지 않는 이상 오답이다.

본문분석

1) Writings on hygiene and health have been accessible for centuries, but (a) <u>never before have books and magazines on these subjects been as numerous as they are today</u>. Most of the information is so general, vague and indefinite that only a few have the time and patience to read the thousands of pages necessary to learn what to do to keep well. The truth is to be found in the archives of medicine, in writings covering a period of over thirty centuries, but it is rather difficult to find the grains of truth.
2) Health is the most valuable of all possessions, for with health one can attain anything else within reason. A few of the great people of the world have been sickly, but it takes men and women sound in body and mind to do the important work. Healthy men and women are a nation's most valuable asset.
3) It is natural to be healthy, but we have wandered so far astray that disease is the rule and good health the exception. Of course, most people are well enough to attend to their work, but nearly all are suffering from some ill, mental or physical, acute or chronic, which deprives them of a part of their power. The average individual is of less value to himself, to his family and to society than he could be. His bad habits, of which he is often not aware, have brought weakness and disease upon him. These conditions prevent him from doing his best mentally and physically.

문단이 나눠진 경우 각 문단별로 주제를 파악해야 한다. 주로 다루고 있는 내용이 무엇인가?

1) 첫 번째 문단

위생과 건강에 관한 글임을 첫 번째 문장에서 알 수 있다. 첫 번째 문단에서 지적하고 있는 바는 위생과 건강에 대한 서적이 그 어느 때보다 넘치지만, 이러한 정보는 'general, vague and indefinite'하다면서 <u>그 문제점을 지적하고 있 다</u>.

2) 두 번째 문단

중심 소재는 건강으로 '건강의 중요성'을 언급하면서 건강한 사람이 국가의 가장 가치 있는 자산이라고 말하고 있다.

3) 세 번째 문단

현상에 대한 설명이 먼저 이어지고 있다. 사람들은 일반적으로 자신의 건강을 잘 돌보지 못해 대부분 어느 정도의 병을 앓고 있다고 지적하면서, 이럴 경우 자신뿐 아니라 가족, 국가에 원래 의도된 가치만큼 인정을 못 받게 된다고 하고 있다. 그리곤, 이러한 것의 원인은 바로 다름 아닌 '나쁜 습관'에서 비롯된다는 원인을 밝히고 있다.

해석 위생과 건강에 관한 글은 수세기 동안 우리 주변에서 접할 수 있었지만, 이 주제에 관한 책과 잡지들이 오늘날만큼 많았던 적은 없었다. 대부분의 정보가 너무 일반적이고 막연하며 분명하지 않아서 건강을 잘 지키기 위해 해야 할 것을 배우기 위해 수천 페이지에 걸친 내용을 시간을 들여 인내심을 가지고 읽을 사람은 거의 없다. 진실은 의학 기록, 30세기가 넘는 기간에 걸친 저서들을 통해 찾아볼 수 있지만, 진실성을 찾기가 그리 쉬운 것이 아니다.

건강은 가지고 있는 모든 것 중 가장 가치 있는 것으로 이는 건강해야만 사리에 벗어나지 않으며, 그 밖의 어떤 일도 이룰 수 있기 때문이다. 위대한 사람들 중에도 병약한 사람이 몇 명 있긴 하지만 중요한 일을 하려면 몸과 마음이 건강해야 한다. 건강한 사람은 한 국가의 가장 중요한 자산인 것이다.

건강한 것은 자연스러운 것이지만 우리가 너무 잘못된 길을 헤매었기에 병이 통치하고 건강은 예외가 되어 버렸다. 물론 대부분 사람들은 자신의 일을 수행할 만큼 건강하지만 거의 모두가 특정한 정신적, 물리적, 급성 또는 만성의 병을 가지고 있는데, 이것은 이들에게 그들이 가지고 있는 힘의 일부를 빼앗는다. 보통 사람들은 자기 자신과 가족 그리고 사회를 실제로 그러한 것보다도 하찮게 여긴다. 자신은 의식하지 못하는 경우가 많은데, 자신의 나쁜 버릇 때문에 허약해지고 병이 생기는 것이다. 이러한 조건은 그가 정신적으로나 신체적으로나 최선을 다하지 못하게 만든다.

어 휘

hygiene n. 위생학; 위생상태
accessible a. 접근하기 쉬운; 이용할 수 있는
numerous a. 다수의, 수많은
vague a. 어렴풋한; 막연한; 모호한
indefinite a. 불명확한; 한계가 없는
archives n. 문서; 기록
sickly a. 병약한; 허약한
wander v. 헤매다; 빗나가다; 길을 잃다
astray a. 길을 잃어; 타락하여
acute a. (병이) 급성의
deprive v. 박탈하다
(of) average a. 평균의; 평범한

[Challenge 2]

문제 1

답 (4)

해설 보기 (4)의 내용은 본문에 언급되어 있지 않으며, 인간의 감각 기관을 통한 외부 정보 감지는 인간의 의지와 관련 없이 발생하는 경우도 많다. 본문에 언급된 'in the fringe of consciousness'의 표현을 참조한다.

문제 2

답 (2)

해설 본문에 비추어 볼 때, 빈칸에 들어갈 단어는 우리 눈에 들어오는 여러 사물이나 사건 중에서 우리의 관심 밖에 있는 것에 대해 우리가 의식적으로 인식하지 않는다는 내용을 전달하는 적절한 표현을 넣으면 된다(They are in the "fringe" of consciousness, and we deliberately ignore them. 참조). '의식적으로 인식하지 않는'에 가장 알맞은 표현은 보기 항 (2)이다. 보기 항 (1)의 경우 '곁눈으로'라는 표현으로 전치사 from을 가져 'from the corner of one's eyes'로 주로 사용한다. 보기 항 (3)은 '의심의 눈초리로'라는 뜻이며, 보기 항 (4)는 '특정한 태도(주로 부정적)를 가지고'라는 뜻이다.

문제 3

답 (1)

해설 우리의 관심 밖 또는 현재의 생각과 관련이 없는 외부의 정보에 대해 우리가 어떤 식으로 반응을 보일지 생각해 본다. 빈칸 문제는 앞뒤의 내용을 철저히 파악한 후 전체 지문의 내용을 염두에 두면서 풀어야 한다. 때로는 바로 앞 또는 뒤에 힌트가 올 수도 있으며, 본문처럼 앞과 뒤 모두에 힌트가 오는 경우도 있다. 답의 힌트는 본문 여기저기 숨겨져 있기에 근거를 찾는 연습을 꼭 해야 한다.

해석 우리가 단지 "반쪽의 눈"으로 보는 많은 것들이 우리 주위에서 일어나고 있다. 이것들은 의식의 "가장자리"에 있으며, 우리는 의식적으로 이러한 것을 무시한다. 우리의 감각 기관을 자극하는 감각 인상의 형태로 많은 일들이 일어나지만, 우리는 수고스럽지 않게 그것들을 무시할 수 있다. 우리는 전혀 이런 것들에 영향을 받지 않으며 의식하지도 않는다. 이는 우리의 삶의 관심사의 선택에 의해 이것들에 대해서 문을 꼭 잠그고 있기 때문이다. 의식의 "가장자리"에 있든지 아니면 완전히 의식 밖에 있든지 어느 경우든 이러한 인식되지 않은 감각은 현재의 사고의 주제와 전혀 관련성 없는 감각 이미지로 나타나게 된다. 그러므로 이런 감각은 우리의 관심을 조금도 이끌어내지 못한다. 마치 우리의 각각의 감각 기관이 몸의 표면을 지속적으로 때리는 수없이 많은 공기의 진동 중에서 그 감각 기관에 조율이 된 속도에 맞는 파장만을 선택하는 것과 마찬가지로, 우리 각자는 하나의 완전한 존재로서 끊임없는 감각 경험에서 현재 또는 습관적 경향의 생각과 어떤 식으로 관련성이 있는 그런 특정한 관심 대상만을 선택한다.

어 휘

fringe n. 가장자리, 주변부
consciousness n. 자각; 의식   **deliberately** ad. 의도적으로
clamorously ad. 시끄럽게, 소란스럽게
assail v. 습격하다, 공격하다
unconscious a. 무의식의; 모르는
unperceived a. 눈에 띄지 않는   **sensation** n. 감각, 지각
sensory a. 감각의; 지각의
multitude n. 다수; 군중; 군집
vibration n. 진동; 떨림; 전율
constantly ad. 변함없이; 항상
velocity n. 속력; 빠르기   **attune** v. 맞추다; 조율하다
integral a. 완전한; 빠트릴 수 없는
stream n. 시내; 흐름; 연속

[Challenge 3]

문제 1

답 (3)

해설 본문은 창조 신화가 무엇인지 그 특징을 중심으로 정의를 내리고 있다.

문제 2

답 (4)

해설 내용 일치 문제는 시간이 걸리지만, 말 그대로 본문의 내용을 정확히 파악해야 한다. 일반적으로 본문과 같이 특정 대상에 대한 특징을 중심으로 정의를 내리는 글을 읽을 땐, 새로운 정보가 나올 때마다 밑줄을 긋거나 표시를 하면서 읽는 것이 좋다. 그래야 나중에 다시 본문을 파악할 때 다시 다 읽어야 하는 번거로움을 피할 수 있다. 보기 항 (4)의 경우 창조 신화는 전혀 역사적 또는 문자적 의미를 가지고 있지 않다고 했지만, 본문에서 'although not always'라고 표현하고 있다.

문제 3

답 (2)

해설 독해형 빈칸 문제는 크게 다음 세 가지로 나눠진다.

1) 글 전체의 문맥을 파악하여 답을 구하는 문제

빈칸의 내용을 전체 문맥과 같은 맥락에서 답을 고르는 유형이다. 일반적으로 글의 주제를 생각하면서, 빈칸에 들어갈 내용이 긍정인지 부정인지를 구별한 후 접근하면 보기 항을 2개로 줄일 수 있는 경우가 많다.

2) 글의 구조에 따라 답을 구하는 문제

글의 구조에 따른 접근 방법은 첫 번째 문장과 마지막 문장 또는 구체적 진술 내 빈칸이 있을 경우이다.

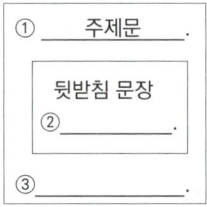

① 첫 번째 문장이 빈칸일 경우 일반적으로 주제문일 가능성이 크다.

② 만약 주제문 뒤에 이어지는 뒷받침 문장의 한 부분이 빈칸 일 경우 다음을 생각한다. 뒷받침 문장은 언제나 글쓴이의 요지를 뒷받침해 주기에, 항상 같은 맥락에서 해석되어야 한다. 또한, 통일성 관점에서 특정 주제문을 뒷받침하는 내용 S1, S2, S3가 나왔을 때, 이들 모두 하나의 주제를 뒷받침하는 같은 맥락의 진술이 되어야 한다 (S1 = S2 = S3).

③ 마지막 문장이 빈칸일 경우 글의 결론에 해당하기에 글의 주장이 드러나는 경우가 많다. 본문의 내용을 바탕으로 가장 적절한 결론을 이끌어낸다.

3) 접속사 문제

일반적으로 문장과 문장 사이의 연결사를 고르는 문제와 문단과 문단을 연결하는 접속사를 고르는 문제로 나뉜다. 어느 경우든 앞에서 진술된 문장과 빈칸이 들어간 문장을 모두 해석한 후 두 문장의 관계를 파악해서 가장 적절한 접속사를 선택한다.

4) 빈칸이 들어간 문장 또는 바로 앞에 나오는 문장과의 관계에서 답을 구하는 문장완성형 문제

문장완성형 문제와 같은 방식으로 푼다. 즉, 논리 정보 장치를 최대한 활용하여 전체 문맥을 감안하면서 빈칸이 주어진 문장 내에서 답안을 고른다.

다시 문제로 돌아가 빈칸이 주어진 문장을 살펴보자.

> the ordering of the cosmos from a state of chaos or _____(a)_____.

우선 빈칸 앞에 위치하는 or는 앞의 단어를 다른 말로 표현하는 기능을 한다. 따라서 chaos와 같은 맥락의 단어를 고르는 문제이다. 문맥을 보면, '우주가 공허 또는 _____ 상태에서 순서대로 발생'한다는 내용이므로 보기 항 (2)의 '무형'이 정답이다.

참고로, 아래는 본문에서 글을 읽으면서 창조 신화에 대한 중요 포인트만을 밑줄 친 것이다. 특히 빨간색 표시된 부분을 잘 확인할 것.

> A creation myth or creation story is a <u>symbolic narrative of a culture, tradition or people</u> that describes their earliest beginnings, how the world they know began and how they first came into it. They are stories expressing, <u>usually through metaphor and imagery</u>, how the world came to be and what humanity's place and role is in it. Creation myths develop <u>in oral</u> traditions, and are the most common form of myth, found <u>throughout human culture</u>. In the society in which it is told, a creation myth is usually regarded as <u>conveying profound truths</u>, although not necessarily in a historical or literal sense. They are commonly, although not always, considered <u>cosmogonical myths</u>— that is they describe the ordering of the cosmos from a state of chaos or amorphousness. They are also commonly, although not always, considered <u>sacred accounts</u>, and can be found in nearly all known religious traditions.

해설 창조 신화 또는 창조 이야기는 가장 초기의 시작, 지금 알고 있는 세계가 어떻게 시작되었는지 그리고 이들이 어떻게 그 안에 존재하기 시작했는지를 기술하는 문화, 전통 또는 사람들에 관한 상징적인 이야기이다. 이것은 주로 은유와 비유적 표현을 통해서 세상이 어떻게 존재하게 되었는지 그리고 그 안에서 인간의 위치와 역할이 무엇인지를 드러내는 이야기이다. 창조 신화는 구전되며, 신화 중에서 가장 일반적인 형태이고, 인간의 문화 전반에서 발견된다. 신화가 전해지는 사회에서 창조 신화는 비록 이것이 반드시 역사적

또는 문자 그대로의 의미가 있는 것은 아니지만 일반적으로 의미심장한 진실을 전달하는 것으로 간주된다. 이것은 항상 그런 것은 아니지만 일반적으로 우주 진화론적 신화로 간주되는데, 다시 말해 이것은 혼돈 또는 무형의 상태에서 우주가 질서를 잡는 순서를 기술한다는 의미에서 그러하다. 이것은 또한 항상 그런 것은 아니지만 일반적으로 신성한 이야기로도 간주되며, 세상에 알려진 거의 모든 종교적 전통에서 찾아볼 수 있다.

어휘

metaphor *n.* 은유, 비유　　**imagery** *n.* 마음의 상, 이미지
oral *a.* 구두의, 구술의　　**profound** *a.* 깊은, 심오한
cosmogonical *a.* 우주 발생의

입은 아이는 양말 없이 신발을 신지만 옆에 있는 아이는 양말을 신고 있다. 그의 양말은 짙은 푸른 옥양목으로 만들어졌으며, 바닥은 촘촘히 짜여 있고, 엄지 발가락을 끼울 공간이 있다. 만약 일본식 신발을 신는다면 양 발가락 사이의 끈이 불편하다고 느낄 것이다. 그러나 이런 종류의 신을 계속 신는 습관으로 인해 엄지는 다른 발가락과 더욱 떨어져 자라며, 엄지와 옆 발가락 사이의 피부는 개나 고양이 발의 피부처럼 단단해진다.

어휘

snowball *n.* 눈뭉치, 눈덩이　　**charcoal** *n.* 숯, 목탄
streak *v.* 줄, 선(바탕을 이루는 부분과 색깔이 다른 기다란 줄 모양의 것)
sink *v.* (눈, 진흙 속에) 빠지다　　**thong** *n.* 가죽 끈
toe *n.* 발가락　　**grass** *n.* 풀, 잔디　　**calico** *n.* 옥양목
weave *v.* 짜다, 엮다　　**paw** *n.* (네 발 짐승의) 발

[Challenge 4]

문제 1

[답] (3)

[해설] 세부 내용 확인에 해당하는 내용 일치 문제이다. 일반적으로 글의 요지를 중심으로 문항이 구성될 때가 있고, 아니면 본문처럼 세부적인 사항을 묘사하는 글에서 국부적인 내용이 나오는 경우도 있다. 글을 읽으면서 특정 사람, 물건의 특징이 나올 경우 항상 표시를 해 두는 연습을 해야 한다. 'The thong is made of grass, and covered with strong paper, or with white or black.' 부분에서 알 수 있듯이, 가죽 끈은 일반적으로 흑백 중 하나의 색상을 취한다.

문제 2

[답] (2)

[해설] 엄지와 다른 발가락 사이에 가죽 끈이 지나가 그곳에 굳은 살이 오른다는 내용이다.

[해석] 남자아이 두 명이 서로 눈덩이를 던지며 놀고 있다. 비록 여기보다 그 나라의 여름은 더 덥지만, 겨울은 여기만큼 춥다. 우리의 아이들과 마찬가지로 사내아이들은 눈이 내리는 것을 좋아하며, 눈을 굴리는 것보다는 눈사람을 만들 때 양 눈에 목탄 공을 붙이고 입에는 석탄으로 선을 그어 표현하는 것을 더 좋아한다. 이 아이들이 밖에서 신는 일반적인 신발은 우리가 겨울에 신는 부츠보다도 눈 오는 날에 더욱 적절한데, 이는 아이들의 발이 눈이 아주 많이 오지 않는 한 눈에 빠지지 않기 때문이다. 이 신발은 나무로 만든 것으로 아이들이 원래보다 3인치 정도 더 커 보이게 만든다. 이 신발은 끈이나 단추는 없지만, 첫 번째와 두 번째 발가락 사이로 지나가는 끈으로 인해 발에 고정된다. 이 끈은 풀로 만들며 튼튼한 종이나 흰색 또는 검은색으로 덮는다. 체크 옷을

[Challenge 5]

문제 1

[답] (3)

[해설] 두 번째 문단까지 사무라이 의식인 할복 자살에 대한 전반적인 설명 후 현대 안락사와의 유사점을 다루고 있다.

문제 2

[답] (4)

[해설] 본문에서 할복 자살을 행하는 과정이 너무나 길고 고통스럽기에 다른 사무라이가 그 고통을 줄이기 위해 의식을 행하는 사무라이의 목을 자른다고 말하고 있다. 'the ritual seppuku usually included a second samurai, an attendant, who would mercifully behead the one practicing seppuku shortly after he had slit open his own stomach.'

참고. 보기 항 (1)은 'length of life was regarded as far less important than honor.'로 보아 옳은 진술이 아니다. 보기 항 (2)의 강조 부사 'solely'와 같은 단어의 쓰임에 주의해야 한다. 본문에 명시되지 않은 이상 'never, only, absolutely'와 같은 단어를 수반하는 문장은 오류 문일 가능성이 크다. 보기 항 (3)과 같은 내용은 본문에 언급이 없고 유추할 수도 없다.

문제 3

[답] (2)

[해설] 콜론 이후의 내용과 가장 유사한 성격을 드러내는 보기 항은 (2)이다.

[해석] 안락사와 자살의 맥락에서 언급할 가치가 있는 것은 바로 사무라이 전통인 할복 자살로, 이는 일종의 의식 자살이

다. 대부분 사무라이들은 선종 불교 신자로, 이들의 전반적 철학은 오래 사는 것이 명예보다 별로 중요하지 않다는 견해이다. 할복 자살은 사무라이들이 포로로 잡히는 불명예를 피하기 위해서 행했으며, 이는 죽음으로 영주를 따름으로 그에게 충성을 표하는 것이며 또한 실패의 참회를 뜻하기도 한다. 본의 아닌 할복 자살 또한 사무라이 계층에게 사형의 수단이었다.

할복 자살을 행하기 위해서 사무라이는 우선 자신의 마음을 가다듬고, 자신의 배를 오른쪽에서 왼쪽으로 의식에 사용하는 칼로 가른다. 이러한 잔인한 방법은 사무라이의 힘과 용맹을 드러내지만, 아주 오랜 고통스런 죽음에 이르게 한다. 따라서 의식적 할복 자살은 일반적으로 자기 자신의 배를 가른 직후 이러한 할복 자살을 행한 자의 목을 자비롭게 베는 보조 사무라이가 있다.

이 보조 사무라이의 자비로운 행동뿐 아니라 할복 자살의 행위 자체는 현대 안락사의 행위와 비교된다. 사무라이의 자살 이유에는 다른 이의 손에 피할 수 없는 죽음을 모면하기 위한 것과 사회의 활동적이고 생산적인 구성원이 되지 못하고 참을 수 없는 고통 또는 심리적 비참함을 오래 겪는 것을 회피하기 위함이었다. 이것은 바로 오늘날 안락사가 요구되는 그런 상황이다.

사무라이의 할복 자살 의식은 안락사와 아주 가까웠는데, 보조 사무라이는 자살한 사람이 빨리 죽음에 이르고 고통스러워하는 시간을 줄이기 위해 목을 벤다. 사무라이의 자살 동기는 안락사를 원하는 사람의 그것과 비슷하다. 전쟁에서 지거나 적에게 죽임을 당하거나, 너무 치명적인 상처를 입어 더 이상 사회의 유용한 구성원이 되지 못한다는 점이다.

어 휘

euthanasia *n.* 안락사 **Zen Buddhist** *n.* 선승
practice *v.* 실행하다, (항상) 행하다; (신앙·이념 등을) 실천하다, 신봉하다
dishonour *n.* 불명예
involuntary *a.* 본의 아닌, 마지못해 하는 **slit** *v.* 세로로 베다
inevitable *a.* 피할 수 없는 **behead** *v.* 목을 베다, 참수하다
stab *v.* (칼 따위로) 찌르다
wounded *a.* 상처 입은, 부상당한; (마음을) 상한

[Challenge 6]

문제 1

답 (2)

해설 일반적으로 제시된 본문 앞에서 전개된 내용에 대한 추론은 거의 첫 번째 문장에서 확인할 수 있다.

> From this analysis we observe that the nitrogenous matter is to the carbonaceous in the proportion of one-sixth, which is the composition of a perfect food.

지시형용사 'this'가 나타내는 바를 추론해야 한다. 제시된 문장에서 특정 음식의 질소와 탄소의 비율이 1대 6이라고 말하고 있다. 바로 이어지는 내용을 보면, 밀 속의 영양 성분을 말하는 것임을 알 수 있다. 보기 항 (2)가 가장 적절하다.

문제 2

답 (4)

해설 본문에서 밀의 장점으로 언급되지 않은 것은 변비라는 의미의 보기 항 (4)이다. 사실 보기 항 (2)와 정반대의 의미를 나타내기에 둘 중 하나는 답이 아니란 것을 보기 항만으로도 알 수 있다.

문제 3

답 (1)

해설 두 번째 문단에서 밀을 어떻게 준비해야 하는지에 관해서 순서대로 자세히 설명하고 있다.

문제 4

답 (4)

해설 본문에서 곡물을 깨끗이 다듬는 과정에서 발생할 수 있는 작은 철 조각을 떼어내기 위해 자석에 통과를 시킨다고 했다. 자석의 사용이 곧 곡물의 질을 높이는 것은 아니다.

해석 이 분석을 통해 우리는 (탄수화물의) 탄소 대 질소의 비가 1:6일 때 가장 완벽하다는 것을 알 수 있다. 게다가 이런 비율의 밀을 살펴보면, 물에 녹지 않기 때문에 장을 통째로 통과하게 되어서 배변에도 도움이 된다. 만약 밀이 그렇게 완벽한 음식이라면, 통밀 빵이 우리의 일용할 음식으로 가장 좋다는 결론을 낼 수 있다. 이것이 사실이라는 것은 모든 면에서 그 증거를 볼 수 있다. 이것을 먹는 사람은 그렇지 않은 사람보다 다른 모든 것이 동일할 때, 더 건강하고, 튼튼하며, 더욱 힘이 넘친다. 통밀 빵은 흰 곡물보다 거의 완벽한 음식의 표준에 가깝다. 발효될 때 전분 일부가 파괴되고 질소의 비율이 약간 증가한다.

다음 질문은 우리가 어떻게 이 곡물을 잘 준비해서 최상의 빵을 만들 것이냐이다. 이것은 곡물을 돌로 잘게 빻아서 이렇게 나온 밀가루를 빵을 만드는 데 사용하게 될 때 가능하다. 우선 이 곡물을 깨끗이 씻고 털어준 다음, 혹시나 다른 과정에서 붙었을 조각이나 철을 떼어내기 위해 자석에 통과시킨 후 곱게 빻는다. 잘 빻았는지를 확실히 하기 위해 항상 가마에서 말리는 것이 좋다. 빻았을 때, 아무 것도 거기에 있어서는 안 되며, 밀가루에 어떤 것도 더 넣어서는 안 된다. 그리고 이렇게 만들어진 가루로 빵을 만들어야 한다.

어휘

nitrogenous *a.* 질소의; 질소를 함유하는
bran *n.* 밀기울, 겨   **insoluble** *a.* 불용해성의
in bulk 대량으로   **bowel** *n.* 창자, 장
laxation *n.* 느즈러짐, 이완; 변통   **wheat** *n.* 밀, 소맥
wholemeal *a.* 통밀로 된
wheaten *a.* 밀의, 밀로 만든
fermentation *n.* 발효 (작용)   **starch** *n.* 녹말, 전분
proportion *n.* 비율; 비례   **nitrogen** *n.* 질소
so as to ~하기 위해   **finely** *ad.* 곱게
flour *n.* 밀가루   **magnet** *n.* 자철, 자철
kiln *v.* (벽돌 등을 굽는) 가마

[Challenge 7]

문제 1

답 (2)

해설 두 번째 문단의 첫 번째 문장에서 어떤 내용을 주로 다루는 글인지 파악할 수 있다. 설명의 글인 통념 비판이며, 구체적 예시를 통해 진술을 뒷받침하고 있다. 세계화가 진행되면서 자국의 회사를 보호하려는 수입 규제가 오히려 일반인의 견해와 달리 자국 회사에 해가 된다는 내용을 전달하는 글이다.

문제 2

답 (4)

해설 'Even when no unfair practices are alleged, the simple claim that an industry has been injured by imports is sufficient grounds to seek relief.'에서 보기 (4)가 정답임을 알 수 있다.

문제 3

답 (5)

해설 앞에서 전개된 내용에 대한 구체적 사례에 해당한다.

문제 4

답 (4)

해설 미국 내 수입 규제를 실시할 경우 외국계 미국 회사가 미국계 외국 회사에 수입 규제를 실시할 수 있다는 점을 경고하고 있다.

해석 안타깝게도, 미국의 많은 기업이 주요 업종으로의 수입 경쟁으로부터 법적 보호를 받는 방법을 모색했다. 1980년 이래 미국의 ITC(미국 상거래위원회)는 외국 정부로부터 받은 보조금으로 혜택을 받은 수입품 때문에 피해를 입었다는 내용의 약 280건에 달하는 불만 사항을 접수했다. 또 다른 340건의 경우 외국 기업들이 미국에서 '정상적인 가격보다 낮은 가격에' 그들의 상품을 '덤핑(국내 가격 이하로 외국 시장에 투매하는 것)' 처리했다고 고소했다. 공정하지 못한 관행이 아니라도, 수입품에 의해 특정 산업이 피해를 입었다는 간단한 주장만으로도 완화 조치를 요구할 근거가 충분했다.

일반적 인식과는 달리, 수입 규제 조치는 많은 기업에 도움보다는 해를 끼쳐왔다. 기업들이 세계화되면서, 마케팅, 생산 및 연구 개발 사이에 복잡한 네트워크가 형성되었다. 이들의 관계가 복잡해지면서 수입 규제 조치 제도가 동일한 모회사 아래 모든 자회사의 전략적 필요성을 충족시키지 못할 가능성이 있다.

국제화가 되면서 수입 규제법이 원래 보호하고자 했던 (국내) 기업들에 오히려 불리하게 작용함에 따라 외국 기업들이 오히려 이 법을 역이용하게 될 위험성이 커졌다. 한 미국 소유의 회사가 특정 제품을 만들기 위해 해외에 공장을 세우고, 이 회사의 경쟁사는 미국에서 동일한 제품을 만든다고 가정해보자. 만약 경쟁사가 수입품으로 인해 피해를 받았다는 것을 증명할 수 있다면, 그리고 그 말인즉, 그 미국 기업이 그 회사의 공장을 외국에 세운 것으로 그곳 정부로부터 보조금을 받았다고 한다면, 이 미국 기업의 제품은 미국에서 경쟁력을 갖지 못하게 될 것이다. 이 회사의 제품이 관세 대상이 되기 때문이다.

아마 가장 노골적이었던 경우는 캐나다 기업들이 도로 제빙에 쓰이는 암염을 덤핑 처리하여 미국의 제염업계에 피해를 끼쳤다는 의혹(주장)을 ITC에서 조사할 때였을 것이다. 이 불만 사항의 특이한 점은 미국이 운영하는 한 외국계 대기업이 외국이 운영하는 미국계 회사에 맞서 도움을 요청했다는 점이다. 피해를 입었다고 주장하는 '미국계' 회사는 네덜란드 대기업의 자회사인 반면, '캐나다' 기업들은 국내 제2 규모의 암염 생산업체인 시카고 회사의 자회사를 포함하고 있었다.

어휘

a line of work 특정 분야의 직업(일)
subsidy *n.* 보조금   **fair** *a.* 공정한
ground *n.* 근거   **relief** *n.* 구제, 도움
intricate *a.* 복잡한, 뒤얽힌
meet the needs of ~의 요구를 충족하다
duty *n.* 조세; 관세
allegation *n.* 주장, 증거 없는 주장
conglomerate *n.* 대기업, 복합 기업
subsidiary *n.* 보조의, 보조금에 의한

[Challenge 8]

문제 1

답 (1)

해설 물질의 기원에 관한 두 가지 관점을 첫 번째 문단에서 기술한 후 두 번째 문단에서 과학이 바라보는 물질의 기원에 관한 견해를 주된 내용으로 삼고 있다.

문제 2

답 (4)

해설 보기 항 (4)는 다음 본문의 내용과 일치하지 않는다.

> "So scientists accept what amounts to the eternity of matter, inconceivable though that is, simply because the only alternative, direct creation, is clearly incredible to them."

해설 비물질에서 물질이 유래한다는 것은 분명 자연적 현상 중 하나는 아닌데, 이는 (다른 것과) 비유적으로 이것을 이해할 수 있도록 돕는 그런 경험이 없는 우리가 생각할 수 없는 현상이기 때문이다. 물질의 시작이 없었다는 것은 우리는 상상할 수 없다. 그리고 물질이 무에서 갑자기 나왔다는 것 또한 상상할 수 없다. 실질적으로 이 두 가지 대안밖에 없으며, 이 두 개는 단순히 상상할 수 없다. 그러나 이 둘 중 하나는 진실이 되어야 한다.

그래서 과학자들은 비록 상상할 수 없지만 물질의 영원성이란 것을 받아들인다. 이는 단순히 이것이 유일한 대안이며 직접적인 창조가 분명 이들에게는 거짓말인 것이 분명하기 때문이다. 다른 말로, 이들은 믿을 수 없는 것이라기보다는 상상할 수 없는 것을 받아들이는데, 이는 이들이 초자연적인 것으로 보는 것보다는 초자연적인 설명을 선호하기 때문이다. 이러한 길을 따라 출발했기에, 이들은 이것을 일관성 있게 따라야 하고, 고로 분명하게, 게다가 독단적으로 신의 개입에 대한 어떠한 개념도 거부하게 될 수밖에 없다. 이들에게 다른 선택이란 없다.

어 휘

natural event 자연 현상
inconceivable *a.* 상상할 수도 없는   phenomenon *n.* 현상
analogy *n.* 비유, 유사점   beginning *n.* 초기, 시작
equally *ad.* 동등하게
alternative *n.* 대안, 선택 가능한 것 *a.* 대체 가능한
eternity *n.* 영원, 오랜 시간
incredible *a.* 믿을 수 없는, 믿기 힘든
supernatural *a.* 초자연적인   explanation *n.* 설명
bound *a.* 꼭 ~할 것 같은
unequivocally *ad.* 명백하게, 분명하게
dogmatically *ad.* 독단적으로

[Challenge 9]

문제 1

답 (2)

해설 본문은 첫 번째 문장에서 문제 제기로 시작하고 있다. 일반적으로 문제 제기는 그 단락의 주제(제목)로 작용하고, 거기에 대한 답변이 글쓴이가 다루고자 하는 중심 내용(Main Idea)이 된다. 문제 제기로 시작하는 전형적인 'G – S'의 구조를 취하면서 본문에선 나열(Listing)의 전개 방법을 취하고 있다. 뒷받침 문장이 전개되는 구체적 진술에서 시그널을 찾아 글의 전체적인 흐름을 따라가면 쉽게 두 번째 답도 추론해낼 수 있다.

* 글의 전체적 구성

주제문	Aristotle's theories might be intrinsically gendered and sexist.
뒷받침 문장	For example, 뒷받침 문장 1
	(Another example), 뒷받침 문장 1
	Finally, 뒷받침 문장 1

문제 2

답 (4)

해설 위 글의 구성을 보면, '주제문(Topic Sentence) – 뒷받침 문장(Supporting Sentence)'으로 구성되고 뒷받침 문장은 나열을 통해서 전개되고 있다. 주제문(T)과 뒷받침 문장(S)의 관계는 쉽게 말해 'T = S'라고 볼 수 있는데 이는 뒷받침 문장은 항상 주제문과 같은 맥락에서 해석이 되어야 한다는 말이다. 또한 글의 통일성에 따라 뒷받침 문장은 모두 주제문과 같은 맥락에서 전개되기에, 'S1 = S2 = S3'가 된다. 즉, 주어진 세 예문이 모두 같은 맥락에서 해석되어야 하기에, 아리스토텔레스가 노예 제도와 여성의 불평등이 존재하는 아테네의 현 상태를 정당화시키는 쪽으로 전개되어야 전체 글의 통일성을 깨지 않게 된다.

해설 아리스토텔레스의 이론이 내재적으로 한쪽 성에 치우쳐 성차별적인가? 그래서 이론 자체를 수정하지 않는 이상 성차별을 제거할 수 없는가? 여러 페미니스트 철학자들이 이러한 논제를 발전시켰다. 예를 들자면, "Woman Is Not a Rational Animal"에서 Lynda Lange는 주장하길 아리스토텔레스의 성별 이론은 아리스토텔레스가 사용한 형이상학적 용어에 모두 포함되어 있으며, 그녀는 "아리스토텔레스의 성차별 이론이 철학 전반의 상태에 대한 고찰 없이 단순히 제거될 수 있는지는 분명하지 않다."고 결론을 지었다. Elizabeth Spelman은 아리스토텔레스의 정치 형이상학은 그의 영혼 이론에 반영되어 있는데, 다시 이것은 정치에서

여성의 복종을 정당화하는데 사용된다고 주장했다. 그리고 마지막으로 Susan Okin은 아리스토텔레스의 형상 기능 이론은 아리스토텔레스가 노예와 여성의 불평등을 포함한 아테네의 정치적 현 상태를 합법화하기 위해서 고안한 것이라고 주장했다.

어 휘

intrinsically *ad.* 본질적으로
metaphysical *a.* 형이상학의
jargon *n.* (동업자·동일 집단 내의) 특수 용어
reflection *n.* 숙고, 심사; 반사, 반영
subordination *n.* 예속시킴; 종속시키기; 경시; 하위
functionalist *a.* 기능주의의
status quo *n.* 현재의 상황

적인 결과가 모두 나오는 것을 보고, 이 이론을 통해서 '정체성 위기'라는 용어를 이끌어 낸다.

어 휘

psychology *n.* 심리학
Psychoanalytic *a.* 정신 분석의
Sigmund Freud 프로이드 (오스트리아의 정신분석학자·의학자; 1856-1939)
psychosexual *a.* 성심리의   **sexual impulse** 성충동
psychosocial *a.* 심리사회적인

[Challenge 10]

문제 1

답 (2)

해설 본문은 Eric Erikson의 생애와 이론에 관한 간략한 설명으로 전기문에 해당한다. 일반적으로 전기의 글은 시간/공간의 흐름에 따른 'Order'의 전개 방법을 취한다. 본문에서 구체적인 연도와 장소의 이동이 있을 경우, 잘 확인해 두어야 내용 일치 문제에서 시간을 절약할 수 있다.

문제 2

답 (4)

해설 본문에서 Erikson이 Sigmund Freud와 다른 이론을 전개한 것은 맞지만, 서로 사이가 좋지 않다는 이야기를 발견할 수 없으며, 더욱이 Erikson은 Freud의 딸 밑에서 수학했다. 고로 보기 항 (1)과 (2)는 옳지 않은 설명이다. 본문에서 명백히 제시되지 않은 점을 이용하여 확대 해석하게 만든 경우로 조심해야 한다. 보기 항 (3)도 같은 맥락이다. 배경지식을 이용하여 '아마도 ~했을 것이다'라는 내용을 이끌어내어 답을 고를 경우 모두 오답이 된다. 보기 항 (4)는 본문 마지막 문장에서 확인할 수 있다.

해석 Erik Erikson은 독일의 프랑크푸르트에서 태어났으며, Vienna Psychoanalytic Institute에서 Anna Freud(프로이드의 딸) 아래서 심리학을 수학했다. 그는 미국으로 이주해 1939년 미국 시민권자가 되고, 거기서 하버드, 예일 그리고 버클리를 포함한 여러 주요 대학에서 교수직을 역임했다. 그는 아동 심리학에 관한 글로 아주 정평이 나 있다. 그는 Freud의 성/심리 발달의 단계와 아주 유사한 단계 이론을 펼치지만, 성적 충동 측면보다는 Erikson의 경우 발달의 사회적 측면에 더욱 관심을 두었다. 그는 인간의 수명을 8단계로 나눈 정신사회 발달 이론을 전개했다. 그는 각 발달 단계에 위기를 조성하면서, 단계마다 부정적이거나 긍정

Day 27

[Challenge 1]

문제 1

답 (1)

해설 이 글은 순서를 베열하는 문제이다. 일반적으로 각 단락의 첫 번째 문장에 힌트가 있다. 두 번째 문장과 세 번째 문장을 먼저 살펴보자.

> The Pyramids, <u>for instance</u>, those huge piles that are still the wonder of the world, were far older than any building now standing in Europe, before Joseph was sold to be a slave in Potiphar's house.
>
> <u>But besides that</u>, it is a land which has a most strange and wonderful story of its own.

빨간 색으로 밑줄 친 접속사(구)를 보았을 때 알 수 있는 사실은 이것으로 시작하는 두 문단 모두 글의 첫 번째 문단에 해당하지 않는다는 것이다(우선 잠정적이긴 하지만 임의적인 순서를 먼저 짜내는 것이 우선이다. 그 이후 다른 문단과의 관계를 고려해서, 틀릴 경우 다시 순서를 정하도록 한다). 그러므로, 보기 항목 (1)만이 (a)로 시작하는 점으로 보아 (1)이 답일 가능성이 크다. (c)에서 (b)로 넘어가는 힌트는 (c)의 마지막에 이집트의 'great temples and tombs'를 소개하고 있으며, 이에 대한 구체적인 예로 (b)에서 피라미드를 언급하고 있다. 이후 잠정적인 글의 순서에 따라 글을 읽으면서 글의 통일성과 응집성에 맞게 잘 구성되어 있는지 생각하면서 답을 선정하도록 한다.

문제 2

답 (2)

해설 본문은 유명한 고대 도시인 이집트의 흥미로운 특징을 소개하는 글이다. 보기 항목 (2)가 가장 적절하다. 이런 글의 구조는 일반적으로 다음의 패턴을 따른다.

```
but 주제문 제시

┌─────────────┐
│ 뒷받침 문장  │
└─────────────┘
```

일반적으로 'but'을 기점으로 글쓴이가 궁극적으로 밝히고자 하는 '주제 + 요지'가 드러난 주제문이 제시되고, 이후 뒷받침 문장이 전개되는 'G – S'의 형태 중 하나이다. 일반적으로 대조의 글에서 종종 발견된다.

문제 3

답 (3)

해설 른 나라 사람들은 이집트의 몇 백 년 된 흥미로운 건물을 보고 놀라움을 금치 못하는 반면, 이집트 사람들은 이것을 거의 새 건물로 취급한다고 했다. 바로 뒤에 이어 나오는 내용에서 알 수 있듯이 이들은 수천 년의 역사를 가진 건물들이 많기 때문이다. 이러한 맥락에서 빈칸에 들어갈 표현을 골라야 한다. 순접의 'and'를 감안하면, 바로 앞의 표현과 같은 맥락 안에서 보기 항목을 골라야 하므로 '거의 새 건물이나 마찬가지여서 별로 신경을 쓰지 않는다.'는 표현이 가장 적절하다.

해석 만약 이 세상에서 가장 흥미로운 국가의 이름을 대라고 한다면, 나는 대부분 사람들이 팔레스타인이라고 말할 것으로 생각하는데, 이 나라 자체가 정말 멋지거나 해서 그런 것이 아니라 여기서 발생했던 위대한 일들 때문이며, 무엇보다 예수님이 탄생한 곳이기 때문이다. 그러나 팔레스타인 다음으로 내가 생각할 수 있는 나라는 바로 이집트이다. 우선, 이집트는 구약의 모든 아름다운 이야기에서 팔레스타인과 아주 밀접한 관련이 있는데, 이 구약은 우리에게 이집트의 총독이 되는 노예 소년인 요셉의 이야기와 파라오 집안의 왕자가 되는 히브리인 모세 그리고 이스라엘 자손들의 위대한 탈출의 이야기를 들려준다.

그러나 이것 말고도 그 자체로 아주 이상하고도 놀라운 이야기를 가지고 있는 땅이다. 다른 어떤 나라도 (이 나라만큼) 위대한 왕, 현인 그리고 용감한 군인의 유구한 역사를 가진 나라도 없다. 그리고 다른 어느 나라에서도 이집트에는 그렇게 많은, 아름답고 놀라운 위대한 건축물들에 비견할 만한 것을 볼 수 없다. 이 나라에는 오랜 역사를 가진 흥미로운 건축물이 있는데, 사람들은 오륙백 년 또는 그 이상 오래된 성당과 성을 보기 위해 먼 길을 마다하지 않고 간다. 그러나 이집트에선 이 정도 역사의 건축물은 거의 새것이나 다름이 없으며, 어느 누구도 이러한 것에는 그리 관심을 보이지 않는다. 왜냐하면 이집트의 많은 사원과 무덤은 정확하게 말하면 성경에서 언급되고 있는 시기보다 약 몇백 년 전의 것이기 때문이다.

예를 들어, 여전히 세계의 불가사의인 피라미드는 엄청나게 거대한 건축물로, 유럽에 현재 서 있는 어떠한 빌딩보다도 훨씬 오래되었으며, 이것은 요셉이 보디발의 집에 노예로 팔리기 전 시기이다. 그리스와 로마에 관한 이야기를 듣기 수백 년 전부터 이집트를 통치하던 위대한 왕들은 자신들의 군대를 시리아와 수단을 정복하기 위해 보내고, 함대를 보내어 미지의 남해를 탐험하게 했으며, 현인들은 우리가 여전히 읽을 수 있는 책을 썼다. 영국이 남해의 섬 주민들만큼이나 광폭하고 무지한 야만인만 살던 야생의 미지의 섬일 때, 이집트는 강대하고 고도로 문명화된 국가로, 웅장한 궁전과 사원이 있는 근사한 도시로 가득했고, 국민들도 현명하고 학식 있는 사람들이었다.

어휘

household n. 가정 **exodus** n. 탈출[이동]
pile n. 웅장한 건물; 쌓아둔 것, 더미
slave n. 노예, 종속장치
reigning a. 군림하는; 세도를 부리는
conquer v. 정복하다, 이기다
civilize v. 개화(교화)하게 하다, 세련되게 하다
cathedral n. 대성당

[Challenge 2]

문제 1

답 (4)

해설 교환(가치)에 대해 기존의 정의와 달리 글쓴이가 주장하는 새로운 정의를 밝히는 글이다.

문제 2

답 (2)

해설 전체 문맥을 감안하면서 빈칸이 들어간 문장과 앞뒤를 확인하고 답을 고르도록 한다.

> When it is said, "<u>Do this for me, and I will do that for you</u>," an exchange of _____(a)_____ is proposed.

밑줄 친 부분은 바로 용역과 용역의 교환으로 볼 수 있다. 따라서 보기 항목 (2)가 가장 적절하다.

문제 3

답 (2)

해설 해설 본문에서 교환 가치의 원리는 바로 용의 교환 안에 있다고 말하고 있다. 즉, 물건 교환은 단순히 물건을 건네주는 <u>물건 자체의 교환이 아니라 용역의 교환</u>으로 보고 있다.

해석 교환이란 정치 경제학의 주된 분야인데, 이는 이것이 이 학문 분야에서 다루는 법칙과 영향력에 대한 자유롭고 자발적인 합의에 따라, 소유물을 전달하는 데 가장 흔히 사용

되는 수단이기 때문이다. 정확히 말하면 교환은 서비스의 상호작용이다. 당사자들은 서로에게 "나에게 그걸 주면 내가 이걸 줄게" 또는 "이걸 해 주면, 내가 저걸 해 줄게"라고 말하는 것이다. 두 번째 형태가 첫 번째 형태에 항상 포함되어 있다고 말하는 것이 당연한 것이다(이는 이것이 가치의 개념을 새롭게 해석하는 것이기 때문이다). "나를 위해 이걸 해 주면 나는 그걸 해 줄게"라고 말하면, 서비스와 서비스의 교환이 제기되는 것이다. 다시 말해 "이걸 주면, 내가 저걸 줄게"라고 말하는 것은 "내가 한 것을 너에게 양도하고, 그 대신 네가 한 것을 나에게 양보하라"는 것과 동일한 것이다. 노동은 현재라기보다 과거이다. 그럼에도 교환은 두 서비스의 상대적 가치에 영향을 받는다. 그러므로 (교환) 가치의 원칙은 제품 자체에서가 아니라 교환된 제품을 위해 주고받은 서비스에 있다고 말하는 것이 맞는 말이다.

어휘

department n. (공공기관의) 부; 분야
reciprocity n. 상호성; 상호의 이익
labour n. 노동; 애씀
comparative a. 비교의, 비교적인, 상당한; 상대적인
valuation n. 평가; 가치평가

[Challenge 3]

문제 1

답 (2)

해설 척추를 잘 관리해야 함의 중요성을 알리는 글이다. 척추에 무리가 가는 행위를 했을 경우, 평생 어깨 또는 등이 굽은 상태로 살아갈 수 있다고 경고하고 있다.

문제 2

답 (2)

해설 보기 항 (2)와 본문의 내용을 같이 살펴보자.

> Bones have cushions in them. ≠ bones with cushions between them

즉, 뼈가 완충물을 가지고 있는 것이 아니라 뼈 사이에 완충물이 존재한다.

문제 3

답 (3)

해석 추는 작은 뼈로 이루어져 있고 사이에 완충물이 있어서 쉽게 구부러지는데, 아이들은 때로 지나치게 구부릴 때가 있다. 책을 읽거나 글을 쓸 때 또는 다른 일을 하면서 앞으로 기대면, 늘어나는 이 완충물이 안쪽 가장자리에서 압박을 받기에 원래 모양으로 다시 돌아오지 않을 수 있다. 이런

식으로 하면, 어깨나 등이 구부정해진다. 이렇게 구부리는 것은 또한 폐를 죄게 되어, 숨을 쉬는 데 필요한 공간을 확보 하지 못하게 된다. 어릴 때는, 뼈가 쉽게 구부러진다. 한 쪽 으로 삐딱하게 서면 한쪽 어깨나 엉덩이가 다른 쪽보다 높 게 된다. 이것은 더 심각한 것인데, 이는 자기도 모르게 삐뚤 게 자라게 되기 때문이다. 이제 뼈가 얼마나 부드러운지 그 래서 얼마나 쉽게 구부러지는지 알았으니 똑바로 앉고 서는 것에 주의를 기울여야 한다. 평생 어깨나 등이 구부정한 재 로 아니면 절름발이인 채로 살지 않고, 곧고 우아한 사람으로 자라고 싶을 테니 말이다. 다리나 팔 또는 어깨를 꼬지 마라.

어 휘

spine *n.* 척추 **cushion** *n.* 완충물 **lean** *v.* 기대다
elastic *a.* 탄력(성)있는
round-shouldered *a.* 등[어깨]이 굽은[구부정한]
hump *n.* (등허리) 군살 **cramp** *a.* 답답한, 비좁은
hip *n.* 엉덩이 **unevenly** *ad.* 평탄하지 않게, 울퉁불퉁하게
crook *v.* 구부리다 *n.* 굽은 것 **lame** *a.* 절름발이의

[Challenge 4]

문제 1

답 (2)

해설 우리가 보통 '피는 못 속인다'라는 말을 하는 것과 마찬가지로 영어로 'It runs in the family'라고 표현한다. 즉, 본문의 'run in families'는 '유전적,' 또는 '생물학적'이란 말과 같은 표현으로 사용되고 있다.

문제 2

답 (3)

해설 빈칸 뒤에 나오는 'That is' 즉, 재진술의 표현을 통해서 빈칸의 내용에 무엇이 들어가면 가장 적절한지 생각한다. 'That is' 이후의 내용은 바로 앞에서 진술된 내용과 반대의 상황을 전개하고 있다.

해석 어떤 종류의 우울증은 가족 내 유전되는 것으로, 우 울증에 대한 생물학적 취약성이 유전될 수 있다는 것을 드러 낸 다. 이것은 특히나 조울증의 경우 더욱 그러한 듯하다. 각 세 대의 가족구성원이 조울증을 앓은 가족을 연구했다. 이 연구 를 통해서 조울증을 앓고 있는 가족구성원은 조울증을 앓고 있지 않은 가족과 약간은 다른 유전자 구성을 가진 것을 알 아냈다. 그러나 반대의 경우는 사실이 아니었다. 다시 말해 조울증에 걸리기 쉬운 유전자 구성을 가진 모든 이가 다 조 울증에 걸리는 것은 아니다. 분명 스트레스를 많이 받는 환 경이라든가 하는 추가적 요소가 조울증의 출현과 관련되며, 보호 요소가 그 예방에 관련된다.

어 휘

vulnerability *n.* 상처받기 쉬움
bipolar *a.* 조울증의
inherit *v.* (유전적으로) 물려받다
makeup *n.* 구성, 조립
apparently *ad.* 보아하니
onset *n.* 시작
protective *a.* 보호하는
prevention *n.* 예방, 방지

[Challenge 5]

문제 1

답 (1)

해설 바로 앞에서 종교는 문관의 사법권 밖에 있다는 표현 을 하면서 비유적으로 개인이 국가의 간섭 밖에 있다는 논리 로 전개하고 있다. 따라서 보기 항 (1)이 가장 적절하다.

문제 2

답 (4)

해설 보기 항 (4)의 경우 본문의 다음 내용과 일치하지 않는다.

> The toleration extended to all others is denied to papists and to atheists; and his <u>inconsistency</u> in this respect has been often and severely criticized.

문제 3

답 (4)

해설 다음 본문에서 보기 항 (4)가 틀린 진술임을 알 수 있다.

> it is clear that Locke made the exception not for religious reasons <u>but on grounds of state policy</u>.

일반적으로 극단적/강조 부사 (solely)가 나올 경우 본문과의 일치성을 잘 확인해야 한다.

해석 Locke에 따르면 교회는 '자유롭고 자발적인 사회단체' 이며, 이것의 목적은 하나님에 대한 공적 예배이다. 예배의 가치는 예배로 인도하는 믿음에 달려 있다. "진정한 종교 의 모든 생명과 힘은 내적이며 온전한 마음의 설득이다." 그 리고 이러한 문제는 온전히 문관의 사법권 밖에 존재한 다. 그러므로 Locke는 (이후 언어로 말한다면) 종교에 주체 적이 있는데, 마치 그가 국가 간섭의 문제에 개인주의적 관 점을 취한 것과 마찬가지다. 그러나 그가 종교 문제에서 개 인주의 입장을 취하는 것에도 예외는 있었다. 모두에게 미 치는 종교적인 관용은 가톨릭 신자 (papist)와 무신론자들 에게는 허락 되지 않았다. 따라서 그의 모순은 이러한 면에 서 자주 심각 하게 비판받았다. 그러나 Locke가 종교적 이 유가 아니 라 국 가 정책적 동기에서 예외를 두었다는 것은 분명하 다. 그는 로마 가톨릭을 사회의 안정에 위험한 것으

로 보았는데, 이는 그가 외국 왕자에게 충성을 공언했기 때문이다. 그리고 무신론자들을 배제했는데, 이는 Locke의 견해에서 마치 모든 도덕적 법은 하나님의 의지에 달린 것과 같이 국가의 존재는 계약과 그 계약의 의무를 따른다고 보았기 때문이다.

어휘

- **voluntary** *a.* 자발적인, 임의적인
- **inspire** *v.* 고무하다, 영감을 주다
- **religion** *n.* 종교
- **consist** *v.* (~로) 이루어져 있다
- **inward** *a.* 마음속의, 내심의
- **jurisdiction** *n.* 관할권, 사법권
- **magistrate** *n.* 치안 판사
- **doctrine** *n.* 교리, 신조, 정책
- **toleration** *n.* 용인, 관용
- **papist** *n.* 가톨릭 신자
- **atheist** *n.* 무신론자
- **inconsistency** *n.* 불일치, 모순
- **severely** *ad.* 심하게, 엄하게
- **on ground of** ~의 이유로, 구실 핑계로
- **profess** *v.* 주장하다, 공언하다
- **allegiance** *n.* 충성

[Challenge 6]

문제 1

답 (4)

해설 보기 항 (4)와 같이 모든 인종이 자신의 출생 배경과 관련없이 모두 학교에 갔다는 사실을 본문만으로 추론할 수는 없다.

해석 아메리카 대륙의 발견과 동인도 제도로 향하는 바닷길이 열려 무역과 탐험의 새로운 지평이 열렸다. 그러나 지적 분야에서는 훨씬 더 광대한 지평이 시야에 들어왔다. 과거의 협소한 한쪽에 치우친 편협함은 불가능하게 되었다. 진실에 도달하기 위해선 모든 과거의 장벽을 무너뜨려야 했다. 모든 혁명적 시대와 마찬가지로 이 시기에는 앎에 대한 불타는 욕구가 있었다.

어휘

- **horizon** *n.* 수평선, 지평선
- **barrier** *n.* 울타리, 장벽, 장애
- **revolutionary** *a.* 혁명의, 혁명적인
- **epoch** *n.* 시대; 신기원

[Challenge 7]

문제 1

답 (2)

해설 본문에서 개인의 시민권과 참정권이 신에게 부여받은 인간의 권리라고 주장한 Locke와 달리 현대는 다른 이의 권리를 존중하는 한 자율적 인간이란 전제 아래 개인의 시민 권과 참정권을 주장하고, 이러한 자율적 인간이란 관점에서 다른 이에게(예를 들어 국회에) 직업, 교육 등에 대해서 요구할 근거가 없다고 말하고 있다.

문제 2

답 (3)

해설 보기 항 (3)과 같이 극단적인 표현 (under any situation)은 오답일 가능성이 크다. 본문에서 조건이 제시되고 있다.

> so long as I similarly respect the civil and political rights of all others

문제 3

답 (4)

해설 바로 앞의 선행사가 'gap'이라는 것을 놓쳐서 안 된다.

> a logical gap here, which no one has successfully ____(a)____ yet

gap과 말뭉치를 이루는 동사는 'bridge'이다.

해설 Locke의 경우 시민권과 참정권은 신으로부터의 선물로 인간에게 생긴 것이었다. 그러나 하나님은 오늘날 1세대의 권리의 정당화를 위해 좀처럼 인용되지 않는다. 대신 이런 권리는 인간이 근본적으로 자율적 인간이라는 관점에 기초한다. 그리고 만약 근본적으로 자율적 인간이라 한다면, 다른 모든 상황이 같을 경우 국가 또는 어느 누구도 내가 다른 모든 이의 시민권과 참정권을 동일하게 존중하는 한 나 자신의 목적과 수단을 선택하는 자유를 제한할 수 없다는 나의 요구를 이해하고 인식하기가 쉽다. 그러나 어떠한 근거에서 자율적 인간이 다른 자율적 인간에게서 제2세대의 권리인 직업, 건강 보험 또는 교육을 요구할 수 있는가? 여기에는 논리적 간격이 존재하며 어느 누구도 성공적으로 이것을 메우지 못했다. 자율적 인간이라는 단순한 전제에서 내가 고용의 권리가 있다는 결론을 이끌어 내지 못한다. 그 이상의 무엇이 필요하지만 근본적으로 자율적 인간으로서 인간의 관점과 충돌하지 않는 그것이 어떤 것인지는 분명하지가 않다.

어 휘

accrue v. 저절로 생기다   **invoke** v. 기원하다; (신 등을) 부르다
autonomous a. 독립적인   **essentially** ad. 본질적으로
appreciate v. 인식하다, 잘 이해하다
ceteris paribus (=other things being equal) 다른 사정이 같다면
abridge v. 단축하다   **conflict** v. 충돌하다, 대립하다

[Challenge 8]

문제 1

답 (1)

해설 'Most publicly-held companies will file under Chapter 11 rather than Chapter 7 because they can still run their business and control the bankruptcy process.'에서 보기 항 (1)을 추론할 수 있다.

해석 연방 파산법은 기업이 파산하거나 심각한 부채에서 회사가 어떻게 회복하는지를 관리한다. 빚이 있는 부도 회사는 파산법 11조항을 이용하여 사업을 '재조정'하고 다시 이윤을 내려고 시도한다. 회사는 그날그날의 사업 운영을 지속 하지만, 기업의 주된 결정은 파산 법원의 승인을 받아야 한다. 대부분의 공기업은 조항 7보다는 조항 11에 준해 신청하는데, 이는 사업도 할 수 있고 파산 절차도 제어할 수 있기 때문이다. 이는 11조항의 경우 쓰러져 가는 회사를 재건하는 절차를 마련해주기 때문이다. 때로 회사가 수익성 회복을 위한 계획을 성공적으로 수행하는 경우도 있지만, 결국 도산하는 경우도 있다. 11조항에 따른 재조정 아래 회사는 일반적으로 사업을 계속 유지하고, 주식과 채권은 주식 시장에서 계속 거래가 되기도 한다.

| 참고 사항 |

정치/경제 지문에 종종 나오는 용어이니 반드시 알아두도록 한다.

챕터 7(Chapter 7)

챕터 7은 한국말로 '청산'으로 표현할 수 있으며, 파산 처리 에 관 한 유형 중 가장 일반적인 형태이다. 챕터 7을 결정하게 되면, 정해진 규정(Chapter 7 of the Title 11 of the United States Code-Bankruptcy Code)에 의해 미국 법이 정하는 파산법(the bankruptcy laws of the United States)에 따른 청산(liquidation)의 절차를 진행하게 된다. 챕터 7에 들어가게 되면, 사업은 중단되고 모든 자산을 매각 하여 채권자들에게 그 순위에 따라 분배하게 된다. 법원은 채 무의 일부 혹은 전체를 면제할 수 있으며, 청산으로 남은 자 산은 채권의 순위에 따라 분배하고, 남은 부분이 회사의 주 인, 즉 주주에게 돌아가게 된다. 남은 자산이 채무보다 적을 경우 주주에게 돌아가는 것은 아무것도 없게 되는데, 만약 청산을 하게 된 회사의 주식을 가지고 있다 면, 말 그대로 휴지 조각이 될 수도 있는 것이다.

챕터 11(Chapter 11)

반면, 챕터 11은 한국말로 '관리 대상'에 가깝다. 챕터 11은 미국 파산법에 따라 채권자의 권리 순서를 재구성하는 규정이다. 챕터 11을 진행하더라도, 대부분의 경우에 채무자들(debtor)은 경영을 할 수 있으나, 모든 것은 법원의 감시와 지도를 받게 된다. 챕터 11 신청 이후에, 채무자가 회생 방안에 대한 계획을 우선 제안하게 되고, 이후에 채권자들도 회생 방안을 제안할 수 있다. 양측의 제안은 모두 법원에서 승인된 규정을 만족해야 하며, 부채의 우선권 조정은 채무자들의 승인을 위한 투표를 거쳐야만 한다. 투표가 부결될 경우, 법원은 챕터 7로 전환하거나 아니면 파산 신청 이전의 상태로 운영을 계속하게 할지를 채무자의 이익을 우선으로 고려하여 결정하게 된다.

어 휘

Federal bankruptcy laws 연방 파산 법
go out of business 폐업하다, 파산하다
crippling debt (회사를) 불구로 만들 정도로 쓰러지게 하는 빚
management n. 경영
day-to-day business operations 그날그날의 기업 운영
file under Chapter 11 챕터 11을 신청하다
be approved by ~에 의해서 승인되다
rehabilitate v. 재건하다, 원상태로 되돌리다, 복원하다
faltering a. 쓰러져 가는
return to profitability 이윤을 내는 상태로 돌아가다
liquidate v. 파산하다   **securities markets** 주식시장
stock and bonds 주식과 채권

[Challenge 9]

문제 1

답 (1)

해설 아이는 특정 물건에 대해서 처음 찾았던 자리에 그 물건이 옮겨진 것을 보았음에도 그 자리에 있을 것(대상 영속 성)이 라 고 생각한다. 이러한 맥락을 가장 잘 표현한 문장은 보기 (1)이다.

해석 A—not—B 오류는 아이의 인지발달 이론을 전개한 피 아제의 연구에 의해서 밝혀진 현상이다. A—not—B 오류 는 감각운동기 내 4단계 시기에 유아가 범하는 특정한 오류 를 말한다. 일반적인 실험은 다음과 같이 진행된다. 실험자 는 아이의 손이 닿는 곳에 있는 박스 A 아래 좋아하는 장난 감을 숨긴다. 아이는 장난감을 찾으면서 박스 A 아래를 보 고는 장난감을 찾는다. 이 행위를 여러 차례 반복적으로 실행 한다(항 상 실험자가 박스 A 아래 장난감을 숨기면서). 그런 다음, 'critical trial'에서 실험자는 박스 B 아래로 장난감을 옮기는 데 이 역시 아이의 손이 닿는 곳에 놓는다. 10개월 이하의 유아의 경우 일반적으로 인내 실수

(perseverance error)를 범하는데, 이것은 아이들이 실험자가 박스 B 아래로 장난감을 움직이는 것을 보았고, 박스 B 또한 A처럼 손에 닿을 만큼 가까이 있음에도 불구하고 박스 A 아래를 살펴본다는 의미다. 이것은 아이가 대상 영속성의 선험적 도식이 없거나 불완전함을 드러낸다. 12개월 이상의 아이들은 일반적으로 이러한 실수를 하지 않는다.

어휘

cognitive *a.* 인식의   infant *n.* 유아
sensorimotor *a.* 감각운동적인   experimenter *n.* 실험자
attractive *a.* 마음을 끄는   perseverance *n.* 끈기
demonstrate *n.* 증명하다, 보여주다
incomplete *a.* 불완전한   schema *n.* 도식; 윤곽
object permanence 대상 영속성

purge *v.* 깨끗이 하다   excessive *a.* 과도한
immutable *a.* 변경할 수 없는
congeal 얼(리)다, 응결시키다[하다]; 굳히다(고기·생선 기름 따 위); 생기를 잃게 하다(사상 따위) 예) Fear congealed my blood. 무서워서 피가 얼어붙는 듯했다.

[Challenge 10]

문제 1

답 (1)

해설 범죄에 대한 기존과는 다른 Durkheim의 새로운 관점을 다루고 있다.

문제 2

답 (4)

해설 Durkheim은 범죄가 사회 정화의 기능이 있다는 측면에서 개혁의 전조로 유용하게 작용할 수 있다는 말은 했지만, 이것을 '범죄 장려'라는 의미로 말하고 있진 않다. 보기 항 (4)는 틀린 표현이다.

해석 범죄에 대한 Durkheim의 관점은 전통적 개념과는 전혀 다른 것이었다. 그는 범죄가 사회생활의 근본적인 조건들과 관련이 있고 사회적인 역할을 수행한다고 믿었다. 그가 말하길 범죄란 "이것은 필요한 변화에 열려있을 뿐 아니라 특정 경우 이것은 직접적으로 이러한 변화를 제안하며, 범죄는 그런 의미에서 개혁의 유용한 전조가 된다." 이러한 의미에서 그는 범죄를 특정한 사회적 긴장감을 완화시키는 작용을 하는 것으로 보았으며, 그래서 사회 정화작용의 기능을 지닌다고 보았다. 그는 나아가 "도덕적 양심의 권위를 지나치게 신봉해서는 안 된다. 그렇지 않으면 어느 누구도 이것을 감히 비판하려 하지 않게 되며, 이것은 너무 쉽게 바꿀 수 없는 형태로 굳어져 버릴 것이다. 진보하기 위해, 개인의 독창성은 반드시 표현될 수 있어야 한다. 심지어 범죄의 독창성조차도 표현될 수 있어야 한다."

어휘

bound up with ~와 묶다
fundamental condition 기본적인 조건
state *n.* 상태
imply *v.* 함축하다   prelude *n.* 전주곡

Day 28

[Challenge 1]

문제 1

답 (2)

해설 보기 항 (1)은 각 경제 주체가 정부에서 할당한 CO2 양보다 많은 양을 배출했을 때(CO2 양을 줄이지 못했을 때) 세금을 부과한다고 나와 있다. 보기 항 (3)의 내용은 본문만으로 알 수 없다. 보기 항 (4)는 본문에 언급이 나와 있지 않을뿐더러 생산 비용의 증가가 어떤 요인에 의해서 발생했는지에 대한 설명도 없기에 보기 항과 같은 영향을 회사에 미칠지 알 수가 없다.

문제 2

답 (1)

해설 부 규제의 'command and control'은 본문에서 다루는 시장 경제 안에서 탄소량을 기업 활동에 참여하는 주체가 스스로 결정하게 하는 것과 대조적인 성격을 띠어야 한다. 그러므로 '규범적인, 이미 정해진'이란 'prescriptive'가 가장 적절하며, 두 번째 빈칸의 경우 역접의 'while'을 활용한다. 앞에서 경제 주체는 자신이 배출하는 탄소를 줄이는 데 비용이 덜 드는 곳은 과감히 삭감을 감행하되, 탄소의 양을 줄이는 것이 오히려 비용이 더 드는 곳은 허용하는 선택을 하게 된다.

해석 경제학자들은 규정된 "명령과 통제" 법규 대신 환경문제에 대처하기 위해서 탄소 무역과 같은 "시장을 기반"에 둔 도구를 사용하라고 주장한다. 명령과 통제를 통한 규제는 지역과 기술적 차이점에 융통적이지 않고 둔감하며 비효율적이라는 측면에서 비판을 받는다. 그러나 탄소 무역은 배출량을 효과적으로 줄이기 위해 한계 설정이 필요하고, 그 한계가 정부의 규제 메커니즘이 된다. 이 한계가 정부의 정치적 과정을 통해 상정이 된 뒤, 개인 회사들은 그들이 배출량을 어떻게 줄일지 또는 줄이지 안 줄일지를 자유롭게 선택하게 된다. 배출량을 줄이지 못하면 종종 정부의 규제 메커니즘에 의해 처벌을 받는데, 생산 비용을 증가시키는 벌금으로 치러진다. 회사는 오염 규제를 만족하면서 가장 적은 비용으로 생산하는 방법을 추구하기 때문에, 비용을 최소화할 수 있는 해결책이 있으면 비용 삭감으로 이어지겠지만, 줄이는 데 비용이 더 들면 탄소 배출을 허용하게 된다.

어휘

geographical *a.* 지리적인
technological *a.* 공업의, 기술의
inefficient *a.* 효과 없는, 무능한
cap *n.* 상한, 최고한도
mechanism *n.* 기계, 기구, 장치
punishable *a.* 벌 줄 수 있는, 처벌할만한

[Challenge 2]

문제 1

답 (4)

해설 본문에서 실존주의자들은 시만큼이나 글로 표현하지 않는 예술 양식(non-discursive arts)을 인간의 지혜를 표현하기에 적합하지 않다고 했다.

> the other non-discursive arts attract almost as little interest as poetry.

문제 2

답 (4)

해설 본문에서 실존주의자들은 색상과 소리를 가지고 만든 예술작품의 경우 이상적 내용이 그 작품의 물질성에 그대로 갇혀 있어, 인간의 자유를 표현하기에 적합하지 않다고 했다.

> Rather, the ideal content in non-linguistic art-forms remains trapped in the materiality of the artwork.

즉, 비언어적 예술 양식에서 사용된 색상과 소리와 인간의 자유를 표현하는 도구인 언어는 서로 같은 것이 아니라는 보기 항 (4)가 실존주의자들의 관점을 가장 잘 드러낸다.

해석 시에 대한 실존주의자들의 관심 부족(사르트르의 경우 특히나 철저하게 거부한다)은 시인들이 언어 사용을 오도한다는 관점에 기반한다. 동일한 이유에서, 다른 비담론적 예술도 시만큼이나 거의 관심을 끌지 못한다. 그러나 이것들을 논의할 때는, 시보다는 더 호의적으로 다뤄지는데, 이는 이것이 언어를 도구로 사용하지 않기 때문이며, 이는 시에 대한 비난과 관련성이 없게 되기 때문이다. 인간의 자유를 표현하는 탁월한 도구로서 언어를 강조하는 것은 이미 헤겔의 미학의 핵심에 존재하는 고전적 주장을 재현한다(실존주의자들은 잘 인식하고 있는 사실). 여기에는 다른 예술들이 이상적인 내용, 의미, 아름다움을 생산하고 전달할 수는 있지만, 언어적 표현만큼 분명하게 접근할 수 없다는 뜻이 함축되어 있다. 오히려, 비언어적 예술 형태에 포함된 이상적 내용은 예술작품의 물질성에 갇혀 있게 된다. 모양(note), 색상, 그리고 형태는 기호가 아니다. 이것은 그 자체 외부에 어떤 것도 지칭하지 않는다. 메를로 퐁티가 인식의 현상학(The Phenomenology of Perception)에서 지적

한 바와 같이, "그것 안에 거하는 아주 희미한 작은 의미는 내재해 있거나 안개와 같이 진동할 뿐이다. 이것은 색상 또는 소리이다."

어휘

existentialist *n.* 실존주의자   dismissal *n.* 묵살, 일축; 해고
misguided *a.* 오도된, 미혹된
discursive *a.* 산만한, 만연한, 종잡을 수 없는; 광범위한
favourably *ad.* 호의적으로
accusation *n.* 비난, 규탄
irrelevant *a.* 부적절한; 무관계한
aesthetics *n.* 미학(美學)
transparently *ad.* 투명하게, 명료하게
Phenomenology *n.* 현상학   dim *a.* 흐릿한; 어스레한
dwell *v.* 살다, 거주하다   immanent *a.* 내재하는
tremble *v.* 떨다, 전율하다

[Challenge 3]

문제 1

답 (2)

해설 본문은 역병이 발생했을 때, 사람들이 어떻게 반응했는지에 대해 대조적인 글 전개 방법(some – others – many others 또는 still others)으로 기술하고 있다.

문제 2

답 (4)

해설 빈칸 문제는 앞뒤 문맥을 잘 파악한 후 가장 적절한 표현을 골라내야 한다. 역병으로 인해 많은 사람이 자신의 집을 버렸기에 사람들이 마음대로 남의 집에 들어가서 사용할 수 있다고 했다. 따라서 집이 '공동 소유'가 되었다는 보기 항 (4)가 가장 적절하다.

해석 어떤 이는 중용의 삶과 과도한 모든 생활을 회피하면 이런 역병(혹사병)에서 자신을 보호할 수 있을 것이라 생각했다. 이들은 소(小)공동체를 조직하여 다른 사람들과 완전히 따로 떨어져 살았다. 이들은 병에 걸릴 일이 없는 집에만 틀어박혀 아주 적절한 양의 가장 좋은 음식을 먹고, 최상의 와인을 마셨으며, 죽음과 병에 관한 소식을 듣거나 이야기하지 않았으며, 음악을 듣거나 이와 비슷한 유희를 즐기며 시간을 보냈다. 다른 이는 이와 전혀 반대의 생각을 했다. 이들은 역병에 대한 확실한 치료법은 마시고, 노래하며, 웃고 즐기는 것이며, 온갖 욕구를 맘껏 풀고, 일어났던 사건에 웃고 농담을 하는 것이라고 생각했다. 이들은 자신의 말을 실천에 옮겨 밤낮으로 이 술집 저 술집을 오가며 무절제하게 술을 마시거나 다른 집에 가 이들을 기쁘게 할 그러한 행위만을 했다. 이들이 이런 일들을 쉽게 할 수 있었던 이유는 누구나 죽을 운명으로 느끼고 자신의 가옥을 이미 버린 상태이기 때문에, 대부분의 집은 공동 소유가 되었으며, 누구든 그 집에 들어가 자신의 집인 마냥 사용했기 때문이다. 그리고 이 모든 무절제한 행위를 통해 이들은 가능한 한 병을 회피하려고 했다. 또한 많은 다른 이는 위에서 기술한 두 방법의 중간의 삶을 선택했다. 이들은 음식을 전자만큼이나 제한하지 않는 동시에 후자만큼 방탕히 먹지 않으면서 적절하게 즐겼다. 이들은 집에 갇혀 지내지 않고, 밖으로 돌아다니며 손에 꽃 또는 향기가 나는 허브 또는 향수를 들고 다녔는데, 이는 이러한 냄새가 뇌를 편안하게 하기에 아주 좋다는 믿음에서였다. 이들이 그렇게 한 이유는 대기가 온통 시체와 병자들과 약 냄새로 오염되었기 때문이다.

어휘

superfluity *n.* 여분, 과다   tavern *n.* 선술집; 여인숙(inn)
immoderately *ad.* 무절제하게
doomed *a.* 운이 다한, 불운의
bestial *a.* 짐승의, 짐승과 같은; 흉포한, 야만스런, 잔인한; 상스러운
midway *a., ad.* 중도의[에], 중간 쯤의[에]
victual *n.* 음식, 양식   dissolute *a.* 방종한, 방탕한, 난봉피우는
perfume *n.* 향료, 향수; 냄새

[Challenge 4]

문제 1

답 (2)

해설 본문에서 남녀 교사 간의 봉급 차이를 없애고 동일한 봉급을 받게 되는 곳은 'Washington county'이며, 학교라는 공간에만 적용되는 이야기이다. 이를 미국 전역으로 확대하여 해석한 보기 항 (2)는 옳지 못하다.

문제 2

답 (4)

해설 remonstrate는 '항의하다, 불평하다'의 뜻이다.

문제 3

답 (3)

해설 아래 문맥을 살펴보자.

> She then refused to pay her taxes. Such was the respect for her in the community, and the sense of justice in regard to the teachers, that the authorities _____(b)_____ , and at the end of the year accepted the proposition

세금 내기를 거부한 그녀의 행위는 공동체 내 그녀에 대한 존중과

선생님과 관련된 정의감으로 받아들여졌다고 했다. 고로 당국은 그녀가 세금을 내지 않는 것을 말리지 않았을 것임을 추론할 수 있다.

해석 1837년 나의 아버지는 워싱턴 카운티의 Union township의 학교 위원회의 멤버로 여성의 동등한 봉급을 보장했다. 그리고 꾸준한 반대에도 불구하고 4년 동안 이것을 지켰다. 여름 학기를 가르친 여성은 겨울 학기를 가르친 남자와 동일한 봉급을 받았다. 아버지가 돌아가시고, 위원회는 다시 옛 제도로 돌아가 여성에게 봉급을 반만 주었다. 결과는 "무능한 선생님들"의 배출이었다. 이는 반대파들이 바라던 '여자는 학교 선생으로 적합하지 않다'는 핑계거리를 마련해 주었다. 어머니는 항의했지만 소용없었다. 그들은 "어떤 일에 대해서도 여자가 남자만큼 돈을 받은 적이 없었다"면서, 게다가 이런 학교 문제는 남자에게 해당하는 것이니 여자들은 참견할 권리가 없다는 답변을 했다. 1842년 어머니는 위원회가 공정하게 그녀의 봉급을 올려 준다면, 무료로 그 지역의 선생님에게 하숙을 제공하겠다고 제안했다. 이들은 비아냥거리면서 그녀의 제안을 받아들였다. 그런 다음 그녀는 세금을 내는 것을 거부했다. 사회에서의 그녀에 대한 신망이 두터웠고, 교사와 관련된 정의감도 인정받아서인지 당국은 세금 미납을 감수했고, 그 해 말에는 이 제안을 받아들였다. 그 이후 수년 동안 그녀는 그 지역의 선생님에게 하숙을 제공하며 그 여성의 순 급여가 남성의 봉급과 동등하게 유지되도록 했다.

어 휘

county *n.* 자치주   incompetent *a.* 무능한
furnish *v.* 제공하다   plea *n.* 변명, 핑계
remonstrate *v.* 항의[불평]하다
interfere *v.* 간섭하다, 참견하다
board *v.* 하숙을 제공하다   district *n.* 지구, 구역
gratis *ad.* 무료로, 거저   proportionally *ad.* 비례해서
proposition *n.* 제의; 일, 문제(과제)
scorn *n.* 경멸, 멸시

[Challenge 5]

문제 1

답 (1)

해설 일반적으로 문장의 순서를 맞추는 문제는 관사, 대명사, 접속사, 동사 등을 보고 힌트를 찾을 수 있다. 우선 각 문장의 앞쪽을 살펴보자. (가)에서 the New York(배)가 다른 배로 향해서 떠내려가다 배에 부딪힐 뻔한 긴박한 상황이 전개되고 있다. 우선 이런 구체적인 사건이 바로 드러나는 경우는 문단 처음에 오지 않는다. 보기 항 (4)는 우선 제외하고, (나)를 볼 경우 다른 항구에서 승객을 추가로 태웠다고 했는데, 앞에서 다른 여러 항구의 이름이 거론되는 곳(가)이 있어야 한다. (다)의 경우 큰 배(타이타닉)가 항구를 빠져나가기 전에 큰 불상사가 있었다고 말하고 있다. 당연히 이에 대한 구체적 설명이 따라야 한다. 이것에 대한 내용이 (라)에서 전개되고 있다. 고로 (다) - (라)임을 알 수 있다. 또한 'the American liner New York'과 'The New York'을 볼 때, 글쓴이는 특정 대상을 처음 소개할 때 Full Name(이름 전체)을 알려주고 이후 간략하게 표현한다는 것을 알 수 있다. 고로 (라) - (가)임을 알 수 있다.

문제 2

답 (1)

해설 (a)는 the American New York Liner를 가리키고, 나머지는 모두 타이타닉호를 지칭한다.

해석 그러나 이 거대한 배(타이타닉 호)에는 사우샘프턴 항구를 빠져나가기도 전에 불운한 기운이 감돌았다. 배가 물살의 흐름을 지나가면서, 이 엄청난 규모의 배는 압도적인 흡입력으로 물을 퍼올리다가 계류 중이던 New York 여객선에 구멍을 낼 뻔했다. 그러자 7개의 굵은 철 밧줄이 실처럼 끊어졌다. New York 선은 White Star 선 쪽으로 떠갔다. 만약 예인선인 Vulcan과 Neptune이 이 배를 멈춰 세워서 부두로 다시 끌고 오지 않았더라면 그새 배를 들이받고 말았을 것이다. 이 거대한 배가 Cherbourg를 거쳐 Queenstown에 기항했을 때 이 배는 다시금 열렬한 박수를 받았다. 수천 명의 사람들이 그 엄청난 크기에 경탄하며 바라보았다. 각 항구마다 손님들을 추가로 태운 뒤에 타이타닉호는 망망대해로 뱃머리를 돌려 첫 항해 기록을 위한 경주를 시작했다.

어 휘

ram *v.* (다른 차량, 선박 등을) 들이받다; 부딪치게 하다
tug *n.* 예인선
tow *v.* 끌다, (배·자동차를) 밧줄[사슬]로 끌다, 견인하다
quay *n.* 선창, 부두; 방파제
ovation *n.* 열렬한 (박수)
stupendous *a.* 엄청난, 굉장한; 거대한
immense *a.* 막대한(enormous, vast), 무한한, 헤아릴 수 없는; 광대한

[Challenge 6]

문제 1

답 (1)

해설 본문은 'G → S'를 취하는 전형적인 두괄식 글이다. 본문 첫 번째 문장이 주제문으로 중심 소재는 수학이 아니라 '수학의 역사'이다. 또한 주제는 '수학 역사의 유용성'이며, 이후 나열을 통해 그 유용성을 뒷받침 문장으로 제시하고 있다.

```
┌─────────────┐
│   주제문    │
│             │
│  뒷받침 문장 │
│    (나열)   │
│             │
└─────────────┘
```

문제 2

답 (1)

해설 문제 1에서도 설명했듯이, 두괄식의 'G → S'이다. 보기 항 (1)이 정답이다.

문제 3

답 (2)

해설 빈칸 문제를 푸는 방법은 다양하다. 본문의 전체적인 문맥에 따라 해석을 바탕으로 문제를 풀 수도 있지만, 글의 구조와 문장의 구조 및 주술관계를 통해서도 풀 수 있다. 여기서 두 가지 방법에 대해서 소개하는데, 우선 가장 빠른 풀이 방법부터 보자.

1) 특정 동사가 가지는 목적어: 빈칸이 들어간 문장을 보자.

> it discourages _____(a)_____ specialization on the part of investigators, by showing how apparently distinct branches have been found to possess unexpected connecting links

우선 보기 항에 들어가는 단어는 부정적인 어감을 전달해야 한다. 이는 본문에서 유용한 정보를 제공하는 '수학의 역사'가 주어(긍정)이고, 동사가 'discourages'이기에 목적어에 해당하는 단어는 부정적인 어감을 전달하는 단어가 와야 한다. 고로 보기 항에서 부정적인 어감을 전달하는 단어는 보기 항 (2)번뿐이다.

2) 두 번째 방법은 글의 전개 방법을 이용하는 것인데, 빈칸에 들어간 문장은 주제문의 뒷받침 문장에 해당한다. 중간에 but과 같은 역접의 접속사가 없으면 앞에서 전개된 뒷받침 문장과 같은 맥락에서 해석되어야 한다. 글의 전개 방법이 이미 익숙한 사람은 답을 쉽게 구할 수 있다.

해석 수학의 역사는 좋아할 만한 것뿐 아니라 교훈적이기도 하다. 이것은 우리에게 우리가 소유하고 있는 것을 상기해 줄 뿐 아니라 우리가 어떻게 우리의 저장고를 늘릴지에 대해서 가르쳐주기도 한다. De Morgan이 말하듯, 수학과 관련된 인간 정신의 초기 역사를 통해 우리가 범한 실수를 지적할 수 있다. 그리고 이러한 측면에서 수학의 역사에 관심을 두는 것은 마땅하다. 수학의 역사는 우리가 성급하게 결론에 이르는 것을 경고해 준다. 수학의 역사는 과학의 발전에 훌륭한 주석의 중요성을 지적한다. 이것은 연구하는 사람의 입장에서 보면, 표면상 뚜렷이 구별되는 분야가 뜻밖의 연결 고리를 가지고 있음을 보여줌으로써 과도한 전문화로 빠지는 것을 막아준다. 이것은 학생이 오래 전에 이미 해결되었을 문제에 시간과 에너지를 소모하는 것을 방지해 준다. 이것은 학생이 다른 과학자가 실패한 동일한 방법으로 해결하지 못한 문제를 풀려고 하는 시도를 막아 준다.

어 휘

instructive *a.* 교훈[교육]적인, 본받을 점이 많은; 메모, 주석
agreeable *a.* 기분 좋은, 마음에 드는
hasty *a.* 황급한, 조급한, 경솔한
notation *n.* 기호법, 표시법; 메모, 주석
discourage *v.* 용기를 잃게 하다(deject), 실망[낙담]시키다
specialization *n.* 특수화, 전문화

[Challenge 7]

문제 1

답 (1)

해설 본문은 첫 번째 문장에서 보다시피 '학습(learning)'의 정의를 시작으로 어떻게 행동주의가 형성되게 되었는지를 기술하고 있다. 이러한 행동주의가 미국의 주된 학적 주류가 되었다는 점과 대표적인 사상가를 함께 거론하고 있다. 이 글은 주로 '학습과 행동주의'에 관한 이야기를 다루고 있다.

문제 2

답 (2)

해설 빈칸에 들어갈 접속사를 넣는 문제이다. 일반적으로 접속사는 앞 문장과 접속사에 걸리는 문장과의 관계를 파악한다. 빈칸 이후의 진술은 바로 앞에 전개된 내용에 대한 재진술에 해당하므로 보기 항 (2)가 가장 적절하다.

문제 3

답 (4)

해설 내용일치 문제의 경우 본문을 읽을 때 중요 정보에 대한 표시를 미리 해 두지 않을 경우 문제풀이 시 본문 전체를 다시 읽어야 하는 상황이 벌어져 상당한 시간적 소모가 발생한다. 평소에 글의 도입부에서 포괄적 주제를 설정하고, 글의 특징에 따라 중요 정보를 표시해 두는 습관이 필요하다. 본문과 같이 일반적으로 특정 (사상)학파가 나올 경우 특징을 정리해 두면서 읽고, 또한 상대적으로 다른 주장을 펼친 학자가 비교/대조되고 있을 경우, 같은 점과 다른 점을 명확하게 정리하면서 각각의 학자의 특징을 파악해 둘 필요가 있다.

해석 학습이란 상대적으로 영구적인 행동 변화 또는 그럴 가능성이 농후한 행동 변화를 이끌어 내는 과정으로 정의할 수 있다. 다른 말로 하자면, 우리가 배우면서, 주변을 인식하고, 거기서 들어오는 자극을 해석한 후 상호작용 또는 행동하는 방법을 바꾸게 된다는 것이다. John B. Watson은 학습 과정이 우리의 행동에 어떻게 영향을 미치는지를 연구

한 첫 번째 사람이었으며, 행동주의라는 학파를 창설하게 된다. 행동주의 이면의 핵심 사상은 단지 관측할 수 있는 행위만이 연구의 가치가 있다는 것인데, 이는 사람의 기분이나 생각과 같은 추상적인 것은 너무 주관적이기 때문이다. 이러한 신념은 미국에서 자그마치 50년간이나 심리학 연구의 주류를 이루었다.

아마도 행동주의자 중에 가장 유명한 사람은 B. F. Skinner일 것이다. 그는 Watson의 대부분의 연구와 결과들을 따랐지만, 내적 상태 또한 외적 자극과 마찬가지로 영향을 미칠 수 있다고 믿었다. 그는 이러한 신념으로 인해 극단적 행동주의 학자로 꼽히지만, 오늘날에는 내외적인 자극 모두가 우리의 행동에 영향을 미친다고 간주한다.

어 휘

define v. (성격·내용 따위를) 규정짓다, 한정하다
behaviorism n. 행동주의
observable a. 관찰할 수 있는, 눈에 띄는, 주목할 만한; 현저한
abstraction n. 추상적 개념
subjective a. 주관적인 **stimuli** n. 자극

[Challenge 8]

문제 1

답 (3)

해설 첫 번째 문단 마지막에 보기 항 (3)에 대한 설명이 분명히 드러난다. 글의 도입부에서 알 수 있듯이 글쓴이는 미국인을 이상주의자라고 부르는 것은 아주 상투적인 말이라고 전하고 있다. 역사적으로 미국은 그 설립 배경에서 종교적 자유와 개인의 자유라는 이상을 국가적 신념으로 삼았다. 이러한 점은 미국의 정치/사회/문화 모든 측면에서 드러난다. 그러나 이러한 측면이 종족 전체가 아닌 자신만의 몫을 생각하는 개인주의로 억제되고 퇴색되었다고 말하고 있다.

문제 2

답 (1)

해설 본문 마지막에 명확히 제시되고 있다. 'so far as the average individual is concerned, with just his share and no more of the race-tendency, this idealism has been suppressed, and in some measure perverted.'

해석 미국인들을 이상주의자라고 말하는 것은 공공연한 상투적인 문구를 말하는 것과 같다. 대부분의 상투적인 말과 같이, 이 말은 한 쪽의 관점에선 논쟁할 수 없이 정당한 말이지만 다른 한 쪽에선 사실과 맞지 않는 것이기에 성가시다. 전통에 관해서라면, 반론의 여지가 없다. 17세기 이후로 미국에 들어온 많은 영향력 있는 이민자들 중 대다수는 적어도 부분적으로라도 이상주의자가 되려는 동기를 가지고 있었다. 만약 그들을 미국으로 오게 만든 것이 종교적 자유에 대한 갈망에서가 아니라면 그들은 아마도 개인적인 자유 추구를 위해서 그랬을 것이다. 물론 이런 동기들은 모두 우리가 미국적이라고 부르는 심신 상태를 자리잡게 하는 데 가장 큰 역할을 한 초기 이민 과정에서 가장 강력하게 작용했다. 나는 이러한 주장을 위해 힘쓸 필요도 없다. 우리의 정치 사회적 역사가 뒷받침해 주기 때문이다. 우리의 최고 문학에서 볼 수 있듯이, 우리가 위대하다고 부르는 작가들 중에 미국의 작가들보다 더 이상주의적인 사람은 없기 때문이다. 에머슨, 소로우, 호손, 휘트먼 — 이상주의가 이들 작가 안에서보다 더 구체화된 적이 있었던가?

그리고 이러한 이상주의는 미국의 전반에 흘러왔다. 이것은 우리 종파에 스며들었고, 그중 몇 가지 종파가 생겨나기도 했다. 이것은 우리의 생각에 색깔을 더했으며, 우리 감정에 더욱 그러했다. 그러나 낙천주의, 부정부패 들추기(드러난 모든 것이 다 그리 보기 좋지는 않다), 사회봉사, 종교, 시, 민주적 개혁은 이상을 추구하려는 미국인들의 선천적인 성향의 활기와 오만함의 증거이다. 1918년에 우리가 이러한 이상주의를 믿었다는 것은 누구도 의심하지 않는다. 그럼에도, 평범한 개인에 있어서, 딱 그 자신만의 몫만 있고 민족적인 성향 이상의 것은 없는 이런 이상주의는 억제되어 있고, 어느 정도는 왜곡되어 있다.

어 휘

thoroughgoing a. 철저한, 완전한, 전적인
platitude n. 단조로움, 평범함, 진부함
indisputably ad. 명백하게
possessed a. 홀린, 쒼, 미친, 열중한
incarnate a. 구체화한
permeate v. 스며들다, 침투하다, 투과하다
manifestation n. 표시, 표명
bumptiousness n. 뽐냄, 자만
pervert v. 왜곡하다, 곡해하다

[Challenge 9]

문제 1

답 (1)

해설 본문은 MRSA가 주로 어떤 경로를 통해서 전염되는지에 대해 설명하고 있다.

문제 2

답 (1)

해설 본문 초반부에 보균자에 관한 내용이 등장한다. 보기 항 (1)은 옳은 설명이다. 본문에서 사람들이 MRSA의 치명성을 잘 인식하고 있다는 이야기는 없다. 오히려 청소년들은 별로 외상을 대수롭지 않게 여겨 MRSA에 걸릴 확률이 높은 대상으로 설

명하고 있다. 'People with pneumonia (lung infection) due to MRSA can transmit MRSA by airborne droplets.'로 보아 보기 항 (3)은 틀린 표현이다.

문제 3

답 (1)

해설 '쇠약해진'의 뜻을 지닌 'depressed'이다.

해설 람들이 MRSA에 감염되는 주된 2가지 경로가 있다. 첫째 MRSA에 감염된 사람이나 MRSA 보균자와 신체적으로 접촉하는 것이다. 두 번째 경로는 MRSA에 감염되었거나 병원균 보유자가 만진 문손잡이, 마루, 개수대 또는 타월과 같은 물건에 묻은 MRSA를 신체적으로 접촉했을 때이다. 사람들의 일반적인 피부 조직에는 MRSA 감염이 발생하지 않는다. 그러나 만약 베인 상처나 염증, 건선(물집이나 발적, 비늘처럼 벗겨지는 피부의 증상을 보이는 만성 염증성 피부병)과 같이 피부에 하자가 있을 경우 번질 수 있다. 이런 증상이 없는 건강한 사람들, 특히 아이나 젊은이들은 작은 상처나 감염을 잘 눈치채지 못하며 신체 접촉에 주의를 덜 기울이는 경향이 있다. 이것이 학교 운동선수, 기숙사 거주자들, 항상 밀접하게 (피부) 접촉을 하는 군인들과 같은 다양한 종류의 사람들에게 MRSA가 발생하는 주요 이유이다.

MRSA에 감염될 위험성이 높은 사람은 뚜렷한 피부 절개를 한 사람(예를 들어 수술이나 외상으로 인한 상처가 있는 환자나, 화상이나 피부 궤양을 가진 병원 환자)과 쇠약해진 면역체계를 가진 사람(아이, 노인 또는 HIV 감염 환자) 또는 만성 질환(당뇨 또는 암)을 가진 환자들이다. MRSA로 인한 폐렴을 겪는 사람은 대기 중 수증기를 통해서 MRSA를 옮길 수 있다. 환자를 돌보는 사람들은 단체로 MRSA에 양성반응을 보인 환자에게 지속적으로 노출되어 적절한 예방조치를 취하지 않을 경우 감염될 확률이 높다. 결과적으로 환자를 돌보고 방문하는 사람들은 일회용 마스크, 가운 그리고 글러브를 사용하여 MRSA에 감염된 환자의 방에 들어가야 한다.

어휘

abrasion n. 찰과상　**flaw** n. 흠집
chronic a. 만성의
inflammatory a. 염증성의
scaly a. 비늘이 있는; 비늘처럼 벗겨지는
proliferate v. 증식[번식]하다; 급격히 늘다
imperfection n. 불완전성, 결함
lax a. (줄 등이) 느슨한, 느즈러진, (정신·덕성 등이) 해이한, 단정치 못한, 방종한
dormitory n. 기숙사　**airborne** a. 공기로 운반되는

[Challenge 10]

문제 1

답 (2)

해설 본문은 환경론에 대한 성경적 입장을 드러내고 있다. 보기 항 (2)가 가장 적절하다.

문제 2

답 (1)

해설 보기 항 (1)은 본문 마지막에 명시되어 있다. (2)의 경우 성경은 인간과 그를 둘러싼 환경에 대한 아주 명확한 관점을 드러내고 있다. 보기 항 (3)의 경우 'it demands faith to deliberately avoid planting or harvesting with only the promise that there will be sufficient food in the sixth year to cover the seventh and eighth years.'에서 알 수 있듯이, 성경에선 7년과 8년차에 식량이 충분할 것이라는 믿음을 요구한다. 이 말은 하나님의 약속에 대한 인간의 확신을 의도적으로 요구하는 것으로 식량이 부족할 때에는 안식년에 해도 된다는 말의 의미로 언급한 것은 아니다. 성경에 유기농 농법이 잘 기록되어 있다는 내용은 없다.

해설 40년 전 내가 여기 언급된 작품 중 어느 것을 읽기 전 또는 환경 문제에 관한 TV 인터뷰를 행하기 전 나는 학생의 신분으로 유기농 정원과 농업을 접하게 되었다. 영국에서 나는 농학을 공부하면서 이런 유기농 전통에 헌신한 사람들과 함께 정원사인 동시에 퇴비사로 일할 특권을 가졌다. 내가 배운 이들이 이렇게 한 것은 바로 이것이 성경적 기반을 갖추고 있기 때문이었다. 예를 들면, 농업 프로그램에 안식년 준수 — 매 7년째 되는 해 땅을 1년 쉬게 함 — 가 포함되어 있었다. 이것은 오래전부터 체계화된 생태학 법칙 중 하나이다. 게다가, 여기에는 7, 8번째 해를 감당할 만큼의 충분한 식량을 6번째 해에는 얻게 될 거라는 약속만으로, 심고 수확하는 것을 일부러 피할 수 있는 믿음도 요구한다. 레위기 25장에서 이 법칙과 약속된 득을 상세히 다루고 있다. Berry가 위에서 가리킨 대로, 우리에게 환경을 보존하고 돌보며, 땅을 사랑하고, 균형과 조화를 이루며, 개인적 성장을 하라는 성경적 가르침이 있다. 아담이 놓여진 정원을 가꾸고 보존하라는 지시에 대한 그의 언급은 성경에 드러난 첫 번째 생태 원칙 중 하나에 대한 언급이다. 인간 기원에 대한 이 책(성경)은 인간을 둘러싼 자연 환경과 어떤 관계를 가져야 하는지에 대한 진술이 드러난다는 점에서 의미심장하다. 'dress'와 'keep'에 해당하는 히브리어는 일하고, 보존하고, 배양하며, 보호한다는 것을 나타낸다. 분명 여기에는 착취와 파괴에 대한 언급은 없다. 종종 인용되는 창세기 1장 26절의 만물을 지배하는 인간에 대한 인용구에서 인간은 모든 피조물을 지배하는 것이 아니라 자비로운 지도자의 역할을 하는 것이라고 언급되어 있다. 인간은 보살핌, 사랑 그리고 지혜를 가지고 이렇게 하도록 되어 있다.

어휘

agronomy *n.* 농업 경제학, 농경학, 경종학
dedicate *v.* (시간·노력을) 바치다, 전념[헌신]하다
spell out ~을 간결하게[자세히] 설명하다
precept *n.* (행동) 수칙, 계율
beneficent *a.* 도움을 주는, 선을 베푸는; 친절한

Day 29

[Challenge 1]

문제 1

답 (2)

해설 필자는 종교가 인간 본성의 내재적 요소라고 언급하고 있다. 즉, 다시 말해 인간이라면 누구나 하나님의 존재에 대한 인식을 가지고 있다는 말이다. 그런데, 본문에서 말하는 바와 같이 때로 인간 중에서 보이지 않는 이런 하나님에 대한 존재감이 없는 것처럼 보이는 이도 있는데, 이것에 대해 글쓴이는 어떤 반론을 제시할 수 있을지 생각해야 한다. 사람은 누구나 볼 수 있는 눈과 들을 수 있는 귀가 있지만 개중에 색맹이거나 음감이 없는 사람도 있다는 비유를 통해서 글쓴이는 반론을 제기할 수 있다.

문제 2

답 (1)

해설 and의 용법은 다양하다. 보기 항 (1)은 'some – others'의 상대적인 내용을 다루는 대조의 역할을 하고 있다. 보기 항 (2)는 순차적인 행위를 나타낼 때 쓰이는 용법이다. 보기 항 (3)의 역할은 동일한 명사를 반복해서 써서 같은 종류의 것들 사이에도 중요한 차이가 있음을 나타낼 때 쓰인다. 보기 항 (4)는 목적의 의미를 전달할 때 쓰이는 to부정사 대용으로 볼 수 있다.

문제 3

답 (4)

해설 본문에서 종교는 유령과 같은 허상이 아닌 경험할 수 있는 실체라고 했다. 보기 항 (4)는 틀린 표현이다.

해석 종교는 경험이다. 이것은 자신의 가장 고귀한 영감에 대한 인간 본성의 반응이다. 종교는 자신과 자신이 속한 세상을 넘어선 존재와의 교제이다. 종교는 일반적인 경험이다. 종교를 비판하는 사람은 이것을 '지울 수 없는 미신'이라 부르고, 종교를 주창하는 사람은 인간은 믿음을 가지고 태어난다고 주장한다. 여기저기 몇몇 사람들이 보이지 않는 존재에 대한 감이 없는 것처럼 보이는 것은 가끔 어떤 사람이 색맹이거나 음감이 없다는 사실을 발견하게 되는 것과 비슷하다. Mr. Lecky는 "종교적인 본능은 우리의 식욕이나 신경처럼 우리의 진정한 본능 중에 하나라는 것은 모든 역사가 증명하는 사실이며, 그러한 것들은 인간의 영혼이 계속적으로 추구하는 보이지 않는 세계의 실체에 대한 가장 강력한 증거이다."라고 썼다. 어떤 이는 종교를 유치함으로 치부하며 깎아내리려 한다. 그들의 말로는, 아기 같은 태도는 이런 의존적인 마음에서 더 자라지 못하고, 의지하는 대상이 보이는 것에서 보이지 않는 것으로 옮겨간 것뿐이라고 한다. 그러나 다른 아이 같은 것, 즉 유령과 요정 같은 것은 없앨 수 있지만, 인간은 '절대 종교를 벗어날 수 없는' 것처럼 보이며, 바로 하느님에 대한 인간의 태도가 미숙해 보이지만, 그들이 보이는 가장 완벽하고 독실한 신앙의 본성만은 전혀 미숙한 기미를 보이지 않는다. 종교의 파괴할 수 없는 생명력은 인간 본성의 내재적 요소이며 불신자는 그 이하의 인간이라는 증거이다.

어휘

intercourse *n.* (인간의) 교제, 교섭, 교류, (신과 사람의) 영적 교통
indelible *a.* 지울 수 없는, 지워지지 않는
assert *v.* 단언하다   instinct *n.* 본성
proof *n.* 증거   discredit *v.* 믿지 않다, 의심하다
childish *a.* 유치한   fairy *n.* 요정
incurably *ad.* 낫지 않을 만큼; 교정할 수 없을 만큼
indestructible *a.* 파괴할 수 없는, 불멸의
vitality *n.* 생명력, 활력   subnormal *a.* 정상 이하의

[Challenge 2]

문제 1

답 (3)

해설 Bruce의 재기의 계기를 마련한 거미와의 만남에서 얻은 교훈을 이야기하고 있다.

문제 2

답 (1)

해설 교훈적 글임.

문제 3

답 (4)

해설 the English 는 "영국 사람들"을 가리키는 표현으로 의미상 복수로 쓰였기에 were 를 was 로 바꾸면 오히려 틀린 표현이 된다

해석 스코틀랜드의 왕 Robert Bruce는 슬픔과 피로로 언덕 사이의 인가가 없는 동굴의 바닥에 누워있었다. 그의 마음은 근심스러운 걱정으로 가득했는데, 이는 그를 죽이거나 잡아서 왕에게 데려가려고 하는 영국의 병사들을 피해 숨어 있었기 때문이었다. 용감한 스코틀랜드인들은 많은 전쟁에서 패했고, Bruce는 그가 다시 자신의 소중한 나라를 자유

롭게 하지 못할 것이라고 근심하기 시작했다. "포기해야겠어."라고 그는 말했다. 바로 그때, 거미 한 마리가 동굴의 천장에서 긴 줄에 매달려 왕의 눈앞을 왔다 갔다 했다. 그는 이 작은 동물이 무엇을 하는지 보기 위해 자신의 우울한 생각을 제쳐두었다. 거미는 천천히 자신의 거미줄을 타고 오르기 시작하며 조금씩 위로 잡아당겼다. 그러나 아주 조금 올라갔을 뿐인데, 거기서 미끄러지고 다시 거미줄 아래 끝으로 떨어졌다. 계속해서 오르기 시작하고 다시 미끄러지고 떨어지기를 6번이나 반복했다. "분명 이 어리석은 작은 동물은 이제 이 아주 가느다란 줄을 오르는 것을 포기할 거야."라고 Bruce는 생각했다. 그러나 거미는 그렇게 하지 않았다. 다시 7번째 위로 향하는 여정을 시작했으며, 이번에는 떨어지지 않았다. 1인치씩 위로 조금씩 더 높이 올라가 마침내 천장에 닿아 안전하게 집에 도착했다. 왕은 "브라보!"라고 외쳤다. "거미가 나에게 큰 교훈을 주었다. 나 또한 이길 때까지 포기하지 않겠다." Bruce는 자신의 약속을 지켰다. 그는 용감한 자신의 부하들을 이끌고 계속해서 전장에 나가 마침내 영국을 자기네 땅으로 쫓아내고 스코틀랜드는 자유롭게 되었다.

어 휘
weary *a.* 피로한, 지쳐있는　　lay *v.* 눕히다
thread *n.* 실; 가느다란 선　　swing *v.* 흔들리다, 진동하다
gloomy *a.* 어둑어둑한, 암흑의

[Challenge 3]

문제 1

답 (2)

해설 본문은 '음악적 상상력'의 중요성을 이야기하고 있다. 즉, 악기를 연주하기 전 소리를 머릿속에 미리 상상해서 기억하게 만든다는 이야기다. 단지 수학과 역사에서만 상상력이 필요한 것이 아니라 음악에서 이런 상상력도 아주 중요한 역할을 한다고 본문 중간에 다루고 있다.

문제 2

답 (3)

해설 보기 항 (3)의 본문에서 말하는 '음악적 상상력'과는 거리가 먼 'rote learning'에 가까운 내용이다.

해석 "소리로 생각"하는 마음의 능력은 한동안 음악적 성취를 위한 중요한 이슈가 되어 왔다. 예를 들어, 트럼펫 개인 교사는 학생이 연주의 질을 높이기 전에 내적으로 음악의 선율을 "듣도록" 장려한다. 일반적인 음악 전문가는 6번째 학급에 나중에 연주할 때 흐름을 비교할 수 있도록 듣기 수업을 하는 동안 음악의 선율을 "기억"하도록 권장한다. 지휘 선생은 학생들이 리허설을 하기 전에 악보의 소리를 "상상"하도록 독려한다. 내적으로 의미 있게 소리를 상상할 수 있는 능력은 음악의 성취와 수렴적 작업(하나의 정확한 답변을 이끌어내도록 고안된 작업)에 중요할 뿐 아니라, 창조적 사고 능력과 특히 발산적 작업(여러 가지 답이 가능한 일)을 위해서도 중요하다. 흥미로운 것은 교실, 리허설 홀 그리고 개인 스튜디오에서 상상과 발산적 사고를 장려한다는 것이다. 창조적 과정에 있어 아주 중요한 역할을 하고 창조성에 관한 정식 연구에 관심이 있는 많은 음악 전문가들의 관심을 모았던 부분이 바로 음악적 소리와 관련된 이런 창의적 문제 해결이다. 모순적이게도 사실적이고 기술 지향적인 내용의 선호로 음악 교사들에 의해 무시되고 강조되지 않는 것도 바로 이런 종류의 사고이다. 사실적 정보는 물론 창의적 사고에 있어 중요한 것은 맞지만 우리는 학생들에게 창조적 작업에 이러한 개념적 이해를 적용할 기회를 제공해 주어야 한다.

어 휘
internally *ad.* 심적으로, 내부적으로　　rehearsal *n.* 예행연습
meaningfully *ad.* 의미 있게, 의의 있게
convergent *a.* 한 점에 모이는, 집중적인
divergent *a.* 분기하는, 갈라지는
ironically *ad.* 반어적으로; 얄궂게도
precisely *ad.* 바로, 꼭, 정확히　　factual *a.* 사실에 기반을 둔
oriented *a.* ~을 지향하는
conceptual *a.* 개념의, 구상의

[Challenge 4]

문제 1

답 (3)

해설 우선 첫 번째 문단은 역사와 전기의 구분이며 이에 대한 정의를 내리는 부분이다. 두 번째 문단이 시작하는 시점은 'The value of the literature'로 시작하는 문장이다. 두 번째 문단의 주제는 '역사와 전기에 필요한 조건'이 된다. 본문에서 이를 'truth'라고 보고 있다. 즉, 실제 일어난 일을 진솔하고, 정확하게 기록해야 역사와 전기는 그 가치를 인정받을 수 있다는 의미다.

문제 2

답 (1)

해설 빈칸이 들어간 문장을 살펴보자.

> The value of the literature included in these two classes depends almost wholly upon truth; that is, upon the precise _____(a)_____ of the statements made with the real facts of the man's life and career.

재진술한 'that is'를 활용해야 한다. 즉, 앞에서 역사와 전기의 필수 조건은 바로 사실성이라고 했다. 이는 다시 말해 역사와 전기에서 다뤄지는 인물의 삶과 성격이 기술된 내용에 얼마나 정

확히 일치하느냐를 말하는 것이다.

해석 위대한 사람의 인생과 업적에 기원을 두는 대부분의 문학은 두 가지 제목 아래 구분할 수 있다. 역사와 전기이다. 그 사람의 행적과 이러한 행적이 민족과 국가의 운명을 형성하는 데 미치는 영향력과 관련된 부분은 바로 첫 번째 구분에 해당한다. 반면, 주로 그 인물의 성격에서 흥미를 이끌어내고 주로 그 행위의 결과가 어떤 정신과 도덕적 특성으로 이루어졌는지를 다루는 부분은 두 번째 구분에 적절히 들어간다. 이 두 가지에 포함된 문학의 가치는 거의 전적으로 진실에 달려있다. 다시 말해 그 인물의 삶과 업적의 실제 사실로 이루어진 진술의 정확한 일치의 여부에 달려있다. 역사 속 사건을 정확하게 연대순으로 기술하지 않으면 이는 무용지물보다 더 나쁜 것이다. 그리고 전기는 개인의 성격을 진실하게 전개하지 못할 때 가치가 없고 오해를 불러온다.

어휘

classify v. 분류[구분]하다   biography n. 전기
chiefly ad. 주로   outcome n. 결과
properly ad. 적절하게   precise a. 정확한, 정밀한
chronicle v. 연대순으로 기록하다
set forth ~을 진술하다

[Challenge 5]

문제 1

답 (1)

해설 주제는 첫 번째 문장에서 나와 있듯이 사회문화 재생산의 과정과 방법을 다루는 글임을 알 수 있다. 이를 바탕으로 전달하려는 요지는 이러한 사회문화 재생산이 바로 공식적인 교육을 통해서 자연스럽게(natural), 즉 특권층의 가정에서 태어나면서 구별된 교육을 통해서 그 문화권의 사상뿐 아니라 행동까지 습득하게 된다는 것이다.

문제 2

답 (4)

해설 본문에서 정식 교육(Formal education)이 사회 제도 내 특정 계급의 위치를 재생산하는 데 아주 중요한 역할을 한다고 언급하고 있기에 보기 항 (1)과 (3)은 같은 맥락에서 옳은 표현이고, 보기 항 (2)는 'Bourdieu regards this 'ease', or 'natural' ability — distinction — as in fact the product of a great social labour, largely on the part of the parents.'에서 언급된 것을 확인할 수 있다. 그러나 공교육을 통해 사회 이동이 수월해진다는 내용은 없으며 본문과는 거리가 있는 내용이다.

해석 부르디외는 자신의 이론을 전개하는 글에서 특정 경제학의 용어를 사용하여 사회문화적 재생산의 과정과 어떻게 다양한 형태의 자본이 한 세대에서 다음 세대로 전이되는 경향을 지니는지 분석한다. 부르디외의 경우 정식 교육이 이러한 과정의 핵심 예로 작용한다. 부르디외에 따르면 교육의 성공은 자세, 옷 또는 액센트와 같이 표면상 비학문적 특징까지 확장하는 전반적 문화 행위를 포함한다. 특권층의 아이들은 자신의 선생이 배웠듯이 이러한 행위를 배운다. 빈곤층 아이들은 이러한 교육을 받지 못한다. 그러므로 특권층의 아이들은 아주 '쉽게' 자기 선생님들의 기대 유형에 맞춘다. 이들은 '잘 길들여져 있다.' 빈곤층의 아이들은 '아주 다루기 힘들며, 상당한 난제'로 인식이 된다. 이들 모두 자신들이 교육받은 대로 행동한다. 부르디외는 이런 "수월함" 또는 "본성적" 능력 — 구별 — 을 주로 부모에 의한 엄청난 사회적 노동의 산물이라고 간주한다. 이것은 아이들에게 교육 체계 속에서 성공할 수 있고 더 폭넓은 사회 제도에서 부모 계급의 위치를 재생산할 수 있다는 확신을 주는 생각뿐 아니라 행위의 성향을 갖추게 해준다.

어휘

terminology n. 전문 용어   reproduction n. 재생; 재현
entail v. 일으키다, 남기다, 수반하다
ostensibly ad. 외견상으로, 표면상으로
gait n. 걷는 모양, 걸음걸이   docile a. 가르치기 쉬운, 유순한
behave v. 행동하다; 작용하다
upbringing n. (유년기의) 양육, 교육
dictate v. 구술하다; 명령하다   distinction n. 구분, 차별; 차이
labour n. 노동   equip v. 준비를 갖춰 주다
disposition n. 성향; 기질

[Challenge 6]

문제 1

답 (2)

해설 빈칸 문제는 일반적으로 다음 두 가지를 활용할 수 있다. 빈칸을 중심으로 전체 글의 주제와의 통일성을 고려하면서 해석을 통한 접근과 문법적 요소를 이용한 빈칸 채우기가 있다. 저자는 시간을 최대한 효율적으로 사용한다는 점에서 두 번째 방법을 추천하고 싶다 (때로 해석으로 접근해야 할 경우도 있지만 일반적으로 문법적 힌트가 거의 제시된다). 빈칸 바로 뒤에 순접의 등위접속사 and가 존재하고 대명사 'they'가 보인다. 고로 앞에 전개된 문장에서 반드시 복수형 명사가 나와야 하는데, 이는 'The second'로 시작하는 문장이기에 앞과는 관련이 없이 새로운 정보가 다시 나오기 때문이다. 고로 보기 항에서 'they'를 받을 수 있는 것은 'surroundings, branches, parents, milestones'이다. 바로 이어지는 'Each of these sciences'라는 표현에서 'These sciences'를 받을 수 있는 것은 'branches'밖에 없다. 이후 보기 항의 표현을 본문에 넣어 다시 한 번 확인하도록 한다.

해석 아이들의 미성숙함과 무지라는 이러한 각각의 사실들

195

은 교육학의 기초로서 작용한다. 첫 번째로 교육학은, 인간의 능력, 그들의 발달과정, 그리고 성장과 행위의 규칙들을 강조한다. 두 번째는, 인간의 다양한 지식 분야에 관한 연구와 어떻게 사람들이 그것을 발견하고 발전시키고 완성하는지를 강조한다. 이러한 학문들은 힘을 연구하는 데 질량을 빼놓을 수 없고(뉴턴의 법칙 F(힘) = 질량 곱하기 가속도), 영향에 관한 연구에서 원인을 꼭 고려해야 하는 것처럼 서로 따로 떼어서 고려할 수 없다.

어 휘

immaturity *n.* 미숙, 미완성　　ignorance *n.* 무지; 무학
serve *v.* 섬기다; 봉사하다; 공급하다　　basis *n.* 기초, 근거
emphasize *v.* 강조하다; 역설하다　　capacity *n.* 능력; 자격
perfect *v.* 완성하다; 수행하다
involve *v.* 연루시키다 (in); 수반하다
effect *n.* 결과; 효과; 영향　　include *v.* 포함하다
survey *n.* 조사, 검사　　cause *n.* 원인; 주의; 주장

[Challenge 7]

문제 1

답 (1)
해설 본문은 전체적으로 중세의 시대가 끝나고 새로운 시대 (현대 유럽)의 도래를 기술하고 있다.

문제 2

답 (4)
해설 아래 본문을 통해 Henry에 관한 구체적 정보를 확인할 수 있다.

> Henry had strengthened his position by alliance with France, Spain, and Scotland.

즉, Henry는 다른 나라와 동맹을 통해 자신의 입지를 견고하게 한 것이지, 힘의 분권화로 이룬 것이 아니다.

문제 3

답 (2)
해설 접속사 문제이다. 앞뒤 문맥을 파악하여 답을 유추해야 한다.

> At the same time feudalism was ruined, because the invention of gunpowder had previously been changing the art of war. _____(a)_____ the King of France, Louis XI, as well as the King of England, Henry VII, had entire disposal of the national artillery; and therefore overawed the barons and armored knights. Neither moated fortresses nor mail-clad warriors, nor archers with bows and arrows, could prevail against powder and shot.

빈칸 앞에 전개된 내용은 화약의 발달로 인해 전쟁의 기술이 모두 바뀌었다고 했다. 뒤에 이어지는 내용은 구체적인 왕을 언급하면서 이들이 전국에 포대를 배치함으로써 남작과 무장한 기사를 위협할 수 있게 되었다고 말하는 동시에 이러한 포대로 이전 중세의 무기를 압도했다고 말하고 있다. 따라서, 빈칸 뒤에 전개되는 내용은 앞에서 전개된 문장에 대한 구체적 진술이 된다.

해석 이 책의 서두에 르네상스, 즉 문예 부흥이라 불리는 유럽 역사의 위대한 격변이 언급되었다. 1453년 터키가 콘스탄티노플을 점령하고, 그리스의 학자들을 이탈리아로 몰아내자, 이곳은 즉시 유럽에서 가장 문명화된 나라가 되었다. 시, 철학 그리고 예술이 그때부터 프랑스, 영국 그리고 독일로 들어갔으며, 인쇄술의 발명에 크게 힘입어 그 당시 이전보다 책을 더 싸게 만들 수 있게 되었다. 동시에 봉건제도가 붕괴되는데, 화약의 발달이 이전의 전쟁의 기술에 큰 변화를 가져왔기 때문이다. 예를 들어, 영국의 왕 헨리 7세와 마찬가지로 프랑스 왕 루이 11세는 전국적으로 포대를 완전 배치했다. 그래서 남작과 무장한 기사를 위압했다. 해자를 두른 성, 쇠미늘갑옷을 입은 전사 또는 활과 화살을 가진 궁수 어느 것도 화약과 포탄을 극복하지 못했다. 중세의 끝이 다가오고 현대 유럽이 태동했다. 영국이 마지막으로 추방되고 왕국의 봉건 제후들이 전부 몰락한 '백년 전쟁'이 종결되면서, 프랑스는 남과 북이 통합되어 중앙집권화가 이루어졌다. 동시에 영국은 근간의 '장미 전쟁'에 의해 귀족들의 통치 체제를 일소하였고 헨리왕은 프랑스, 스페인 그리고 스코틀랜드와의 동맹을 통해 자신의 입지를 강화했다. 스페인은 1492년 Granada에서 무어 일파를 추방함으로써 Castile에서 Leon에 이르는 이사벨라의 왕국과 Aragon에서 Sicily에 이르는 퍼디난드 왕국의 통합으로 처음으로 강력한 하나의 국가로 중앙집권화가 이루어졌다.

어 휘

reference *n.* 말하기, 언급　　upheaval *n.* 격변, 대변동
scholar *n.* 학자　　refuge *n.* 피난(처), 피신(처)
at once 즉시, 동시에　　feudalism *n.* 봉건 제도
gunpowder *n.* 화약　　artillery *n.* 대포, 포병대
overawe *v.* 위압하다　　baron *n.* 남작
armor *v.* ~에게 갑옷을 입히다, 장갑시키다
moated *a.* 해자로 둘러싸인　　archer *n.* 궁수

abolition n. 폐지   feudatory a. 봉건 가신(家臣)
alliance n. 연합, 동맹

[Challenge 8]

문제 1

답 (4)

해설 본문에서 말하는 생활 수준의 향상은 바로 생산성의 증가로 좀 더 나은 삶을 사는 것을 말한다. 첫 번째 문단에서 생산성을 높이기 위한 가장 확실한 방법은 교육과 건강관리이다. 두 번째 문단에서는 자본의 증가를 통한 노동력의 질적 향상을 들고 있다. 인구 증가가 반드시 삶의 질을 향상시키는 것은 아니라고 말하고 있다.

문제 2

답 (3)

해설 본문 마지막에 명시되어 있다.

> an increase in the supply of capital means that each worker has more tools to work with, and can be more productive. That can lead to a higher standard of living — to economic growth.

문제 3

답 (1)

해설 아래 밑줄 친 부분이 서로 어떤 관계인지 생각해 보자.

> So increase of the population ... lead to a declining standard of living instead   (나)   , an increase in the supply of capital ... lead to a higher standard of living — to economic

인구 증가와 자본의 증가는 서로 대조적인 결과를 가져온다는 것을 볼 수 있다.

해석 우리가 스스로를 변화시켜 미래에 더 생산적인 직원이 되게 만들거나 또는 미래에 다른 방식으로 우리가 이익을 얻는 모든 것은 인간 자본의 투자가 된다. 아주 흔한 예가 바로 교육이다. 또 다른 예로 예방 차원의 건강관리가 있다. 우리가 미래에 더 건강할 수 있게 건강 관리를 해 직장을 덜 빠지는 것이 바로 더욱 생산적인 것이다(미래에 더욱 삶을 즐긴다). 이것이 바로 인간 자본의 투자이다. 생산성을 높이는 한 가지 방법은 이용할 수 있는 자원의 양을 늘리는 것이다. 세 가지 자원 중에서, 노동과 자본의 공급은 늘릴 수 있다. 대조적으로 지구상의 토지와 천연자원의 양은 늘릴 수가 없다. 콜럼버스와 같이 이 지구상의 새로운 농경지의 공급처를 찾지는 못한다고 하더라도 더 많은 천연 자원을 발견할 수 있다는 점은 사실이다. 그러나 발견은 생산과 동일한 것이 아니다. 우리는 발견할 수는 있지만 더 많은 토지와 자원을 만들어 낼 수는 없는 것이다. 우리는 더 많은 자본과 노동력을 만들어 낼 수 있다. 인구 증가는 노동력 공급의 증가를 의미하지만 소위 말하듯이 사람이 한 명 증가할 때마다 추가적으로 먹여야 할 입도 증가하는 것이다. 그래서 인구 증가가 그 자체로 높은 생활 수준, 즉 더 부유한 나라에 이르는 것이 아니다. 이것은 오히려 생활 수준의 하락으로 이어질 수도 있다. 반면, 자본의 증가는 각 노동자가 일을 할 때 사용하는 도구의 증가이며 이를 통해 더 많이 생산할 수 있게 된다. 이것을 통해 더 나은 생활 수준, 즉 경제 성장에 이를 수 있다.

어 휘

investment n. 투자   obvious a. 명백한, 명료한
preventive a. 예방의, 예방하는
agricultural a. 농업의, 경작의   give birth to ~을 낳다

[Challenge 9]

문제 1

답 (4)

해설 보기 항 (1)의 내용과 같이 부처가 직접 했는지는 본문에 언급이 없다. 참고로, 보통 석가모니를 높여 부처(꼭 석가모니가 아니라도 열반의 경지에 오른 사람은 부처라 부름)라 부르는데, 그는 기원전 6세기경 사람이다. 보기 항 (2)의 경우 첫 번째 문장 "(According to Chinese historians Buddhism was officially recognized in China about 67 A.D.)"에서 알 수 있듯이 틀린 진술이다. 본문에서 중국의 왕실도 불교를 반겼다는 내용이 드러나 있는 것으로 보아 보기 항 (3)은 잘못된 진술이다. 보기 항 (4)는 본문 마지막에 드러난 중국의 이민 정책에서 알 수 있다.

문제 2

답 (4)

해설 우선 제시된 문장에서 처음에 나오는 'in fact'의 역할을 살펴보자. 크게 두 가지 기능이 있다. (1) 앞에 제시된 내용의 추가 부연 (2) 앞에 제시된 내용과 역접의 내용을 전개함. 본문은 'in fact'의 첫 번째 기능으로 관료 중 한 명이 불교를 도입하기 전부터 이 종교의 신봉자가 되었다는 내용이 추가적으로 제시되고 있으므로 앞에는 중국이 불교에 대해 호의적인 반응을 보이고 있었다는 내용이 전개되면 된다.

문제 3

답 (2)

해설 다른 나라를 정복하는 군사 활동, 수많은 사절단 그리고 폭넓은 무역은 그 나라의 종교를 접하게 되는 불가피한 행위이다. 즉, 불교와의 접촉은 이런 행위의 부산물이라는 것을 알 수 있다.

해석 중국의 역사학자들에 따르면 불교는 서기 67년경에 중국에서 공식적으로 인정되었다. 몇 년 후, Ming-Ti 황제는 꿈에서 그의 궁전 위를 떠도는 후광이 비치는 거대한 금색의 형상을 보았다. 벌써 이 새로운 종교에 의심 없이 호의적이었던 그의 몇몇 고문들은 이 꿈의 형상을 바로 인도의 위대한 현인인 부처의 형상이라고 해석했다. 이들의 충고를 따라 황제는 불교에 대한 모든 것을 연구하고 오라고 사절단을 보냈다. 이 사절단은 두 명의 인도 수도승과 함께 부처의 많은 고전을 가져왔다. 백마를 타고 왔기 때문에, 황제가 이 수도승들과 이들 이후에 온 사람들을 위해 지은 수도원을 백마 수도원이라 불렀다. 이 건물의 갓돌은 오늘날까지 전해진다고 한다.

이 꿈 이야기는 반복해서 언급할 가치가 있는데, 이는 불교가 아주 이른 시기에 알려졌다는 것뿐 아니라 중국의 왕실에서 받겼다는 점을 보여주기 때문이다. 사실, 이 꿈과 관련된 동일한 역사에서 이 꿈이 발생하기 몇 년 전 불교의 신봉자가 되었다는 한 관료의 전기가 들어 있다. 이것이 그리 놀라운 일이 아닌 것은 군사 활동, 수많은 사절단 그리고 이들 나라와의 넓은 교역으로 불가피하게 알게 될 수밖에 없던 것이 바로 불교였다. 그러나 중국에 불교가 도입된 것은 특히나 중국 정부가 중국의 서부 쪽에 위치한 나라들의 정복한 민족들을 중국으로 이주시키려는 그 당시 정부의 정책에 의해서 장려되었다. 이 정복당한 민족들은 자신의 종교를 함께 가져왔다. 현재의 Shansi 지방에는 한때, 대부분 사람들이 불교도인 Hsiung-nu가 이렇게 거주했었다.

어휘

- **buddhism** *n.* 불교
- **emperor** *n.* 황제
- **halo** *n.* 후광
- **hover** *v.* 멤돌다, 서성이다
- **sage** *n.* 현자, 철인
- **embassy** *n.* (대사가 이끄는) 사절단
- **monk** *n.* 수도자, 수도승
- **quantity** *n.* 양, 수량, 분량
- **classic** *n.* 고전; 고전 문학
- **monastery** *n.* 수도원
- **tablet** *n.* 갓돌
- **acquaintance** *n.* 면식, 친숙함; 지식
- **inevitable** *a.* 불가피한, 필연적인
- **vanquish** *v.* 완파하다
- **province** *n.* 주, 지방
- **populate** *v.* 살다, 거주하다

[Challenge 10]

문제 1

답 (2)

해설 'depression self-test'와 1차 치료 의사들의 'screening tools'를 통한 우울증 진단에 관한 내용이다.

문제 2

답 (3)

해설 앞뒤 문장이 원인적 관계를 가진다.

문제 3

답 (2)

해설 보기 항 (2)번과 같이 다그치는 내용의 질문은 적절하지 못하다. 우울증은 심리적인 증상의 일종으로 감정적으로 다가가 치료하려는 것은 오히려 상황을 악화시킬 수 있다.

해석 자신이 우울증이 있는지 여부에 관해 건강 전문가에게 이야기를 해야 할지 모르는 사람의 경우 우울증 증상에 대한 질문으로 구성된 우울증 자가 테스트를 할 것을 고려해 볼 수 있다. 우울증에 대한 의학 조언을 언제 구해야 할지에 대해서 고려할 때, 우울증을 앓고 있는 환자는 이런 슬픈 감정이 2주 이상 지속되고 있는지, 아니면 이러한 감정이 심각하게 집, 학교, 직장 그리고 인간관계를 수행하는 능력을 심각하게 방해하고 있는지를 고려하면 도움이 된다. 적절한 치료를 구하는 첫 번째 단계는 정확한 진단인데, 이것은 환자가 우울증 증상을 가지고 있는지와 그렇다면 어떤 종류인지를 결정하는 완벽한 신체적, 심리학적 평가를 요구한다. 이미 언급했듯이, 특정 의학적 상태뿐 아니라 약품 또한 우울증 증상을 유발할 수 있다. 그러므로 검사 담당 의사는 면담, 신체 검사 그리고 실험실 시험에서 이러한 가능성을 철저하게 배제해야 한다. 많은 1차 진료 의사들은 우울증을 확인하기 위해 검사 도구를 사용하는데, 이것들은 일반적으로 우울증 증상을 갖고 있고 자세한 정신 감정을 받아야 할 필요가 있는 사람들을 식별하는 데 도움을 주는 설문지이다.

어휘

- **medication** *n.* 약[약물]
- **symptom** *n.* 증상, 징후
- **examine** *v.* 조사[검토]하다
- **rule out** 배제하다, 제외시키다
- **exclude** *v.* 제외[배제]하다
- **screening** *n.* (질병 등을 찾기 위한) 검사[심사]
- **questionnaire** *n.* 설문지

Day 30

[Challenge 1]

문제 1

답 (3)

해설 제목을 고르는 문제이다. 주의할 점은 본문의 부분적인 내용만을 드러내는 제목은 답이 될 수 없다는 것이다. 예를 들어, 보기 항 (1)은 본문에서 중반 이후에 다뤄지는 내용이며, 보기 항 (2)의 경우는 본문 초중반에 나오는 이야기이다. 본문은 곰에 관한 특정 주제를 다루기보다는 다양한 측면에서 곰에 관한 이야기를 하고 있다. 고로 보기 항 (3)이 가장 적절하다.

문제 2

답 (4)

해설 빈칸을 중심으로 앞뒤의 내용을 파악하여 답을 골라야 한다.

> Bears will often continue on the road in front of the palanquin for a mile or two, tumbling and playing all sorts of antics, as if _____(a)_____. But I believe it is their natural disposition; for they certainly are the most amusing creatures imaginable in their wild state.

바로 뒤에 'but'이 이어지면서 인과의 부연인 세미콜론도 볼 수 있다. 우선 'but' 뒤에 나오는 내용은 곰이 앞에서 언급한 모든 종류의 재주는 타고난 성향이라고 말하고 있다. 그럼 앞에서 전개 된 내용은 이와 상반된 내용이 와야 한다. 고로, 본성적으로 자연스럽게 익힌 것과 반대되는 보기 항 (4)가 가장 적절하다.

해석 곰은 종종 길 위의 가마 앞에서 1~2마일을 구르며 온갖 종류의 익살맞은 행동을 하는데, 마치 이들이 그렇게 하라고 교육을 받은 듯이 한다. 그러나 나는 이것이 이들의 타고난 성향이라 믿는다. 이는 분명 이들이 야생의 상태에서 가장 재미있는 동물이기 때문이다. 그래서 원숭이와 함께 이들은 인간을 즐겁게 하기 위해 지도를 받는가 보다. 익살 스럽기도 하지만 이들이 거친 바위를 오르고 벼랑을 굴러 떨어지는 것은 놀랍기 그지없다. 만약 이들이 말을 탄 사람에 의해서 공격을 받으면, 이들은 자신의 뒷다리로 서서 날카로운 흰 이를 드러내며 쨰지는 소리를 낸다. 만약 말이 가까이 오면, 이들은 다리로 잡으려 하고, 놓치게 되면, 여러 번 반복해서 구른다. 곰은 가까이 갈 만큼 대담한 말을 탄 사람에 의해서 창에 찔리기 쉽다.

어휘

disposition *n.* 성질; 기질
astonish *v.* 놀라게 하다; 깜짝 놀라다
ludicrous *a.* 익살맞은, 우스운
tumble *v.* 넘어지다; 몸부림치며 뒹굴다; (가격 따위가) 폭락하다
precipice *n.* 절벽; 벼랑   erect *a.* 똑바로 선; 곧추선
cackle *v.* 꼬꼬댁 울다; 낄낄 웃다

[Challenge 2]

문제 1

답 (2)

해설 강수를 땅에 저장하는 것만이 땅에 수분을 공급하는 유일한 방법이라는 이야기는 없다.

해석 정원에는 충분한 수분을 공급해 주어야 한다. 이러한 공급을 확보하는 첫 번째 노력은 바로 빗물을 저장하는 것이다. 적절한 준비와 경작으로 토지가 강수를 잘 담아 둘 수 있는 그런 조건이 되도록 해야 한다. 아주 딱딱하고 탄탄한 땅은 물을 흡수하지 못하는데, 특히나 이것이 경사지 거나 표면에 식물이 없는 경우 더욱 그러하다. 만약 딱딱한 경반층 (hard-pan)이 표면 근처에 있을 경우, 이런 토지는 물을 많이 흡수하지 못하고 비가 보통 정도로 와도 물이 넘쳐흐르게 되거나 표면에 웅덩이가 생긴다.

어휘

liberal *a.* (양이) 많은, 풍부한   tillage *n.* 경작(지); 농작물
compact *a.* 조밀한, 촘촘한   shed *v.* (물 등을) 튀기다; 흘리다
sloping *a.* 경사진; 비탈진   overflow *v.* 넘쳐흐르다; 넘치다
puddle *n.* 웅덩이

[Challenge 3]

문제 1

답 (4)

해설 이들이 가는 길에 벽이 있었다는 내용은 본문에 없다.

문제 2

답 (4)

해설 'trust to'는 '의탁하다'의 뜻이다.

문제 3

답 (2)

해설 '가파른'이란 뜻을 가진 단어는 보기 항 (2)다.

문제 4

답 (3)

해설 빈칸이 들어간 문맥을 살펴보자.

> For they expected to be able to cross without hindrance, and then, in consequence of the suddenness of their inroad, to be able to ravage all the country around; but they had _____ (c) _____.

우선, 빈칸 앞에 위치한 'but'을 활용해야 한다. 즉, 빈칸의 내용은 앞에서 전개된 내용과 상반된 의미를 전달함을 알 수 있다. 앞에서 이들은 아무 문제 없이 그날 모든 주변을 다 황폐화시킬 수 있을 거라 기대했다고 말하고 있다. 이와 대조되는 상황은 예상 밖에 큰 고난을 맞았다는 보기 항 (3)이다.

해설 그러므로 전속력으로 서둘러 이들이 움직인다는 모든 소문을 미리 막기 위해(anticipate) 신속한 움직임으로 자신들의 체력과 움직임에 맡기고 구불구불한 길을 따라가다가 그들은 산 정상 고지에 도착했는데, 가파른 경사로 인해 이들의 진군은 예상했던 것보다 더디어졌다. 그리고 마침내 산의 모든 어려움을 극복해 오른 후, 이들은 Melas의 가파른 기슭(bank)에 도달했는데, 아주 깊은 강으로 위험한 물살이 가득했으며, 이곳은 그 지역을 감싸고 있어 (wind round) 벽처럼 그곳 거주민을 보호하고 있었으며, 밤이 엄습해오고 그들의 두려움이 커지자 그들은 잠시 길을 멈추고 날이 밝기를 기다렸다. 이들은 아무런 장애 없이 건널 수 있을 것이라 생각하고 갑자스럽게 침투를 감행하면 온 국토를 유린할 수 있을 거라 기대했다. 하지만 엄청난 고난에 부딪혀 (모든 것이) 헛수고가 되었다 (to no purpose).

어휘

hasten v. 서두르다   exceeding a. 엄청난
anticipate v. 예기하다
winding road 구불구불한 길   steepness n. 가파름
march n. 행진   surmount v. 극복하다
precipitous a. 험한   halt v. 멈춰서다
hindrance n. 방해   consequence n. 결과
suddenness n. 급작스러움   inroad n. 침입
ravage v. 황폐하게 하다

[Challenge 4]

문제 1

답 (1)

해설 보기 항 (2)의 경우 진공 상태라고 본문에 나와 있으며, (3)의 경우 본문 마지막에 그 공식이 소개되고 있다. (4)의 경우 본문 초반에 나온 실험을 통해서 알 수 있다. 보기 항 (1)에 관련 내용은 본문만으로 알 수가 없다.

해설 든 물체는 공기의 저항이 없다면 같은 속도로 떨어지는데, 이는 진공 리시버의 위에서 깃털과 기니(동전)를 떨어뜨리는 실험에서 보인 바와 같이 동시에 바닥에 도달한다. 떨어지는 물체의 속도는 알려진 법칙에 따라 균등하게 가속화된다. 떨어지는 물체의 높이가 주어지면, 떨어지는 마지막 지점에서 얻은 속도는 쉽게 계산할 수 있다. 피트 단위의 높이의 제곱근을 8.021로 곱하면 속도가 나온다는 것은 실험에 의해서 밝혀졌다.

어휘

velocity n. 속도, 빠르기   exhaust v. 다써버리다, 지치게 하다
guinea n. 기니(영국의 구 금화)   at the same time 동시에
accelerate v. 가속화하다   uniformly ad. 한결같이, 균일하게
descent n. 하강, 내리기; 가계, 혈통
compute v. 계산(측정)하다; 평가하다   square root n. 제곱근

[Challenge 5]

문제 1

답 (3)

해설 호주 낙농업의 최근 눈에 띄는 성장세를 소개하는 글이다.

문제 2

답 (1)

해설 endemic은 "어떤 생물지리역에 한정되어 있는"이라는 뜻으로 밑줄 친 indigenous와 가장 유사한 의미를 지닌다.

문제 3

답 (4)

해설 (1)은 열악한 환경과 전혀 반대의 상황이다. (2)는 이후 'dramatic change'에 대한 구체적 언급이 따라와야 한다. 이 문장은 현재 호주의 낙농업 환경이 안 좋다는 것을 전제로 하고 있어 답이 될 수 없다. (3)의 경우, 현재 호주의 낙농업은 그 시초 단계에 있지만 환경의 호조건으로 인해 최근 장족의 발전을 했다는 점과 점차 그 시장이 넓어지고 있다는 것을 파악하면 오답임을 파악할 수 있다.

문제 4

답 (3)

해설 기름진 다양한 토양, 영양적 가치가 높은 토착 풀, 온화한 기후 등의 훌륭한 자연적 이점을 가지고 시작한 호주의 낙농업은 장족의 발전을 이루었다. 농부 스스로가 소유하고 운영하는 협동 공장의 메인 지역 전역의 시설과 냉동 저장소의 도입은 이러한 성장을 크게 가속화시켰다. 지난 10년 동안 그 성장세는 놀랄 만했다. 호주의 낙농업은 세계 시장을 기반으로 하고 있다. 매년 호주와 다른 낙농과 농장 제품에 대한 여러 나라의 수요는 증가하고, 거대한 국내 시장 또한 확장하고 있다. 관리, 처리, 운송 시설이 개선되고 있으며, 오늘날 호주의 낙농업자들은 자국의 농산물에 대해 국내와 국외 시장 모두에서 높은 가격을 받고 있다.

어휘
splendid *a.* 아주 좋은   **a wide range of** 다양한
fertility *n.* 비옥함   **indigenous** *a.* 토착의
congenial *a.* (~에) 알맞은   **dairy** *n.* 낙농업
remarkable *a.* 주목할 만한
be based on ~을 기반으로 하다
farmyard *n.* 농가의 마당   **supervision** *n.* 관리, 감독
dairyman *n.* 낙농업자

[Challenge 6]

문제 1

답 (3)

해설 본문은 일을 하는 임산부는 출산을 하기 전에 휴식을 취해야 함을 강조하는 글이다.

문제 2

답 (3)

해설 박스 안에 제시된 문장에서 지시대명사 'This'와 본문 (c)의 'For' 접속사를 잘 활용하도록 한다.

문제 3

답 (2)

해설 산모가 아이를 가졌을 때 적절한 휴식을 취하도록 조치를 취하지 못하고, 오히려 이후 잘못된 아이가 나왔을 때 방비하는 모습을 담고 있는 내용의 속담을 고르도록 한다.

해설 충분한 양의 산모의 휴식이 없다면, 보육도 없다. 한 인간을 만들어 내는 일은 한 여성의 최선의 에너지 전부를 필요로 하는데, 아이를 낳기 전 3개월 간은 특히나 더 하다. 이것은 육체적, 정신적 노동이나 심지어 힘든 사회적 의무나 오락에 수반되는 강도에 지워지는 부담보다 부차적인 것이 될 수 없다. 최근 몇 년 간 산부인과, 특히 프랑스에서 이루어진 수없이 많은 실험과 관측을 통해 산모의 현재와 미래의 건강과 해산의 고통 완화뿐 아니라 아이의 발육도 임신 마지막 달에 취한 휴식에 크게 영향을 받는다는 것을 확고히 보여주었다. "모든 일하는 여성은 임신 마지막 3개월 간은 휴식을 취할 권리가 있다." 이 말은 1900년에 국제 위생 위원회에 의해 채택이 되었지만, 이것은 전 공동체의 협력이 없이는 실질적으로 실행될 수 없다. 왜냐하면 여성이 임신 기간 중 휴식을 취해야 한다고 말하는 것만으로는 충분하지 않기 때문이다. 바로 이러한 휴식이 적절히 보장되도록 하는 것은 공동체 모두의 일이다. 아이를 가진 여성 스스로와 고용주는, 확신하건대 공동체를 속이려 최선을 다 할 것이지만, 사실 경제적으로나 도덕적으로 여성이 열등한 아이를 낳았을 경우 손해를 보는 쪽은 공동체이기에, 공동체 자신을 위해 고용주와 피고용주를 관리할 수밖에 없다. 우리는 "오늘 인간 종의 찌꺼기 즉, 맹인, 청각 장애인, 성도착자, 신경 과민증 환자, 부도덕자, 백치, 정신 박약자, 크레틴병 환자, 간질 환자가 임신한 여성보다 더 잘 보호되고 있다"는 말이 더 이상 Bouchacourt의 말에서 들리지 않도록 해야 한다.

어휘
nursery *n.* 육아실; 탁아소   **subordinate** *a.* 부수[종속]하는
manual *a.* 육체노동의   **mental** *a.* 마음의, 정신의
strenuous *a.* 힘이 많이 드는   **social duty** 사회의무
amusement *n.* 즐거움; 오락   **numerous** *a.* 다수의, 수많은
confinement *n.* 분만, 해산
immensely *ad.* 엄청나게, 대단히
duly *ad.* 정식으로, 정당하게   **deaf-mute** *n.* 농아자
degenerate *a.* 타락한; 퇴화한
vicious *a.* 사악한, 악의 있는, 나쁜   **idiotic** *a.* 백치의; 천치의
imbecile *a.* 저능한, 우둔한
cretin *n.* 크레틴병 환자; 백치, 천치
epileptic *a.* 간질의 *n.* 간질 환자

[Challenge 7]

문제 1

답 (3)

해설 지칭 대명사 'this'를 놓치지 말아야 한다. 그리고 대명사 'they'를 받을 수 있는 대상이 둘 이상 나와야 하기에, 서로 다른 두 학계(circle)임을 알 수 있는 동시에 어떤 것에 관한 의견의 일치점과 관련된 내용이 앞에 전개되어 있어야 한다.

문제 2

답 (3)

해설 화제의 전환이 이루어지는 곳을 찾도록 한다. 과학자와 기독교인들이 일치하는 내용(첫 번째 문단의 화제)을 다루다 서로의 의견이 상반되는 내용(두 번째 문단에서 다루는 화제) 즉, 역접의 접속사를 넣어야 할 곳이 어디인지를 찾아보도록 한다.

해석 지구 표면의 특징이 현재의 형태에 도달하기 위해 일련의 순서를 가진 단계를 거쳤다는 것과 이런 상태가 되기까지 아주 오랜 시간이 걸렸을 것이라는 증거에 대해 전문 지질학자들 간에 상당한 일치점을 보인다. 이것은 생명체들의 연속적 순서와도 일치했는데, 이들은 현재 일반적으로 인정된 기간 중 더 나중에 나타나기 시작했지만, 인간의 역사의 기간에 비교했을 때 아주 오랜 시간 계속 진행되었다. 지구의 과거의 역사에 대한 엄청난 연구를 바탕으로 이끌어 낸 이 두 개괄적인 결론은 많은 정통 기독교인들과 자질 있는 대부분의 지질학자와 생물학자들 모두 받아들이고 있다. 이것이 사실이라는 것을 장담하진 못한다. 그러나 분명 이것은 두 진영 내 현재의 의견의 일치를 드러내는 것은 확연하다. 우주는 아주 오랜 기간 동안 존속했을 것이며, 생명은 아주 오래 전에 시작했고, 단순함에서 복잡함으로 순서에 따른 진행을 보인다. 우리는 단지 연속적 형태의 물질에 대해서만 이야기하는 것이지 이러한 형태의 것이 다른 형태의 선형적 진화를 거쳤다는 이야기를 하는 것이 아니다.

일련의 지질학적, 고생물학적 사건들에서 끌어낸 이런 것들을 고려해 볼 때, 우리는 과학자들 사이에서도 의견 일치가 안 되고 있고, 정통 기독교인들 사이에서도 그런 것을 볼 수 있다. 사실은 이 증거는 한 가지 방법 이상으로 해석될 수 있기에 선호하는 해석은 항상 어떤 기본적이고 일반적으로 설명되지 않는 가정에 기반을 둔다. 이러한 가정은 자연의 법칙이 과거의 모든 사건을 설명하기에 충분한 것인지 아니면 이것들 중 특정한 것만 가능한 것인지에 대한 질문에 따라 정해진다.

어 휘

presently *ad.* 현재, 지금　　time frame *n.* 시간[기간]
span *n.* 기간, 시간　　succession *n.* 연속, 잇따름
linear *a.* 선의, 선으로 된　　immensely *ad.* 엄청나게, 대단히
sequence *n.* 연속적인 사건들
paleontological *a.* 고생물학의　　unstated *a.* 말로 하지 않는
assumption *n.* 추정, 상정
hinge upon 전적으로 ~에 달려있다
account for ~을 설명하다, 처리하다

[Challenge 8]

문제 1

답 (4)

해설 본문에서 토마스 페인은 국민들이 원하는 소망을 글로 쓰지 않았다. 이는 대부분 국민들이 당시 복잡한 정치적 글을 이해할 수 없을 뿐 아니라 종종 많은 이들이 글을 모르는 문맹이었기 때문이다. 그는 문제의 핵심을 아주 단순한, 이해하기 쉬운 언어로 말했다고 본문에 언급되어 있다.

문제 2

답 (3)

해설 앞에서 언급한 내용에 추가적인 정보를 제공하는 세미콜론과 앞뒤의 문맥을 잘 살펴야 한다.

> The superstructure of scholarship and experience upon his own poverty enabled him to talk to plain and often barely literate people, to expound the most complex of political ideas in straightforward, understandable, and dramatic language. He did this ____(a)____ ; he simplified by going directly to the heart of the matter, to the crux of the issue, not by writing in pidgin English.

문제 1에서도 언급했듯이 대부분의 국민이 문맹이라는 점과 뒤의 부연진술에서 영어로 쓰지 않았다는 것에서 'without writing down'을 추론할 수 있다.

해설 토마스 페인의 위대한 여러 재능 중 하나는 사람들 사이에 이미 존재하는 생각과 행위의 경향에 민감했다는 점이다. 그는 자신의 의견을 주장하지 못하는 대중들의 원초적인 갈망과 열망이 놀랍게도 오롯이 전달되도록 했다. 그 자신의 빈곤 위에서 세워진 학문과 경험의 상부 구조는 그가 평범하고 종종 글을 잘 모르는 사람과 대화를 나눌 수 있는 배경을 제공했으며, 가장 복잡한 정치적 개념을 직접적으로 이해하기 쉽고 인상적인 언어로 표현할 수 있게 해 주었다. 그는 이것을 글로 쓰지 않고 해냈다. 그는 피진 영어로 쓰지 않고 문제의 핵심에 직접 다가감으로 단순화시켰다.

어 휘

inchoate *a.* 이제 막 시작한, 초기의
longing *n.* 동경, 갈망, 열망
inarticulate *a.* 똑똑히 말을 못하는, 발음이 분명치 않은
beginning *n.* 처음, 최초
marvelously *ad.* 불가사의하게, 기적적으로
articulate *a.* 분명히 발음된, (생각, 감정을) 잘 표현할 수 있는
superstructure *n.* 상부 구조
barely *ad.* 간신히, 가까스로; 거의 ~않다
literate *a.* 읽고 쓸 수 있는, 학식 있는
expound *v.* 상술하다, 해설하다
straightforward *a.* 똑바른; 정직한
dramatic *a.* 극적인, 인상적인
crux *n.* 중요한 점, 핵심　　pidgin *n.* 혼합어

[Challenge 9]

문제 1

답 (1)

해설 본문은 아일랜드를 중심으로 유로권 국가들의 금융 위기를 다루고 있다.

문제 2

답 (3)

해설 보기 항 (1)은 'when Europe's problems disrupted interbank lending and dented U.S. growth'에서 확인할 수 있다. 보기 항 (2)는 'Investors' concern about the credit-worthiness of highly indebted euro zone countries will make it hard for some states to finance hefty debt repayments in the first half of 2011, even as new issuance in the bloc falls.'에서 확인할 수 있다. 'the interest rates investors are demanding pose a burden that may become unsustainable for the likes of Spain and Portugal.' 부분에서 알 수 있듯이, 스페인과 포르투갈도 현재 금융 위기로 몸살을 앓고 있다. 보기 항 (3)은 틀린 표현이다. 보기 항 (4)는 'Moody's, the ratings agency, slashed Dublin's credit grade'에서 확인할 수 있다.

해설 지난주에 더욱 격해진 것처럼 보이는 유럽의 재무로 인한 붕괴의 모습이 조금씩 드러나기 시작하고 있다. 아일랜드 국회가 유럽 연합과 IMF에서 850억의 구제 금융을 받기로 승인한 바로 이틀 후, IMF는 대출을 갚을 능력에 영향을 미칠 만큼의 큰 위기에 여전히 직면해 있다고 아일랜드에 경고했다. 평가 기관인 무디스는 더블린의 신용등급을 깎았으며 유럽 은행들은 아일랜드 자산에 손실이 생길 것이라고 경고했다. 많은 빚을 지고 있는 여러 유로권 국가들의 신용에 대한 투자자들의 불안 심리로 인해 통화 공급이 원활하지 못한 관계로 특정 국가들은 2011년 전반기 이자를 갚기 위한 자금 융통이 어려울 것으로 보인다. 유로권 국가들은 2011년엔 작년보다 채권시장에서 돈을 덜 빌릴 것으로 예상되지만, 투자자들이 요구하는 금리는 스페인과 포르투갈 같은 나라에게는 감당할 수 없는 짐이 된다. 유럽의 문제가 은행 간의 대출을 방해하고, 미국 성장을 악화시킨 봄과 달리 이러한 영향이 최근에는 느껴지지 않는다. 하지만 분석가들은 이러한 위기가 여전히 실질적으로 남아있다고 말하고 있다.

어휘

loom v. 어렴풋이 보이다, 아련히 나타나다
convoluted a. 뒤얽힌, 매우 복잡한
parliament n. 의회   repay v. (아무에게 돈을) 갚다, 상환하다
slash v. 대폭 줄이다   hefty a. 거대한, 막대한
issuance n. 발행, 발포(發布); 배급, 베포

[Challenge 10]

문제 1

답 (2)

해설 새로운 연구에서 발견한 사실인 '마취는 잠보다 혼수 상태에 가깝다'는 것을 제목으로 삼은 보기 항 (2)가 가장 적절하다.

문제 2

답 (4)

해설 앞에서 마취는 혼수상태와 비슷하다고 했다. 곧 마취 환자가 어떻게 깨어나는지에 대한 연구는 혼수상태의 환자가 빠져나오는 단계에 대한 예측에 도움을 줄 수 있다고 볼 수 있다.

문제 3

답 (4)

해설 While sleeping usually involves moving through a series of phases, in general anesthesia(잠에 해당하는 내용이므로 보기 항 (1)은 틀린 표현), patients are typically taken to a specific phase or state and kept there during the surgery(보기 항 (4)는 옳은 진술이다). This phase most closely resembles a coma(보기 항 (3)은 틀린 표현). "The brain is becoming very, very quiet. The activity of the neurons is being dampened dramatically(보기 항 (2) 는 틀린 표현)"

해설 미국의 연구자들은 마취가 깊은 잠이라기보다는 약에 의한 혼수상태에 더 가깝다고 말했다. 뉴잉글랜드의 의학 저널에 발표된 이들의 연구 결과에는 잠, 마취 그리고 혼수상태의 유사점과 차이점에 관한 3년간의 연구가 드러난다. 의사와 환자는 일반적으로 전신 마취를 잠이 드는 것으로 해석하는 반면, 이 두 상태는 아주 깊은 잠의 상태와 마취의 가장 가벼운 단계 사이에 약간의 중복만 있는 큰 차이점이 있다. 잠은 일반적으로 일련의 단계를 거쳐 이동하는 반면, 전신 마취의 경우 환자는 일반적으로 특정 단계 또는 상태에 이르게 되고, 수술이 진행되는 동안 거기서 계속 머무르게 된다. 이 단계는 혼수상태와 아주 유사하다. "뇌는 아주 조용해진다. 뉴런의 활동은 급격히 늦어진다."고 전화 인터뷰에서 Schiff는 말했다. "이것은 혼수상태일 때도 마찬가지다." Schiff는 혼수상태 회복 전문가로 뇌의 부상은 어떤 것이든 같은 경우는 없는 반면, 사람들이 마취에서 빠져나오는 방법 연구는 혼수상태에서 빠져나오는 단계를 예측할 수 있는 모델로 활용될 수 있다고 말했다. 이것은 혼수상태의 사람이 어떤 단계의 회복기에 있는지를 평가하는 도구와 진단을 파악할 수 있게 하며, 의사들이 환자들의 의식을 되찾을 수 있도록 도와주는 새로운 방법을 개발하는 데 사용될 수 있다. 또한 뇌의 회로 메커니즘에 대해 더 많이 파악하게 되면 연구원들이 특정 뇌 회로를 조작할 수 있는 약을 개발하는 데도 도움을 줄 수 있을 것이라고 Schiff 박사는 덧붙였다. 그리고 이 연구는 전신마비를 이해하는 데 새로

운 통찰력을 제공해 줄 것이라고 전신마취 전문가인 Brown이 한 보고서에서 밝혔다.

어휘

anesthesia *n.* 마취, 마비
reversible *a.* 거꾸로[전도, 전환]할 수 있는; 뒤집을 수 있는
-induced *a.* ~이 야기된
pharmacological *a.* 약리학의   coma *n.* 혼수상태
findings *n.* 결과, 결론   exploration *n.* 조사, 연구, 탐구
imilarities and differences 유사점과 차이점
general anesthesia *n.* 전신 마취   overlap *n.* 겹침
the deepest states of sleep 가장 깊이 잠든 상태
through a series of phases 일련의 단계를 거쳐
during the surgery 수술을 하는 동안   resemble *v.* 닮다
dampen *v.* (물에) 축이다; 풀이 죽게 하다, 기를 꺾다
come out of ~에서 나오다   monitor *v.* 감시하다, 검토하다
diagnostics *n.* 진단(법)
bring patients back to consciousness 환자가 의식의 상태로 돌아오게 하다
brain circuit mechanism 뇌순환 메커니즘
tweak *v.* 수정하다, 조작하다
lend new insight into ~에 새로운 관점을 조명하다

퍼펙트 독해
PERFECT READING

| 문제가 깔끔하고 보기편하게 정리되어있어 공부하기 유용해요! - 독자 서평 (bo******* - 교보문고)

| 독해의 완성은 이책을 본 이후입니다. 아주 좋습니다. 추천합니다. - 독자 서평 (rb***** - 교보문고)

| 쉬운 지문부터 어려운 지문까지 설명이 잘 되어있고 구성이 좋은 책이라고 생각해요 - 독자 서평 (he******** - 교보문고)

| 편입공부시 필수적인 책이라 판단되어 구매하게 되었습니다! 홧팅! - 독자 서평 (so***** - 교보문고)

| 학습에 도움이 되는 책입니다. - 독자 서평 (sj****** - 교보문고)

| 오우 이렇게 수준있고 좋은 문제로 구성된 퍼펙트 독해 강추합니다! 편입 막바지 준비하고 있는 이 시점에 적절한 교재라고 생각합니다. 독학하는 사람에게도 적합합니다 꼭 보세요 꼭!!! - 독자 서평 (qo***** - 교보문고)

| 내용이 탄탄해서 공부하는데 도움이 돼요. - 독자 서평 (tl***** - 교보문고)

| 좋아요, 방법론과 예시가 많아 독학하기에 좋습니다. 다만 더 지문이 어려워도 괜찮을듯. - 독자 서평 (st***** - 교보문고)

| 좋습니다!!!명불허전 편입 ㅎㅎ - 독자 서평 (cj******* - 교보문고)

| 편입 준비 하면서 어려운 독해를 찾으시면 이거 사세요 실제로 어려워서 정말 눈물이 났던 기억이 나네요 ㅋ 한 달(30day) 완성 목표 문제구성이고 중·상위권 대학 출제경향 반영 문항 수로 구성하였고, 편입 등, 기타 기출 문제를 배제한 예상문제를 수록했어요. 다방면에 걸친 다양한 주제로 된 원문이에요 후회는 안하실거같아요 단어도 잘 설명해줘요. 배송 빠름. - 독자 서평 (k****y - yes24)

| 편입 독해 분야에서 유명하다고 들어서 사봤습니다 - 독자 서평 (d********1 - yes24)